# INTERPRETING CANADA'S PAST

## ✑A POST-CONFEDERATION READER

### FOURTH EDITION

Edited by:
J.M. Bumsted, Len Kuffert, and Michel Ducharme

OXFORD

UNIVERSITY PRESS

# OXFORD

UNIVERSITY PRESS

Oxford University Press is a department of the University of Oxford.
It furthers the University's objective of excellence in research, scholarship, and education by publishing worldwide.
Oxford is a registered trade mark of Oxford University Press in the UK and in certain other countries.

Published in Canada by
Oxford University Press
8 Sampson Mews, Suite 204,
Don Mills, Ontario  M3C 0H5 Canada

www.oupcanada.com

First Edition published in 1986
Second Edition published in 1993
Third Edition published in 2005

**Library and Archives Canada Cataloguing in Publication**

Interpreting Canada's past / edited by J.M. Bumsted, Len Kuffert and Michel Ducharme.—4th ed.

Includes bibliographical references.

Contents: [v. 1]. A pre-Confederation reader—[v. 2]. A post-Confederation reader.

ISBN 978-0-19-542779-0 (v. 1 ).—ISBN 978-0-19-542780-6 (v. 2)

1. Canada—History—Textbooks. 2. Canada—History—Sources.

I. Bumsted, J. M., 1938– II. Kuffert, L. B. (Leonard B.) III. Ducharme, Michel, 1975–

FC170.I57 2011      971      C2011-900505-0

Cover image: ADRIEN HÉBERT, R.C.A. (1890-1967)
"Christ Church Anglican Cathedral at Burnside, Montreal", 1927
Oil on canvas 33" x 23"
Reproduced with permission of Bruno Hébert. Image provided by Galerie Walter Klinkhoff.

This book is printed on permanent acid-free paper ∞.

Printed and bound in Canada.

3 4 – 16 15

# Contents

# Six | The First World War    173

# Seven | Marketing the Nation    210

# Preface

As with the Third Edition of *Interpreting Canada's Past*, it remains our intention to provide students of Canadian history with a collection of primary and secondary sources, a collection that represents the material historians use daily. Paying attention to current scholarship is essential, and bearing in mind the not-so-current interpretations of a particular theme is likewise part of the historian's job. The privilege of setting aside the work of historians and encountering voices from the eras we are studying is another perk not usually available to students in lecture courses. We wanted once again to give those using the readers an opportunity to see how our understanding of the past is built upon evidence, carefully sifted and handled, and how sometimes these bits of evidence can lead historians to offer conclusions that prompt still more questions.

Accordingly, even though the volumes have been streamlined considerably based on student and instructor feedback, the emphasis is again on *interpretation*. The primary documents have been chosen so that students will take those first steps toward generating the kind of questions that are useful even outside the discipline of history: What does this document mean? Why did its creator want to express the ideas it contains? How reliable is it? What does it tell us about change? The secondary source selections have been simplified in this edition, with the assumption that students can dig deeper into each article or excerpt, dealing with less in terms of who-did-what-when, but discovering more in terms of connections with the primary sources and the overall theme of each section. On the basis of user comments and classroom experience, we have retained some of the more popular selections and added more that are entirely new, also altering our lists of topics.

We thank the staff at Oxford, and Jack Bumsted, for his vision for the readers and commitment through three editions.

Michel Ducharme, University of British Columbia
Len Kuffert, University of Manitoba

# Chapter 1

# Debating Confederation

## READINGS

### Primary Documents

### Historical Interpretations

### Introduction

Historians of Canada have devoted much attention to explaining how Canada's four original provinces were brought together. The partnership was not an equal one, nor was it a harmonious arrangement in the beginning, given the variety of backgrounds and interests represented (even then) among the new partners. Debate over how the new provinces were to co-operate continued after the deal was made. Some, like the wary Nova Scotians, who were the first to raise the possibility of leaving the federation, were afraid of becoming 'sub-species' within the larger Dominion, valuing their roles as more autonomous members in a 'family' of imperial outposts. Their provincial Assembly debated the possibility of repealing the British North America Act and leaving Confederation—a threat that was not issued idly and did not go away for almost a generation. Despite Nova Scotians' discontent with their new status, the new federation could not pause to address such internal tensions. These tensions arose at least partly because Canada was a nation created by politicians and was not held together by one language, one religion, or a unifying experience like a successful revolution against colonial rule. Canada entered a phase of 'adolescence' with the added pressure of growing up next to a boisterous and dynamic neighbour. Within its first decade, the young federation expanded, taking control of the vast North-West Territories, from which Manitoba was carved in 1870. British Columbia joined in 1871, and Prince Edward Island in 1873. The effect was to answer the prayers of expansionists, who viewed these additions as Canada's destiny, and to set off a wave of speculation as to what Canada would do with all this land. Our selections here reflect this contentious period, first with the Nova Scotia debate over nullifying the Confederation pact, and then with a hymn of praise to British Columbia. In the former case, the Attorney General Wilkins speaks of the 'rival and discordant interests' that Confederation cannot reconcile, while lauding the ingenuity and perfection of the British parliamentary system. In the latter, Lt.-Col. Coffin tells us that the metal mining potential of British Columbia is its greatest asset. Or is it coal? No, wait, timber's the thing! No, the ocean! But finding out how the new province was to prove its worth would probably have to wait until the much-anticipated Canadian Pacific Railway was finished. In our first selection from a historian, Forrest Pass addresses the same sort of question, but with a great deal more hindsight. Parliamentarians asked: Was British Columbia going to be Canada's western window on the world, or was acquiring it going to be an expensive folly? The debates over these 'competing conceptions of Canada' and concerns about how newly acquired territory would benefit the new nation reveal how unsettled public and elite opinions were at the time. Peter Russell's comprehensive discussion of provincial rights outlines how Canada moved away from Prime Minister Macdonald's ideal of a more unified system toward one in which the provinces became more comfortable asserting their needs and desires. Though Macdonald was a masterful acquirer of land, the newer provinces were especially successful at acquiring a greater measure of control over their own fates.

## QUESTIONS FOR CONSIDERATION

1.  Why does Martin Wilkins mention the United States and its constitution?
2.  Why did Coffin consider it important to report on British Columbia's prospects, even though the province had already joined Confederation?
3.  We now recognize that Canada has distinct regions with differing interests. Why might this have been a difficult admission for some Canadians to make right after Confederation?
4.  If you were debating the British Columbia Terms of Union, would you have sympathized with the 'commercialists' or the 'agrarians'? Why?
5.  Quebec played an extraordinary role in the struggle over provincial autonomy during the first few decades after Confederation. What impact did it have?

## SUGGESTIONS FOR FURTHER READING

Forrest Duncan Pass, 'Pacific Dominion: British Columbia and the Making of Canadian Nationalism, 1858–1958', Ph.D. Dissertation (History), University of Western Ontario, 2009.

Kenneth G. Pryke, *Nova Scotia and Confederation 1864–74* (Toronto: University of Toronto Press, 1979).

Paul Romney, *Getting It Wrong: How Canadians Forgot Their Past and Imperilled Confederation* (Toronto: University of Toronto Press, 1999).

A.I. Silver, *The French-Canadian Idea of Confederation, 1864–1900* (Toronto: University of Toronto Press, 1997).

Garth Stevenson, *Ex Uno Plures: Federal–Provincial Relations in Canada, 1867–1896* (Montreal and Kingston: McGill-Queen's University Press, 1993).

Robert Vipond, *Liberty and Community: Canadian Federalism and the Failure of the Constitution* (Albany: State University of New York Press, 1991).

## PRIMARY DOCUMENTS

**1** From Martin Isaac Wilkins, 'Attorney General's Speech', Nova Scotia, House of Assembly, *Debates on the Resolutions* Relative to Repeal of the 'British North American Act' in the House of Assembly of Nova Scotia, 1868. (Halifax: Nova Scotia House of Assembly, 1868), 3–16.

Debate on the Repeal Resolutions
Monday, Feb 10

HON. ATT. GENERAL'S SPEECH.

Hon. ATTORNEY GENERAL addressed the House as follows— [ . . . ] I am about to lay before the members of the House, before the people of this country, and probably before the people of England, the facts of one of the most important political cases that ever arose in the Colonies, and in order to do so satisfactorily I shall endeavour to show the true condition in which this country was placed before certain political changes took place in its constitution. I shall endeavour in the first place to show that Nova Scotia was a well governed and law respecting, a contented and a happy country. She was well governed because her institutions were moulded in miniature on the model of the British constitution, which is the finest political system by which any nation was ever governed—a system calculated to maintain order and harmony among all orders of people—a system under which obedience to law and the necessary result of obedience to law, liberty, have been better maintained than in any other country; for, sir, however paradoxical it may seem, it is a literal truth that the highest degree of freedom consists in obedience to law. It is obedience to law which preserves to me my rights and liberties, my property and my life; and therefore, however inconsistent it may seem, it is actually true that the highest degree of liberty consists in obedience to law; and that country which possesses institutions calculated to produce that result, must be the happiest nation on earth. Now the constitution of Nova Scotia was based upon the principles of the British Constitution—those principles which best suit the genius of the people. Its whole condition was different from those of any other country on the Continent of America, and the constitution which was granted to the people of this province by King George II, and which had been enlarged and greatly improved by his successors on the throne of England, was a well working constitution. It was as much like the British constitution as it was possible to make things which are different in their nature. [ . . . ]

When we compare our constitution in Nova Scotia with that of the Great Republic, the contrast must be favourable to this province. We admire the people of that country, we have sincerely sympathised with them in their recent distress and troubles. We feel towards them all the emotions of fraternal affection, but we do not approve of their constitution. We consider that their institutions are possessed of two fatal defects—the one is democracy, the second Confederation. We consider that having our little constitution moulded upon the monarchial institutions of England makes it infinitely superior to that of the United States, although the latter is a master work of human hands, and the finest piece of composition ever prepared by men for political purposes. It was manufactured by men who were really statesmen—by men who loved their country—by men who had been educated in an English school—by men who had sense enough to perceive the beauties of the British constitution—by men who endeavoured with the utmost imaginable pains and skill to apply the principle of the British constitution to a democratic system and form of government; but the people of the United States were unfortunate, after having separated from England in 1783, in the political system which they instituted. Had they combined in a legislative union—had they incorporated all the States into one Legislature, having one set of laws and revenues, they would undoubtedly, at this time, be the greatest nation upon the earth. They certainly would not have been second to any other; but, unfortunately, they chose Confederation, and that Confederation has resulted as every Confederation must result, for it is impossible so to adjust the rival and discordant interests of different countries under a Confederation as to maintain permanent harmony. It is not in the nature of things that they should continue as separate and individual countries, having separate legislatures and individualities, without clashing with one another at some time or other. We have seen, notwithstanding the skill with which that famous constitution of the United States was made—notwithstanding the intelligence of that people, that great evils have made their appearance already. The Confederation was broken, an internecine civil war deluged their land with blood, and they expended in three years more than probably three times the amount of the national debt of England, in money, and the destruction of their property; and sir, at this moment there is no man on earth who is able to say what is to be the result of the political affairs of that great country. An earthquake is growing under their feet, and no man can tell when and where the volcano is to burst, bringing with it destruction and ruin. I make these observations with the greatest possible regret, for I believe that every man in Nova Scotia wishes well to the people of the United States, although the people of this province have no desire to be connected with them. They are too wise, too sensible to desire for a moment to part with their own well-working public institutions, and enter into Union with the States.

I shall now turn your attention to another Confederation—the Confederation of Canada—and contrast it with the United States, and show you that if it be not desirable to enter into the Union with the United States, Confederation with Canada is absolutely hateful and detestable to the people of this country. We object to a union with the American States, because we disapprove of *Democracy* and *Confederation*, but there is a worse political combination, that is *Oligarchy* and *Confederation*. If we dislike the constitution of the United States we are bound to hate and detest the constitution which the Confederation Act has prepared for the people of those fine colonies. If we were to join the United States, Nova Scotia would possess all the freedom that every State of the Union possesses. We would have the choice of our own Governors, of our Senators, of our Legislators; we would have the power of self-taxation and self-government in the highest degree; but what would be our position if we suffered ourselves to be dragged into this hateful union with Canada, where would Nova Scotia's freedom be? Before the British America Act was imposed upon us Nova Scotia was as free as the air. How could the people of this country be taxed? There was no power to tax them except this House, their own servants, whom they commissioned to tax them. Is that the state of things now? Have we any power over the taxation of this country? Does not the Act in question confer upon Canada the fullest power of taxing all the property of Nova Scotia at their arbitrary will? What is our control over that Legislature? We have but a paltry voice of 19 members in the popular branch, but a single one in the other. We have, therefore, to protect the rights of this country from spoliation, only 19 members out of 253. If we should continue in Confederation we should not be governed by the people, as is the case in the United States, but by a little knot of Executive Councillors in Canada. Therefore we have no disposition to unite with the one or the other—neither with the United States nor with Canada; and, sir, if we were driven to the necessity of making a choice between the two calamities, we would be bound to choose the least, and that would be, to join the United States of America, and participate in their liberty and prosperity rather than submit to the tyranny of Canada. We would have to prefer the democratic tyranny of the one country to the oligarchical tyranny of the other, and there would be no difficulty in making a choice; but thank Heaven we are not called upon to choose between them. We have a constitution of our own, and that belongs to the people of Nova Scotia; and I am going to show you that the constitution they enjoy is their own property—that the Parliament of England had no power to take it away from them—that the British America Act is entirely unconstitutional—that Nova Scotia has never been legally confederated with Canada—and it rests with her to say whether she will ever be so or not.

Before I come to look to the constitution of this country, I must make a few remarks with regard to England. We intend to send to the mother country certain gentlemen authorized to present to the Queen our humble address, praying Her Majesty to relieve us from this Confederation with Canada. We go in the most perfect confidence that our prayer will be heard. We know to whom we are going to appeal. We are not placed in the condition that the old thirteen colonies were in under old King George III. We have a very different person to deal with in Queen Victoria. We have to approach ministers very different from those of the last century. We have no stubborn King like George III; we have no prejudices of the royal mind to counteract; we have not the infatuation of his ministers to meet. We have the greatest princess that ever adorned a human throne—a most virtuous Queen, who, when she accepted the sceptre, took the oath that she would rule the country according to the laws, customs and statutes of the realm. She has most nobly fulfilled her obligations, and, in answer to the prayers of her own church, 'she has been endued most plenteously with heavenly gifts'. In her person she is an example of every virtue; her obedience to the laws exalts her above all monarchs.—Her personal virtues are brighter than all the gems which adorn her Imperial diadem. It is to a Queen like this that the people appeal. Have the people no right to present themselves before their Sovereign Queen? Has not this ever been the most loyal portion of her dominions? Did not our forefathers flee from their country because they would not participate in rebellion? Did they not leave their property for their king's sake? I have seen a resolution passed by the Legislature of Nova Scotia at the time the thirteen colonies rebelled actually petitioning the King to impose taxes upon the Province to assist the Empire in its extremity. From that time to this the people of Nova Scotia have been the most loyal that ever dwelt in any part of Her Majesty's dominions. They will have confidence in presenting themselves before the Queen, and asking to be restored—to what? To anything that they have no right to demand? Simply to get their own. Can any man suppose for a moment that they will be rejected by a Sovereign like ours? We need be under no apprehension. We are pursuing the proper course to obtain a legitimate end, and there is no power on earth that can prevent the people from being restored to their rights but downright tyranny, and that we cannot expect from the hands of the Queen and her Government. Do not let the loyalty of Nova Scotia be suspected. Has any one a right to suspect it? Look at the injuries done to this Province within the last six months. See their liberties taken away, see them taxed by a foreign and alien Legislature; see their property taken from them,—all their customs handed over to others, collected by strangers before their very eyes. See stamp duties and tea duties imposed upon them. Those very acts which forced the old thirteen colonies to rebellion have been imposed upon Nova Scotia with the same extraordinary fatuity. And yet have the people rebelled? I have heard of no movement of agitation on the part of the people beyond the simple burning in effigy of one of the delegates. [ . . . ]

Now, having made these preliminary remarks, I shall turn your attention to the history of our Constitution. I have heard men assert that we have no valid constitution—that it is made up of despatches. I have been at the pains of examining into this question, and can show you that Nova Scotia has had a chartered constitution, an irrevocable constitution—one that no power on earth can take away except by force or violence. Neither the Queen nor Parliament of England has any right to touch or abrogate that constitution. [ . . . ] In 1747 [Nova Scotia] came into the hands of George II, and he, being desirous of having it settled by English subjects, promised the people of England who would undertake the settlement of the country that he would give them the British Constitution in miniature. Accordingly he ordered a patent to be drawn up, with the Great Seal—a Seal larger than the crown of a hat—for Lord Cornwallis, by which he granted to the people of Nova Scotia the constitution they were to possess. I shall call your attention briefly to the words of that part of the patent which refers to the establishment of a Legislative Assembly in the Province. He established by this patent a Governor in the place of King, a Council in the place of Lords, and a House of Assembly in the place of Commons, and made the constitution of the colony as nearly like that of Great Britain as he could. 'And we do hereby (this patent is dated 6th May, 1747,) give and grant unto you (Edward Cornwallis) full power and authority, with the advice and Consent of our said Council, from time to time, as need shall require, to summon and call general assemblies of the freeholders and planters within your jurisdiction according to the usage of the rest of our plantations in America, and that you, the said Edward Cornwallis, with the advice and consent of our House of Assembly or the major part of it, shall have full power and authority to make and ordain (here is power given to the Legislature) laws, statutes and ordinances for the public peace, and welfare, and good government of our said Province and of the people and inhabitants thereof, and such measures as shall tend to the benefit of us and our successors, which said laws and ordinances are not to be repugnant, but as nearly agreeable as possible to the statutes of this our said Kingdom of England'.

This solemn deed and covenant cannot be repudiated. [ . . . ] The King having given the charter in question, had no power to make laws. Wherever a country is conquered, the conqueror to whom it is ceded has the power to do as he or she pleases in its management. He may, if he chooses, allow the inhabitants of that country to make their own laws, or put them all to death, or he may send them a code of laws made by himself, and allow his Governors to execute them within the country. But if he confers upon the country any privileges, the deed is obligatory upon himself and heirs, and he cannot annul it, he is bound to submit to it. It is just the same with an individual, as soon as he signs a deed for a piece of land to his neighbour, neither he nor his heirs can afterwards dispute that seal. The day the King signed that deed and appended the seal to the commission of the Governor, he conceded the power to make laws. Both his Attorney and Solicitor Generals tell him, we have looked at Lord Cornwallis' patent, and you have not the power to make such laws. No law can be binding upon the people of Nova Scotia except such as are passed in accordance with that charter. [ . . . ]

Now, Mr. Speaker, I shall endeavour to bring this argument to a close by inviting the attention of the House, and of the people of England to whom I am speaking at this moment, to the great importance of Nova Scotia to the British Empire. This is a subject which has never been well considered. The old colonies are the most valuable portions of the earth—by the stubbornness of a British King and the stupidity of his Ministers they were lost to the Empire; and that dismemberment was the most serious that ever befell the British nation. Lord Chatham actually died protesting against it. Nova Scotia stands on the front of the American continent just as England does in that of Europe. She possesses great mineral wealth, the source of England's greatness. Her coal and iron, with the energy of her people, have brought the mother country to her present high condition. We possess the same advantages—we too are almost an island. If Nova Scotia were lost to England she might bid adieu to New Brunswick, to Prince Edward Island, and to Newfoundland. These four Maritime Provinces together have a territory similarly situated to the British Isles, and are capable of sustaining a population equal to theirs. Now Great Britain has been to Nova Scotia a very affectionate parent. She has been most kind to us, but we sometimes hear the statesmen of England grumbling a little about the expense incurred in defending these colonies. I must confess I cannot see what that expense is. Great Britain is a maritime nation and a military power. She must have the best navies on the ocean and one of the strongest armies in the field. Where could she maintain her troops and navy more economically than in these Colonies. The climate is a very healthy one; the statistics show that mortality here is less than in any other part of the world. The people of England would never consent to a standing army remaining in their own country. Therefore the scattering of the troops through the colonies has been a kind of necessity. Therefore, so far from those colonies costing England anything they are little or no expense to her. She was always a kind mother although not a wise one at times. When she adopted her trade policy in 1848 she left these colonies entirely unprotected; she left the trade of Nova Scotia to be managed by people who knew nothing about it. She had up to that time managed our trade herself; she withdrew her fostering care and left us to walk alone. We have managed to live very happy and contentedly, but she did not act wisely towards these colonies. Since 1848 no less than six millions of people have left England, Ireland and Scotland; where have they gone to? They have gone directly past us into the United States. If England had been a judicious foster mother she would have diverted the emigration into these colonies. If she had encouraged the commercial advantages of Nova Scotia and the agricultural capabilities of Canada we would now be a strong nation instead of having only four millions of souls in our midst. We would have a population of nine or ten millions, and instead of being afraid of invasion the people of the United States would be pleased to think during their internecine war that such was the peaceful character and orderly disposition of Her Majesty's Colonies in America that there was no danger to be apprehended from them.

I believe there is no time that a parent knows the value of the child he loves until he hears the cold earth falling upon the coffin, and the sad words, 'earth to earth, ashes to ashes, dust to dust'. Let England transfer this little province to the United States, and she will, after a few years' time, wake up to the loss she has sustained. If the people of the United States succeed in restoring the union, in healing the differences between the North and the South, and in concentrating their tremendous energies, she must become one of the greatest powers of the world. She is now a great naval power, but give her the harbour of Halifax,—which in her hands could be made just as impregnable as Gibraltar. Give her the coal, iron, and fisheries of Nova Scotia, and her power will be largely increased, and millions of people will pour into this country. The fisheries alone of these provinces would be to the United States a nursery for a million or a million and a half of seamen. How long would England then boast of her maritime supremacy? When the Americans had only a few miserable ships they brought more disgrace upon the British flag than any other nation ever succeeded in doing. What would they be if, when challenged to the test by Great Britain, they had possession of the Colonies in addition to their ordinary strength? Suppose in the order of things France, another great naval power, should combine her energies with those of the United States, against England, in what position would the mother country be? How could she contend with such maritime nations as these? Therefore the loss of these Colonies might lead to the degradation of England, and instead of standing at the head of nations she might be lowered to the condition of a secondary state, if indeed she were not converted into a province of France.

I shall now very briefly call the attention of the House to the resolutions before it. They develop the arguments on which we ask for a repeal of the Union. The first clause contends that the Legislative Assembly of Nova Scotia had no power to change the constitution; they had none except what was given them in the charter. Parliament had no power over this country—it never had any. This country belonged to the Queen of England, and our Assembly had no constitutional right to consent to or make the slightest alteration in the constitution under which they were elected to make laws. That is the position which we take, and I would like to see the British constitutional authorities examine this subject, for I am convinced they will acknowledge that I am correct. The second resolution is to the effect that the only authority which the Delegates had was derived from the Assembly, who had no power to give any such authority at all. Even this authority, however, they disregarded. Their authority simply extended to the negotiation of the terms of a Federal union between all the British North American Colonies. They had no power to select three provinces and confederate them, and therefore in that respect they did not act up to their authority. Then, sir, their delegation was not legally constituted. [ . . . ] No constituent assembly was constituted—it could make no constitution, or do any act until all the delegates were present. [ . . . ]

The sixth resolution states that no change can be made without an appeal to the people. Here is a self-evident proposition. The constitution belongs to whom? To the House of Assembly? No. To the Legislative Council? No. It is the property of the people of Nova Scotia—every man, woman and child are the owners, and it cannot be taken away from them without their consent. Even the arbitrary monarchies of Europe admit that principle. When Napoleon seized upon the Empire what did he do? At all events he went through the ceremony of sending around the ballot box, and asking the people whether they were willing to change their constitution. The other day two States of Italy, Nice and Savoy, were transferred after the Austrian campaign, and what was done? Did one king sit down and cede the country to the other? No; the people were called upon to decide whether they were prepared to accept the change of constitution or not. No constitution can be lawfully and constitutionally taken away without consulting the people who own the constitution. This is a self-evident proposition—just as evident as the fact that no man can have his farm taken away from him without his consent.

These resolutions go on to argue that the people of Nova Scotia were never consulted until the 18th September, 1867, after the British North America Act had passed the Parliament, and the Queen had given it force by her proclamation. They were then for the first time asked whether they were willing to accept the change of constitution. Then did the people answer emphatically that they would have nothing to do with it. These resolutions state that the preamble of the Imperial Statute is false, and I believe that when the Quebec scheme went home no such words were in it. But no sooner did the crown officers cast their eyes over it than they, knowing the constitutional course in all such matters, perceived that it was impossible for the Imperial Government to legislate upon the question without the consent or request of the people of these colonies. Accordingly they added the preamble declaring that 'whereas the people of Canada, Nova Scotia and New Brunswick desire to be federally united, &c.' That statute could not have been placed before the Imperial Parliament unless it had these words in it, for it would be unconstitutional unless the people of these colonies had testified their assent to it. Therefore the preamble being false, the statute is unconstitutional and falls to the ground.

The resolutions go on to say that the people were not only not consulted, but that they were purposely and designedly prevented from being consulted. Is not that a true statement? What did the House of Assembly who recently sat upon these benches, with no great credit to them, do in the month of March last? When it was moved that the people of Nova Scotia had a right to be consulted at the polls, whether they would consent to be confederated or not, that resolution was negatived by 32 against 16 representatives of the people. Whose servants were these 32 persons? The servants of the Executive Council; they ignored the authority of the people, and said that the constitution of Nova Scotia belonged to Dr Tupper and a few others. Then I think we have asserted strictly in accordance with the fact that the people of Nova Scotia were systematically and perseveringly kept from passing upon the subject of confederation. We have also stated with truth that the last election turned entirely upon confederation. I have heard men venture to assert that other issues entered into that election, but men who say this will state anything. No man living before or during the election, can venture to deny the fact that confederation was the great question which excited the people from one end of the province to the other. [ . . . ]

We shall pass these resolutions and we may, if necessary, add one or two more; and when we have done so, it is the design of the Government and House to send Delegates to England as soon as we can, to submit to the Queen a humble Address, embracing the substance of these resolutions; and I have much pleasure in announcing, so far as I am able to judge, my belief and conviction that the Delegation cannot possibly fail of success.

2   From Lieutenant-Colonel Coffin, 'Our New Provinces: British Columbia', *The Canadian Monthly and National Review*, 3(5) (May 1873). (Toronto: Adam, Stevenson, 1873), 361–72.

Mr. Langevin's Report, as Minister of Public Works, is an exception to the general wearisomeness of blue books. Divested of its externals it rises, as read, in the opinion of the reader. As being the result of five weeks of laborious and well directed enquiry, it is most creditable—terse, yet not dry; compendious, replete, suggestive. It comes too, most opportunely, when the popular mind in Canada craves for information on the subject of British Columbia, and it comes *ex cathedra*. We know that, if we can rely upon anything, we can rely upon this, for the writer has achieved a reputation for truthfulness and discrimination, and from the position he occupies is, therefore, doubly trustworthy. [ . . . ]

We shall have occasion, by and by, to revert to this leading feature in Mr. Langevin's picture, but among the accessories we may note, first, the agreeable climate of Vancouver Island, which resembles that of England without its humidity; where the summer is dry and warm, the autumn bright and balmy, the winter and spring open, though wet; where, in seasons exceptionally severe, ice forms to the thickness of a penny piece, but where, in compensation, gooseberry buds open in February, early plants burgeon in March, and strawberries bloom in the middle of April. The littoral, both of the Island and of the mainland—British Columbia proper—partakes of these characteristics, but the interior of both is mountainous and highly picturesque, intersected by valleys, deep and fertile, by elevated and extensive plateaux, where in winter the snow does not impede travelling, and the pasture is such—a species known as bunch grass—that animals thrive well at all seasons.

[ . . . ]

These conditions of climate operate exuberantly on a soil whereon flourishes, in great abundance, the Douglas pine, rising often to 150 and 175 feet, without knot or branch; and turns out logs which would make the mouth of an Ottawa lumberman water—say 80 feet long by 6 in diameter—and yet, by the side of this sylvan giant, and other noble forest trees, common to Canada, do not disdain to grow cabbages, carrots, turnips and potatoes, equal to any in the Dominion; and even at a level of 2,700 feet above the sea, on the plateaux before adverted to, were seen fields of wheat, oats and barley, which, aided by an ingenious system of artificial irrigation, presented the finest possible appearance, proclaiming, as it is prettily put, 'in their mute language, that those who believed that Columbia was a land of mountains, unfit for cultivation and destined to prove a source of expense to Confederation, had made a great mistake'.

[ . . . ]

But the hidden riches of this picturesque country far exceed those which meet the eye. In the bowels of the earth, in the waters under the earth, on the rocky shores of the inland seas, in the beds of rivers, nature has been prodigal of gifts. Gold and silver, copper and coal, crop out, geologically, all over the country. Near the town of Hope, on the Fraser River, Mr. Langevin saw specimens of silver of such richness as to justify the construction of extensive works, including a road from Hope to the mine itself; and there is every reason to believe that the silver region extends through the range of mountains in which this mine is situated. Of the copper little is said, but Governor Douglas, in a report communicated to the Colonial Office, dated August 27, 1852, stated that he had 'procured a rich specimen of copper ore found in a distant part of Vancouver Island', and manifestations of the existence of this metal have reproduced themselves since; but when gold can be had for the trouble of picking it up, but little of research will be vouchsafed to the inferior metals. The auriferous regions extend over the whole Province, from the United States frontier to the 53rd degree of north latitude. For a width of from one to two hundred miles gold is found, but specially in the beds of the great rivers, the Fraser and the Thomson, the Peace and the Ominica, and in the rivers and creeks flowing into them. The *detritus*, borne down by freshets, had created banks and bars, which on the subsidence of the water were found to abound with gold. The precious metal was literally to be had for the 'picking of it up'. The wonder was how it should have remained so long undiscovered, for the Indian, now as keen and as greedy as the white man in his quest for gold, must for ages have passed it by unnoticed. [ . . . ]

Happily for the country, the days of surface diggings, of washings and scrapings, of easy gains and wicked waste, have passed away, and have been succeeded by systematic mining and the employment of capital, scientific skill, and steady labour. Mr. Langevin speaks cheeringly of the prospects of mines at the extremity of the Cariboo road: 'At a depth of from 100 to 150 feet under ground, and with shafts communicating with galleries, each more than 200 feet long, is the "Lane & Kurtz" mine, owned by an American company with a capital of $500,000, which, though stopped for a time by subterranean inundation, is expected yet to reward great sacrifices by a rich harvest of gold'. The Columbian Blue Book for 1870 gives the yield of gold for the year from the mines of Cariboo, Silionet, Columbia, Gale and Lytton, at $1,333,745, without counting the quantity of gold carried out of the country in private hands.

The golden shower which immortalized Dame gave, at first, but a doubtful reputation to British Columbia. In either case less of greed, and far less of guilt, might have accomplished better things. For a mining population will, of itself, never make a country; the gold which is not squandered in waste and wassail, is carried out of it. We find by authentic returns, that from 1862 to Sept. 1871, gold to the extent of $16,650,036 has been shipped from British Columbia by banks, registered and known, to which amount should be added at least $5,000,000 carried out of the country by miners themselves. This outflow might be arrested, and utilized *in transitu*, as suggested by Mr. Langevin, by the re-establishment of a mint, the machinery for which, originally imported by the Government of Columbia, is carefully preserved. The constructors of our Canadian Pacific Railway will, no doubt, direct it in the direction of our eastern enterprises, manufactures and products. [ . . . ]

But the great promise of the future of British Columbia lies deep seated in its coal measures. Coal has been found, of excellent quality, to lie on Vancouver's Island and on the main. In 1859 coal was obtained outcropping in Coal Harbour of Burrard's inlet, and was critically used on board of H.M. ship *Plumper*, with most favourable results. Coal abounds all over the north end of Vancouver Island. It has been found of good quality a little way to the northward of Fort Rupert. But the present chief source of supply, the most practical and the most convenient, is Nanaimo. This place is 75 miles north of the capital, Victoria, on the Gulf of Georgia. The harbour is good, and there is no difficulty in making it. The coal is found handy to the ships' side. It is highly bituminous and well suited to the manufacture of gas. For economic purposes it is most valuable, resembling in quality the varieties of coal produced in the central coal fields of England, and it has been remarked at Nanaimo that the deeper the workings have been carried the better the quality becomes. For domestic consumption and for use in factories, it is thought to be equal to that brought from the Welsh mines. It is considered to be better steam coal than that of Newcastle. The English ships of war stationed at Esquimault are all supplied with it. It can be laid down alongside the ship at from $5 to $6 per ton. It is sold at San Francisco at from $12 to $15 per ton, where English coal costs from $20 to $35. [ . . . ]

Anthracite coal has been found in the interior of Columbia, on the River Nicolas, 160 miles from the sea, of a very superior quality to that produced on the coast, although this mineral exists on Queen Charlotte's Island in vast quantities, and is considered to be equal, for smelting purposes, to the Pennsylvanian anthracite; but the price should be reduced below $10 per ton at the mouth of the pit, to make it marketable. This commodity has already attracted the attention of capitalists. Mr. Langevin speaks of one company which had expended $80,000, which, from distance of markets, cost of labour and a depleted purse, had been compelled to abandon both mines and capital. These enterprising individuals have probably been ahead of the times, but the day cannot now be far distant when this traffic must revive, and the real difficulty will be to supply the wants of the immense and increasing steam-fleets, military and commercial, which frequent the coasts of Eastern Asia, and throng the Pacific seaboard from Cape Flattery to Cape Horn. There can be no doubt but that the heavy import duty imposed by the American tariff on Canadian coal prejudices grievously the trade between British Columbia and its nearest market, San Francisco. Though we are satisfied that the American consumer is the greater sufferer, though he pays us our price for our commodity, and thus, 'to gain his private ends', taxes himself to boot; still, it is beyond question that, were the duty removed, we should sell two tons where we now sell one, and it is only to be the more deplored that the Canadian House of Commons, in the session of 1870, should by precipitate action, and showing its hand too soon, have played the game of foreign manipulators, and by emasculating the Washington Treaty, have deprived the Dominion of 'free coal', which had been freely tendered by the American High Commissioner as a pendant to 'free fish'. [ . . . ]

But the real treasury of British Columbia is in the ocean—the untold and immeasurable wealth of its fisheries. The waters of the Gulf of Georgia are alive with fish, proper for the food of man, while the Northern Pacific abounds in the *cetaceae* and other deep sea species known to commerce. The whale, the 'right whale' of Scoresby, the whale of train-oil and whalebone, the porpoise and the dog-fish, all oil-producing, have given birth to enterprises which, though still in their infancy, present an infancy full of promise. In 1871 three whaling expeditions were in successful operation. The most prominent was the 'British Columbia Whaling Company'. They had already secured 20,000 gallons of oil and expected 10,000 more. The value of this oil is 37 cts. per gallon. In England it is worth £35 per ton of 252 gals., or about 2s. 9d. per gallon. Dog-fish oil, worth 55 cents the gallon in California, is produced in large and increasing quantities; it is stated that the catch exceeds, in importance, that of the whale. In 1870, 50,000 gallons were rendered, and at that time this branch of commerce was steadily improving. These oils, under the operation of the Treaty of Washington, will find at San Francisco not only a ready market but an increased demand. The price may or may not increase, but the demand will be doubled. [ . . . ]

The Gulf of Georgia swarms with salmon, cod, (the true cod,) herring and houlican, each in its season, with halibut, sturgeon, smelt, haddock and sardines. The salmon begin to enter the river in March, species after species following each other in regular succession. The spring or silver salmon is the first and the most valuable arrival. They vary from 4 to 25 lbs. in weight, and have been known to reach 75 lbs. These fish, instinct-driven, force their way in myriads up the Fraser river and its tributaries to the distance of a thousand miles from the sea, and at times, exhausted by their labour, are stranded in such numbers as to heap the shores with their remains and poison the air with their exhalations. [ . . . ]

Then we have the houlican, the Indian name given to a small fish, about the size of a sprat, which produces oil of superior quality and delicate flavour, to which is ascribed all the sanative virtues of cod-liver oil, free from its nauseousness. So oily is its nature that, when dried, the fish may be lighted and will burn like a candle. Our great navigator, Cook, who, by the way, while giving a name to Cape Flattery ignored the existence of the Straits of Fuca, eat houlican at Nootka Sound. He calls them 'sardines', and lauds highly the quality both of the fish and of the oil. The houlican swarm in millions. By means of a rude apparatus the full of a canoe may be taken in two hours. If these fish are sardines (the flavour is pronounced to be delicious), and can, like others of their class, be preserved in tins, we have here a most lucrative article of commerce.

[ . . . ]

Providence has been bountiful to the hardy Norsemen in either hemisphere. The riches of the sea redress the rigour of clime. The hardy fisherman of Newfoundland, contending with the tempest and a winter of intense severity, supplies the Catholic markets of France and Spain, Portugal and the Brazils; the West Indies share in the dispensation; but the produce of the Grand Bank will not stand a voyage round Cape Horn. It must be salted until it loses all savour or it perishes. Within the Tropics, the fish, parti-coloured and picturesque in aspect, will not bear curing, and would hardly be worth it if it did. The Southern Pacific, therefore, looks to its Northern waters and to Vancouver Island for the same stores and supplies which the Atlantic and Mediterranean derive from Newfoundland. Both islands, so diverse in climate, lie in the same latitude. The Line 49° bisects each. Both islands,—the one the glory and the other the hope of this Dominion,—command and minister to one great need of the Catholic world; and beyond all peradventure the fisheries of British Columbia, rightly cultivated, will create a market, unrivalled, producing more of wealth than the gold mines of Ominica and Cariboo, and a wealth still more inappreciable in a vigorous growth of stalwart native seamen.

[ . . . ]

We have thus far touched but superficially on the great staple of the country, the great staple indeed of this continent, which, disappearing rapidly elsewhere, abounds throughout

British Columbia. It is stated that the supply of timber from British Columbia has been barely tapped, hardly enough to make any impression upon these vast forests. The white pine and the yellow pine, and that most valuable species of all, the Douglas pine, are universally found on the sea coast and up to the Cascade range of mountains. Cedar and hemlock attain an enormous growth; oak, pine, poplar and maple are chiefly used for fuel. The river and the inlets of the sea coast afford unbounded water power and immense facilities for the development of a trade which must command the markets both of the Pacific sea coast and of the Eastern Ocean. [ . . . ] It would be difficult to follow Mr. Langevin through the diversity of subjects which crowd a report at once exhaustive and instructive, but the number and the character of the population, and the social status of British Columbia, demand observation. The exotic population of British Columbia, the whites and the Chinese, increased by a long-drawn process of immigration, does not exceed 15,000. It must be kept in mind that this country, the existence of which was doubted by Cook in 1778, which was only explored superficially by Vancouver in 1792, was practically unknown to civilization until 1857, and then became first known to the crews of a small British exploring squadron. The previous knowledge of the Hudson's Bay Company was limited to the quantity and quality of its peltries, and their policy ignored all further knowledge. The country was, in fact, from remoteness, inaccessible, while other countries, nearer and as attractive, were, moreover, easier of access. [ . . . ] In 1857, contemporaneous with the surveys, came the rush for gold. This discovery brought down an avalanche, which on its subsidence left a rough *moraine*; but amid the wreck remained a very large amount of building material. The work of reconstruction dates from the advent of Confederation. In the interval the country has become known and is appreciated, and the completion of the Canadian Pacific Railway will find it populous and make it wealthy. Among the relics of the wreck were left men of education and ability, of settled habits and social standing in the land from whence they came. They have given an impulse to intellectual progress, and united with the families of officials in civil life, and of officers of the British army and navy, constituting a society which embellishes and refines, and which, for elegance and geniality, is unsurpassed in any part of this Dominion. We have had, recently, in Ottawa, in the Grand Columbian Ball, an entertainment second to none ever seen in the metropolis—an evidence of the princely spirit which presides among those who represent the social element of British Columbia.

But the scarcity of labour is a great drawback to the enjoyments of society and the wants of life. So long as the white man can get $5 a day, and the Chinaman and Indian $3.50, at the gold mines, they can hardly be expected to delve for coal, or dig in gardens, at a lower figure. Seeing, too, that the female population is, in number, less than one half of the male, it will easily be understood that the ministering angel is angelic in its dispensations. They are few and far between. Female 'help' is almost unattainable, and the simple-minded man who soars above sentiment, whose tastes take a practical turn, would starve were it not for the intervention of the opportune Chinaman.

Of this class of the population Mr. Langevin speaks very favourably. The Chinese are pronounced to be thrifty, clean, docile and industrious, not popular with the whites, because they work cheaper, and are a living antidote to 'strikes'; saving of what they make and careful of what they spend, but still consumers. They travel 'first class' on steamers and stages, take their meals with others and pay for them, cook well, and make good domestic servants. We trust that under British rule they will increase and multiply and replenish the land, to the discomfiture of a generation of cooks who spoil our victuals, and of laundresses who destroy our clothes. Let the Chinaman feel that he is safe and respected; that upon British soil he becomes a British subject, with the rights, privileges and aspirations of a British subject, and we shall secure a valuable class of settlers, an invaluable aid in the construction of our great public works, and at some future day, possibly, a successor not unworthy of Mr. Pope in the Bureau of Agriculture.

The Indian problem admits of a solution more honourable to humanity in British Columbia than has been achieved in other parts of this continent. The Indian population does not exceed 35,000 souls, decreasing annually from causes almost beyond human control or cure, but not from want of food. In the Plains, the progress of civilization is fatal alike to the Indian and to the buffalo; the destruction of the one entails the destruction of the other, but the tribes which inhabit British Columbia, both the coast tribes and the tribes of the interior, are, to a great extent, supported on fish, and the supply is inexhaustible. They are all imbued with a profound respect for the British name and character. They are not averse to labour. With a strong passion for acquiring property they combine a mania for squandering it; a love of wealth and generosity of disposition, however morbid, are ductile elements of character. They form communities, and live in permanent dwellings, crowded and filthy, and rife with disease, and yet they give ear to the voice of reason and religion, and have greatly amended their ways under the teaching of missionaries, both Catholic and Protestant. The Catholic establishments 'though small and restricted as to means, have been productive of very satisfactory results'. They are conducted on the principle of 'schools industrial and agricultural; where ten children are lodged, boarded and clothed, where they acquire regular habits of order and discipline, and a taste and liking for work, receiving elementary instruction at the same time'. Their exertions among adults have also been eminently successful, but the system above devised is the true groundwork of permanent improvement.

[ . . . ] Thus speaks Chief Justice Begbie of these tribes, a witness beyond peradventure: 'The Indian admires and desires to acquire our stores of knowledge and our means of wealth. He appreciates our comforts, of clothes and food, and dwellings. But his inborn capacity for enduring hardship, the very qualities which render him useful as a hunter and a pioneer, make him tire of steady industry and less influenced by the results. Accordingly, after years of cultivation, he constantly relapses, for a time at least, into the painted savage, and goes hunting, and fishing, or starving, for relaxation'.

The Indian of the interior is not the nomadic horseman of the plains, whose vagrant habits and plundering propensities, like those of the Arab, are probably ineradicable. The tribes of the North have something of the Yorkshireman about them. They have an eye to the main chance, are good judges of horseflesh, breed horses for sale, obtain employment in 'packing' or forwarding goods and merchandise, and as 'common carriers' are perfectly trustworthy. [ . . . ]

These Indian tribes lean with implicit faith on the honour, truthfulness and superior knowledge of 'King George's men'. In their simple way they plead for protection and guidance. May the people of our great Dominion discharge this most sacred duty constantly and well. Provide tenderly for the guardianship and management of these children of the wilderness. Look upon them as wards in the Chancery of Heaven, as the greatest national trust that could be confided to the hands of men. Watch over them, instruct them, and guide them, improve and elevate them in the scale of humanity, and be assured that, as you do your duty by these helpless ones, so will God toward you.

But to enjoy as well as to admire, we must find a way. To work out the great future of British Columbia, material as well as moral, to apply its wealth, to develop its resources, we must surmount inaccessibility and remove distance. We must conquer time and space, and this has been the great object of Mr. Langevin's mission. [ . . . ]

The Canadian Pacific Railway Company had become a 'fixed fact' in public opinion and in law, long before Mr. Langevin illustrated the subject by his experiences, but the terminus of the road, on the Pacific coast, second only to the construction of the road itself; had not yet been decided upon. It is impossible to overestimate the importance of this decision, and a recent event, the award of the Emperor of Germany on the San Juan arbitration, has added to its cogency. Upon this point—the dominating idea of the whole report—Mr. Langevin has evidently bestowed grave thought, and expresses himself with becoming caution. He deals with the subject generally, both in a military and commercial aspect. He discusses the passes through the Rocky Mountains; he details, with great fairness, the claims of the different harbours of our West to outvie the olden glories of Alexandria and Venice in the East. [...]

Finally, we thank Mr. Langevin very heartily for his excellent report, faulty alone in externals. Had it been even *relié en rouge* it would have circulated better. He has brought out, in strong relief, the wealth and resources of British Columbia. He holds up to light that gem of the Pacific, Vancouver Island—a diamond, uncut but of the first water, and destined to be the brightest jewel in the diadem of this Dominion.

# HISTORICAL INTERPRETATIONS

3    From Forrest D. Pass, 'Agrarian Commonwealth or Entrepôt of the Orient? Competing Conceptions of Canada and the BC Terms of Union Debate of 1871', *Journal of the Canadian Historical Association* 17(1) (2006): 25–53.

'All hail Columbia! not least though last.' So the Rev. Aeneas McDonell Dawson opened his 1871 ode, 'British Columbia Becomes a Province of the Canadian Confederation'. Over sixty-one lines, the Ottawa Roman Catholic priest—and brother of the well-known surveyor and expansionist, Simon James Dawson—extolled British Columbia's resources and, more importantly, the position its acquisition would soon give the fledgling Dominion of Canada.[1] Dawson was not alone in waxing poetic on the riches that Canada would accrue through its annexation of British Columbia. For Dominion Day 1869, a verse in the Belleville, Ontario *Daily Intelligencer* eagerly anticipated the extension of the Dominion's borders to the Pacific, 'where the stormless waves have no angry crest / As they wash our barques to the gorgeous East'.[2] Two years later, the *Intelligencer*, the organ of North Hastings MP and Conservative cabinet minister Mackenzie Bowell, supported unequivocally the Terms of Union admitting British

Columbia to Confederation.[3] The transcontinental railway promised as one of the Terms of Union would, the paper predicted in an editorial of 1 April 1871, 'be certain to become the great artery for [the] great traffic' between China and Liverpool.[4] In extolling the value of Asiatic commerce, Dawson and the *Intelligencer* positioned themselves firmly on one side of the fierce debate over the admission of British Columbia, a debate which provides an intriguing insight into the competing conceptions of the new Canadian nation that prevailed in the years immediately following 1867.

Historians have explained satisfactorily the motivations of British Columbians in seeking federation with Canada, but the eastern Canadian parliamentary and press discussion of British Columbia's entry into Confederation has received considerably less scholarly attention.[5] The authors of the national surveys have presented the Terms of Union as a 'Made-in-BC' solution to local economic problems, a solution eagerly endorsed by an expansionist parliament.[6]

Though these historians have downplayed the significance of the debate, the proposed Terms of Union sharply divided the Canadian parliament and press. Even if, as Ormsby suggests, Canadians believed in a manifest destiny they disagreed on whether this destiny included British Columbia: the Pacific colony's admission to the union was a considerably more divisive question for Canadian parliamentarians and journalists than the purchase of Rupert's Land two years earlier, the *Manitoba Act* the previous year, or the Prince Edward Island Terms of Union two years later. Both government and opposition commentators recognized the British Columbia debate as one of the keenest fought battles in Canada's short parliamentary history.[7] The financial cost of the Terms, and of the promised railway in particular, figured prominently in the discussion, as Ormsby correctly noted. 'It wouldn't pay Canada to take many British Columbias at this price', the Orangeville, Ontario *Sun* opined, and most opponents of the Terms were inclined to agree.[8] However, it is simplistic to characterize the debate as merely a conflict between government patriotism and opposition parsimony. Rather, the debate on the Terms was so contentious because it enflamed a pre-existing ideological conflict over the source of Canada's future prosperity. For those, generally opposition Liberals or Reformers, whose conception of Canada was inspired by the agrarian ideal, distant, barren, and sparsely settled British Columbia was an expensive and unnecessary liability, and its population failed to conform to their ideal of the upstanding yeoman-citizen. On the other side were those, including Rev. Dawson and the staff of the Belleville *Intelligencer*, who saw Canada's future prosperity in its emergence as a nexus of international commerce. British Columbia, already rich in mineral wealth, was well situated to control the trade of the Pacific, and the construction of a Canadian Pacific railway would make Canada the entrepôt between Europe and the Orient. The division I posit between the commercial and agrarian camps was not perfect. Commercialist Conservatives were certainly concerned about agriculture and frequently sought to reassure the opposition that parts of British Columbia were indeed arable. For their part, Liberal agrarians asserted, often formulaically, their commitment to the eventual consummation of a transcontinental union and even to the desirability of expanding trade with Asia. Party allegiance certainly informed the final division on the Terms, but we should not dismiss partisanship as a mere antipathy between the 'ins' and the 'outs'. Rather, the parties that emerged in the decade after Confederation were themselves products of competing conceptions of Canada's economic and political future. Ben Forster in particular has emphasized the importance of the tariff question, which divided farming and business interests, in defining the political landscape of the 1870s.[9] That the debate on the Terms of Union was so acrimonious, especially when compared to the relative bi-partisanship that had typified discussions of other expansionist legislation, suggests an important role for the agrarian-commercial dichotomy generally, and the British Columbia debate specifically, in defining Canada's early two-party system. Considering the Terms of Union debate as a contest between two competing conceptions of Canada's ideal economic foundation accounts for the debate's contentiousness.

[ . . . ]

The debate on the British Columbia resolutions concerned not only the political future of a far-off colony, it also served as an opportunity for Canadians to discuss once again the nature and future of their 'new nationality'.

The circumstances and provisions of the British Columbia Terms of Union are well known to most students of British Columbian and Canadian history. In the years following the union of British Columbia and Vancouver Island in 1866, rival factions emerged favouring either federation with Canada or annexation to the United States as a means of alleviating the depopulation and economic recession that followed the Cariboo gold rush. Meanwhile in Canada, Prime Minister Macdonald lobbied the Colonial Office to replace British Columbia's anti-Confederationist Governor, Frederick Seymour, with someone more favourable to union.[10] After Seymour's sudden death at Bella Coola in June of 1869, the Colonial Office complied with Macdonald's request and dispatched Anthony Musgrave, the Governor of Newfoundland, to Victoria. Frustrated with the divisions among the colony's pro-Confederationists, Musgrave presented draft terms, as a motion of the Government, to the colony's unicameral legislature during the winter of 1870.[11] Upon the legislature's ratification, with some minor modifications, of the Governor's proposed Terms, a delegation of three under the *de facto* leadership of the colony's Commissioner of Lands and Works, Joseph Trutch, travelled to Ottawa to negotiate with the Dominion government. Macdonald's Quebec lieutenant and fellow leader of the great coalition, Sir George-Etienne Cartier, acted for the Dominion, famously offering the British Columbians a transcontinental railway when only a wagon road had been requested. The revised Terms, ratified by the colonial legislature in January 1871, included a *per capita* subsidy for the maintenance of the provincial government; representation in Parliament by six members and three senators; and, most importantly and controversially, a promise to commence construction of a transcontinental railway within two years, for completion within ten.[12] Trutch then returned to Ottawa, where British Columbia's political future now lay in the hands of Canada's parliamentarians.

Cartier introduced the address to the Queen embodying the British Columbia Terms of Union in the House of Commons on 28 March 1871.[13] For the governing party, the admission of British Columbia was simply the culmination of the road to nationhood embarked upon at Charlottetown in 1864. Cartier reminded the House that the former

Colonial Secretary, Sir Edward Bulwer Lytton, had predicted as early as 1858 that the colonies of British North America would one day form a united empire from the Atlantic to the Pacific, and he marvelled at the speed with which Lytton's prediction had been accomplished. The progress of the Dominion evoked favourable comparisons with the American experience: expansion to the Pacific had taken the Americans six decades, Cartier remarked, but Canada had accomplished it in less than ten years, indeed in less than five.[14] Canada's development ought to mirror or even overtake that of the United States, for it was the new Dominion's duty and destiny to establish a British empire in North America.[15] If a transcontinental empire was the 'ulterior object' of Confederation, as Postmaster General Alexander Campbell suggested on introducing the Terms of Union in the Senate on 3 April 1871, certainly the admission of British Columbia was integral to the success of the project.[16]

The supporters of the Terms of Union looked beyond expansion to the Pacific. Cartier's speech only briefly alluded to the purpose for which Canada should acquire a Pacific seaboard. English history, he suggested, demonstrated the 'splendid position' that could be achieved through maritime power, and access to the Pacific was critical 'if ever this Dominion was to be a powerful nation in the future'.[17] In conversation with the British Columbia delegates, Cartier had expressed his belief that Quebec, as a manufacturing centre, and British Columbia, as the inlet for the Pacific trade, would become the most important sections of the Dominion, and his Montreal organ, *La Minerve*, was quick to develop the theme of maritime commercial power.[18]

[ . . . ]

Conservative MPs and newspapers from Ontario also looked forward to Canada's emergence as the world's leading commercial power. The member for Russell County, Dr James Alexander Grant, spoke in terms very similar to *La Minerve*. Like the nations of classical antiquity and more recent commercial centres, British Columbia was destined to become the new centre of Asian trade. When he considered the geography of the Strait of Georgia basin, Grant saw a series of harbours 'set apart by a special Providence as a depot for the shipping of the East, and as an entrance to the great highway of all nations across the British American continent.'[19] The national prosperity that Oriental trade would bring was worth the price the British Columbians demanded. Equally enthused was Alexander Morris. The Inland Revenue minister and member for Lanark South had been among the earliest proponents of transcontinental Confederation. His 1858 lecture on 'The Hudson's Bay and Pacific Territories' foresaw the emergence of a 'Great Britannic Empire of the North' that would become the thoroughfare for the trade of China and Japan.[20]

For some years Maritimers had eagerly anticipated that the trade of the Orient flowing into British North America through British Columbia would flow out through Halifax and Saint John.[21] Cartier had predicted that the merchant communities of the lower provinces would make common cause with the British Columbians, and indeed many Maritime MPs and newspapers came out in favour of the British Columbia resolutions.[22] The member for the City of Saint John, former New Brunswick premier Sir Samuel Leonard Tilley, spoke to the commercial benefits for eastern Canadian ports. He argued that, unlike a railway that ended at the eastern foothills of the Rocky Mountains, as some in the opposition proposed, an interoceanic line would capture not only local but also through traffic, and this trade could only benefit the terminal cities of the St Lawrence and the Atlantic seaboard.[23] [ . . . ] Maritime newspapers sympathetic to the federal ministry also saw the Canadian national destiny in global terms. 'We have entered upon an era of great public works', predicted the Halifax *Daily Reporter*, 'all tending to give British North America its true

position in the British Empire as the great central link uniting the three Islands that constitute the "Motherland" with those great dependencies of India, Australasia and New Zealand and forming the great highway over which traffic and travel to and from these dependencies shall pass by the shortest and speediest route'.[24]

[ . . . ]

Cartier himself linked the admission of British Columbia with the national aspirations of French Canada in a speech at a banquet for Joseph Trutch.[25] One Anglophone paper melded *La Minerve*'s French Canadian interpretation with the British imperialist view. According to the *Ottawa Times*, the railway was a significant imperial concern, insofar as it would strengthen Great Britain's military and commercial position in the Pacific. However, in recounting Cartier's speech at Trutch's banquet, the paper deemed it noteworthy that the opening of a western route to Asia would be the work of a 'lineal descendant' of Jacques Cartier, who had also sought 'Oriental splendour' up the St Lawrence.[26] In the centuries-old quest for the Northwest Passage, the commercialists found common ground for French and English Canadians.

*La Minerve*'s appeals to see the admission of British Columbia as the culmination of a long history of Canadian progress were not, of course, shared by all French Canadian commentators. A rival Montreal paper, *Le Franc-Parleur*, argued that in considering only the commercial side of the Terms, the government would increase the national debt and thus compromise Canada's future.[27] In the House of Commons, the most vocal French Canadian opponent of the Terms of Union was Henri-Gustave Joly de Lotbinière, ironically the man Wilfrid Laurier would later appoint as British Columbia's Lieutenant-Governor. Ever fond of illustrating his contentions with the fables of Lafontaine, Joly compared the Canadian expansionists with the frog who, aspiring to be as large as an ox, inhaled air until he exploded.[28] He ridiculed in particular the notion that Canada might become a highway to Asia. 'It was very fortunate', he observed sarcastically, '[that] the Pacific made a boundary to the land to be annexed, although it was true [that] China and Japan were beyond, and perhaps the Pacific might yet be made a Canadian sea'.[29]

Joly was joined by English Canadians in dismissing the notion of a Canadian empire built on commerce. The Toronto *Globe* acknowledged that Canadians were interested in Eastern trade and were therefore willing to offer prudent and economical inducements to British Columbia.[30] Others in the English Canadian opposition were less charitable. For Montreal Centre MP Thomas Workman, the notion that merchants would send Oriental goods over the Pacific Railway was ridiculous because long distance travel by rail would damage fragile items.[31] William Miller might profess that Canadian expansionism had goals more just and more noble than mere self-aggrandizement, but both Thomas Workman and Ontario Senator William McMaster saw in the resolutions and the speeches of their proponents a 'spread-eagleism' more characteristic of American than Canadian nationalism.[32] [ . . . ] In Loyalist Ontario, no comment against a policy could be so damning as the suggestion that it reeked of Americanism.

Opponents of the Terms argued that the ministry's American precedents were not apt because British Columbia and the American West were at different stages of development. Senator David Wark of New Brunswick observed that there was already a substantial population and a rich economy in California before the Americans contemplated a railway.[33] To the opposition, British Columbia lacked a critical feature necessary for nation-building, namely the presence of, or even the potential to attract, a significant and permanent population. The mining colony's population was composed largely of transient sojourners, who rarely stayed long in one location and felt no compunction against quitting British Columbia when the mines

ceased to be profitable. For Canadians, as for others, mining was a valuable pursuit insofar as it garnered attention for new fields for colonization, but it was not in itself a viable economic foundation for a new nation.[34] A railway intended to carry through-traffic was a purely speculative venture and no more a suitable basis for national stability than gold mining. Agriculture alone was the basis for lasting prosperity. The Canada the opposition envisioned was a nation of thrifty yeoman farmers, with a fiscally prudent legislature constituted strictly upon the principle of representation by population to protect them from the excesses of corrupt ministers and monopolistic corporations. [ . . . ]

The alleged agricultural sterility of British Columbia underpinned much of the opposition to the Terms of Union, and the proponents of the resolutions worked vigorously to refute it. Although the commercialists had presented the British American West as a 'passage to India', they also subscribed to the second great myth of the west, the myth of the 'Garden of the World'.[35] Lacking personal experience of the colony, politicians on both sides of the floor drew on anecdotal and published sources for their information about the colony's productivity. On the basis of Trutch's reports, Alexander Morris stated that British Columbia encompassed almost as much agricultural land as Ontario.[36] Others sidestepped the issue of British Columbia's fertility to emphasize its other resources. Cartier himself in introducing the resolutions suggested that the land offered to the railway company would be 'not merely agricultural land, but mineral land', and *Le Journal des Trois-Rivières* noted the colony's mineral and timber wealth, citing Trutch as its source.[37] [ . . . ] Senator James Ferrier of Quebec drew attention to the colony's mines and fisheries, while William Miller, acknowledging the 'uneven ground', spoke of rich supplies of coal and timber, as well as the prospect of a thriving trade in fish between British Columbia and Catholic South America.[38] In addition to its strategic importance for the Pacific trade, the commercialists saw in British Columbia the resources necessary for diverse economic pursuits, including agriculture.

For the opposition, however, the lack of agriculture loomed large. In addition to trade statistics printed in the sessional papers, opponents of the Terms drew, albeit selectively, on the reports of Canadians who had first-hand knowledge of the far West. David Christie related to the Senate his recent personal conversation with Malcolm Cameron, the Sarnia politician and newspaperman who had visited the Pacific colonies in 1862. Cameron's initial reports from British Columbia to eastern newspapers had been favourable, emphasizing the colony's mineral wealth and dismissing Canadians who had returned home prematurely and now denigrated British Columbia's resources as 'not worthy sons of the men who made Canada'.[39] Indeed, like the Macdonald-Cartier government six years later, Cameron predicted in an 1865 speech that political unification of British North America would make Canada the great commercial emporium of the world.[40] However, as Christie emphasized, Cameron had been only lukewarm in his assessment of the colony's agricultural potential. [ . . . ]

To the opponents of the Terms of Union, the government's suggestions that British Columbia would attract settlers, and consequently that sales of land in the province could finance railway construction, were absurd. 'If you could not derive a revenue from the fertile lands [of Ontario and Quebec], how could you expect to do so from this miserable region of the West?' inquired Senator Benjamin Seymour. Timothy Warren Anglin, member for Gloucester County, New Brunswick, made much the same point, asking why settlers who would not take lands in Ontario would choose to settle in a 'sea of mountains' where 'it would be difficult to find those vast tracts of fertile country spoken of by Hon. Members opposite'.[41] In Anglin's view, perpetual landslides and avalanches would frustrate efforts to construct railways and farms in British Columbia's 'sterile mountains' and gloomy canyons.[42] For Quebec nationalists Antoine-Aimé Dorion and Luc Letellier de St Just, the money necessary to build 'a railway in a barren and mountainous country' would be better spent to improve transportation networks in the proven agricultural districts of the St Lawrence Basin.[43] Without an agricultural base, critics of the Terms of Union feared British Columbia would never enjoy significant population growth.

The small size of the present and projected population of British Columbia was a significant concern for opponents of the Terms. The resolutions estimated British Columbia's population at 60,000 for the purposes of determining its per capita subsidy and parliamentary representation, and, accordingly, granted the province six members in the House of Commons. However, if British Columbia did have a population of 60,000, even by the most generous estimates only one quarter of that population was white, the rest comprising Aboriginal peoples and Chinese.[44] The British Columbia government was most concerned about the population estimate as it affected the subsidy.[45] The Canadian press and parliament, however, were most concerned about the apparent violation of the principle of representation by population. To Ontarians in particular, the constitutional violation, which followed a dangerous precedent established by the *Manitoba Act* the previous year, threatened to reignite sectional hostility.[46] The Goderich *Huron Signal* calculated that British Columbia would have one member of parliament for every 2,000 white citizens, while Ontario had but one member for every 20,000 citizens.[47] In his memoirs, Richard Cartwright, the member for Lennox, speculated that in admitting British Columbia the ministry had sought to compensate for projected electoral losses in the East with new, safely Conservative seats in the far West.[48] In Parliament, member after member rose to challenge the representation formula.[49] [ . . . ]

For the opposition, permanent landed settlement, almost certainly agricultural, was the only basis for political participation. In their view, agriculture determined not only the size but also the moral quality of a population.[50] Governor Musgrave himself gave the opposition ample evidence that the nature of British Columbia's economy indeed produced moral degradation. 'The white inhabitants', Musgrave had written to Governor-General Young, 'are chiefly male adults of wasteful and expensive habits', and the Canadian opposition seized upon this characterization.[51] A people so un-Canadian in their morality were only fit for an un-Canadian form of government. Senator Sanborn thought it humiliating that 'a country like [Canada], enjoying responsible Government and representative institutions for many years—with a superior system of colleges and schools, with a territory and resources in a high stage of development', should have terms dictated to it by a despotism such as British Columbia.[52] For those opponents of the Terms who did accept the principle of extending the Dominion's boundaries to the Pacific, the American model of territorial administration was preferable, both economically and politically, to the admission of full provinces in the West. Inexpensive to administer and represented only by a nonvoting delegate, territories were only admitted to statehood when they reached a certain population threshold and a concomitant level of infrastructure development and political maturity.[53]

If the opposition saw the white population as degraded by their economic circumstances, they were even more indignant at the suggestion that Aboriginal peoples be included in the population for the purpose of calculating subsidies and parliamentary representation. This was further evidence of the government's intention to undermine representation by population; why else, the opponents wondered, should British Columbia's Indians be included in the population estimates if Ontario's were not?[54]

Musgrave acknowledged that the population included 'a large number of Indians', but he also noted that they were consumers.[55] If one accepted his contention that contribution to revenue was an appropriate basis for representation, and if the Aboriginal population participated in a taxable market economy, then there was, ironically enough, no contradiction in including Aboriginal peoples in the representation formula. The opposition, however, mocked the government's presentation of the Aboriginal population. Senator Christie suggested instead that the Indians in question were 'perfectly worthless', and, according to Arthur Harvey's *Statistical Account of British Columbia*, contributed nothing to the labour force.[56] The most damning assessment of British Columbia's racial composition came, however, from the Halifax *Morning Chronicle*, which warned that 'the "fellow countrymen" we would meet at the end of the [Pacific railway] would be mostly Digger Indians and "Heathen Chinees"'.[57] While the prospect of having 'heathen Chinees' as compatriots was probably offensive enough to white Canadian sensibilities, the American term 'Digger Indian' connoted all that was undesirable about the indigenous peoples of the Pacific Slope.[58] Lazy, dirty, and simian to the settler's eye, the Digger Indians of California were seen as the lowest, most degraded form of humanity, much lower in the hierarchy of races than the First Nations to the east of the continental divide.[59] In California, the degradation of the Digger Indian justified expansion and dispossession. For Canadian opponents of the British Columbia Terms of Union, the presence of degraded western Aboriginal peoples, combined with the lax mores of the settler population and the sterility of the soil to present British Columbia as quintessentially un-Canadian space.

[ . . . ] Increasing the size of the union could only increase the scope for government patronage, and indeed the opposition contended that this had been the cynical aim of Confederation in the first place. 'Injurious as has been the effect of Confederation to the best interests of this province', opined the *Canadian Gleaner*, 'it has yielded rich fruits to Cartier and his colleagues. It has enriched and aggrandized them in every way. They look for greater results from this admission of British Columbia'.[60] After all, the paper predicted, the Pacific Railway would provide considerably more opportunities for corruption than the Intercolonial Railway, a remarkably prescient observation considering the scandal that would sweep the government from office two years later. [ . . . ]

The opposition was particularly concerned that the principal beneficiaries of the government's new railway patronage would be large private interests. Fear of corporate capitalism had been a strong feature of pre-Confederation reform ideology, as Allan Greer has demonstrated, and the prospect of a privately constructed but state-subsidized transcontinental railway rejuvenated these concerns.[61] Where the proponents of the union and of the railway saw the fulfillment of the dream of the Northwest Passage, the opposition remembered a previous gamble on the value of Pacific trade, the South Sea Bubble of 1720, in which rampant speculation had ruined many an investor.[62] Now the investor that faced ruin was the State. Numerous politicians and newspapers feared that cost overruns in the construction of the Pacific railway would drive the Dominion to bankruptcy. Aside from the ministers who would profit from patronage, the only beneficiaries of the railway speculation would be large capitalists, who would receive substantial land grants to finance the project. The government presented the proposed land grants as a means of financing railway construction without spending public funds, but the opposition saw it as a massive giveaway of public property to private interests. [ . . . ] The anti-corporate sentiment that inspired opposition to the railway scheme, also led the leader of the opposition to dismiss the economic attractions of British

Columbia. 'The gold mines have certainly proved remunerative', granted Alexander Mackenzie, 'but they are carried on by large companies', so presumably little of the wealth they produced went to the ordinary miner.[63] The virtuous Ontario yeoman who settled in British Columbia, unable to draw a living from the land, could only hope to become the degraded wage slave of a mining conglomerate.

The opposition's arguments failed ultimately to influence the will of Parliament. The division in the Commons was 91 in favour (56.9 per cent) to 69 opposed, while in the Senate the resolutions were passed by a slightly larger margin of 36 (63.2 per cent) to 21. [ . . . ]

The commercialists' conception of Canada carried the day, and British Columbia was admitted to Confederation with the hope that the barques of 'the gorgeous East' would soon ply the province's harbours and the transhipment of their wares would enrich the entire nation. [ . . . ]

The parliamentary and press debates on the British Columbia Terms of Union were about much more than the future of British Columbia. For the government and its supporters, swift extension of the Dominion's boundaries to the Pacific promised to make the new country the centre of international commerce, with the Canadian Pacific Railway cutting thousands of miles off the voyage between Asian and European ports. For the opposition, however, the extravagant promises made to secure the admission of a barren, under-populated colony threatened Canada's future as a nation of virtuous, self-governing yeoman farmers. Thus, Canadian politicians used the proposed admission of British Columbia as an opportunity to rearticulate their visions of Canada's future, and in its ideological underpinnings the Terms of Union debate represents a continuity from earlier discussions on British North American union, and a foreshadowing of discussions yet to come. This analysis of the Terms of Union discussions suggests we must expand our definition of what constitutes the 'Confederation Debates' to include the parliamentary discussions about the admission of the latecomer provinces, for it is in the significances Canadians attached to territorial expansion that their aspirations and anxieties concerning their new nation were most evident. Pitting the opposition's conception of Canada as an agrarian commonwealth against the government's dream of becoming the entrepôt of the Orient, the debate on the admission of British Columbia clearly demonstrated that, in the first years of Confederation, a longstanding conflict over Canada's character and future remained unresolved.

# NOTES

1. Aeneas McDonell Dawson, 'British Columbia Becomes a Province of the Canadian Confederation', in his *The North-west Territories and British Columbia* (Ottawa: C.W. Mitchell, 1881), 218; Doug Owram, *Promise of Eden: The Canadian Expansionist Movement and the Idea of the West, 1856–1900* (Toronto: University of Toronto Press, 1980), 39.

2. 'Land of the Maple Leaf', *Daily Intelligencer* (Belleville) (3 July 1869), 4, col. 1.

3. P.B. Waite, 'Sir Mackenzie Bowell', *Dictionary of Canadian Biography*, www.biographi.ca/EN/ShowBio.asp?BioId=41353.htm, (viewed 16 January 2007).

4. 'Admission of British Columbia', *Daily Intelligencer* (1 April 1871), 2, col. 2–3.

5. Margaret Ormsby, *British Columbia: A History* (Toronto: Macmillan, 1958), 245–9, 257; Jean Barman, *The West Beyond the West* (Toronto: University of Toronto Press, 1996), 96; Patricia Roy and John Herd Thompson, *British Columbia: Land of Promises* (Don Mills: Oxford University Press, 2005), 49–50.

6. Arthur Lower, *Colony to Nation: A History of Canada*, 4th rev. edn (Don Mills: Longmans, 1964), 361; W.L. Morton, *The Kingdom of Canada: A General History from Earliest Times*, 2nd edn (Toronto: McClelland & Stewart, 1969), 338; Desmond Morton, *A Short History of Canada*, 5th edn (Toronto: McClelland & Stewart, 2001), 104–5.

7. Alexander Morris to Sir John A. Macdonald, 1 April 1871, cited in Donald Grant Creighton, *John A. Macdonald*, vol. 2 (Toronto: Macmillan, 1955), 105; 'The British Columbia Resolutions', *Perth Courier* (7 April 1871), 2, col. 3.

8. 'The Resolutions to Admit British Columbia . . . ' *Sun* (Orangeville) (6 April 1871), 2, col. 1.

9. Ben Forster, *A Conjunction of Interests: Business, Politics, and Tariffs, 1825–1879* (Toronto: University of Toronto Press, 1986), 147–64.

10. Public Record Office (hereafter PRO), CO 537, Colonial Office Secret Supplementary Correspondence, 1832–1922, /100, no. 204, John A. Macdonald to Sir John Young, 23 May 1869.

11. PRO, CO 60, British Columbia, Original Correspondence, 1858–1871, /38, no. 11, Anthony Musgrave to Sir John Young, 20 February 1870.

12. *Terms of Union, 1871* (Victoria, BC: Queen's Printer, 1981).

13. Macdonald was in Washington as part of the British delegation negotiating a new fisheries treaty with the Americans. The absence of references in his papers suggests that he had little involvement in the British Columbia debate.

14. Canada. House of Commons, *Debates of the House of Commons, 1871* (Ottawa: Queen's Printer, 1871), 663.

15. See, for example, the speeches of Col. John Hamilton Gray, Hector-Louis Langevin, and William Miller. Canada. House of Commons, *Debates, 1871,* 692, 700; Canada. Senate, *Debates, 1871,* 179.

16. Canada. Senate, *Debates, 1871,* 151–2.

17. Canada. House of Commons, *Debates, 1871,* 663.

18. Quoted in John Sebastian Helmcken, Dorothy Blakey Smith, ed., *The Reminiscences of Doctor John Sebastian Helmcken* (Vancouver: University of British Columbia Press, 1975), 358; 'La Colombie et le chemin du Pacifique', *La Minerve* (Montreal) (29 March 1871), 2, col. 2–5.

19. Canada. House of Commons, *Debates, 1871,* 675.

20. Alexander Morris, *Nova Britannia: or Our New Canadian Dominion Foreshadowed* (Toronto: Hunter, Rose and Co., 1884), 88.

21. T.T. Vernon Smith, *The Pacific Railway, and the Claims of Saint John, New Brunswick, to Be the Atlantic Terminus Read before the Mechanics' Institute of Saint John, February 7, 1859* (Saint John: W.L. Avery, 1859), 19–20, 28–9.

22. Quoted in Helmcken, *Reminiscences*, 358.

23. Canada. House of Commons, *Debates, 1871*, 668, 671.

24. 'Marching On', *Daily Reporter and Times* (Halifax) (1 April 1871), 2, col. 1.

25. *British Columbia and the Pacific Railway, Complimentary Dinner to the Hon. Mr. Trutch, Surveyor-General of British Columbia, Given at the Russell House, Ottawa, on Monday, 10th April, 1871* (Montreal: Gazette, 1871), 4.

26. '"The Star of Empire Glitters in the West"', *Times* (Ottawa) (13 April 1871), 2, col. 1–2.

27. Adolphe Ouimet, 'La Colombie Anglaise et le chemin defer du Pacifique', *Le Franc-Parleur* (Montreal) (6 April 1871), 314–16.

28. Canada. House of Commons, *Debates, 1871*, 696; Janet Azjenstat, et al., eds., *Canada's Founding Debates* (Toronto: Stoddart, 1999), 138–9; 'British Columbia', *Owen Sound Advertiser* (6 April 1871), 2, col. 2; 'An Outrageous Proposition', *Norfolk Reformer* (Simcoe) (6 April 1871), 2, col. 1; 'The Dominion Parliament', *Weekly Dispatch* (St Thomas) (6 Apr 1871), 2, col. 1–2.

29. Canada. House of Commons, *Debates, 1871*, 696.

30. 'The British Columbia Resolutions', *Globe* (Toronto) (30 March 1871), 2, col. 1.

31. Canada. House of Commons, *Debates, 1871*, 723.

32. Canada. House of Commons, *Debates, 1871*, 723; Canada. Senate, *Debates, 1871*, 247.

33. Canada. Senate, *Debates, 1871*, 224.

34. 'An English Gentleman . . .', *Globe* (Toronto) (5 September 1865), 2, col. 2–3.

35. John Logan Allen, *Passage through the Garden: Lewis and Clark and the Image of the American Northwest* (Urbana, IL: University of Illinois Press, 1975); Henry Nash Smith, *Virgin Land: The American West as Symbol and Myth*, Reissue edn (Cambridge: Harvard University Press, 1978); Doug Owram, Promise of Eden.

36. Canada. House of Commons, *Debates, 1871*, 714.

37. Canada. House of Commons, *Debates, 1871*, 662; 'Parmi les mesures ...', *Le Journal des Trois-Rivières* (17 April 1871), 2, col. 2.

38. Canada. Senate, *Debates, 1871*, 172–3, 227.

39. Quoted in 'Hon. M. Cameron on British Columbia', *Globe* (Toronto) (14 November 1862), 2, col. 2.

40. Malcolm Cameron, *Lecture Delivered by the Hon. Malcolm Cameron to the Young Men's Mutual Improvement Association, the Lord Bishop of the Diocese in the Chair* (Montreal: G.E. Desbarats, 1865), 21.

41. Canada. House of Commons, *Debates, 1871*, 718, 720.

42. This characterization of British Columbia's geography does not appear in the official record of the Commons debate but it does appear in at least one press account of Anglin's speech. See 'The Dominion Parliament', *Weekly Dispatch* (St Thomas) (4 April 1871), 2, col. 1–2.

43. Canada. Senate, *Debates, 1871*, 165; Canada. House of Commons, *Debates, 1871*, 729.

44. Several estimates of the white population were posited, ranging from 10,000 to 17,000. Canada. House of Commons, *Debates, 1871*, 665, 696, 718,729.

45. Helmcken, *Reminiscences*, 348–9; British Columbia Archives, GR-0441, Premier's Papers, Box 4, File 4, Item 579/96, Alexander Begg to Premier John Herbert Turner, 26 October 1896.

46. 'A Hundred Million Dollars, and a Hundred Million More', *Huron Signal* (Goderich) (6 April 1871), 2, col. 1.

47. Richard J. Cartwright, *Reminiscences* (Toronto: W. Briggs, 1912), 94.

48. Canada. House of Commons, *Debates, 1871*, 666, 672, 680, 698, 702, 727; Canada. Senate, *Debates, 1871*, 164, 250, 257.

49. PRO, CO 60, /38, no. 20, Musgrave to Granville, 23 February 1870.

50. Adele Perry, *On the Edge of Empire: Gender, Race, and the Making of British Columbia, 1849–1871* (Toronto: University of Toronto Press, 2001), 3–19.

51. PRO, CO 60, /38, no. 11, Musgrave to Young, 20 February 1870.

52. Canada. Senate, *Debates, 1871*, 184.

53. Canada. House of Commons, *Debates, 1871*, 666; Canada. Senate, *Debates, 1871*, 251–2.

54. Canada. House of Commons, *Debates, 1871*, 672, 698.

55. PRO, CO 60, /38, no. 11, Musgrave to Young, 20 February 1870.

56. Canada. Senate, *Debates, 1871,* 252; Arthur Harvey, *Statistical Account of British Columbia* (Ottawa: G.E. Desbarats, 1867), 9.

57. 'British Columbia', *Morning Chronicle* (Halifax) (3 April 1871), 2, col. 1.

58. Allan Lönnberg, 'The Digger Indian Stereotype in California', *Journal of California and Great Basin Anthropology* 3, no. 2 (1981): 215–6.

59. Ibid., 219; William Penn Adair, 'The Indian Territory in 1878', *Chronicles of Oklahoma* 4, no. 3 (1926): 258–9.

60. 'The Admission of British Columbia', *Canadian Gleaner* (Huntingdon) (6 April 1871), 2, col. 5–6.

61. Allan Greer, 'Historical Roots of Canadian Democracy', *Journal of Canadian Studies* 34, no. 1 (Spring 1999): 18–22.

62. Canada. Senate, *Debates, 1871,* 166.

63. Canada. House of Commons, *Debates, 1871,* 672.

4    From Peter H. Russell, 'Provincial Rights', *Constitutional Odyssey: Can Canadians Become a Sovereign People?* (Toronto: University of Toronto Press, 2004), 34–52.

The great conceit of constitution-makers is to believe that the words they put in the constitution can with certainty and precision control a country's future. The great conceit of those who apply a written constitution is to believe that their interpretation captures perfectly the founders' intentions. Those who write constitutions are rarely single-minded in their long-term aspirations. They harbour conflicting hopes and fears about the constitution's evolution. The language of the constitution is inescapably general and latent with ambiguous possibilities. Written constitutions can establish the broad grooves in which a nation-state develops. But what happens within those grooves—the constitutional tilt favoured by history—is determined not by the constitutional text but by the political forces and events that shape the country's subsequent history.

Canada's constitutional development in the decades immediately following Confederation is a monument to the truth of these propositions. Although a majority of the Fathers of Confederation favoured a highly centralized federation, it soon became apparent that their aspirations would not be fulfilled. Instead, the most effective constitutional force in the new federation was the provincial rights movement.

Far from moving towards a unitary state, Canada, by the end of the nineteenth century, had become a thoroughly federal country.

One might have expected the stiffest challenge to Macdonald's centralism to have come from Nova Scotia or Quebec. Nova Scotians, as we have seen, voted against Confederation in the provincial and federal elections of 1867. Immediately following Confederation a significant secessionist movement was developing in the province.[1] In 1868 Joseph Howe led a delegation to London seeking a repeal of the union. Nova Scotian opposition to Confederation, however, was not based on a desire for stronger provincial powers. In the end, Nova Scotian separatism was quelled by persuading Howe to join the federal cabinet and by offering Nova Scotia better terms, not through a constitutional amendment but by bringing its debt allowance into line with New Brunswick's.

From the very beginning, the Province of Quebec, in the words of A.I. Silver, 'was seen as the geographical and political expression of the French-Canadian nationality, as a French-Catholic province and the French-Canadian homeland'.[2] It was not just the *rouge* opponents of Confederation who championed the cause of provincial autonomy and resisted federal interference in provincial affairs. The *Bleus* had promoted Confederation in Quebec largely on the grounds that it would give the French majority in Quebec exclusive control over matters basic to their culture. A *bleu* paper in 1872, for example, claimed that 'as Conservatives we must be in favour of provincial rights and against centralization'.[3]

It was not Quebec but Ontario that spearheaded the provincial rights movement. Ontario would seem the least likely province to play this role. After all, support for Confederation had been stronger in Ontario than in any other province. With the largest and fastest-growing population, Ontario was expected to be able to dominate national politics. Why at this formative stage in the federation's history should its provincial government be in the vanguard of the provincial rights movement?

The answer is to be found in the pattern of partisan politics that developed soon after Confederation and has endured ever since. Even before Confederation, the Great Coalition of Conservatives and Reformers had broken up. The first federal government after Confederation was headed by the Conservative leader John A. Macdonald. As Ontario Reformers and Quebec Liberals began to organize a competing national party, they naturally took up the provincial cause. In the words of Christopher Armstrong, 'If Macdonald's Conservatives were the party of centralism, then its opponents would become the party of localism and provincialism, recruiting the anti-Confederates of the Maritimes to the Reform cause'.[4]

The Conservatives dominated the first 30 years of federal politics, holding office in Ottawa for all but four of those years. During that same period the Liberals were having their greatest success at the provincial level. Nowhere was this more true than in Ontario, where Oliver Mowat's Liberals won six successive elections between 1875 and 1896. While Mowat found Liberal allies in other provincial capitals, notably Quebec's Honoré Mercier, he was in office the longest and built the strongest record of provincial rights advocacy. Mowat's championing of this cause is remarkable in that he began his professional career as a junior in John A. Macdonald's law office, was a Father of Confederation, and had moved the Quebec Resolutions setting forth the division of powers between the two levels of government.[5]

The pattern of politics in which one party dominates at the federal level while its main opposition gathers strength in the provincial capitals has been repeated several times in Canadian history. For a long stretch of the twentieth century the Liberals dominated the federal scene while the Conservatives and other opposition parties won in the provinces. The reverse has been developing since the Mulroney Conservatives came to power in Ottawa in 1984. The fact that the largest national parties have gone through long periods in which their experience in government has been concentrated at the provincial level has done much to make provincial rights a cause that transcends partisan politics.

Although this phenomenon is one that stems from the fluctuating fortunes of partisan politics, it is closely tied to the Canadian system of parliamentary government. Responsible government tends to concentrate power in the hands of the prime minister and the cabinet. After Confederation it soon became apparent that this concentration of power would occur in the provincial capitals as well as in Ottawa. In Canada, provincial premiers emerged as the strongest political opponents to the federal prime minister. State governors in the United States, hemmed in by an elaborate system of checks and balances, are political pygmies compared with provincial premiers who perform as political giants on the national stage. Canadians, without any conscious design, found their liberal check and balance not *within* the national or provincial capitals but in the rivalry and tensions *between* those capitals.

The success of the provincial rights movement cannot be attributed to weak governments at the national level in Canada's formative years. Quite to the contrary, federal administrations presided over by John A. Macdonald, who was prime minister of Canada for 19 of the country's first 24 years, were strong nation-building governments not at all shy about asserting federal power. Under Macdonald's leadership, Canada's 'manifest destiny' of becoming a continental nation-state was quickly fulfilled. In 1869 the Hudson's Bay Company's territories covering the prairies and the far north were purchased and added to Canada. A year later, following military suppression of the Métis led by Louis Riel, the Province of Manitoba was carved out of the North-West Territories. In 1871 Canada was extended to the Pacific, when British Columbia became a province on terms agreeable to its colonial government. Prince Edward Island became the seventh province, agreeing to join Confederation in 1873. To this expanding national territory Macdonald's Conservatives applied a National Policy, completing the transcontinental rail link, erecting tariff walls to protect manufacturing, and stimulating immigration to populate the west and provide a market for the protected industries.[6]

Important as the achievements of Macdonald's governments were in building the material conditions of nationhood, they contributed little to a Canadian sense of political community. Nor did they translate into constitutional gains for the federal government. The Conservatives' economic nationalism, as Reg Whitaker has observed, relied 'on elites and on their exclusively economic motives'.[7] It did not have much emotional appeal at the mass level. Government in far-away Ottawa had difficulty competing with provincial governments for the allegiance of citizens in the new provinces. During these years it was the provinces, not Ottawa, that seized and held the initiative in constitutional politics.

The first objective of the provincial rights movement was to resist and overcome a hierarchical version of Canadian federalism in which the provinces were to be treated as a subordinate or junior level of government. An early focal point of resistance was the office of provincial lieutenant-governor. From a Macdonald centralist perspective, the lieutenant-governors were essentially agents of the federal government in provincial capitals. In the 1870s, however, Ontario, under Mowat's leadership, began to insist that lieutenant-governors had full Crown powers in matters of provincial jurisdiction and that they exercised these powers on the advice of provincial ministers. [ . . . ] Implicit in the provincial claim was an assertion of the provinces' constitutional equality with the federal government.

No element of the Constitution was potentially more threatening to provincial autonomy than the federal powers of reservation and disallowance. These powers derived from an imperial rather than a federal structure. Under the reservation power, the lieutenant-governor of a province could refuse to sign a bill that had passed through the provincial legislature and could reserve it for consideration by the federal cabinet. If, within a year, the lieutenant-governor was not instructed to give royal assent, the bill would die. Disallowance was simply a veto power under which the federal government could render null and void any provincial law within a year of its passage by the provincial legislature. These federal powers mirrored powers of reservation and disallowance over federal legislation that the imperial government retained and that were also written into the BNA Act.[8] The only difference was that the British government had two years rather than one to decide whether to block Canadian legislation.

The powers of reservation and disallowance are classic examples of how a shift in political sentiment and principle can render formal legal powers unusable. Well before Confederation, the British government had greatly reduced the use of its imperial powers of control over the British North American legislatures. Soon after Confederation these powers fell into desuetude. In the first decade a few Canadian bills were reserved, but royal assent was always granted and there were no reservations after 1878. Only one Canadian act was disallowed, in 1873, and the act in question was clearly unconstitutional.[9] At imperial conferences in the late 1920s declarations were made that these imperial powers would never be used and that steps would be taken to remove them from Canada's Constitution. Although the latter step was never taken, no one really cares that the powers remain formally in the Constitution because there is a clear political understanding—a constitutional convention—on both the British and Canadian sides that the powers are completely inoperative.[10] This convention of desuetude was established because use of the imperial powers was incompatible with the principle of Canadian self-government, a principle which, at least in matters of domestic policy, was so firmly in place by the 1870s that breach of it would have had the gravest political consequences.

A similar process occurred with respect to the federal government's powers of reservation and disallowance. Over time, the principle of provincial autonomy—self-government in those areas constitutionally assigned to the provincial legislatures—became so strongly held in the Canadian political system that the federal powers of reservation and disallowance, though remaining in the Constitution, became politically unusable. This did not happen all at once. It occurred only because the idea that the provinces are not subordinate to but coordinate with the federal government became the politically dominant conception of Canadian federalism.

At first federal governments—not only Macdonald's but the Liberals too when they were in power in the 1870s—made extensive use of the powers of reservation and disallowance.[11] Macdonald's first administration withheld assent on 16 of 24 provincial bills reserved by lieutenant-governors. Between 1867 and 1896, 65 provincial acts were disallowed by the federal government. Although the powers continued to be used, they came under increasing attack from the provinces, and from no province more than Ontario. Even when, as was most often the case, the rationale for using these powers was the federal government's view that the legislation was outside the province's jurisdiction, provincial rights advocates were inclined to argue that questions concerning the division of powers should be settled in the courts, not by the federal cabinet. When the Macdonald government in 1881 disallowed Ontario's Rivers and Streams Act primarily to protect the interests of a prominent Conservative, Mowat decided to fight back. He promptly had the legislation re-enacted. After being disallowed and re-enacted three more times, the legislation was allowed to stand. The courts had the final say when the Judicial Committee of the Privy Council upheld the provincial law in 1884.[12]

Abolition of the federal disallowance power topped the list of constitutional proposals emanating from the Interprovincial Conference of 1887. The conference was called by Honoré Mercier, premier of Quebec, who had come to power largely on the strength of Quebec's resentment of the use of federal power in the hanging of Louis Riel. Macdonald and the Conservative premiers of British Columbia and Prince Edward Island declined Mercier's invitation. Delegates from the Liberal governments of the four original provinces and from Manitoba's Conservative administration, 'angered by repeated disallowances of their railway legislation',[13] met for a week under Mowat's chairmanship behind closed doors. The 22 resolutions that they unanimously endorsed amounted to a frontal attack on the centralist conception of Confederation. Besides calling for the abolition of federal disallowance and an increase in federal subsidies, the conference proposed that half of the federal Senate be chosen by the provinces. Once these proposals had been approved by the provincial legislatures, they were to be submitted to London for enactment as constitutional amendments by the imperial Parliament.

In the end, nothing concrete came of these proposals. Only the lower houses of New Brunswick and Nova Scotia sent them on to London. The imperial authorities refused to act without having heard from the federal government or the other provinces.[14] Nonetheless, the 1887 conference is a significant landmark in Canada's constitutional politics, for it clearly demonstrated that the constitutional initiative had passed to the provinces. Strong centralist voices could still be heard, not least John A. Macdonald's, but the centralist view was losing its ascendancy in both French and English Canada.

During the first 30 years of Confederation, the provinces made their most tangible constitutional gains not through the process of formal constitutional amendment but through litigation in the courts. Their judicial victories were achieved in London before the Judicial Committee of the Privy Council. The Supreme Court of Canada had been created by the federal Parliament in 1875, but it was supreme in name only. Although the Liberal government which had sponsored the Supreme Court Act aimed at making the court Canada's highest tribunal, the Conservative opposition and the Colonial Office were able to thwart this objective.[15] The right of appeal to the highest court in the British Empire, the Judicial Committee of the Privy Council, was retained in Canada until 1949.

Retaining the Judicial Committee as Canada's highest court had significant consequences for the development of the Canadian Constitution. [ . . . ]

It did not take long for the English law lords who manned the Judicial Committee of the Privy Council to reverse the Supreme Court's approach to the Constitution. By the 1880s a steady stream of constitutional cases was being taken on appeal to London. The fact that so many constitutional questions were coming before the courts gives the lie to the pretension of the Fathers of Confederation to have settled all questions of jurisdiction. [ . . . ]

Between 1880 and 1896 the Judicial Committee decided 18 cases involving 20 issues relating to the division of powers. Fifteen of these issues (75 per cent) it decided in favour of the provinces. What is even more important, as Murray Greenwood has observed, is that in these decisions the committee reversed 'every major centralist doctrine of the [Supreme] Court'.[16] [ . . . ]

The theory espoused by the Judicial Committee of The Privy Council is often called the theory of 'classical federalism'.[17] There can be no doubt that Macdonald and many of Canada's constitutional founders did not think of the country they were building as a classic federation. Some of the Fathers of Confederation, however, especially Quebec leaders like Cartier and Taché, were apprehensive of the centralist view and hoped that the provinces would be autonomous in the areas of law making reserved for them. The Quebec supporters of Confederation realized they could not retain their political support if they portrayed Confederation publicly in centralist terms. The political coalition that put Confederation together never came to a clear and explicit accord on federal theory.[18] What the Judicial Committee did was to give official legal sanction to a theory of federalism congenial to those who, at the time of Confederation and afterwards, could not accept centralism.

The impact of the Judicial Committee's constitutional decisions demonstrates a fundamental feature of constitutional development which is still, at most, only dimly understood by the Canadian public. In countries with written constitutions stipulating the powers of government and the rights of citizens, and in which the constitution is taken seriously, judges will play an important role in enforcing the constitution. The process through which judges play that role is called 'judicial review'. In performing the function of judicial review, judges review the acts of the executive and legislature and rule null and void those that do not conform with the constitution. Through these determinations, especially those of the highest court, the meaning of the constitution's general terms is fleshed out. This process of judicial review has been so important in the United States that it is said that 'the constitution is what the judges say it is'.[19]

The Fathers of Confederation did not discuss judicial review. Although some of them were aware of the important role the Supreme Court was playing in the United States, they did not see that there would be an immediate need for a Canadian Supreme Court.[20] Their constitutionalism was much more British than American, and hence more attuned to an unwritten constitution. They were accustomed to having the Judicial Committee of the Privy Council, as the highest imperial court, review colonial laws for their conformity with imperial law. Since the Canadian Constitution took the form of an act of the imperial Parliament, it was logical that this mechanism of imperial judicial control would apply to the BNA Act. For enforcing the rules of federalism internally, within Canada, it is evident that the Fathers of Confederation looked more to the federal executive using its powers of reservation and disallowance than to the judiciary. Also, it was to the federal executive, not the judiciary, that the BNA Act directed minorities to appeal if they believed a province had infringed their constitutional right to denominational schools.[21]

Federal government enforcement of the Constitution made sense, of course, so long as Canadian federalism was viewed primarily as a hierarchical, quasi-imperial structure in which the provinces were a junior level of government. From this perspective, the objective of constitutional enforcement was to keep the provinces from exceeding their powers. John A. Macdonald never contemplated that Canadian courts would find federal laws unconstitutional.[22] Once however, the hierarchical view of federalism began to be eclipsed by the theory of classical federalism and dual sovereignty, it was much

more logical for a judicial tribunal independent of both levels of government to exercise the primary responsibility for applying the Constitution. [ . . . ]

The success of the provincial rights movement did not mean that in terms either of governmental power or of citizens' allegiance the provincial political realm had come to surpass the federal. Laurier, after all, was a national leader whose government would pursue important initiatives in domestic and international politics. Indeed, Laurier and other Quebec leaders, by supporting the rights of French Catholics outside Quebec, were encouraging Quebecers, in the words of A.I. Silver, to look beyond 'the still-special home of Quebec' and see that 'all Canada should yet be a country for French-Canadians'.[23] Since the 1890s there have been shifts back and forth in the balance of power between the two levels of government, but there has always been a balance; neither level has been able to dominate the other. Canada's citizens have been thoroughly schizophrenic in their loyalties, maintaining strong associations with their provincial governments as well as the federal government. In this sense Canada, despite the ambiguities and contradictions in its Constitution, became, as Donald Smiley put it, 'in the most elemental way a federal country'.[24]

One measure of how ingrained the balanced view of federalism has become is the fate of those imperial powers of reservation and disallowance which the federal government held over the provinces. They are still in the Constitution, but they are simply not used any more. Disallowance has not been used since 1943. The last time a lieutenant-governor reserved a provincial bill was 1961, and then his action was totally repudiated by the federal prime minister, John Diefenbaker, as violating the basic principles of Canadian federalism.[25] When the Parti Québécois came to power in Quebec in the 1970s and enacted Bill 101, the Charter of the French Language, the Trudeau government in Ottawa, which bitterly opposed this legislation, did not ever indicate that it would disallow it. [ . . . ] By the 1980s political parties and leaders of all persuasions, like Laurier and the Liberals a century earlier, would not protect minority rights at the cost of violating provincial rights.

The sovereignty at issue in the struggle for provincial rights was not the sovereignty of the people but the sovereignty of governments and legislatures. The sovereignty claimed and won for provincial legislatures and governments within their allotted sphere of jurisdiction was primarily a top-down kind of sovereignty.[26] Canadian constitutional politics continued to be highly elitist, with federal and provincial leaders contending against each other in intergovernmental meetings and the courts. Still, traces of a more democratic constitutionalism were beginning to appear in the rhetoric, if not the reality, of the constitutional process. [ . . . ]

Out of this rhetoric and the political success of its authors was born the myth of Confederation as a compact entered into by sovereign provincial communities. According to the compact theory, the provinces as the founding, constituent units of the federation retained the right to alter the terms of their original union.[27] This was the theory promulgated by Honoré Mercier and the other provincial premiers who attended the 1887 Interprovincial Conference: 'the conference represented all of the original parties to the compact of 1864, and the partners should now assess the state of their joint enterprise'.[28] Not surprisingly, the theory found its most articulate spokesmen in Quebec, where the notion of the province as a founding community could be infused with a sense of ethnic nationalism.

What is meant in referring to the compact theory as a 'myth' is that its validity depends not on its historical accuracy but on its capacity to serve as a set of 'beliefs and notions that men hold, that they live by or live for'.[29] Confederation, as we have seen, did involve a two-stage agreement, first between English- and French-Canadian politicians and then between Canadian and Maritime politicians. Leading participants in the agreement, including John A. Macdonald and George-Etienne Cartier, as well as some of the imperial authorities, frequently referred to the Quebec Resolutions as a treaty or pact. But it is not clear that when they used this terminology they had the same thing in mind. It is most unlikely that when John A. Macdonald talked of a treaty he meant that the parties to the agreement exercised and retained sovereign political authority.

From a strictly legal point of view, the founding colonies in 1867, as colonies, did not have sovereign powers to retain. They did not formally sign or give legal authority to the Constitution. Further, given the elitist quality of the process and the failure, indeed the disinclination, to seek a clear popular mandate for the Confederation deal, it is a total fabrication to maintain that the peoples of the founding provinces had covenanted together to produce the Canadian federal union. This fabrication flies in the face of the top-down process whereby new provinces were added—especially the two provinces carved out of the North-West Territories in 1905. As Arthur Lower observed, 'there was not the slightest vestige of a "compact" in the Acts of Parliament that created the provinces of Alberta and Saskatchewan in 1905'.[30]

Nor was the compact theory strictly followed in constitutional practice. If the Canadian Constitution was a compact or treaty among the provinces, then no changes should have been made to it without the consent of all the provinces. Formally constitutional changes, as amendments to the BNA Act, were enacted by the British Parliament, but that body would act only on a request from Canada. During the period that the compact theory was gathering force, however, several amendments were made to the BNA Act at the request of the federal government and Parliament without consulting the provinces or seeking their consent. While none of these amendments directly affected the powers of the provinces, two of them related to the structure of the federation: one empowered the federal Parliament to create new provinces and the other provided for the representation of territories in the federal Parliament.[31] Prior to the 1907 amendment,[32] which revised the subsidies paid to the provinces, Laurier did hold a federal-provincial conference and eight of the nine provinces (British Columbia held out for better terms) agreed to the federal proposal. But the provinces were not consulted on the 1915 amendment that redefined the divisions of the Senate, forming a new section out of the four western provinces.[33]

Even though the compact theory was not consistently observed in the constitutional amendment process, it had become a powerful constitutional ideal by the turn of the century. Provincial rights and the compact theory had, as Ramsay Cook put it, 'attained a position close to motherhood in the scale of Canadian political values. It would be difficult to find a prominent politician who was not willing to pay lip-service to the principle of provincial rights and its theoretical underpinning, the compact theory'.[34] As a constitutional doctrine, the compact theory may have contained ambiguities and lacked precision, but its strength as a political value in Canada meant that the Canadian political community that was forming would be complex and deeply pluralist. Canada would take its place in the world as an interventionist state and its nationwide activities would take on increasing significance in the lives of its citizens, but the provinces would nonetheless endure as strong constituent elements of the Canadian community.

The ambiguities of the compact theory were intensified by the co-existence of two competing versions of the compact: a compact of founding provinces and a compact of founding peoples.[35] The latter contended that Canada was founded on the basis of a covenant between English Canadians and French Canadiens. In the final analysis, the making of Canada in 1867 was 'the free association of two peoples, enjoying equal rights in all matters'.[36] These were the words of Henri Bourassa, the theory's most eloquent spokesman and founder of the great Montreal newspaper Le Devoir in 1910. Again, the significance of this theory in Canada's constitutional politics rests not on its historical accuracy but on its potency as a political myth. It is easy to show that neither in law nor in politics was the BNA Act a formal agreement between the French and English people of British North America. Nonetheless, that constitutional settlement depended, as we have seen, on English- and French-Canadian leaders agreeing to a federal structure with a province in which the French Canadians would remain a majority. For many English Canadians, assent to this agreement was only grudgingly given; for French Canadians it represented liberation from Lord Durham's scheme to assimilate them into a unicultural English political community, the triumph of their cultural survival—and, indeed for many, of national survival. The expectations on the French side flowing from that agreement gave rise to the theory that Confederation was based on a compact between two founding peoples.[37]

As originally espoused by Bourassa and other French Canadians, the two founding peoples theory was applied to all of Canada. Indeed, it was advanced as the theoretical underpinning for a pan-Canadian nationalism that viewed all Canada in dualist terms. Its exponents defended the rights of the French minorities outside Quebec and of the English minority in Quebec. In this sense, it may have provided 'moral support for minimizing the consequences of the compact of provinces' and of provincial rights.[38] At the same time, this dualist view of Canada always retained a special place for the province of Quebec. As the homeland of one of the founding peoples, it had the right to be secure against intrusions into its culture by the general government answerable to an English-speaking majority.

Lurking within these rival compact theories were deep-seated differences on the nature of Canada as a political community. The idea that Quebec has a special place in Confederation as the only province in which one of the founding peoples forms the majority would collide with the doctrine of provincial equality. More fundamentally, the idea of a Canada based on the English and the French as its two founding peoples would be challenged at the end of the twentieth century by Canadians who were neither British nor French in their cultural background and by the Aboriginal peoples.

So long as Canadians were not interested in taking custody of their Constitution into their own hands, this conflict over the nature of Canada as a political community was of no great political importance. It was bound, however, to become salient once that condition changed. The time arrived in 1926, when the Balfour Declaration declared Canada and the other self-governing dominions to be 'autonomous Communities' within the British Commonwealth.[39] Canada's political leaders then faced the challenge of arranging for Canada to become constitutionally self-governing.

# NOTES

1. W.P.M. Kennedy, *The Constitution of Canada, 1534–1937: An Introduction to Its Development, Law and Culture*, 2nd edn (London: Oxford University Press 1938), 318–20.

2. A.I. Silver, *The French-Canadian Idea of Confederation, 1864–1900* (Toronto: University of Toronto Press 1982), 111.

3. Ibid., 121.

4. Christopher Armstrong, *The Politics of Federalism: Ontario's Relations with the Federal Government, 1867–1942* (Toronto: University of Toronto Press 1981), 14.

5. A. Margaret Evans, *Sir Oliver Mowat* (Toronto: University of Toronto Press for The Ontario Historical Studies Series 1992).

6. Craig Brown, 'The Nationalism of the National Policy', in Peter H. Russell, ed., *Nationalism in Canada* (Toronto: McGraw-Hill 1966), 155–63.

7. Reginald Whitaker, 'Democracy and the Canadian Constitution', in Keith Banting and Richard Simeon, eds., *And No One Cheered: Federalism, Democracy and the Constitutional Act* (Toronto: Methuen 1983) 250.

8. Sections 55–7.

9. R.M. Dawson, *Government of Canada* (Toronto: University of Toronto Press 1947), 142.

10. Peter W. Hogg, *Constitutional Law of Canada*, 2nd edn (Toronto: Carswell 1985), 38.

11. Gerard V. LaForest, *Disallowance and Reservation of Provincial Legislation* (Ottawa: Department of Justice 1965).

12. Paul Romney, *Mr. Attorney: The Attorney General for Ontario in Court, Cabinet and Legislature, 1791–1899* (Toronto: University of Toronto Press 1986), 255–6.

13. Armstrong, *Politics of Federalism*, 29.

14. See Paul Gérin-Lajoie, *Constitutional Amendment in Canada* (Toronto: University of Toronto Press 1950), 142–3.

15. Frank MacKinnon, 'The Establishment of the Supreme Court of Canada', *Canadian Historical Review* 27 (1946): 258–74.

16. F. Murray Greenwood, 'Lord Watson, Institutional Self-Interest and the Decentralization of Canadian Federalism in the 1890's', *University of British Columbia Law Review* 9 (1974): 267.

17. K.C. Wheare, *Federal Government*, 4th edn (London: Oxford University Press 1963).

18. P.B. Waite, *Life and Times of Confederation, 1864–1867: Politics, Newspapers, and the Union of British North America*, 2nd edn (Toronto: University of Toronto Press 1962), chap. 8.

19. A.T. Mason and W.M. Beaney, *American Constitutional Law* (Englewood Cliffs, NJ: Prentice-Hall 1959), 3.

20. Jennifer Smith, 'The Origins of Judicial Review in Canada', *Canadian Journal of Political Science* 16 (1983): 115–34.

21. Section 93(4).

22. Peter H. Russell, *The Supreme Court of Canada as a Bilingual and Bicultural Institution* (Ottawa: Queen's Printer 1969), chap. 1.

23. Silver, *French-Canadian Idea of Confederation*, 243

24. D.V. Smiley, *Canada in Question: Federalism in the Eighties*, 3rd edn (Toronto: McGraw-Hill Ryerson 1980), 1.

25. See Edwin Black, *Divided Loyalties: Canadian Concepts of Federalism* (Montreal and London: McGill-Queen's University Press 1975), 132–5.

26. Whitaker, 'Democracy and the Canadian Constitution'.

27. Ramsay Cook, *Provincial Autonomy, Minority Rights and the Compact Theory, 1867–1921* (Ottawa: Queen's Printer 1969).

28. Black, *Divided Loyalties*, 154.

29. R.M. MacIver in *The Web of Government* (New York: Macmillan 1947), 4.

30. Arthur R.M. Lower, *Colony to Nation: A History of Canada*, 4th edn (Toronto: Longmans 1964), 432.

31. Guy Favreau, *The Amendment of the Constitution of Canada* (Ottawa: Queen's Printer 1965).

32. The British North America Act of 1907.

33. The British North America Act of 1915.

34. Cook, *Provincial Autonomy*, 44.

35. Filippo Sabetti, 'The Historical Context of Constitutional Change in Canada', *Law and Contemporary Problems* 45 (1982): 11–32.

36. Quoted ibid., 21.

37. Daniel J. Elazar, 'Constitution-making: The Pre-eminently Political Act', in Keith G. Banting and Richard Simeon, eds., *Redesigning the State: The Politics of Constitutional Change in Industrial Nations*' (Toronto: University of Toronto Press 1985), 245–6.

38. Sabetti, 'Historical Context of Constitutional Changes in Canada', 20.

39. Dawson, *Government of Canada*, 63.

# Chapter 2

# Establishing a New Order

## READINGS

### Primary Documents

1   From 'An Act Respecting the Administration of Justice, and for the Establishment of a Police Force in the North West Territories', *Acts of the Parliament of the Dominion of Canada, 1873*

2   'Articles of a Treaty made and concluded near Carlton . . .' (Treaty No. 6, 1876)

### Historical Interpretations

3   From '"A Splendid Spirit of Cooperation": Churches, Police Forces, and the Department of Indian Affairs', in *Liberalism, Surveillance, and Resistance: Indigenous Communities in Western Canada*, Keith D. Smith

4   From 'Creating "Semi-Widows" and "Supernumerary Wives": Prohibiting Polygamy in Prairie Canada's Aboriginal Communities to 1900', in *Contact Zones: Aboriginal and Settler Women in Canada's Colonial Past*, Sarah A. Carter

### Introduction

As Chapter 1 indicated, Confederation did not bring harmony or homogeneity to the former British North American colonies. Yet, the young Dominion had to exert authority over a huge land base and a variety of people, many of whom, especially in the North-West, had little experience as citizens in the European or colonial sense. This was also the age of railways and of restless capitalists envisioning cities where others saw only wilderness. They were eager to build quickly, but they also wanted to project a sense of decorum and civility, and conquering the wilderness would be easier if the process could be rendered more predictable. They fondly wished that before long Canada would gain status as a young lion of the Empire, an Empire that was not yet ready, as Prime Minister Macdonald would find out, to allow Canada a free hand in its dealings with other nations. Still, there was more than enough for the Canadian government to do at home as it experienced first-hand the difficulties of managing a kind of 'internal empire'. Each new province added to the federation held the promise of new resources for Canada, but this rapid expansion also meant further expenditure to maintain control over the newly added land and those living on it. Dominion also meant the informal process of defining who (or what) represented order, and ensuring that the legal and moral standards of faraway places like Montreal or London were at least loosely adhered to on the frontier. This resulted in treaties with Aboriginal peoples and the establishment of institutions and infrastructure, most famously the North West Mounted Police (NWMP) and the transcontinental railway. The abrupt changes brought about as these arms of the state reached into the lives of long-time residents are what concern us most here. The first primary source sets out the composition of the well-known mounted police force, but also gives us a distilled version of the laws that were considered most important for the territory. The new force accompanied federal government officials whose job was to conclude treaties with various First Nations in the Territories. We have included parts of Treaty Six, one of the 'numbered' treaties that lumped First Nations living in particular geographical areas together for the purposes of negotiation and administration. The treaty shows what was expected of the Aboriginal signatories, and what they could expect in return. It makes few, if any, allowances for Aboriginal conceptions of possession, as the treaty expected that the First Nations involved would make way for the inevitable. The secondary sources both deal with the impact of treaties and the more formalized relationships created by the treaties. Keith Smith's contribution shows how the federal government, churches, and police forces controlled the movements of Aboriginal people and their relationships with settlers so that a liberal order could take hold in the West. Sarah Carter addresses the state's responses to polygamy in Aboriginal communities, noting that condemnation of the practice allowed authorities to reach deep into the family unit to reconfigure (or at least attempt to reconfigure) the lives of individuals.

## QUESTIONS FOR CONSIDERATION

1.  Considering the various provisions in the act establishing the NWMP, what sort of vision did the Canadian government have for the West?
2.  Why do you think Treaty Six was between Queen Victoria and the First Nations named in the treaty?
3.  What seemed to be the purpose of exerting all the effort to 'civilize' Canada's newest territory?
4.  Smith describes the Department of Indian Affairs' dealings with the churches. Why did these two parties sometimes have their differences?
5.  Why did the Department care that some bands included families that had more than one wife?

## SUGGESTIONS FOR FURTHER READING

Sarah Carter, *The Importance of Being Monogamous: Marriage and Nation Building in Western Canada to 1915* (Edmonton: University of Alberta Press, 2008).
——, *Lost Harvests: Prairie Indian Reserve, Farmers and Government Policy* (Montreal and Kingston: McGill-Queen's University Press, 1990).
Olive Patricia Dickason, *Canada's First Nations: A History of Founding Peoples from the Earliest Times*, 3rd edn (Toronto: Oxford University Press, 2002).

Cole Harris, *Making Native Space: Colonialism, Resistance, and Reserves in British Columbia* (Vancouver: UBC Press, 2003).

John Sutton Lutz, *Makuk: A New History of Aboriginal–White Relations* (Vancouver: UBC Press, 2009).

J.R. Miller, *Compact, Contract, Covenant: Aboriginal Treaty-Making in Canada* (Toronto: University of Toronto Press, 2009).

——, *Shingwauk's Vision: A History of Native Residential Schools* (Toronto: University of Toronto Press, 1996).

Arthur J. Ray, Jim Miller, and Frank Tough, *Bounty and Benevolence: A Documentary History of Saskatchewan Treaties* (Montreal and Kingston: McGill-Queen's University Press, 2000).

Jill St. Germain, *Indian Treaty-Making Policy in the United States and Canada, 1867–1877* (Toronto: University of Toronto Press, 2001).

# PRIMARY DOCUMENTS

1 From 'An Act Respecting the Administration of Justice, and for the Establishment of a Police Force in the North West Territories' (1873) *Acts of the Parliament of the Dominion of Canada . . . first session of the second Parliament, begun and holden at Ottawa, on the fifth day of March, and closed by prorogation on the thirteenth day of August, 1873* (Ottawa: B. Chamberlin, 1873), 110–18.

## CHAP. 35.

An Act respecting the Administration of Justice, and for the establishment of a Police Force in the North West Territories.

[Assented to 23rd May, 1873.]

HER MAJESTY, by and with the advice and consent of the Senate and House of Commons of Canada, enacts as follows:—

1. The Governor may from time to time appoint, by commission under the Great Seal, one or more fit and proper person or persons to be and act as a Stipendiary Magistrate or Stipendiary Magistrates within the North West Territories, who shall reside at such place or places as may be ordered by the Governor in Council; and the Governor in Council shall assign to any such Stipendiary Magistrate a yearly salary not exceeding three thousand dollars, together with his actual travelling expenses.

2. Every Stipendiary Magistrate shall hold office during pleasure; and shall exercise within the North West Territories, or within such limited portion of the same as may be prescribed by the Governor in Council, the magisterial, judicial and other functions appertaining to any Justice of the Peace, or any two Justices of the Peace, under any laws or Ordinances which may from time to time be in force in the North West Territories.

3. Any Stipendiary Magistrate shall further have power to hear and determine, in a summary way and without the intervention of a jury, any charge against any person or persons for any of the following offences alleged to have been committed within the North West Territories, as follows:—

1. Simple larceny, larceny from the person, embezzlement, or obtaining money or property by false pretences, or feloniously receiving stolen property, in any case in which the value of the whole property, alleged to have been stolen, embezzled, obtained or received, does not, in the judgment of such Stipendiary Magistrate, exceed one hundred dollars; or

2. Having attempted to commit larceny from the person or simple larceny; or

3. With having committed an aggravated assault, by unlawfully and maliciously inflicting upon any other person, either with or without a weapon or instrument, any grievous bodily harm, or by unlawfully and maliciously cutting, stabbing or wounding any other person; or

4. With having committed an assault upon any female whatever, or upon any male child whose age does not, in the opinion of the magistrate, exceed fourteen years, such assault, if upon a female, not amounting, in his opinion, to an assault with intent to commit a rape; or

5. Having assaulted, obstructed, molested or hindered any Stipendiary Magistrate, Justice of the Peace, Commissioner or Superintendent of Police, a policeman, constable or bailiff, or Officer of Customs or Excise, or other officer, in the lawful performance of his duty, or with intent to prevent the performance thereof;

And upon any conviction by such Stipendiary Magistrate, the person so convicted may be sentenced to such punishment as he thinks fit, by imprisonment for any period less than two years in any gaol or place of confinement, with or without hard labour, and with or without solitary confinement, or by fine, or by such imprisonment and fine.

**4.** The Chief Justice or any Judge of the Court of Queen's Bench of the Province of Manitoba, or any two Stipendiary Magistrates sitting together as a Court, shall have power and authority to hear and determine within the North West Territories, in a summary way and without the intervention of any Grand or Petty Jury, any charge against any person or persons for offences alleged to have been committed within the North West Territories, and the maximum punishment for which does not exceed seven years imprisonment; and such Court shall be a Court of record; and if imprisonment in a penitentiary be awarded in any such case, the Court may cause the convict to be conveyed to the penitentiary in the Province of Manitoba; and he shall undergo such punishment therein as if convicted in the Province of Manitoba.

**5.** Any Justice of the Peace, or any Stipendiary Magistrate or any Judge of the Court of Queen's Bench of the Province of Manitoba, shall have power and authority to commit and cause to be conveyed to gaol in the Province of Manitoba, for trial by the said Court of Queen's Bench according to the laws of criminal procedure in force in the said Province, any person or persons at any time charged with the commission of any offence against any of the laws or Ordinances in force in the North West Territories, punishable by death or imprisonment in the penitentiary: and the Court of Queen's Bench and any Judge thereof, shall have power and authority to try any person arraigned before the said Court on any such charge; and the jury laws and laws of criminal procedure of the said Province shall apply to any such trial; except that the punishment to be awarded, upon conviction of any such person, shall be according to the laws in force in the North West Territories: and the sentence may be carried into effect in a penitentiary or other place of confinement in the said Province, as if the same were in the North West Territories.

[ . . . ]

**7.** Where it is impossible or inconvenient, in the absence or remoteness of any gaol or other place of confinement, to carry out any sentence of imprisonment, any Justice of the Peace or Stipendiary Magistrate, or any two Stipendiary Magistrates sitting together as aforesaid, or any Judge of the Court of Queen's Bench of Manitoba, may, according to their several powers and jurisdictions hereinbefore given, sentence such person so convicted before him or them, and sentenced, as aforesaid, to such imprisonment, to be placed and kept in the custody of the Police of the North West Territories, with or without hard labour,—the nature and extent of which shall be determined by the Justice of the Peace or Stipendiary Magistrate or Stipendiary Magistrates, or Judge, by or before whom such person was convicted.

8. The Governor in Council may cause to be erected in any part or parts of the North West Territories any building or buildings, or enclosure or enclosures, for the purposes of the gaol or lock-up, for the confinement of prisoners charged with the commission of any offence, or sentenced to any punishment therein; and confinement or imprisonment therein shall be held lawful and valid.

9. Whenever in any Act of the Parliament of Canada in force in the North West Territories, any officer is designated for carrying on any duty therein mentioned, and there shall be no such officer in the North West Territories, the Lieutenant Governor in Council may order by what other person or officer such duty shall be performed; and anything done by such person or officer, under such order, shall be valid and legal in the premises: or if it be in any such Act ordered that any document or thing shall be transmitted to any officer, Court, territorial division or place, and there shall be in the said North West Territories no such officer, Court or territorial division or place, then the Lieutenant Governor in Council may order to what officer, Court or place such transmission shall be made, or may dispense with the transmission thereof.

## Mounted Police Force

10. The Governor in Council may constitute a Police Force in and for the North West Territories, and the Governor may from time to time, as may be found necessary, appoint by commission, a Commissioner of Police, and one or more Superintendents of Police, together with a Paymaster, Surgeon and Veterinary Surgeon, each of whom shall hold office during pleasure.

[ . . . ]

12. The Governor in Council may, from time to time, authorize the Commissioner of Police to appoint, by warrant under his hand, such number of Constables and Sub-Constables as he may think proper, not exceeding in the whole three hundred men; and such number thereof shall be mounted as the Governor in Council may at any time direct.

13. No person shall be appointed to the Police Force unless he be of a sound constitution, able to ride, active and able-bodied, of good character, and between the ages of eighteen and forty years; nor unless he be able to read and write either the English or French language.

[ . . . ]

15. The Commissioner and every Superintendent of Police shall be *ex-officio* a Justice of the Peace; and every constable and sub-constable of the Force shall be a constable in and for the whole of the North West Territories; and may execute the office in any part thereof, and in Manitoba in the cases hereinbefore mentioned and provided for.

[ . . . ]

17. The Governor in Council may, from and out of any of the lands of the Dominion in the Province of Manitoba or in the North West Territories, make a free grant not exceeding one hundred and sixty acres, to any constable or sub-constable of the said force, who, at the expiration of three years of continuous service in the said Force, shall be certified by the Commissioner of Police to have conducted himself satisfactorily, and to have efficiently and ably performed the duties of his office during the said term of three years.

[ . . . ]

**19.** It shall be the duty of the Force—

1. To perform all duties which now are or shall be hereafter assigned to constables in relation to the preservation of the peace, the prevention of crime, and of offences against the laws and Ordinances in force in the North West Territories, and the apprehension of criminals and offenders, and others who may be lawfully taken into custody;

2. To attend upon any Judge, Stipendiary Magistrate or Justice of the Peace, when thereunto specially required, and, subject to the orders of the Commissioner or Superintendent, to execute all warrants and perform all duties and services in relation thereto, which may, under this Act or the laws and Ordinances in force in the North West Territories, lawfully be performed by constables;

3. To perform all duties which may be lawfully performed by constables in relation to the escort and conveyance of convicts and other prisoners or lunatics, to or from any Courts, places of punishment or confinement, asylums or other places,—

And for these purposes, and in the performance of all the duties assigned to them by or under the authority of this Act, they shall have all the powers, authority, protection and privileges which any constable now has or shall hereafter by law have.

**20.** The Governor in Council may, from time to time, make rules and regulations for any of the following purposes, viz:—To regulate the number of the Force, not exceeding in the whole the number of three hundred men as hereinbefore provided; to prescribe the number of men who shall be mounted on horseback; to regulate and prescribe the clothing, arms, training and discipline of the Police Force; to regulate and prescribe the duties and authorities of the Commissioner and Superintendents of the Force, and the several places at or near which the same, or the Force or any portions thereof may from time to time be stationed; and generally all and every such matters and things for the good government, discipline and guidance of the Force as are not inconsistent with this Act: and such rules and regulations may impose penalties, not exceeding in any case thirty days' pay of the offenders, for any contravention thereof, and may direct that such penalty when incurred may be deducted from the offender's pay: they may determine what officer shall have power to declare such penalty incurred, and to impose the same; and they shall have force as if enacted by law.

[ . . . ]

**22.** Any member of the Force may be suspended from his charge or dismissed by the Commissioner or by any Superintendent to whom the Commissioner shall have delegated the power to do so; and any Superintendent may be suspended from office by the Commissioner until the pleasure of the governor in Council shall be known; and every such suspension or dismissal shall take effect from the time it shall be made known either orally or in writing to the party suspended or dismissed.

**23.** Any Superintendent or any member of the Force suspended or dismissed shall forthwith deliver up to the Commissioner or to a Superintendent or to any constable authorized to receive the same, his clothing, arms, accoutrements and all property of the Crown in his possession as a member of the Force or used for police purposes; or in case of his refusing or neglecting so to do, shall incur a penalty of fifty dollars.

**24.** Whenever the Commissioner shall deem it advisable to make or cause to be made any special enquiry into the conduct of any Superintendent or of any member of the Police Force, or into any complaint against any of them, he, or the Superintendent whom he may appoint for that purpose, may examine any person on oath or affirmation on any matters relative to such enquiry, and may administer such oath or affirmation.

[ . . . ]

**28.** The Governor in Council may also from time to time regulate and prescribe the amounts to be paid, for the purchase of horses, vehicles, harness, saddlery, clothing, arms and accoutrements, or articles necessary for the said Force: and also the expenses of travelling, and of rations or of boarding or billeting the force and of forage for the horses.

**29.** The Governor in Council may make regulations for the quartering, billeting and cantoning of the Force, or any portions or detachments thereof; and for the furnishing of boats, carriages, vehicles of transport, horses and other conveyances for their transport and use, and for giving adequate compensation therefor; and may, by such regulations, impose fines not exceeding two hundred dollars for breach of any regulation aforesaid, or for refusing to billet any of the said Force, or to furnish transport as herein mentioned. But no such regulations shall authorize the quartering or billeting of any of the Force in any nunnery or convent of any Religious Order of females.

**30.** All sums of money required to defray any expense authorized by this Act may be paid out of the Consolidated Revenue Fund of Canada.

[ . . . ]

**32.** All regulations or Orders in Council made under this Act shall be published in the *Canada Gazette*, and shall, thereupon have the force of law from the date of their publication, or from, such later date as may be therein appointed for their coming into force; and a copy of any such regulations purporting to be printed by the Queen's Printer shall be *prima facie* evidence thereof.

**33.** The Department of Justice shall have the control and management of the Police Force and of all matters connected therewith; but the Governor in Council may, at any time order that the same shall be transferred to any other Department of the Civil Service of Canada, and the same shall accordingly, by such order, be so transferred to and be under the control and management of such other Department.

**34.** The Commissioner and every Superintendent of Police, shall be *ex-officio* a Justice of the Peace, within the Province of Manitoba; and the constables and sub-constables of the Police Force shall also have and exercise within the Province of Manitoba, all the powers and authority, rights and privileges by law appertaining to constables under the laws of the Dominion, for the purpose of carrying the same into effect.

**35.** The Governor in Council may from time to time enter into arrangements with the Government of the Province of Manitoba for the use or employment of the Police Force, in aiding the administration of justice in that Province and in carrying into effect the laws of the Legislature thereof; and may, in any such arrangement, agree and determine the amount of money which shall be paid by the Province of Manitoba in respect of any such services of the said Police Force.

**2**    'Articles of a Treaty made and concluded near Carlton . . .' (Treaty No. 6, 1876), in Canada, *Indian Treaties and Surrenders from 1680 to 1890 in Two Volumes*, Vol. 2 (Ottawa: Brown Chamberlin [Queen's Printer], 1891), 35–43.

ARTICLES OF A TREATY made and concluded near Carlton on the 23rd day of August and on the 28th day of said month respectively, and near Fort Pitt on the 9th day of September, in the year of Our Lord one thousand eight hundred and seventy six, between Her Most Gracious Majesty the Queen of Great Britain and Ireland, by Her Commissioners, the Honourable Alexander Morris, Lieutenant Governor of the Province of Manitoba and the North-West Territories, and the Honourable James McKay, and the Honourable William Joseph Christie, of the one part, and the Plain and Wood Cree and the other Tribes of Indians, inhabitants of the country within the limits hereinafter defined and described by their Chiefs, chosen and named as hereinafter mentioned, of the other part.

Whereas the Indians inhabiting the said country have, pursuant to an appointment made by the said Commissioners, been convened at meetings at Fort Carlton, Fort Pitt and Battle River, to deliberate upon certain matters of interest to Her Most Gracious Majesty, of the one part, and the said Indians of the other.

And whereas the said Indians have been notified and informed by Her Majesty's said Commissioners that it is the desire of Her Majesty to open up for settlement, immigration and such other purposes as to Her Majesty may seem meet, a tract of country bounded and described as hereinafter mentioned, and to obtain the consent thereto of Her Indian subjects inhabiting the said tract, and to make a treaty and arrange with them, so that there may be peace and good will between them and Her Majesty, and that they may know and be assured of what allowance they are to count upon and receive from Her Majesty's bounty and benevolence.

And whereas the Indians of the said tract, duly convened in council, as aforesaid, and being requested by Her Majesty's said Commissioners to name certain Chiefs and Headmen, who should be authorized on their behalf to conduct such negotiations and sign any treaty to be founded thereon, and to become responsible to Her Majesty for their faithful performance by their respective Bands of such obligations as shall be assumed by them, the said Indians have thereupon named for that purpose, that is to say, representing the Indians who make the treaty at Carlton, the several Chiefs and Councillors who have subscribed hereto, and representing the Indians who make the treaty at Fort Pitt, the several Chiefs and Councillors who have subscribed hereto.

And thereupon, in open council, the different Bands having presented their Chiefs to the said Commissioners as the Chiefs and Headmen, for the purposes aforesaid, of the respective Bands of Indians inhabiting the said district hereinafter described.

And whereas, the said Commissioners then and there received and acknowledged the persons so presented as Chiefs and Headmen, for the purposes aforesaid, of the respective Bands of Indians inhabiting the said district hereinafter described.

And whereas, the said Commissioners have proceeded to negotiate a treaty with the said Indians, and the same has been finally agreed upon and concluded, as follows, that is to say:—

The Plain and Wood Cree Tribes of Indians, and all other the Indians inhabiting the district hereinafter described and defined, do hereby cede, release, surrender and yield up to the Government of the Dominion of Canada, for Her Majesty the Queen and Her successors forever, all their rights, titles and privileges, whatsoever, to the lands included within the following limits, that is to say:

Commencing at the mouth of the river emptying into the north-west angle of Cumberland Lake; thence westerly up the said river to its source; thence on a straight line in a westerly direction to the head of Green Lake; thence northerly to the elbow in the Beaver River; thence down the said river northerly to a point twenty miles from the said elbow; thence in a westerly direction, keeping on a line generally parallel with the said Beaver River (above the elbow), and about twenty miles distant therefrom, to the source of the said river; thence northerly to the northeasterly point of the south shore of Red Deer Lake, continuing westerly along the said shore to the western limit thereof; and thence due west to the Athabasca River; thence up the said river, against the stream, to the Jaspar House, in the Rocky Mountains; thence on a course south-eastwardly, following the easterly range of the mountains, to the source of the main branch of the Red Deer River; thence down the said river, with the stream, to the junction therewith of the outlet of the river, being the outlet of the Buffalo Lake; thence due east twenty miles; thence on a straight line south-eastwardly to the mouth of the said Red Deer River on the south branch of the Saskatchewan River; thence eastwardly and northwardly, following on the boundaries of the tracts conceded by the several treaties numbered four and five to the place of beginning.

And also, all their rights, titles and privileges whatsoever to all other lands wherever situated in the North-West Territories, or in any other Province or portion of Her Majesty's Dominions, situated and being within the Dominion of Canada.

The tract comprised within the lines above described embracing an area of 121,000 square miles, be the same more or less.

To have and to hold the same to Her Majesty the Queen and Her successors forever.

And Her Majesty the Queen hereby agrees and undertakes to lay aside reserves for farming lands, due respect being had to lands at present cultivated by the said Indians, and other reserves for the benefit of the said Indians, to be administered and dealt with for them by Her Majesty's Government of the Dominion of Canada; provided, all such reserves shall not exceed in all one square mile for each family of five, or in that proportion for larger or smaller families, in manner following, that is to say: that the Chief Superintendent of Indian Affairs shall depute and send a suitable person to determine and set apart the reserves for each band, after consulting with the Indians thereof as to the locality which may be found to be most suitable for them.

Provided, however, that Her Majesty reserves the right to deal with any settlers within the bounds of any lands reserved for any Band as She shall deem fit, and also that the aforesaid reserves of land, or any interest therein, may be sold or otherwise disposed of by Her Majesty's Government for the use and benefit of the said Indians entitled thereto, with their consent first had and obtained; and with a view to show the satisfaction of Her Majesty with the behaviour and good conduct of Her Indians, She hereby, through Her Commissioners, makes them a present of twelve dollars for each man, woman and child belonging to the Bands here represented, in extinguishment of all claims heretofore preferred.

And further, Her Majesty agrees to maintain schools for instruction in such reserves hereby made as to Her Government of the Dominion of Canada may seem advisable, whenever the Indians of the reserve shall desire it.

Her Majesty further agrees with Her said Indians that within the boundary of Indian reserves, until otherwise determined by Her Government of the Dominion of Canada, no intoxicating liquor shall be allowed to be introduced or sold, and all laws now in force, or hereafter to be enacted, to preserve Her Indian subjects inhabiting the reserves or living elsewhere within Her North-West Territories from the evil influence of the use of intoxicating liquor, shall be strictly enforced.

Her Majesty further agrees with Her said Indians that they, the said Indians, shall have right to pursue their avocations of hunting and fishing throughout the tract surrendered as hereinbefore described, subject to such regulations as may from time to time be made by Her Government of Her Dominion of Canada, and saving and excepting such tracts as may from time to time be required or taken up for settlement, mining, lumbering or other purposes by Her said Government of the Dominion of Canada, or by any of the subjects thereof duly authorized therefor by the said Government.

It is further agreed between Her Majesty and Her said Indians, that such sections of the reserves above indicated as may at any time be required for public works or buildings, of what nature soever, may be appropriated for that purpose by Her Majesty's Government of the Dominion of Canada, due compensation being made for the value of any improvements thereon.

And further, that Her Majesty's Commissioners shall, as soon as possible after the execution of this treaty, cause to be taken an accurate census of all the Indians inhabiting the tract above described, distributing them in families, and shall, in every year ensuing the date hereof, at some period in each year, to be duly notified to the Indians, and at a place or places to be appointed for that purpose within the territory ceded, pay to each Indian person the sum of $5 per head yearly.

It is further agreed between Her Majesty and the said Indians, that the sum of $15 per annum shall be yearly and every year expended by Her Majesty in the purchase of ammunition, and twine for nets, for the use of the said Indians, in manner following, that is to say: In the reasonable discretion, as regards the distribution thereof among the Indians inhabiting the several reserves, or otherwise, included herein, of Her Majesty's Indian Agent having the supervision of this treaty.

It is further agreed between Her Majesty and the said Indians, that the following articles shall be supplied to any Band of the said Indians who are now cultivating the soil, or who shall hereafter commence to cultivate the land, that is to say: Four hoes for every family actually cultivating; also, two spades per family as aforesaid; one plough for every three families, as aforesaid; one harrow for every three families, as aforesaid; two scythes and one whetstone, and two hay forks and two reaping hooks, for every family as aforesaid, and also two axes; and also one cross-cut saw, one hand-saw, one pit-saw, the necessary files, one grindstone and one auger for each Band; and also for each Chief for the use of his Band, one chest of ordinary carpenter's tools; also, for each Band, enough of wheat, barley, potatoes and oats to plant the land actually broken up for cultivation by such Band; also for each Band four oxen, one bull and six cows; also, one boar and two sows, and one hand-mill when any Band shall raise sufficient grain therefor. All the aforesaid articles to be given once for all for the encouragement of the practice of agriculture among the Indians.

It is further agreed between Her Majesty and the said Indians, that each Chief, duly recognised as such, shall receive an annual salary of twenty-five dollars per annum; and each subordinate officer, not exceeding four for each Band, shall receive fifteen dollars per annum; and each such Chief and subordinate officer, as aforesaid, shall also receive once every three years, a suitable suit of clothing, and each Chief shall receive, in recognition of the closing of the treaty, a suitable flag and medal, and also as soon as convenient, one horse, harness and waggon.

That in the event hereafter of the Indians comprised within this treaty being overtaken by any pestilence, or by a general famine, the Queen, on being satisfied and certified thereof by Her Indian Agent or Agents, will grant to the Indians assistance of such character and to such extent as Her Chief Superintendent of Indian Affairs shall deem necessary and sufficient to relieve the Indians from the Calamity that shall have befallen them.

That during the next three years, after two or more of the reserves hereby agreed to be set apart to the Indians shall have been agreed upon and surveyed, there shall be granted to the Indians included under the Chiefs adhering to the treaty at Carlton, each spring, the sum of one thousand dollars, to be expended for them by Her Majesty's Indian Agents, in the purchase of provisions for the use of such of the Band as are actually settled on the reserves and are engaged in cultivating the soil, to assist them in such cultivation.

That a medicine chest shall be kept at the house of each Indian Agent for the use and benefit of the Indians at the direction of such agent.

That with regard to the Indians included under the Chiefs adhering to the treaty at Fort Pitt, and to those under Chiefs within the treaty limits who may hereafter give their adhesion thereto (exclusively, however, of the Indians of the Carlton region), there shall, during three years, after two or more reserves shall have been agreed upon and surveyed be distributed each spring among the Bands cultivating the soil on such reserves by Her Majesty's Chief Indian Agent for this treaty, in his discretion, a sum not exceeding one thousand dollars, in the purchase of provisions for the use of such members of the Band as are actually settled on the reserve and engaged in the cultivation of the soil, to assist and encourage them in such cultivation.

That in lieu of waggons, if they desire it and declare their option to that effect, there shall be given to each of the Chiefs adhering hereto at Fort Pitt or elsewhere hereafter (exclusively of those in the Carlton district), in recognition of this treaty, as soon as the same can be conveniently transported, two carts with iron bushings and tires.

And the undersigned Chiefs on their own behalf and on behalf of all other Indians inhabiting the tract within ceded, do hereby solemnly promise and engage to strictly observe this treaty, and also to conduct and behave themselves as good and loyal subjects of Her Majesty the Queen.

They promise and engage that they will in all respects obey and abide by the law, and they will maintain peace and good order between each other, and also between themselves and other tribes of Indians, and between themselves and others of Her Majesty's subjects, whether Indians or whites, now inhabiting or hereafter to inhabit any part of the said ceded tracts, and that they will not molest the person or property of any inhabitant of such ceded tracts, or the property of Her Majesty the Queen, or interfere with or trouble any person passing or travelling through the said tracts, or any part thereof, and that they will aid and assist the officers of Her Majesty in bringing to justice and punishment any Indian offending against the stipulations of this treaty, or infringing the laws in force in the country so ceded.

IN WITNESS WHEREOF, Her Majesty's said Commissioners and the said Indian Chiefs have hereunto subscribed and set their hands at or near Fort Carlton, on the days and year aforesaid, and near Fort Pitt on the day above aforesaid.

Signed by the Chiefs within named in presence of the following witnesses, the same having been first read and explained by Peter Erasmus, Peter Ballendine and the Rev. John McKay.

ALF. JACKES, *M.D.*,
JAS. WALKER, *N.W.M.P.*
J.H. McILLREE, *N.W.M.P.*
PIERRE LEVAILLER, his X mark
ISADORE DUMOND, his X mark
JEAN DUMOND, his X mark
F. GINGRAS,
J.B. MITCHELL, *Staff Constable N.W.M.P.*

[other witnesses and councillors . . .]

ALEXANDER MORRIS, *L. G. N. W. T.*
JAMES McKAY, *Indian Commissioner.*
W.J. CHRISTIE    *do*

*Head Chiefs of the Carlton Indians*

MIS-TO-WA-SIS, his X mark
AH-TUK-UK-KOOP, his X mark

PEE-YAHN-KAH-NICHK-OO-SIT, his X mark
AH-YAH-TUS-KUM-IK-IM-AM, his X mark
KEE-TOO-WA-HAW, his X mark
CHA-KAS-TA-PAY-SIN, his X mark
JOHN SMITH, his X mark
JAMES SMITH, his X mark
CHIP-EE-WAYAN, his X mark

*Chiefs*

# HISTORICAL INTERPRETATIONS

**3** From Keith D. Smith, '"A Splendid Spirit of Cooperation": Churches, Police Forces, and the Department of Indian Affairs', in *Liberalism, Surveillance, and Resistance: Indigenous Communities in Western Canada* (Edmonton: Athabasca Press, 2009), 51–91.

The precise techniques applied by liberal Canadian institutions to 'de-Indianize' Indigenous populations were neither uniform nor consistent across time or geography. Rather, the specifics were a fluid array of disciplinary techniques that were constantly adjusted to meet local conditions. Increased pressure on land as the result of an influx of non-Indigenous settlers, localized resistance to a particularly offensive policy or official, stubborn refusal to readily accept the dogma of the newcomers, or the need to explain previous policy failures might necessitate an adjustment in strategy or a change in tactics. Liberalism, as it was applied to Indigenous people in western Canada, was creative and adaptable. The feature common to all of these shifting schemes that ranged from education in various forms to military force and from legislation to morally reprehensible actions that had no basis in law, was that they were informed and reinforced by surveillance. Surveillance was the primary means of normalization. On 'Indian reserves', as in the other disciplinary institutions, the smallest details of activity were supervised and recorded. In this way normalization was disseminated through day-to-day activity and secured through relentless monitoring.

The importance of surveillance was well understood by those concerned with 'civilizing Indians' in the late nineteenth century. When, in 1875, well-known Anglican lay missionary and founder of the Metlakatla settlement, William Duncan, offered his suggestions on policy that should be followed in the new province of British Columbia, he wrote under the leading head, 'surveillance',

'[t]his I conceive to be the proper starting point for commencing a right policy in Indian affairs; for without surveillance no satisfactory relationship can ever exist between the Government and the Indians'.[1] Hayter Reed, Indian Commissioner for the North-West Territories, spoke more specifically when he told all agents under him that 'closer supervision would ensure better results' in agricultural pursuits.[2]

The surveillance of Indigenous people in western Canada was primarily the responsibility of the DIA [Department of Indian Affairs] and it is the DIA that gets most of the attention in this study. Additionally, though, there were many other groups and individuals engaged in scrutinizing Indigenous people. While their tactics may have varied and their specific objectives may have differed, there was considerable collaboration between and within groups watching, judging, and set on reforming Indigenous people. Additionally, these groups and individuals were actively involved in observing the activities of each other. Policemen watched DIA employees, missionaries watched policemen, DIA employees watched missionaries, farmers watched policemen, and individuals within each of these groups observed and judged their colleagues.

## MISSIONARY SURVEILLANCE AND SURVEILLANCE OF MISSIONARIES

Protestants and Catholics watched each other carefully and jealously guarded any advances they made into First Nations communities.[3]

This jealousy extended not only to the building of churches and schools, but also to the provision of on-reserve health services.[4] The *Calgary Herald* declared, 'something should be done to prevent the agents of the denominations from interfering with each other's labors' in 'their efforts to elevate the Indians of the North West in the scale of civilization'.[5] The DIA monitored all missionary activity on reserves and in Indian schools and each year published information on these activities in its Annual Reports. At the same time, missionaries observed the activities of the department's employees and did not hesitate to articulate their concerns when they believed their interests in relation to other denominations were in jeopardy[6] or when they felt their moral influence and example were compromised by the department or one of its employees.[7] Occasionally, to the dismay and indignation of the DIA, church representatives went to the media and allowed their criticisms to enter the public's field of view.[8]

[ . . . ]

Despite local conflicts, it is clear that the department at Ottawa went to some length to maintain friendly relations with all denominations and to protect its public image of religious equality. The glowing report of Frederick Abbott, Secretary to the U.S. Board of Indian Commissioners, attests to the success of the department's public relations efforts when the author wrote that a 'splendid spirit of cooperation exists between the various religious denominations in Canada and the government'.[9] The churches too, went some way to maintaining good relations with Ottawa so that, for example, when Anglican missionary A.E. O'Meara, a vocal advocate for Indigenous rights, was critical of the DIAs inability to fulfill its written promises and objectives and publicly labelled 'one of its officers a liar . . . he was called to order very strongly by the Primate' of the Anglican Church.[10]

In addition to the DIA, the police too, particularly the NWMP [North West Mounted Police], were interested in the activities of various churches, especially if they believed that public peace was in jeopardy. When, for example, the Siksika voiced their dissatisfaction regarding compulsory attendance at the school on their reserve, Anglican missionary J.W. Tims recommended 'a force of 200 or more men located on the border of the Reserve as a check to their present behaviour'.[11] It is unlikely that such a large proportion of the force would ever be committed to such an assignment, but soon it was not necessary. A week later NWMP Commissioner Herchmer was able to report that the 'departure of Rev. Tims has removed all cause of complaint and Indians are now perfectly quiet'.[12] The same year, when NWMP Superintendent S.B. Steele found that children at the school at St. Paul's Mission on the Kainai reserve were being locked in at night, he warned the priest/principal that if lives were lost in the event of a fire, he would be tried for manslaughter.[13]

There was sectarian discord, differences in opinion regarding tactics within various denominations, and disputes between individual missionaries and police, and missionaries and DIA employees. There were few in either region, though, who presented any serious challenge to what was believed to be the natural correctness of individual land tenure and property ownership, to the belief that Indigenous people were not yet advanced enough to be permitted to reap any benefits liberalism had to offer, or that adherence to Christianity was a necessary prerequisite not only for civilization but for human development. Further, missionaries were employed by government officials to pacify Indigenous residents. For example, in preparation for the arrival of NWMP Policemen and American troops into their territories to mark off the boundary between the United States and Canada, missionary John McDougall was sent to the Blackfoot to advise them of 'the good will of the Queen' and to ask them 'to regard the Force with a friendly eye'.[14] On a larger scale, adherence to Christianity seems to have gone some way toward the DIA objective of fostering quietude. As Chief at Cayuse Creek, a Lil'wat community, reported to missionary and DIA employee McDougall in 1910:

> We never leased land. We never gave away our right to game and salmon. They, the white men, took it from us. We did not get mad. The white people did all this. We did not get mad. No—Christ said 'do not get mad'.[15]

## POLICE SURVEILLANCE

Though there were other police and investigative bodies involved with law enforcement in western Canada, these duties fell mainly to the NWMP east of the Rockies, and to the British Columbia Provincial Police [BCPP] to the west. Like the representatives of the various churches, the BCPP and the NWMP observed the movements and activities of First Nations peoples within their jurisdictions.

The BCPP formed in 1858, 16 years before the NWMP, was the first territorial police force in Canada. While the immediate impetus for the creation of the force was the need to control the tens of thousands of gold seekers that arrived in the Fraser River watershed in 1858, it had a myriad of law enforcement duties during its existence.[16] That the British Columbia police were primarily responsible for ensuring the orderly development of liberal capitalism is evident from the particular attention it paid to working-class people, especially union organizers and the unemployed.[17] Undoubtedly, the increased surveillance of these individuals is a direct result of the demands of settlers, businessmen, and their political representatives for increased policing.

The provincial government felt that since 'Indians' were a federal responsibility the cost of their surveillance should be borne by the government at Ottawa. Nevertheless, the BCPP continued to keep a watch on Indigenous people.[18] Indeed, the 1901 diary of a constable stationed in the southern Okanagan includes such regular entries as: 'watched actions of party of half breeds', 'large gathering of Indians on reserve', and 'patrolled reserve all day'.[19] Similarly, 10 years later, the constable in the district visited at least some reserves once a week.[20] The BCPP was also active in locating and returning truant students to boarding schools for Indigenous children including the Kamloops Indian Residential School.[21]

Job actions by Indigenous people, in concert with white workers, also brought them more directly under the supervisory gaze of lawmakers and police in the early twentieth century. The Fraser River fishery strikes of 1900 and 1901 are cases in point. As was reported to the Attorney General 'over forty white and [I]ndian patrol boats, manned by ten men each now on the river intimidating destroying property and preventing fishing'.[22] Here, as in the province's coal mines, Asian workers were co-opted into acting as strike breakers. This strategy, coupled with the declaration of martial law and the employment of special constables, militia men, and the BCPP to protect the Japanese fishers and so the interests of the cannery owners, ultimately defeated the action taken by striking Indigenous and white fishers.

It was not only overt resistance, however, that caused Indigenous people to be singled out as the primary reason for requesting additional policing. As one settler argued:

> [m]y contention in this matter is, that the Govt.—in localities like this where the halfbreed element and Siwash element so largely prevail—should consider itself bound to see that the whites who keep up the country with their enterprise and taxes are allowed to live in comparative comfort and freedom from annoyance.[23]

For a short time, there was also a provincial police force in Alberta. When the RNWMP, apparently unwilling to enforce provincial prohibition regulations, cancelled its contract with the Province in 1916, Alberta established its own provincial police which operated until the RCMP [Royal Canadian Mounted Police] reassumed policing responsibilities in 1932. While there was some surveillance of the First Nations of southern Alberta by the Alberta Provincial Police [APP], the continued responsibility of the Mounties for matters concerning Indigenous people insured that these activities were even less substantial than those of the provincial police in British Columbia.[24]

[ . . . ]

John A. Macdonald began preparing the ground for the formation of a mounted police force as the situation in the prairie west began to deteriorate in 1869, partly as a result of the lack of consultation with First Nations and Métis inhabitants regarding the transfer of Rupert's Land from the Hudson's Bay Company to Canada. The force began to take shape with an order-in-council in April 1870 in which provision was made for a mounted force which, like the Royal Irish Constabulary, would be under the central control of Ottawa and not territorial or regional governments.[25] While the resistance centred at Red River was over in 1870, the desire to establish Canadian authority over the west remained. In September of 1873, nine commissioned officers were appointed to a 'Mounted Police Force for the North-West Territories' and by November 3 a further 150 men were recruited to the force.[26] In 1874, 300 Mounties marched west and arrived in the area that became southern Alberta to establish Fort Macleod in 1874 and Fort Calgary in 1875. The conspicuous expansion of Anglo-Canadian liberal values in this region and the formal surveillance network in preparation for the western settlement was initiated in advance of any treaty or agreement with resident First Nations.

The NWMP were an essential part of Macdonald's national policies.[27] In turn, the success of the national policies took precedence over not only treaty promises but also the basic human rights of Indigenous people.[28] The primary role of the Mounted police was to facilitate the peaceful occupation of the west by Anglo-Canadians and to allay their fears of Indigenous people once they arrived. Without farmer-settlers both the railway and the NWMP themselves would be redundant.[29]

Even more than the BCPP, the NWMP and its successors were required to fulfill a host of enforcement responsibilities at different times: from the *Leprosy Act* to the *Explosives Act* and from the *Bank Act* to the *Canada Temperance Act*. The Mounted police also, of course, enforced the *Indian Act* and other pieces of legislation both on and off the reserves. Further, despite the extent of the panoptic machinery that the DIA had in place, the NWMP and its successors provided them with a myriad of services.[30] They were a major force in laying the ground work for the acceptance of Treaty 7 and were a presence, along with their cannon, at the negotiations for the treaty.[31] In the years that followed they also provided an escort for the annuity money guaranteed in 1877.[32] The Mounted police could be called in at short notice at the request of the department to enhance its capacity in the case of a perceived threat. As occurred at the signing of the treaty, the Mounted police, by patrolling or merely by being visibly present, provided a show of force that could be very persuasive in 'encouraging' Indigenous people to meet their will and that of the DIA.

[ . . . ]

The relationship between the police and the DIA, both institutionally and at the local individual level, was not always smooth, but both agencies had the same long-term objectives. Both were primarily interested in paving the way for non-Indigenous settlement and advancing Anglo-Canadian cultural and economic interests. Neither believed it necessary, or even feasible, to extend the rights and freedoms apparently guaranteed by liberalism to Indigenous people.

## THE PASS SYSTEM

The restriction on the right of Indigenous people to travel freely provides perhaps the clearest illustration of the operation of exclusionary liberalism in western Canada. This restriction is best seen as a matrix of laws, regulations, and policy meant to 'elevate' Indigenous people while simultaneously securing the interests of non-Indigenous newcomers. Like colonialism itself, this restrictive complex was creative and adaptable and so could adjust as political, economic, or social conditions changed. The most notorious element of this network was the 'pass system', a DIA policy that had no legal basis, but nonetheless required reserve residents to secure a pass from their Indian agent before leaving their reserve for any reason.

The restriction of Indigenous movement seems to have originated with a NWMP concern regarding the potential consequences of cross-border movement by Canadian Indigenous people to hunt buffalo and steal horses. In the late 1870s, the NWMP was concerned primarily with proving they were able to exercise authority over Canadian territory and especially over Indigenous people. The worry was that Canada might provide a staging area for military action against the US army, which could then result in a US military incursion into Canadian territory in retribution. Brian Hubner confirms that the NWMP built forts Walsh and Macleod to this end.[33] By 1882, correspondence between the US and Canada led to the passage of an Order in Council in April by which Canada would propose to the US 'that individual permits be granted by the authorities of both nations to their respective Indians who may wish to cross the border'.[34]

In 1882 as well, NWMP Commissioner Irvine specifically recommended that Indian agents be vigilant in preventing large groups from leaving their reserves.[35] In November 1883, Deputy Superintendent General of Indian Affairs [DSGIA] Vankoughnet wrote to Macdonald to express his concern about Indigenous women camped near towns in the North-West and suggested that the problem could be rectified 'in a very simple manner by the Mounted Police . . . requiring that the owner of any tepee produce a permit from the local Indian agent for his or her

having the tepee at that point'.[36] Macdonald agreed that the presence of women, especially near settler towns and villages, needed to be restricted. In his annual report for that year Macdonald offered the opinion that the location of the Tsuu T'ina so close to Calgary 'operates detrimentally, to their improvement' and causes 'demoralization of their women'. In view of formulating a strategy 'for checking this evil' Macdonald ordered the establishment of a dialogue between the Indian Commissioner for the North-West Territories and the Commissioner of the NWMP 'with a view to the adoption of some plan to prevent the indiscriminate camping of Indians in the vicinity of towns and white settlements in the North-West Territories. . . . '[37]

The correspondence of the early 1880s indicates that there was desire and action at all levels of both the DIA and NWMP hierarchies to restrict Indigenous movement prior to 1885, but that a universally applied pass system as such did not yet have official approval. In 1885, though, 'the [North West] Rebellion brought the pass system to life with a jolt'.[38]

In May 1885, Major-General Frederick Middleton asked Dewdney '[w]ould it not be advisable to issue proclamation warning breeds and Indians to return to their Reserves and that all those found away will be treated as rebels. I suppose such a proclamation would be disseminated without difficulty'. Dewdney responded immediately that he had 'issued a notice advising Indians to stay on Reserves and warning them of risks they run in being found off them but have no power to issue proclamation as you suggest'.[39] The notice warned 'all good and loyal Indians should remain quietly on their Reserves where they will be perfectly safe and receive the protection of the soldiers and that any Indian being off his Reserve without special permission in writing from some authorized person, is liable to be arrested on suspicion of being a rebel, and punished as such'.[40]

By June, with the resistance mostly subdued, Dewdney wrote of the futility of attempting to restrict Indians to reserves 'when, if they do leave them, there is no law by which they can be punished and our orders enforced'.[41] This does not necessarily mean that he was opposed to restricting Indigenous movement, only that, in his opinion, without supporting legislation, the pass system was inoperable. The Indian Commissioner then turned to his assistant, Hayter Reed, and requested that he put into writing some suggestions regarding 'the future management of the Indians in the North West Territories'.[42]

Following the instructions of his superior, and as Dewdney confirmed 'only after careful consultation between myself and my assistant', Reed made 15 proposals. Of special interest here is Reed's seventh recommendation that 'no rebel Indian should be allowed off the Reserves without a pass signed by an ID [Indian Department] official'.[43] Significantly, Reed's suggestions were amplified as they moved up the DIA hierarchy. Indian Commissioner Dewdney, supported Reed's recommendation and suggested that 'another year' legislation might be enacted in support.[44]

Apparently encouraged by Dewdney's support, Reed reported from Battleford in August, 'I am adopting the system of keeping the Indians on their respective Reserves + not allowing any leave them without passes—I know this is hardly supportable by any legal enactment but one must do many things which can only be supported by common sense and by what may be for the general good—I get the Police to send out daily and send any Indians without passes back to their Reserves'. Reed complained though 'unless one is at their heels Police duties here are done in a half hearted manner'.[45]

In June of 1886 Dewdney was sent 'a form of pass proposed to be given to Indians when allowed to absent themselves from their Reserves' and in September he was sent the 50 books of passes that he had apparently requested. The following month Reed sent out the books of passes to Indian agents and the pass system was officially launched.[46]

Throughout the remainder of the 1880s the DIA and NWMP generally co-operated to apply the policy in the Treaty 7 area as they did in the prairie west to the east despite the fact that no Treaty 7 First Nation participated in the events of 1885.

[ . . . ]

In 1890, the DIA acquiesced to NWMP requests to make the pass system more restrictive. Vankoughnet assured NWMP Comptroller White that agents would be told to issue passes only to those who convinced the agent that the reason for requesting leave was 'a legitimate one'.[47] He pledged further that Kainai Agent Pocklington would be instructed to withhold passes from anyone who was previously found using alcohol when away from the reserve.[48] The NWMP were particularly concerned about the Kainai, who Superintendent Deane admitted the police were unsuccessful in restricting to their reserve. According to Deane '[t]he Bloods think that they are the cream of creation, and it is time for them to begin to imbibe some modification of the idea'.[49]

The pass system was part of a coercive and flexible matrix meant to restrict Indigenous movement in the interests of white settlers and it must be seen in that light. It took time for the pass system to find its place within this network and within the larger complex of exclusionary liberalism. Even though Canada never had the capacity to forcibly restrict all off-reserve movement, the will of both the police and the DIA to do what they could in this regard is evident, even if some in the upper echelons of the former were sometimes uncomfortable. There were cases of Indigenous people forcibly returned to their reserve, but even when passes were used solely as instruments of surveillance or as demonstrations of state control, they remained bereft of any legal justification. Both the DIA and the mounted police wanted to be seen as responding to settler fears, first of the military threat, and later the annoyance, posed by Indigenous people.

## RESTRICTION OF MOVEMENT IN BRITISH COLUMBIA

In British Columbia, there was no operational pass system nor was there the same degree of restriction of movement generally as there was in the prairie west. Secwepemc elders confirm that the period under discussion here is before 'Indian Affairs had really taken hold of the Indians' in this area.[50] Since the 'demands of war [World War I] coupled with our remoteness delayed the full effect of the system until a decade after the war', the Secwepemc were 'just beginning to come under the domination of the Indian agent' at the end of this period.[51] For example, at various times the agent at Kamloops and Okanagan had to send advance notice of his coming to ensure that residents would be present on their reserve when he arrived. Sometimes he even met community leaders in hotels in town.[52] As British Columbia's Indian Superintendent Arthur Wesley Vowell reminded DSGIA Frank Pedley in 1903, '[i]n connection with the Indians in British Columbia it is well to recollect that they consider themselves as a self-supporting people, mixing freely wherever they please, and may expect to find profitable employment, amongst the whites, as independent so long as they obey the laws governing the Dominion and the Province'.[53] As noted, there were only a few treaties in British Columbia and none in the southern interior. As a result there were no annuity payments, programs of farm instruction, or regular provision of foodstuffs and, coupled with the absence of the mounted police and far fewer DIA employees, there was less opportunity for coercion.

This does not mean that disciplinary surveillance was not applied in aid of the expansion of liberalism in British Columbia. Rather the point is only that the official structures to facilitate it were not as well developed nor as well staffed as they were in southern Alberta, at least in the period under discussion here and especially away from southern Vancouver Island and the Lower Mainland. As was the case in the prairie region, though, even those few First Nations who entered into the Douglas Treaties in the 1850s found that guarantees for freedom of movement in pursuit of economic activity were gradually eroded.[54]

As in the Treaty 7 region as well, special attention was paid in the interior of British Columbia to the movements and activities of Indigenous women.

Most attention appears to have been directed at keeping Indigenous women away from settler population centres of Victoria and the Lower Mainland. To this end, Indian Superintendent A.W. Vowell wrote to coastal steamship companies the following spring and requested that they 'refuse passage to all Indian women unless they have permits from their Agents to take passage on the Steamer or other boats, to certain points of destination'. While the initial responses from these companies seemed to indicate that they were willing to comply, as long as the other firms did as well, Superintendent Vowell reported that 'so long as an Indian woman is able and willing to pay her fare upon any of these boats passage will not be denied her'.[55] Like many east of the Rockies, Agent Pidcock remained in favour of a generalized restriction akin to the pass system but Superintendent Vowell argued that such a system would be 'practically inoperative and the cause of much disquietude to all the Indians in the Province' since 'many bands of Indians are beyond the reach of the Agents, who are the only representatives of the law known in some of these out of the way places, as far as the exercise of any immediate supervision over their actions is concerned'.[56] This position was accepted by SGIA Thomas Mayne Daly who recognized that the distance between Indigenous people and their agents in British Columbia would make it impractical to obtain a pass before leaving their reserve to obtain work.[57]

Pidcock changed tactics and had a petition apparently signed by 31 Kwakwaka'wakw men stating 'we are not able to stop the shameful traffic with Indian women without the assistance of the law' and requested that steamers only be allowed to transport women with the approval of the agent or designate. To this, the department responded that its employees would always help, 'when requested by the husband or brother or any one having proper authority, to stop a woman from going away'.[58] It is impossible to know for sure the circumstances that led to the creation of this document or the actual feelings of the community regarding the sentiments expressed in it. It seems unlikely though that any community would willingly turn over the right of its members to move freely to an outside authority and the incident involving the forcible restraint by the BCPP supports this interpretation. Women's freedom of movement was still an issue in 1909 when J.E. Rendle, a missionary on the coast, requested that the DIA 'order the Indians to all live in their village'. While the DIA passed on their own concerns to British Columbia, the Province's attorney general reported that things were 'not in such a bad state as the Indian Department would lead us to believe'.[59]

## MOUNTED POLICE

In both these regions of western Canada, racialized constructions of liberalism, which served to fundamentally exclude Indigenous people from land ownership, were backed up by the force of direct military intervention when necessary. For, as Reverend George McDougall confirmed before the arrival of the NWMP in western Canada, 'experience has taught us that Proclamations without a civil force to enforce them are not worth the paper they are written on'.[60] But such interventions were extremely rare in the history of Canada. The main disciplinary mechanism and the principal reformatory apparatus was unquestionably, in fact could only be, surveillance.

While everyone in liberal Canada was under observation at some level, no single group experienced the intensity or continuity of surveillance that Indigenous people did. In addition to those groups and individuals mentioned above, who clearly made the observation of First Nations people a priority, only those defined as 'Indians' had an entire government department dedicated to observing their actions and behaviour, and relieving them of their land and resources, while at the same time was charged with minimizing 'the risk of a rebellion or of great dissatisfaction'.[61]

## NOTES

1.   Appendix C of 'Report of the Government of British Columbia on the Subject of Indian Reserves' in British Columbia, *Papers Connected to the Indian Land Question, 1850–1875, 1877* (1875 and 1877). Rpt. 1987, 14.

2.   Hayter Reed, Circular, 9 February 1891, Library and Archives Canada (LAC), RG 10, vol. 1137.

3.   Harry W. Gibbon Stocken to Baring-Gould, 21 February 1899. See also, H.G.W. Stocken's *Among the Blackfoot and Sarcee* (Calgary: Glenbow Institute, 1976), v, vii, xii.

4.   For an example of the conflict in relation to a proposed hospital on the Nakoda reserve see correspondence in LAC RG 10, vol. 3993, file 186,790.

5.   'Indian Proselytism', *Calgary Herald*, 15 April 1891. 'Why Not More Co-operation among the Churches', *Calgary Herald*, 8 June 1895.

6.   Alex, Archbishop of St. Boniface, O.M.I. to Governor General in Council, 28 July 1889, LAC, MG29 E106, vol. 16, file 'Church-Dept. Relations, 1887–1895'.

7.   Hayter Reed to Lucas, Indian Agent, Bears Hills, 18 December 1888 M699/4; Dewdney to Rev. Canon Newton, Edmonton, 31 May 1890, M699/4 and Lucas to Alonzo Wright, M.P. Ottawa County, 21 January 1891, M699/5, Glenbow, Lucas Family Fonds.

8.   'Correspondence Regarding Communications Made to Newspapers by Ministers of the Gospel Criticizing Indian Affairs Government

Officials in the Northwest Territories', LAC, RG 10, vol. 3753, file 30,613.

9.  From the Report of Frederick Abbott, Secretary to the U.S. Board of Indian Commissioners, in regard to the relations between the church and government in Canada, Frederick H. Abbott, *The Administration of Indian Affairs in Canada* (Washington, DC: n.p., 1915), 25.

10. S.H. Blake to DSGIA Frank Pedley, 19 October 1908, LAC, RG 10, vol. 4024, file 289,032-2.

11. Tims to Indian Commissioner, 27 June 1895, LAC, RG 18, vol. 110, file 517-95.

12. Herchmer to Comptroller, telegram, 3 July 1895, LAC, RG 18, vol. 110, File 517-95. On Tims' unpopularity see J.R. Miller, *Shingwauk's Vision: A History of Native Residential Schools.* (Toronto: University of Toronto Press, 1996), 129–30.

13. Comptroller Frederick White to Commissioner L.W. Herchmer, 16 October 1895, LAC, RG 18, vol. 112, file 665-95.

14. Alexander Morris to John McDougall, 20 June 1874, LAC, MG 29 C23.

15. 'Minutes of meeting held with Indians of Bonaparte, Pavilion and Fountain reserves on the 11th, 12th, 13th, and 14th August, 1910', LAC, RG 10, vol. 3750, file 29858-11.

16. British Columbia Archives (BCA), GR-0099, box 4, file K-18 and Hatch 'The British Columbia Police', 1–18.

17. BCA GR-0056, box 12, file 12.

18. Lynne Stonier-Newman, *Policing a Pioneer Province: The B.C. Provincial Police 1858–1950* (Madeira Park, BC: Harbour Publishing, 1991): 38.

19. Entries for 30 April, 8 June and 9 June 1901, BCA, GR-1728, vol. 2.

20. See, for example, entries for 5, 11, and 24 May 1911; 3, 10, 28, and 30 September and 3, 6, 10, and 17 November 1911, BCA, GR-1728, vol. 3.

21. Daily Journal, 1914, entries for 25, 26, and 27 1914 and Daily Journal, 1915, entry for 11 November, 1915. LAC, RG 10, vol. 1325.

22. H. Bell Irving, W. Farrel to D.M. Eberts MPP, telegram, 8 July 1901, BCA, GR-0429, box 7, file 3, item 2314/01. See also F.S. Hussey to D.M. Eberts, AG, telegram, 8 July 1901, item 2317/01.

23. H.D. Phen Armthrop to Hussey, 25 October, 1904, BCA, GR-0063, box 2, file 5.

24. Zhiqiu Lin and Augustine Brannigan, 'The Implications of a Provincial Police Force in Alberta and Saskatchewan', in *Laws and Societies in the Canadian Prairie West, 1670–1940*, eds. Louis A. Knafla and Jonathan Swainger (Vancouver: UBC Press, 2005), 1, and Howard Palmer with Tamara Palmer, *Alberta: A New History* (Edmonton: Hurtig Publishers, 1990), 176.

25. S.W. Horrall, 'Sir John A. Macdonald and the Mounted Police Force for the Northwest Territories', *Canadian Historical Review*, LIII, 2 (June 1972): 183.

26. Horrall, 'Sir John A. Macdonald', 195–6.

27. R.C. Macleod, *The North-West Mounted Police and Law Enforcement, 1873–1905* (Toronto: University of Toronto Press, 1976): 3.

28. John Jennings, 'The North West Mounted Police and Indian Policy After the *1885 Rebellion*', in *1885 and After: Native Society in Transition*, eds. F. Laurie Barron and James B. Waldram (Regina, SK: Canadian Plains Research Center, University of Regina, 1986): 315; Sarah Carter, *Lost Harvests: Prairie Indian Reserve Farmers and Government Policy* (Montreal and Kingston: McGill-Queen's University Press, 1990): 155.

29. Gerald Friesen, *The Canadian Prairies: A History.* (Toronto and London: University of Toronto Press, 1993): 181; and Sarah Carter, *Lost Harvests: Prairie Indian Reserve Farmers and Government Policy* (Montreal and Kingston: McGill-Queen's University Press, 1990): 52.

30. Scott to Stewart, 28 October 1927, LAC, RG 10, vol. 6822, file 494-1-2 pt. 1.

31. R.C. Macleod, *The North-West Mounted Police and Law Enforcement, 1873-1905* (Toronto: University of Toronto Press, 1976): 28; and Treaty 7 Elders and Tribal Council with Walter Hildebrandt, Dorothy First Rider, and Sarah Carter. *The True Spirit and Original Intent of Treaty 7* (Montreal and Kingston: McGill-Queen's University Press, 1996), 80, 117, 136–7, and 378–9.

32. NWMP, 'Annual Report for 1883', paper no. 12 in Canada, Sessional Papers, 1884, 15.

33. Frederick White in 'North-West Mounted Police', Appendix D of Report of the Secretary of State in Canada, *Sessional Papers*, 1877, 21; Jennings, 'The North West Mounted Police',

228; and Brian Hubner, 'Horse Stealing and the Borderline: The NWMP and the Control of Indian Movement, 1874–1900', *Prairie Forum* 20, 2 (Fall 1995): 286–288.

34. Copy of Order in Council, 24 April 1882, Canada, DIA, *Annual Report, 1882,* xliv-xlv. John A. Macdonald's annual report as SGIA for that year indicates his early support for the idea of passes to restrict Indigenous movement, DIA, *Annual Report, 1882,* xi.

35. Commissioner A.G. Irvine in 'North-West Mounted Police Force', Part III of *Annual Report of the Department of the Interior, 1882* in Canada, Sessional Papers, 1883, 11–12.

36. Vankoughnet memorandum to Macdonald, 15 November 1883, LAC, RG 18, vol. 1009, file 628.

37. DIA, Annual Report, 1883, lii. Macdonald's report is dated 1 January 1884.

38. Jennings, 'The North West Mounted Police', 290–291.

39. Middleton to Dewdney, 6 May 1885 and Dewdney to Middleton, 7 May 1885, LAC, Dewdney Papers, MG 27 I C4, vol. 4, pages 1658–1660. See also B. Bennett, *Study of Passes for Indians to Leave Their Reserves* (N.P.: Treaties and Historical Research Centre, 1974), 1–2 and Carter, *Lost Harvests,* 150.

40. Dewdney 'Notice', 6 May 1885, LAC, RG 10, vol. 3584, file 1130.

41. Dewdney to J.M. Rae, Agent at Battleford, 23 June 1885, LAC, Dewdney Papers, MG 27 I C4, vol. 5, pages 1948–1949. See also Bennett, 'Passes for Indians', 3; and Carter, *Lost Harvests,* 150.

42. Dewdney to Macdonald, 1 August 1885, LAC, RG 10, vol. 3710, file 19550-3.

43. Dewdney to Macdonald, 1 August 1885 and Reed 'Memorandum for the Hon[ble] the Indian Commissioner relative to the future management of Indians', 20 July 1885, LAC, RG 10, vol. 3710, file 19550-3.

44. Reed's Memorandum of 20 July 1885, LAC, RG 10, vol. 3710, file 19550-3. Carter, *Lost Harvests,* 146 and F. Laurie Barron, 'The Indian Pass System in the Canadian West, 1882–1935', *Prairie Forum* 13, 1 (Spring 1988): 27–8.

45. Reed to Dewdney, 16 August 1885, LAC, Dewdney Papers, MG 27 I C4, vol. 5, pages 2076–2087. Quote at 2078–2079.

46. Unsigned letter to Dewdney, 4 June 1886 and unsigned Memorandum to McNeil, 1 September 1886, vol. 3710, file 19550-3. The date written on the first letter is 1866 but this must be an error. Bennett, 'Passes for Indians', 3–4.

47. Vankoughnet to White, 21 October 1890, LAC, RG 18, vol. 44, file 784-90.

48. Vankoughnet to White, 17 October 1890, LAC, RG 18, vol. 44, file 782-90.

49. NWMP, *Annual Report, 1889,* 42.

50. Harvey Jules, interview with author Joyce Dunn at Chase, British Columbia 1983. Copy of tape recording in author's possession.

51. George Manuel and Michael Posluns, *The Fourth World: An Indian Reality* (New York: Macmillan Publishing Co., 1970): 54, 1.

52. Kamloops Agent Daily Journal, 1898, entries for 30 March and 17 May 1898; Daily Journal for 1912, entries for 8 March, 29 June, and 1 July 1912 and Daily Journal, 1913, entries for 20 May 17, 18, and 23 June, LAC, RG 10, vol. 1325.

53. Vowell to Pedley, 30 June 1903, LAC, RG 10, vol. 3944 file 121698-54.

54. For an example of restrictions on fishing imposed on the Lekwungen (Songhees) near Victoria see John Lutz, Makúk: *A New History of Aboriginal-White Relations* (Vancouver: UBC Press, 2008), 257–62.

55. A.W. Vowell, I Supt to Capt J.D. Warren, Victoria, 3 March 1890; Warren to Vowell, 21 March 1890; Jno Irving to Vowell, 11 March 1890 and Vowell to Vankoughnet, DSGIA, 25 March 1890, LAC, RG 10, vol. 3816, file 57,045-1.

56. Pidcock to Vowell, n.d, (marked received 4 March 1891) LAC, RG 10, vol. 3816, file 57,045-1.

57. T. Mayne Daly to Senator W.J. Macdonald, 10 May 1895, LAC, RG 10, vol. 3816, file 57,045-1.

58. Vowell to DSGIA, 11 May 1895 and DSGIA to Vowell, 20 May 1895, LAC, RG 10, vol. 3816, file 57,045-1.

59. J.E. Rendle, Methodist missionary, Quatiaski Cove, BC to Vowell, 29 October 1909, BCA, GR-0063, box 5, file 3.

60. George McDougall to D.A. Smith, 8 January 1874, LAC, RG 10, vol. 3609, file 3278.

61. Blake to Oliver, 6 February 1907, LAC, RG 10 vol. 4023, file 289,032-1.

4   From Sarah A. Carter, 'Creating "Semi-Widows" and "Supernumerary Wives":
Prohibiting Polygamy in Prairie Canada's Aboriginal Communities to 1900', in
M. Rutherdale and K. Pickles, eds. *Contact Zones: Aboriginal and Settler Women
in Canada's Colonial Past* (Vancouver: University of British Columbia Press, 2005):
131–159.

Historically and culturally specific meanings of masculinity and femininity, and grave concern about alternate meanings of these, profoundly shaped the policies that Canada's Department of Indian Affairs (DIA) devised to 'civilize' Aboriginal people living on reserves in western Canada in the post-1870 era. Legal, political, and missionary authorities shared the view that a particular marriage model—of lifelong monogamy in the tradition of the Christian religion and English common law—symbolized the proper differences between the sexes and set the foundation for the way both sexes were to behave. Sustained efforts were made to introduce and perpetuate this marriage model, and this endeavour is clearly illustrated in the 1890s resolve of the DIA to abolish polygamy.[1] Yet there were limitations and challenges to the authorities' ability to impose and enforce one marriage model. Aboriginal marriage law proved tenacious, because of the determination of Aboriginal people, but also because of the limited capacity of the state to control the domestic domain. While constrained and never fully accomplished, however, these interventions caused considerable turmoil and rupture in Aboriginal communities.

Prohibiting polygamy among the Aboriginal people of western Canada was not an isolated, or unique development, and this study points to the concerns Canadian colonizers shared with the broader colonizing world about the 'intimacies of empire'.[2] In other colonial settings, polygamy was similarly condemned, but the nature, timing, purpose, and outcomes of programs of intervention varied widely. In western Canada,

as in other colonial contexts, ideologies of gender and sexuality were a foundation of the colonial regime, but this was an unstable foundation.

Plains Aboriginal marriages were varied and complex, and they were not well understood by newcomers to western Canada.[3] The ceremonies and protocol involved differed from the Christian and English common-law model. In Plains societies, marriage was more of a process than a particular defining moment. Among the Blackfoot, marriages were family affairs—both sets of relatives had to give their consent. The relationship involved reciprocal obligations among the sets of relatives. The marriage was validated, and the reciprocal obligations of both parties established, through an exchange of gifts that could be initiated by either set of relatives. It became a matter of pride for the family receiving the first gifts to return gifts of greater value. Obligations were ongoing; they did not end with a defining wedding moment.

There were a variety of ideal types of conjugal union, not just one as in Euro-Canadian society. Lifelong, monogamous unions were common, but there were other kinds of marriages, seen not as a departure from a norm, but as a desirable family unit. Many of the leading men in Plains societies had more than one spouse. The term 'polygamy' does not have a parallel in the Cree or Blackfoot languages, suggesting that it was not seen as a separate, distinct departure from a norm but as one of several possible forms of marriage. Often sisters were married to the same man. A man might also marry his deceased brother's widow, adopting the children and preserving the relationship with the grandparents and extended family. Only hardworking men of wealth could maintain these large households, so parents sought these marriages for their daughters.

Cree and Blackfoot sources indicate that subsequent wives were brought into a family generally after consultation with, and with the approval of, the first wife. These domestic arrangements provided economic assistance, companionship, and enhanced status for the senior wife. In 1891 Chief Red Crow of the Kainai (Blood) of southern Alberta described marriage practices to Indian agent R.N. Wilson, saying that the first wives seldom objected to the presence of other wives and that it was very often they who proposed that sisters or other relatives become second or third wives.[4]

Cree Chief Fine Day provided a detailed description of marriage practices in his 1934 sessions with anthropologist David Mandelbaum.[5] Fine Day's father had two wives, his mother being the second wife, and he said that the two got along well. Fine Day stressed that permission was required from the first wife, and that the acquisition of a second wife was a joint decision in recognition of the needs of the first wife. According to Fine Day, if a wife required assistance running her household, the husband would say, 'How would you like to have a helper?' If she said yes, they then both would pick out some likely girl. He would ask her again, 'Would you be kind to her?' She would say, 'Yes, that's why I want her.' Then he would go and get the other woman. But the first wife was always the boss.[6] Fine Day stressed the authority of the wives to determine the size and nature of the family unit:

> It was not a man's abilities as a hunter that determined the number of wives he had, but upon the arrangements he made with his wife. Both a man and his wife paid for the second wife. Young girls would not want to be married to a man

that was of no account. They wanted to marry a Worthy Man because they know that there would be no quarrelling—he would stop it.

> If a man wanted to take a third wife, his first would usually agree but his second would often say no. That usually would settle it.[7]

If the permission of the wives had not been obtained there were consequences. Fine Day noted that if a man married a third wife without the permission of his first two, they would never be friendly toward her. According to Red Crow, if a husband brought home a second wife to the disgust of the first, she would 'keep up a continual row until the newcomer was sent away'.[8]

Kainai historian Beverly Hungry Wolf wrote that women did a tremendous amount of work, and it was thought to be desirable for a young woman to marry a prominent man with several wives as this eased the burden of work.[9] Work was divided. A 73-year-old Blackfoot woman, Middle Woman No Coat, who was interviewed in 1939, recalled the division of labour in her father's household with five wives. The first two wives 'are older and do all the tanning. Younger wives do the cooking. In winter, all take turns getting wood; someone always present to take care of the fire'.[10] Other advantages for the co-wives were that women in polygamous marriages tended to have fewer children, and the mothers of the sister co-wives were often part of the household.[11]

Among the Blackfoot the first and generally the oldest wife was known as the 'sits-beside-him' wife, and this was a position of honour. She was the female head of the household and she had an important role in ceremonies such as those involving sacred bundles. She accompanied her husband to feasts and ceremonies, and she directed the other wives in their work. The other wives did not have as high a standing in the community as the 'sits-beside-him' wife. These marriages were not always successful, but such incidents seem to have been the exception in an environment in which co-operation and sharing was vital, and in a society where women did almost all of their work communally. [ . . . ] According to Beverly Hungry Wolf, there were occasions when a younger wife in a large household and with a much older husband suffered from loneliness and a desire to be loved. She noted that some older husbands sanctioned outside relationships as long as they were discreet and brought no public disgrace.[12]

Church, government, political, and legal authorities severely censured what they understood as polygamy in Aboriginal societies. It was seen as deviant and morally depraved. Polygamy became a towering example of the shortcomings of Aboriginal societies, which were understood to subordinate women, in contrast to the ideal of monogamous marriage, cherished by Europeans as an institution that elevated women. Polygamy was viewed as a system that exploited and degraded women, depriving them of respect and influence. It was thought that jealousy and friction among the wives was inevitable. The husbands were seen as idle, debauched, and tyrannical. The sexual desires of the husband were seen as a main motivation for polygamy. Missionaries were among the most outspoken critics. They were deeply concerned about the propriety of a host of customs involving sexuality, marriage, and divorce. Aboriginal marriage, even when monogamous, was misunderstood and condemned as a heartless business transaction without love, courtship, or ceremony—a commodity simply changed hands.[13] But polygamy topped the list of forces that allegedly degraded women. As Methodist missionary John Semmens wrote in his 1884 memoirs, multiple wives were 'general slaves, subject to the behests of the most thoughtless and relentless of taskmasters'.[14]

These views were common throughout the imperial world in the late nineteenth century. In a book entitled *Women of the Orient*, Rev. R.C. Houghton described his thoughts on polygamy: 'Deceit, bickerings, strife, jealousies, intrigues, murder and licentiousness have followed in its train; true love has, in its presence, given place to sensual passion, and woman has become the slave, rather than the companion of man. The word home, as symbolical of confidence, sympathy, rest, happiness and true affection, is not found in the vocabulary of polygamous lands. Polygamy is subversive of God's order; and, beginning by poisoning the very sources of domestic and social prosperity, its blighting influences are felt and seen in every department of national life'.[15]

While missionaries and other reformers were ostensibly concerned with what they depicted as the despotism and degradation that Aboriginal women had to contend with from the men who were their 'ruthless taskmasters', there was at the same time a contradictory and muted recognition that these women had some freedoms and privileges not enjoyed by non-Aboriginal women. Sexual freedom before marriage was tolerated. Divorce was relatively easy. People separated and divorced for reasons of incompatibility, physical abuse, laziness, or lack of support. Among the Blackfoot a marriage was dissolved when a wife left, returning to her parents or an older brother, taking her property, which included the tipi, with her. Children normally stayed with the mother following a divorce.[16] [ . . . ] Esther Goldfrank concluded that Blackfoot women had considerable power and influence, emphasizing also their central role in sacred ceremonies. Women 'enjoyed a comparatively strong position . . . a woman could lead a war party; she could own property, receive and exercise medicine power, and give names. She was a necessary part of every ceremonial transfer; she was the custodian of the bundles that her husband bought. The pubic initiation of the Horn Society still dramatized the man's dependence. It is the wife who receives the power from the seller. Her husband can only gain possession from her'.[17]

In contrast to widely held assumptions about their servitude and misfortunes, Aboriginal wives enjoyed more options and autonomy than Canadian women of the nineteenth century married under English common law. Legal historian Constance Backhouse has described this form of marriage as 'very rigid, overbearing [and] patriarchal'.[18] Husbands were expected to wield all the power, and wives were denied independence or autonomy. Under the 'doctrine of marital unity', the very existence of the wife was legally absorbed by her husband. Her property became his property. Divorce was almost unknown; marriages were regarded as virtually indissoluble. Divorce was also expensive, and it carried a social stigma, attached strongly to the divorced woman regardless of the cause of marital breakdown. If a divorce did occur, the woman risked the loss of custody of children.

It was the missionaries in western Canada who made the first efforts to discourage polygamy. Their methods, however, and the enticements at their disposal (refusal to baptize, excommunication) were not particularly compelling. Missionaries were also uncertain about how best to proceed, and there was concern especially for the 'discarded' wives and their children. These perplexing issues were discussed at the highest church levels. Anglican missionaries of the Church Missionary Society (CMS) were instructed not to baptize any man who had more than one wife, but the wives, perceived as victims, could be baptized. Although the policy was confirmed at the Lambeth Conference of 1888, it was not without considerable discussion of perplexing conundrums that might arise. [ . . . ]

Missionaries in western Canada were not in agreement about how to proceed when dissolving polygamous marriages. Which wife should be retained? How should the 'semi-widows' or 'abandoned' wives and children be provided for? Methodist missionary E.R. Young regretted the fate of the abandoned ones, but claimed in his memoirs that he felt obliged to enforce the rule that the first wife must take precedence over a later one, even if the first was childless and the later wife had a larger family.[19] John Semmens, however, felt that while the rule favoured the claim of the senior wife, there were 'many instances . . . in which the right is waived voluntarily in favour of the younger women'.[20] He felt the husband should care for the younger children, permitting the abandoned wives to earn a living. The Hudson's Bay Company, he noted, felt charitable toward these 'semi-widows', allowing them job opportunities where others were refused. The children of a first wife, Semmens wrote, would be grown up and able to support their mother. In his memoirs of missionary life, Anglican John Hines wrote that he 'followed no definite rule in deciding which wife should be retained, but that those with the greatest number of small children had the strongest claim'.[21] Hines found that it was generally the eldest wife who left the marriage, moving to the homes of grown-up daughters.

While missionaries sought to eradicate polygamy from the beginning of their work on western Canadian Indian reserves after the 1870s era of treaties, federal government administrators were, until the 1890s, hesitant, even reluctant, to pursue any concerted efforts. The Indian agents, farm instructors, inspectors, school officials, teachers, and bureaucrats in Regina and Ottawa worked within the legal framework of the *Indian Act* and pursued a cluster of policies that together were to have the effect of imposing gender roles and identities drawn from the experiences of the colonizers. Men were to be yeoman farmers, and for a time the residential and industrial school system trained them for other trades such as shoemaking or blacksmithing. Women were to be farm homemakers, undertaking their tasks of butter-making, sewing, cleaning, and cooking individually in permanent (not mobile) homes. (Women were also to be mothers, but their capacity in this regard was viewed by authorities as suspect, necessitating the residential school system.) These homes were to house nuclear families, and there would be decent partitions allowing privacy.

As part of this program, administrators wanted to impose what they regarded as legal, permanent, and monogamous marriages. The *Indian Act* was of some assistance in imposing this model of marriage. Under this legislation a widow could inherit her husband's property only if she could prove she was of good moral character and had lived with her husband until he was deceased.[22] A DIA official, most likely the Indian agent, would decide whether the widow was 'moral' and so qualified. Also helping to impose the patriarchal and monogamous model of marriage was a clause of the act which stipulated that annuities (annual payments promised under treaties) and any interest money (which might arise from the sale of reserve land) could be refused any Indian 'who may be proved, to the satisfaction of the Superintendent-General, to have been guilty of deserting his or her family and the said Superintendent-General may apply the same towards the support of any family, woman or child so deserted'. The superintendent-general could also 'stop the payment of the annuity and interest money of any woman having no children, who deserts her husband and lives immorally with another man'.[23] These laws, which reflected a range of stereotypes about Aboriginal women, particularly their potential for 'immorality', were aimed at keeping women within monogamous, lifelong marriages.

Based on legal advice from the Department of Justice, however, DIA authorities found that it was not possible to simply impose their marriage model. Indian agents expressed grave concern about what they perceived as a tenuous, invalid, impermanent form of marriage, as divorce was permitted. Yet they could not abolish or prohibit Aboriginal marriage. Not to recognize these as marriages, to proclaim them all invalid, would mean that married persons would feel free to consider their relationships null and void. The children would be illegitimate. There was also no one to perform civil or Christian marriages in many regions of the West. The superintendent

inspector for Manitoba, Ebenezer McColl, complained in 1893 that couples were 'living illegally together, according to the unorthodox custom of their pagan ancestors', but he was forced to admit that people did not have the money to obtain licences, and that the visiting missionary seldom remained long enough to enable the banns to be published the requisite number of times to legalize a marriage. 'Hence', wrote McColl, 'they have either to postpone indefinitely the regular consummation of their nuptials or live unlawfully together without having any authorized wedding ceremony performed'.[24]

The resistance of Aboriginal people, who showed a preference for their own marriage laws, also hampered any program of intervention. According to the Fort Macleod *Gazette*, the first marriage of an Aboriginal couple in southern Alberta to be solemnized through obtaining a marriage certificate took place in 1895.[25] Two years later on the Blackfoot reserve, the first marriage of a Siksika couple at that mission was performed according to the rites of the Catholic Church, over 50 years after the first Catholic missionaries arrived on the prairies, and after twenty years of reserve life.[26] The DIA could do little to impose a new regime, although officials were instructed to work to end 'tribal customs and pagan views', and to facilitate an understanding of the 'true nature and obligations of the marriage tie'.[27]

An 1888 Department of Justice opinion on Indian marriage and divorce established the policy that the DIA would pursue well into the twentieth century. '[Marriages of] Pagan Indians which have been contracted in accordance with tribal customs should be treated by your Department as *prima facie* valid and the issue of such marriage as legitimate', wrote a law clerk in 1888. 'If, however, an Indian so married deserts the woman who is recognized or is entitled to recognition as his wife, and during her life time lives with and has children by another woman, the Minister does not think that such cohabitation should in any case be recognized as marriage, unless there has been an actual divorce from the first wife. The resulting issue should therefore be treated as illegitimate and as having no right to share in the annuities of the band'.[28]

By about 1900 a complicated situation had emerged in which Aboriginal marriage law was recognized as valid if both parties were of that ancestry, and if the marriage conformed to the ideal of a monogamous, lifelong bond. Aboriginal divorce law was not regarded as valid. This policy, and the way in which it was interpreted by many reserve administrators, caused upheaval and instability in a society that had easily permitted remarriage in the event of marriage breakdown. Those who were divorced or deserted by their spouses were without their former option of forming a new family. 'Legal' divorce was a virtual impossibility for reserve residents, and it was rare at this time for all Canadians.[29] Indian agents had tremendous power to decide which couples were legally married, which were living together 'immorally', in their view, and which children were legitimate. For the purposes of annuity payments, the agents decided what constituted a valid family unit. Agents gave and denied permission for couples to marry, and they also refused permission for people to remarry in the event of divorce according to Aboriginal law. At times agents, the North West Mounted Police, and school principals took concerted action to break up what they saw as illegal marriages.[30]

DIA officials took few steps to abolish polygamous marriages until the early 1890s, and even then no action was taken against those who had entered into treaty in these circumstances. Annuity paylists indicate that leading men had two, three, or four adult women in the household. It was hoped that the practice would die naturally under the influence of missionaries and under the new conditions of reserve life. Officials did take steps to discourage any new polygamous marriages. An 1882 departmental circular established a policy that was intended to achieve this goal. Indian superintendent J.F. Graham wrote: 'There is no valid reason for perpetuating polygamy by encouraging its continuance in admitting any further accessions to the number already existing, and I [illegible] to instruct you not to recognize any additional transgressions by allowing more husbands to draw annuities for more than their legal wives'.[31] There is no indication that Indian Affairs officials were aware that until 1890 no statute existed that explicitly asserted that polygamy was illegal in Canada; a comprehensive antipolygamy bill was only introduced in 1890 in response to the arrival of Mormons in Alberta.

Why did the DIA decide that more active intervention was necessary by the early 1890s? In other colonial settings, programs of intervention were motivated by economic factors and the desire for Indigenous labour. In Natal and southern Rhodesia, for example, colonial authorities argued that married men would not be compelled to work while they were permitted to live 'idly' at home with their wives doing all the work for them. Thus polygamy was understood to deprive the settler colony of African male labour, undermining the economic progress of the region. Men would have to seek wage labour if they could no longer accumulate many wives.[32] In the US West, punishing polygamists was a means of undermining the authority of many of the leading Native American men. The Court of Indian Offenses, established in 1883, took aim at polygamy. Judges were to be selected from among the leading men of the reservations, but a polygamist could not serve as a judge. Polygamists were to be fined or to serve time with hard labour. As historian John D. Pulsipher has written, the Court of Indian Offenses was designed to strike at the heart of the power of Native American male leaders: 'As with Mormons, polygamists in Native groups were usually the leading men of their tribes. By barring polygamists from judicial service—monogamy being the only qualification for serving on the bench—and actively prosecuting any-one who tried to take multiple wives, the Bureau could hope to subvert the existing tribal power structures and replace them with structures which were properly sub-sumed under federal authority'.[33]

In western Canada there was little demand for the labour of Aboriginal males, so this factor can be ruled out. By the late nineteenth century in Canada, however, there was a widespread fear that the nuclear family and the home, the central institutions of the social order, were disintegrating in the wake of industrialization, rural depopulation, and urbanization. Reformers and leaders in Canada took steps to reinforce the institu-tion of marriage. As historian James G. Snell has written, 'in particular, Canadian lead-ers pressed for a stronger role by the state in defending marriage and in punishing any deviations from the moral code and social order associated with marriage'.[34] The forces of industrialization, rural depopulation, and urbanization were somewhat remote from western Canada in the 1890s, when policy-makers remained desperate to attract agri-culturalists. But in this new region of the Dominion, the imperative to reinforce the institution of lifelong monogamous mar-riage took on added dimensions and urgency. The nuclear family, centring on a husband and wife, was to be the basic building block of the West. This goal was embedded in the *Dominion Lands Act* and the homestead system that established the economic and social foun-dation of the prairie West. Yet there were chal-lenges to this marriage and family model, not only from Aboriginal residents, but also from recent immigrants. In the late 1880s, mission-aries had publicly voiced concern about the morality of some of the white men of the West who had a sequence of Aboriginal wives and were not supporting their children.[35] Some prominent men had cast aside women married according to Aboriginal law and had remar-ried newly arrived white women. Immigrants had marriage customs and domestic units that

departed from the cherished single model. These multiple definitions posed a threat, endangering convictions about the natural-ness or common sense of the European family formation. The arrival of the Mormons in southern Alberta in the late 1880s, however, combined with the Blackfoot's open resist-ance to and defiance of interference in their domestic arrangements, altered the situation. Charges of polygamy also in some cases per-mitted DIA authorities to depose, or threaten to depose, chiefs who challenged government authority.

The presence of the Mormons in Canada caused fear and anxiety. They also had sup-porters, as they were viewed as excellent dry land farmers, but support fell away after their request to continue in their polygamous mar-riages.[36] There was concern that Canadian men might be tempted to join up, and these fears seemed to be realized in 1889 when Anthony Maitland Stenhouse, a member of the British Columbia legislative assembly, tendered his resignation, renounced his own faith, and joined the Mormons in southern Alberta. He vocally and vigorously defended polygamy in the press (although he himself remained unmarried).[37] It was Stenhouse who read the Canadian statutes and discovered a loophole: marrying two wives at the same time did not violate existing laws.[38] Other concerns were that the Mormons would pros-elytize, dragging young non-Mormon girls into lives of degradation. But polygamy was seen as a deeper threat to the very fabric of the young nation. As one Ontario Liberal parlia-mentarian declared in the House of Commons during the 1890 debate on 'An Act respect-ing Offences relating to the Law of Marriage', polygamy was 'a serious moral and national ulcer'.[39]

Amendments to Canadian law, passed in 1890, imposed a five-year prison sentence and a fine of $500 on any person guilty of entering into any form of polygamy, any kind of con-jugal union with more than one person at the same time, or what the 'persons commonly called Mormons' knew as 'spiritual or plural marriage'. Any kind of ceremony, rite, or form practised by any society, sect, or denomination, religious or secular, or mere mutual consent could qualify—a binding form of marriage recognized by law did not have to have taken place.[40]

[ . . . ]

Given the public attention to the issue of polygamy, the widespread anxiety about the disintegration of the nuclear family, the proximity of the Mormons to a reserve community where polygamy was practised, and the new legislation that specifically prohibited polygamy, the time had come for the DIA to act. Also motivating action was evidence that new polygamous marriages were being contracted. A final factor to be considered is that in the early 1890s in western Canada, the land on fertile Indian reserves was being subdivided at great expense into 40-acre lots that were to be the small-scale farms and homes of nuclear families.[41] This plan was inspired in part by the US *Dawes Severalty Act*, as well as by Canada's *Dominion Lands Act*, but it was not precisely the same as either. It was similar, however, in that the ideal of a self-sufficient, independent family in which the male was the breadwinner and the farm wife his helpmate served as a rationale for the scheme. Large extended families of several wives, grandmothers, and many children could simply not survive on these miniature farms. In the United States, the implementation of the *Dawes Act* became an effective method of undermining polygamous households.

Yet measures aimed at eradicating polygamy remained reluctant and hesitant: In 1892 Indian Commissioner Hayter Reed asked his Ottawa superior for an opinion from the Department of Justice on questions that could guide a possible criminal prosecution 'to suppress polygamy among our Indians', as cases still continued to occur 'and the question arises whether some more stringent measures than heretofore resorted to should not now be adopted'.[42] Not receiving a reply,

Reed wrote in a similar vein the next year, saying that 'their pernicious practices' were 'far from showing sign of the gradual eradication which was expected', and asking for an opinion on questions including: 'Is an Indian liable to criminal prosecution, if, in accordance with the customs of his Band, he lives with more than one wife?'[43]

In a December 1893 circular letter, each of the Indian agents in western Canada was asked to report on the state of polygamy in their agencies by ascertaining the numbers, and recording the names, of husbands and wives and recording the number of years of marriage. Agents were also to fully explain the law on the subject. In preparing the lists, Assistant Commissioner Amedée Forget emphasized 'the necessity for the utmost carefulness, in order that injustice may not be inadvertently done to anyone named therein'.[44] What Forget may have meant was that there was great potential for misunderstanding in drawing up these lists; not all of the households with more than one adult woman were necessarily polygamous. [ . . . ]

The initial lists of polygamous families were submitted to Ottawa in September 1894, but any action was delayed as bureaucrats there asked that further information be supplied as to the 'ages of the Indians shown to have added to the number of their wives since entering into Treaty'.[45] [ . . . ]

The people of southern Alberta's Treaty 7, however, stood out from the others in the persistence of polygamy. There were 76 polygamous families on the Blood Reserve, and 49 on the Blackfoot Reserve.[46] The list of polygamous marriages entered into since the treaty were 23 Blood, 41 Blackfoot, and 49 Peigan.[47]

Resolve to take legal action was strengthened when new cases of polygamous marriages continued in the Blood agency, despite the fact that in the summer of 1894 the people had been notified that no plural marriages would be permitted for the future.[48] Indian agent James Wilson reported that marriages were defiantly continuing.[49] Two young men had taken second wives and 'upon [Wilson's] ordering them to obey instructions of the Department they refused'. Wilson had warned them they were liable to be sent to prison, and he was refusing the families rations until they obeyed. He wanted to send them up before a judge and felt that 'a little coercion' was necessary now to 'put a stop to what is probably one of the greatest hindrances to their advancement'. Threats of legal action and withholding rations worked in two cases, but a man named Plaited Hair refused to give up his second wife. Wilson sought permission to place the second wife in a residential school, and Forget agreed with this course of action.[50] Forget stated that threats of prosecution had been made for years, that regard for the 'prestige of the law' would be lessened if they did not proceed, and that their wards might be emboldened by what would seem to them to be evidence of weakness if no action was taken.[51]

In all the correspondence concerning the eradication of polygamy, DIA officials expressed almost no concern about the fate of the 'semi-widows' who would be the result of a successful policy or prosecution. There is no indication of the kind of discussion of the conundrums that bedevilled the missionaries, such as which wife would be regarded as legitimate and which would have to go, and were they able to remarry. The records also contain almost no indication of the thoughts or reactions of the wives. Concern that women were treated within their own society as chattels, to be moved about at will, seems hollow when officials were prepared to remove them from their homes and place them in residential schools without any apparent consultation or permission. A central rationale for eradicating polygamy was that women were to be saved from lives of slavery, yet if the initiatives were successful, the 'semi-widows' or 'supernumerary wives' and children were to be abandoned.

[ . . . ]

DIA administrators became ever more determined to take stringent measures as new cases of polygamy arose. It was also reported that girls were being promised in marriage as a means of preventing them from being sent to residential schools.[52] Before proceeding with the uncertain criminal prosecution, consideration was given to the tactic of placing girls in residential schools under the compulsory education clauses of the *Indian Act*. In 1895 Forget was wondering whether this might be more successful, causing 'less friction than by proceeding to prosecute for bigamy under the Criminal Code'. The linking of the residential school program with the campaign to abolish polygamy further inflamed protests on reserve communities of southern Alberta.

[ . . . ]

By the late 1890s, DIA officials were worried about the determination of the Blackfoot to resist interference in their domestic relations. Chief Red Crow of the Kainai continued to live with his four wives despite the fact that in 1896 he was baptized into the Roman Catholic Church and was married in a Catholic ceremony to his youngest wife, Singing Before. [...]

As evidence of new cases of polygamy accumulated in 1898, Indian Commissioner Forget wrote the new Deputy Superintendent General of Indian Affairs, James Smart, requesting 'a definite and unqualified authorization to take measures of repression. Department's sanction of proceedings in such cases having hitherto been so qualified as to practically nullify same'.[53] J.D. McLean, acting secretary, replied that the department was willing to leave the matter in his hands. Newcombe's 1895 opinion was quoted, and Forget was told that if he felt it was in the best interests of the Indians, and of public morality, he could take the necessary proceedings.[54] Forget was determined to take action, as he was convinced that 'unless severe measures are taken it will be many years before the evil is eradicated'.[55] In 1898 Indian agent James Wilson reported that notwithstanding all his efforts on the Blood reserve, six or seven young men had taken second wives, and he felt others would follow this example.[56]

In the Treaty 4 district, Cree Chief Star Blanket was reported in the fall of 1898 to have taken another wife.[57] The File Hills Indian agent informed the chief that more was expected of him as he had only recently been reinstated as chief. According to the agent, Star Blanket said that 'he would rather give up the Chiefship [sic] than give the woman up'.[58] After several months, Star Blanket complied with DIA policy to some extent by giving up his first wife, who appealed to the department for assistance as she was in a state of destitution.[59] Star Blanket was regarded as 'difficult' to handle as he was opposed to policies on schools. It was recommended that he be deposed.

Forget decided to focus on the Blood Reserve after first giving the parties reasonable notice that they would be prosecuted unless they abandoned polygamy. He hoped that with firmness and the 'hearty co-operation' of the police, the law would be enforced. In August 1898 Forget instructed agent Wilson to collect and submit information regarding all the new cases of polygamy to the Crown prosecutor, C.F. Conybeare of Lethbridge.[60] [ . . . ]

The Kainai were determined to resist. By November 1898 [the Crown prosecutor] Wilson could report no changes, despite numerous meetings on the subject. He tried another tactic by refusing to pay the wives their annuities.[61] Wilson explained to Forget that the *Indian Act* 'gave power to refuse payment to women who deserted their families and lived immorally with another man, and that as these women knew what they were doing they were equally guilty with the men'. Wilson told Red Crow that the paylist books would be kept open for ten days, and that during that time the chief was to hold a meeting with the women to persuade them to give up their marriages. A meeting was held, but it was reported that Red Crow's position was that the new rules about marriage should apply only to the graduates of the schools.[62] Wilson declared that the young people were

bound to obey and that Red Crow should insist they obey. The chief refused to do this. Once again the young men were given one month to withdraw from the position they had taken. Wilson reported that the tactic of holding back annuities worked with a number of the wives, but three refused to comply or to give up their marriages. Wilson sought permission to continue to withhold annuities. In his view, these women were 'living immorally' as they had 'undoubtedly' left their families to reside with another married man. Two of the women were widows with children when they remarried. Forget permitted Wilson to withhold the annuities of the women who 'still persist to live immorally'.[63]

By December 1898 Wilson was determined that legal proceedings should be taken to 'enforce the law as those young men still refuse to obey'.[64] In consultation with Coneybeare, he decided to proceed against Bear's Shin Bone, a scout for the North West Mounted Police and the man who had most recently entered into a polygamous marriage. Bear's Shin Bone was brought before Judge C. Rouleau at Fort Macleod on 10 March 1899 on a charge of practising polygamy with two women, an offence under Section 278 of the Criminal Code.[65] His wives were Free Cutter Woman and Killed Herself, and there is no indication that any evidence was taken from them during the trial. To do so would have raised the question of whether they were competent to, or could be compelled to, testify against their husband. If, as in *Regina v. Nan-e-quis-a-ka*, the second wife was found not to be a valid wife, the case for the prosecution for polygamy would be weakened. Coneybeare had to prove that there was a form of contract between the parties, which they all regarded was binding upon them. M. McKenzie for the defence argued that this section of the statute was never intended to apply to Indians (as discussed earlier, it was originally designed to address Mormon polygamy).[66] The court held that the law 'applied to Indians as well as whites', and that the marriage customs of the Bloods came within the provisions of the statute and were a form of contract, recognized as valid by the case of *Regina v. Nan-e-quis-a-ka*. Both marriages had to be recognized as valid in order to invalidate the second marriage. This anomaly was recognized in the local newspaper's coverage of the case, in which it was noted that 'Bare-Shin-Bone, the Blood Indian charged with polygamy, was convicted and allowed to go on suspended sentence, being instructed to annul his latest marriage (?) and cleave to his first spouse and none other'.[67] If he did not, he would be brought up at any time for sentencing.[68]

The DIA regarded this as a test case, with the goal being not to punish, but to make the prisoner and the others obey the law. The DIA agreed to pay for the defence barrister, even though the Kainai had raised a sum of money for that purpose. Wilson also sought and received permission to pay arrears for the 1898 annuities withheld from the women who refused to give up their marriages. Wilson further sought permission to have the children listed as legitimate, allowing them to draw rations and annuities. These measures would, in Wilson's view, 'help to allay the feeling of soreness which one or two of them feel at having to give up their second wives'.[69] Permission was granted, and newly appointed Indian commissioner David Laird was advised from Ottawa that the offspring of these marriages would be considered legitimate and not only rationed, but also placed on the paylist.[70] DIA accountant Duncan Campbell Scott endorsed these measures,

writing in a memorandum that 'the right of the women themselves to payment of annuity is not impugned by the relation referred to, and if we were to consider the offspring of such unions illegitimate it would hardly be possible to advance just grounds for our decision, as a great number of adult Indians and children throughout Manitoba and the North West are the fruit of such marriages. The effect of leniency in these cases will assist in furthering an easy transition to civilized ways of matrimony'.[71]

The 1890s flurry of activity aimed at prohibiting polygamy, which culminated in the Bear's Shin Bone case, did not entirely result in the desired goal. There was much 'unfinished business'. The 1901 census for the Blood Reserve indicated over thirty polygamous families.[72] Not all of these would have been marriages contracted before or at the time of Treaty 7, as some involved younger men and women. Indian agents continued to report polygamous marriages, although concerns about divorce and cases of bigamy became the more frequent complaints.[73] The 1890s prohibition campaign was one chapter in a lengthy saga of efforts, using diverse tactics, rewards, and punishments, which were aimed at imposing monogamous morality and 'proper' gender roles. The concerted resistance and defiance demonstrated by the Kainai did not continue after Bear's Shin Bone, but Aboriginal people continued to challenge and contest interference in the domestic domain. Although unfinished and not always successful, however, these interventions continued well into the twentieth century.

# NOTES

1. The term 'polygamy' embraces both 'polygyny' (one husband taking multiple wives) and 'polyandry' (one wife taking multiple husbands). Plains Aboriginal societies practised polygyny (as did the Mormons), but non-Aboriginal people at the time and since have referred to this as polygamy. In Blackfoot

and Cree there are no words for polygamy, polygyny, or polyandry.

2. Ann Laura Stoler, 'Tense and Tender Ties: The Politics of North American History and (Post) Colonial Studies', *The Journal of American History* 88, 3 (December 2001): 829–65.

3. Jane Fishburne Collier, *Marriage and Inequality*

in *Classless Societies* (Stanford, CA: Stanford University Press, 1988).

4. R.N. Wilson Papers, vol. 1, edited and annotated by Philip Godsell, p. 118, Glenbow Archives.

5. David G. Mandelbaum field notes, Fine Day # 1B, 6 August 1934, pp. 4–5, Canadian Plains Research Center.

6. Ibid., 4.

7. Ibid., 5.

8. Glenbow Archives, Wilson Papers, 118.

9. Beverly Hungry Wolf, *The Ways of My Grandmothers* (New York: Quill, 1982), 201.

10. Sue Sommers Dietrich typescript of 1939 interviews on the Blackfoot Reservation, Montana, p. 4, Marquette University Archives. Thanks to Alice Kehoe for this reference.

11. John H. Moore, 'The Developmental Cycle of Cheyenne Polygyny', *American Indian Quarterly* (Summer 1991): 311–28, at 311.

12. Hungry Wolf, *Ways of My Grandmothers*, 27.

13. Sarah Carter, *Capturing Women: The Manipulation of Cultural Imagery in Canada's Prairie West* (Montreal and Kingston: McGill-Queen's University Press, 1997), 163–6.

14. John Semmens, *The Field and the Work: Sketches of Missionary Work in the Far North* (Toronto: Methodist Mission Rooms, 1884), 163.

15. Rev. Ross C. Houghton, *Women of the Orient: An Account of the Religious, Intellectual and Social Condition of Women* (Cincinnati: Hitchcock and Walden, 1877), 190–1.

16. L.M. Hanks Jr. and Jane Richardson, *Observations of Northern Blackfoot Kinship*, Monographs of the American Ethnological Society, no. 9, ed. A. Irving Hallowell (Seattle: University of Washington Press, 1944), 23.

17. Esther Goldfrank, *Changing Configurations in the Social Organization of a Blackfoot Tribe during the Reserve Period*, Monographs of the American Ethnological Society, no. 8, ed. A. Irving Hallowell (Seattle: University of Washington Press, 1944), 47.

18. Constance Backhouse, *Petticoats and Prejudice: Women and Law in Nineteenth-Century Canada* (Toronto: Women's Press, for the Osgoode Society, 1991), 176.

19. John Webster Grant, *Moon of Wintertime: Missionaries and the Indians of Canada* (Toronto: University of Toronto Press, 1984), 235.

20. Semmens, *The Field and the Work*, 166.

21. John Hines, *The Red Indians of the Plains: Thirty Years' Missionary Experience in the Saskatchewan* (Toronto: McClelland, Goodchild and Stewart Ltd., 1916), 158–9.

22. Sharon H. Venne, ed., *Indian Acts and Amendments, 1868–1975: An Indexed Collection* (Saskatoon: University of Saskatchewan Native Law Centre), 94.

23. Ibid., 139–40, Sections 72 and 73.

24. Canada, 'Ebenezer McColl's report on the Manitoba Superintendency, 18 October 1893', in 'Department of Indian Affairs report for 1893', *Sessional Papers*, no. 14, vol. 27, 45.

25. *Macleod Gazette*, 25 January 1895.

26. M.B. Venini Byrne, *From the Buffalo to the Cross: A History of the Roman Catholic Diocese of Calgary* (Calgary: D.W. Friesen and Sons, 1973), 50.

27. Canada, 'Annual Report of the Superintendent-General of Indian Affairs', in 'Department of Indian Affairs Report for 1898', *Sessional Papers*, no. 14, vol. 33, xxv.

28. 'Questions on Indian Marriage', pp. 3–4, Records of the Department of Justice, Record Group (RG) 13, vol. 2406, file 1299–1914, Library and Archives Canada (LAC).

29. James G. Snell, *In the Shadow of the Law: Divorce in Canada, 1900–1939* (Toronto: University of Toronto Press, 1991).

30. See Records of the Department of Indian Affairs, RG 10, vol. 3559, file 74, pt. 4, LAC.

31. Circular letter of J.F. Graham, 24 July 1882, Records of the Department of Indian Affairs, RG 10, vol. 3602, file 1760, LAC.

32. Diana Jeater, *Marriage, Perversion and Power: The Construction of Moral Discourse in Southern Rhodesia, 1894–1930* (Oxford: Clarendon Press, 1993), 78.

33. John D. Pulsipher, 'The Americanization of Monogamy: Mormons, Native Americans and the Nineteenth-Century Perception that Polygamy Was a Threat to Democracy' (Ph.D. dissertation, University of Minnesota, 1999), 162.

34. James G. Snell, '"The White Life for Two": The Defence of Marriage and Sexual Morality in Canada, 1890–1914', in *Canadian Family History: Selected Readings*, ed. Bettina Bradbury, 381–400 (Toronto: Copp Clark Pitman Ltd., 1992), 381.

35. Sarah Carter, 'Categories and Terrains of Exclusion: Constructing the "Indian Woman" in the Early Settlement Era in Western Canada', *Great Plains Quarterly* 13 (Summer 1993): 147–61, at 150.

36. Ibid.

37. Robert J. McCue, 'Anthony Maitland Stenhouse, Bachelor Polygamist', in *American History and Life* 23, 1 (1990): 108–25.

38. Dan Erickson, 'Alberta Polygamists? The Canadian Climate and Response to the Introduction of Mormonism's Peculiar Institution', *Pacific Northwest Quarterly* 86, 4 (Fall 1995): 160.

39. Quoted in Brian Champion, 'Mormon Polygamy: Parliamentary Comments, 1889–90', *Alberta History* 35, 1 (Spring 1987): 10–17, at 13.

40. Ibid., 16.

41. Sarah Carter, *Lost Harvests: Prairie Indian Reserve Farmers and Government Policy* (Montreal and Kingston: McGill-Queen's University Press, 1990), 193–236.

42. Hayter Reed to Deputy Superintendent General of Indian Affairs (DSGIA), 8 September 1892, Records of DIA, RG 10, vol. 3881, file 94-189, LAC.

43. Reed to DSGIA, 25 September 1893, ibid.

44. Circular letter, Assistant Commissioner Amedée Forget to Indian Agents, 19 December 1893, ibid.

45. M. McGirr to A. Forget, 26 September 1894, ibid.

46. These figures are from the copies of the 1893 agents' reports prepared by A. Forget. The statements for the Peigan are incomplete and unclear (ibid.).

47. These ligures are from the 'Statement showing ages of Indians who have entered into polygamous relations since taking treaty', ibid.

48. J. Wilson to A. Forget, 21 January 1895, ibid.

49. Ibid.

50. Wilson to Forget, 20 February 1895, ibid.

51. Forget memo, n.d., ibid.

52. Magnus Begg to Forget, 23 March 1895, Records of DIA, RG 10, vol. 3881, file 934, 189, LAC.

53. Forget to J. Smart, 15 April 1898, Records of DIA, RG 10, vol. 3881, file 934, 189, LAC.

54. J.D. Mclean to Forget, 22 April 1898, Records of DIA, RG 10, vol. 3559, file 74, pt. 3, LAC.

55. Forget to McLean, 8 August 1898, Records of DIA, RG 10, vol. 3881, file 934, 189, LAC.

56. Wilson to McLean, 23 July 1898, ibid.

57. Forget to the Secretary, DIA, 13 September 1890, Records of DIA, RG 10, vol. 3559, file 74, pt. 6, LAC.

58. Ibid.

59. Forget to Indian agent, File Hills agency, 20 January 1899, ibid.

60. Forget to Wilson, 18 August 1898, Records of DIA, RG 10, vol. 3559, file 74, pt. 3, LAC.

61. Wilson to Forget, 4 November 1898, ibid., file 74, pt. 19.

62. Ibid.

63. Forget to Wilson, 10 December 1898, ibid.

64. Wilson to Forget, 6 December 1898, ibid.

65. Brian Slattery, *Canadian Native Law Cases*, vol. 2, 1870–1890 (Saskatoon: University of Saskatchewan Native Law Centre, 1981), 513. See also Backhouse, *Petticoats and Prejudice*, 26.

66. Wilson to Forget, 13 March 1899, Records of DIA, RG 10, vol. 3559, file 74, pt. 19, LAC.

67. *Macleod Gazette*, 11 March 1899.

68. Wilson to Forget, 13 March 1899, Records of DIA, RG 10, vol. 3559, file 74, pt. 19, LAC.

69. Ibid.

70. S. Stewart, Secretary, to Indian Commissioner David Laird, 1 April 1899, ibid.

71. Duncan Campbell Scott, memorandum, 29 March 1899, ibid.

72. 1901 Census Data, Canada Census Records, Glenbow Archives.

73. Records of the Department of Indian Affairs, RG 10, vol. 3559, file 74, part 3-30, LAC.

# Chapter 3

# Resisting the New Order

## READINGS

### Primary Documents

### Secondary Documents

### Introduction

Canada's rush to take hold of its new possessions during the generation or so after Confederation brought a determined response from the Métis and, to a less spectacular extent, from settlers and Aboriginal residents in the territory. In 1869–70 at Red River, and again in 1885 in the Saskatchewan River country, the Métis questioned the authority of the Canadian government. Both instances culminated in sending an armed force to quell the resistances; in 1885, these troops saw action. The enigmatic and charismatic Louis Riel played a significant role in the dramas, setting up provisional governments on both occasions. In 1870, a deal was worked out to create the province of Manitoba, and to preserve at least some of the rights the Métis valued. Land was allocated for them, and significant numbers went north and west to take it up. By 1885, they had formed communities in these new spaces, and their interest in consolidating what they had eventually meshed with Canadian settlers' desire for stronger representation in Ottawa and with Cree convictions that the treaties signed in the 1870s were inadequate. The primary sources here come from the two resistance periods. J.S. Dennis was a surveyor charged with the task of imposing a grid system on Red River land in 1869, and his report is that of the dutiful public servant, even though his actions were at least part of the reason why people in the Red River colony were prepared to prevent the new Lieutenant Governor from assuming his post. The narrative of two white women captured by some men from the band of

Mistahimaskwa (Big Bear) occurs on the fringes of the resistance in 1885, as Aboriginal agitation to renegotiate the treaties of the 1870s finds expression but is not coordinated with Métis efforts. The women refer to some of the military engagements between the NWMP/Canadian forces and the Métis, but these events take second place to their own predicament. Even though the battles raged nearby, the captives were most concerned with escape and rescue, and less willing to explain the nature of the alliance between their captors and the Métis. In the first of our secondary sources, Tom Flanagan looks at the scene(s) of resistance through a legal lens, contending that Riel et al. viewed themselves as unsatisfactorily compensated parties in a complex negotiation. The Canadian government was not inclined to give them all they wanted. The law features again in the final secondary source from Ted McCoy, who highlights the ways in which resistance was punished. The courtroom dramas that played out in the summer and fall of 1885 show how ideas long present in the British legal tradition—for example, mercy—could be significantly reinterpreted in the light of racial and cultural differences, as well as the goals of the still-young Dominion.

# QUESTIONS FOR CONSIDERATION

1.  Did Dennis sympathize with Red River residents that opposed his presence, or did he dismiss their concerns? Why?
2.  What seem to be the greatest fears of the women held captive by Big Bear's band?
3.  Why were the Métis the ideal group to articulate a wide range of concerns with the way settlement was proceeding in the period after Confederation?
4.  In what ways did Métis notions of title to land combine European and Aboriginal concepts of use or ownership?
5.  What did the punishments handed out to First Nations men participating in the 1885 resistance tell us about the way that 'mainstream' Canada viewed the West and the Aboriginal people living there?

# SUGGESTIONS FOR FURTHER READING

Albert Braz, *The False Traitor: Louis Riel in Canadian Culture* (Toronto: University of Toronto Press, 2003).

J.M. Bumsted, *Louis Riel v. Canada: The Making of a Rebel* (Winnipeg: Great Plains Publications, 2001).

Sarah Carter, *Capturing Women: The Manipulation of Cultural Imagery in Canada's Prairie West* (Montreal and Kingston: McGill-Queen's University Press, 1997).

Thomas Flanagan, *Louis 'David' Riel: Prophet of the New World* (Toronto: University of Toronto Press, 1996).

Frits Pannekoek, *A Snug Little Flock: The Social Origins of the Riel Resistance of 1869–70* (Winnipeg: Watson and Dwyer, 1991).

Jennifer Reid, *Louis Riel and the Creation of Modern Canada: Mythic Discourse and the Postcolonial State* (Albuquerque: University of New Mexico Press, 2008).

A.I. Silver, 'Ontario's Alleged Fanaticism in the Riel Affair', *Canadian Historical Review* 69(1) (1998): 21–50.

George F.G. Stanley, *The Birth of Western Canada. A History of the Riel Rebellions* (London and New York: Longmans, Green and Co., 1936).

Blair Stonechild and Bill Waiser, *Loyal Till Death: Indians and the North-West Rebellion* (Calgary: Fifth House, 1997).

# PRIMARY DOCUMENTS

**1** From J.S. Dennis, 'Memorandum of Facts . . .', *Correspondence and Papers Connected with Recent Occurrences in the North-West Territories* (Ottawa: I.B. Taylor, 1870), 7–9.

## FORT GARRY, *11th October, 1869.*

*Memorandum of facts and circumstances connected with the active opposition by the French half-breeds in this settlement to the prosecution of the Government surveys.*

This day about 2 p.m. a messenger arrived, Mr. Farmer, chain-bearer of Mr. Webb's party employed in surveying the base line or parallel of latitude, between Townships 6 and 7 east of the Meridian, on which service the party left a week ago to-day, bringing the unwelcome information from Mr. Webb, that his further progress with the survey had been stopped by a band* of some 18 French half-breeds, headed by a man named Louis Riel.

Mr. Webb had projected the line to about the fourth section, in Township 7, 2nd range east, and being within say 2½ miles of the Red River, when this occurrence took place.

He was ordered by the leader of the party at once to desist from further running the line, and in fact notified that he must leave the country on the south side of the Assinniboine, which country the party claimed as the property of the French half-breeds, and which they would not allow to be surveyed by the Canadian Government.

No arms were seen with the party, but by standing on the chain and using threats of violence if the survey was persisted in, it became evident that to go on with the survey would probably have led to a collision, and Mr. Webb, in accordance with written instructions, which I had previously given him to provide for any such contingency, discontinued his work, and as the half-breeds would not allow him to remain encamped where he was, moved his camp out to the main road on the Red River, waiting for orders, having sent off in the meantime Mr. Farmer, as above stated.

I at once waited on Dr. Cowan, the chief magistrate in the settlement, and laying the facts of the case before him, requested that he would consult with the Governor, or such other magistrate as he might think desirable to call in, and take such further steps with regard to this outrage, as he and they might think called for under the circumstances.

I remarked to Dr. Cowan at the same time that I question whether, owing to the unsettled state of the land tenure as regarded the half-breeds and Indians, and the peculiar irritation or

---

* NAMES OF BAND. *Louis Riel, Leader.* De Sangré and Son, Baptiste Taureau and Three Sons, François Charest, Edward Morin, Janvier Ritchot. Other names not legible.

sensitiveness that existed on the part of the French half-breeds in view of the transfer of the Territory and the assumption of the Government by Canada, it would be politic to take harsh measures towards the offenders in this case, but stated that as he and his brother magistrate knew the temper and feeling of the people in the settlement generally, that I left the matter in their hands, satisfied that they would do what would seem most advisable under the circumstances.

Before I left Dr. Cowan it was settled that he would call in another magistrate, Mr. Goulet, and consult with him as to what course to take.

### Tuesday, 12th October, 1869.

I waited on Dr. Cowan this morning, about 11 o'clock, and was informed that he and Mr. Goulet had thought it best to send for Riel, the leader, and ascertain what the party means by this proceeding, and explain to him and them the serious character of the offence of which they have been guilty, and endeavour quietly to obtain a promise that no further opposition should be made to continuing the survey.

The magistrates had done so accordingly but had failed either to extract from him any rational excuse for their proceeding (beyond the assertion that the Canadian Government had no right to make surveys in the Territory without the express permission of the people of the settlement), or any promise that their opposition would be withdrawn.

Dr. Cowan stated further, that Riel was to be back at 2 o'clock, when he, the Doctor, if Riel refused to listen to reason, would bring in the influence of Governor McTavish, whose health being in a critical position, he had desired should not be troubled if it could be avoided.

### Wednesday, October 13th.

Dr. Cowan informed me this morning that the interview of himself and Governor McTavish with Riel, which had taken place yesterday, had been in no respect satisfactory, that Riel still persisted that injustice was being done by the Canadian Government, and utterly refused to withdraw from the position he and those under him had taken.

Dr. Cowan said he should now apply to the Father Superior Lestanc, in charge of the Diocese during the absence of Bishop Taché, and that he felt sanguine that the Rev. Father, if so disposed, could put a stop to trouble at once.

It being important that I should no longer delay visiting another of my parties under Mr. Hart, engaged in projecting the meridian up near Shoal Lake (on which service, had this trouble not occurred, I would have left on the afternoon of the 11th instant). I determined to leave to-day, desiring Dr. Cowan, after consulting with Father Lestanc, to send a note to my office, stating the result, and instructing Mr. Webb; accordingly I started on the service above mentioned.

### October 14th to 20th, both inclusive.

Absent at Shoal Lake and examining country between that Lake and Lake Manitoba.

### October 21st.

Having returned to the settlement late last night, found Dr. Cowan's efforts with Father Lestanc had been without avail, the Rev. Father declining to attempt to use any influence with the party of half-breeds in question.

Dr. Cowan informed me that the Rev. Father, in explanation of his refusal, said that any such attempt in consequence of an idea that possessed the half-breeds that the Company was in collusion with the Canadian Government, would have a tendency to impress them with the idea that the Church also was in sympathy with the Government, and so might lead to weakening their influence over the people in a religious point of view.

Dr. Cowan had written a note, (see same dated 15th October,) announcing the entire failure of his endeavours to get over the opposition of the French Settlers to the survey, in consequence of which Mr. Webb, according to my instructions in such event, had withdrawn his party to the north side of the Assinniboine, and was proceeding with the surveying of the settlement north of Fort Garry, to which no opposition was offered. Such is the present condition of affairs.

## Same day, 4 o'clock P.M.

The High Constable, Mulligan, has just come to inform me, as a matter of duty, that a meeting took place yesterday, at a house of a French half-breed, named Bruce, on the other side of the river, by a number of the disaffected French party, among whom the man Riel was conspicuous.

That at such meeting it was resolved, to send an armed party to meet the Governor, whom they expected to come in to-morrow, and to prevent at all hazards, his entering the settlement.

Under these circumstances, not wishing to identify myself with any one of the three parties into which the people in the village are evidently divided, and who have no sympathy with each other, either socially or politically, I called in the council of two Canadian gentlemen, Messrs Sanford and Turner, of Hamilton, who had accompanied Mr. Howe on his visit, and remaining behind that gentleman were still in the settlement.

He considered that the circumstances called for immediate and vigorous action on the part of the Authorities, and it was arranged that Mr. Turner and I should wait upon Judge Black, and inform him of the intended outrage.

We found Judge Black at his residence, some four (4) miles down the settlement, and laid the matter before him, and it was arranged that he should wait upon the Governor and Dr. Cowan, early to-morrow morning, to concert measures to defeat the object of the refractory half-breeds.

On our return, there were reports confirmatory of the statements we had heard.

## Friday, October 22nd.

I met Judge Black, Governor Mr. McTavish, and Dr. Cowan this morning at the Fort by appointment, when the matter was fully discussed in all its bearings, and in view of the serious aspect of affairs, the Governor thought it only proper that a meeting of the Council of the Colony should be convened with the least possible delay, and upon their advice and action such further steps should be promptly taken as should effectually prevent the perpetration of the gross outrage intended.

In evidence of the object intended by this armed party, reference is called to the affidavit of *   *   * , a copy of which is hereto annexed, which was made during the afternoon, the original having been sworn to before Dr. Cowan, and remaining in his possession.

This affidavit was further corroborated by a statement made about 4 p.m., by Mr. *   * , who, on his way from Pembina to-day, found a body of armed men in possession of the roadway near the crossing of the river Sale, across which they had thrown a barricade, through which barricade they were not allowed to pass without explanation, and without giving satisfactory assurances that a stranger who formed one of the party was not connected with the Canadian Government.

The meeting of Council, Governor McTavish called for Monday, the 25th inst., it being stated that some of the members resided at such a distance that it could not be convened at an earlier date.

J. S. DENNIS.

Red River Settlement,
October 23rd, 1869.

2    From Theresa Delaney and Theresa Gowanlock, *Two Months in the Camp of Big Bear* (Regina: Canadian Plains Research Center, 1999), 14–22, 30–1, 33–5, 68–9, 71–5. Reproduced courtesy of the Canadian Plains Research Center Press, University of Regina, Regina, Saskatchewan, Canada.

[from Theresa Gowanlock's account]

## THE MASSACRE

Now come the dreadful scenes of blood and cruel death. The happy life is changed to one of suffering and sorrow. The few months of happiness I enjoyed with the one I loved above all others was abruptly closed—taken from me for ever—it was cruel, it was dreadful. When I look back to it all, I often wonder, is it all a dream, and has it really taken place. Yes, the dream is too true; it is a terrible reality, and as such will never leave my heart, or be effaced from off my mind.

The first news we heard of the Duck Lake affair was on the 30th of March. Mr. Quinn, the Indian Agent, at Frog Lake, wrote a letter to us and sent it down to our house about twelve o'clock at night with John Pritchard, telling my husband and I to go up to Mr. Delaney's on Tuesday morning, and with his wife go on to Fort Pitt, and if they saw any excitement they would follow. We did not expect anything to occur. When we got up to Mr. Delaney's we found the police had left for Fort Pitt. Big Bear's Indians were in the house talking to Mr. Quinn about the trouble at Duck Lake, and saying that Poundmaker the chief at Battleford wanted Big Bear to join him but he would not, as he intended remaining where he was and live peaceably. They considered Big Bear to be a better man than he was given credit for.

On the 1st of April they were in, making April fools of the white people and shaking hands, and they thought I was frightened and told me not to be afraid, because they would not hurt us. My husband left me at Mr. Delaney's and went back to his work at the mill, returning in the evening with Mr. Gilchrist. We all sat talking for some time along with Mr. Dill, who had a store at Frog Lake, and Mr. Cameron, clerk for the Hudson's Bay Company. We all felt perfectly safe where we were, saying that as we were so far away from the trouble at Duck Lake, the Government would likely come to some terms with them and the affair be settled at once. The young Chief and another Indian by the name of Isador said if anything was wrong among Big Bear's band they would come and tell us; and that night Big Bear's braves heard about it and watched them all night to keep them from telling us. We all went to bed not feeling in any way alarmed. About five o' clock in the morning a rap came to the door and Mr. Delaney went down stairs and opened it, and John Pritchard and one of Big Bear's sons by the name of Ibesies were there.

Pritchard said 'There trouble'.

Mr. Delaney said 'Where?'

Pritchard '*Here!* Our horses are all gone, the Indians deceived us, and said that some half-breeds from Edmonton had come in the night and had taken them to Duck Lake, but Big Bear's band has taken them and hid them, I am afraid it is all up'.

My husband and I got up, and Mrs. Delaney came down stairs with a frightened look. In a few minutes Big Bear's Indians were all in the house, and had taken all the arms from the men saying they were going to protect us from the half-breeds, and then we felt we were being deceived. They took all the men over to Mr. Quinn's, and my husband and I were sitting on the lounge, and an Indian came in and took him by the arm saying he wanted him to go too; and he said to Mrs. Delaney and I 'do not to be afraid, while I go with this Indian'. We stopped in the house, and while they were gone some of the Indians came in and went through the cupboard to find something to eat. They opened the trap door to go down cellar, but it was very dark, and they were afraid to venture down. Then the men came back and Mrs. Delaney got breakfast. We all sat down, but I could not eat, and an Indian asked Mr. Gowanlock to tell me not to be afraid, they would not hurt us, and I should eat plenty. After breakfast they took us out of the house and escorted us over to the church; my husband taking my arm, Mr. and Mrs. Delaney were walking beside us. When we got to the church the priests were holding mass; it was Holy Thursday, and as we entered the door, Wandering Spirit sat on his knees with his gun; he was painted, and had on such a wicked look. The priests did not finish the service on account of the menacing manner of the Indians; they were both around and inside the church. We were all very much frightened by their behaviour. They then told us to go out of the church, and took us back to Mr. Delaney's, all the Indians going in too. We stopped there for awhile and an Indian came and told us to come out again, and my husband came to me and said 'you had better put your shawl around you, for its [sic] very cold, perhaps we will not be gone long'. We all went out with the Indians. They were going through all the stores. Everything was given to them, and they got everything they could wish for and took us up the hill towards their camp. We had only gone but a short distance from the house when we heard the reports of guns, but thought they were firing in the air to frighten us; but they had shot Quinn, Dill and Gilchrist, whom I did not see fall. Mr. and Mrs. Delaney were a short distance ahead of my husband, I having my husband's arm. Mr. Williscraft, an old grey-headed man about seventy-five years of age came running by us, and an Indian shot at him and knocked his hat off, and he turned around and said, 'Oh! don't shoot! don't shoot!' But they fired again, and he ran screaming and fell in some bushes. On seeing this, I began crying, and my husband tried to comfort me, saying, 'my *dear* wife be *brave* to the end', and immediately an Indian behind us fired, and my husband fell beside me his arm pulling from mine. I tried to assist him from falling. He put out his arms for me and fell, and I fell down beside him and buried my face on his, while his life was ebbing away so quickly, and was prepared for the next shot myself, thinking I was going with him too. But death just then was not ordained for me. I had yet to live. An Indian came and took me away from my dying husband [sic] side, and I refused to leave. Oh! to think of leaving my *dear* husband lying there for those cruel Indians to dance around. I begged of the Indian to let me stay with him, but he took my arm and pulled me away. Just before this, I saw Mr. Delaney and a priest fall, and Mrs. Delaney was taken away in the same manner that I was. I still looking back to where my poor husband was lying dead; the Indian motioned to where he was going to take me, and on we went. I thought my heart would break; I would rather have died with my husband and been at rest.

## WITH THE INDIANS

Hardly knowing how I went or what I did, I trudged along in a half conscious condition. Led a captive into the camp of Big Bear by one of his vile band. Taken through brush and briar, a large pond came to view, we did not pass it by, he made me go through the water on that cold 2nd of April nearly to my waist. I got so very weak that I could not walk and the Indian pulled me along, in this way he managed to get me to his tepee. On seeing Mrs. Delaney taken away so far from me, I asked the Indian to take me to her; and he said 'No, No', and opening the tent shoved me in. A friendly squaw put down a rabbit robe for me to sit on; I was shivering with the cold; this squaw took my shoes and stockings off and partly dried them for me. Their tepees consisted of long poles covered with smoke-stained canvas with two openings, one at the top for a smoke hole and the other at the bottom for a door through which I had to crawl in order to enter. In the centre they have their fire; this squaw took a long stick and took out a large piece of beef from the kettle and offered it to me, which I refused, as I could not eat anything after what I had gone through.

Just then Big Bear's braves came into the tent; there were nearly thirty of them, covered with war paint, some having on my husband's clothes, and all giving vent to those terrible yells, and holding most murderous looking instruments. They were long wooden clubs. At one end were set three sharp shining knife blades. They all looked at me as I eyed those weapons (and they well matched the expression of their cruel mouths and develish [sic] eyes) thinking my troubles would soon be over I calmly awaited the result. But they sat down around me with a bottle full of something that looked like water, passing it from one Indian to the other, so I put on a brave look as if I was not afraid of them. After this they all went out and the most bloodcurdling yells that ever pierced my ears was their war-whoop, mingled with dancing and yelling and cutting most foolish antics.

[ . . . ]

After I had been there for four hours, Louis Goulet and Andre Nault came in, and Goulet said to me 'Mrs. Gowanlock if you will give yourself over to the half-breeds, they will not hurt you; Peter Blondin has gone down to where the mill is, and when he comes back he will give his horse for you'. I asked them to interpret it to the Indians in order to let me go to Pritchard's tent for awhile, and the Indians said that she could go with this squaw. I went and was overjoyed to see Mrs. Delaney there also. After getting in there I was unconscious for a long time, and upon coming to my senses, I found Mrs. Pritchard bathing my face with cold water. When Blondin came back he gave his horse and thirty dollars for Mrs. Delaney and me. He put up a tent and asked me to go with him, but I refused; and he became angry and did everything he could to injure me. That man treated me most shamefully; if it had not been for Pritchard I do not know what would have become of me. Pritchard was kinder than any of the others.

After I had been a prisoner three days, Blondin came and asked me if could ride horse back, and I said 'yes', and he said if I would go with him, he would go and take two of the best horses that Big Bear had and desert that night. I told him I would *never* leave Pritchard's tent until we all left, saying 'I would go and drown myself in the river before I would go with him'. [ . . . ]

## PROTECTED BY HALF-BREEDS

On the 3rd of April Big Bear came into our tent and sitting down beside us told us he was very sorry for what had happened, and cried over it, saying he knew he had so many bad men but had no control over them. He came very often to our tent telling us to 'eat and sleep plenty, they would not treat us like the white man. The white man when he make prisoner of Indian, he starve him and cut his hair off'. He told us he would protect us if the police came. The same day Big Bear's braves paid our tent another visit, they came in and around us with their guns, knives and tomahawks, looking at us so wickedly.

Pritchard said, 'For God sake let these poor women live, they can do no harm to you; let them go home to their friends'.

The leaders held a brief consultation.

An Indian stood up and pointing to the heavens said, 'We promise by God that we will not hurt these white women; we will let them live'.

They then left the tent.

Every time I saw one of Big Bear's Indians coming in, I expected it was to kill us, or take us away from the tent, which would have been *far worse* than death to *me*.

But they did not keep their word.

On the third night (Saturday, the 4th April,) after our captivity, two Indians came in while all the men and Mrs. Delaney were asleep, I heard them, and thought it was Pritchard fixing the harness, he usually sat up to protect us. A match was lighted and I saw two of the most hedious [sic] looking Indians looking over and saying where is the *Monias* squaw, meaning the white women. I got so frightened I could not move, but Mrs. Delaney put out her foot and awakened Mrs. Pritchard, and she wakened her husband, and he started up and asked what they wanted, and they said they wanted to take the white women to their tent, and I told Pritchard they could kill me before I would go, and I prayed to God to help me. Pritchard and Adolphus Nolin gave their blankets and dishes and Mrs. Pritchard took the best blanket off her bed to give to them and they went off, and in the morning the Wood Crees came in and asked if those Indians took much from us, and Pritchard told them 'No'; the Indians wanted to make them give them back. After that Pritchard and other half-breeds protected us from night to night for we were not safe a single minute.

During the two days which had passed, the bodies of the men that were murdered had not been buried. They were lying on the road exposed to the view of everyone. The half-breeds carried them off the road to the side, but the Indians coming along dragged them out again. It was dreadful to see the bodies of our *poor dear* husbands dragged back and forth by those demoniac savages.

On Saturday the day before Easter, we induced some half-breeds to take our husbands' bodies and bury them. They placed them, with those of the priests, under the church. The Indians would not allow the other bodies to be moved. And dreadful to relate those inhuman wretches set fire to the church, and with yelling and dancing witnessed it burn to the ground. The bodies, I afterwards heard, were charred beyond recognition.

Upon seeing what was done the tears ran profusely down our cheeks and I thought my very heart would break. All the comfort we received from that unfeeling band was, 'that's right, cry plenty, we have killed your husbands and we will soon have you'. [ . . .]

## THEY TAKE FORT PITT

[ . . . ]

On Sunday the 12th of April they returned from the Fort flush with victory. They had captured that place, killed policeman Cowan, taken the whites prisoners, and allowed the police to escape down the river, all without loosing [sic] an Indian or half-breed. The prisoners were brought in while we were at dinner. Mr. and Mrs. Quinney came to our tent. Mrs. Quinney said she was cold and wet. She sat down and put her arms around me and cried. I gave her a cup of hot tea and something to eat. Shortly after the McLeans and Manns came in. It was a great relief to see white people again.

It was not long before they moved camp about two miles from Frog Lake. Mrs. Delaney and I, walking with Mrs. Pritchard and family, through mud and water: my shoes were very thin, and my feet very wet and sore from walking. The Indians were riding beside us with our horses and buckboards, laughing and jeering at us with umbrellas over their heads and buffalo overcoats on. We would laugh and make them believe we were enjoying it, and my heart ready to break with grief all the time. When we camped, it was in a circle. A space in the centre being kept for dancing.

I asked Blondin if he had any of our stockings or underclothing in his sacks. He told me no, and shortly afterwards took out a pair of my husband's long stockings and put them on before me, he would change them three and four times a week. He had nearly all my poor husband's clothes. Two men came in one time while Blondin was asleep and took one of my husband's coats out of his sack and went out; Blondin upon missing it got very angry and swore before me, saying that some person had come in and taken one of his coats, and all the time I knew whose coat it was they were quarrelling over. I wished then I could close my eyes and go home to God. [ . . . ]

## ANOTHER BATTLE

Was it the distant roar of heaven's artillery that caught my ear. I listened and heard it again. The Indians heard it and were frightened.

A half-breed in a stage whisper cried, 'a cannon! a cannon!'

An Indian answered, 'a cannon is no good to fight'.

I looked at them and it showed them to be a startled and fear-stricken company, notwithstanding that they held the cannon with such disdain as to say 'cannon no good to fight'. That night was full of excitement for the Indians; they felt that the enemy was drawing near, too close in fact to be safe. The prisoners were excited with the thought, that perhaps there was liberty behind that cannon for them, and taking it all round, there was little sleep within the tepees.

The next morning I awoke early with hopefulness rising within my breast at the thought of again obtaining my liberty. The first sound I heard was the firing of cannon near at hand; it sounded beautiful; it was sweet music to my ears. Anticipating the prospect of seeing friends once more, I listened and breathed in the echo after every bomb.

The fighting commenced at seven o'clock by Gen. Strange's troops forcing the Indians to make a stand. It was continued until ten with indifferent success. The troops surely could not have known the demoralized condition of the Indians, else they would have compelled them to surrender. The fighting was very near, for the bullets were whizzing around all the time. We thought surely that liberty was not far away. The Indians were continually riding back and fro inspiring their followers in the rear with hope, and we poor prisoners with despair. At last they came back and said that they had killed twenty policemen and not an Indian hurt. But there were two Indians killed, one of whom was the Worm, he who killed my poor husband, and several wounded. We were kept running and walking about all that morning with their squaws, keeping out of the way of their enemies, and our friends. We were taken through mud and water until my feet got so very sore that I could hardly walk at all.

The Indians ordered us to dig pits for our protection. Pritchard and Blondin dug a large one about five feet deep for us, and they piled flour sacks around it as a further protection; but they dug it too deep and there was two or three inches of water at the bottom. They then threw down some brush and we got into it, twenty persons in all, with one blanket for Mrs. Delaney and me. McLean's family had another pit, and his daughters cut down trees to place around it. Mr. Mann and family dug a hole in the side of the hill and crawled into it. If I had my way I would have kept out of the pit altogether and watched my chance to escape.

We fully expected the troops to follow but they did not; and early in the morning we were up and off again. Some of the Indians went back to see how about the troops, and came back with the report that the 'police' (they call all soldiers police) had vanished, they were afraid. When I heard it, I fairly sank, and the slight spark of hope I had, had almost gone out. Just to think that succor was so near, yet alas! so far. But for Mrs. Delaney I would have given way and allowed myself to perish. [ . . . ]

## HOPE ALMOST DEFERRED

Almost a week afterwards, on a Saturday night, the fighting Indians gathered around a tepee near ours and began that never ending dancing and singing. It was a most unusual thing for them to dance so close to our tent. They had never done so before. It betokened no good on their part and looked extremely suspicious. It seemed to me that they were there to fulfil the threat they made some time previous, that they would put an end to us soon. The hour was late and that made it all the more certain that our doom had come. I became very nervous and frightened at what was going on. When all at once there was a scattering, and running, and yelling at the top of their voices, looking for squaws and children, and tearing down tents, while we two sat in ours in the depths of despair, waiting for further developments. I clung to Mrs. Delaney like my own mother, not knowing what to do. The cause of the stampede we were told was that they had heard the report of a gun. That report was fortunate for us, as it was the intention of the Indians to wrench us from our half-breed protectors and kill us.

[ . . . ]

## OUT OF BIG BEAR'S CAMP

Monday morning, May 31st, was ushered in dark and gloomy, foggy and raining, but it proved to be the happiest day we had spent since the 31st of March. As the night was passing, I felt its oppressiveness, I shuddered with the thought of what another day might bring forth; but deliverance it seems was not far away; it was even now at hand. When the light of day had swallowed up the blackness of darkness, the first words that greeted my ears was Pritchard saying 'I am going to watch my chance and get out of the camp of Big Bear'. Oh! what we suffered, Oh! what we endured, during those two long months, as captives among a horde of semi-barbarians. And to think that we would elude them, just when I was giving up in despair. It is said that the darkest hour is that which preceedes [sic] dawn; weeping may endure for a night, but joy cometh in the morning. So with me, in my utter prostration, in the act of giving way, God heard my prayer, and opened a way of deliverance, and we made the best of the opportunity.

'No foe, no dangerous path we lead,
Brook no delay, but onward speed'.

Some of the Indians it seems had come across General Strange's scouts the night before, and in consequence, all kinds of rumors were afloat among the band. They were all very much frightened, for it looked as if they were about to be surrounded. So a move, and a quick one, was made by them, at an early hour, leaving the half-breeds to follow on. This was now the golden opportunity, and Pritchard grasped it, and with him, five other half-breed families fled in an opposite direction, thereby severing our connection with the band nominally led by Big Bear.

We cut through the woods, making a road, dividing the thick brush, driving across creeks and over logs. On we sped. At one time hanging on by a corner of the bedding in order to keep from falling off the waggon. Another time I fell off the waggon while fording a stream; my back got so sore that I could not walk much. On we went roaming through the forest, not knowing where we were going, until the night of June 3rd the cry was made by Mrs. Pritchard with unfeigned disgust, 'that the police were coming'. Mrs. Delaney was making bannock for the next morning's meal, while I with cotton and crochet needle was making trimming for the dresses of Mrs. Pritchard's nine half-breed babies.

I threw the trimming work to the other end of the tent, and Mrs. Delaney called upon Mrs. Pritchard to finish making the bannocks herself, and we both rushed out just as the scouts galloped in.

## RESCUED

Rescued! at last, and from a life worse than death. I was so overjoyed that I sat down and cried. The rescuing party were members of General Strange's scouts, led by two friends of my late husband, William McKay and Peter Balentyne of Battleford. We were so glad to see them. They had provisions with them, and they asked us if we wanted anything to eat. We told them we had bannock and bacon, but partook of their canned beef and hard tack. It was clean and good; and was the first meal we enjoyed for two months.

I could not realize that I was safe until I reached Fort Pitt. The soldiers came out to welcome us back to life. The stories they heard about us were so terrible, that they could scarcely believe we were the same.

The steamer was in waiting to take us to Battleford. Rev. Mr. Gordon took my arm and led me on board. The same gentleman gave us hats, we had no covering for our heads for the entire two months we were captives. We were very scant for clothing. Mrs. Delaney had a ragged print dress, while I managed to save one an Indian boy brought me while in camp. Upon reaching Battleford we were taken to the residence of Mr. Laurie.

Coming down on the steamer, on nearing a little island, we saw a number of squaws fishing and waving white flags. All along wherever we passed the Indians, they were carrying white flags as a token that they had washed off their war paint and desired rest.


[from Theresa Delaney's account]


Up to this point, I might say, the Indians showed us no ill-will, but continually harped upon the same chord, that they desired to defend and to save us from the half-breeds. So far they got everything they asked for, and even to the last of the cattle, my husband refused nothing. We felt no dread of death at their hands, yet we knew that they were excited and we could not say what they might do if provoked. We now believed that the story of the half-breeds was to deceive us and throw us off our guard—and yet we did not suspect that they meditated the foul deeds that darkened the morning of the second of April, and that have left it a day unfortunately, but too memorable, in the annals of Frog Lake history.

When I now look back over the events, I feel that we all took a proper course, yet the most unfortunate one for those that are gone. We could have no idea of the murderous intentions on the part of the Indians. Some people living in our civilized country may remark, that it was strange we did not notice the peculiar conduct of the Indians. But those people know nothing either of the Indian character or habits. So far from their manner seeming strange, or extraordinary, I might say, that I have seen them dozens of times act more foolishly, ask more silly questions and want more rediculous [sic] things—even appear more excited. Only for the war-paint and what Big Bear had told us, we would have had our fears completely lulled by the seemingly open and friendly manner. I have heard it remarked that it is a wonder we did not leave before the second of April and go to Fort Pitt; I repeat, nothing at all appeared to us a sign of alarm, and even if we dreaded the tragic scenes, my husband would not have gone. His post was at home; he had no fear that the Indians would hurt him; he had always treated them well and they often acknowledged it; he was an employee of the Government and had a trust in hand; he would never have run away and left the Government horses, cattle, stores, provisions, goods, &c., to be divided and scattered amongst the bands, he even said so before the council day. Had he ran [sic] away and saved his life, by the act, I am certain he would be then blamed as a coward and one not trustworthy nor faithful to his position. I could not well pass over this part of our sad story without answering some of those comments made by people, who, neither through experience nor any other means could form an idea of the situation. It is easy for me to now sit down and write out, if I choose, what ought to have been done; it is just as easy for people safe in their own homes, far from the scene, to talk, comment and tell how they would have acted and what they would have done. But these people know no more about the situation or the Indians, than I know about the Hindoos, their mode of life, or their habits.

[ . . . ]

Imagine yourself seated in a quiet room at night, and every time you look at the door, which is slightly ajar, you catch the eye of a man fixed upon you, and try then to form an idea of my feelings. I heard that the human eye had power to subdue the most savage beast that roams the woods; if so, there must be a great power in the organ of vision; but I know of no object so awe-inspiring to look upon, as the naked eye concentrated upon your features. Had we but the same conception of that 'all seeing eye', which we are told, continually watches us, we would doubtlessly be wise and good; for if it inspired us with a proportionate fear, we would possess what Solomon tells us i[s] the first step to wisdom—'The fear of the Lord is the beginning of wisdom'.

But I never could describe all the miseries I suffered during those few weeks. I was two months in captivity; and eight days afterwards we heard of Major-General Strange's arrival, I managed to escape. The morning of our escape seemed to have been especially marked out by providence for us. It was the first and only time the Indians were not upon the close watch. Up to that day, we used to march from sunrise to sunset, and all night long the Indians would dance. I cannot conceive how human beings could march all day, as they did, and then dance the wild, frantic dances that they kept up all night. Coming on grey dawn they would tier [sic] out and take some repose. Every morning they would tear down our tent to see if we were in it. But whether attracted by the arrival of the soldiers—by the news of General Strange's engagement—or whether they considered we did not meditate flight, I cannot say—but most certainly they neglected their guard that day.

Some of them came in as usual, but we were making tea, and they went off. As soon as the coast was clear we left our tea, and all, and we departed. Maybe they did not know which way we went, or perhaps they were too much engaged with their own immediate danger to make chase, but be that as it may, we escaped. It was our last night under the lynx-eyed watchers. We went about two miles in the woods, and there hid. So far I had no covering for my head, and but scant raiment for my body. The season was very cold in April and May, and many a time I felt numb, chill, and sick, but there was no remedy for it; only 'grin and go through'. In the last part of my captivity, I suffered from exposure to the sun. The squaws took all my hats, and I could not get anything to cover my head, except a blanket, and I would not dare to put one on, as I knew not the moment we might fall in with the scouts, and they might take me for a squaw. My shawl had become ribbons from tearing through the bush, and towards the end I was not able to get two rags of it to remain together. There is no possibility of giving an idea of our sufferings. The physical pains, exposures, dangers, colds, heats, sleepless nights, long marches, scant food, poor raiment, &c., would be bad enough,—but we must not loose [sic] sight of the mental anguish, that memory, only two [sic] faithful, would inflict upon us, and the terror that alternate hope and despair would compel us to undergo. I cannot say which was the worst. But when united, our sad lives seemed to have passed beneath the darkest cloud that could possibly hang over them.

[ . . . ]

After our escape, we travelled all day long in the same bush, so that should the Indians discover us, we would seem to be still with them. We had nothing to eat but bread and water. We dare not make fire as we might be detected by the savages and then be subjected to a stricter *surveillance*, and maybe punished for our wanderings. Thus speaking of fire makes me think of the signals that the bands had, the beacons that flared from the heights at stated times and for certain purposes. Even before the outbreak, I remember of Indians coming to my husband and telling him that they were going on a hunt, and if such and such a thing took place, they would at a certain time and in a certain direction, make a fire. We often watched for the fires and at the stated time we would perceive the thin column of smoke ascend into the sky. For twenty and thirty miles around these fires can be seen. They are made in a very peculiar manner. The Indian digs a hole about a foot square and in that start the flame. He piles branches or fagots up on a cone fashion, like a bee-hive, and leaving a small hole in the top for the smoke to issue forth, he makes a draught space below on the four sides. If the wind is not strong, that tiny column of blue smoke will ascend to a height often of fifty or sixty feet. During the war times they make use of these fires as signals from band to band, and each fire has a conventional meaning. Like the *phares* that flashed the alarm from hill-top to hill-top or the tocsin that sang from belfry to belfry in the Basse Bretagne, in the days of the rising of the Vendee, so those beacons would communicate as swiftly the tidings that one band or tribe had to convey to another. Again, speaking of the danger of fire-making, I will give an example of what those Indians did with men of their own tribe.

A few of their men desired to go to Fort Pitt with their families, while the others objected. The couple of families escaped and reached the opposite side of a large lake. The Indians did not know which direction the fugitives had taken until noon the following day, when they saw their fire for dinner, across the lake. They started, half by one side and half by the other side of the lake, and came up so as to surround the fugitives. They took their horses, blankets, provisions, and camps, and set fire to the prairie on all sides so as to prevent the unhappy families from going or returning. When they thus treated their own people, what could white people expect on their hands?

[ . . . ]

It was upon Friday morning that we got into Fort Pitt, and we remained their [sic] until Sunday. On Friday night the military band came down two miles to play for us. It was quite an agreeable change from the 'tom-tom' of the Indians. Next day we went to see the soldiers drill. If I am not mistaken there were over 500 men there. Sunday, we left per boat, for Battleford, and got in that night. We had a pleasant trip on the steamer 'The Marquis'. While at Fort Pitt we had cabins on board the very elegant vessel 'North West'. We remained three weeks at Battleford, expecting to be daily called upon as witnesses in some cases. We travelled overland from Battleford to Swift Current, and thence by rail to Regina. At Moose Jaw, half way between Swift Current and Regina, we were greatly frightened. Such a number of people were collected to see and greet us, that we imagined it was Riel and his followers who had come to take us prisoners. Our fears were however, soon quelled. We remained four days at Regina; thence we came to Winnipeg. There we remained from Monday evening until Tuesday evening. Mostly all the people in the city came to see us, and I cannot commence to enumerate the valuable presents we received from the open-hearted citizens. We stoped [sic] with a Mrs. Bennett; her treatment to us, was like the care of a fond mother for her lost children.

We left on Thursday evening for Port Arthur, and thence we came by boat, to Owen Sound. A person not in trouble could not help but enjoy the glorious trip on the bosom of that immense inland sea. But, although we were overjoyed to be once more in safety, and drawing nearer our homes, yet memory was not sleeping, and we had too much to think off [sic] to permit our enjoying the trip as it could be enjoyed. From Owen Sound we proceeded to Parkdale by train. Parkdale is a lovely spot just outside of Toronto. I spent the afternoon there, and at nine o'clock that night left for home. I said good-bye to Mrs. Gowanlock; after all our sorrows, troubles, dangers, miseries, which we partook in union, we found it necessary to separate. And although we scarcely were half a year acquainted, it seemed as if we had been playmates in childhood, and companions throughout our whole lives. But, as we could not, for the present, continue our hand-in-hand journey, we separated merely physically speaking—for 'time has not ages, nor space has not distance', to sever the recollections of our mutual trials.

I arrived home at 6 o'clock on Monday morning. What were my feelings as I stepped down from the hack, at that door, where three years before I stepped up into a carriage, accompanied by my husband! How different the scene of the bride leaving three years ago, and the widow returning today! Still, on the first occasion there were tears of regret at parting, and smiles of anticipated pleasure and happiness—on the second occasion there are tears of memory, and yet smiles of relief on my escape, and happiness in my safe return.

# HISTORICAL INTERPRETATIONS

**3**   From T. Flanagan, *Riel and the Rebellion: 1885 Reconsidered*, 2nd edn (Toronto: University of Toronto Press, 2000), 85–97.

## ABORIGINAL TITLE

[Editors' note: Flanagan explains in the previous chapter that Métis people had been compensated in land and, more importantly, in money for their land after 1870.]

Why did the North-West Rebellion occur, if the government responded to the grievances of the Métis? Of course, other factors contributed to the alienation of the Métis. They were bitter over the events in Manitoba, which had left them a marginal minority in their own homeland. Having moved farther west, they could see themselves once again being outnumbered by white settlers. Another consideration was the decline of the Métis economy.

The buffalo vanished after 1878, adversely affecting several lines of business in which the Métis had made their living: buffalo hunting, trading with the Indians for pemmican and robes, and transporting these goods to market. The Métis cart trains and boat brigades also suffered from the advent of railways and steamboats. Deprived of their income from traditional occupations, the Métis had to rely more on agriculture. As they started to make the transition, they were struck, as were all western farmers, by the economic depression and fall in grain prices that began in 1883. For the Métis of St Laurent, this economic malaise was aggravated by the decision to build the Canadian Pacific Railway through Regina instead of Prince Albert. The Métis lost out on jobs and contracts that would have been created by a construction boom in northern Saskatchewan.

All these factors help explain the prevailing mood in St Laurent, yet none really accounts for the outbreak of the Rebellion, for similar factors were equally at work in other Métis settlements which remained peaceful. The unique fact about St Laurent was the presence of Louis Riel. His great prestige made him a prism refracting all information from the outside world to the Métis. He made the government's concessions seem like provocations. Any explanation of why the rising occurred must focus on Riel. What motivated him to take up arms?

First was his brooding resentment over the aftermath of 1869–70. Thinking himself the natural leader of his people, Riel had expected a quick amnesty followed by a successful career in politics. Instead he received exile, loss of his Commons seat, and penniless obscurity. His own misfortunes paralleled those of the Métis as they were submerged in Manitoba politics and went into voluntary emigration. Riel's bitterness lay behind the efforts he made in the winter of 1884–5 to obtain a cash payment from the federal government. The failure of these efforts to show any tangible result strengthened his readiness for extreme measures.

A second factor was Riel's religious 'mission'. As I have shown in Louis 'David' Riel: 'Prophet of the New World', he believed himself to be a divinely inspired prophet, even after his 'cure' in the insane asylums of Quebec. His mission of religious reform was only in abeyance, awaiting a signal from God to be made public. The longer he stayed with the Métis, the more ostentatious Riel's piety became. He argued with the Oblate missionaries over points of politics and theology, until the exasperated priests threatened him with excommunication. The notebook of prayers he kept over the winter of 1884–5 shows an ascending curve of spiritual confidence culminating in readiness for action.[1] Riel launched the Rebellion partly to reveal his new religion to the world, beginning his first major speech to the Métis with the words, 'Rome has fallen'.

In spite of this religious dimension, Riel's rising was a political phenomenon whose causes must also be sought at the political level, where Riel's views on aboriginal rights were crucial. He held that the Métis were the true owners of the North-West, that their entry into Confederation had been conditional upon fulfillment of the Manitoba 'treaty', and that they were legally free to secede from Canada since (in his view) Canada had not kept the 'treaty'. In this sweeping tableau, grievances over river lots and scrip were petty complaints, useful in mobilizing local support but peripheral to the real issues. Pre-existing local grievances were only pawns in a complex series of manoeuvres aimed at vindicating Métis ownership of the North-West as a whole. This explains the apparent paradox that the Métis launched an insurrection immediately after the government granted their demands. Under Riel's leadership, they were fighting for stakes far transcending river lots and scrip. They may have only dimly perceived what the real goals were, but these are plain enough in Riel's writings.

## CONFLICTING VIEWS OF ABORIGINAL RIGHTS

Riel's interpretation of the Red River Resistance was quite different from that prevailing in official circles in Ottawa or London. To see the magnitude of this difference, we must first sketch the official view. Here, a word of caution is required. What I call the 'official view' was not fully articulated until the St Catherine's Milling Case, decided by the Judicial Committee of the Privy Council in 1888. But the theory of aboriginal title developed in this case was implicit in the documents and practice of the previous decades, including the Royal Proclamation of 1763, the acquisition of Rupert's Land by Canada in 1870, and subsequent dealings with Indians and Métis.

To the rulers of Britain and Canada as well as to the proprietors of the Hudson's Bay Company, the acquisition of Rupert's Land was a complicated real-estate conveyance. In return for compensation from Canada, the company surrendered its land to the crown, which in turn passed it to Canada by act of parliament and royal proclamation. The transaction was founded on the property rights conferred on the company by the royal charter of 1670: ' . . . the sole trade and commerce of all those seas, straights, bays, rivers, creeks and sounds in whatsoever latitude they shall be that lie within the entrance of the straights commonly called Hudson's Straights together with all the lands and territories upon the countries, coasts, and confines of the seas, bays, lakes, rivers, creeks, and sounds aforesaid that are not already actually possessed by or granted to any of our subjects or possessed by the subjects of any other Christian prince or state'.[2] Canada had accepted the company's ownership rights only reluctantly and after years of putting forward the different theory that Rupert's Land ought to belong to Canada because of explorations undertaken from New France. But the Colonial Office refused any measures to diminish the company's rights, and in the end the sale went through on the assumption that the company was the rightful owner of this immense territory.

When the Red River Métis showed signs of resistance, the Canadian government refused to take possession, much as a purchaser might refuse to take possession of a house that had undergone damage between signing of contract and date of transfer. The imperial government doubted the legality of Canada's position but did not force the issue. Canada invited the inhabitants of Red River to send a delegation to Ottawa to make their concerns known. Having discussed matters with the three delegates (Father N.-J. Ritchot, Alfred Scott, and John Black), the Canadian government drafted the *Manitoba Act* to respond to the desires of Red River, including provincial status, responsible government, official bilingualism, and protection of customary land rights. Importantly, the *Manitoba Act* was a unilateral action of the Canadian parliament, not a treaty between independent partners (although it was probably *ultra vires* of the Canadian parliament and had later to be confirmed by imperial statute).[3] Payment for Rupert's Land was made in London after the company delivered the deed of surrender to the Colonial Office; and the imperial government, by order-in-council of 23 June 1870, annexed Rupert's Land to Canada, effective 15 July.

It was always assumed by both governments that aboriginal rights would be respected. Indeed section 14 of the order-in-council of 23 June 1870 specified that 'any claims of Indians to compensation for lands required for purposes of settlement shall be disposed of by the Canadian Government in communication with the Imperial Government'.[4] The Métis were not explicitly mentioned, but the Canadian government recognized in the *Manitoba Act* that they had inherited a share of aboriginal title from their Indian forebears.

Native title was not seen as sovereignty in the European sense. Only a state could claim sovereignty, and the North American Indian tribes had never been organized as states. Hence the validity of claims to sovereignty made by European states on the basis of discovery, settlement, and conquest. Nor was Indian title understood as ownership in fee simple, for the nomadic tribes of North America had never marked off plots of land according to European notions of private property. Indian title was interpreted as an encumbrance upon the underlying title to the land held by the sovereign. Indians had a real and enforceable right to support themselves on this land as they had from time immemorial. This right could be surrendered only to the sovereign, not to private parties; and compensation would normally be paid for surrender, according to the ancient principle of common law that there should be no expropriation without compensation.

[ . . . ] To explain aboriginal title, judges resorted to the concept of usufruct, which in Roman law was the right to use and enjoy the fruits of property—usually slaves or a landed estate—without actually owning it. Holders of usufructuary rights could enjoy the property undisturbed during their lifetime but could not sell or otherwise alienate the property. At the expiration of the usufruct, the property reverted to the owner. Canadian and British courts, seeking to interpret aboriginal title as it had developed over the centuries, used the concept of usufruct as an analogy. They cast the sovereign in the role of owner and the natives in the role of holders of 'a personal and usufructuary right' to occupy the land and support themselves from its produce. This limited right stemmed from the benevolence of the sovereign, who had not yet chosen to make use of the land in other ways. It was a domestic concession made by the sovereign as part of Indian policy, not a right to be claimed under the law of nations by Indian tribes as if they were sovereign nations.

Title, thus, was vested in the crown. The aboriginal right to use the land was an encumbrance on that title which had to be extinguished before the crown could alienate the land to private owners. Extinguishment normally required compensation, which might take the form of land reserves, money payments, educational or medical services, and so on. Logically, the situation was not different from real-estate conveyances where an encumbrance existed upon a title, as from mortgage or other debt. Title had to be cleared before transfer was completed.

The Canadian government acted on this basis to extinguish aboriginal rights in Rupert's Land. The Indians were dealt with in the numbered treaties of the 1870s, and a land grant of 1,400,000 acres was divided among the Métis children of Manitoba while their parents received scrip redeemable in Dominion Lands. The only anomaly concerned the Métis of the North-West Territories, where delay ensued for various reasons. But on the eve of the Rebellion, the government announced that it would also deal with them, although the precise form that compensation would take was still undecided. This sequence of actions should have wiped the slate clean, according to the official view. All encumbrances to title should have been removed, all aboriginal rights extinguished. Without injustice to Indian or Métis, the government could open the land for homesteading, make land grants to railways or colonization companies, and in general act as a landlord with a clear title.

It is crucial to appreciate the intellectual framework within which the government acted. From offering to purchase through taking possession and finally clearing title, everything was based on the validity of the HBC charter and on the contemporary understanding of aboriginal rights. The quarrel with Riel arose in large part because his view of the situation diverged at fundamental points. He never expressed his view completely and systematically, but it may be put together from various writings and utterances.

Riel explicitly denied the validity of the HBC charter because of its monopolistic provisions. The company's sole right to trade 'unjustly deprived the North-West of the advantages of international trade and the rest of humanity, especially neighbouring peoples, of the benefit of the commercial relations with the North-West to which they were entitled'.[5] The result was impoverishment and oppression of the native inhabitants, both Indians and Métis. Riel coined the term *haute trahison internationale* to describe the situation,[6] which we might translate into today's idiom as 'a crime against humanity'. The charter was void, as was any sale based upon it; for the company could not sell what it did not own. The most Riel would admit was that the company had an interest in the land which it had sold to Canada;[7] but that transaction did not affect the natives, who were the true owners of the land. Riel saw aboriginal rights not as a mere encumbrance on the title but actual ownership—not individual ownership in fee simple, perhaps, but a collective ownership by the Métis as a nation and by the Indians as tribes. In effect, he reversed the official view, according to which the HBC was the true owner of the land and the natives possessed the usufructuary right of subsistence. Riel made the natives the owners of lands in which the company possessed the interest of being allowed to trade. They owned their land in the same way as all other nations owned their lands under the law of nations; their title was not merely a limited right of occupancy dependent on the grace of the sovereign.

Riel had argued in a slightly different way when he established the provisional government on 8 December 1869. Then he issued a declaration that somewhat grudgingly conceded the legitimacy of the company's regime while remaining silent about the question of ownership: 'This Company consisting of many persons required a certain constitution. But as there was a question of commerce only their constitution was framed in reference thereto. Yet since there was at that time no government to see to the interests of a people already existing in the country, it became necessary for judicial affairs to have recourse to the officers of the Hudson's Bay Company. Thus inaugurated that species of government which, slightly modified by subsequent circumstances, ruled this country up to a recent date'. Although this government 'was far from answering to the wants of the people', the Métis 'had generously supported' it. But now the company was abandoning its people by 'subjugat[ing] it without its consent to a foreign power'; and according to the law of nations, a people abandoned by its government 'is at liberty to establish any form of government it may consider suitable to its wants'.[8] Thus the provisional government was legitimate according to the law of nations, and the Hudson's Bay Company had no right to transfer to Canada the land and people it had abandoned. Canada would have to deal with the provisional government if it was going to annex Rupert's Land.

Riel's original position of 1869 was that it violated the law of nations (or 'international law', as we would say today) to transfer a population without seeking its consent. In 1885 he added the argument that the company did not own Rupert's Land because its charter was void. Both arguments led to the same conclusions, that the sale to Canada was invalid until the inhabitants of Rupert's Land gave their consent, and that they had the right to form their own government to negotiate the terms of sale.

Riel also tried to show that both Canada and Britain had recognized the provisional government. Ministers of the Canadian government had invited the insurgents to send delegates to Ottawa and had conducted negotiations with them. The governor general had promised an amnesty, both directly and through intermediaries. Thus both Canada and Britain had recognized the provisional government de facto, even if there had not been a formal exchange of ambassadors according to international protocol.[9]

The legitimacy of the provisional government was essential to Riel because it determined his interpretation of the *Manitoba Act* and of the entry of Manitoba into Confederation. His frame of reference was the law of nations (*droit des gens*), because negotiations had been carried out between independent entities, Canada and Red River. Rupert's Land had not been purchased; rather its inhabitants, acting through their government, had decided to join Canada. Union with Canada was not the result of unilateral action in Ottawa; it had required the assent of the provisional government, which was formally given after Father Ritchot returned from Ottawa to report on the terms offered by Canada. After the vote, Riel's 'secretary of state' wrote to Canada's secretary of state that 'the Provisional Government and the Legislative Assembly, in the name of the people of the North-West, do accept the 'Manitoba Act', and consent to enter into Confederation on the terms entered into with our delegates . . . The Provisional Government and the Legislative Assembly have consented to enter into Confederation in the belief, and on the understanding, that in the above mentioned terms a general amnesty is contemplated'.[10] The arrangement was a 'treaty' in the sense of an international agreement between states. The treaty had two parts: the written text of the *Manitoba Act* and the oral promise of amnesty for all acts committed over the winter of 1869–70. This explains the final lines of Riel's pamphlet on the amnesty question: 'Ce que nous demandons, c'est l'amnistie: C'est l'exécution loyale de l'acte de Manitoba. Rien de plus, mais aussi rien de moins' [What we request is amnesty—the fulfillment in good faith of the *Manitoba Act*—nothing more, but also nothing less].[11]

Riel literally meant that the annexation of Rupert's Land was the result of a 'solemn treaty'[12] which, like all treaties, would become void if it were not observed. Hence the annexation was reversible. The people of Rupert's Land, which had become the province of Manitoba and the North-West Territories, could remove themselves from Canada if the treaty was broken in either of its branches: the amnesty or the *Manitoba Act*.

In Riel's view, Canada had betrayed its obligations under both headings. We will not go into the amnesty question here because, although never far from Riel's mind, it would not have sufficed to raise the flag of revolt among the Métis in 1885. This purpose was served by Riel's interpretation of the *Manitoba Act*, particularly of section 31, which authorized the Métis land grant. At its time of entry into Confederation, Manitoba consisted of approximately 9,500,000 acres. With the 1,400,000 acres set aside by section 31 for the 'children of the half-breed heads of families', the government thought to equip the young Métis with enough land to make them economically self-sufficient. It was the same principle as the one that calculated Indian reserves at the rate of a quarter-section of land per family of five. The government was thinking in terms of the future needs of a special group among the population.

Riel, on the contrary, viewed the 1,400,000 acres as the sale price of the 9,500,000 acres comprised in Manitoba. In his mind, this ratio set a precedent for the rest of the North-West. As subsequent acres were opened for settlement, the Métis of those areas should receive a similar price, in order to extinguish their aboriginal title, namely one-seventh of the land or the financial value of the one-seventh. This would amount to about 176,000,000 acres for the North-West outside the original boundaries of Manitoba.[13]

Riel gave his single best explanation of this theory in his final trial speech. It must be read carefully, for his English phrasing was awkward, even though the ideas were clear:

But somebody will say, on what grounds do you ask one-seventh of the lands? In England, in France, the French and the English have lands, the first was in England, they were the owners of the soil and they transmitted to generations. Now, by the soil they have had their start as a nation. Who starts the nations? The very one who creates them, God. God is the master of the universe, our planet is his land, and the nation and the tribes are members of His family, and as a good father, he gives a portion of his lands to that nation, to that tribe, to everyone, that is his heritage, that is his share of the inheritance, of the people, or nation or tribe. Now, here is a nation strong as it may be, it has its inheritance from God. When they have crowded their country because they had no room to stay anymore at home, it does not give them the right to come and take the share of all tribes besides them. When they come they ought to say, well, my little sister, the Cree tribe, you have a great territory, but that territory has been given to you as our own land, it has been given to our fathers in England or in France and of course you cannot exist without having that spot of land.

This is the principle God cannot create a tribe without locating it. We are not birds. We have to walk on the ground, and that ground is encircled of many things, which besides its own value, increases its value in another manner, and when we cultivate it we still increase that value. Well, on what principle can it be that the Canadian Government have given one-seventh to the half-breeds of Manitoba? I say it must be on this ground, civilization has the means of improving life that Indians or half-breeds have not. So when they come in our savage country, in our uncultivated land, they come and help us with their civilization, but we helped them with our lands, so the question comes: Your land, you Cree or you half-breed, your land is worth to-day one-seventh of what it will be when the civilization will have opened it? Your country unopened is worth to you only one-seventh of what it will be when opened. I think it is a fair share to acknowledge the genius of civilization to such an extent as to give, when I have seven pair of socks, six, to keep one. They made the treaty with us. As they made the treaty, I say they have to observe it, and did they observe the treaty? No.[14]

The statement justifies the surrender of land by aboriginal peoples in return for compensation. To that extent, it is compatible with the official Indian policy of Britain and Canada. Beyond that, however, lie some marked differences. Riel seems to challenge the unilateral assumption of sovereignty undergirding British rule in North America. In any case, he certainly does not accept the principle of unilateral extinguishment of aboriginal title through legislation. The land grant of section 31 was valid compensation for surrender of land only inasmuch as it was part of a treaty approved by both sides. Furthermore, the basis of compensation was a *quid pro quo*

as in any sale. Because the advantages of civilization could multiply the value of land seven times or more, the Métis would be at least as well off by surrendering six-sevenths of their land and adopting civilized ways while retaining one-seventh (or its money equivalent). It was not a matter of government allocating a certain amount of land to each Métis individual. In another text, Riel derided this approach as a 'sophism' designed to let the government 'evade its obligations' and 'frustrate the Métis, as a group or nationality, of their seventh of the lands'.[15]

Riel's insistence on the principle of 'the seventh' nicely illustrates the difference between his position and the official view. According to the latter, aboriginal title was a 'personal and usufructuary right' of the natives to gather subsistence from the land. If it was to be extinguished, it was logical to compute compensation according to the number of persons who would now have to subsist in other ways. Riel, however, maintained that the natives were the true proprietors of the soil in the full sense of ownership. Thus compensation for expropriation should be based on the value of the land, not on the number of people affected. To use a modern analogy, if a provincial government has to expropriate land for a hydroelectric transmission line, it must compensate owners according to the fair market value of the asset, not according to the size of their families. Riel's understanding of the nature of aboriginal title drove him to demand analogous treatment for the Métis.

The government grudgingly agreed to a new issue of scrip to provide for the relatively few Métis who had not participated in the Manitoba land grant. But in Riel's mind, the whole North-West outside Manitoba still belonged to the Métis. The HBC had sold whatever interest it had, and the Indians had signed land-surrender treaties. It was still necessary to extinguish the Métis title, but that could not be done with a few pieces of scrip. It would require payment of the value of one-seventh of the whole North-West, following the precedent solemnly established in the 'Manitoba Treaty'. And if that treaty continued to be broken, the Métis would no longer be part of Canada. According to the law of nations, they could once again form a provisional government and undertake negotiations with other governments. There might be a new treaty with Canada, or perhaps the North-West would become a separate colony within the Empire, or perhaps it would even ask for annexation to the United States, as Riel did after his trial. Everything was possible. It is this train of thought, and only this, that makes the North-West Rebellion intelligible.

## NOTES

1. George F.G. Stanley et al., eds., *The Collected Writings of Louis Riel*, 5 vols. [hereafter *CW*] (Edmonton: University of Alberta 1985), 3–194.
2. Cited in Peter A. Cumming and Neil H. Mickenberg, *Native Rights in Canada* (Toronto: General Publishing 1972), 138. I have modernized the orthography.
3. 34 and 35 Vict., c. 28 (UK).
4. Cumming and Mickenberg, *Native Rights in Canada*, 148.
5. Louis Riel, Mémoire sur les troubles du Nord-Ouest, *CW* 3–157, 295.
6. Ibid.
7. Interview with C.B. Pitblado, *Winnipeg Sun*, 3 July 1885, *CW* A3–011.
8. Louis Riel, 'Declaration of the People of Rupert's Land and the North West', *CW* 1–023.
9. Louis Riel, *CW* 3–157; and Petition 'To His Excellency [Grover] Cleveland . . . ', [August–September 1885], *CW* 3–095.
10. Cited in G.F.G. Stanley, *The Birth of Western Canada* (Toronto: University of Toronto Press 1961), 124.
11. Louis Riel, *L'Amnistie* (Montreal: Bureau du 'Nouveau Monde' 1874), 22. The last words, 'Rien de plus . . . ', may have been added by the publisher; see *CW* 3–188 n.1.
12. Ibid.
13. Louis Riel to J.W. Taylor, 2–3 August 1885, *CW* 3–083; Riel, Manifeste à ses concitoyens américains, August–November 1885, *CW* 3–161.
14. Desmond Morton, ed., *The Queen v Louis Riel* (Toronto: University of Toronto Press 1974), 358–9.
15. Riel, Manifeste à ses concitoyens américains, *CW* 3–161.

---

4   From Ted McCoy, 'Legal Ideology in the Aftermath of Rebellion: The Convicted First Nations Participants, 1885', *Histoire sociale/Social history*, 42(83) (May 2009): 175–201.

IN EARLY OCTOBER 1885, Winnipeg's train depot played host to an unusual arrival. Hundreds of curious onlookers crowded the platform and surged forward as the train pulled in. Excitement peaked as a large group of First Nations men disembarked in shackles. Among them were the famous Cree chiefs Big Bear, Poundmaker, and One Arrow. Many of the men still wore traditional dress, including blankets drawn closely around their bodies. A newspaper reporter suggested that their appearance did not disappoint the thrill-seeking crowd: 'a more lawless looking set can hardly be imagined'.[1] The men were taken to a local provincial jail before being transported by wagon to Manitoba Penitentiary the next day.

These men were Cree, Assiniboine, Dakota, and Blood individuals who had been tried and convicted for their participation in the 1885 North-West Rebellion. The legal aftermath of the Rebellion played out in three primary settings: in the courtroom, on the gallows at Fort Battleford, and inside the walls of Manitoba Penitentiary (also known as Stony Mountain). The events in each of these settings demonstrate a response to First Nations defendants that was informed by British legal ideology and transformed by the unique colonial setting of the Canadian North-West, and they reveal sites of struggle between First Nations people and the Canadian state that enhance our understanding of the early legal history of Western Canada. At these sites of trial and punishment, First Nations defendants and their kin negotiated the legal ideologies of majesty, justice, and mercy in a setting in which these elements of the Canadian law were far from established or understood. Judicial and religious rhetoric and ritual invoked the majesty and mercy of the law, while capital punishment and penitentiary sentences revealed these ideologies in practice.

[ . . . ] Events demonstrate that legal ideology must be understood in specific historical, colonial, and geographic contexts. It will come as no surprise to Canadian historians that justice in Regina and Battleford required unique adaptations of the British legal customs and traditions on which Canadian law was based. However, interrogating the legal proceedings and punishment that followed the North-West Rebellion reveals a unique social context in which the law unfolded. [ . . . ]

In many ways, discussion of the Rebellion's aftermath reveals an emergent hegemony in Western Canada. Though the post-Rebellion period is but one small part of this wider history, we must also uncover the instances in which this early domination was challenged and resisted by First Nations people. To do so, we must see more than pure terror, look beyond the majesty, justice, and mercy of the Canadian courts, and understand the social relations between the Canadian state and the First Nations as something more

complex than an ever-expanding 'subjugation'. As E. P. Thompson suggests, hegemony does not impose an 'all embracing domination upon the ruled', eclipsing the possibility of resistance or correction.[2] The experience of the convicted First Nations participants in 1885 is one example of how this hegemony played out on the stage of the criminal law. Uncovering examples of this experience, even in the darkest days of the post-Rebellion North-West, suggests the possibility of resistance in all areas of the relationship between First Nations people and colonial authorities.

If we are to understand why law and punishment operated as they did in the aftermath of the Rebellion, it is useful to look back to the Bloody Code of eighteenth-century England. Though separated by a century from the establishment of Canadian law in the North-West, the legal ritual and ideology underlying Canadian law can be found in this history. Douglas Hay proposes that majesty, justice, and mercy were at the centre of the law's power in eighteenth-century England. Enforced by the Bloody Code, which featured the death penalty us its moral centre, the division of property by terror was effective and resonated with the population because it was complemented by ideologies of majesty, justice, and mercy. These ideologies were expressed in rituals that enriched and mystified the law and gave it emotional and psychic grounding. These rituals helped define contemporary social and class relations to help ensure a broader political conformity in England.[3] It would be obvious to state that the same ideological constructs resonated differently as they were translated into the colonial setting of British North America, but the historical facts demonstrate that British legal authorities attempted such a translation repeatedly in the nineteenth century. [ . . . ]

Theorists in the eighteenth century argued that the law must be structured in certain ways to establish its legitimacy. It should be 'known and determinate, instead of capricious and obscure'.[4] This permanence and impartiality supported the fiction that social class played no role in the operation of the law. This gave the law an important ideological weapon even when it did not operate uniformly. In nineteenth-century Canada, particularly in colonial settings, the concept of justice was adapted to the purpose of introducing the Queen's law to First Nations people in an evenhanded and non-biased way. The very idea of justice thus became an important colonial tool. However, historians of colonial contexts argue that the law takes on different forms to maintain the legitimacy of its underlying ideology. [ . . . ] Tracking the contradictory and unusual applications of the law in this way has allowed historians to examine justice as a legal ideology. Closely related and central to the experience of First Nations people meeting British law was the ideology of mercy.

In eighteenth-century England, mercy gave legal authorities the power of discretion to take into consideration, for instance, poverty or other extenuating circumstances. Rather than diminishing the terror and authority invested in capital punishment, legal discretion gave authorities an extra measure of power over the letter of the law by 'creating the mental structure of paternalism' towards the condemned. Incidences of mercy helped to validate capital punishment to the poor by demonstrating the supposed sensibility of the law to mitigating circumstances.

[ . . . ]

Most accounts of the First Nations' participation in the North-West Rebellion focus on the role played by Big Bear's Plains Cree, who had been wintering northeast of Edmonton at Frog Lake. Although Métis leader Louis Riel was in contact with Cree leaders throughout late 1884, the events involving Big Bear's band were among the first instances of serious conflict involving a First Nations group. Big Bear returned to Frog Lake in early April 1885 to find a horrifying scene.[5] While he had been away on a solitary hunting trip, his war chief Wandering Spirit and other young men,

including Miserable Man and Imasees (Big Bear's son), planned to take hostages from the tiny settlement of Frog Lake and obtain desperately needed food and supplies. The plan was quickly derailed when Indian Agent Thomas Quinn refused to agree to the Cree demands. A standoff ensued between Quinn and Wandering Spirit, which escalated into a bloody *mêlée*. Big Bear pleaded for peace, but the situation spiraled towards a violent resolution. Nine white men were killed by Cree warriors who then took the survivors prisoner and burned Frog Lake to the ground. This debacle occurred days after the Métis victory against the North West Mounted Police (NWMP) at Duck Lake and sparked fears across the country of a First Nations uprising inspired by Louis Riel. The government responded to news of the Frog Lake uprising with extreme military force. Three militia columns were deployed across the North-West to stamp out the rebellion.

As fear gripped the region, residents of the Fort Pitt and Battleford districts wired for help from inside barricaded forts and waited for the militia to arrive. The hysteria throughout the North-West also drew Cree chiefs Poundmaker and One Arrow into armed conflict. After terrifying the residents of Battleford (barricaded inside Fort Battleford) with the mere presence of his band, Poundmaker found his camp attacked three weeks later by an overzealous militia column under the command of Colonel W.D. Otter.[6] From this point, Poundmaker's band became more deeply embroiled in the events of the uprising, finding themselves in the middle of a massive confrontation between the Métis and the Canadian militia. While the primary militia column under General Middleton fought Riel's Métis forces at Batoche, the remaining columns pursued Cree chiefs Big Bear and Poundmaker. After a summer of being pursued by the militia, the majority of the exhausted Cree surrendered or were captured. In the summer and fall of 1885 the Rebellion participants encountered the Canadian legal system in a series of criminal trials.

The government prepared cases against the captured and surrendered First Nations men throughout the summer of 1885 and charged 81 people with various crimes, ranging from arson and murder to treason-felony. The initial trials took place in Regina before the senior court in the North-West Territories, presided over by Stipendiary Magistrate Hugh Richardson. At the centre of the government prosecution were Cree chiefs Poundmaker, Big Bear, and One Arrow, all charged with treason-felony for their roles in the uprising. Following the treason-felony trials, the venue moved to Battleford, where Stipendiary Magistrate Charles Rouleau presided over murder trials for those men accused of the Frog Lake murders as well as other isolated murder trials. During the trials, the judges invoked majesty through the spectacle of legal ritual and the use of rhetoric by which, as Hay notes about English law, 'the powers of light and darkness [were] summoned into the court'.[7] When First Nations defendants came before the court at Regina, this metaphor stood for the invocation of colonial authority.

Judge Rouleau excelled at lecturing in these tones, admonishing Itka and Man Without Blood at their murder trial: 'you were foolish enough to rebel against the government, foolish because the government could send soldiers here until they were numerous as mosquitoes'.[8] At the trial of Bad Arrow and Miserable Man, Rouleau expanded on these themes in an elaborate speech explaining the need for peace between whites and the First Nations. He asked the prisoners, 'what object had you in killing the whites? If the whites withdrew from the country you would starve in a year, but the white man could live without the Indians'.[9] Rouleau repeatedly invoked emotional language that gave his courtroom speeches the element of a religious sermon preached in the secular realm. Although the entire community of Battleford felt the events of the Rebellion personally,

Rouleau's emotionalism was likely heightened when he received a telegram in April from Indian Commissioner Edgar Dewdney laconically informing him, 'your house burnt by Indians yesterday'.[10] When Rouleau summoned colonial paternalism at the sentencing of Wandering Spirit, it was clear that he was addressing the multitude of First Nations groups in the North-West as well as whites who badly needed reassurance about the stability of government authority throughout the region. Rouleau lectured:

> You were murdering while others were burning houses and committing other crimes. You could not expect any good results to follow your acts. . . . Instead of listening to wise men, you preferred to listen to the advice of bad men who were as poor as yourselves, and who could not help you if they wanted to, and who only got you in trouble. The Government do not want to destroy the Indians, but they wish to help them to live like white men but as far as murderers in cold blood are concerned, the Government has no pity for them. If a white man murders an Indian he must hang, and so must an Indian if he kills a while man.[11]

Here the eighteenth-century concept of justice, originally intended to inure the ruling class from suggestions of favouritism, was adapted to explain to a First Nations population that culture or race bore no influence on the operation of law. After the Rebellion, this left First Nations people at a distinct disadvantage because many of the defendants, including Poundmaker and Big Bear, defended themselves in court based on their particular circumstances or cultural misunderstandings.[12]

This raises a question about how such legal rhetoric was received by the First Nations defendants. Is it possible to gauge the effectiveness of such ideological categories through the limited sources detailing the reaction of those men who came before the court? We can make some assumptions and believe, as E.P. Thompson suggested, that people are not so stupid as to be mystified by the first man to don a wig.[13] It is not clear that First Nations defendants were awed by these paternalist messages or the larger majesty of the law. In all likelihood, the messages contained in Rouleau's courtroom rhetoric were not novel to most of the Cree defendants. [...]

Some of the convicted men were despondent when sentenced. When Little Runner was sentenced to four years for horse-stealing, he replied, 'I am glad to hear that. I have been longing to know what was to be done with me'.[14] Though his execution was later commuted, Louison Mongrain responded to his death sentence, 'I am not guilty of the charge, and hope God will receive me, as the charges against me are not true; I prepare myself to be resigned to my fate. After I am sentenced I would like to write to my mother and wife; I have no children, for which I am thankful. I pity the old man who was sentenced today'.[15] Other defendants were belligerent or offhanded. Big Bear addressed the court for nearly an hour at his sentencing, ending with a plea for the welfare of his people.[16] Clearly aware that he was responding to a legal official vested with the full power of the Canadian state, Big Bear used the opportunity to deliver the last serious speech of his political career. Poundmaker responded to his accusers with a poignant majesty of his own. 'I am a man', he said. 'Do as you like. I am in your power. You did not catch me'.[17] As he was sentenced to three years in the penitentiary, his offhandedness boiled over, and while being dragged from the court he shouted. 'I would rather be hung than put in that place'.[18] These responses, particularly Big Bear's, exemplified their defiance, despite their position of subjugation to the Canadian courts. Others would speak as forcefully or eloquently as their political leaders, but the limited number of recorded responses demonstrates that the defendants understood with some subtlety the court's

majesty and were not merely overwhelmed by it, placing their experience beyond the realm of 'awe'.

Several other elements contributed to the haphazard nature of the trials and compromised the sense of majesty and justice surrounding them. At Regina, most of the men had no legal representation before the court and could not understand the proceedings in English. One Arrow famously responded to the translation of his treason-felony charge by asking, 'are you drunk?'[19] Catholic priest Louis Cochin was disgusted by the impossible position of the defendants. After One Arrow's trial he complained, 'The poor old man didn't understand a word of it'.[20] Cochin was further distressed at reports that the prosecutors and the judge were determining the sentences between themselves beforehand and then applying them to each defendant at trial. Missionaries on the scene counseled the men to plead guilty to all charges, effectively forfeiting any claim to a fair trial. 'Does the government know of this?' Louis Cochin demanded in a letter to the Archbishop. 'Or if it does know of it, how can it put up with such things?'[21] As the trials concluded, the government made plans to execute eight First Nations men at Fort Battleford.

In the aftermath of the North-West Rebellion, the death penalty was intended not only to punish, but to reassert government authority throughout the region. It is not clear that the one-time event of mass execution at Battleford terrorized First Nations people as Canadian legal and government authorities had intended. Evidence from the courtrooms and the scene of execution indicates that the hangings, carried out as public spectacle, were met with a mix of ambivalence, sadness, and outrage by First Nations defendants and their kin.[22] Peter Linebaugh notes that public hanging in Britain represented a rare meeting of many levels of government united with church and legal authorities for a common purpose.[23] The Battleford hanging signified an important moment of this convergence in Western Canada. Although it was the first execution under Canadian authority in the North-West, the common elements shared with hangings in other British and American jurisdictions indicate that the Canadian authorities were familiar with the script of the execution pageantry. In the weeks leading up to the execution, the original plan to hang the men two at a time was altered so that all eight men would die at once.

The hanging was carefully planned as a public spectacle at Fort Battleford to demonstrate visibly the government's power over First Nations people. Prime Minister John A. Macdonald, also Minister of Indian Affairs, informed Dewdney, 'the executions . . . ought to convince the Red Man that the White Man governs'.[24] Assistant Indian Commissioner Hayter Reed agreed with the prime minister and suggested to Dewdney that First Nations people must witness the hanging as confirmation of their 'sound thrashing'. The hanging would 'cause them to meditate for many a day and besides have ocular demonstration of the fact'.[25] Curiously, government officials drew the line at what constituted *too much* intimidation. Indian Commissioner Edgar Dewdney stipulated that the execution could not occur on Cree reserves near the site of the crimes for fear that superstition would overtake the people and cause them to abandon their settlements.[26] The government's plan to intimidate and demoralize the Cree was not simply a response to the Rebellion but part of a longer pattern of Cree 'subjugation' stretching back to the signing of the numbered treaties. In the year before the Rebellion, Cree efforts at organization and political solidarity had alarmed Indian Affairs officials so much that they quietly planned the arrest and immobilization of dissident Cree leaders like Big Bear and Poundmaker in the fall of 1884.[27] If it is generally accepted that in 1883 and 1884 the government executed a campaign of intimidation and subordination of the Plains Cree, the execution appears as a final and decisive blow to Cree political efforts.

[ . . . ]

[ . . . ] As newspapers across Canada justified the impending execution scheduled for November 24, at Fort Battleford the dialogue between the clergy and the prisoners centred on more personal and religious matters.

In the days before the hanging, Catholic priests A.H. Bigonesse and Louis Cochin attempted to convert the condemned men to Christianity. Their ministry is chronicled in *The Reminiscences of Louis Cochin*, published more than 40 years after the events.[28] Though clearly embellished, the narratives of the priests portray a conversion experience that demonstrates the role of religion in the pageantry of death frequently seen before the execution of First Nations people under British law. In their accounts, the priests strove to infuse the experience of the Cree and Assiniboine men with religious meaning. Christianity was depicted as the force bridging civilization and savagery in the face of the awesome power of capital punishment. [ . . . ] Religious writers in . . . the post-Rebellion North-West employed religious solemnity as a powerful narrative tool to demonstrate the centrality of capital punishment in the developing relationship between the state and First Nations people. In Cochin's narrative, Wandering Spirit filled the role of the terrible savage against which Christianity's redemptive power was pitted. The War Chief was well suited to the part, as the press and government recognized him as the murderous leader of the Frog Lake Massacre. At his sentencing, Judge Charles Rouleau called Wandering Spirit 'the greatest killer ever to walk on two legs in America'.[29] A popular account of the final days of the prisoners, written by eye-witness William Cameron, repeated many of the savage portrayals of Wandering Spirit. Cameron's account frequently described the War Chief as 'cruel' and 'evil' in an attempt to sensationalize his role in the events of 1885. According to Bigonesse, Wandering Spirit refused to acknowledge the priests until the day before execution when he experienced a spiritual awakening.[30] Wandering Spirit finally accepted Christianity, thus shedding the savagery that had characterized his path to condemnation.

However, other evidence suggests that Wandering Spirit was deeply remorseful over the events at Frog Lake, and his interest in Christianity may have sprung from the grief that overtook him during the summer of 1885. Elizabeth McLean, taken prisoner by Big Bear's Cree at Fort Pitt, described Wandering Spirit as a deeply dejected and depressed individual who morosely asked them, 'what would your God do to a man who had done what I did?'[31] McLean described the sight of a solitary and sad Wandering Spirit walking slowly into the camp of the Wood Cree prior to his capture, his hair turned from deep black to almost totally white.[32] He attempted to kill himself shortly after his capture and spent his final days dejectedly protesting his minor role in the uprising, telling Cameron, 'I fought against it. Imasees nor the others would not let me go . . . it seemed it was to be—I was singled out to do it'.[33] Unsurprisingly, this regret is never noted by the priests' narratives. Instead, their account emphasizes the power of conversion to effect change by highlighting the contrition of the Cree and Assiniboine prisoners.

In fact, although some of the men made conciliatory remarks from the gallows before their deaths, Little Bear and Itka both shouted menacing last words. They urged the people gathered in the square at Fort Battleford to remember how the whites had treated them and to make no peace. Further, they urged the spectators to show their contempt for the punishment they were about to witness. This scene certainly did not fit the script of conversion and contrition offered in the priests' version of the execution.

As the eight men ascended the scaffolding to be hanged, one of them allegedly said to Cochin, 'Father, we do not know any Christian hymns, but we are anxious, however, to die singing. I pray you, allow us to sing in our own fashion'. Cochin stated that

he allowed them to do this 'with good heart'.[34] Cochin thus constructed another important element of the execution pageantry in his narrative—the confession. What other writers identified only as Cree and Assiniboine death chants and songs, Cochin transformed into improvised Christian prayers. When the trap dropped, Cochin saw it not as sending the men to their death, but sending them 'together into eternity, where we have the sweet confidence they rejoiced in the favour of the infinite mercy of God'.[35] The punitive elements of the execution that characterized government rhetoric fell away in these descriptions as the priests suggested a majesty rooted in Christian solemnity.

However, there are strong indications that this majesty and the terror it accompanied were not as immediately apparent to either the condemned men or the First Nations people who witnessed the hanging. While the government may have wanted the Cree to witness the execution, it is likely the Cree people from surrounding reserves would have been at the event for their own personal reasons. The singing of traditional death songs from the gallows is another strong indication of the specific First Nations understanding of these events. At the hanging of 38 Dakota men following the Minnesota Uprising in December 1862, the *St. Paul Pioneer* noted that upon the scaffold the hooded and bound men grasped for each other's hands and sang out their own names and the names of their friends as if to say 'I'm here ! I'm here!'[36] At Battleford many of the condemned men sang to assembled family members and friends present at the execution.[37] One newspaper claimed the predominating sound was the 'wails of the wives of the condemned braves'.[38] These reports complicated the notion of the terror created by the Battleford hanging by demonstrating that First Nations people attended the execution for their own personal reasons. The spectators may well have been terrorized by the traumatic scene, but their role in the event was more than a passive one. A similar perspective should be employed for the actions of the condemned men. In a position of ultimate subordination and helplessness, they remained more than either characters in a spiritual passion play or signifiers of government power and authority.

Historians have examined the process of mercy following the Rebellion less frequently than they have commented on the terror of the executions, but it formed an important feature of the legal landscape in the case of capital convictions. Three of the eleven men sentenced to death by Judge Rouleau did not hang in 1885. The practical application of state terror was sometimes mediated in subtle ways. In the aftermath of the Rebellion, a sensitivity to Cree culture determined the process of mercy for the defendants Dressy Man and Charlebois. The two men were in Big Bear's camp following the uprising, during which time a woman named She-wins turned into a Windigo.[39] When the woman warned the camp that she was 'bent on eating human flesh before the sun went down', Dressy Man, Charlebois, and a man named Bright Eyes agreed to murder She-wins, and the act was witnessed by 40 or 50 of Big Bear's men as well as Hudson's Bay Company factor William McLean. At the murder trials, Judge Rouleau attempted to instruct the jury on the differences between the charges of murder and manslaughter in an effort to accommodate some consideration of the Cree spiritual beliefs that had motivated the crime. He cautioned jury members that they could only convict for murder if they decided the crimes surrounding the Cree spiritual beliefs had been committed with malice. The jury deliberated for 20 minutes and brought back murder verdicts for Dressy Man and Charlebois and manslaughter for Bright Eyes. Dressy Man and Charlebois were sentenced to death and Bright Eyes to 20 years at Manitoba Penitentiary.[40] Two weeks before the Battleford hanging, the Governor General commuted the death sentences for the Windigo killers to life imprisonment in Manitoba Penitentiary.[41]

This sensitivity to First Nations cultural considerations suggests a number of questions surrounding the operation of mercy. When Judge Rouleau instructed the Frog Lake Massacre suspects that they would be treated without bias, he invoked a concept of justice based on equality before the law for First Nations people. To create a perception of impartiality to racial differences, it was essential that the court be seen to treat First Nations offenders with the same severity as whites. This was one example of how justice was regarded as 'the great equalizer'.[42] For both ideological and practical reasons, Canadian law was concerned with not only the appearance of impartiality, but also the transmission of British values throughout the North-West. The magisterial rhetoric from the bench was premised on this notion, and it precluded sensitive consideration of the meaning of murder based on racial factors.

However, there are also numerous historical examples in which considerations of cultural differences played an important role in the exercise of mercy in capital trials of First Nations people.[43] This occurred not at the trial stage but at the executive level. As Loo argues, cultural considerations were not given formal weight in reaching verdicts, but were used in recommendations of mercy and addressed in post-trial reports written by magistrates.[44] Although he had lectured on the impartiality and justice of the law, in the case of Dressy Man and Charlebois, Rouleau was able to see the need for both impartial justice and mercy based on mitigating cultural circumstances. The judge's and politicians' cultural sensitivity in the Rebellion aftermath resembled what Loo dubbed 'savage mercy', confirming racial differences between whites and the First Nations by granting judges and the executive the power to decide which cultural elements to consider, a process heavily dependent upon stereotypes.[45] Further, the murder of a Cree woman by Cree offenders was easier to pardon than the murder of settlers or government officials because it did not threaten the emerging Canadian order in the North-West. The Windigo murder remained in the realm of the 'savage', and this helps to explain the unique instances of government mercy. Making similar conclusions on the pardon of the Windigo killers, Carolyn Strange argues, 'capital punishment could be an instrument of racist terror, yet selective mercy toward First Nations capital offenders was no less racially informed or politically hued'.[46] When mercy appeared in this way, it could only help to reinforce the 'mental structure of paternalism' towards First Nations people, ironically aided by attention to their specific cultural circumstances. Although the Windigo killers were spared by the prerogative of mercy, their commutation sent them to Stony Mountain Penitentiary and placed the men into the grip of a different form of legal punishment.

[ . . . ]

In the late 1870s and 1880s, an increasing number of First Nations men in the North-West were sentenced to federal penitentiaries. By the time the Rebellion prisoners arrived in late 1885, the prison administration at Manitoba Penitentiary had experience with First Nations inmates and offered a programme of instruction not dissimilar to government industrial schools for younger First Nations boys. In the late 1870s, Warden Samuel Bedson adopted the view that the penitentiary could be used as an instrument of 'civilization' and instituted a special education programme for First Nations prisoners. Some of the programmes reveal how the 'civilizing' nature of the penitentiary, more than any other post-Rebellion punishment, attempted to integrate First Nations people into the hegemonic landscape of white settlement in the North-West. If First Nations people crudely understood the subtleties of majesty, justice, and mercy in other forms of legal ritual and terror, the officials at Manitoba Penitentiary possessed the means to make these messages more direct.

[ . . . ]

In spite of the intentions of penitentiary authorities, the structural deficiencies and sanitary conditions at Stony Mountain undercut positive efforts at education and reform. Manitoba Penitentiary was a ramshackle building barely completed by the Department of Public Works before the first federal inmates moved to the site in 1877. The Inspector of Penitentiaries visited Manitoba two years after it opened and reported, 'anything more unsuited to the purpose of a penitentiary it were difficult to conceive'.[47] The worst shortcomings found by the inspector involved matters of cleanliness and hygiene. [ . . . ]

The 44 First Nations prisoners who arrived at Manitoba Penitentiary in October 1885 along with 36 Métis prisoners caused an immediate problem of overcrowding.[48] Respiratory disease infected the Rebellion prisoners soon after their arrival. Overcrowding forced the men to share tiny cells or to sleep in hallways, which made segregation of the sick impossible. In any case, the penitentiary had no formal hospital facilities, and sick prisoners were confined to 'hospital' within their cells mixed with the general population. The Rebellion prisoners succumbed to disease in far greater numbers than the white prisoners for a number of possible reasons. The men likely entered the penitentiary in depleted health after a year of hardship, starvation, and military confrontation.[49] A pattern of vulnerability among First Nations prisoners was noted in prison records throughout the 1880s. The prison recorded the first death of a First Nations inmate in 1882, when a 19-year-old man named Ka-Ka-wink died of debility caused by scrofula.[50] Within the next two years, three more First Nations men, all under the age of 30, died in the Manitoba Penitentiary. [ . . . ]

[ . . . ] Despite intimate knowledge of the dreadful sanitary condition within penitentiaries, officials relied on stock Victorian ideologies regarding the degenerated health of the First Nations to explain higher than normal incidences of disease and mortality.[51]

Transmittable (and preventable) respiratory disease re-imagined as racial defect became the standard response to First Nations' sickness within the penitentiary and formed the basis of a powerful stereotype about the way they reacted to imprisonment. [ . . . ]

Mercy played a role again as the government began to consider pardons for the Rebellion prisoners in 1886, largely as a result of their failing health. Anger surrounding the Rebellion had subsided considerably by 1886, and the majority of prisoners ceased to be perceived as threatening or politically relevant. In these cases, political pragmatism carried the day over cultural considerations, particularly as officials realized throughout 1886 that many of the prisoners were terminally ill. The first 11 Rebellion prisoners, including Chief Poundmaker, were released in March of 1886.[52] Catholic priest Albert Lacombe broke the news to the pardoned prisoners at Stony Mountain and recalled later, 'they were so happy, like little children'.[53] For the most part, the fear of political scandal over prisoners' deaths motivated these pardons. The press noted that the released men were very weak and sickly, and some were even unable to walk. Among the men released that spring was Chief One Arrow, who made it only as far as St. Boniface before dying four days later.[54]

The inclusion of Poundmaker in the first group of pardoned prisoners also reveals the influence of political considerations. [ . . . ]

The fear of a future insurgency among the Blackfoot caused government officials to treat Poundmaker with unusual deference. Dewdney wrote to the prime minister just after Poundmaker's trial expressing the anxiety that something more might come of the personal relationship: 'I hope no understanding will be come to between the Crees & Blackfeet through Poundmaker—that is what I have been afraid of, but I think the light sentence will prevent that . . .'.[55] The politics surrounding Poundmaker . . . foretold the treatment he would receive from prison and government officials throughout

his incarceration.[56] Indeed, some newspapers interpreted Poundmaker's treatment on his release in March 1886 as adulation. Once again, Poundmaker's relationship with Crowfoot served him well. Dewdney received a telegram from the prime minister in late February 1886 informing him that Poundmaker was to be released 'at Crowfoot's intercession'.[57] The penitentiary organized a banquet to celebrate the first release of the Rebellion prisoners, and Warden Bedson presented Poundmaker with a gold watch. The unusual fêting of the pardoned prisoners made the event seem more like a graduation ceremony than a release from a federal penitentiary. Poundmaker was granted a meeting with Indian Commissioner Edgar Dewdney the day of his release, and, after leaving the prison, the men slept at the mansion of Archbishop Taché before beginning the trip back to the Treaty 6 area.[58] [ . . . ] However, Poundmaker did not escape the disease endemic to Stony Mountain. He died at the age of 45, three months after his pardon. [ . . . ]

In striking contrast, First Nations politics in the North-West worked against Big Bear during his time at Stony Mountain. Big Bear languished at Manitoba Penitentiary throughout 1886 with several other Cree prisoners. Although about two dozen additional Rebellion prisoners were quietly released from prison in the summer of 1886, Big Bear was not among them. In early 1887, Cree chiefs including Mistiwasis, Ahtakakoop, James Twatt, and John Smith petitioned the government for Big Bear's release. The petition paid tribute to the government and gave assurances that the chiefs considered that the prison sentences would have 'the happy effect of deterring other evil disposed persons from attempting to disturb the peace of the country in the future'.[59] [ . . . ] Playing a deft political card, the chiefs emphasized the 'loyal' status bestowed upon them by Hayter Reed following the Rebellion.[60] Significantly, the language of the petition also marginalized Big Bear's standing among Cree leaders in the

North-West by emphasizing their disapproval of his crimes.

However, Dewdney and Reed showed little interest in a pardon for Big Bear. Following the Rebellion his band was scattered, and several of his followers sought sanctuary from the law in Montana.[61] Writing to the Superintendent of Indian Affairs, Reed initially rejected the petition based on the fear that the former members of Big Bear's band would leave their present settlements to join him. Evidently, the government still feared the political viability of Big Bear and opted to keep him imprisoned.[62] Reed also considered that Big Bear would need to be released eventually and suggested to the Superintendent, '[If] the Authorities decide to release him, I beg to suggest that the release should be made prominently to appear as having been obtained through the exertions of the loyal chiefs, since that tends to give them more influence with Big Bear'.[63] Vankoughnet agreed that the release of Big Bear in 1887 would be premature and that a pardon should be deferred. Authorities were left with little choice only a month later when Big Bear's failing health caused the penitentiary surgeon to urge his release as soon as possible.[64] Big Bear was released in February 1887 and died less than a year later on the Little Pine reserve.

Big Bear's release put a symbolic bookend on the entire legal aftermath of the North-West Rebellion. The thunderous rhetoric of law and order, punishment and revenge that characterized the legal response to the Rebellion ended in this way, with the slow degeneration of an elderly former chief waiting for government mercy. What transpired in between is a demonstration of the mutability of these ideological categories. Although government and legal authorities grounded their actions and responses in the ideological tenets of English law, the process revealed something quite different: a paternalist regime willing to

resort to striking brutality in its response to opposition. [ . . . ] Although the North-West Rebellion violence ended in the early spring of 1885, the government did not hesitate to open a new front against First Nations people in the legal realm. In this way the government used punishment to decapitate politically the most oppositional First Nations bands in the North-West.

Canada's legal response to the convicted First Nations participants suggests that, beneath an overarching colonial agenda, the law operated in complex and contradictory ways. The Rebellion court cases, capital punishment, and penitentiary sentences reveal a process of colonization in which the majesty, justice, and mercy of the law unfolded, although seldom in the manner legal authorities intended. Elements of punishment, including executions and incarceration, demonstrate the different ways law and punishment were used to subordinate First Nations people. However, this subordination did not occur as directly as some writers have suggested. Domination was far from absolute in the shattering days after the North-West Rebellion. Productive and colonial relations were badly shaken by the uprising. In the aftermath, we see these relations reconstituted not only by brute state force but through the mediating effect of the ideological tenets of law. This legal response and the complex ways in which it unfolded tell us much about the emerging colonial relationship that figured forcefully in precipitating the Rebellion and even more about an emergent Canadian hegemony afterward. The experience of the convicted First Nations participants of the North-West Rebellion is found in the midst of this history. Revealing their participation in these sites of struggle provides an essential contribution to our understanding of how Canadian hegemony in the North-West was challenged.

# NOTES

1. Prince Albert *Times,* October 9, 1885.
2. E.P. Thompson, 'Eighteenth-Century English Society: Class Struggle Without Class?' *Journal of Social History* (May 1978), pp. 133-165, quoted in Bryan Palmer, *The Making of E.P. Thompson: Marxism, Humanism, and History* (Toronto: New Hogtown Press, 1981), p. 95.
3. Douglas Hay, 'Property, Authority, and the Criminal Law', in Douglas Hay, Peter Linebaugh, John G. Rule et al., *Albion's Fatal Tree* (New York: Pantheon Books, 1975), p. 49.
4. Ibid., p. 33.
5. Big Bear was a chief of the Battle River Cree. This group hunted in the Fort Pitt area of present-day Saskatchewan. Declining to sign Treaty 6 in 1876, Big Bear instead waged a political campaign against government for the next six years to obtain better terms for the settlement of First Nations people into the colonial relationship. Believing the Cree should speak in a single voice, Big Bear attracted other discontented Cree throughout the 1870s and 1880s. Although he signed Treaty 6 in 1882, he continued to refuse settlement on a reserve until late 1884, when his followers, numbering nearly 500, were reluctantly settled alongside the Wood Cree at Frog Lake, northeast of Edmonton, in present-day Alberta (Hugh Dempsey, *Big Bear: The End of Freedom* (Vancouver: Greystone Books, 1984), chap. 5 and 6). [ . . . ]
6. Blair Stonechild and Bill Waiser, *Loyal 'till Death: Indians and the North-West Rebellion* (Calgary: Fifth House Ltd., 1997), chap. 7, 'Making History', pp. 126-145.
7. Hay, 'Property, Authority, and the Criminal Law', p. 27.
8. *Saskatchewan Herald,* October 5, 1885.
9. *Saskatchewan Herald,* October 12, 1885.
10. Library and Archives Canada [hereafter LAC], MG27, IC4 Volume 7, E. Dewdney to C. Rouleau, April 24, 1885.
11. *Saskatchewan Herald,* September 28, 1885.
12. See Bingaman, 'The Trials of Poundmaker and Big Bear': Waiser and Stonechild, *Loyal 'till Death,* chap. 10, 'Snaring Rabbits', pp. 214-237.
13. E.P. Thompson, *Whigs and Hunters: The Origins of the Black Act* (New York: Pantheon Books, 1975), p. 262.
14. *Saskatchewan Herald,* September 28, 1885.
15. Ibid.
16. William B. Cameron, *Blood Red the Sun* (Calgary: Kenway Publishing Company, 1926), p. 199.
17. *Saskatchewan Herald,* September 7, 1885.
18. Quoted in Bingaman, 'The Trials of Poundmaker and Big Bear', p. 86.
19. Quoted in Stonechild and Waiser, *Loyal 'till Death,* p. 200.
20. Saskatchewan Archives Board [hereafter SAB], Taché Papers, R–E3641, L. Cochin to A. Taché, August 14, 1885, Regina. Some accounts of One Arrow's courtroom experience expand on his difficulty with English. According to Waiser and Stonechild, when the charge for treason was translated to the chief, he understood he was accused of 'knocking off the Queen's bonnet and stabbing her in the behind with a sword' (*Loyal 'till Death* p. 200).
21. SAB, Taché Papers, R–E3641, L. Cochin to A. Taché, August 14, 1885.
22. The idea of the terrible spectacle of the death penalty has been best studied by Peter Linebaugh and Michel Foucault, among many others. Peter Linebaugh, *The London Hanged: Crime and Civil Society in the Eighteenth Century* (Cambridge: Cambridge University Press, 1992), and 'The Tyburn Riot Against the Surgeons' in Hay et al., eds., *Albion's Fatal Tree,* pp. 65-119; Michel Foucault, *Discipline and Punish: The Birth of Prison,* trans. Alan Sheridan (New York: Vintage Books, 1995).
23. Linebaugh, *The London Hanged,* pp. xx-xxi.
24. Glenbow Archives [hereafter GA], Dewdney Papers, box 2, f.38, 587-88, J.A. Macdonald to E. Dewdney, November 20, 1885.
25. GA, Dewdney Papers, box 2, f.57, H. Reed to E. Dewdney, September 6, 1885.
26. SAB, Macdonald-Dewdney Correspondence. R–70, E. Dewdney to J.A. Macdonald, September 3, 1885.
27. This argument is found in Tobias, 'Canada's Subjugation of the Plains Cree, 1879–1885', and echoed in Stonechild and Waiser, *Loyal 'till Death.*
28. Louis Cochin and A. Bigonesse, *The Reminiscences of Louis Cochin, O.M.I.: a veteran missionary of the Cree Indians and a prisoner in Poundmaker's camp in 1885* (Battleford: North-West Historical Society, 1927).

29. *Saskatchewan Herald,* October 26, 1885.

30. There are at least two other accounts recording the spiritual conversion of Wandering Spirit. According to prison records, he was baptized by Catholic priest G. Cloutier of Stony Mountain Penitentiary while serving a sentence for horse-stealing in 1884 (*Sessional Papers,* 1885, No. 15, S.L. Warden Samuel Bedson, *Annual Report of the Wardens,* 'Report of the Roman Catholic Chaplain [translation]', p. 80). Cameron's book also notes that Wandering Spirit was baptized in captivity after the Rebellion three weeks prior to his execution.

31. Elizabeth M. McLean, 'The Siege of Fort Pitt', *The Beaver,* December 1946, pp. 22-41.

32. Stonechild and Waiser, *Loyal 'till Death,* p. 211.

33. Cameron, *Blood Red the Sun,* p. 207.

34. Cochin and Bigonesse, *The Reminiscences of Louis Cochin,* p. 42.

35. Ibid., p. 40.

36. *St. Paul Pioneer,* December 28, 1862.

37. Cameron, *Blood Red the Sun,* p. 80.

38. *New York Times,* November 28, 1885.

39. Among a variety of First Nations groups, including Cree and Ojibwa, the Windigo is thought to be an anthropomorphic monster that feeds on human flesh. The Windigo is traditionally destroyed by a spiritually powerful individual. In the late nineteenth and early twentieth century, Canadian courts heard a number of cases involving the murder of Windigos. See Sidney Harring, *White Man's Law: Native People in Nineteenth Century Jurisprudence* (Toronto: University of Toronto Press, 1998), chap. 8.

40. Stonechild and Waiser, *Loyal 'till Death,* pp. 261-263.

41. LAC, RG13, Series B–1, Volume 1423, File 206A, 'Charlesbois, Charles (alias: Ducharme) (also: Dressy Man)'.

42. Hay, 'Property, Authority, and the Criminal Law', pp. 32-40.

43. These two interpretations are explored in articles by Tina Loo. See 'The Road From Bute Inlet' and 'Savage Mercy: Native Culture and the Modification of Capital Punishment in Nineteenth-Century British Columbia', in Carolyn Strange, ed., *Qualities of Mercy: Justice, Punishment, and Discretion* (Vancouver: University of British Columbia Press, 1996), pp. 104-129.

44. Loo, 'Savage Mercy', p. 108.

45. Ibid., p. 110.

46. Carolyn Strange, 'The Lottery of Death: Capital Punishment in Canada, 1867–1976', *Manitoba Law Journal,* vol. 23, no. 3 (1996), pp. 593-619.

47. 'Third Annual Report of the Inspector of Penitentiaries of the Dominion of Canada For The Year 1878', *Sessional Papers,* 1879, No. 27, p. 15.

48. The approximate inmate population of Manitoba Penitentiary before the arrival of the Rebellion prisoners was 100.

49. Additionally, most of the Plains Cree were unable to obtain much-needed buffalo resources throughout the 1880s and particularly in the era after their settlement on reserves. Several accounts note that the winter of 1884–1885 had been particularly difficult for the Cree, as they tried to obtain what wild game they could in the midst of widespread cutbacks in government rations throughout the North-West.

50. 'Return of Deaths In Manitoba Penitentiary Hospital', *Sessional Papers,* 1883, No. 29, p. 133.

51. Anne McClintock explores the discourse of degeneration in an imperial context. She argues that social crisis in Britain in the 1879s and 1880s caused a eugenic discourse of degeneration predicated upon the fear of disease and contagion. Ruling elites classified threatening social groups (working-class and racialized people) in biological terms that pathologized their perceived shortcomings and potential to threaten the riches, health, and power of the 'imperial race'. Anne McClintock, *Imperial Leather: Race, Gender, and Sexuality in the Colonial Contest* (New York: Routledge, 1995), pp. 46-51.

52. *Saskatchewan Herald,* March 8, 1886.

53. Katherine Hughes, *Father Lacombe: The Black-Robe Voyageur* (New York: Moffat Yard and Company, 1911), pp. 308-309.

54. *Saskatchewan Herald,* August 30, 1886.

55. SAB, R70, Macdonald-Dewdney Correspondence, E. Dewdney to J.A. Macdonald, August 23, 1885.

56. Chief Crowfoot had adopted Poundmaker for a time in his youth to replace a son lost in

battle. This was a customary reciprocity between warring tribes. After the last hostilities between the Cree and Blackfoot ended, the adoptive relationship between the two chiefs forged a strong political alliance. Although the Blackfoot did not participate in the Rebellion, the government understood that feelings within Blackfoot communities were strongly in favour of the Cree participants.

57. SAB, R70, Macdonald-Dewdney Correspondence. J.A. Macdonald to E. Dewdney, February 24, 1886.

58. *Saskatchewan Herald,* March 8, 1886.

59. LAC, RG10, Vol. 3774, File 36846, 'Petition of Cree Chiefs Requesting Big Bear's Release', January 15, 1887.

60. Following the Rebellion, Hayter Reed compiled a list of 'band behaviour' in which he detailed the activities of each First Nations group and branded them as either 'loyal' or 'disloyal'. The designations had wide-ranging implications and determined levels of assistance, government monitoring, and permission to possess firearms.

61. A large number of Big Bear's followers, including his son Imasees, fled the North-West for Montana following the Rebellion. Imasees stood trial in the 1890s for his role in the Frog Lake Massacre, but was not convicted. Despite American military attempts to dislodge them from Montana, the Cree under Imasees never returned permanently to Canada. Michel Hogue, 'Disputing the Medicine Line', *Montana,* vol. 52, no. 4 (2002), pp. 2-17.

62. LAC, RG10, Vol. 3774, File 36846, H. Reed to Superintendent of Indian Affairs, January 29, 1887.

63. Ibid.

64. Quoted in Dempsey, *Big Bear,* p. 195.

# Chapter 4

# Britishness at the Margins

## READINGS

### Primary Documents

### Historical Interpretations

### Introduction

After the Conquest of New France, much of the territory that would become Canada was unambiguously *British* North America. Loyalist migrations and a determination to maintain a colonial presence only bolstered the sense of British identity that grew most vigorously in Upper Canada (Ontario) and the Atlantic colonies. As the Empire became larger and stronger, more prosperous and more diverse, social and cultural institutions in Canada developed in imitation of British ways. A parliamentary political system and support for British economic power were also clear evidence of how much Canadians valued 'Britishness', even after 1867. Throughout the later part of the nineteenth century and into the twentieth, immigrants from the British Isles continued to account for a significant proportion of those coming to Canada. Their degree of attachment to the 'old country' may have varied, but they knew they were coming to a place where it was relatively easy to retain their Britishness. Indeed, remaining culturally British was expected of them. Though situated next to a bustling republic, Canada was still part of the British 'family' of nations and colonies, which valued the imperial connection, and Canadian society reflected this orientation. Protestants dominated, and ensured that their traditions and sympathies would dominate as well, encouraging contentment with one's social position and with Canada's role in the imperial scheme of things. Because of this, dissenters like Goldwin Smith were all the more noticeable. Smith, a Briton who had lived in both Canada and the United States, penned our first primary source, 'Canada and the Canadian Question', to show that Canadians had already fallen too far behind Britain and had grown too close to the Americans to resist annexation to the US. Despite the energetic pragmatism of people like Smith, sentimental attachments to Empire remained, bursting forth when the Empire faced a threat or when the monarch needed to be celebrated. Margaret Yarker's poem in praise of Canadian volunteers fighting for 'England's cause' (defending Britain's interests in the Boer War) is a prime example of the sort of stirring call to loyalty designed to convince readers that Canada could play a leading role in the Empire. One did not need to be of British origin to participate, as Kurt Korneski explains. Even a relatively young city like Winnipeg could be a site for displaying and reproducing Britishness, because the growth of the Dominion and the economic progress of even its newest residents reinforced the power of those at the centre of Empire. Finally, Sheila Andrew turns to the Maritime margins to relate the curious case of Acadian support for things British, including Queen Victoria's 1887 Jubilee. Expelled by British colonial authorities more than a century earlier, Acadians had little reason to cultivate a positive attitude toward the Empire, yet Andrews notes that, at least in the pages of *Le Moniteur Acadien*, Britishness found unlikely allies far from London's metropolis.

# QUESTIONS FOR CONSIDERATION

1. Did Goldwin Smith like anything about Canada?
2. How does Yarker combine Canadian pride and imperial loyalty in her poem?
3. Why does an empire sometimes inspire sacrifice or deference from people living in imperial outposts? Shouldn't they rebel, or resist it?
4. How does Korneski think Britishness was reinforced in Winnipeg?
5. How do you account for the *Moniteur's* sunny attitude toward Britain?

# SUGGESTIONS FOR FURTHER READING

Damien-Claude Belanger, *Prejudice and Pride: Canadian Intellectuals Confront the United States, 1891–1945* (Toronto: University of Toronto Press, 2011).

Carl Berger, *The Sense of Power: Studies in the Ideas of Canadian Imperialism, 1867–1914* (Toronto: University of Toronto Press, 1970).

Phillip Buckner and R. Douglas Francis, eds., *Canada and the British World: Culture, Migration and Identity* (Vancouver: UBC Press, 2006).

Lisa Chilton, *Agents of Empire: British Female Migration to Canada and Australia, 1860s–1930* (Toronto: University of Toronto Press, 2008).

Colin Coates, ed., *Imperial Canada, 1867–1917* (Edinburgh: University of Edinburgh Press, 1995).

Sylvie Lacombe, *Rencontre deux peuple sélus: Comparaison des ambitions nationale et impériale au Canada entre 1896 et 1920* (Quebec: Presses de l'Université Laval, 2002).

R.O. Moyles and Doug Owram, *Imperial Dreams and Colonial Realities: British Views of Canada, 1880–1914* (Toronto: University of Toronto Press, 1988).

Katie Pickles, *Female Imperialism and National Identity: Imperial Order Daughter of the Empire* (Manchester: Manchester University Press, 2002).

## PRIMARY DOCUMENTS

**1**   Margaret G. Yarker, 'A Nation's Welcome', *Echoes of Empire* (Toronto: W. Briggs, 1900), 29–32.

Slow circling round, the year has rolled away
Since from our midst, 'neath Autumn's golden ray,
Through banner'd streets ye marched, amid our cheers
That rent the skies, yet bore the sound of tears.

Our hearts' proud beating, measured by our pain,
As from our sight ye passed with martial strain,
A people's faith and honour forth to bear,
Your footsteps followed by a people's prayer.

Well kept your gage! Our name ye bravely bore
Before the world on Afric's distant shore,
To shine from Paardeberg's unfading day,
Where Death stood scorn'd upon your dauntless way.

What reck'd ye? Nay! ye onward rushed to dare
The Transvaal's Lion in his cavern'd lair,
And 'mid the storm of battle's hail and flame,
Ye wreathed the Maple with the Flower of Fame.

In that brief hour for some, alas! fulfill'd
Life's dream, ere age their bounding pulse had chill'd
In youth eternal, resting where they fell;
Fame's flower for them the 'pale-hued asphodel.'

Then from our coasts, like Centaurs springing forth,
Leaped out the Riders of 'the faithful North'
To plant the Standard by their comrades' side,
Upon the heights that Britain's power defied.

On, on, the stubborn foe in flight they press
O'er river-drift and rock-bound wilderness;
'Mid bursting shell and deadly bullet sting,
They hear the rushing wind of Azrael's wing

Unfaltering, for they hold the soldier's creed,
'Not years we live in, but heroic deed',
Yet must we mourn the sons who sleep afar,
Though wrapped in honour, 'neath the Southern Star.

Their names are sounded in the triumph song,
To live remembered, long as time is long.
Our high acclaim perchance afar they hear
In air-borne echoes waved from sphere to sphere.

For now, brave Keepers of our Faith! ye come,
Amid the trumpet blare, the roll of drum;
With cheers that thunder through the cannon's roar,
The Nation greets her heroes to her shore.

The streaming colours leap to light the air,
With welcome flung from street and spire and square,
And proudly wave the folds, upon the breeze,
Ye bore to victory across the seas.

Ye, with your comrades, England's cause upheld;
Ye, with your comrades, widen as ye weld
And forge with willing hands the chain of Might
That lifts a Land of Darkness into Light,

And links yet closer, 'neath the flag unfurled,
One people with one will around the world,
Who look to God, high-purposed, strong and free,
Beneath the Crown of Britain's sovereignty.

TORONTO, December, 1900.

---

2 From Goldwin Smith, *Canada and the Canadian Question* (Toronto: Hunter, Rose and Company, 1891), 24–5, 27–38, 42–3, 47–56.

## THE BRITISH PROVINCES

Ontario, formerly Upper Canada, and better designated as British Canada, was the nucleus and is the core of the Confederation. It will be seen on the map, running out between Lake Ontario and Lake Erie on one side, and Lake Huron and the Georgian Bay on the other, Windsor on its extreme point being almost a suburb of Detroit, though separated from that city by the Detroit river. That great tongue of land is its garden, but it has also fruitful fields along the Upper St Lawrence. It reaches far back into a wilder and more arctic country, rich however in timber, and still richer in minerals. The minerals would yield great wealth if only the treasure-house in which an evil policy keeps them locked could be opened by the key of free-trade. 'Rich by nature, poor by policy,' might be written over Canada's door. Rich she would be if she were allowed to embrace her destiny and be a part of her own continent; poor, comparatively at least, she is in striving to remain a part of Europe. At present the great industry of Ontario is farming. It is so still, in spite of the desperate efforts of protectionist legislators to force her to become a manufacturing country without coal. The farmers are usually freeholders, but leaseholders are growing more common. Not a few of the farms are mortgaged, as are a good many of the farms in the United States. Let this be noted by those who fancy that to make a happy commonwealth they have only to do away with landlords and divide the land among small proprietors. The mortgagee is a landlord who never resides, never helps the tenant, never reduces the rent. Much of the money, however, borrowed in Ontario has been spent in clearing or improving farms in a new country, and has proved an excellent investment to the borrower.

[ . . . ]

In British Canada, as in the United States, we see that the world gets on without the squire or any part of the manorial system. In Canada, as in the United States, the rich live in cities; they have no country houses; they go in summer to watering-places on the Gulf of the St Lawrence, or more commonly in the United States, to Europe, or to the cottages which stud the shores and islets of the Muskoka Lakes. Not that the total absence of the manorial system does not make itself felt in American civilisation. Wealth, at all events, is the worse for having no rural duties.

A yeoman proprietor of one or two hundred acres, let the agrarian reformers of England observe, is not a peasant proprietor or of kin to the peasant characters of Zola. Let them observe also that America has been organised for the system from the beginning. In England to introduce peasant proprietorship you would have to pull down all the farm buildings and build anew for the small holdings. In France you had only to burn the chateaux.

In this fundamental respect of yeoman proprietorship, without a landed gentry, the structure of society in British Canada is identical with its structure in the United States. It is identical in all fundamental respects. Canadian sentiment may be free from the revolutionary tinge and the tendency to indiscriminate sympathy with rebellion unhappily contracted by American sentiment in the contest with George III; but it is not less thoroughly democratic. In everything the pleasure and convenience of the masses are consulted. In politics everybody bows the knee to the people. Where there is wealth there will be social distinctions, and opulence even at Toronto sometimes ventures to put a cockade in the coachman's hat. Titled visitors who come either to Canada or to the United States have too much reason to know that the worship of rank is personal, and can survive under any social system. But aristocracy is a hateful word to the Canadian as well as to the American ear. It is politically a word wherewith to conjure backwards. Any exhibition of the tendency would be fatal to an aspirant. If a citizen has a pedigree, real or factitious, he must be content to feed his eyes on it as it hangs on his own wall.

Wealth everywhere is power, and everywhere to a certain extent commands social position. This is the case in Toronto and the other cities of British Canada. But wealth in Toronto society has not everything quite its own way. There is a circle, as there is a circle even at New York, which it does not entirely command. Nor does a young man forfeit his social position by taking to any reputable calling. In that respect we have decidedly improved on the sentiment of the Old World.

One sign of the pervading democratic sentiment is the servant difficulty, about which a continual wail from the mistresses of households fills the social air. The inexperience of masters and mistresses who have themselves risen from the ranks, the dulness of small households which makes servants restless, and the rate of wages in other employments, may in part be the causes of this; but the main cause probably is the democratic dislike of service. Rarely, if ever, will you see a native American servant, and in Canada the domestics are chiefly immigrants. The work in the factory may be much harder, and the treatment less kind than in the household; generally they are; but the hours of work over, the girl calls no one mistress, and she can do what she likes in the evenings and on Sundays. In the household the democratic scorn of service is unpleasantly apt to display itself by mutiny. Ladies complain that the parts of mistress and servant are reversed, and that it is the servant that requires a character of the mistress. People begin to wonder how the relation is to be kept up, and they talk of flats, hotels, and restaurants, a recourse to which would be very injurious to domestic life and affection. It has been suggested that the children of families may have again, as they did in former days, to help in the housework. They would probably like anything which gave vent to their bodily energies almost as well as play. Dishonesty on the other hand among domestics appears to be rare, and a Canadian servant is less punctilious than an English servant in mixing different kinds of work. Another unattractive manifestation of the democratic spirit is the behaviour, in cities at least, of the lower class of Canadian boys, of which even the most silver-tongued of governors-general could not bring himself to speak with praise. Neither the schoolmaster nor anybody else dares effectually to correct the young citizens. Something may perhaps be due to the extensive and increasing employment, from economical motives, of women as teachers. There are those at least who think that this practice is not favourable to subordination or to the cultivation of some manly points of character; while others contend that the gentler influence is the stronger. The question as to the effect likely to be produced on the character of a nation by the substitution of the schoolmistress for the schoolmaster is at all events worthy of consideration. Apart however from any special cause, no one can be surprised at hearing that in a new and crude democracy there is a want of respect for authority, and of courage in exercising it, which makes itself felt throughout the social frame, and on which the young rowdy soon learns to presume. No wonder juvenile crime is on the increase.

[ . . . ]

A city in British Canada differs in no respect from an American city of the second class. It is laid out in straight streets crossing each other at right angles, with trams for the street car—the family chariot of democracy, which by carrying the working man easily to and from his work enables him to live in the suburbs, where he gets a better house and better air. Nor does city life in Canada differ from that in the United States. It is equally commercial, and though the scale is smaller than that of Wall Street the strain is almost as great. People are glad to escape to the freshness of something like primitive life on a Muskoka islet, or even to get more entirely rid of civilisation and its cares by 'camping out' on a lake side. Of late there has been in Canada as elsewhere a great rush of population to the cities. Toronto has grown with astonishing rapidity at the expense of the smaller towns and villages, and fortunes have been made by speculations in real estate. The cause of this is believed to be partly education, which certainly breeds a distaste for farm work. Another cause is the railway, which brings the people to the cities first to shop or see exhibitions, and, when they have thus tasted of city pleasures and shows, to live. The passion for amusement and excitement grows in Canada as fast as elsewhere. Railways, moreover, have killed or reduced some country employments, such as those of carriers and innkeepers. This tendency to city life is universal, and it may be said that what is universal is not likely to be evil. But the people cannot afford to be so well housed in the city as they are in the village; their children grow up in worse air, physical and moral; and though they have more of crowd and bustle they have really less of social life, because in the village they all know each other, while in the city they do not know their next-door neighbour. In the cities the people will be brought under political influences different from those of the country, and a change of political character, with corresponding consequences to the commonwealth, can hardly fail to ensue.

[ . . . ]

The Public School system in Canada is much the same as in the United States, and as in the United States is regarded as the sheet-anchor of democracy. The primary schools are free; at the High Schools a small fee as a rule is paid.[1] At Toronto University there are no fees for University lectures, but the youth during his course has to board himself, so that except to the people of the University town the education cannot be said to be free. If it were we should be in danger of having a population of penniless and socialistic graduates. As it is there are more than graduates enough. In the city of Toronto in one year $600,000 were levied for Public Schools, including the expenditure on sites, buildings, and repairs, besides the sum expended on High Schools and Separate Schools, amounting to nearly $100,000 more. Grumblers then began to challenge the principle of the system, and to ask why the man who has one child or none should be called upon for the schooling of the man who has six, when three-fourths probably of the people who use the schools are able to pay for themselves. The answer is that with a popular suffrage ignorance is dangerous to the commonwealth. Unluckily there is reason to believe that of the class likely to be dangerous a good many escape the operation of the system. It appeared from a recent report of the Minister of Education that 25 per cent of the children are not in school at all, while of those on the register the attendance was not more than half the roll. The attendance is higher in cities than it is in the country, where the weather in the winter season is a serious obstacle; but in the cities and towns it is only about 60 per cent. Attendance is legally compulsory, but the law is a dead letter; nor is the well-to-do artisan anxious to have the ragged waif in the school at his child's side. [ . . . ]

The Public Schools, saving the Separate Schools for Roman Catholics, are secular. To satisfy the religious feelings of the people some passages of Scripture of an undogmatic character are read without comment. This in strictness is a deviation from the secular principle: thoroughgoing secularists object, and there has been a good deal of controversy on the subject. The practice is defended on the ground that the moral code of the community is a necessary part of education, and that the ethics of the gospel, apart from anything dogmatic, are still the moral code of the community. Clergymen are by law allowed access at certain hours, but this privilege is not used. The organ of religious education is the Sunday School. Of these there are said to be in Ontario nearly 4,000, more than half of the number being Methodists, with 40,000 unpaid teachers. The Sunday School is made attractive by entertainments, picnics, and excursions.

The New World has produced no important novelty in religion. Universalism, the only new sect of importance, is but Methodism with Eternal Punishment left out. Upon that doctrine in almost all the Churches, as well of Canada as of the United States, the humanitarianism of democracy has acted as a solvent. Perhaps the Presbyterian Church should be excepted. At least a very eminent preacher of that church in Toronto, who had breathed a doubt some years ago, was compelled to explain, after a debate in Knox Church which recalled the debates of the primitive councils. The two Presbyterian Churches had just united, but their distinctive characters were still visible, like those of two streams which have run together yet not perfectly commingled, and the men of the Free Kirk exceeded those of the Old Kirk in orthodox rigour. Freedom from an Establishment begets tolerance as well as equality: the co-operation of the ministers, of all Protestant Churches at least, in good works is almost enforced by public opinion; dogmatic differences are softened or forgotten, and among the masses of the laity practically disappear. There is even talk of Christian union. Old-standing organisations, with the interests attached to them, are in the way; but economy may in time enforce, if not union, some arrangement which, by a friendly division of the spiritual field, shall enable a village, which neither knows nor cares anything about dogma, to feed one pastor instead of starving three. Of the Protestant Churches in Ontario the largest and the most spreading is Methodism, strong in its combination of a powerful clergy with a democratic participation of all members in church work; strong also in its retention of the circuit system, which saves it from the troubles bred in other voluntary churches by the restlessness of congregations which grow weary of hearing the same preacher. [ . . . ] Neo-Catholicism gains ground fast among the clergy; even a college founded by Low Churchmen to stem the movement finds itself turning out High Churchmen. The Mass, the Confessional, the monastic system, Protestants say, are creeping in. Still the English of the wealthier class, whatever their opinions, generally adhere to their old Church: so do the English of the poorest class, who are unused to paying for their religion, and among whom the Anglican clergy are very active. All the Protestant Churches, even that of the Baptists, have relaxed their Puritanism of form and become aesthetic: church architecture, music, flowers, have generally been introduced. The metropolitan church of the Methodists at Toronto is a Cathedral. There is a tendency also in preaching to become lively, perhaps sensational. The most crowded church on Sunday evenings in Toronto is one in which the preacher handles the topic of the day with the freedom of the platform, and amidst frequent applause and laughter. The Church of Rome, of course, stands apart with the Encyclical and Syllabus in her hand waiting till the time for putting them in execution shall arrive. In Ontario she is mainly the church of the Irish, the race which is now nearly her last hope. She does not appear to gain by conversion. [ . . . ]

In the streets of Toronto the drum of the Salvation Army is still heard. Other revivals have for the most part quickly passed away, but this endures. So far at all events it has in it the genuine spirit of Christianity that it points the road to excellence and happiness not through the reform of others, much less through dynamite, blood, and havoc, but through self-reform.

Wherever books find their way criticism and scepticism must now go with them. There is in Toronto an Agnostic circle, active-minded and militant. What is at work in minds beyond that circle nobody can tell. But there is no falling off in the outward signs of religion. Churches are built as fast as the city grows; their costliness as well as their number increases, and they are wonderfully well filled. Sunday is pretty strictly kept, though there is an agitation for Sunday street cars and the strong Sabbatarians have failed to put down Sunday boats. With regard to the whole of the American continent this appearance not only of undiminished but of increased life in the Churches while free inquiry is making inroads, of which those who read cannot help being conscious, on old beliefs, is an enigma which the result alone can solve. Revision of creeds is in the air, and it is probable that among the laity of all the Protestant Churches there has been formed a sort of Christian Theism in which many, without formulating it, repose. The tide of scepticism does not beat so fiercely against Free Churches as against an Establishment. To suppose that all the religion is hollow or mere custom would be absurd. We must conclude that people in general still find comfort in worship. Nor can it be doubted that belief in God and in conscience as the voice of God is still the general foundation of Canadian morality.

[ . . . ]

Toronto is said to be English, and likes to have that reputation. Of the leaders of society some are English by birth, and all of them keep up the connection by going a good deal to England. This habit grows with the shortening of the passage and the cheapness of the sojourn; not with the best results to Canada, for unless the chiefs of society everywhere will remain at their posts and do their duty, the edifice cannot stand. Canadian boys and youths are sometimes sent to the public schools and universities of England, but seldom, it is believed, with good results. What the boy or youth gains by superior teaching he is likely to lose by estrangement from the social and industrial element in which his life is to be spent, and by contracting tastes suitable rather to the mansions of the British gentry than to Canadian homes. English fashion perhaps presses rather heavily on us. We are apt to outvie London in the heaviness of our dinners and the formality with which they are exchanged, and the once pleasant afternoon tea has become a social battue. Mrs Grundy has too much power. The easy sociability, however, which delights and refreshes is everywhere with difficulty attained. The man who said that others might make the laws of a nation if they would let him make its ballads ought to have bargained also for the making of the games. English games and sports are the fashion in Canada, as indeed they are among the young men of wealth in the United States. Cricket is kept up in face of great difficulties, for in a commercial community men cannot afford to give two days to a game, while Canadian summer scorches the turf, and there are few school playing-fields and no village greens. Baseball, which is the game of the continent, is played in two hours, and requires no turf. Lacrosse is called the Canadian game, but it is Indian in its origin, and some think that to Indians it belongs. Football is also much played, and under the regular English rule, everything being kicked except the ball. In Toronto the red coat of the English fox-hunter is seen, though it is not to be supposed that foxes can be preserved among democratic hen roosts or freely chased over democratic farms. At Montreal, under the theocracy, you may see a real fox chased over fences as stiff as an English fox-hunter could desire. The Turf, the gambling table of England, has its minor counterpart in her colony. Yachting and rowing are popular, and Toronto has produced the first oarsman of the world: unhappily these also have brought betting in their train. The Scotchman keeps up his Scotch love of curling and of golf. Imitations are generally unsuccessful, and it was not likely that an imitation of the British sporting man or anything British would be an exception to the rule. But Anglomania, whatever it may be worth either to the imitators or to the imitated, is as strong among the same class in the United States as it is in Canada. It angers the loyal Republican and draws from him bitter jests. Nor can the rich men of Toronto be fonder of tracing their pedigrees to England than are the rich men of the United States.

[ . . . ]

Canada is a political expression. This must be borne in mind when we speak of Canadian Literature. The writer in Ontario has no field beyond his own Province and Montreal. Between him and the Maritime Provinces is interposed French Quebec. Manitoba is far off and thinly peopled. To expect national literature is therefore unfair. A literature there is fully as large and as high in quality as could be reasonably looked for, and of a character thoroughly healthy. Perhaps a kind critic might say that it still retains something of the old English sobriety of style, and is comparatively free from the straining for effect which is the bane of the best literature of the United States. The area is not large enough to support a magazine, though the attempt has more than once been made. It is hardly large enough to support a literary paper. Ontario reads the magazines of the United States, especially the illustrated magazines in which New York leads the world. Canada has been at a disadvantage alongside of the United States in falling under British copyright law and also in having her booksellers cut off by the tariff from their natural centre of distribution at New York. To fill an order at once a double duty must be paid. Let it be remembered also that it is difficult for the sapling of Colonial literature to grow beneath the mighty shadow of the parent tree. It is not so long since the United States were without writers of mark. Even now have they produced a great poet?

To make a centre of Art is still harder than to make a literary centre, because art requires models. There can barely be said to be an art centre in the United States. For art, people are likely long to go to Europe. Of millionaires Canada has not many, and such as there are can hardly be expected to give high prices for pictures and statues where they have no connoisseurs to advise them. Ontario, however, has produced a school of landscape painters the merit of which has been recognised in England. For subjects the painter has to go to the Rocky Mountains, the more poetic Selkirks, the magnificent coast-scenery of British Columbia, the towering cliffs of the Saguenay, or the shores and shipping of Nova Scotia and New Brunswick. Ontario has pleasant spots, but little of actual beauty or of grandeur, if we except Thunder Bay, with some other points on the shore of Lake Superior, and the unpaintable Niagara. [ . . . ] In a new country there can be few historic or picturesque buildings, so that the painter's landscape must lack historic or human interest. Nor can there be anything like the finished loveliness of England. The gorgeous hues of Canadian autumn and the glories of Canadian sunset are nearly all, and these often reproduced will tire. That the love of beauty and the desire to possess objects of beauty are not wanting, the stranger may learn by a glance at the display in the Toronto stores or at the house architecture of the new streets, which, whether the style be the best or not, unquestionably aspires to beauty and does not always miss its aim. The rows of trees planted along all the streets and the trim little lawns are proof of taste and refinement which cannot fail to please.

Science, as well as literature and art, has its centres in old countries. But from these, unlike literature and art, it can be imported by the student. Medical science is imported into Canada, as is believed, in full perfection. Canadian surgery performs the most difficult operations with success. The traveller who is borne safely on the Canadian Pacific Railroad along the gorges and over the chasms of the Rocky Mountains will acknowledge the skill and daring of the Canadian engineer as he will acknowledge in all details of the service the excellence of Canadian railway administration. [ . . . ]

Canada, when the value of the connection is under discussion, is always set down as a place where an Englishman can find a home. A sudden change has come over the attitude of the occupants of the American continent on the subject of Emigration. Till lately the portals were opened wide and all the destitute of the earth were bidden to come in. It was the boast of America that she was the asylum of nations. Now the door is half shut, and there are a good many who, if they could, would shut it altogether. Malthus has his day again. The world has grown afraid of being over-peopled. Moreover, the Trade Unions want to close the labour market. They have forced the Canadian Government to give up assisting emigration, and they watch with a jealous eye anything like assistance to emigration on the other side of the water. There is, however, still a demand in Canada for farm labourers, and the labourer if he is steady and industrious will do well and earn wages which in a few years will enable him to own a farm. There is a demand also for domestic servants, if they come prepared to be useful, and not with the notion that a colony is a place of high wages and no work. For teachers or clerks, it has already been said, there is absolutely no room unless they have been engaged beforehand. The Trade Unions declare that there is no room for mechanics and take everyone by the throat who says that a good mechanic may still do well. Setting the cost of living against the higher rate of wages, it is doubtful whether a British mechanic improves his lot by coming to Canada. House rent is high, clothes are dear, and a great deal of fuel is required. The difference in the cost of fuel would soon equal the difference between the price of a ticket to Canada and a ticket to New Zealand.

[ . . . ]

The notion that an Englishman enjoys a preference in Canada is pleasant, but not well founded. He is rather apt to be an object of jealousy. Anything like favour shown to him gives umbrage. The appointment of three English Professors in Toronto University roused a feeling which lingered long. From the political abuse of England which constantly offends an Englishman in the American Press, and which is largely a homage paid to Irish sentiment, the Canadian Press of course is free; but social allusions may be sometimes seen not of a friendly kind. If the writers are Irish or Socialists, still the allusions appear. The jealousy is, perhaps, a legacy of the times when most of the high places and good things were in the hands of emigrants from the Imperial country. At all events, it has been with truth said that in any candidature no nationality is so weak as the English. In the United States, on the contrary, while there is a traditional prejudice against England, against the individual Englishman there is none. He is perfectly welcome to any employment or appointment that he can get. However, an Englishman intending to emigrate had better turn his thought first to Australia and New Zealand where there is no prejudice either against him or his country, and the Irish are not so strong. These remarks have reference, of course, only to the emigrant who goes to a colony to push his fortunes in competition with the natives, not to him who goes to live on his own patrimony or the farm which he has bought, seeking nothing beyond. Nor does what has been said apply to Manitoba, and the recent settlements of the North-West. There all alike are newcomers, and no one has to encounter any jealousy or prejudice whatever.

Lord Durham said in his famous Report on Canada: 'There is one consideration in particular which has occurred to every observant traveller in these our colonies, and is a subject of loud complaint within the colonies. I allude to the striking contrast which is presented between the American and the British sides of the frontier line, in respect to every sign of productive industry, increasing wealth, and progressive civilisation. By describing one side, and reversing the picture, the other would be also described.' That this was so in Lord Durham's day was not the fault of Canadian hands, brains, or hearts. It is not the fault of Canadian hands, brains, or hearts if the contrast, though softened, still exists and is noticed by the stranger who passes from the southern to the northern shore of Lake Ontario and the St Lawrence, as he compares Windsor, Hamilton, London, Kingston, and even Toronto, with Detroit, Buffalo, Rochester, and Oswego. The cause is the exclusion of Canada from the commercial pale of her continent, and the result would be the same if an equal portion of England were cut off from the rest. The standard of living and of material civilisation is necessarily higher in the wealthier country. Let the traveller make due allowance for this if he misses an air of homelike comfort in a Canadian house or if he does not find luxury in a Canadian country inn.

[ . . . ]

From British as well as from French Canada there is a constant flow of emigration to the richer country, and the great centres of employment. Dakota and the other new States of the American West are full of Canadian farmers; the great American cities are full of Canadian clerks and men of business, who usually make for themselves a good name. It is said that in Chicago there are 25,000. Hundreds of thousands of Canadians have relatives in the United States. Canadians in great numbers—it is believed as many as 40,000—enlisted in the American army during the civil war. There is a Lodge of the Grand Army at Ottawa. A young Canadian thinks no more of going to push his fortune in New York or Chicago than a young Scotchman thinks of going to Manchester or London. The same is the case in the higher callings as in the lower: clergymen, those of the Church of England as well as those of other churches, freely accept calls to the other side of the Line. So do professors, teachers, and journalists. The Canadian churches are in full communion with their American sisters, and send delegates to each other's Assemblies. Cadets educated at a Military College to command the Canadian army against the Americans, have gone to practise as Civil Engineers in the United States. The Benevolent and National Societies have branches on both sides of the Line, and hold conventions in common. Even the Orange Order has now its lodges in the United States, where the name of President is substituted in the oath for that of the Queen. American labour organisations, as we have seen, extend to Canada. The American Science Association met the other day at Toronto. All the reforming and philanthropic movements, such as the Temperance movement, the Women's Rights' movement, and the Labour movements, with their conventions, are continental. Intermarriages between Canadians and Americans are numerous, so numerous as scarcely to be remarked. Americans are the chief owners of Canadian mines, and large owners of Canadian timber limits. The railway system of the continent is one. The winter sports of Canada are those of the United States. Canadian banks trade largely in the American market, and some have branches there. There is almost a currency union, American bank-bills commonly passing at par in Ontario, while those of remote Canadian Provinces pass at par only by special arrangement. American gold passes at par, while silver coin is taken at a small discount: in Winnipeg even the American nickel is part of the common currency. The Dominion bank-bills, though payable in gold, are but half convertible, because what the Canadian banks want is not British but American gold. Canadians go to the American watering-places, while Americans pass the summer on Canadian lakes. Canadians take American periodicals to which Canadian writers often contribute. They resort for special purchases to New York stores, or even those of the Border cities. Sports are international; so are the Base Ball organisations; and the Toronto 'Nine' is recruited in the States. All the New-World phrases and habits are the same on both sides of the Line. The two sections of the English-speaking race on the American continent, in short, are in a state of economic, intellectual, and social fusion, daily becoming more complete. Saving the special connection of a limited circle with the Old Country, Ontario is an American State of the Northern type, cut off from its sisters by a customs line, under a separate government and flag.

## NOTE

1. The trustees have the option of remitting the fee, and this is commonly done as a reward for proficiency in the public school.

## HISTORICAL INTERPRETATIONS

3   From Kurt Korneski, 'Britishness, Canadianness, Class, and Race: Winnipeg and the British World, 1880s–1910s', *Journal of Canadian Studies* 41(2) (Spring 2007): 161–84.

In 1882, George Bryce, author, Presbyterian minister, and founder of Manitoba College, explained to readers of his then recently published history of Manitoba that 'the traveller, on crossing the line at Emerson as he enters Manitoba from Minnesota, is reminded not only by the appearance of the Union Jack that he is again on British soil, but by many other things as well. The dress of the people is more English, [as are] their manners and custom, and speech' (1882, 358). Bryce not only reported the habits and practices of some Manitobans, but himself imagined the Canadian nation as a 'British American nation', and in this he was far from unusual (Bryce 1896, 1909, 1910). Whether advocates of imperial federation like lawyer John L. Thompson and prominent reformer Minnie J.B. Campbell (Thomson 1905, 25–6; Campbell 1911, 1–2), autonomists[1] like *Manitoba Free Press* editor J.W. Dafoe and lawyer John S. Ewart (Dafoe 1909, 6–8; Ewart 1906, 19), or 'progressive' social gospel ministers such as J.S. Woodsworth and William Ivens (Woodsworth 1972, 234; Ivens 1909, 24), many middle-class Winnipeggers agreed that Canada was what Bryce dubbed a 'Brito-Canadian' nation (Bryce 1910, xvi; Wardaugh 1997). Moreover, there is evidence to suggest that in Canada generally from Confederation up through to the middle of the twentieth century, a large number of men and women imagined themselves as 'Britishers'. So ingrained was this notion that even when Paul Martin Sr. and other legislators developed a *Canadian Citizenship Act* to provide a legal basis for Canadian citizenship after the Second World War, they felt compelled to state that all Canadian citizens were British subjects. As Martin recalled, 'if Canadians' status as British subjects had been done away with in my Bill, it would not have passed' (1993, 74).

The centrality of Britishness to Canadian national imaginings from the mid-nineteenth to the mid-twentieth centuries reflected the fact that most observers, historians included, understood the Dominion as an integral part of the British Empire, and many lauded that fact. Since the mid-twentieth century, the study of the colonies of settlement among imperial historians and the willingness of Canadian historians to acknowledge Canada's imperial past have faded, just as the British Crown and the empire have increasingly been supplanted by imagery that emphasizes Canada's independence, its biculturalism and multiculturalism, and its resolutely North American character. In recent years, a number of scholars have suggested that this shift has led us to under-appreciate important aspects of imperial and Canadian history, and they have set out to bring colonies like Canada back into imperial history and to bring the empire back into the history of Canada (Buckner and Francis 2005, 9–20; Perry 2003; Limerick 2001, 2004).

[ . . . ]

This essay focusses primarily on writers, ministers, editors, club women, and other middle-class cultural producers in Winnipeg from the late nineteenth century to the period before the outbreak of the First World War. It should not be read as a purely local study of the social or intellectual history of imperialism in Winnipeg. Rather, it is a critical assessment of the 'British world' strategy for bringing the empire back into Canadian history and for bringing Canada back into imperial history. The focus is on Winnipeg rather than some other 'edge of empire' because conditions in the city in the period under consideration make it suggestive of broader trends in the nation at large. Winnipeg was western Canada's most populous and industrial city (Bellan 1978, 159–82). It also stood as the 'gateway' to a region that had yet, to use the contemporary language, to be fully 'civilized'. The tensions inherent in living in a centre on the periphery were manifestations of important dynamics facing middle-class nationalists as they set out to realize an imperialist national project. Capturing tensions that were central to nation-building efforts in northern North America more generally in these years, Winnipeg provides an entry point into the identities and imaginings that those tensions produced.

The Winnipeg case suggests that there is much to be said for the British world perspective. A close examination of the meanings Britishness held and the ways Winnipeggers used it indicates that the identity was pliable, and that diverse men and women shaped it to suit their own situation and aims; yet the notion that the widespread acceptance of a British identity in settlement colonies like Canada shows that consensus, rather than coercion, violence, and disparate power relations, was responsible for the appeal and pervasiveness of that identity is questionable. To the contrary, the Winnipeg situation indicates that coercion, violence, and dispossession on global, national, and local levels was important for the appeal of Britishness in the city. When the literary elites who are at the centre of this essay spoke of Britishness, they did not refer to qualities of life on the British Isles. Rather, Britishness appealed largely because the geopolitical situation in the late nineteenth and early twentieth centuries enabled them to legitimate their visions of the future by reference to it. The appeal of the identity, then, was contingent on a long history of violence, dispossession, and coercion that produced and sustained the geopolitics in relation to which Winnipeggers understood themselves. Moreover, part of the appeal of the identity lay in the fact that it allowed advocates of the national project to come to terms with the fact that, even though Aboriginal peoples comprised a comparatively small population that was weakened by disease and conflict, violence against and dispossession of these peoples was still important for nation building in northern North America. Finally, it is essential to understand the pervasiveness of Britishness among a diverse settler population both as a product of consent and as a function of disparate power relations within Canadian capitalism. That is, many of those who migrated to the city from non-British points of origin and who formed a significant portion of Winnipeg's working class embraced a British identity because they believed that doing so would allow them access to better and higher paying jobs and would afford them a better quality of life. For many local Winnipeggers, there were market-driven reasons for choosing Britishness over, or in addition to, some other identity.

## I

Up until the mid-nineteenth century, the site that became Winnipeg was part of a fur-trade hinterland that most observers viewed as uninhabitable and unappealing (Owram 1980, 48). After that time, many Britons and Euro-Canadians began to name, to divide, and to view this colonial space differently. What once was of marginal value became central to the vision of a prosperous, populous liberal-capitalist society. The shift is worth reflecting on, for it signalled important changes within the longstanding, mutually determining processes of material and ideological transformation that linked colonizing centres and their peripheries. Rebellions in Jamaica, India, and New Zealand around the middle of the nineteenth century, combined with a slightly later economic crisis, meant that for imperial officials 'the settlement of British peoples in colonial spaces emerged as an expedient way of securing Britain's interests abroad and of relieving pressures at "home"' (Perry 2007, 12).

As British world scholars have suggested, in northern North America the Aboriginal population was comparatively small and weakened by disease and war. That the mid-century rebellions caused imperial officials to question whether Native populations could become self-governing peoples within the empire had less significance in Canada than it did elsewhere. Nevertheless, many Britons and Canadians did view the region as a 'vast empty space' that could receive settlers, and as the site of a future nation that could help Britain to meet the challenge of American ascendency (Cain and Hopkins 2001, 270–83; Naylor 1972, 15). The will to develop a northern North American nation that encompassed a vast territory made the visions of Canadian expansionists realistic, reasonable, and relevant (Owram 1980, 34–8, 57). From Confederation onward, nation builders hoped to ensure economic vitality for Britain and the new Canadian nation by reproducing and extending a liberal-capitalist politico-economic system among a newly settled population in the periphery. [ . . . ]

It is likely that Winnipeg would have developed into little more than a modest town had its business elite not convinced the

Canadian Pacific Railway to route its main-line through their city. After a struggle with their neighbours in Selkirk in the mid-1870s, however, Winnipeggers did ensure that their city was the site through which the railway would pass. From that point on, Winnipeg became the gateway to the West, and virtually everything and everyone who travelled to or from the interior had to pass through it (Artibise 1975, 61–76). This strategic location produced urban, industrial, and commercial growth, and soon the city was the regional metropolis. Winnipeg firms supplied settlers with the products and equipment they needed for farming and processed settlers' grain and livestock; the city also functioned as a clearing house for labour needed in work and construction camps to the west and north of the city (Bellan 1978, 53–80; Friesen 1987, 274–8).

## II

The ministers, authors, club women, journalists, and others who are at the centre of this essay came west as a part of this imperialist national project. Most supported the empire and spent a great deal of time, energy, and money expressing their devotion to the Crown. For example, they built and named schools after important imperial figures, greeted visiting royals with lavish celebrations, raised monuments to commemorate important figures and events, undertook and wrote and read about pilgrimages to the 'heart of the empire' (London), and held Empire Balls and Pageants. They also distributed Union Jacks to settlers, undertook speaking tours on Empire Day, and played 'British sports'. Even though most middle-class men and women embraced the 'British connection', however, Britain and many British peoples, as Congregationalist minister J.L. Gordon observed, 'had a bad reputation in Canada' (1911, 6). Indeed, they not only had a bad reputation, but many nationalists actually viewed them as a threat. In the 'lessons' that Charles Gordon taught through his social gospel novels characters

who represented sources of corruption, like the mine manager in *Black Rock* (1905, 95) or 'the Kid' in *The Prospector* (1904, 195), were often upper-crust Britons. Similarly, while men like Dafoe and J.S. Woodsworth could find desirable qualities even amongst those, like the Doukhobours, whose 'strange habits' unnerved many of their counterparts, they lumped 'the English with the cockney accent' with Asians, African Americans, the 'Levantine races', and others whom they viewed as totally unsuited to life in Canada (Woodsworth 1972, 46–50, 137–60).

These reservations, as Phillip Buckner and R. Douglas Francis have pointed out, were linked with nationalists' objections to parts of the social system in the British Isles, and especially its class structure (2005, 16). In part a carry-over from the aristocratic tradition and in part a product of modern economic concentration, the class system was seen by many as the cause of two major problems. On the one hand, as John Dafoe explained, 'by the operation of social and commercial conventions . . . the making of a competence [had] become almost a privilege' (1901). The lack of opportunity for social mobility produced a debased and demoralized populace of men and women who lived in squalor and who had been reduced to a 'state of dependence'. These were the East Londoners, 'the Englishmen with the cockney accent' (1905). On the other side of the class divide were those who, as George Chipman complained, 'came from the great nation to which Canada owes its greatness today' and 'would refuse a "job" but wanted a position' (1909, 411–12). These were the men who in Britain had enjoyed the benefits of the 'social and commercial conventions'. They were men who held positions of authority, or at least enjoyed a reasonably comfortable existence, because of their ancestry rather than their own personal merits.

This simultaneous embracing of the British connection and the rejection of life in, and often of men and women from, the British Isles was not a contradiction. Britishness was not primarily about the perceived realities of life on the British Isles, the present, or even necessarily the corporeal world. Instead, it reflected and spoke to geopolitics, spiritual qualities, politico-ethical principles, and visions of the future. Thus, when Dafoe adulated the 'British connection' and 'British institutions', he discussed neither the formal political landscape in Britain nor the contemporary quality of life on the British Isles. Rather, he directed his attention to general laws of social development. He mused that the dominant position of the 'Anglo-Saxon race' that had sprung from the British Isles was explained by its suitability to those laws (1901; 1902; 1906). Charles Gordon and businessman and senator Charles Boulton professed the belief that British global predominance reflected that 'Britishers' were particularly in tune with a divine plan that supposedly guided human history (Boulton 1896; Gordon 1914). Others did not provide such intricate explanations. Minnie Campbell, for example, noted that Canada was a 'land of promise' where 'life, liberty and property are safe'. It was, as such, part of the inexorable spreading of the 'British race' (1911). Similarly, Congregationalist minister J.B. Silcox argued that the Canadian state had a duty to prepare its children for citizenship by making sure that they 'speak one language, read one literature, swear allegiance to one flag, and make a united Dominion from Atlantic to Pacific'. The language, he noted, 'should be English and the literature and flag British'. In this language and literature were 'imbedded the ethical and political principles that have made and will keep our nation great'. It 'is a significant fact', he continued, 'that our language and literature are girdling the globe' (Silcox 1911, 13–14).

As Campbell's comments about liberty and property suggest, liberalism and liberal institutions were central to middle-class Winnipeggers and their vision of the nation. Even though these men and women defined Britishness in liberal terms, they did not hope to build a replica of the liberal society that existed in Britain itself. Rather, Canada's frontier offered abundant resources and a bracing climate that would 'breed and maintain the most virile community of Anglo-Saxons in the world' (Dafoe 1906). Individual property holders, pursuing their respective self-interests on the level playing field of the Canadian prairies, would provide the foundations for a society that functioned according to what was 'natural' to the human condition. It would transform the men and women who travelled to it by freeing them from 'the restraints of custom and surrounding' and allowing them to 'shed all that was superficial in their make-ups' (Gordon 1899, 26–7). Canada provided a setting not for a 'little Britain', but for a 'better Britain' (Belich 1996, 2001). It would be a society in which the qualities, traits, and/or politico-ethical principles that explained the vastness of the empire in the first place could find their fullest expression.

## III

Understanding that Britishness was about politico-ethical principles rather than about the particulars of a geographical region is important for a variety of reasons. For example, it explains what otherwise appear as striking inconsistencies in late nineteenth- and early twentieth-century nationalist thought. That is, it explains why men like J.W. Dafoe and J.S. Ewart could demand independence for Canada and also proclaim that they were not advocates of 'independence if by that is meant separation from the British crown'. Canada, in their view, would be 'a nation, in the truest sense of that term'. It would be 'self-existent, autonomous, [and] sovereign'. It would also be 'a nation with the British King as its only and all-sufficient head' (Ewart 1906, 19). The problem with having men in the British Isles in control of policies that affected Canada was that they were not British enough. Although the spiritual qualities and some of the institutions that captured their essence were vital to 'Brito-Canadianism', the policies of the

Canadian nation had to be determined by those who had been freed of the artifices that plagued Britain itself. Only 'better Britons' could consistently understand what was best and necessary for a 'better Britain' (Dafoe 1908; Ewart 1907, 1911).

That Britishness was about a spiritual essence, and as such was both flexible and contestable, was important for the appeal and pervasiveness of the identity. This flexibility allowed the middle-class men and women to deal with tensions rooted in applying the concept of 'the nation' to northern North America. As Benedict Anderson has pointed out, after nationalism came into existence as a way of thinking about community and belonging, it became a cultural artefact (1991, 4). It was, at least broadly speaking, a distinctive form of thinking about humans and their relationships to one another. One defining characteristic of nationalism, as is well known, is that it was about 'imagined communities'. Less recognized is that nationalism in the nineteenth century also involved an emphasis on what Anthony Smith has called a core 'ethnie' (1986, 30). That is, those who were part of 'the nation' conformed to the language (particularly the written language), 'traditions', and spiritual qualities (however they were defined) of a core group whose presumed timeless past stood as the 'primordial foundations of national culture and the matrices of the national mind' (Hobsbawm 1992, 54).

In Canada, and especially in the West and in Winnipeg, it was obvious, and often deeply unsettling, to many middle-class observers that a large number of settlers were from an array of kingdoms and countries. Britishness defined in the ways mentioned above was appealing because, even though there may have been no obvious core 'ethnie', nationalists could maintain that with a measure of diligence on their part, a still-developing, linguistically and ethnically uniform, fixed Canadian type would be British, meaning that it would conform to the politico-ethical principles that were common to the most 'advanced' and globally

predominant segments of humanity. They could hold that the diverse collection of men and women within Canada could be 'refined' into Britishers, meaning that they could be infused with the qualities necessary to realize the ideally functioning liberal-capitalist society nationalists envisaged. Indeed, they even surmised that various 'lesser' peoples could contribute efficacious aspects of their national groups to the 'Better Britons'. Scandinavians, for example, were a source of heroism (Dafoe 1911, 34). Slavs showed a 'devotion to ideals, and constancy in the face of persecution', and could 'bring a fine strain of idealism into our Canadian character'. Mennonites brought sturdiness and commitment to education. Jews or 'Hebrews' were 'naturally religious, temperate, home-loving, intelligent, industrious and ambitious'. Italians were committed to family (Woodsworth 1972, 88, 129, 134). The 'coming race' would be 'the glory and triumph of which every nation whose name is on the map of the world, at the present time, [would] make a contribution' (J.L. Gordon 1914, 3). As Dafoe told an audience at the Fort William Canadian Club, 'the many strains of nationality in Canada', if the Brito-Canadians 'on the ground are true to themselves, while they may modify the type, will not destroy, but will strengthen and improve it' (1911, 34).

[ . . . ]

The flexibility of the identity was also well suited to the social divisions that became more pronounced as the city developed into a regional metropole. Competitive pressures within the global economy of the day meant that as the tide of goods and people flowing to and from the West swelled, and as the city became an industrial and commercial hub, local capitalists had to replicate forms of ownership and production that existed elsewhere (Burley 1998). In doing so, they reproduced attendant social consequences, including increased material inequity. The tendency to class polarization was reflected in Winnipeg's social and residential structure.

Natural barriers and limited transportation meant that early in its history the city was relatively socially diverse and centralized. With the bridging of the Assiniboine and Red rivers, and the advent of streetcars, bicycles, and automobiles in the very late nineteenth and early twentieth centuries, the city's more affluent residents began to migrate out of the increasingly overcrowded original centre around the intersection of Main Street, Portage Avenue, and Notre Dame Avenue to build homes on or near the banks of the Assiniboine. By the turn of the century, there was the increasingly sharp divide between the park-like setting of primarily Anglo-Canadian bourgeois enclaves near Rosyln Road and Wellington Crescent and in Armstrong's Point, and the sometimes unimaginably poor, working-class North End (Hiebert 1991).

Especially during the first decades of the twentieth century, this social polarization fostered an increasingly potent class identity among members of the city's expanding urban proletariat. Even in times of bitter social conflict, the question for many of the city's Anglo-Canadian working-class men and women was not whether they were British: it was how to define Britishness. According to many working people, a British society was one in which all citizens were guaranteed the right to a certain level of material comfort and to protection from oppressive employers and government officials. To much of the city's bourgeoisie, it meant the defence of the liberal-capitalist 'civilization' in which they enjoyed a privileged social standing.

## IV

Recognizing that a wide variety of men and women could press for their aims under the banner of Britishness provides an alternative to what Jane Connors has characterized in a different context as explanations of collective identity that stress 'manipulation from on high and an audience of "cultural dopes" down below' (1993, 382). That is, it places popular agency at the centre of identity formation and the success of particular collective imaginings. To acknowledge that popular agency was important to identity formation, however, does not mean that coercion, dispossession, and violence were not also central to the identity and its popularity. In a general sense, for example, when Winnipeggers thought of themselves as part of the empire, they did not just think of themselves in terms of their particular locality. Rather, they developed modes of conceptualization as agents who were enmeshed in a web of social relations that enveloped the globe itself. They were embedded within and observers of a social reality that, though always in flux, was also defined by long-term, if contingent, patterns. In the late nineteenth and early twentieth centuries, the social reality of which nationalists were part included a tremendous amount of inequity and the tendency of those in the industrial West to carve up and dominate the non-Western, non-industrial world. The centrality of this state of affairs for Canadian national imaginings is apparent. Britishness appealed to Canadian nationalists partly because they could refer to an extensive British empire to evidence their claims that Divine or natural laws or unnamed principles governed the history of humanity. Thus, nationalists were not separate from coercive relationships. Rather, they existed in, made sense of themselves through, and embraced identities that were possible and appealing because those identities took form within an imperial context—a context that was at least partly produced and sustained by coercion and oppression. The empire of coercion made possible the modes of imagining communities that stood as the basis for the empire of consent.

Moreover, it is true, as British world scholars suggest, that the relationship between colonized and colonizing in settler societies differed markedly from those in dependent colonies. In the latter, there tended to be large, disease-resistant, centralized populations. Confronted with such realities, imperialists usually tried to extract profits from indigenous labour through some form of collaboration. Where the indigenous populations were small, decentralized, and often ravaged by European diseases, however, the aim was, as Patrick Wolfe, Donald Denoon, and others have pointed out, to displace indigenes from, or to 'replace' them on, the land (Wolfe 1999, 1; Denoon 1983, 1–6).

Even though the Aboriginal population was comparatively small, decentralized, and weakened by disease and war, the coercion involved in re-placing Aboriginal peoples was still significant for the form and appeal of Brito-Canadianism. Discussions of the 'better Britain', for example, were premised on the idea that the territory over which local European-descended men and women sought dominion was devoid of history and tradition. It was this presumption that allowed nationalists to dream of a 'better Britain'; yet these ways of speaking about the world did not imply that the interior actually was devoid of people. Many of Winnipeg's early residents witnessed and sometimes participated in putting down the Riel rebellions. They also continued to engage with the history of Aboriginal peoples and dealt with lower-level resistance on a more quotidian basis. In this setting, musings about Brito-Canadianism were not divorced from concerns about the Aboriginal population, dispossession, and coercion. Rather, they were a nationalist discourse that allowed settlers to deal with dispossession by refusing to acknowledge the existence, historicity, or full humanity of those who stood as obstacles to their national project. That is, Brito-Canadianism was a nationalist discourse whose 'deafening silences' worked to deal with Aboriginal people and their resistance. As Anthony Moran has pointed out in a different context, such formulations are a part of an ideological project in which 'colonizers do not take stock of the colonized as men and women, but treat them as part of the natural landscape' (2002, 1023). Erasing Aboriginality from the landscape does not

show that 'Brito-Canadianism' was divorced from coercion of the Aboriginal population. Rather, it was a way of speaking that provided an implicit justification for the forced removal of large numbers of men and women from the interior of the continent. To paraphrase Moran, when indigenous people were seen as parts of, rather than fully human residents in, the wilderness, taming nature meant taming indigenous peoples (2002, 1023).

While silences and omissions in constructions of Brito-Canadianism were important, Britishness also was appealing as an identity because it enabled middle-class Winnipeggers to explain dispossession even when they did acknowledge that the interior of northern North America was not a blank slate. When middle-class nationalists in Winnipeg discussed Aboriginal men and women, they portrayed them, as J.S. Woodsworth put it, as 'belated survivors of an earlier age' (1972, 159). We have already seen that advocates of Brito-Canadianism found Britishness appealing in part because they could use the fact of an extensive British empire as evidence for laws of human social development. We have also seen that those laws were constructions that naturalized a particular envisioned future. It is also evident that these laws explained dispossession. If the advanced nature of 'British civilization' (however it was defined) ensured that it would, according to the dictates of laws of social development, sweep across the globe, then the supplanting of 'lesser races' became a necessary, if unfortunate, result of the 'slow and inevitable turning of the wheels of progress'. It followed that if Britishness was at the core of Canadianness, then the dispossession that was inherent in Canadian nation building became natural and inevitable. Aboriginal peoples and/or their cultures disappeared like 'mist before the rising sun' (Bryce 1884, 1).

While the lopsided relationships between colonized and colonizer are significant, another sort of inequity is also important. As has been suggested above, part of the reason that Britishness could work as a way of imagining the 'Canadian community' was that it was flexible enough to allow a range of men and women to push for what were viewed as the proper goals of social change. That a host of men and women could accept this identity and define it in ways that suited their aims and interests, however, does not mean that the range of disparate aims articulated by reference to Britishness found expression in actual patterns of social, political, and economic life in the Dominion. Indeed, as the land settlement policy mentioned above indicates, middle-class men and women could express their liberal definition of Britishness with greater force than others. That is, they not only articulated a definition of what 'type' of people Canadians were and what they should become through their definition of Britishness, but they also were able to convince and compel a large number of men and women to act and interact in ways that made their social vision central to social practice.

[ . . . ]

A central impetus for the Canadian national project in the first place was the economic crisis that grew out of that economic system. In particular, the Canadian national project, at its core an imperial endeavour, became reasonable and appealing to capitalists in the world's foremost industrial and colonizing centre because they saw it as a way to preserve the privileged standing (within their own society and within the world) in the face of the twin threats of stagnation and social unrest. An important part of the reason that Britishness, defined in liberal terms, prevailed was that it suited the interests of powerful men and women who could lend force to Britishness defined in these ways. They could do so, in turn, because it was they who benefitted from the extraction of surplus from a large number of men and women engaged in the production process. Put differently, Britishness (defined in liberal terms) had force in Canada because it was the ideology embraced by and reinforcing those who held a monopoly on social power derived ultimately from sometimes brutal exploitation of the subaltern classes within and outside of capitalist hubs.

Moreover, that liberalism reinforced and reflected capitalism meant that in establishing a 'British society' defined in liberal terms, bourgeois men and women (wittingly or not), worked to establish a society in which men and women in Canada, like their counterparts in the centres, ordered their lives in ways that made further accumulation possible. It was to create a nation governed by a state that ensured (by force if necessary) that conditions that allowed purely economic force—the 'imperative of the market'—to coerce men and women into allowing a net transfer of their productive powers. As the suppression of strikes and other socialist and labour initiatives in Winnipeg suggests, force did become central to sustaining a social order of the type prescribed in bourgeois definitions of Britishness.

The fact that settler societies like Canada were also capitalist societies was important for a different reason as well. While some working-class men and women embraced Britishness, the fact that the city was home to a working class that was not only growing but also culturally diverse created particular dynamics within the locality. Particularly significant for our purposes is the fact that divisions between workers and employers and amongst workers themselves inspired a rejection, or at least only a grudging acceptance of, Britishness among many working-class men and women. While, as we have seen, some immigrants with no personal or ancestral ties to the British Isles accepted a British identity, a portion of these groups were also disinclined to do so. The bulk of newly arrived, non-Anglo-Canadian immigrants in Winnipeg were not simply working-class men and women, but were the 'lumpen proletariat'; they found themselves the object of ridicule from two different directions. On the one hand, Anglo-Canadian working-class men and women tended to view them as potential competitors who would drive down wages and undermine their ability to earn the living wage to which they, as 'true

Britishers', were entitled. On the other hand, middle-class men and women tended to blame the indigence and social dislocation entailed by increasingly large industrial and commercial concerns on ethnicity.

Taken together, these pressures from Anglo-Canadians on both sides of the class divide encouraged non-British immigrants in the city to develop organizations that expressed both their class standing and their alternate—i.e., non-British—ethnic identity, a tendency that is evidenced by the organization of language-based locals of broader political movements and the construction of institutions like the Ukrainian Labour Temple (Yuzyk 1953; McCormack 1972–3; 1977, 65–7, 71–5; Stone 2003). It is also suggested by the fact that some male youths who were either immigrants or the children of immigrants, as John Marlyn recalled, sometimes joined working-class street gangs composed of other young men of their own ethnic background—gangs whose members, it is worth pointing out, viewed 'the British', particularly in the south end of the city, as totally divorced from themselves (Marlyn 1957).

Even those who did not see themselves as British still often publicly embraced the identity. Their reasons for doing so, however, had less to do with a sense of belonging to a 'Greater Britain' than they did with material necessity. The fact that middle-class nationalists held a comparatively privileged standing in Canadian society, and that they had, or had access to, political and economic authority, meant that structures of opportunity tended to reward acceptance of the form and type of identity that they championed. As labour and working-class historians have long noted, many immigrants Anglicized their names so that they might conform to, be accepted into, and receive the higher wages and better jobs afforded to 'Britishers' (Klymasz 1960; Avery 1979). As Ukrainian immigrant Michael Harris (his actual name was Michael Hrushka) recalled, 'no matter how you measure success in the sense of amassing a fortune, securing a good job with good pay, gain friendship and a happier life' (n.d., 49), it was necessary to be British. While the pervasiveness of Britishness may not have been produced by malevolent elites on high, prevailing social relations allowed some men and women to define their identity in the ways they saw fit with greater force than other groups. Although Britishness may have been one among a large number of identities made possible by an extant cultural repertoire, there were market-driven reasons for choosing Britishness in addition to, or over and above, other possibilities.

## NOTE

1. I have used the term 'autonomist' to differentiate proponents of a formally independent Canadian nation-state from advocates of imperial union. I have chosen 'autonomist' rather than 'nationalist' because, as Carl Berger demonstrated long ago (1970), both imperialists and autonomists were nationalists.

## REFERENCES

Anderson, Benedict. 1991. *Imagined Communities: Reflections on the Origins and Spread of Nationalism*. New York: Verso.

Artibise, Alan. 1975. *Winnipeg: A Social History of Urban Growth*. Montreal and Kingston: McGill-Queen's University Press.

Avery, Donald. 1979. *'Dangerous Foreigners': European Immigrant Workers and Labour Radicalism in Canada, 1896–1932*. Toronto: McClelland & Stewart.

Belich, James. 1996. *Making Peoples: A History of New Zealand from Polynesian Settlement to the End of the Nineteenth Century*. Honolulu: University of Hawaii Press.

———. 2001. *Paradise Reforged: A History of the New Zealanders from the 1880s to the Year 2000*. Honolulu: University of Hawaii Press.

Bellan, Ruben. 1978. *Winnipeg, First Century*. Winnipeg: Queenston House.

Berger, Carl. 1970. *The Sense of Power: Studies in the Ideas of Canadian Imperialism, 1867–1914*. Toronto: University of Toronto Press.

Boulton, Charles. 1896. 'Extract from Hansard: A Permanent International Tribunal'. MG 14 B20, box 3, file 7. Archives of Manitoba, Winnipeg, MB.

Bryce, George. 1882. *Manitoba: Its Infancy. Growth and Present Condition*. London: Sampson Low, Marston, Searle and Rivington.

———. 1884. *'Our Indians': Address Delivered Before the Y.M.C.A. of Winnipeg, December 1st 1884*. Winnipeg: Manitoba Free Press.

———. 1896. *Great Britain as Seen by Canadian Eyes*. Winnipeg: Winnipeg Free Press.

———. 1909. *The Romantic Settlement of Lord Selkirk's Colonists*. Toronto: Musson.

———. 1910. *The Canadianization of Western Canada*. Ottawa: The Royal Society of Canada.

Buckner, Phillip, and R. Douglas Francis. 2005. Introduction to *Rediscovering the British World*, eds. Philip Buckner and R. Douglas Francis, 9–20. Calgary: University of Calgary Press.

Burley, David. 1998. 'The Social Organization of Self-Employment in Winnipeg, Manitoba, 1881–1901'. *Histoire Sociale/Social History* 31: 35–69.

Cain, P.J., and A.G. Hopkins. 2001. *British Imperialism, 1688–2000*. London: Longman.

Campbell, Minnie J.B. 1911. 'The Supremacy of the Flag'. Minnie J.B. Campbell Papers. P2503, folder 13. Archives of Manitoba, Winnipeg, MB.

*Canadian Citizenship Act*, Statutes of Canada 1946, c.15.

Chipman, George. 1909. 'Winnipeg: The Melting Pot'. *Canadian Magazine* 33 (5): 409–46.

Connors, Jane. 1993. 'The 1954 Royal Tour of Australia'. *Australian Historical Studies* 25 (100): 371–82.

Dafoe, John W. 1901a. 'Growth in the West's Political Strength'. *Manitoba Free Press*, 19 August, 4.

———. 1901b. 'The Stranger Within Our Gates and His Treatment'. *Manitoba Free Press*, 19 September, 4.

———. 1901c. 'Colonization by Settlements'. *Manitoba Free Press*, 16 October, 4.

———. 1902a. 'The Waning of Evil'. *Manitoba Free Press*, 3 February, 4.

———. 1902b. 'More Attacks on Galicians, Etc.' *Manitoba Free Press*, 20 January, 4.

———. 1902c. 'Canada a Home For All'. *Manitoba Free Press*, 26 April 1902, 4.

———. 1902d. 'The Doukhobors'. *Manitoba Free Press*, 10 November, 4.

———. 1905a. 'Last Year's Immigration'. *Manitoba Free Press*, 2 August, 4.

———. 1905b. 'Immigration'. *Manitoba Free Press*, 5 April, 4.

———. 1906. 'The Day of the Anglo-Saxon'. *Manitoba Free Press*, 16 June, 4.

———. 1908. 'The Restriction of Undesirable Immigration'. *Manitoba Free Press*, 13 April, 4.

———. 1909. *The Imperial Press Conference*. Winnipeg: *Winnipeg Free Press*.

Denoon, Donald. 1983. *Settler Capitalism: The Dynamics of Dependent Development in the Southern Hemisphere*. Oxford: Clarendon Press.

*Dominion Lands Act*, Statutes of Canada 1872 (35 Vict.), c. 23.

Ewart, J.S. 1906. *Report of the Canadian Club of Winnipeg*. Papers of the Canadian Club of Winnipeg. P2739. Archives of Manitoba, Winnipeg, MB.

———. 1907. 'The Canadian Flag: A Suggestion for Canadian Clubs'. *Canadian Magazine* 30 (6): 332–5.

———. 1911. 'Canadian Independence'. *Canadian Magazine* 37 (3): 33–40.

Friesen, Gerald. 1987. *The Canadian Prairies: A History*. Toronto: University of Toronto Press.

Gordon, C.W. [Ralph Connor]. 1899. *The Sky Pilot: A Tale of the Foothills*. Toronto: Revell.

———. 1904. *The Prospector: A Tale of the Crow's Nest Pass*. Toronto: Westminster.

———. 1905. *Black Rock: A Tale of the Selkirks*. New York: A.L. Burt.

———. 1914. 'How a Nation Wins its Right to Live'. Charles W. Gordon Papers. MSS 56, box 28, folder 12. University of Manitoba Archives and Special Collections, Winnipeg, MB.

———. 1925. 'Presenting a Problem Through Characters'. Gordon Papers. MSS 56, box 1, folder 12. University of Manitoba Archives and Special Collections, Winnipeg, MB.

Gordon, J.L. 1911. 'An Englishman In Canada'. J.L. Gordon Papers. PP 17, folder h. United Church of Canada Archives, Winnipeg, MB.

———. 1914. 'The Coming Race'. J.L. Gordon Papers. PP 17, folder h. United Church of Canada Archives, Winnipeg, MB.

Harris, Michael. n.d. 'Excerpts from Michael Harris's Autobiography'. Michael Harris Papers. MG 9 A 43, folder 1. Archives of Manitoba, Winnipeg, MB.

Hiebert, Daniel. 1991. 'Class, Ethnicity, and Residential Structure: The Social Geography of Winnipeg, 1901–1921'. *Journal of Historical Geography* 17 (1): 56–86.

Hobsbawm, Eric. 1992. *Nations and Nationalism since 1780: Programme, Myth, Reality*. New York: Cambridge University Press 1992.

*Homestead Act*, 43 United States Code §§ 161–284 (1862).

Ivens, William. 1909. 'Canadian Immigration'. M.A. thesis, University of Manitoba.

Klymasz, Robert. 1960. 'Canadianization of Slavic Surnames: A Study in Language Contact'. M.A. thesis, University of Manitoba.

Limerick, Patricia. 2001. 'Going West and Ending Up Global'. *Western Historical Quarterly* 32 (1): 5–24.

———. 2004. 'Empire and Amnesia'. *Historian*, 66 (3): 532–38.

Marlyn, John. 1957. *Under the Ribs of Death*. Toronto: McClelland & Stewart.

Martin, Paul. 1993. 'Citizenship and the People's World'. In *Belonging: The Meaning and Future of Canadian Citizenship*, ed. William Kaplan, 64–78. Montreal and Kingston: McGill-Queen's University Press.

McCormack, A. Ross. 1972–3. 'Radical Politics in Winnipeg, 1899–1915'. *Historical and Scientific Society of Manitoba Transactions*, 3rd ser., 29: 81–97.

———. 1977. *Reformers, Rebels, and Revolutionaries: The Western Canadian Radical Movement, 1899–1919*. Toronto: University of Toronto Press.

Moran, Anthony. 2002. 'As Australia Decolonizes: Indigenizing Settler Nationalism and the Challenges of Settler/Indigenous Relations'. *Ethnic and Racial Studies* 25 (6): 1013–42.

Naylor, R.T. 1972. 'The Rise and Fall of the Third Commercial Empire of the St. Lawrence'. In *Capitalism and the National Question in Canada*, ed. Gary Teeple, 1–42. Toronto: University of Toronto Press.

Owram, Douglas. 1980. *Promise of Eden: The Canadian Expansionist Movement and the Image of the West, 1856–1900*. Toronto: University of Toronto Press, 1980.

Perry, Adele. 2003. 'Canada and the Empires of Past'. *History Compass* 1 (1): 1–4.

———. 2007. 'Whose World Was British? Rethinking the "British World" from an Edge of Empire'. In *Britishness Abroad: Transnational Movements and Imperial Culture*, eds. Patricia Grimshaw and Stuart Macintyre, 1–26. Melbourne: University of Melbourne Press.

Silcox, J.B. c1911. 'Our Schools'. J.B. Silcox Papers. PP 50, folder b. United Church of Canada Archives, Winnipeg, MB.

Smith, Anthony. 1986. *The Ethnic Origins of Nations*. New York: Basil Blackwell.

Stone, Daniel. 2003. *Jewish Life and Times. Vol. 3, Jewish Radicalism in Winnipeg, 1905–1960*. Winnipeg: Jewish Heritage Centre of Western Canada.

Thomson, John L.M. 1905. 'The Relation of imperial to Colonial Government'. M.A. thesis, University of Manitoba.

Wardaugh, Robert. 1997. '"Gateway to Empire": Imperial Sentiment in Winnipeg, 1867–1917'. In *Imperial Canada, 1867–1917*, ed. Colin Coates, 206–19. Edinburgh: University of Edinburgh.

Wolfe, Patrick. 1999. *Settler Colonialism and the Transformation of Anthropology: The Politics and Poetics of an Ethnographic Event*. London: Cassell.

Woodsworth, J.S. 1972. *Strangers within Our Gates*. Toronto: University of Toronto Press.

Yuzyk, Paul. 1953. *The Ukrainians in Manitoba: A Social History*. Toronto: University of Toronto Press.

4    From Sheila Andrew, 'More than a Flag of Convenience: Acadian Attitudes to Britain and the British Around the Time of Queen Victoria's 1887 Jubilee', *History of Intellectual Culture* 5, 1(2005).

Although the term Acadian refers to the French-speaking population of the Maritime provinces, the focus of this study is New Brunswick. In 1763, Acadians were permitted to return from the Deportation of 1755, but when the Loyalist supporters of the British crown arrived from the United States in 1783, government policy encouraged concentration of Acadians in the fringe areas of New Brunswick. This degree of isolation allowed Acadians to retain their particular language, religion, and culture. By 1887, the Acadian population of New Brunswick was the centre of a Maritime Canadian French-speaking nationalist movement with its own hymn, flag, and convention meetings. Improved communications, education, and expanded employment opportunities in government established a growing Acadian middle class, yet opposition to Acadians was still expressed, based on language and religion. These factors were crucial to the self-image that made Acadians a voting, buying, and productive power, enthusiastically fostered by the priests, politicians, and some merchants eager to benefit from Acadian support. Similar to many colonized people in the British Empire, the Acadians also constructed part of their self-image on resentment of the imperial power. During the Seven Years War, thousands of Acadians in the Maritimes had been deported, on the orders of the governor appointed by the British authorities. The resulting tragedies and the struggle to survive as a separate people after they were allowed to return were the focus of Acadian history in the nineteenth and early twentieth centuries.

In light of these developments, it is interesting that the Acadian newspaper, *Le Moniteur Acadien*, claimed in 1887 that [t]he world admits there are no more loyal subjects of the British Crown than the Acadians.[1] The Acadian community in Shediac, where the newspaper was published, proceeded to celebrate the jubilee with enthusiasm along with other Acadian communities in the region. The *Moniteur* continued to publish approving articles about Queen Victoria, The Prince of Wales, and other members of the royal family as well as providing an image of Britain as increasingly pro-Catholic and increasingly favourable to the use of the French language. The other New Brunswick Acadian newspaper of the time, *Le Courrier des Provinces Maritimes*, published in Bathurst, showed far less interest in the monarchy or British society, but still reflected a basically positive attitude toward the British connection.[2]

Historians of other pro-British minorities have suggested several possible explanations for this attitude, and some fit the Acadian situation. Many French-Canadian leaders and historians recognized that British parliamentary institutions had given francophone males access to political power.[3] Trade with the British Empire was still valuable to the Maritime Provinces and the imperial connection could have provided some reflected glory.[4] Professed loyalty to the Crown was a possible accommodation with the powerful anglophone elite that allowed Acadians to maintain their religious and linguistic individualism.[5] By careful choice of news items, it was also possible to use the distant image of Britain to belabour local elites who professed the same loyalty but opposed the disadvantaged Acadian elite's ambitions.[6] Analysis of the *Moniteur* suggests, however, a more subtle Acadian creation of a British identity that balanced it against not only anglophone Canada but also against France, the United States, and even Quebec. By careful choice of metropolitan images, Acadians were looking to find their own place in the modern world.[7]

The *Moniteur* did not necessarily reflect the views of all Acadians and the darker side of the British image established by the Deportation continued to cast the occasional shadow both in the *Moniteur* and the other New Brunswick French language newspaper founded in 1885, *Le Courrier des Provinces Maritimes*. The *Moniteur* catered to a substantial section of the Acadian elite, however, particularly in the southern counties of the province. It presumably reflected the views of this influential section of the Acadian population.[8] The *Moniteur* was the first French language newspaper founded in the Canadian Maritimes and had survived since 1867, eventually outliving its rival. By 1887, it was publishing two issues a week. The *Courrier* was founded in Bathurst to represent the interests of Acadians further north in the province.[9]

Historians agree that both these newspapers were supporters of Acadian nationalism, religion, and language, but took a confrontational approach to issues before 1890.[10] Both newspapers were patronized by the clergy, liberal professions, and merchants, including local English-speaking merchants, and they had to respond to the views of their clientele.[11] The *Courrier* showed little of the *Moniteur's* optimism for Britain or interest in its royalty and aristocracy, or even in British internal affairs. This may have been because the British were seen as a direct and immediate threat in the northern area where Crown lands, that the Acadian elite hoped to populate with francophones, were being taken over by British settlers. The *Courrier* may have been more pessimistic due to the increased sensitivity to Irish Catholic readers of the Bathurst region as compared to the Protestant anglophone merchants who advertised in the *Moniteur*.[12] The *Courrier's* indifference and occasional hostility to aspects of Britishness may have indeed represented some Acadian views of Britain, but the *Moniteur* was a powerful instrument of the Acadian nationalist movement and represented a significant proportion of the elite.

The *Moniteur's* positive image of Britain included British parliamentary institutions, although the editor saw little need to comment on this. Catholics had been able to vote in New Brunswick since 1810 and to stand for office since 1830. The first Acadian member of the provincial assembly had been elected in 1846 and the first francophone member of the federal parliament from New Brunswick was elected in 1870. The newspaper, however, was willing to push the image of 'Britishness' beyond the institution to moral principle as a part of its created image of Britain. Elections in New Brunswick were hotly contested and the candidates' religion and language were often issues. In one effort to get the Acadian candidate elected, the editor wrote '[l]et British Fair Play and Acadian Fair Play be the same', claiming this required that all minorities and classes should be given a voice in the management of the affairs of the country. The number of Acadian members of parliament should be directly related to the number of Acadians in the province.[13]

The *Moniteur's* attitudes toward Britain's Imperial role were more ambivalent. Trade with the British Empire was useful and no doubt encouraged the positive image. In 1887, England, the British West Indies, and Newfoundland were the major export markets for the port of Shediac, bringing $74,220 into the local economy, while the United States provided $51,765, and the French colony of St-Pierre and Miquelon $7,216.[14] However, little reference was made to reflected glory from the British Empire. The newspaper was fond of statistics and it informed the readers of the number of French and English speakers in the world and the square miles of various European Empires. It took no particular pride in this;[15] on the contrary, it added that the dominance of the English language could vanish as easily as Greek and Chaldean, and the reason why the sun never set on the British Empire was because it wanted 'to see what the rascals were up to now'![16]

Neither newspaper was willing to adopt the protective colouring of imperial jingoism at the expense of the self-image of neutral Acadians. British campaigns in Africa in 1889 and 1890 never made headlines and the *Moniteur* even referred to them as the 'so-called' war.[17] A passionate article on 6 December 1887 called wars an example of human stupidity and requested heads-of-state to go away and play with wooden soldiers to settle their disputes.[18] Looking ahead, the *Moniteur* wholeheartedly condemned the Spanish-American War and reported official dispatches on the Boer War without any expressions of sympathy for either side.[19] As might be expected, the *Courrier* was even clearer. It accompanied a tribute to the bravery of Canadian troops in the war with a fervent wish for their swift return, along with an angry comment on the previous arrogance of British officers, now forced to recognize Canadian valour. A separate article on the front page of the same issue reported British parliamentary concerns over imperial policy that was entering a 'period that was strange and full of uncertainty', recommending that Canada avoid closer ties with Britain even if the British were concerned.[20]

Although the *Moniteur* was ambivalent in reporting imperial campaigns, its enthusiasm for the royal family and particularly for the Queen and Prince of Wales was evident.[21] This was an area where sharing celebrations with the anglophone population could be good for business. The Acadians involved in organizing the 1887 celebrations in Shediac were young members of the business community who worked with their more established English counterparts. The most prominent Acadian merchant, Fidèle Poirier, flew a large Union Jack outside his store. Floats in the procession were flagrantly commercial, including one from the *Moniteur* itself with the printer giving out pamphlets. The militia, with no mention of Acadian members, gave a twenty-one gun salute and both communities took enthusiastic part in the Polymorphian costume procession and games. The Queen was loudly cheered and the report finishes with an editorial cry of Vive Shediac.[22] More restrained celebrations of the Queen's birthday followed in other years.

The relationship of the *Moniteur* to Queen Victoria was particularly interesting as she was adopted into an Acadian image of the ideal woman. The 21 June 1887 tribute to her reign described her as a young woman with a cultivated spirit carefully raised by her mother in devotion to her country. Apart from the careful omission of any reference to religion, this image could have been lifted from an Acadian convent brochure. When Victoria was driven by circumstances into public life, the article was sympathetic to her for the loss of tranquility, but grateful for her achievements and relieved that she was guided by men of superior talents. The newspaper rejoiced in her nine children and claimed that anglophone royalists did not know her family name, but every francophone knew that she was also Mrs Wettin.[23]

Acadian women also identified with Victoria as they often assumed active roles in business and community life while dually being ornaments in the parlour. Older women had an integral role in community formation.[24] The achievements of Victoria's reign were listed mainly in terms of economic progress and greater tolerance for Jews and Catholics. Her wealth was described with the same joy in prosperity that the *Moniteur* showed when describing Acadian wedding presents or houses, and her charity was frequently noted.[25] Victoria's religious politics that the newspaper chose to portray, however, was more unusual. As presented by the *Moniteur*, she wanted an end to the persecution of Catholics in Ireland and sought an audience with the Archbishop of Savoy when she was taking the waters at Aix-les-Bains. The Archbishop published the Pope's response, noting Queen Victoria's goodwill towards Catholics and his esteem for her since he met her when he was papal nuncio in Belgium.[26] Indeed, a hopeful touch was evident in reports of the Queen's increasing frailty and possible abdication.

The *Moniteur's* laudatory approach to the monarchy extended to the reporting of the Prince of Wales and the conversion from Protestant to Catholic of Princess Louise and Princess Helen. The Prince was proudly said to speak French as well as he spoke English.[27] His interest in Paris and French culture was noted with approval, especially when he gave a generous donation towards rebuilding a Catholic church.[28] Princess Louise apparently went to Rome in spite of disapproval from the British Protestant press in 1888 and was charmed by the Pope at an audience in 1890.[29] Princess Helen's imminent conversion was reported as a fact in 1888.[30]

The newspaper also offered its own interpretation of language and religion in English society. It was seen as increasingly pro-Catholic and pro-French. Favourable statistics were given on the conversion rate within the country—the English aristocracy seemed attracted to Catholicism.[31] French was the most popular second language in England and the English army was encouraging its officers to learn French as a mark of civilization.[32] One unidentified English newspaper was even proposing a union between France and England.[33] Notably, no positive references were made to Scottish Catholicism or to the 'Auld Alliance' between Scotland and France. Anti-Catholic riots by the Orange Order in Glasgow were bitterly reported. The mob demanded the removal of Papists from Ireland and accused Gladstone of being a Jesuit.[34] In Manchester, however, the Protestant crowd applauded warmly as 15,000 Catholics carried a life-size statue of the Virgin Mary through the streets of the city in procession.[35]

Judging by the *Moniteur's* attitude between 1887 and 1890, this was a time of optimism for Acadians. The newspaper saw some progress towards the realization that assimilation had not worked. Displays of Canadian patriotism were limited. Whether the Shediac shops would be shut on Confederation Day in 1888 was not clear, and the only Acadian celebration of that day seemed to be a ball in Arichat.[36] Despite a perceived growing appreciation of French language and culture,[37] anglophone Canadians were not entirely welcoming. The news of Princess Helen's imminent conversion was a response to francophobe and anti-Catholic articles in the *Toronto Mail*.[38] News that English army officers were learning French was followed by the comment that not all Englishmen were like the notorious opponent of Catholic education D'Alton McCarthy. More often, the critical reports on anti-French and anti-Catholic prejudice in Canada went without obvious comparison, but the reports clearly implied that Canadian anglophones posed a greater threat than anglophones in England.

The roughly positive image of Britain benefitted from changes in France. The revolution of 1789 brought Royalist priests to Acadia, further bolstering the ideal of Acadia as a vibrant French society. This image was promoted by priests exiled by the 1870 revolution. The influential Acadian Senator Pascal Poirier and the Acadian Jesuit Fidèle Belliveau considered Acadians as the faithful younger daughter of the Church, showing ungrateful France the error of abandoning religion.[39] According to the *Moniteur*, this infidelity led to a drop in the French birth rate, while the Acadian increase in population was evidence of faith.[40] French historian Edmé Rameau de St-Père's enthusiasm for the colonization movement that would have seen Acadians returned to the primitive simplicity of pioneer farming met with less enthusiasm in both newspapers. St-Père saw Acadia as the last remnant of traditional European French values that had disappeared in his home country. He wanted to conserve these values by keeping Acadians away from the industrialized towns but this well-meant European French effort at rurification was given only lip service in both newspapers.[41] The *Moniteur* preferred to see Acadians as the heirs to French *joie de vivre*, French hospitality, and even courtly manners with the hope that France would return to Catholicism; however, the barrier posed by France's conversion into a godless republic was too high for many of the Acadian elite.[42] The use of the tricolour in the Acadian flag was still a source of dispute, in spite of reassurance from a correspondent that the star of Mary added to it showed the triumph of religion over the principles of 1789.[43]

Distant Britain was also a positive factor when compared with the immediate threat of cultural and possible political assimilation with the United States. Seasonal workers and permanent immigrants were leaving Acadian regions in large numbers. Those who left were at risk of losing their religion, language, and ethical values; those who returned were a cause for concern because they might bring with them changed cultural values. A letter published in 18 May 1888 said young men of Cocagne were returning with new clothes and with 'the English of a negro. Soaked in United States' liberty, they forget religion and the taste for agriculture'. The Americans who came north were often reported as scam artists and confidence tricksters.[44] The American movement to ensure the dominance of the English language in the Catholic church was also considered dangerous. Irish and Scottish priests in the Maritimes could see the advantages of this.[45] The *Moniteur* applauded the Polish women in Buffalo who defended their church against efforts to force an anglophone priest upon them.[46]

Some Americans even suggested the annexation of Canada. The newspaper found continuing participation in Canadian Confederation a better option. In 1888, it quoted speeches by Governor General Frederick Stanley to the Société-St-Jean-Baptiste and by a Dr. De Beers of Montreal expressing pride in not being subject to the 'curse of presidential elections' and being part of an Empire that covered a fifth of the habitable globe. 'Under the protection of the British Empire', Dr. De Beers explained, 'French Canadians had experienced progress and become heirs to vast and various privileges'.[47] When a speaker in Waterville, Maine stressed the obvious advantages of uniting Canada and the United States as a logical union of English-speaking people, the Moniteur retorted that 'Canada was not in favour and Quebec was not seeking protection from the star-spangled banner when it gets it so generously from England'.[48] Like Canadians elsewhere in the country, the *Moniteur* was prepared to cheer on the British empire when opposed to United States domination.[49]

Fear of United States domination and influence did not prevent both newspapers from rejoicing in the economic achievements of Acadians who emigrated south. The *Moniteur* had a profound respect for prosperity. It tempered its views, however, of American ideals by reporting the failures as well as the successes of Americans and of Acadians who went to the United States, in contrast to giving numerous general statistics on the riches of the British aristocracy and monarchy.[50] American riches were noted, but the newspaper countered these with statistics about American liquor and tobacco consumption. Several articles suggested that Acadian and French Canadian political influence was growing in the United States, and the Acadian national mission was to bring in the Catholicism, courtesy, hospitality, and hard work that Americans associated with Acadians.[51]

Just as the Acadians could not be totally North American, neither could they identify totally with Catholics. Local hostility from the Irish and Scottish Catholic church hierarchy who opposed the increasing power of the Francophones and the French language in the church made the image of distant Britain look preferable. The anti-nationalist movement within the Catholic church included Canadian supporters who argued for the convenience of one unifying language in the North American Church. In 1889, The Archbishop of Halifax proposed an end to Church divisions that were based on language and nationality. This was perceived as a devastating attack on the self-image the Acadian elites, and the *Moniteur* retorted that the Bishop was trying to make the Catholic Church an 'Irish stew of Irish, Scots and Acadians, with a dash of negro and savage to taste just like an English Canadian and we will all have a feast for the Grand Manitou'.[52]

Looking to Quebec as the metropolis was a threat to the Acadian sometimes fragile self-image. The Acadian national convention movement, which was developing in the 1880s, encouraged every Acadian parish to send representatives to meetings where Acadian aims and image were discussed. This was inspired by the Société Saint-Jean-Baptiste meetings, but after some acrimonious dispute with Quebec-born priests and their allies, the Acadian conventions chose their own feast day, flag, and national hymn. Some French-Canadians were aware of the breach between Acadia and Quebec, as indicated in the *Moniteur's* long article reprinted from the Quebec newspaper, *L'Évènement*, 6 and 9 December 1889. This supposed dialogue between a French-Canadian and an Acadian suggested Acadians felt that Quebec had failed to support them during the Deportation and, secure in its own French-language Church dominance, was conspicuously absent in the Acadians' struggle with the Irish and Scottish anglophone hierarchy. As well, the *Courrier* suggested that Quebecers who overreacted to perceived slights were raising anglophone hostility and making francophones look ridiculous.[53] Even sympathetic French-Canadian historians such as H.R. Casgrain were considered a threat. They were able to publish their version of Acadian history before historical scholarship was established in Acadia.[54] Acadian scholarship later developed and disagreements on interpretation began.[55]

Britain, and particularly the English, took a place in the various metropoles used by the Acadians to construct a self-image. This,

however, did not mean complete loyalty or identification with Britishness. The Acadians looked to France for their literary heritage but when they considered scientific thinking as a racial characteristic, they would attribute it to English Canada—not Britain.[56] As well, although British middle-class customs were adopted, they were likely to utilize English-Canadian examples. Advertisements for women's fashions occasionally mentioned England, but more often referred to France or the United States. The mind-numbing boredom of the English Sunday was mentioned: 'nobody speaks, they barely eat . . . and a glass of wine will cost you 3 guineas because of the fines'.[57] No explicit contrast was made with the Acadian gift for innocent amusement that the newspaper had claimed earlier, but the mental comparison could have been made.[58] The *Moniteur* made socio-economic distinctions, seeing the British working class as a different 'other' and more disturbing than the upper classes. Industrial problems in Britain, such as strikes or serious accidents, were a favourite filler for the 'Bulletin Étrangère' section. Labour may have been considered a threat to the image of class stability that the Acadian elites understandably hoped to establish. Fear of domestic instability would also explain the many references to the underfunding of the British army and navy.[59]

[ . . . ]

The shadow of the Deportation remained a problem in the Acadian image of Britain and this was reflected in the jokes' portrayal of perceived British insensitive arrogance. The wound was reopened in November 1886, when G.A. Archibald made a speech in Halifax, Nova Scotia, blaming the Deportation on Acadian ingratitude and infidelity. Both the *Moniteur* and the *Courrier* published Pierre-Amand Landry's angry response that the British were clearly to blame.[60] The *Moniteur*, however, worked towards a solution that would permit continued loyalty to its image of Britain. In 19 June 1888, while Quebec historian H.R. Casgrain was blaming the Deportation on the British government, the *Moniteur* claimed that 'everyone knows it was a plot born in New England'. In 1890, in its reporting, the newspaper offered another strategy in support of Britishness: a strong condemnation of the English by R.P. François-Xavier-Joseph Michaud described 'the Acadians, [who were] pursued by the English like savage beasts; their goods stolen; their churches burnt. This was the English task in times past: not a record a civilised nation should envy'. The newspaper added a further quote by Michaud, however, that 'before those hordes of barbarians, Acadians hid in the forest, established families, built churches where they adored the God of Love and Charity who commands us to love our neighbours as ourselves and forgive our enemies'.[61] The Deportation was moved into the past to form part of the Acadian self-image of neutrality, survival, and fidelity, and the Acadians showed their moral superiority through forgiveness, eclipsing any focus on British oppression. The pioneer Acadian historian Placide-P Gaudet later followed this up and placed the blame squarely on Governor Charles Lawrence as a representative of American greed and materialism.[62]

The *Courrier* never bothered to shift the blame for the Deportation to American influence and in that newspaper, the wound was clearly not healed. When forced to acknowledge the Jubilee of 1887, the *Courrier* gave no account of the celebrations and published an account of the Queen's reign from the *Official Gazette of Vienna* that described British aggression in earlier wars and British manipulation of the problems of others so her own empire could be expanded. The *Courrier* likened Victoria to the Empress Maria Theresa of Austria because of her personal efforts to keep the peace.[63]

For some late nineteenth-century Acadians, particularly the elite of south-eastern New Brunswick, the threat from America seemed immediate; in contrast, the threat from Britain was in the past. France still represented the past but also possibly future ideals of Catholicism and civilization that could be balanced against the power of the English language. Britain provided examples of increasing Catholicism and appreciation of French that was used to counteract English-Canadian opposition and weaken the potentially overwhelming influence of Quebec institutions. Canada, beneficiary of British parliamentary institutions, was an effective shelter from American influence.

The picture, however, is incomplete, without more information on regional differences and closer analysis of the readership of the *Courrier* and *Moniteur* at this time. By selective use of editorial comment, however, the *Moniteur* created its own positive version of Britishness that was cultivated in a region dominated by a parliamentary system and a monarchy that were increasingly favourable to the French language and Catholic religion. This fit neatly into the national self-image of the south-eastern elite, portraying Acadians as a French-speaking civilization, Catholic yet firmly influenced by aspects of British society. Thus, at a banquet in honour of federal judge Pierre-Amand Landry, the most distinguished member of the south-western New Brunswick Acadian elite at that time and former Member of the Legislative Assembly and of the federal parliament, the assembled could sing the Acadian national hymn 'Stella Mans' and drink to Acadia, the 'Marseillaise' and drink to France, and then finish the proceedings with a rousing version of 'Dieu Sauve la Reine' and health to Her Majesty Queen Victoria.[64]

# NOTES

1. *Moniteur Acadien*, 4 May 1887. All translations are the author's.

2. Gérard Beaulieu, 'Les médias en Acadie', in Jean Daigle, ed., *L'Acadie des Maritimes*

(Moncton: Chaire d'Études acadiennes, 1993), 518.

3. François-Xavier Garneau, *Histoire du Canada depuis sa découverte jusqu'à nos jours* (Québec and Montreal: Aubin, Frechette and Lovell 1854–52).

4. J.M. Beck, *Joseph Howe: Anti-confederate* (Ontario: Canadian Historical Association, 1965); Margaret R. Conrad and James K. Hillier, *Atlantic Canada: A Region in the Making* (Don Mills, Ontario: Oxford University Press, 2001), 110.

5. Jesse Palsetia, *The Parsis of India: Preservation of Identity in Bombay City* (Leiden, Boston and Koln: Brill, 2001).

6. Michael O. West, *The Rise of an African Middle Class: Colonial Zimbabwe, 1898–1965* (Bloomington and Indianapolis: University of Indiana Press, 2002), 5.

7. J.M.S. Careless, 'Frontierism and Metropolitanism in Canadian History', *Canadian Historical Review*, vol. 35, 1 (1954): 1–21.

8. Sheila Andrew, *The Development of Elites in Acadian New Brunswick 1861–1881* (Montreal and Kingston: McGill-Queen's University Press, 1996), 170–81.

9. Gérard Beaulieu, 'Les Médias en Acadie', in Jean Daigle, ed., *L'Acadie des maritimes* (Moncton: Chaire d'études acadiennes, Université de Moncton, 1993), 512–19.

10. Raymond Mailhot, 'La Renaissance acadienne 1864–1888, L'interprétation traditionelle et le Moniteur acadien'. Thèse de Diplôme en Études Supérieures, Département d'histoire, Université de Montréal, 1969. Phyllis LeBlanc, 'Le Courrier des provinces Maritimes et son influence sur la société acadienne 1885–1903'. Thèse de M.A. (Histoire), Université de Moncton, 1978.

11. Nicolas Landry, 'Le Moniteur Acadien et sa perception des relations entre Acadiens et Anglophones', la société historique acadienne, *les cahiers*, 14,1 (1983): 22–32.

12. *Courrier des Provinces Maritimes*, 19 May 1887.

13. *Moniteur Acadien*, 25 July 1890.

14. *Moniteur Acadien*, 30 December 1887.

15. *Moniteur Acadien*, 18 March 1890; and 7 Aug. 1888.

16. *Moniteur Acadien*, 5 March 1889.

17. The word used was 'pretendu'. *Moniteur Acadien*, 10 May 1889; and 7 Feb. 1890.

18. The article was by the French astronomer Camille Flammarion, and came from an unacknowledged European French newspaper.

19. *Moniteur Acadien*, 20 July 1899 for the Spanish-American War. See also 26 October and 9 November 1899.

20. *Courrier*, 18 August 1900. Issues are missing from 21 September 1899 to 2 August 1900, making it unclear if this was always the newspaper's attitude.

21. Up to 1899, however, no evidence in the *Moniteur* shows support for the monarchy as the logical successor to royalist France; and LeBlanc, 'Le Courrier des provinces Maritimes et son influence sur la société acadienne 1885–1903', found none in the *Courrier*.

22. *Moniteur Acadien*, 24 May and 17 June 1887; 5 July 1887.

23. *Moniteur Acadien*, 5 August 1890. Taken from *La Patrie* of Montreal.

24. See, for example, the mythical Pierette presiding over the growth of the rising town of Bouctouche (*Moniteur Acadien*, 23 October 1888) or the achievements of Adèle Michaud Lebel in Madawaska, (*Moniteur Acadien*, 6 June 1890).

25. See, for example, *Moniteur Acadien*, 18 February 1887.

26. *Moniteur Acadien*, 22 March 1887; and 27 June 1890.

27. *Moniteur Acadien*, 27 March 1888.

28. *Moniteur Acadien*, 30 October 1888; and 7 September 1888.

29. *Moniteur Acadien*, 7 September 1888; and 16 May 1890.

30. *Moniteur Acadien*, 31 August 1888.

31. *Moniteur Acadien*, 17 July 1890.

32. *Moniteur Acadien*, 21 June 1889; and 17 December 1889.

33. *Moniteur Acadien*, 21 June 1889.

34. *Moniteur Acadien*, 19 July 1887.

35. *Moniteur Acadien*, 22 July 1890.

36. *Moniteur Acadien*, 5 July 1888; and 12 July 1887.

37. *Moniteur Acadien*, 24 January 1888, as cited in an article from the *Saint John Globe*; and 12 April 1889 is cited the Toronto *Empire*.

38. *Moniteur Acadien*, 31 August 1888. The news came from an editorial by Joseph Tassé in *La Minerve*.

39. Edmé Rameau de Saint-Père, *La France aux colonies: développement de la race française hors*

de l'Europe, Paris: Jouby, 1859. Pascal Poirier, L'Origine des Acadiens, Montréal: Eusèbe Sénécal, 1874.

40. Moniteur Acadien, 18 July 1890.
41. LeBlanc, 'Le Courrier des provinces Maritimes et son influence sur la société acadienne 1885–1903', found that less than 1% of the articles in the Courrier dealt with colonization or emigration.
42. Moniteur Acadien, 23 August 1889; 8 November 1889.
43. Moniteur Acadien, 20 August 1899; Perry Bidiscombe, 'Le tricolore et l'étoile; The Origin of the Acadian National Flag, 1867–1912', Acadiensis, XX, 1, (Autumn 1990): 120–147.
44. Moniteur Acadien, 10 February 1888.
45. Martin Spigelman, 'Race et réligion, les acadiens et la hiéarchie catholique irlandaise du Nouveau-Brunswick'. Revue de l'histoire de l'amerique française, 29, 1 (1975): 69–85.
46. Moniteur Acadien, 18 February 1890.
47. Moniteur Acadien, 11 November 1888, reported on the Governor General's speech, and Dr. De Beer's speech was included in the 30 November 1888 issue.
48. Moniteur Acadien, 16 July 1889.
49. Douglas Owram, 'Canada and the Empire', Ch. 8 in The Oxford History of the Brtisih Empire (Oxford: Oxford University Press, 1998), 152.
50. The Moniteur Acadien's editor seemed to love these column fillers. See, for example, 27 September 1887.
51. Moniteur Acadien, 10 February, 30 March, 26 June, and 5 July 1888; 13 June 1890.
52. Moniteur Acadien, 24 December 1889.
53. Courrier, 9 June 1887.
54. H.R. Casgrain, 'Les Acadiens après leurs dispersion, 1755–1775', Revue Canadienne, 23(1887): 237–246, 280–289, 413–421, and 459–467. See also the fictional work of Napoléon Bourassa, 'Jacques et Marie, souvenirs d'un peuple dispersé', Revue Canadienne (July 1865–August 1866). Both were favourably reviewed in Moniteur Acadien, 11 February 1887.
55. See the acrimonious disputes between Placide-P Gaudet and Quebec historians in L'Évangéline, 16 March to 22 June, 1922.
56. This does not fit Andrew Porter's image of the 'Britishness' exported in 'Empires of the Mind', Cambridge Illustrated History of the British Empire, P.J. Marshall, ed. (Cambridge: Cambridge University Press, 1996), 185–223. The attribution of scientific thinking to English Canadians comes from a speech of Pascal Poirier on university education. See Moniteur Acadien, 28 February 1888.
57. Moniteur Acadien, 15 November 1887.
58. Moniteur Acadien, 24 January 1888.
59. For example, see Moniteur Acadien, 21 December 1888.
60. Courrier, 6 January, and 13 January 1887. Moniteur Acadien, 19 November 1886.
61. Moniteur Acadien, 22 April 1890.
62. In particular, see L'Évangèline, 16 March to 25 June 1922.
63. Courrier, 23 June 1887.
64. Moniteur Acadien, 13 May 1890.

# Chapter 5

# Canadians at Work

## READINGS

## Introduction

Although we could describe today's capitalist economy more elaborately, much of it involves people selling either commodities or services (like physical or mental labour) in the marketplace. Regulations and trade agreements have tamed the marketplace somewhat, but the basic pattern of people working for compensation has only been reinforced over time. In the nineteenth century, when a much larger proportion of the Canadian population was involved in activities like farming and fishing, today's social 'safety net' was still a distant dream, and the wage worker's best protection against unfair labour practices was to join a union. Most employers resisted attempts to unionize and did not view keeping employees healthy and well-paid as a necessary cost of doing business. Between the unions that managed to bargain on behalf of their members and governmental measures to set minimum labour standards, working conditions generally improved, but these advances did not materialize for all workers at the same time or to the same degree. Working life also intersected with workers' leisure and community pursuits. Just as their jobs determined how workers spent their wage-earning time, the money they had available and the social pressures of their class and neighbourhood determined how they lived while away from the shop floor. It was, therefore, difficult to escape the constraints of the wage economy, even in the saloon or in church. Our primary sources address working conditions in two fundamentally different ways: from the perspective of what the worker might expect on the job (hours, breaks, etc.) and from the perspective of what was to be done for the worker. In the first instance, Jean Thomson Scott's report on labouring women in Ontario, we see in some detail what was expected of workers in the last decade of the nineteenth century. The existing regulations are perhaps more notable because Scott observes ways in which the regulations were not followed. (In our other example, Stephen Leacock's gaze fell on Western society's problems in the wake of the First World War, and his solution was ambitious: doing away with inequality of opportunity. Central to his scheme for reform was the re-making of the workplace through minimum wages and a shortened workday. Historians of labour have lately focused less often on working conditions and more on working-class culture.) In the secondary sources featured here, Craig Heron and Melissa Turkstra tackle opposing ends of this culture: booze and religion. In Heron's piece, the working men of Hamilton resist efforts to control where and when they drink, and in doing this reinforce their identities as 'boys', regardless of their ages. Unmarried men, especially, allowed the culture of going out after work for a couple of drinks to define their social routines. Turkstra also discusses Hamilton (and other places in Ontario) examining how workers related to religion, particularly the act of worship. At times, workers thought that churches were not doing enough to encourage employers to behave in a Christian fashion, yet those same workers had grown up in a Christian society and drew inspiration from the gospel message, especially when the gospel called for the fair and equitable treatment of one's fellow man.

# QUESTIONS FOR CONSIDERATION

1.  What were some of the factors motivating workers or employers to bend the labour regulations that Scott describes?
2.  Do Leacock's plans for social reform seem practical?
3.  Has the way we determine or define social class changed much since the period covered by these sources?
4.  Based on Heron's account, why was drinking such a popular activity for bachelors?
5.  Why was religion so important to the labour movement when labour's main goal was changing the material lives of workers?

# SUGGESTIONS FOR FURTHER READING

Bettina Bradbury, *Working Families: Age, Gender, and Daily Survival in Industrializing Montreal* (Toronto: University of Toronto Press, 2007).

Christina Burr, *Spreading the Light: Work and Labour Reform in Late-Nineteenth-Century Toronto* (Toronto: Toronto University Press, 1999).

Terry Copp, *The Anatomy of Poverty: The Condition of the Working Class in Montreal, 1897–1929* (Toronto: McClelland and Stewart, 1974).

Ruth A. Frager and Carmela K. Patrias, *Discounted Labour: Women Workers in Canada, 1870–1939* (Toronto: University of Toronto Press, 2005).

Judy Fudge and Eric Tucker, *Labour Before the Law: The Regulation of Workers' Collective Action in Canada, 1900–1948* (Toronto: University of Toronto Press, 2004).

Craig Heron, *The Canadian Labour Movement: A Short History* (Toronto: Lorimer, 1996).

——and Steve Penfold, *Workers' Festival: A History of Labour Day in Canada* (Toronto: University of Toronto Press, 2005).

Gregory S. Kealey, *Workers and Canadian History* (Montreal and Kingston: McGill-Queen's University Press, 1995).

——and Bryan D. Palmer, *Dreaming of What Might Be: The Knights of Labour in Ontario, 1880–1900* (Cambridge: Cambridge University Press, 2005).

Ian McKay, *Reasoning Otherwise: Leftists and the People's Enlightenment in Canada, 1890–1920* (Toronto: Between the Lines, 2008).

Suzanne Morton, *Ideal Surroundings: Domestic Life in a Working-Class Suburb in the 1920s* (Toronto: University of Toronto Press, 1995).

Mariana Valverde, *The Age of Light, Soap, and Water: Moral Reform in English Canada, 1885–1925* (Toronto: McClelland & Stewart, 1991).

# PRIMARY DOCUMENTS

1   From Stephen Leacock, *The Unsolved Riddle of Social Justice* (Toronto: S.B. Gundy, 1920), 124–52.

## WHAT IS POSSIBLE AND WHAT IS NOT

Socialism, then, will not work, and neither will individualism, or at least the older individualism that we have hitherto made the basis of the social order. Here, therefore, stands humanity, in the middle of its narrow path in sheer perplexity, not knowing which way to turn. On either side is the brink of an abyss. On one hand is the yawning gulf of social catastrophe represented by socialism. On the other, the slower, but no less inevitable disaster that would attend the continuation in its present form of the system under which we have lived. Either way lies destruction; the one swift and immediate as a fall from a great height; the other gradual, but equally dreadful, as the slow strangulation in a morass. Somewhere between the two lies such narrow safety as may be found.

[ . . . ]

When we view the shortcomings of the present individualism, its waste of energy, its fretful overwork, its cruel inequality and the bitter lot that it brings to the uncounted millions of the submerged, we are inclined to cry out against it, and to listen with a ready ear to the easy promises of the idealist. But when we turn to the contrasted fallacies of socialism, its obvious impracticality and the dark gulf of social chaos that yawns behind it, we are driven back shuddering to cherish rather the ills we have than fly to others we know not of.

Yet out of the whole discussion of the matter some few things begin to merge into the clearness of certain day. It is clear enough on the one hand that we can expect no sudden and complete transformation of the world in which we live. Such a process is impossible. The industrial system is too complex, its roots are too deeply struck and its whole organism of too delicate a growth to permit us to tear it from the soil. Nor is humanity itself fitted for the kind of transformation which fills the dreams of the perfectionist. The principle of selfishness that has been the survival instinct of existence since life first crawled from the slime of a world in evolution, is as yet but little mitigated. In the long process of time some higher cosmic sense may take its place. It has not done so yet. If the kingdom of socialism were opened to-morrow, there are but few fitted to enter.

But on the other hand it is equally clear that the doctrine of 'every man for himself,' as it used to be applied, is done with forever. The time has gone by when a man shall starve asking in vain for work; when the listless outcast shall draw his rags shivering about him unheeded of his fellows; when children shall be born in hunger and bred in want and broken in toil with never a chance in life. If nothing else will end these things, fear will do it. The hardest capitalist that ever gripped his property with the iron clasp of legal right relaxes his grasp a little when he thinks of the possibilities of a social conflagration. In this respect five years of war have taught us more than a century of peace. It has set in a clear light new forms of social obligation. The war brought with it conscription—not as we used to see it, as the last horror of military tyranny, but as the crowning pride of democracy. An inconceivable revolution in the thought of the English speaking peoples has taken place in respect to it. The obligation of every man, according to his age and circumstance, to take up arms for his country and, if need be, to die for it, is henceforth the recognized basis of progressive democracy.

But conscription has its other side. The obligation to die must carry with it the right to live. If every citizen owes it to society that he must fight for it in case of need, then society owes to every citizen the opportunity of a livelihood. 'Unemployment', in the case of the willing and able becomes henceforth a social crime. Every democratic Government must henceforth take as the starting point of its industrial policy, that there shall be no such thing as able bodied men and women 'out of work', looking for occupation and unable to find it. Work must either be found or must be provided by the State itself.

Yet it is clear that a policy of state work and state pay for all who are otherwise unable to find occupation involves appalling difficulties. The opportunity will loom large for the prodigal waste of money, for the undertaking of public works of no real utility and for the subsidizing of an army of loafers. But the difficulties, great though they are, are not insuperable. The payment for state labor of this kind can be kept low enough to make it the last resort rather than the ultimate ambition of the worker. Nor need the work be useless. In new countries, especially such as Canada and the United States and Australia, the development of latent natural assets could absorb the labor of generations. There are still unredeemed empires in the west. Clearly enough a certain modicum of public honesty and integrity is essential for such a task; more, undoubtedly, than we have hitherto been able to enlist in the service of the commonwealth. But without it we perish. Social betterment must depend at every stage on the force of public spirit and public morality that inspires it. So much for the case of those who are able and willing to work. There remain still the uncounted thousands who by accident or illness, age or infirmity, are unable to maintain themselves. For these people, under the older dispensation, there was nothing but the poor-house, the jail or starvation by the roadside. The narrow individualism of the nineteenth century refused to recognize the social duty of supporting somebody else's grandmother. Such charity began, and ended, at home. But even with the passing of the nineteenth century an awakened sense of the collective responsibility of society towards its weaker members began to impress itself upon public policy. Old age pension laws and national insurance against illness and accident were already being built into the legislative codes of the democratic countries. The experience of the war has enormously increased this sense of social solidarity. It is clear now that our fortunes are not in our individual keeping. We stand or fall as a nation. And the nation which neglects the aged and infirm, or which leaves a family to be shipwrecked as the result of a single accident to a breadwinner, cannot survive as against a nation in which the welfare of each is regarded as contributory to the safety of all. Even the purest selfishness would dictate a policy of social insurance.

[ . . . ]

The attitude of the nineteenth century upon this point was little short of insane. The melancholy doctrine of Malthus had perverted the public mind. Because it was difficult for a poor man to bring up a family, the hasty conclusion was reached that a family ought not to be brought up. But the war has entirely inverted and corrected this point of view. The father and mother who were able to send six sturdy, native-born sons to the conflict were regarded as benefactors of the nation. But these six sturdy sons had been, some twenty years before, six 'puling infants', viewed with gloomy disapproval by the Malthusian bachelor. If the strength of the nation lies in its men and women there is only one way to increase it. Before the war it was thought that a simpler and easier method of increase could be found in the wholesale import of Austrians, Bulgarians and Czecho-Slovaks. The newer nations boasted proudly of their immigration tables. The fallacy is apparent now. Those who really count in a nation and those who govern its destinies for good or ill are those who are born in it.

It is difficult to over-estimate the harm that has been done to public policy by this same Malthusian theory. It has opposed to every proposal of social reform an obstacle that seemed insuperable,—the danger of a rapid overincrease of population that would pauperize the community. Population, it was said, tends always to press upon the heels of subsistence. If the poor are pampered, they will breed fast: the time will come when there will not be food for all and we shall perish in a common destruction. Seen in this light, infant mortality and the cruel wastage of disease were viewed with complacence. It was 'Nature's' own process at work. The 'unfit', so called, were being winnowed out that only the best might survive. The biological doctrine of evolution was misinterpreted and misapplied to social policy.

But in the organic world there is no such thing as the 'fit' or the 'unfit', in any higher or moral sense. The most hideous forms of life may 'survive' and thrust aside the most beautiful. It is only by a confusion of thought that the processes of organic nature which render every foot of fertile ground the scene of unending conflict can be used to explain away the death of children of the slums. The whole theory of survival is only a statement of what is, not of what ought to be. The moment that we introduce the operation of human volition and activity, that, too, becomes one of the factors of 'survival'. The dog, the cat, and the cow live by man's will, where the wolf and the hyena have perished.

[ . . . ]

The fundamental error of the Malthusian theory of population and poverty is to confound the difficulties of human organization with the question of physical production. Our existing poverty is purely a problem in the direction and distribution of human effort. It has no connection as yet with the question of the total available means of subsistence. Some day, in a remote future, in which under an improved social system the numbers of mankind might increase to the full power of the natural capacity of multiplication, such a question might conceivably disturb the equanimity of mankind. But it need not now. [ . . . ]

I lay stress upon this problem of the increase of population because, to my thinking, it is in this connection that the main work and the best hope of social reform can be found. The children of the race should be the very blossom of its fondest hopes. Under the present order and with the present gloomy preconceptions they have been the least of its collective cares. Yet here—and here more than anywhere——is the point towards which social effort and social legislation may be directed immediately and successfully. The moment that we get away from the idea that the child is a mere appendage of the parent, bound to share good fortune and ill, wealth and starvation, according to the parent's lot, the moment we regard the child as itself a member of society—clothed in social rights—a burden for the moment but an asset for the future—we turn over a new leaf in the book of human development, we pass a new milestone on the upward path of progress.

It should be recognized in the coming order of society, that every child of the nation has the right to be clothed and fed and trained irrespective of its parents' lot. Our feeble beginnings in the direction of housing, sanitation, child welfare and education, should be expanded at whatever cost into something truly national and all embracing. The ancient grudging selfishness that would not feed other people's children should be cast out. In the war time the wealthy bachelor and the spinster of advancing years took it for granted that other people's children should fight for them. The obligation must apply both ways.

[ . . . ]

Few of us in mind or body are what we might be; and millions of us, the vast majority of industrial mankind known as the working class, are distorted beyond repair from what they might have been. In older societies this was taken for granted: the poor and the humble and the lowly reproduced from generation to generation, as they grew to adult life, the starved brains and stunted outlook of their forbears,—starved and stunted only by lack of opportunity. For nature knows of no such differences in original capacity between the children of the fortunate and the unfortunate. Yet on this inequality, made by circumstance, was based the whole system of caste, the stratification of the gentle and the simple on which society rested. In the past it may have been necessary. It is not so now. If, with all our vast apparatus of machinery and power, we cannot so arrange society that each child has an opportunity in life, it would be better to break the machinery in pieces and return to the woods from which we came.

Put into the plainest of prose, then, we are saying that the government of every country ought to supply work and pay for the unemployed, maintenance for the infirm and aged, and education and opportunity for the children. No modern state can hope to survive unless it meets the kind of social claims on the part of the unemployed, the destitute and the children that have been described above. And it cannot do this unless it continues to use the terrific engine of taxation already fashioned in the war. [ . . . ]

But all of this deals as yet only with the field of industry and conduct in which the state rules supreme. Governmental care of the unemployed, the infant and the infirm, sounds like a chapter in socialism. If the same regime were extended over the whole area of production, we should have socialism itself and a mere soap-bubble bursting into fragments. There is no need, however, to extend the regime of compulsion over the whole field. The vast mass of human industrial effort must still lie outside of the immediate control of the government. Every man will still earn his own living and that of his family as best he can, relying first and foremost upon his own efforts.

One naturally asks, then, To what extent can social reform penetrate into the ordinary operation of industry itself? Granted that it is impossible for the state to take over the whole industry of the nation, does that mean that the present inequalities must continue? The framework in which our industrial life is set cannot be readily broken asunder. But we can to a great extent ease the rigidity of its outlines. A legislative code that starts from sounder principles than those which have obtained hitherto can do a great deal towards progressive betterment. Each decade can be an improvement upon the last. Hitherto we have been hampered at every turn by the supposed obstacle of immutable economic laws. The theory of 'natural' wages and prices of a supposed economic order that could not be disturbed set up a sort of legislative paralysis. The first thing needed is to get away entirely from all such preconceptions, to recognize that the 'natural' order of society, based on the 'natural' liberty, does not correspond with real justice and real liberty at all, but works injustice at every turn. And at every turn intrusive social legislation must seek to prevent such injustice.

[ . . . ] Let us take, as a conspicuous example, the case of the minimum wage law. Here is a thing sternly condemned in the older thought as an economic impossibility. It was claimed, as we have seen, that under free contract a man was paid what he earned and no law could make it more. But the older theory was wrong. The minimum wage law ought to form, in one fashion or another, a part of the code of every community. It may be applied by specific legislation from a central power, or it may be applied by the discretionary authority of district boards, or it may be regulated,—as it has been in some of the beginnings already made,—within the compass of each industry or trade. But the principle involved is sound. The wage as paid becomes a part of the conditions of industry. Interest, profits and, later, the direction of consumption and then of production, conform themselves to it.

True it is, that in this as in all cases of social legislation, no application of the law can be made so sweeping and so immediate as to dislocate the machine and bring industry to a stop. It is probable that at any particular time and place the legislative minimum wage cannot be very much in advance of the ordinary or average wage of the people in employment. But its virtue lies in its progression. The modest increase of to-day leads to the fuller increase of to-morrow. Properly applied, the capitalist and the employer of labor need have nothing to fear from it. Its ultimate effect will not fall upon them, but will serve merely to alter the direction of human effort.

Precisely the same reasoning holds good of the shortening of the hours of labor both by legislative enactment and by collective organization. [ . . . ] Seven o'clock in the morning is too early for any rational human being to be herded into a factory at the call of a steam whistle. Ten hours a day of mechanical task is too long: nine hours is too long: eight hours is too long. I am not raising here the question as to how and to what extent the eight hours can be shortened, but only urging the primary need of recognizing that a working day of eight hours is too long for the full and proper development of human capacity and for the rational enjoyment of life. [ . . . ]

The shortening of the general hours of work, then, should be among the primary aims of social reform. There need be no fear that with shortened hours of labor the sum total of production would fall short of human needs. This, as has been shown from beginning to end of this essay, is out of the question. Human *desires* would eat up the result of ten times the work we now accomplish. Human *needs* would be satisfied with a fraction of it. But the real difficulty in the shortening of hours lies elsewhere. Here, as in the parallel case of the minimum wage, the danger is that the attempt to alter things too rapidly may dislocate the industrial machine. We ought to attempt such a shortening as will strain the machine to a breaking point, but never break it. This can be done, as with the minimum wage, partly by positive legislation and partly collective action. Not much can be done at once. But the process can be continuous. The short hours achieved with acclamation to-day will later be denounced as the long hours of to-morrow. The essential point to grasp, however, is that society at large has nothing to lose by the process. The shortened hours become a part of the framework of production. It adapts itself to it. Hitherto we have been caught in the running of our own machine: it is time that we altered the gearing of it.

The two cases selected,—the minimum wage and the legislative shortening of hours,—have been chosen merely as illustrations and are not exhaustive of the things that can be done in the field of possible and practical reform. It is plain enough that in many other directions the same principles may be applied. The rectification of the ownership of land so as to eliminate the haphazard gains of the speculator and the unearned increment of wealth created by the efforts of others, is an obvious case in point. The 'single taxer' sees in this a cure-all for the ills of society. But his vision is distorted. The private ownership of land is one of the greatest incentives to human effort that the world has ever known. It would be folly to abolish it, even if we could. But here as elsewhere we can seek to re-define and regulate the conditions of ownership so as to bring them more into keeping with a common sense view of social justice.

But the inordinate and fortuitous gains from land are really only one example from a general class. The war discovered the 'profiteer'. The law-makers of the world are busy now with smoking him out from his lair. But he was there all the time. Inordinate and fortuitous gain, resting on such things as monopoly, or trickery, or the mere hazards of abundance and scarcity, complying with the letter of the law but violating its spirit, are fit objects for appropriate taxation. The ways and means are difficult, but the social principle involved is clear.

We may thus form some sort of vision of the social future into which we are passing. The details are indistinct. But the outline at least in which it is framed is clear enough. The safety of the future lies in a progressive movement of social control alleviating the misery which it cannot obliterate and based upon the broad general principle of equality of opportunity. The chief immediate direction of social effort should be towards the attempt to give to every human being in childhood adequate food, clothing, education and an opportunity in life. This will prove to be the beginning of many things.

2    From Jean Thomson Scott, *The Conditions of Female Labour in Ontario* (Toronto: Warwick & Sons, 1892), 9–31.

Victor Hugo has fitly called the present age the 'Women's Century'; for although the annals of history have always contained the names of great women yet the position of women as a factor in the economic conditions of social life seems peculiar to recent times.

In this paper some attempt will be made to discuss the conditions under which women are working in the Province of Ontario; referring, perhaps, more particularly to the city of Toronto, which has afforded the most convenient field for observation.

When Harriet Martineau visited America in 1840, she relates that she found only seven employments open to women; namely, teaching, needlework, keeping boarders, working in cotton mills, type-setting, work in book-binderies and household service. Although women still retain their positions in these employments, they have vastly extended the number of their vocations. According to the latest census returns in the United States, women have now secured a footing in 4,467 different branches of various industries. While Ontario can not boast of such large numbers, the various callings entered by women in this Province are rapidly increasing in number. In some cases the establishment of new industries, especially within the last fifteen years, has led to their further employment. In others they have entered fields hitherto, for the most part, occupied by men. New employments are continually opening up with advancing civilization, which require but slight experience and seem adapted for women.

There are various reasons why women are ready for the numerous occupations which are continually offering themselves. In a large number of instances, circumstances make it a matter of necessity for them to earn their living. Often a desire to live up to a certain standard of comfort will lead girls, for a short time at least, to go into employments in which, while living at home, they can partially support themselves, or at least supply themselves with pin-money. Again, the social conditions of life in Canada are such that women find it necessary to prepare themselves for emergencies: they often begin to learn some occupation so as to be prepared for future risks, and then their circumstances and the occupation becomes a permanent one.

For these and other reasons we find a large and increasing number of women employed as wage-earners; and Ontario, following the example of older countries, has found it necessary to subject their labour to various restrictions in order to protect the interests of society.

## SECTION I.—LEGISLATION IN ONTARIO

(1.) The employment of women and girls in *manufacturing* establishments in Ontario is regulated by the *Ontario Factory Act* of 1884 and the *Amendment Act* of 1889.

In passing such Acts Ontario was but following the example of older countries. Factory legislation in Great Britain has been in existence for more than half a century, and has been codified by the *Factory and Workshops Act* of 1878, with subsequent amendments. The example of Great Britain has been followed by other countries; in Europe by Austro-Hungary, in 1859; by France, in 1874; by Switzerland, in 1877; and by Germany, in 1878. In America factory legislation has been of very recent growth, but, although recent, it has been rapid. Massachusetts was the pioneer state in this respect, having passed a *Factory Act* providing for inspection in 1882. Ohio followed in 1884; so that Ontario compares favourably, in point of time, with the various states of the Union.

The principal sections of the *Ontario Factory Acts* which are pertinent to this enquiry may be summarized as follows:—

1. Under the word 'Factory' only *manufacturing* establishments are included.
2. In order to come under inspection, there must be at least *six* persons employed in a factory.
3. No boy under *twelve* and no girl under *fourteen* shall be employed in any factory.
4. No child (defined as a person under the age of fourteen) or female shall be employed more than *ten* hours in one day, or more than *sixty* hours in one week; unless a different apportionment of the hours of labour per day has been made for the sole purpose of giving a shorter day's work on Saturday.
5. If the inspector so directs, meals shall not be eaten in the work-rooms, but in suitable rooms to be provided for the purpose.
6. Boys under twelve and girls under fourteen may be employed during the months of July, August, September and October in any year in such gathering-in and other preparation of fruits and vegetables for canning or desiccating purposes as may be required to be done prior to the operation of cooking, or other process of that nature requisite in connection with the canning of fruits or vegetables.
7. Employers shall allow each child, young girl and woman not less than one hour at noon of each day for meals, but such hour shall not be reckoned in the ten hours to which labour is restricted.
8. Children and women are not allowed to clean machinery while in motion.
9. Where the exigencies of certain trades require that women should be employed for a longer period than above stated, an inspector may give permission for such exemption, under the

following limitations:—(*a*) No woman, young girl or child shall be employed before six o'clock in the morning, nor after the hour of nine in the evening (*i.e.*, while employed during the day). (*b*) The hours of labour shall not exceed twelve hours and a half in any one day, nor more than seventy-two and a half in one week. (*c*) Such exemption shall not comprise more than six weeks in any one year. (*d*) During the continuance of such exemption, there shall, in addition to the hour for the noon-day meal, be allowed to every woman, young girl or child so employed to an hour later than seven o'clock, not less than forty-five minutes for another meal between five and eight o'clock in the afternoon. (*e*) Women only may be employed to a later hour than nine, where the work relates to the canning or desiccating of fruits or vegetables, for twenty days during the summer months.

10. Provision is made for separate conveniences for women, and for the proper ventilation of the work-rooms.
11. A register of the children, young girls and women employed in any factory shall be kept by the employer for the reference of the inspector.
12. Notices of the hours between which children, young girls and women are to be employed shall be hung up in a conspicuous place in the factory.

After the passing of this Act it was found necessary to provide means for seeing that it was carried out, and in 1887 three inspectors were appointed in Ontario under the Act.

As has been intimated, the *Factory Act* in Ontario deals exclusively with those employed in manufacturing establishments, and not with those in mercantile or mechanical employments.

[ . . . ]

# SECTION II.—EFFECTS OF LEGISLATION AND INSPECTION

## *1. Limitations of Inspection*

The provisions of the 'Factories Act' do not apply (*a*) to any factory employing not more than *five* persons; (*b*) where children, young girls or women are employed at home in a private dwelling, wherein the only persons employed are members of the family dwelling there. Originally the limit was placed at twenty; but as soon as the inspectors entered on their work it was found that the smaller places of business were more in need of inspection than the larger; and on their recommendation the Act as amended placed the limit at *five*.

Thus there are numerous small places of business employing four and five women, particularly small dressmaking and millinery establishments, which are excluded from the benefits of the Act. But it cannot be doubted that some system of inspection is needed for *all* places where women and children are employed. There is no reason why some places should be inspected and others not. That only one or two women are employed in any capacity is no reason why they should be subject to whatever conditions their employers see fit to impose. It would be advisable to do away with the number-limit altogether.

## *2. Child Labour*

Section 6 prohibits the employment of boys under twelve and girls under fourteen in any factory coming under the Act; and in the case of boys under fourteen the employer is obliged to keep a certificate signed by the parent or guardian of the birth-place and age of each child, or else the written opinion of a registered physician that such child is not under age. But boys and girls under age are allowed to work during the summer months in such gathering in and other preparation of fruits and vegetables for canning or desiccating purposes as may be required to be done prior to the operation of cooking or other processes of that nature. Such employment is, of course, only temporary, owing to the perishable nature of the material; and, as the employment is light, children are as well able to do it as older persons, but whether it is really as profitable to employ them is a matter for the employers to decide. In some cases, such as the operation of shelling peas, machinery has taken the place of manual labour, thus lessening the employment of children.

That some legislation was necessary to limit the employment of children in Ontario was seen long before the passing of the Act. In 1881 the Dominion Government appointed a Commission to make inquiry into the working of mills and factories in Canada and the labour employed therein. The Commission visited and reported upon 465 factories, in which over two thousand children under fourteen years of age were found, and nearly two hundred of these were under *ten* years of age. The Commissioners state that considerable difficulty was found in obtaining with accuracy the ages of the children; for there was no record required to be kept, and in many instances the children, having no education, were unable to tell their ages—this more particularly among the very young children of eight and nine years. It was found, too, that wherever children were employed they invariably worked as many hours as the adults, and if not compelled were at least requested to work overtime; so that the condition of the young workers in the latter part of the day, especially during the warm summer weather, was anything but desirable. In some cases they were obliged to be at work as early as 6.30 a.m., necessitating their being up much earlier for their morning meal and walk to work, and this in winter as well as in summer. This was unquestionably too heavy a strain on growing children, and was condemned by all except those who were directly benefited. As late as 1886–7 the Royal Labour Commission reported that child labour under legal age was still largely employed, the *Factory Act* not having got into working order. That the enforcement of this Act has been the means of largely decreasing the amount of child labour may be seen from the Inspectors' Reports. Wherever boys and girls under age have been found the employer has been notified; and when the practice has been continued they have been prosecuted. In the report for the Western District for 1888 there were found about two hundred and fifty boys between twelve and fourteen, while in the report for the ensuing year only one hundred and sixty-nine were recorded. One reason given for the decrease was that the canning factories were not as active in the latter year. In some cases the employers preferred not to employ the children because of the trouble attached to procuring certificates. The chief resistance indeed comes from the parents of the children who, either from necessity or greed, are so anxious to get employment for them that they will sometimes furnish false certificates.

Sometimes children under legal age were employed by persons who took contracts for work and who, although working in a factory, argued that because the number they employed was less than constituted a factory under the law they were exempt from its provisions, although the total number of persons employed in such factory would cause it to be classed under the Act.

In some cases where children under age were found it was pleaded as an excuse that they were only a month or two under the required age. Parents too, complained that their children would not go to school, and were better at work than running about in the streets.

Of the boys between twelve and fourteen quite a number work in saw-mills where dangerous machinery is used. The Inspector for the Eastern District has suggested that the legal age for boys employed in saw-mills be raised to fourteen. In Quebec the legal age for boys in saw-mills is sixteen. Seeing that the whole number of boys between twelve and fourteen employed in factories is comparatively small, it would be no great revolution to raise the age for boys employed in any kind of factory to fourteen, and also prohibit their employment in any kind of dangerous work before sixteen. It would simplify the labours of the Inspectors considerably in the matter of requiring certificates, and also diminish the responsibility of the employers, who, in many cases, are importuned by the parents or even by the children themselves to give employment. A saving clause might be added to allow a boy to work where it could be shown that such work was necessary either for his own support or for the support of his family.

The factories found employing girls under age at the first visit of the Inspectors were principally cotton, woollen and knitting mills, which are run generally the full sixty hours a week, and where the work is purely mechanical as well as extremely monotonous. For a girl of fourteen or thereabouts to work continuously for ten hours a day and six days a week cannot but prove injurious to her health. Where factories are running for ten hours a day no girls under sixteen ought to be employed, or if they are, only for a short period. In Quebec the employment of boys under sixteen and girls under eighteen is prohibited in any factory named for that purpose by the Lieutenant-Governor in Council as unhealthy or dangerous. The list at present contains the names of twenty-eight kinds of manufactures which are considered dangerous on account of the dust, obnoxious odours, or danger from fire. Among these are tobacco factories and saw-mills; and boys under fourteen and girls under fifteen are altogether prohibited from working in cigar factories.

Scarcity of labour cannot be pleaded as an excuse for the employment of children as long as able-bodied men are seeking employment; and, of course, the gradual restriction of child labour widens to some extent, if not in the same proportion, the field for adult labour.

While child labour is thus partially restricted in Ontario in factories, there is still not the slightest restriction set upon their employment in shops and offices. Numerous children find employment as cash and parcel boys and girls in retail stores. This evil, however, does not exist now to the same extent as formerly owing to the introduction of machinery for carrying cash and even parcels to the desks and wrapping counters. Boys in Toronto find employment in selling newspapers on the street; but although girls did engage in such employment at one time they are now, very properly, prohibited from doing so.

It is to be hoped that the restrictions under the *Factories Act* in regard to child labour will be applied to their employment in mercantile and mechanical establishments as soon as possible. If child labour is to be effectually restricted the compulsory school law and the *Factories Act* must work together. If the school law compels all children between eight and fourteen to be in attendance at some school it is plain that they cannot be employed in any work during school hours. But to carry out the *Education Act*, far more abundant and efficient inspection must be provided than at present, and school accommodation, even if of a temporary character, must be promptly furnished in growing suburbs.

### 3. Hours of Labour

Sub-section 3 of section 6, of the *Factory Act* enacts that no child, young girl or women shall be employed in a factory for more than *ten* hours a day or more than *sixty* hours in any one week; unless a different apportionment of the hours of labour per day has been made for the sole purpose of giving a shorter day's work on Saturday. Sub-section 4 requires that every employer shall allow each child, young girl and women not less than one hour at noon of each day for meals.

In addition to these regular hours for work, exemptions may be granted by the Inspectors, where the exigencies of certain trades demand it, for working overtime; but in such cases no child, young girl or women shall work longer than twelve and a half hours a day or seventy two and a half in any one week; and such exemption shall not comprise more than six weeks in any one year, nor shall the time fixed for meals be diminished. During the period of such exemption, every child, young girl or woman, employed in any factory to an hour later than seven in the evening shall be allowed not less than forty-five minutes for an evening meal between five and eight o'clock in the evening. While working overtime, women are not to be employed before six in the morning, nor later than nine in the evening, except in canning factories where they may work later than nine in the evening for not more than twenty days in a year.

In those places coming under the *Factories Act* where women are employed comparatively few work for the full sixty hours a week. In a list comprising eighty factories in Toronto, only ten worked for sixty hours a week; fourteen worked less than sixty but over fifty-five; thirty worked from fifty to fifty-five hours; and the remainder from forty-four to fifty. One cause of the reduction of hours in Toronto is the general adoption of the Saturday half-holiday. Outside Toronto it is not so general, and the hours of labour per week reach a higher average. It is to be hoped that fifty-five hours will be made the limit instead of sixty; and so cause the hours of labour to be nine hours a day, or else five and a half days a week.

The clause in the Act which allows a different apportionment of the hours per day in case of shorter hours on Saturday is an unfortunate one, because it would permit an average of eleven hours a day for five days in the week,—far too long a period for women to work.

Those factories which work the full sixty hours are principally cotton, woollen and knitting mills, where expensive machinery is employed.

Before the *Factories Act* came into force many factories worked longer than ten hours a day; so that the results of inspection have been thus far beneficial.

Another loop-hole in the law is the clause concerning the noon meal hour. It reads, 'the employer shall allow not less than one hour at noon,' which has been interpreted to mean that the employees may take less if they choose, and in some cases this has been done, either in order to stop work earlier in the evening or to lessen the hours of work on Saturday. It need hardly be said that shortening the meal hour is poor economy in the way of preserving one's health. In this matter the girls themselves are not the best judges; for the majority of them would even prefer to take only a half hour at noon if by so doing they could stop working in the evening. In some cases where girls made such a request the employers wisely advised against it; and in one case a compromise of three-quarters of an hour was effected. It would be better if the law were more absolute in the matter, especially where the full ten hours a day is insisted on.

Still another matter in which the law is indefinite is that of night labour for women and children. The law *does* state that where, under the exemption women work longer than ten hours a day they are not to be employed before six in the morning nor later than nine in the evening, but it does not prohibit night labour *per se*. As a matter of fact girls in Toronto have been employed for a few months from eleven o'clock in the evening till five or six in the morning in setting type at the Central Press Agency for the cable despatches to country newspapers. The Deputy Attorney-General was appealed to for the interpretation of the law, but it was decided that nothing in the Act prevented the night employment of women. Fortunately for the women themselves, in the case referred to they found the work too arduous, and have ceased working (since September 18th, 1891).

The *Factory Law* in Switzerland is more definite in this matter and states that 'under no circumstances shall women work on Sunday or at night work.' The law of Massachusetts is 'no corporation or manufacturing establishment in this commonwealth shall employ any minor or women between the hours of ten o'clock at night and six in the morning.' The *Quebec Factories Act* as amended states 'that the day of ten hours work shall not commence before six in morning nor end after nine in the evening.' According to the new English Act, the employment of women must now be brought within a specified period of twelve hours, taken between 6 a.m. and 10 p.m., with an hour and a half off for meals, except on Saturday, when the period is eight hours with half a hour off. It is to be hoped that the law in Ontario will be so amended that night labour for women will be prohibited.

Complaint has frequently been made to the Inspectors that women in millinery and dress-making establishments are employed over ten hours a day; but of course as long as the legal limit of sixty hours per week is not exceeded by any one employee, the Inspector cannot interfere. It seems usual during the busy season to ask part of the staff to remain after six o'clock, the usual hour for closing, one part taking turn with another. There is generally no allowance made for an evening meal in such cases, the girls preferring to work till they finish rather than go home and come back again; but to work from one till eight or nine in the evening without food is certainly not conducive to health. Legislation on the subject seems to be called for. According to the English *Factory Act* no women can be employed for more than four and a half hours without an interval of half an hour at least for a meal. The overtime occurs only during the busy season or on Saturdays. Employers argue that it is not always possible to foresee what work is coming in, and that in order to oblige their customers they have to promise the work at a certain time. Some establishments make it a rule never to work overtime; and when urgent work comes in, other work is put aside for a time. It would be well if all would make this the rule. A little more forethought too, on the part of customers would lessen the evil. Ladies could often wait a day or two for a bonnet or gown; or, if not, could give their order earlier. Conversation with those in the business reveals the fact that it is not orders for dresses for weddings or funerals which cause overtime—but those for balls and parties, this of course in establishments doing a trade of that kind. The general desire again on the part of many to have a new gown or bonnet for Sunday makes Saturday the busiest day for dressmakers and milliners. In England no woman can be employed in such establishments after 4 p.m. on Saturdays. It is not customary to pay for such overtime in Toronto. The matter seems to be looked on as only occasional, but there is a danger of too much of it being done if some restriction is not placed on the length of time in any one day during which a woman may be employed.

All that has been said hitherto in regard to the hours of labor only applies to manufacturing establishments where girls and women are employed.

The *Factories Act* in Ontario does not include mercantile or mechanical employments in its provisions. The *Shops Regulation Act* however prohibits the employment of boys under fourteen and girls under sixteen for a longer period than twelve hours a day including meal hours, or than fourteen hours a day on Saturday also including meal hours. *Such an enactment makes no regulations whatever for girls over sixteen as far as the hours of work are concerned, and as the majority of girls employed in shops are over that age the Act is not very far-reaching.* As has been already stated there is no system of inspection under this Act. In some towns the shopdealers have combined under the early closing by-law and close their shops at seven in the evening; but this is not as general as could be wished.

# HISTORICAL INTERPRETATIONS

3  From Craig Heron, 'The Boys and Their Booze: Masculinities and Public Drinking in working-class Hamilton, 1890–1946', *The Canadian Historical Review* 86, 3 (September 2005): 411–51.

In 1924 a working man in Hamilton, ON, took pen in hand to express his opposition to arguments in a local newspaper about the harmfulness of alcoholic beverages. He signed himself 'One of the Boys'. Two decades later, another wrote to Ontario's Liquor Control Board on behalf of some 'pals that works with me' to complain about conditions they had found in the Homeside Hotel when they dropped in for a drink after work. He signed the anonymous message 'A Bunch of Working Boys'. By this point in the history of industrial capitalism, these 'boys' would certainly have been full-grown men, not children, yet this was not an unusual way for male wage-earners to refer to themselves. A working man was always, to some degree, 'one of the boys'. It is time to take seriously their own labelling of their group identity and its significance in working-class communities.[1]

When grown men who worked for wages called themselves 'boys', they were invoking at least four parts of their boyhood experience—the fraternal solidarity that bound them together with their young male peers, the privilege to enjoy a relative freedom and independence within the daily responsibilities to the working-class family economy that was rarely available to their sisters, the spirit of hedonistic, transgressive playfulness that filled their lives, and the anti-authoritarian posture of outlaws. As these men grew older, those elements of boyhood carried through into the prolonged bachelorhood that most of them experienced before marriage and, for many, into their lives outside the household after marriage. Their 'boyishness' found expression in a variety of social practices and settings, which, in turn, became alternatives to the harsh indignities of the capitalist workplace, the constraints of bourgeois moral and cultural codes, and the responsibilities of the family household. They were central to the shaping of their masculine identities.

One of those practices was drinking with other men in a public space. The customs and rituals developed around the consumption of booze symbolized a collective defiance of bourgeois efforts to control them, as well as the privilege to participate in a public life that was closed to most women in their communities. This essay traces how, [in the early twentieth century,] many working-class men made their participation in these drinking cultures an important part of their evolving expression of their masculinities and how they interacted with the new regulatory regimes that aimed at controlling them.

## BOYS WILL BE BOYS

[ . . . ] In early twentieth-century Hamilton, as in most other industrial centres across North America, working-class masculinities faced daunting challenges on many fronts—the formal schooling that tied working-class boys to school desks for much more of their childhood and adolescence, the campaigns to tame working-class youth, the rising importance of imperialism and 'whiteness' as central to the new hegemonic definition of 'manliness', the relentless insecurities of the workplace that challenged notions of skill and shop-floor autonomy, the uncertainties of breadwinning created by spiralling retail price inflation and lengthening cycles of unemployment', the new voices of first-wave feminism and the new aggressiveness of women in public space, the emergence (in larger cities) of a homosexual subculture, the crusades against allegedly immoral male behaviour (including drinking, gambling, and sexual dalliance), and the growing intervention of the state to support many of these initiatives.

To appreciate how masculinities persisted and changed in the face of these upheavals, it is important to follow working males through their lifecycle, so that we can appreciate the evolving formation of their masculine identities. It is important to identify the four sites where a working-class boy would learn what it was to be a man. First, in the family household, males and females were expected to shoulder specific responsibilities within the working-class family economy, including particular tasks for boys. Second, in Sunday school and then elementary schools, which in this period in Ontario became compulsory for working-class children up to the age of 14 (after 1920 up to age 16), the lessons were about moral probity, the hegemonic masculinity of empire, and, for working-class boys, the importance of orderly behaviour and deference to authority and expertise. Third, in the streets, bonds of male solidarity with their peers became central to young male lives, as boys spent increasing time outside adult supervision in loosely structured gangs, where they cultivated important and often apparently contradictory attitudes and behaviours—intense loyalty, aggressive display, personal toughness, competitiveness, peer recognition through performance, and the disowning of any 'feminine' tendencies. The fourth arena of gender formation was, of course, the paid workplace, which in Hamilton was most often a factory.

The interaction among these four sites of activity would establish the dominant forms and central dynamics of masculine norms and practices among working-class males in industrial cities like Hamilton. In particular, in contrast to middle-class experience, the relative freedom that young working-class males carved out for themselves between boyhood and young bachelorhood gave them a reference point for coping with all kinds of authority, including bosses. But it also had to bend to the demands of the family economy, which expected each boy to contribute work at home or in the paid labour market. That fundamental tension in the working-class male between irresponsibility and obligation within the structures of wage-earning, domestic life, and community was at the core of proletarian masculinities.

Bachelorhood was a key moment in this process. In their mid-teens, virtually all working-class boys growing up in Hamilton shifted from school to more-or-less full-time employment, where they began to participate in all-male occupational cultures, and, individually and collectively, to find new forms of validation within industries that no longer showed much respect for craft skill. At the same time, they began to renegotiate their relationships with family and friends to become more independent bachelors, a phase of male experience that has had relatively little scholarly attention. Since they typically did not marry until their mid- to late twenties, young men in Hamilton emerged from a transitional phase of teenaged wage-earning into a prolonged period of bachelorhood, which was most often spent in their family household. The large number of newcomers born in Britain followed a similar path, while those arriving from southern and eastern Europe or Asia had generally had less schooling but were otherwise on a similar life-course of wage-earning before marriage.

The earnings of Hamilton's working-class men in their early twenties tended to rise quickly to approach adult levels. So, like their fathers, they could take pride in being providers for their parents and siblings. In some households, a young working man might even do better than his father if the older man's trade was being eroded by industrial transformations, or if frailties or disabilities hindered his wage-earning capacities. How much of this income a young man turned over to his family and how much he kept was a subject of ongoing negotiation and inevitable conflict. If he was white and Canadian-born, naturalized, or a British subject, once a young man in his early twenties reached the status of full citizenship, he may have had a stronger sense of his rights to greater autonomy. Yet his family obligations increased if anything happened to his father's ability to earn an income. But although parents still often expected to get most of a young man's wages, they must have conceded him more spending money as a guarantee that he would not leave home completely. Moreover, he might distance himself from the family household. Whether as a part of a conscious family strategy, a form of resistance to family obligations, a search for adventure, or simply frustration with local employment prospects, some young men would strike out on their own to look for work or better wages elsewhere in North America. Many washed up in Hamilton on such a quest and boarded with other families or in larger boarding houses. These young transient workers were the most likely to have coins jingling in their pockets, but even those living at home probably had enough spending money to allow for some personal indulgences. Their sisters never had as much mobility or this much financial independence.[2]

So, in the first half of the twentieth century, young men in working-class Hamilton enjoyed a lengthy time where their responsibilities to their family households were diminishing, their workplace identities were solidifying, their disposable income was rising, and, while under their parents' roof or in a cheap boarding house, their living expenses were limited. This material reality gave them the opportunity—and the privilege—to participate in a vibrant leisure-time culture of young bachelorhood. They gathered on street corners and jeered at passersby, burned up energy in amateur sport and spontaneous fights, and frequented pool halls, bar-rooms, vaudeville and movie theatres, and skating and roller rinks. Some were drawn into the recreational programs of church groups or the YMCA, where they might find an outlet for their energy and passion in 'muscular Christianity'. Yet the difficulty that these more earnest programs had in attracting and holding young working-class men reflected their failure to catch the fundamentally transgressive quality of what went on among the 'boys'—the point was to be at least a little 'bad'.

Bachelor life was built on the solidarities these men had developed at a younger age with other boys. In particular, it celebrated a personal independence and freedom from responsibility or obligation, the closeness and loyalty but also, sometimes, competitiveness of men together, the superiority of men over women (even a misogynistic distrust of women), and self-expression through the body. Like the revelry of boyhood, the practices and institutions of bachelor life were a refuge from the increasing harshness of capitalist industry and the responsibilities and constraints of domesticity—a zone of physical expressiveness, boisterousness, and flamboyant swaggering, shouting, whistling, singing, swearing, and farting in deliberate performance.

Bachelors generally preferred the company of other men, but, at some stage, most young men began to cross the gender divide and to move through courtship into marriage. At that point, they reached another Rubicon in their lives. Setting up a new household and starting a family brought breadwinning responsibilities and expectations that a man would turn his back on the excesses of bachelorhood. In practice, during their married lives, working-class men seemed to fall somewhere along a continuum of behaviour. At one extreme, they withdrew completely from the rowdiness and carousing of young adulthood. They stayed home in their leisure time and took their families on excursions to local parks or beaches on special occasions.[3] At the other extreme, men who remained restless and unwilling to accept the domestic constraints of being a husband and father might have a life punctuated with frequent drunkenness, gambling, absenteeism from work, or violent behaviour.[4] Or married men might instead maintain some middle ground where they occasionally enjoyed the all-male camaraderie of their bachelor haunts—an afternoon at the ballpark, a day spent fishing in the harbour, a few hours sharing drinks at a saloon or illegal 'dive'—but tried not to let those outings disrupt their domestic lives or wage-earning potential. These men might also participate in the apparently more sedate homo-social culture of fraternal societies, unions, or veterans' clubs. This time with the 'boys' required potentially difficult negotiation with their spouses, though many men probably expected their wives and children to accept without question how they used their own leisure time and the money needed to support it.

In the first half of the twentieth century, then, working-class men of all ages participated in public activities developed and defined by the bachelor experience. This loosely structured bachelor culture was often disorderly and free-spirited, but it made no direct challenges to the capitalist and patriarchal social order. While working-class men easily identified themselves as 'one of the boys', they never staked their claims to entitlements as wage-earners or citizens on that identity. Indeed it was inward-looking and profoundly conservative in its defence and celebration of the working man's right to time, space, and material resources apart from his family. In contrast to the public outrage at women who attempted to enjoy themselves in the same ways ('women adrift', they were often called), the general tolerance of what the 'boys' got up to was encapsulated in the all-forgiving phrase 'boys will be boys'.

## I'LL DRINK TO THAT

For generations, public drinking of alcoholic beverages had been central to bachelor life, and excessive drinking and disruptive drunkenness among young men had a long history.[5] Since the 1820s, a succession of temperance movements had tried to convince such tipplers to abandon the bottle,[6] but booze remained the lubricant of much bachelor-based sociability at the turn of the twentieth century.[7] Its impact was nonetheless changing. On the one hand, many working-class drinkers insisted that consumption in moderation did no damage to their respectability, while, on the other, the onslaught of Prohibition threatened to shut down all sites of public drinking.

Alcohol was consumed in private households, both as medicine or tonic and as refreshment. In the years before the war, brewers and distillers played to these popular consumption patterns in their advertising. Hamilton's own Regal beer was said to be 'a real tonic, a harmless beverage, a stimulant to digestion'.[8] It is difficult to know how much and how often working-class people drank at home. Temperance tracts denounced the practice without much real investigation. Bringing home a pail of beer (known as 'rushing the growler') seems to have been as common here as elsewhere, and, when they could afford it, some men picked up a bottle or two for after-hours drinking. Police constables commonly noted the drunkenness on Sundays that they claimed resulted from taking a bottle home. They also turned their sights on drinking practices in immigrant boarding houses, where landlords liked to lay in booze for their boarders but ran into trouble for having more than the legal limit for a private residence. The police and the local provincial liquor inspector—the aptly named James Sturdy—raided them regularly. Many families, it seemed, also expected to have alcoholic drinks for such special celebrations as weddings or christenings or at such festive times as Christmas and New Year's (when the city newspaper blossomed with advertising for booze).[9]

Outside the home, there was still some drinking in the workplace, despite decades of efforts to stop this practice. Many men insisted that alcoholic beverages helped them through arduous labour in a smoky foundry, steel plant, or glass works. A steel company foreman told a parliamentary committee in 1910 that 'if he stopped the men from drinking during working hours . . . half of them would walk off the job'. As the firm's historian later discovered, 'Every Saturday night the plant policeman would disappear while a wagon and team loaded with beer kegs and whisky cases was run right into the plant'. Foundrymen also grumbled that moulders slipped out of the sweltering heat of their factories to enjoy a quick drink at a nearby tavern. Industrialists often tried to ensure that there were no saloons near their plants.[10]

By far the greatest amount of drinking, however, seems to have taken place after work in licensed, publicly visible saloons, virtually all of them attached to hotels. In the early 1900s, Hamilton's drinkers found their access to these watering holes restricted in three ways by provincial regulation.[11] First, the recurrent pressure to reduce the number of licensed premises cut the number of liquor shops from 20 in the 1890s to 16 by 1915, and the taverns from 75 to 55.[12] Second, the location of these licensed outlets was increasingly confined to the downtown core. No affluent neighbourhoods had them, and many of the new East-End working-class suburbs were similarly dry as a result of the local licensing board's biases.[13] And third, the hours of operation were being curtailed. Well before the war, earlier closing times were sending drinkers home by 7 PM on Saturday. One consequence of these changes was the growth of more illicit 'blind pigs' run by bootleggers. Inspector Sturdy cracked down particularly hard on alleged bootleggers in the 'foreign colonies' of recent European immigrants near the major factory districts, who, he and the police alleged, ran the 'great majority' of the more than 200 blind pigs estimated to be active in the city by 1916.[14]

The saloons were the centre of much controversy in the decade before the war, notably in the spring of 1913. At that point, Bryce M. Stewart arrived in Hamilton as the key figure in a cross-country series of 'preliminary social surveys' jointly sponsored by the Methodist and Presbyterian Churches, to collect information on poverty, public health, housing, moral purity, and other features of contemporary urban life in Canada. One Saturday night in April, Stewart and a small team of volunteer investigators fanned out across the city to visit the city's 57 bar-rooms in the hour before closing that evening (that is, between 6 and 7 PM). The investigators stayed in each saloon 'just long enough to make the inspection' before moving on to the next, and later produced what they called a 'census' of these establishments based on their observations. Although annoyingly vague, their report gives us a rare glimpse through the saloon window. The churchmen claimed to have counted up 1,775 drinkers and estimated that probably three times that number would have passed through the bar-rooms during that hour.[15]

Whom did they find in front of Hamilton's bars? First, they did not report seeing any women, or any well-dressed businessmen or professionals. These were spaces for working men alone. A century earlier, it had still been common to find a mingling of social classes and men and women in taverns,[16] but well before the end of the nineteenth century bourgeois women had retreated into the gentility of their households, and bourgeois men had either eliminated the 'demon rum' from their lives or withdrawn into expensive hotels or exclusive social clubs. The social life of turn-of-the-century saloons, then, was shaped by male wage-earners. Not surprisingly, many North American commentators in this period captured the class and gender dimensions of the saloon by referring to it as the 'working man's club'.

By the early 1900s, as several American historians have documented, these watering holes met many needs among working men— food, toilets, telephones, news about possible jobs, and even accommodation for those separated from families.[17] But they were much more as well. As the timing of the investigators' visit suggests, these wage-earners were stopping in on their way home from work, at the end of a six-day week (studies in other Canadian cities showed little business in saloons during the day, and most at the end of the week). They were in a moment of transition between the speeded-up labour in the large new plants of the city's Second Industrial Revolution[18] and relaxation at home. Alcohol became the lubricant for the passage between wage labour and leisure, and the moments spent with workmates or neighbours allowed for the sociability that working days in the workplace usually constrained severely.[19] The survey found no children in the bar-rooms, but worried about the 37 'very young' men who they thought 'might be minors'. Evidently younger workers were eventually finding their way into saloon life, despite a new 1907 provincial law that raised the legal drinking age to 21.[20]

The 'working man's club' was an egalitarian place for those who frequented it. A worker could find there an informal, relatively open community of sociability. In 1909, in the midst of a campaign to reduce the number of licences, a hotel-keeper explained that for many wage-earners— 'the main patrons of the bar', he claimed—a saloon was 'a social solvent and center'. In contrast, he argued, the local YMCA would require that the worker 'change his clothes and "wash up," . . . and then walk a mile or so', all of which was too much for 'the working man who has spent ten hours on hard, laborious work'. Moreover, he argued, 'the YMCA is unfortunately full of caste feeling, that feeling which finds expression in so many subtle ways. The working man feels this, and strongly resents it'.[21]

Of course, in practice, this sociability was not always easily accessible to everyone. The community of men who gathered in one saloon tended to draw on those living in the immediate neighbourhood or working in plants nearby. An unwanted visitor could soon get the cold shoulder. Three years later, the owner of the Terminal Hotel was brought to court for allegedly serving alcohol to First Nations people and, when asked to identify the two Natives, said, 'This first fellow I might take for a nigger; the other one looks like a Chinaman to me. Neither of them would get service at my bar'. That probably helps to explain why the Methodist and Presbyterian investigators found the 'non-English speaking' patrons clustered in eight saloons close to the city's 'foreign colonies'.[22]

Once accepted into the flow of saloon life, a man would find that these places helped to affirm important strands in his working-class masculine identity. Saloon patrons shared an experience of selling their labour for wages to their bosses and bonding with their workmates. That included pride in physical labour but often resentments about the ways that the changing work world of capitalist management was eating away at their independence, creativity, and dignity on the job. In front of the bar, these men could plot a strike, or simply try to forget their long hours of paid labour and find others ways to build working-class masculine identities in their leisure time. The continuing ritual of 'treating' each other to drinks symbolized the bonds of mutuality and intensified the camaraderie.

These were spaces that nourished a 'boyish' freedom from control. Beneath pictures of scantily clad women and scenes of hunting and sporting events, the discussions could range over such exclusively male activities as hunting and fishing, sports, politics, or, inevitably, relations with women. Conversations were sprinkled with the 'lewd and profane' language that horrified the prim Protestant investigators in 1913. In these places, these men could smoke, spit, swear, whistle, sing, fart, tell off-colour jokes, laugh loudly and shout, ridicule women, and generally ignore the civilizing constraints of domesticity. There was a cockiness that comes through in the surviving photographs of bodies arched against the bar, one hand wrapped around a drink, the other on the hip, one foot on the brass rail. Here they were 'one of the boys'.[23]

Broadly speaking, consuming alcohol allowed the working men gathered in saloons to play out two different forms of behaviour. One was the boisterous, competitive, potentially violent version that emerged with heavy drinking. This was unquestionably a performance with familiar scripts for the benefit of fellow drinkers,[24] and seems to have been associated with more free-spirited bachelors (both young and old) and sometimes with the seasonally unemployed. The men often roamed between hotel bar-rooms on a Saturday night or a public holiday, extending the stage for their loud performances onto the street. In their drunkenness, they could brag expansively, insult or offend others, and easily take offence—expressing racist comments about blacks, confronting a strikebreaker, defending the honour of their womenfolk or their own reputations. 'He called me names, and made me out to be a rogue', one Hamilton man argued in defending himself. The behaviour was deliberately loud and aggressive—for example, according to the local press, 'shouting and swearing' at 2 AM, 'swearing in broken English' on a street corner, favouring passersby with a 'little iligant [sic] music on a mouth organ', singing hymns at the train station, 'dancing in the middle of the road', offering 'to run any man in Hamilton a 100 yard race', 'chasing girls and women and frightening them', and 'accosting passers-by and trying to stop automobiles by standing in front of them'. Some drunks stood accused of petty theft or more destructive behaviour, including smashing windows. It was not uncommon for their highly theatrical braggadocio to erupt into fights. A few young men even attacked their parents violently. Sometimes, if men became too obstreperous or pugnacious, they earned a trip to police court and, usually, a stiff fine. At that point, they might well claim that the alcohol had blotted out their memory, though the local magistrate never accepted such excuses. The police also targeted unemployed men with no apparent disposition to work, who spent too much of their days hanging about bar-rooms and pool halls, got drunk too frequently, and thus faced charges of vagrancy.[25]

Most often, these drunks were single men. [ . . . ] Two-thirds of the just over a thousand tipplers who faced the police magistrate on charges of public drunkenness (and, in some cases, 'disorderliness') in a 12-month period in 1909–10 were bachelors and widowers. It is not surprising that in the spring of 1910 the magistrate handed down stiffer fines on the rising tide of bachelor drunks. Although the many young men who flocked to Hamilton in the decade before the war were prominent in

their ranks, those under the age of 30 comprised only a third of the unmarried drunks. In that 1909–10 period, more than 400 bachelors and widowers in their thirties, forties, and fifties still made heavy drinking in the city's saloons such a central part of their leisure time that they ended up in police court.[26]

Getting married did not necessarily break that pattern. As suggested earlier, some men tried to carry their bachelor ways into married life and, in at least some cases, fell into debilitating heavy drinking. In that 1909–10 period, a third of the court cases involved married men. All too often, it seems, the men could create havoc with family finances and sometimes attacked their wives and children. Every week women brought abusive husbands to police court on charges of assault or non-support. A good proportion of these cases involved ongoing marital strife or separation. For some time her husband had been 'drinking too heavily and abusing her', one wife told the magistrate in 1910, 'but last night he had beaten her something fierce'; when she fled, 'he wreaked his vengeance on the furniture and dishes destroying nearly everything in the house'. Smashing furniture and crockery seemed to be a ritual act of violence against the demands of domesticity in a number of these cases.

The Prohibition movement, whose discourse blanketed public media in the early twentieth century, made out that these drunkards were the typical patrons of the saloon. Those claims, however, were belied by a second, more restrained pattern of drinking. In 1913 the Methodist and Presbyterian investigators reported that they had spotted only 217 intoxicated men on their Saturday-evening survey—a mere 12 per cent of those tallied in the hour before closing. Given that these teetotallers slinking around the smoky interiors of the city's saloons might have had difficulty distinguishing an extroverted personality from a drunk, this is a remarkably low total—far fewer than temperance rhetoric would have prepared the public to expect. The much larger numbers of drinkers they saw were evidently practising restraint and drinking more moderately. These were arguably men who enjoyed the company of friends and workmates, who understood the limitations of a family budget (national consumption always dropped when the economy took a nosedive),[27] and who doubtless would defend their behaviour as perfectly respectable and not 'rough'. Indeed, there is reason to assume that some of them were churchgoers, especially since the Anglican and Catholic churches had no problems with moderate consumption.[28] Arguably, in the context of extremely limited income and relentless critiques of their leisure time spent in saloons, many working men were informally and collectively taming their time and space apart with the 'boys', in order to preserve an important realm of working-class masculine expression by making it more respectable. Hotel-keepers played to this spirit of restraint with the elaborate decor of their establishments. By the early twentieth century a worker entering a saloon generally stood in front of a long, gleaming mahogany bar and saw himself reflected in huge mirrors framed by ornate woodwork and glass and crystal. The distillers' and brewers' advertising that hung on the walls around him and appeared in local newspapers reinforced his sense that drinking was not necessarily disreputable.[29]

So a common assumption in some historical writing that saloons were simply a repository of 'rough' culture, a pre-industrial remnant in opposition to the rigid disciplines of industrial capitalism, can mislead attempts to understand early twentieth-century working-class male leisure pursuits and masculine identities.[30] Drinking in a city such as Hamilton, it seems, could help to sustain two distinct (and overlapping) forms of working-class masculinity: bachelor-driven expressiveness and more restrained sociability. Of course, the boundaries between these groups must have been as fluid as their beverages and as unstable as their blood-alcohol levels, especially at more celebratory moments. And it is

difficult to know how the moderate drinkers tolerated or distanced themselves from the rowdy drunks. It is nonetheless clear that both forms of male behaviour could extend into married life. To use terms common in working-class Britain at the time, a 'good' husband was a man who used a small part of his pocket money to share a few glasses of beer at the end of the working week and headed home with most of his wages intact, while a 'bad' husband ignored the needs of his family and indulged himself in the saloon culture he had come to enjoy before marriage.[31]

It would be misleading to suggest that even the more respectable version of public drinking was acceptable to all working men. Within the local craft-union movement, division of opinion on temperance and Prohibition was so strong that the Hamilton Trades and Labor Council always refused to take a position on the issue before 1918. A pro-temperance strain in local working-class culture had a long history in the city, running back to the days of the Knights of Labor in the 1880s, reformist coalitions with social reformers in the Royal Templars of Temperance in the 1890s, and the ongoing public program of the Gospel Reform Temperance Club, whose membership and featured speakers included working men, among them William Barrett, a socialist painter and perennial candidate for public office in Hamilton. Alan Studholme, the elderly stove-mounter who was elected to the Ontario Legislature under the Independent Labour Party banner repeatedly between 1906 and 1919, was a committed teetotaller who often spoke out against the evils of drink. Many skilled craftworkers similarly identified sobriety with working-class independence, and drunkenness with undermining the family economy and the wage-earner's ability to engage in collective acts of solidarity. The pre-war editor of the Hamilton *Labor News* presented a dry slant on most public debates about alcohol, and in 1914 published an alternative perspective on manliness—a paean to the responsible breadwinner, 'The Hero of the Payroll', who was 'the worker with a weakness for John Barleycorn who, knowing what happens on pay night, when he stops at the corner saloon to take "just one drink with the boys," bravely marches past, goes straight to his little home, throws his arms around the missus, uptips her chin for a smashing kiss, and then hands over the pay envelope unopened'. This, the editor proclaimed, took 'moral courage, unflinching sacrifice of self'.[32]

Yet most of these dry voices in working-class Hamilton were uncomfortable with the coercive thrust of the mainstream Prohibition movement, which by the turn of the century had set its sights primarily on 'banishing the bar'. Most preferred moral suasion for dealing with heavy drinkers. Wage-earning temperance supporters resented the class bias of much of the rhetoric and the targeting of the 'working man's club', rather than the rich man's social club or wine cellar. Although in 1907 the Canadian labour movement had made a strategic alliance with the moral-reform forces by joining the Social and Moral Reform Council of Canada and its provincial counterparts, craft-union leaders grew increasingly uncomfortable with the prohibitionist orientation of the organization and its failure to tackle pressing issues of concern to working-class communities, and withdrew in 1915. A few years earlier, southern Ontario's regional labour paper, the *Industrial Banner*, had engaged in 'Some Plain Talk' about temperance politics that captured the frustration of many dry labour leaders: 'Our temperance friends' needed 'a broader vision and a larger horizon, to recognize that the high cost of living is not due to the sale of liquor, that the white slave traffic and the social evil, the exploitation of men and women and children is not due to drink', the writer argued. 'We have no patience with the Pharisceasical which shuts its eyes and absolutely refuses to recognize that greater and infinitely more horrible poverty that exists because men and women are exploited in mine, mill and factory and robbed of the fruits of their labor'.[33] During the First World War, these hesitations would help to swing even many of these teetotallers behind a policy of moderation in opposition to complete Prohibition.

## Boys and their Booze

A working man's 'manhood' was a complex package. In early twentieth-century working-class Hamilton, as in many other industrial centres, it began to take shape during boyhood in fluid relationships among the family home, schoolroom, street corner, and factory. Parents, teachers, police officers, and bosses expected boys to learn to subordinate themselves to authority and to shoulder responsibility, and most boys did, to varying degrees. But they also likely participated in the relative freedom and collective defiance practised by their young male friends. Well into adulthood, working-class men still nurtured that kind of solidarity and independence in homosocial activities inside and outside the workplace—determined to still be 'one of the boys'. As much as their experience was preparing them to become breadwinners for their own families, it also provided them with an active critique of such staid domesticity, learned in the long years of bachelorhood. Their masculinities, then, regularly displayed an inherent tension that pulled them between the poles of collective responsibility for family survival within the economic uncertainties of capitalism and the gendered privilege to find among 'the boys' their own comforts and compensations for the harsh indignities of wage-earning.

While some sought out the earnest pleasures of the YMCA or young men's church groups, far more in a city like Hamilton, it seems, turned to saloons or beverage rooms as refuges from the demands of domesticity, wage-earning, and prim morality. Some turned these sites of public drinking into stages for outlandish drunken performances of swaggering bravado and occasional violence. That behaviour connected with two crucial features of the making of working-class 'manhood'.

One was that proving oneself involved so many activities in semi-public spaces in front of audiences of male peers—fights on streets or in schoolyards, games on vacant lots or playing fields, courtship in amusement parks or dance halls, and skill or muscular strength executed on shop floors. The other was that so much that a working man had to do to confirm his masculine identity required him to use his body to the fullest. As Robert Connell has argued, the social construction of gender and the material reality of an actual male body meet as masculinities are worked out through body action in 'reflexive body practices'.[34] In the case of public drinking, the consequences could be seriously debilitating, not simply for the neglected family waiting for him to bring home his wages, but also for the body of the drinking worker, whose liver might well be deteriorating and whose altered motor skills could lead to injuries (just as 'tough' men could wear themselves out in factory labour, or sexual adventurers could succumb to disease). The regulatory apparatuses of post-Prohibition 'liquor control' were aimed at restraining this kind of bodily expressiveness.

Most working men in early twentieth-century Hamilton did not put on such exaggerated displays, however. The conviviality and bonds of comradeship were more important and required different rituals—treating or storytelling, for example. Working-class drinkers seem to have developed a custom of more restrained consumption, which they (and perhaps most of their spouses) interpreted as a small reward for breadwinning and which they generally curtailed if employment became less certain. The purpose of the activity and the setting in which it took place did not change, but the behaviour was arguably more moderate and, in their eyes, undoubtedly respectable. Prohibition changed all that by depriving working men of their neighbourhood gathering places and making consumption much more expensive. Social drinking continued, though much more furtively and probably less frequently. For the first time, the local labour movement spoke out in defence of moderation and respectability, demanding the return of a more palatable beverage. They fought on sporadically until public drinking returned in 1934.

# NOTES

1.  *Hamilton Spectator* [hereafter cited as *HS*], 20 Oct. 1924, 5; Homeside Hotel, 15 Nov. 1945, RG 26-8 (Liquor Control Board of Ontario, Establishment Files), Archives of Ontario [hereafter cited as AO]. A few weeks later, another letter on the same subject arrived in the same file from the 'Boys from the Glass Works'.

2.  Canada, *Census*, 1921, 142, 153–4; Synge, 'Young Working Class Women in Early 20th Century Hamilton: Their Work and Family Lives', in *Proceedings of the Workshop Conference on Blue-collar Workers and Their Communities . . .* , ed. A.H. Turritin (Toronto, 1976), 137–45 ; and 'Transition from School to Work: Growing Up Working Class in Early 20th Century Hamilton, Ontario', in *Childhood and Adolescence in Canada*, ed. K. Ishwaran (Toronto: McGraw-Hill Ryerson, 1979), 249–69.

3.  By the turn of the century, the public holidays on the Canadian calendar consisted of New Year's Day, Easter, Victoria (or Empire) Day, Dominion Day, Labour Day, and Christmas. See Craig Heron and Steve Penfold, *The Workers' Festival: A History of Labour Day in Canada* (Toronto: University of Toronto Press, 2005).

4.  Annalee Golz, '"If a Man's Wife Does Not Obey Him, What Can He Do?" Marital Breakdown and Wife Abuse in Late Nineteenth Century and Early Twentieth Century Ontario', in *Law, Society, and the State: Essays in Modern Legal History*, ed. Louis Knafla and Susan W.S. Binnie (Toronto: University of Toronto Press, 1995), 323–50.

5.  Edith I. Burley, *Servants of the Honourable Company: Work, Discipline, and Conflict in the Hudson's Bay Company, 1770–1879* (Toronto: Oxford University Press, 1997); Peter

DeLottinville, 'Joe Beef of Montreal: Working Class Culture and the Tavern, 1869–1889', *Labour/Le Travailleur* 8–9 (Autumn 1981/ Spring 1982): 9–40; Craig Heron, *Booze: A Distilled History* (Toronto: Between the Lines, 2003), 30–49.

6. Sharon Anne Cook, *'Through Sunshine and Shadow': The Woman's Christian Temperance Union, Evangelicalism, and Reform in Ontario, 1874–1930* (Montreal and Kingston: McGill-Queen's University Press, 1995); Heron, *Booze*, 51–77, 145–63; Jan Noel, *Canada Dry: Temperance Crusades before Confederation* (Toronto: University of Toronto Press, 1995); Ruth Elizabeth Spence, *Prohibition in Canada* (Toronto: Ontario Branch of the Dominion Alliance, 1919).

7. The most revealing statement about this bachelor drinking in North America was Jack London's *John Barleycorn* (Toronto: Bell and Cockburn, 1913).

8. *HS*, 11 Nov. 1909, 19; 13 Dec. 1909, 10; 15 Dec. 1909, 6, 10; 18 Dec. 1909, 15; 3 Dec. 1910, 17; 6 Nov. 1912, 2; Heron, *Booze*, 191.

9. *HS*, 18 June 1900, 8; 6 Oct. 1910, 14. For examples of police raids on blind pigs and boarding houses, see *HS*, 29 Apr. 1907, 12; 2 June 1913, 1; 10 May 1916, 16; June 1916, 15; *Hamilton Herald* [hereafter cited as *HH*], 6 Jan. 1910, 9; 14 Feb. 1910, 10; 20 Apr. 1910, 1; 18 May 1910, 1; 2 June 1910, 1; 3 June 1910, 2; 3 Aug. 1910, 2; 23 Aug. 1910, 10; 14 Sept. 1910, 1; 19 Sept. 1910, 1; 26 Oct. 1910, 1; 1 Nov. 1910, 3; 3 Dec. 1910, 1.

10. William Kilbourn, *The Elements Combined: A History of the Steel Company of Canada* (Toronto: Clark, Irwin, 1960), 120; Canada, Royal Commission on the Liquor Traffic, *Minutes of Evidence* (Ottawa: Queen's Printer, 1895), vol. 4, pt. 1, 181, 209.

11. *HS*, 30 Sept. 1898, 8; 5 Dec. 1902, 10; 7 Jan. 1913, 1; 2 Jan. 1915, 1; *HH*, 18 Nov. 1908, 10; 3 Jan. 1911, 6; 21 Apr. 1911, 1; Canada, Department of Agriculture, *Statistical Year-Book of Canada, 1900* (Ottawa: Government Printing Bureau, 1901), 567.

12. Ontario, *Report of the Operation of the Liquor License Acts* (Toronto: King's Printer, 1916), 49.

13. Methodist Church of Canada, Department of Temperance and Moral Reform, and Presbyterian Church of Canada, Board of Social Service and Evangelism, *Report of a Preliminary and General Social Survey of Hamilton* (n.p., 1913) [hereafter cited as Methodist-Presbyterian, *Social Survey*].

14. *HS*, 29 Mar. 1900, 8; 8 Sept. 1900, 8; 12 Jan. 1910, 12; 23 June 1910, 12; 3 Aug. 1910, 12; 23 Aug. 1910, 10; 14 Sept. 1910, 12; 21 Sept. 1910, 12; 27 Oct. 1910, 16; 30 Nov. 1910, 4; 7 Dec. 1910, 14; 29 Dec. 1910, 11; June 1916, 15 (see also reference in n. 6).

15. Methodist-Presbyterian, *Social Survey*, 19–21.

16. H. Julia Roberts, 'Taverns and Tavern-Goers in Upper Canada: The 1790s to the 1850s' (Ph.D. diss., University of Toronto, 1999).

17. Madelon Powers, *Faces along the Bar: Lore and Order in the Workingman's Saloon, 1870–1920* (Chicago: University of Chicago Press, 1998).

18. The term is used to denote a distinctly new phase of industrial-capitalist development that began in Canada at the turn of the century and incorporated new managerial schemes, technology, and labour-recruitment practices into much larger, corporate-controlled workplaces.

19. Joseph R. Gusfield, 'Passage To Play: Rituals of Drinking Time in American Society', in *Constructive Drinking: Perspectives on Drink from Anthropology*, ed. Mary Douglas (New York: Cambridge University Press, 1987), 73–90.

20. The fact that some hotels ran poolrooms adjacent to the barrooms probably allowed younger drinkers to slip in. *HS*, 30 Dec. 1909, 5; Robert E. Popham, *Working Papers on the Tavern, 2: Legislative History of the Ontario Tavern, 1774–1974* (Toronto: Addiction Research Foundation, substudy no. 809, 1976), 7, 29.

21. *HS*, 21 Dec. 1909, 11.

22. *HH*, 8 Sept. 1916, 2; Methodist-Presbyterian, *Social Survey*, 20.

23. Methodist-Presbyterian, *Social Survey*, 20; London, *John Barleycorn*; Powers, *Faces along the Bar*. For samples of saloon photographs, see Heron, *Booze*, 84–116.

24. C. MacAndrew and R.B. Edgerton, *Drunken Comportment* (Chicago: Aldine, 1969).

25. These behaviour patterns are evident in newspaper reports of police-court proceedings during 1900, 1910, and 1920.

26. Hamilton Police, Annual Reports, series A,

1900–1905, 1909, 1912–13, 1915, RG 10, Special Collections, Hamilton Public Library [hereafter cited as HPL]; Police Registers, series M, 1909–10; *HS*, 4 Mar. 1910, 4; 9 May 1910, 14; 6 June 1910, 12; 11 June 1910, 1.

27. Canada, Inland Revenues, *Report* (Ottawa: King's Printer, 1917), pt. 1, xvi.

28. Heron, *Booze*, 194–6; Edward Arthur Warwick Smith, 'The Dialectics of Faith: Laity, Clergy, and Church Life in Three Hamilton Anglican Parishes, 1889–1914' (Ph.D. diss, University of Guelph, 1999). Hamilton Trades and Labor Council, Minutes, 3 Oct. 1913, 321–2, Special Collections, HPL.

29. Robert Elwall, *Bricks and Beer: English Pub Architecture, 1830–1939* (London: British Architectural Library, 1983); Mark Girouard, *Victorian Pubs* (London: Studio Vista, 1975).

30. This is the thrust of DeLottinville's excellent article on the late nineteenth-century tavern, 'Joe Beef of Montreal'.

31. Andrew Davies, *Leisure, Gender, and Poverty: Working-class Culture in Salford and Manchester, 1900–1939* (Buckingham: Open University Press, 1992).

32. Craig Heron, 'Working-class Hamilton, 1895–1930' (Ph.D. thesis, Dalhousie University,

1981), 588–93, and 'Alan Studholme', *Dictionary of Canadian Biography, Volume 14: 1911 to 1920* (Toronto: University of Toronto Press, 1998), 976–80; Brian Paul Trainor, 'Towards a Genealogy of Temperance: Identity, Belief, and Drink in Victorian Ontario' (Ph.D. diss., Queen's University, 1993), 190–250; Samuel Walker, 'Terence V. Powderly, the Knights of Labor, and the Temperance Issue', *Societas 5* (Autumn 1975): 279–93; Gregory S. Kealey and Bryan D. Palmer, *Dreaming of What Might Be: The Knights of Labor in Ontario, 1880–1900* (New York: Cambridge University Press, 1982); Ronald Morris Benson, 'American Workers and Temperance Reform, 1866–1933' (Ph.D. diss., University of Notre Dame, 1974); Hamilton *Labor News*, 23 Jan. 1914, 4.

33. Heron, *Booze*, 213–24; London *Industrial Banner*, Apr. 1912, 1; see also 10 Mar. 1916, 2; 24 Mar. 1916, 2.

34. Robert W. Connell, *Masculinities* (Berkeley and Los Angeles: University of California Press, 1995), 45–66. Joy Parr, 'Notes for a More Sensuous History of Twentieth-Century Canada: The Timely, the Tacit, and the Material Body', *Canadian Historical Review 82* (Dec. 2001): 720–45.

4  From Melissa Turkstra, 'Constructing a Labour Gospel: Labour and Religion in Early Twentieth-Century Ontario', *Labour/Le Travail* 57 (Spring 2006): 93–130. Reprinted by permission of the publisher.

On 14 December 1900, just under 50 working men gathered in the lecture hall of James Street Baptist Church in Hamilton, Ontario, to meet with its pastor, Rev. J.L. Gilmour. Rev. Gilmour's primary objective in organizing this meeting was to solicit the opinion of workers in order to gain a better understanding of why more working men did not attend church. What is most striking about this meeting is how animated and frank these men were in their responses to the minister. Most of the men conceded that the church did have a message for workers; one worker even admitted that, in his opinion, Christianity was the

only answer for the current social and labour problems while another quoted from the Bible to demonstrate that it had many relevant messages for workers. At the same time, the general consensus was that the churches were not successfully reaching the masses. Part of the problem, the men claimed, was the presence of 'unchristian' manufacturers in the high offices of the church. Long hours and hard work were also cited as key factors keeping men from attending church. The men offered several suggestions of how the churches could amend this situation. First, ministers had to concentrate less on the spiritual welfare of the people and more on their temporal welfare. This meant, for example, that church leaders needed to join in the fight for the shorter workday and denounce the present competitive system. Ministers also had to return to the simple practical doctrine preached by Christ. Despite these criticisms, it was clear that working men were not completely alienated from the church. One worker questioned why working men were being singled out because, in his opinion, they were just as likely to regularly attend church as professionals and businessmen. Another worker stated that the working class had a responsibility to attend church even if it did have faults. Samuel Landers, future editor of the Hamilton *Labor News*, acknowledged that there were a few churches that attracted working men and attributed this to two factors: the attentiveness of these churches to workers' needs, and the concerted effort made by the pastors of these churches to visit their congregants. Probably the most remarkable statement at the conference was the response to Rev. Gilmour's concluding question; he asked, 'How do men, who never attend church, know what is going on inside of them?' He was informed that the men discuss the sermons in the workshop.[1]

The views that were expressed at the working men's conference in Hamilton in 1900 were not exceptional. Both moderate and radical labour leaders voiced similar ideas in various labour publications in early twentieth-century Ontario. Like the working men at the Hamilton conference, these labour leaders were not shy about revealing where the churches had failed when it came to the working class. In the labour press, editors did not hesitate to portray the established churches as symbols of capitalist wealth and clergymen as puppets controlled by their wealthy constituents. They were also quick to point out that their strong critique of the churches did not imply a rejection of Christianity by carefully distinguishing between a true Christianity and a hypocritical 'Churchianity'.[2] While they underlined this distinction, this did not mean there was no

interaction between labour leaders and the churches. Some labour leaders praised and co-operated with those clergymen who were willing to denounce the injustices of the industrial capitalist system and champion labour issues.

[ . . . ]

The purpose of this paper is not only to provide examples of the presence of religion in the formally organized labour movement in early twentieth-century Canada, but to consider why religion continued to influence the thought and actions of labour leaders during this period. It will first explore labour leaders' disillusionment with the established churches and look at what changes they required the churches to make if they hoped to establish stronger ties with labour. It will then examine the non-sectarian, activist Christianity articulated by many labour leaders and consider how these beliefs helped them frame the issues they were concerned about. It will conclude with a close look at the alliances that developed between church and labour bodies at the national level and between labour-friendly clergy and a small group of labour leaders in industrial centres in Southern Ontario. It will carefully look at who in the labour movement was most committed to building these cross-class alliances, determine what they hoped to achieve from this co-operation, and examine the irreparable cracks in the foundation of these alliances as a result of the opposing positions of the churches and labour on a number of important issues. While this labour gospel helped moderate and radical labour leaders in interpreting and constructing the issues they were concerned about, any rapprochement between organized labour and the churches during this period was modest.

To better understand the relationship between organized labour and religion, I have examined a number of labour newspapers including the *Industrial Banner*,[3] *Tribune*,[4] the Hamilton *Labor News*,[5] and the *Labor Leader*,[6] as well as *Cotton's Weekly*,[7] the official organ of the Social Democratic Party of Canada [SDP].[8] The Annual Report of the Proceedings of the Trades and Labor Congress of Canada has been particularly helpful in understanding the alliances that developed between the churches and labour leaders at the national level. With the exception of the socialist *Cotton's Weekly* and the more conservative labour weekly, the *Labor Leader*, which were national publications, the other papers were regional and local Ontario labour newspapers. In the pages of these newspapers, readers were informed about the social and economic injustices of the industrial capitalist system like child and female labour, unemployment, Chinese immigration, and poverty. They could learn about workers who were striking for better wages and shorter hours, the labour reforms organized labour was fighting for, the appeal of trade unionism, and party platforms. For the editors of these papers, including the radical, anti-capitalist W.A. Cotton, these publications were an important vehicle to promote working-class solidarity and teach workers that through trade unionism and the ballot workers could achieve their goals.[9] Although these labour publications are a useful window through which to examine the relationship between labour and religion, it is important to note that in looking at these papers I am, for the most part, analyzing the voices of the organized, articulate, and earnest intellectual leadership of the labour movement, not the rank-and-file. I am also focusing on a particular group of leaders within the labour movement. In many cases, the leaders I refer to were from Southern Ontario. They were class-conscious craftworkers who had a particular idea of how the labour movement would evolve. They were moderate labour reformists who sought to secure a respected place for labour within industrial capitalist society through collective bargaining and labour representation in legislative bodies. These labourists, along with some socialists in the SDP, believed that social transformation would take place gradually through reforms, not revolution. With respect to religion, these men repeatedly insisted that it was not their role to intervene in the religious lives of workers because

religion was a private matter and churches private institutions.[10] Despite the avowed policy of the labour press to avoid this subject, it was not difficult to find references to religion in the pages of their newspapers. It is also important to point out that the references to religion very rarely differentiated between denominations or even between the Protestant and Catholic churches. They discussed the Christian 'church' broadly speaking. It is clear, however, that labour leaders were really concerned with the Protestants, particularly the Methodists, Presbyterians, and Congregationalists, to whom they turned for alliances.[11]

## LABOUR, CHRISTIANITY, AND THE CHURCHES

Like the Knights of Labor and other labour movements before them, labour leaders in the early twentieth century characterized the established churches as symbols of capitalist wealth and, therefore, part of the exploitive industrial capitalist system they were working so arduously to change.[12] What they found particularly appalling were the wealthy capitalists who had monopolized the churches and used their power to control ministers. As one worker in a letter to the editor of the *Tribune* resentfully explained, 'There is no getting away from the fact that the Church at present is for the class, not the mass'.[13] Joseph Marks, editor of the *Industrial Banner*, voiced a similar complaint at a 1906 Labor Forward meeting, arguing that the working class was absent from the church because it catered to wealthy congregants.[14] In a letter to the editor of the *Industrial Banner* in 1913, an observer characterized the religion in the churches as a charity religion that was becoming increasingly dependent on the contributions of wealthy congregants who, as a natural consequence, guided the policy of the churches and silenced its ministers. The writer complained, 'The church practically teaches that God made this world not for the children of men, but for a special few, so that these favourites could live by the sweat of their neighbour's face'.[15]

[ . . . ]

Also contributing to labour's disillusionment with the churches was the apathy of clergymen with regard to labour issues. One trade unionist expressed his disappointment to the editor of the *Tribune*, writing, 'of the twelve years that I have been a trade unionist, I have never seen a clergyman come and ask to be allowed to have a five minute conversation with them on any of their meeting nights, yet they wonder why the large majority do not attend the church'.[16] [ . . . ]

If the churches wanted to mend relations with labour, they would have to do more than just show an interest in labour issues; labour believed it was the duty of the churches and its ministers to join labour in its fight for more just conditions for workers. The *Industrial Banner* questioned why the preachers of Toronto were not supporting the strike of female operatives at the Adams Shoe Company in 1912 who, without notice, received a serious reduction in wages. It noted the hypocrisy in this silence: 'What can be said of the kind of civilization that can stand for it in a city where hundreds of church spires point upward to the skies, and where peace upon earth and good will towards men is openly proclaimed from its myriad pulpits on every Sabbath morn'.[17] In addition to supporting strikes, labour expected churches to endorse labour legislation. An article entitled 'The Church's Opportunity' invited churches in Ontario to take an interest in the workmen's compensation for injuries act because it was essentially a moral and religious question. Such legislation was necessary, it argued, because hundreds of workers were sacrificed every year as a result of industrial accidents and the widows and children of these workers deserved protection from destitution. [ . . . ]

Although labour was clearly frustrated with the inaction of churches, it believed that the churches were not only capable of but had a vital role to play in eliminating the injustice pervading society. Articles explicitly set out what changes the churches had to make if they were sincerely interested in amending their relationship with labour. Instead of remaining neutral in matters that concerned capital and labour, it was the duty of the churches to be involved in and publicize important moral and religious issues that affected the welfare of the people. The issues the churches were expected to address were quite progressive and included increases in wages and a decrease in hours of work, the abolition of child labour in factories, and equal pay for men and women for equal work or service.[18] This assistance also meant action. Churches had to take an aggressive stance against exploitive capitalists and make social and economic issues a priority. An article published in *Cotton's Weekly* in 1913 summoned the churches 'to prepare the rich man for Heaven by condemning a system that allows some men to get rich while other men are starving', insisting that 'the church has got to go into economic conditions or go out of existence'. It proceeded to call on ministers 'to go into the workshop as Christ did and condemn the owners of the slave pens'.[19] [ . . . ]

The labour press, in the early twentieth century, described to their readers what it believed was wrong with the present state of the churches. The fundamental obstacle impeding the churches' relations with workers was the inability of the churches to detach themselves from the exploitive industrial capitalist system. The labour press portrayed the churches as synonymous with this system; the control of the churches and its ministers by wealthy capitalists was simply an extension of capitalists' abusive power. This did not mean that the churches were dismissed completely; it just meant that they were on trial. The message labour editors wanted to convey to their readers regarding the established churches was that they were a useful but not a necessary tool in workers' efforts to secure a more equitable economic and social system.

## CHRISTIANITY IN LABOUR'S MESSAGE

Whether the established churches did or did not join with organized labour in its fight to establish a more just society had little bearing on its view of religion. The labour press made a conscious effort to distinguish between rejecting the 'churchianity' it identified with the churches and the true Christianity that gave meaning to the daily struggles of workers.[20] The *Labor News*, for example, explained that workers were vacant from the pews not because they were infidels and materialists but because they saw the church 'as a tool of the employing class'.[21] And irregular church attendance, according to the *Labor Leader*, did not automatically qualify a person as a non-Christian.[22] [ . . . ]

Not only did labour leaders reject the notion that it was anti-religious, they articulated a radical social gospel that applied their interpretation of Christian teaching to workers' struggles and insisted that social and economic regeneration precede individual regeneration.[23] This labour gospel was both a direct assault on the unrestrained individualism of laissez-faire capitalism and the individualist gospel that focused on the relationship between God and man.[24] For workers, particularly skilled workers whose craft traditions and autonomy were being threatened during this period by dramatic industrial changes like the concentration of capital, new scientific management practices, technological innovations, and new manufacturing industries that relied on huge pools of unskilled and semi-skilled immigrant labour, this labour gospel helped to frame the issues they were concerned about.[25] [ . . . ]

The majority of religious references in the labour press were centred, not on the divinity of Jesus, but on the temporal significance of his life.[26] Labour newspapers emphasized Jesus' working-class origins. Articles in labour newspapers pointed out the parallels between the life of Jesus and the lives of workers,

noting that he was born into poverty and that his trade until the age of 30 was that of a hard-working carpenter.[27] An article printed in the Christmas issue of the *Labor Leader*, entitled 'Jesus in Overalls', asked readers to remember that the clothes they stripped from his body before he was nailed to the cross were the clothes of a working man: 'What! Jesus in overalls? Sure! He wore them. His overalls smelled of human sweat, and the soil of untarrying toil was upon them'.[28] Jesus was an ideal representative of the working class. It was because of his authentic experience as a worker that Jesus was able to honestly understand workers' struggles, needs, and goals.[29]

In addition to establishing his working-class origins, the labour press depicted Jesus as a heroic social reformer and the first great successful labour leader and invoked his ethical teachings and bold actions to fuel opposition to modern-day social and economic problems.[30] Exploitive employment practices, for example, were inimical to Jesus' teaching. An article entitled 'The People Want to Know' questioned what the Christian life meant in the twentieth century and asked 'if the Saviour of mankind, Who blessed little children, would approve of their exploitation by Christian employers who confine them in unsanitary factories' or 'if a Christian employer who pays his female help one half the wages paid to men for the same work is honest or actuated by the spirit of his Master'.[31] Labour leaders also looked to Christianity to frame their critique of the use of immigrant labour and workplace safety. Demonstrating the deep ethnic division in the labour movement during this period, labour leaders characterized the efforts made by the Canadian Manufacturers' Association to overstock the labour market by giving bonuses to immigration agencies and transportation companies as 'neither Christian, civilized, nor decent'.[32]

Labour leaders also drew on Jesus' ethical teachings to target the unequal distribution of wealth. These teachings were often used to garner support for the single tax, the panacea for land monopolization.[33] The *Industrial Banner*, for example, printed several speeches by W.A. Douglas, a vociferous proponent of the single tax, who often drew on the example of Jesus to reinforce his attacks on land speculation. In 1913, Douglas used the pulpit of King St. Methodist Church in Toronto to speak out against those land owners who had amassed their wealth from land monopoly. He queried, 'What would Christ's answer be to the question, "What is the greatest obstacle to the progress of the kingdom of God?" If he were to come, do you think he would be the guest at the homes of the very rich?' Jesus, Douglas continued, would probably ask, 'Where is that brotherhood I came to this world to found?' and respond with the statement, 'I cannot see it as I go among the people. In every city that I visit, the mansions at one end are like the palaces of princes, while the homes of the hard working people who produce the abundance of the wealth are of the poorest character'.[34]

Labour leaders also drew on Jesus' teachings and other biblical lessons and characters to illustrate the effectiveness of labour unions and to underline that workers themselves were the agents that would effect a more just and equitable society. An article entitled 'Trade Unionism Stands for the Open Door' tried to impress upon wage earners the need to join trade unions by noting the similarities between unionism and the early church. Both were wide open to new members; trade union organizers were the missionaries preaching the benefits of affiliation; both provided better improved conditions through brotherly co-operation and mutual assistance; both uplifted moral standards; and both faced the malevolence of and persecution by bitter opponents.[35] While labour leaders did not hesitate to identify with the early churches, they argued that the present churches, while providing important theories like the Golden Rule and the law of love, lacked legitimacy because they were not solving social and economic problems. Trade unionism, on the other hand, was a legitimate institution because it was acting out the teachings of the

Bible. For example, by emancipating children from exploitive labour practices, trade unionism was obeying the command, 'Inasmuch as ye have done it unto one of the least of these my brethren, ye have done it unto me'; 'Suffer little children, and forbid them not to come unto me; for of such is the kingdom of Heaven'.[36]

Socialists also drew on an activist Christianity to frame their calls for an alternative society. *Cotton's Weekly*, on several occasions, identified socialism with Christianity, stating that 'socialism is simply applied Christianity. The golden rule applied to every day life'[37] or that socialism 'has for its foundations the very elements of Christianity'.[38] It also noted that 'the ethics of socialism are identical with the ethics of Christianity'[39] and 'socialism is Christianity put into practice'.[40] [ . . . ]

Religious discourse was present in the labour press in early twentieth-century Canada because moderate and radical labour leaders understood that one way they could effectively reach workers with their message was through religion. The activist Christianity that labour leaders drew on to interpret and construct labour issues helped make workers aware of the injustices of the industrial capitalist system and cultivate in them a desire to change this system. [ . . . ] In the early twentieth century, labour leaders articulated an activist Christianity that helped them frame the social and economic problems that were of concern to them. This labour gospel was distinctive to the working class and became part of these leaders' attempts to change the industrial capitalist society.

## THE CHURCHES AS LABOUR'S ALLIES

In 1911 the *Industrial Banner* acknowledged the friendship between organized labour and the churches when it responded to a letter published in the *Globe* by Moses Baritz, organizer for the Socialist Party of Canada. Baritz had challenged the statement of Methodist

Superintendent S.D. Chown that socialism was founded upon the teachings of Christ. Not only was socialism opposed to all religions, according to Baritz, but all religions would be abolished with the establishment of a socialist regime. While the *Industrial Banner* assured its readers that Baritz was entitled to his private opinion, it chastised him for antagonizing the church, a force that was friendly to the labour movement.[41] This defensive response by the *Industrial Banner* is not surprising given that its editor was among the few labour leaders who saw building alliances with progressive clergymen in the Protestant churches as a practical and effective way to secure middle-class support for labour reforms.[42] While the presence of this cross-class alliance must be appreciated, it is important to point out that the labour leaders I refer to below were, for the most part, from Southern Ontario, their efforts to build an alliance was most evident in the years leading up to World War I, and their alliance with the churches was tenuous as a result of deep divisions between labour and the churches on a number of issues.

Before World War I, the Trades and Labor Congress of Canada [TLCC] and labour leaders in Southern Ontario allied with various church bodies and clergymen because they saw this collaboration as an opportunity to assist the advancement of labour. One of the first examples of co-operation between organized labour and the churches was between the TLCC and the Lord's Day Alliance [LDA], an organization formed by the Protestant churches in 1889 which sought legislation to secure the day of rest. Seeing that both groups had similar aims, labour wanted workers to have one free day from work and the Alliance wanted one free day to worship, organized labour not only lent a supportive voice but several prominent labour advocates were members of the alliance which was successful in securing the passage of the *Lord's Day Act* in 1906.[43] Co-operation between these two groups continued after this legislation was passed.

Although labour exchanged fraternal delegates with the LDA and expressed enthusiasm for its support of labour initiatives, labour leaders made it clear that their support of one day free from work was based on economic not religious grounds.[44] Commenting on legislation to secure the day of rest, the *Industrial Banner* in 1906 stated that this legislation was 'absolutely necessary for the welfare of the working masses'. This legislation should be supported, it continued, not on religious grounds but because workers have a right to have one day of rest to spend as they desire.[45] [ . . . ] The *Industrial Banner* was trying to be neutral on the question of religion as labour unions were made up of Protestants, Catholics, a large number of non-Christians like Jews who regarded Saturday as their sacred day, adherents of other religions, as well as free thinkers.[46]

Co-operation between labour leaders and the church continued in the church-led Moral and Social Reform Council of Canada [MSRCC].[47] Like the LDA, several prominent labour leaders were members of the MSRCC.[48] Clergymen representing the MSRCC were also welcomed at the annual meetings of the TLCC. Labour leaders also attended the meetings of various local church bodies and used church platforms to publicize and educate people on labour issues. [ . . . ]

In addition to co-operating with labour-friendly church bodies and clergymen, the labour press praised enlightened ministers who aggressively spoke out against the social injustices in society. [ . . . ] Before World War I, labour leaders in the Southern Ontario labour movement built an alliance with progressive clergymen at the national and local levels; in the years directly following the war, these leaders were becoming more convinced that the churches, with their call for industrial democracy, were sincere in their sympathy for workers and their struggles. The resolutions of the Methodist Church in 1918 which called for a co-operative system of service to replace the present competitive system of profits elicited the most optimistic response from these leaders. An article in the 18 October 1918 issue of the *Labor News* entitled 'Methodists Out for the Common People' and the headline of a 17 January 1919 issue of the *Industrial Banner*, 'Far Reaching Pronouncement Outlines a Basis for Economic Reconstruction: A Great Church Insists That Business Shall Be Run No Longer For Corporation Profits',[49] demonstrated that organized labour was encouraged by the radical recommendations of the Methodist Church.[50] Labour leaders believed this call for social reconstruction would not only result in future co-operation with the churches but would inevitably lead to great political, economic, and industrial changes.[51] That some of these leaders viewed the churches' statements with optimism was also evident in a statement in the *Labor News*: 'If the Methodist ministers follow up the platform laid down by the Conference some of us fellows might have to start going to church again'.[52]

The alliance that was being built between progressive clergymen in the Protestant churches did not include all members of the labour movement, however; there were deep divisions between labour and the churches on a number of important issues. There were differences between organized labour and the churches on the Sabbatarian issue starting in the late nineteenth century. Although the TLCC initially endorsed the prohibition of Sunday street cars in Toronto in 1891, it was the conservative wing of the TLCC that joined forces with the LDA; workers in Toronto were strongly opposed to this prohibition. When the question of street cars arose again in subsequent years, the TLCC listened to their followers and did not support the Sabbatarian cause.[53] After the *Lord's Day Act* was passed in 1906, and especially after World War I, the differences between the two sides became apparent. Organized labour firmly believed that Sunday was a day for workers to do what they wanted, like attend sports.[54] Organized labour, in fact, became one of the major critics

of the Alliance because of the Alliance's insistence on enforcing legislation and restricting recreation on Sundays.[55]

An even greater obstacle undermining this alliance was the powerful opposition of radical members of the TLCC in the West. As early as 1911 these members demonstrated that they were a serious force to be reckoned with, when they almost ended the Congress' affiliation with the MSRCC. At the annual meeting in Calgary in 1911, delegate McVety of the Vancouver Trades and Labor Congress and delegate Stubbs proposed an amendment to end affiliation with the Council. The amendment was narrowly defeated by a vote of 50 to 52.[56] Just four years later, at the annual meeting in Vancouver, the Congress again voted to withdraw from the Council. Despite the strong opposition from James Simpson, the recommendation was adopted by a vote of 72 to 66.[57] Although the formal separation between the TLCC and MSRCC was a definite setback for those labour leaders who saw the practical advantages of an alliance with the churches, the most potent force preventing any long-term cooperation between these two groups was prohibition.

Prohibition was the most hotly contested form of moral critique of working-class life. While prohibition was one of the great moral crusades of the Protestant churches, for organized labour, it was an issue where there was a distinct difference of opinion. A number of labour leaders applauded the sober morality of Protestant religion, speaking out against drinking in saloons and some even supporting prohibition, particularly those who were members of the MSRCC.[58] Other labour leaders, however, resented the temperance societies that ignored the economic and social causes of drinking. Those who worked in the alcohol business were especially opposed to prohibitive measures like the reduction of licences because they feared losing their jobs. Many leaders also saw prohibition as class-biased legislation that targeted the social lives of working men. The only option for working men, they argued, was to drink in hotel saloons because they could not afford to drink at home or in private clubs. By World War I, organized labour vocally opposed prohibition and by 1919 was rallying around the demand for beer.[59] Organized labour's fight to drink moderately and responsibly collided with the demand by the Protestant churches for a dry regime and was another example of the divisions between churches and the labour movement.

If Sabbatarianism, prohibition, and East-West divisions in the Canadian labour movement led to increasing tension between the churches and the labour movement by World War I, the deterioration of the relationship between organized labour and the churches in the immediate post-war period can be attributed to the inability of the churches to act on their proclamations and a resurgent labour movement that relied less on middle-class support for labour's cause. [ . . . ]

The widening rift between organized labour and the churches came at a time when labour was more confident, united, and class conscious than ever before. Starting in 1916, and for the next four years, union membership rose rapidly and workers joined together in an unprecedented number of strikes.[60] The Winnipeg Strike and the general strikes taking place across Canada in May, June, and July of 1919 were a testament to the wave of nation-wide resistance. This was also a period of increased radicalism in the labour movement, especially in the West, where at the Calgary Labour Conference in the early spring of 1918, the One Big Union was formed.[61] This resistance was accompanied by a renewed interest in independent political action. There was a significant increase in the number of independent labour parties at both the municipal and provincial level. In Ontario, the Independent Labour Party joined the United Farmers of Ontario to form a coalition government in 1919.[62]

The 1921 Toronto printers' strike was the final blow that ended the alliance between the churches and labour. [ . . . ] At the centre of this conflict were the Methodist Book Room and its intransigent superintendent, S.W. Fallis, who refused to give in to the printers' demand for a 44-hour week. [ . . . ] That this strike caused irreparable damage to the alliance between labour and the churches was clear. The *Labor News* argued that the actions of the Methodist Book Room contradicted the 1918 Methodist General Conference resolutions. The *Industrial Banner* stated, 'The position of the Methodist Book Room in the strike of the printing trades is nothing less than tragic. It is a position from which the Church will not recover during its lifetime, and which can only be partly effaced when Church union is brought about and a new name is given to the united churches'.[63] The noticeable decline in the number of references to the churches in the labour press also attests to the negative impact the strike had on the relationship between organized labour and the churches.[64]

[ . . . ]

## CONCLUSION

In early twentieth-century Canada, labour leaders were not reticent in their denunciations of the churches, which they saw as symbols of capitalist wealth. Nor were they afraid to excoriate clergymen who were indifferent or openly hostile to labour's cause. This deep resentment did not mean, however, that they abandoned religion. The labour movement during this period may not have been imbued with religiosity like the Knights of Labor in the late nineteenth century, but religion was present. Both moderate reformist and radical labour leaders believed in an activist Christianity and interpreted and constructed social and economic problems in light of these beliefs. This labour gospel helped make workers better understand these problems, build opposition to the present industrial capitalist system, and attract workers to their respective movements.

In addition to drawing on an activist Christianity to frame the issues they were concerned about, this paper has looked at the alliances that developed between labour leaders in Southern Ontario and the churches. The examination of these alliances suggests a richer relationship between the churches and labour than the work of other historians would suggest. While future research must look at alliances in other regions of Canada, it is evident that labour leaders in Southern Ontario co-operated with church bodies at national and local levels, sang high praises for those socially conscious churches and clergymen who championed the cause of labour, and readily admitted the benefits of the alliances with the churches.[65] Yet, support for a cross-class alliance was not shared by all members of the labour movement. This can be attributed to the deep divisions between the churches and labour on issues like Sabbatarianism and prohibition, but also to regional differences and the national and regional dynamics and diversity of the Canadian labour movement.

The purpose of examining labour leaders' criticism of established churches, their promotion of an activist Christianity, and the alliances they formed with various church bodies and clergymen has not been to measure the extent of religious belief of organized labour. Some labour leaders were churchgoers, but certainly not all were. Some rejected organized religion but espoused an activist Christianity. Some were non-believers, but supported Christian principles. What is evident from this examination of labour publications is that, while labour leaders may have had a diverse range of religious beliefs or even non-belief, Christianity was present in the labour movement.

# NOTES

1. *Hamilton Spectator*, 13 December 1900; *Hamilton Evening Times*, 13 December 1900.
2. 'Churchianity' was a term used to describe the church's obsession with creed, ritual, and wealth. See *Cotton's Weekly*, 28 January 1909.
3. Kevin Brushett, 'Labour's Forward Movement: Joseph Marks, the *Industrial Banner* and the Ontario Working-Class, 1890–1930', (M.A. thesis, Queen's University, 1994), 21, 66, 146; Ron Verzuh, *Radical Rag: The Pioneer Labour Press in Canada* (Ottawa 1988), 97–98; *McKim's Canadian Newspaper Directory* 1920, 87.
4. The *Tribune* was the mouthpiece of the Toronto District Labor Council.
5. James Naylor, *The New Democracy: Challenging the Social Order in Industrial Ontario, 1914–1925* (Toronto 1991), 67–68.
6. *The Labor Leader*, 18 December 1925; 17 December 1926.
7. Edward Penton, 'The Ideas of William Cotton: A Marxist View of Canadian Society, 1908–1914', (M.A. thesis, University of Ottawa, 1978), 14.
8. Janice Newton, *The Feminist Challenge to the Canadian Left, 1900–1918* (Montreal and Kingston 1995), 32.
9. Brushett, 'Labour's Forward Movement';

Penton, 'The Ideas of William Cotton'; and *Dictionary of Hamilton Biography*, vol. 2, 1992, 'Samuel Landers', by Craig Heron.
10. *Industrial Banner*, November 1911; *Labor News*, 10 March 1916; *Labor Leader*, 26 September 1924; *Cotton's Weekly*, 21 January 1909.
11. Jacques Rouillard, *Histoire de la CSN, 1921–1981* (Montreal 1981).
12. Gregory S. Kealey and Bryan D. Palmer, *Dreaming of What Might Be: The Knights of Labor of Ontario, 1880–1900* (Toronto 1987), 311; Lynne Marks, 'The Knights of Labor and the Salvation Army: Religion and Working Class Culture in Ontario, 1882–1890', *Labour/Le Travail*, 28 (Fall 1991), 108; Lynne Marks, *Revivals and Roller Rinks: Religion, Leisure, and Identity in Late-Nineteenth-Century Small Town Ontario* (Toronto 1996), 63.
13. *Tribune*, 4 November 1905.
14. *Industrial Banner*, March 1906.
15. *Industrial Banner*, 6 June 1913.
16. *Tribune*, 4 November 1905.
17. *Industrial Banner*, 29 November 1912.
18. *Industrial Banner*, August 1904, October 1904, October 1907.
19. *Cotton's Weekly*, 12 June 1913.

20. Ian McKay, *For a Working-Class Culture in Canada: A Selection of Colin McKay's Writings on Sociology and Political Economy, 1897–1939* (St. John's 1996), 6.

21. *Labor News*, 25 October 1918.

22. *Labor Leader*, 13 February 1920.

23. McKay, *For a Working-Class Culture in Canada*, 56, 67; Peter Campbell, *Canadian Marxists and a Search for a Third War* (Montreal and Kingston 1999), 128.

24. Gene Homel, 'James Simpson and the Origins of Canadian Social Democracy', (Ph.D. thesis, University of Toronto, 1978), 66; McKay, *For a Working-Class Culture in Canada*, 6–7.

25. Naylor, *The New Democracy*, 4–5, 16–17; Brushett, 'Labour's Forward Movement', 54.

26. Kealey and Palmer, *Dreaming of What Might Be*, 312.

27. *Cotton's Weekly*, 24 December 1908; *Labor Leader*, 25 May 1928.

28. *Labor Leader*, 26 December 1924.

29. *Industrial Banner*, 19 March 1912, 29 August 1913.

30. *Industrial Banner*, November 1908. Several historians have similarly noted that labour leaders and socialists invoked Christ's example in their fight against societal injustices. See Norman Knowles, 'Christ in the Crowsnest: Religion and the Anglo-Protestant Working Class in the Crowsnest Pass, 1898–1918', in Michael Behiels and Marcel Martel, eds., *Nation, Ideas, Identities* (Don Mills 2000), 67; McKay, *For a Working-Class Culture in Canada*, 6–7; W.W. Knox, 'Religion and the Scottish Labour Movement c.1900–1939', *Journal of Contemporary History*, 23 (1988), 615.

31. *Industrial Banner*, May 1906.

32. *Industrial Banner*, February 1906.

33. The 'single tax', which taxed unearned land values, was an important issue for organized labour well into the twentieth century. See Allen Mills, 'Single Tax, Socialism and the Independent Labour Party of Manitoba: The Political Ideas of F.J. Dixon and S.J. Farmer', *Labour/Le Travailleur*, 5 (Spring 1980), 33–56.

34. *Industrial Banner*, 2 May 1913.

35. *Industrial Banner*, January 1906, October 1911.

36. *Industrial Banner*, October 1911.

37. *Cotton's Weekly*, 25 February 1909.

38. *Cotton's Weekly*, 4 March 1909.

39. *Cotton's Weekly*, 11 March 1909.

40. *Cotton's Weekly*, 13 February 1913. See also Homel, 'James Simpson and the Origins of Canadian Social Democracy', 278.

41. *Industrial Banner*, January 1911.

42. Craig Heron, 'Labourism and the Canadian Working Class', *Labour/Le Travail*, 13 (Spring 1984), 64; Homel, 'James Simpson and the Origins of Canadian Social Democracy', 390.

43. Sharon Meen, 'The Battle for the Sabbath: The Sabbatarian Lobby in Canada, 1890–1912', (Ph.D. thesis, University of British Columbia, 1979), 318; *Industrial Banner*, January 1906, November 1911.

44. Christopher Armstrong and H.V. Nelles, *The Revenge of the Methodist Bicycle Company* (Toronto 1977), 62; Meen, 'The Battle for the Sabbath', 42, 119; Homel, 'James Simpson and the Origins of Canadian Social Democracy', 280.

45. *Industrial Banner*, January 1906.

46. *Industrial Banner*, January 1906, August 1908.

47. The MSRCC was later named the Social Service Council of Canada in 1913. Nancy Christie and Michael Gauvreau, *A Full-Orbed Christianity: The Protestant Churches and Social Welfare in Canada, 1900–1940* (Montreal and Kingston 1996), 198, 208–9.

48. NA, Canadian Council of Churches, Moral and Social Reform Council of Canada Minutes; NA, Canadian Council of Churches, Minutes of the Annual Meeting of the Social Service Council.

49. *Industrial Banner*, 17 January 1919.

50. *Labor News*, 18 October 1918.

51. *Industrial Banner*, 14 March 1919.

52. *Labor News*, 25 October 1918.

53. Armstrong and Nelles, *The Revenge of the Methodist Bicycle Company*, 61–3, 102, 177; Meen, 'The Battle for the Sabbath', 120–1.

54. See Barbara Schrodt, 'Sabbatarianism and Sport in Canadian Society', *Journal of Sport History*, 24 (Spring 1977), 22–33; Homel, 'James Simpson and the Origins of Canadian Social Democracy', 282.

55. Meen, 'The Battle for the Sabbath', 272.

56. *Report of the Proceedings of the Annual Trades and Labor Congress of Canada 1911*, 96.

57. *Report of Proceedings of the Annual Meeting of Trades and Labor Congress of Canada 1915*, 106–7.

58. Homel, 'James Simpson and athe Origins of Democracy', 283–4.

59. See Craig Heron, *Booze: A Distilled History* (Toronto 2003), 219–31; Homel, 'James Simpson and the Origins of Canadian Democracy', 283–93.

60. Douglas Cruikshank and Gregory Kealey, 'Canadian Strike Statistics, 1891–1950', *Labour/Le Travail*, 20 (1987), 85–145; Heron, 'National Contours: Solidarity and Fragmentation', in Craig Heron, ed., *The Workers' Revolt in Canada 1917–1925* (Toronto 1998), 269–70.

61. Tom Mitchell and James Naylor, 'The Prairies: In the Eye of the Storm', in Craig Heron, ed., *The Workers' Revolt in Canada 1917–1925* (Toronto 1998), 177.

62. James Naylor, 'Striking at the Ballot Box', in Heron, ed., *The Workers' Revolt*, 155–63.

63. *Industrial Banner*, 8 July 1921.

64. Christie and Gauvreau, *A Full-Orbed Christianity*, 211–12.

65. Lynne Marks, 'Exploring Religious Diversity in Patterns of Religious Participation', *Historical Methods*, 33 (Fall 2000), 247–54.

# Chapter 6

# The First World War

## READINGS

### Primary Documents

### Historical Interpretations

### Introduction

Commitment to an undertaking such as war is both collective and personal, so it should not be surprising that the First World War had national and regional political repercussions and also deeply affected the families that sent troops overseas and tried to manage at home without their sons, husbands, and fathers. Committing to war did not always bring with it harmony or goodwill, despite the fact that fighting a war would be easiest if longstanding grievances, animosities, or anxieties could be set aside. One of the most important things students of history can do when looking at war and wartime life is to recognize that the deployment of troops, the tactics of battle, and coping with casualties were only part of the experience. First World War participants suffered during and after the war from the shock of living at the centre of battle for months on end, and new approaches to understanding the war continue to yield stories and historical data that testify to a transformation of the entire society along with the more frequently cited transformation of Canada's foreign and domestic relations. On the home front during the First World War, the struggle to keep Canadians enlisting and producing highlighted ongoing divisions. One of these, the gulf between Quebec and English-speaking Canada, became wider over the issue of conscription, and is illustrated by our primary sources. Henri Bourassa was to deliver the speech presented here late in 1914, a time of relative optimism about the war, before Canadians had heard much about the early fighting. Bourassa questions Canada's participation in the war, urging his audience to think critically about leaping headlong into the conflict and scolding the Canadian government for putting out a special call to French speakers. Prime Minister Borden's speech, although not presented as a direct response to Bourassa, shows he was convinced of the righteousness of war against Germany and its allies, and did not wish to acknowledge that there was much difference of opinion about war, either within Canada or the Empire. The secondary works here deal with two widely separated aspects of wartime life. Tim Cook brings the question of underage soldiers into focus, examining the reasons the young men may have joined (not always patriotic), and showing how Canada's need for soldiers could trump concern for the innocence of youth. In Tarah Brookfield's article, we see campaigners for women's suffrage both elated and troubled by the achievement of a limited vote for female relatives of men on active service. Wartime could bring the agenda of the state together with those who had been working for decades to overcome resistance to change, and it could also fragment a formerly united women's organization. The emergency of war rearranged the priorities of families, clubs, and the larger society as the threat of the external enemy prompted stark choices in the military and at home.

# QUESTIONS FOR CONSIDERATION

1.  What were Bourassa's main objections to the way the First World War was being 'sold' to Canadians in various parts of the country?
2.  Borden pointed to Germany's nineteenth-century history to justify Canada's participation in the war? Why?
3.  What seems to be the main social or cultural factors that motivated Canada to increase its participation in the war?
4.  How do you account for the way that the Montreal Council of Women's president was treated?
5.  What were some of the forces pushing adolescents to enlist?

# SUGGESTIONS FOR FURTHER READING

Tim Cook, *At the Sharp End: Canadians Fighting the Great War, 1914–1918* (Toronto: Viking Canada, 2007).

Sandra Gwyn, *Tapestry of War: A Private View of Canadians in the Great War* (Toronto: HarperCollins, 1992).

Geoffrey Hayes, Andrew Iarocci, and Mike Bechthold, eds., *Vimy Ridge: A Canadian Reassessment* (Waterloo: Wilfrid Laurier University Press, 2007).

Gregory S. Kealey, 'State Repression of Labour and the Left in Canada, 1914–1920: The Impact of the First World War', *Canadian Historical Review* 73(3) (1992): 281–314.

David Mackenzie, eds., *Canada and the First World War: Essays in Honour of Robert Craig Brown* (Toronto: University of Toronto Press, 2005).

Susan Mann, *Margaret Macdonald: Imperial Daughter* (Montreal and Kingston: McGill-Queen's University Press, 2005).

Desmond Morton, *Fight or Pay: Soldiers' Families in the Great War* (Vancouver: UBC Press, 2004).

Desmond Morton, *When Your Number's Up: The Canadian Soldier in the First World War* (Toronto: Random House, 1993).

Robert Rutherdale, *Hometown Horizons: Local Responses to Canada's Great War* (Vancouver: UBC Press, 2004).

Jonathan F. Vance, *Death So Noble: Memory, Meaning, and the First World War* (Vancouver: UBC Press, 1997).

# PRIMARY DOCUMENTS

1   From Henri Bourassa, 'The Duty of Canada at the Present Hour: An Address Meant to Be Delivered at Ottawa in November and December 1914, but Twice Suppressed in the Name of "Loyalty and Patriotism"', Montreal, January 1915.

Canada, an Anglo-French community, bound to Great Britain and France by a thousand ties, ethnical, social, intellectual and economic, has a vital interest in the preservation of France and Britain, in the maintenance of their prestige, power and action in the world. It is therefore the national duty of Canada to contribute in the measure of her resources and by such means of action as she may command, to the success and above all to the *endurance* of the combined efforts of France and Great Britain. But if we want our contribution to be effective, if we mean to keep up the effort, we must face with clearsighted resoluteness the grim realities of the situation; we must calculate the exact measure of our means of action, and secure first the internal safety of Canada, before we attempt to settle the affairs of the world.

Whether Canada has or has not a strict obligation to help, directly or indirectly, the cause of France and England, one fact is indisputable: the effects of this tremendous conflict will be deeply felt in Canada as in the rest of the world. It will be particularly disastrous in Canada on account of certain local and accidental causes: intense immigration in late years, exclusive dependence upon British capital, extravagant speculation, excessive borrowings by public bodies and individuals, etc., etc. Canadians are just on the point of realising how poor Canada is, financially speaking. They are just beginning to perceive that they have been living extravagantly on borrowed money, which they are called upon to pay back at the very moment they are unable to do it. The crushing weight of the burden will be increased in proportion to our direct contribution to the war: the larger that contribution the greater the strain upon our meagre financial resources, not to speak of the stoppage of our industries and the weakening of our military forces, which may be needed to preserve internal peace.

If a general collapse is to be avoided, these aspects of the situation call for the immediate attention and co-operation of all men of good will. And they must be viewed primarily from the point of Canada's interests.

## CANADA FIRST

To some, the Empire is all and every thing; others think of France only; another category, logical but narrow in their Canadian exclusiveness, see nothing beyond the borders of Canada: they seem to ignore our most conspicuous world's responsibilities.

These various feelings indicate a singular absence of a truly national patriotism. They show a marked contrast with that strong and practical sentiment which binds in one solid mass the people of other countries, the moment the vital interests of the nation are at stake. Since the outbreak of the war, the country has been flooded with 'patriotic' speeches and writings; but those words have been followed with very few deeds for the good of Canada.

This marks all the difference between the thoughtful action of sovereign peoples, masters of their destinies, conscious of their responsibilities, and the thoughtlessness of a child-nation, deprived of international status, unable to measure the consequences of its actions and even to foresee the repercussions of the movements of other nations, including that from which it depends.

Everyone speaks of the duties of Canada to Great Britain or France. Who has thought of the duties of Canada to herself?

It may be objected that it is too late to consider the question: the parliament and people of Canada have decided upon it, emphatically and unanimously; the active participation of Canada in the European war is settled; to pursue that participation with full strength and celerity is all that remains to be done.

The answer to that objection is that it is never too late for nations or individuals to think of the consequences of their actions.

We are yet at the beginning of the war. If, as generally asserted and as decreed by parliament with apparent unanimity, Canada is bound to share actively in this war, it is assuredly the duty of the Canadian government to make our participation as efficient as possible, and to minimise the grave effects of that participation upon the economic and social life of the country.

It is also the duty of all citizens to help the government with such advice and information as may guide its movements. In all national crises, the government is not to be considered as a mere group of politicians of doubtful or diverse ability, temporarily invested with authority. The men in office represent the power of the nation. They ought to be enlightened, informed and advised. They must even be supported till they are guilty of betrayal. National accord demands the adjournment of party quarrels and acrimonious discussions; it does not however impose silence in face of danger, nor complicity in any crime or error; nor does it call for any sacrifice of principle.

## ECONOMIC ASPECTS OF THE WAR

When a country means to make war, or to share in war, the first duty of its rulers is to take the necessary steps to keep up the economic life of the country. 'Battles are won with pounds sterling as much as with bullets', as was very truly said by the genial Chancellor of the Exchequer. That they are won with wheat sheaves still, more than with gold, he might well have added,— had he not meant, of course, that with her enormous wealth and reserve of gold, Great Britain is well able to purchase corn and other foodstuffs.

There is something ludicrous and painful at the same time in contrasting the ineffectiveness of war preparation in Canada with the practical and effective methods followed in the countries of Europe.

In France and England,—not to speak of Germany where it was carried to the point of perfection—, no single regiment was put on foot, no man-of-war despatched for action, before the most elaborate and effective measures had been adopted and put into execution in order to maintain the credit of the country and its financial institutions, to provide for the storing of foodstuffs, to prevent the cornering of food and the rise of prices, to keep up the trade and industries of the country, and even to profit by the exclusion of German trade from foreign markets.

In this peaceful, mercantile and rural community, apart from a few measures of finance, nothing has been done except a tremendous display of wordy patriotism, with a view to enlisting as many men as possible, fit or unfit for warfare.

The determination of the Canadian Government, as enunciated in Winnipeg by the Solicitor General, is to bankrupt Canada to save the Empire. Considering that practically all the creditors of Canada are London bankers, and that the British government is most anxious to maintain the credit of the United Kingdom, the execution of that patriotic program would hardly contribute to the strength, glory and prestige of the Empire.

[ . . . ]

To keep up the credit and the prosperity of Canada, first, for the sake of Canada, and, secondly, for the benefit of Great Britain and her allies, ought to be the main object of every level headed and truly patriotic Canadian.

It is but a few weeks since one of the most authoritative London journals, the *Westminster Gazette*, was obliged to remind us that we could render better service to the Motherland and the Empire by growing wheat than by raising soldiers.

In the first weeks of the war, one of the most thoughtful and practical statesmen of the Empire, Lord Milner, warned Great Britain, the British Empire, and the world at large, of the dire menace of famine, which is sure to follow in the footsteps of war.

[ . . . ]

## 'GET BACK TO THE LAND!'

'Get back to the Land!' Such is the timely and pressing advice given by many patriotic politicians and publicists, though in no greater hurry to go and till the soil than they are of shouldering their muskets for war, in spite of their tremendous efforts to induce other people to enlist.

The advice is excellent; but if it is to be followed by any large number of unemployed city dwellers, it requires something more than verbal commendations. In so far as it applies to the great rural provinces west of Lake Superior, where the production of wheat could be increased on the largest scale, the situation has been aptly illustrated in a cartoon published in the *Grain Growers' Guide*. One unfortunate city man, attracted by the cry: 'Get back to the Land!' starts in search of a farm lot. He climbs to the top of a telegraph post along the track of the Canadian Pacific Railway. As far as his sight can reach, he is unable to find one single foot of free land. On each lot is planted a post with a sign: '*Canadian Pacific Railway Lands*',—'*Hudson's Bay Company Lands*' ,'*Canadian Northern Railway Lands*'—and the whole series of grabbing firms and so-called Colonisation Societies, created during the last quarter of a century by our politicians, much to their own profit. At the foot of the telegraph post, a patriotic cur yaps and yelps to its heart's content: '*Get back to the Land!*'

[ . . . ]

## UNEMPLOYMENT AND FOOD PRODUCTION

If the government and parliament are sincere in their wish to help Great Britain, France and Belgium, if they really want to bring our people *back to the land*, to diminish unemployment and misery, and stimulate the production of food, they have a clear duty to perform: let them put the State, temporarily at least, and without disbursement, in possession of a portion of the immense waste lands cornered by the CPR, the CNR, the Hudson's Bay Company and the multitude of real estate companies, most of which include among their directors, shareholders and profit grabbers, a large portion of our *patriotic* statesmen, politicians and publicists. That being done, efficient and strong measures should be adopted to enlist and organise the 'civil army'. This was the first care of the Patriotic Committee in France; it was immediately followed with practical action and fruitful results. The unemployed of our large cities should be enrolled and put in active service on the land. That army should be equipped with building material and farm implements *made in Canada*, with horses and cattle, seed, etc. Naturally, it cannot be hoped that this work could be accomplished without a certain waste of money and boodle,—though less, I think, than in the raising of an army; for, in military organisation, the exigencies of 'loyalty' and 'patriotism' forbid any inquiry into, or the slightest comment upon, the profitable operations performed under shelter of devotion to the Empire.

Such or similar measures of practical patriotism should have been taken the very first day war was declared, whether Canada participated in it or not. They have been rendered more imperative on account of the enormous expenditure connected with our participation, and the consequent increase of the economic disturbance of the country. Were they adopted immediately, in spite of the deplorable loss of so many weeks of precious time, numerous and fruitful results would accrue.

## THE RESULTS

First, the production of food being largely increased, both the consumers of Canada and those of the allied nations would be partially protected against the frightful inflation of prices which is bound to take place within a few months.

Last year, the government and parliament thought it necessary to create a Commission of enquiry in order to ascertain the cause of the then growing cost of living. Is nothing to be done when the people of this country are face to face with the certainty of a much higher cost synchronizing with general stagnation in business, unemployment of labour and financial stringency?

The second good result of these measures would be the decongesting of large centres. The burden upon municipal exchequers and private charity would be materially alleviated. Thousands of unproductive consumers, threatened with hunger and misery, an easy prey to the temptations of debauchery and disorder, would be turned into active and contented producers. Let there be no delusion: if nothing is done in that sense, there will be riots in more than one Canadian city, before one year or even six months are over.

A third result would be to stimulate several industries, now at a standstill.

The construction of cottages, barns and stables would require building material of various sorts: timber, lumber, bricks, cement, corrugated or galvanised iron-sheeting, etc., etc. Most of those articles would come from our soil and forests, and pass through the various manipulating processes of our factories. Before they were used by the rural producer, their extraction and fabrication would have given bread to the woodman, the brickmaker and the factory labourer; our carrying trade would be enhanced by their transportation.

Those farm implements, shovels, picks, axes, etc., would be the output of our factories.

In August last, the Massey-Harris firm, excluded from its vast European markets, temporarily threw out of employment 5,000 Canadian employees and labourers. If the Federal government, with the help and co-operation of the governments of Alberta, Saskatchewan and Manitoba, undertook to stock five, ten or fifteen thousand new farms the farm implement factories could keep running during the whole winter and save from misery thousands of Canadian men, women and children.

And what about the permanent and ultimate result? By the placement, in the midst of the virgin prairie, of ten or fifteen thousand new homesteads, the State expenditure would be eventually paid back a hundredfold. This would be true national colonisation, far more useful than the wholesale import of foreign immigrants, carried on at a very high cost for the last fifteen years. A similar effort could be attempted on a smaller scale, in their respective spheres of action, by the governments of Ontario, Quebec, New Brunswick and British Columbia, where vast stretches of land could be opened to settlement.

[ . . . ]

## 'KEEP THE FACTORIES RUNNING'

In order to face the grave situation confronting the country, another series of practical measures should have been devised and could yet be adopted with a view to keeping up industrial production and fostering the export of manufactured goods. Naturally, to be fruitful, such measures require the active co-operation of public powers and leaders in finance, industry and trade. In this respect, as in the matter of agricultural production, there has been much talk but very little action. Just as the employed were advised to get back to the land without anything being done to give them land and help them in putting those lands in a state of production, likewise, our talking economists have limited their activities to empty words: *'Capitalists, keep your factories running'*—*'Consumers, curtail your expenses, and buy nothing but home-made goods'*. Very good mottoes, no doubt; but the pious and patriotic warning to be frugal and buy nothing but home-made goods, is singularly weakened by the knowledge that the Canadian volunteers were supplied, at the expense of Canada, with razors made in Germany and purchased at a cost considerably higher than the retail price before the war!

As to the demand that factories be kept running, it must not be forgotten that factories cannot be operated with patriotic expostulations: manufacturers need money as well as raw materials; they need also a consuming market for their goods, and means of transportation to reach those markets.

[ . . . ]

## THE NUMBER OF MEN

As to the number of men, it is more than doubtful if the Canadian government acted wisely in pledging themselves to send to the front one, and perhaps two or three hundred thousand men. Such an effort surpasses, in proportion, what is being done by Great Britain herself. In his parliamentary statement of the 17th of September, Lord Kitchener declared that the total number of British forces then at the front was 'rather more than six divisions of infantry and two divisions of cavalry'. That was equivalent to about eighty-five thousand men; let us say one hundred thousand.

If Canada sends 100,000 men, out of a population of 8,000,000, the United Kingdom, with its 46,500,000 people should keep at least 600,000 men at the front. This is precisely double the figure which Lord Kitchener, on the 25th of August, indicated as the total to be reached the month of February or March.

What are the available military resources of the United Kingdom?

Before the war broke out, the Regular Army stationed in the British Isles counted in round numbers 300,000 men; the Territorial, a trifle less. In his last speech in the House, on the 16th of November, Mr. Asquith declared that 700,000 new recruits had joined the Regulars, and 300,000, the Territorials. This would place the total land forces of the United Kingdom at nearly 1,600,000 men, out of which less than 15 per cent are fighting at present on the battlefields of Europe.

[ . . . ]

## THE DUTY OF 'FRENCH CANADA'

With regard to the decision of parliament to bring Canada into this war, I have little to say at present, except this, that the question should never have been placed on the ground of races.

To make a direct and special appeal to the French Canadians, because French and English are fighting side by side in Europe, is to pave the way to most dangerous possibilities. If the French Canadians are led to believe that they have a special duty to perform, because of the casual co-operation of their two 'motherlands',—as England and France are now called in the Province of Quebec—where will they be the day England is again the enemy of France, as she has been during seven centuries, as she was yet in the days of Fashoda?

If this unfortunate appeal to racial feelings is persisted in, let it be done at least with something akin to truth and justice.

All sorts of nasty comments have been passed upon the small proportion of French Canadians enlisted at Val Cartier. If this and all future Canadian contingents are to be classified by races and nationalities, a distinction should be established, not only between French and English-speaking volunteers, but also between Canadian-born and British-born. If all British-born soldiers were counted out from the first contingent, it would be found that French-speaking Canadians enlisted in larger proportion than English-speaking Canadians. Out of less than 6,000 Canadian-born recruits, over, 2,400 were French. If English Canada is to be credited with all the English-speaking soldiers gone from Canada, then French Canada has the right to count to her credit all the Frenchmen and Belgians, residents of Canada, who have joined their colours or enlisted in their native lands. They are Canadians, just as much as the newcomers from the British Isles. It may be objected that, under the military laws of France, all Frenchmen living in Canada were *obliged* to go and serve. But apart from the fact that those laws could not reach them here, the objection has no value in the mouth of those Imperialists who claim that all Canadians have a strict duty to participate in this war.

Whatever the duty of Canada in this grave contingency, that duty commands the whole of the Canadian people, irrespective of race, creed or language.

## CONSTITUTIONAL ASPECT

Another point of great importance has been raised, in connection with Canada's participation in the war. It has been stated, in Parliament and out of it, that Canada, as part of the British Empire, is in duty bound to participate actively in every conflict in which Great Britain may be drawn.

That doctrine is contrary to all traditions, to the basic principals upon which rests our constitution, to the long standing agreement between the motherland and her self-governing colonies.

Canada, as a mere irresponsible dependency of Great Britain, has no moral or constitutional *obligation*, nor any *immediate interest* in the present war.

Great Britain has entered the conflict of her own free will, in consequence of her entanglements in the international situation. She has framed her policy and decided her action with a sole view to her own interests, without consulting her colonies or considering in any respect their peculiar situation and local interests.

The territory of Canada is not exposed to the attacks of any of the belligerent nations. An independent Canada would be to-day in absolute safety. The dangers to which her trade may be exposed result from the fact that she is a British possession, subject to the consequences of British policy and the risks of a military intervention decided by the Imperial government upon their exclusive authority and responsibility. It is therefore the duty of Britain to defend Canada and not the duty of Canada to defend Britain. Such was the doctrine laid down in 1854, in 1862, in 1871, by Sir John A. Macdonald, Sir George Cartier, Sir Alexander Campbell. It still holds good, in law and in fact.

Besides, in protecting the territory and trade of her colonies, Great Britain makes sure of her own subsistence.

2    Robert Laird Borden, 'Canada Will Answer the Call: Sir Robert Borden's Inspiring War-Message to the Canadian People: Speech Delivered at Toronto, Dec. 5th, 1914', Ottawa: Federal Press Agency, [1914?].

Mr Chairman and Gentlemen,—

Today there is but one thought in our hearts, and it is fitting that I should speak to you of the appalling struggle which has been forced upon our Empire. I say forced upon us, because I am convinced that no nation ever desired peace more sincerely than the nations which compose the British Empire; that no statesmen ever wrought more to avoid war than the statesmen of Great Britain in the weeks which immediately preceded the conflict.

There is not time, nor is it necessary that I should dwell upon the occurrence which determined the issue. The great events which brought about the establishment and consolidation of the German Empire under Prussian domination are well known to you. Bismarck foreshadowed in a famous phrase the policy of the future. 'The great questions are to be settled', he said in 1862, 'not by speeches and majority resolutions, but by blood and iron'. Then came, in quick succession, the war against Denmark in 1864, the downfall of Austria in 1866, and the overthrow of France in 1870. The policy of blood and iron seemed to consummate the realization of that which has been the dream of Germany for centuries. Germany became an Empire; the King of Prussia became its Emperor. The military spirit of Prussia dominated German thought and German ideals. The intoxication of victory aided by a propaganda preached to every child and every young man by the foremost thinkers of Germany imposed on its people an ideal and ambition which included the dominance of Europe, and, indeed, of the world.

## INSIDIOUS TEACHING OF THE WAR ADVOCATES

The world has only recently come to realize the astonishing teaching to which the German people have listened for the last half century. Among many others, Treitschke, a great professor of history, whose influence upon the young men of Germany cannot be over-estimated, and Bernhardi, his disciple, have preached the religion of valour and might. War has been glorified as a solemn duty for the cause of national development. They proclaimed that the State is not only justified, but bound to put aside all obligations and to disregard all treaties insofar as they may conflict with its highest interest.

'War', said Bernhardi, 'is in itself a good thing. It is a biological necessity of the first importance. . . . War is the greatest factor in the furtherance of culture and power; efforts to secure peace are extraordinarily detrimental as soon as they influence politics. . . . Efforts directed toward the abolition of war are not only foolish, but absolutely immoral, and must be stigmatized as unworthy of the human race. . . . Courts of arbitration are a pernicious delusion. The whole idea represents a presumptuous encroachment on natural laws of development which can only lead to the most disastrous consequences for humanity generally. . . . The maintenance of peace never can be or may be the goal of a policy. . . . Efforts for peace would, if they attained their goal, lead to degeneration. . . . Huge armaments are in themselves desirable. They are the most necessary precondition of our national health'.

## GERMANY HAS LONG BEEN A WORLD-MENACE

The profound influence of this teaching upon the German people may be realized from their unquestioning support of the enormous increase in their military and naval forces. Beyond question Germany is the greatest military power in the world. Without any such need as makes a great fleet imperatively necessary to ensure the safety and even the existence of the British Empire, she has built up in ships, personnel, dockyards, and all other essentials a powerful navy designed to challenge conclusions with that of Great Britain. What ambitions would not be open to Germany, what tribute could she not exact, if dominating Europe with her army she could wage a successful naval campaign against Britain.

Within the past ten years the peace of Europe has been threatened by Germany on no less than three occasions. In 1905 France, at her dictation, was obliged to dismiss her Foreign Minister. In 1909 Germany shook her mailed fist and compelled Russia to bow to her will. In 1911, as the history of the Agadir incident recalls, she again attempted to coerce and humiliate France, and the situation was saved only by the interposition of Great Britain. Germany receded on that occasion from her first pretensions, but only to abide her time, which came in 1914.

## CANADA'S OFFER MADE BEFORE WAR WAS DECLARED

The military autocracy of Germany have taught their people for more than twenty years that the British Empire stood chiefly in the path of German expansion, and that war was inevitable. No one could predict the exact occasion which would be seized but no one could doubt the intention of the Prussian militarists. There was the lesson of Denmark and Austria and France. In the end the storm broke suddenly and the country was confronted with responsibilities greater than those which it had ever faced. The situation demanded action; it demanded immediate and unhesitating action beyond the authorization of the law as it then stood; it was impossible for the Government to wait, and by Order-In-Council we promulgated necessary measures in advance of the meeting of Parliament. The people of Canada loyally acquiesced in these measures, and our course has been ratified by the necessary legislative sanction. On the first of August I sent to the British Government a secret telegram announcing Canada's desire to send an expeditionary force if war should ensue. The offer was not accepted until the 6th of August, but in the meantime steps in anticipation were taken and the raising and equipment of troops for such a force was authorized. On the 7th of August the suggested composition of the force was received from the British authorities, and was immediately sanctioned by Order-in-Council.

Recruiting in the meantime had already commenced, and on the 6th of August the preparation of the Valcartier Camp was begun. I visited that camp four weeks from the day on which work commenced, and I am proud that we possess in Canada the ability to achieve within so limited a period all that was accomplished within that month. [ . . . ]

## TREMENDOUS WORK OF ORGANIZATION

I venture the assertion that the organization and arrangements of Valcartier Camp have not been excelled in any part of our Empire since the commencement of this war. It is unnecessary to describe in detail all the equipment, arms, accoutrements and other necessaries furnished. To equip the force sent forward and to make some provision for future contingents 290,000 pairs of boots and shoes have been provided; 100,000 forage caps, 90,000 great coats, 240,000 jackets and sweaters of various types, 235,000 pairs of trousers, 70,000 rifles, 70,000 bayonets, 80,000 oil bottles, 70,000 water bottles, 95,000 sets of valise equipment, and so on in like proportion over a list of sixty-six different articles. With the first expeditionary force we sent to Great Britain 21 thirteen-pounder quick-firing guns, 96 eighteen-pounder quick-firing guns, 10 breach-loading sixty-pounder guns, a large number of machine guns, motor lorries, transport wagons and vast quantities of ammunition. The force was ready for embarkation within six weeks from the outbreak of war, and could have been then despatched if arrangements for escort had been immediately possible. You, perhaps, do not realize how great an undertaking it was for a non-military country to assemble, organize, train, equip and despatch so large a force within that brief period. It is, I believe, the largest military force that ever crossed the Atlantic at one time. In the great Armada, which threatened the shores of Great Britain three centuries ago, there were less than 20,000 soldiers. The force which we have sent across the Atlantic is nearly 50 per cent greater than the total number of British troops under Wellington's command at Waterloo.

## MUST BE HIGHLY TRAINED AND SEASONED

It would be not only useless, but unjust and cruel as well, to send untrained men to the front against highly trained and seasoned troops. They must also be hardened by exercise in the duties of a soldier's life until their physical condition will enable them to endure the hardships of active service. Thus our troops are receiving in Great Britain the same tests of training and of exercise which are prescribed for the volunteer army of the Mother Country. That they will acquit themselves worthily no one can doubt who saw them at Valcartier. In physique, in spirit, in courage, and in all qualities that are necessary for the soldier they will be found second to none.

If the training of a soldier is important, the training, the skill, and the experience of the men who command them are even more essential and imperative. The officers of the Canadian militia have all the necessary qualities that could be desired. They have given ungrudgingly of their time and their energy to fit themselves as far as possible for the duties of active service. But for them even more than for the men the training and experience at Valcartier and on Salisbury Plain are not only invaluable, but absolutely essential before they lead their men into action. In this grim struggle our forces will face the most highly organized military machine in the world.

## SECOND CONTINGENT BEING PREPARED NOW

I have spoken of what Canada has done. The call of duty has not fallen upon unheeding ears in this country. East and west, every province and practically every community has responded with an ardour and spirit which emphasizes the strength of the ties that bind together the Dominions of this Empire. When the first contingent sailed from Canada we immediately announced that another would follow. During the delay which ensued before the War Office, in pressure of multitudinous affairs, could suggest its composition, it was announced that in addition to 8,000 men engaged in garrison and outpost duty, we would enlist and train 30,000 men; and that from these a second contingent would be despatched as soon as the necessary arms and equipment could be provided and as soon as the War Office would be prepared to receive them. The number under training has recently been increased to 50,000 men and it is arranged that as soon as each contingent goes forward a corresponding number of men will be enlisted to take its place. This will proceed regularly and continuously until peace is achieved, or until we are satisfied that no more men are needed. Our forces under arms in Canada and abroad will soon exceed 100,000 men. That number has frequently been mentioned in the press. In this war which we are waging against the most powerful military organization the world ever knew, I prefer to name no figure. If the preservation of our Empire demands twice or thrice that number, we shall ask for them, and I know that Canada will answer the call. But remember that men cannot be sent forward more rapidly than the British authorities are prepared to receive them and to undertake their final training. Moreover, we have not in Canada, as in countries organized on a military basis, great stores of equipment, arms, accoutrements, ammunition and guns. These must be provided, and they are being provided with all possible expedition. Both here and in Great Britain these requisites are lacking upon the tremendous scale which is now necessary. Without thorough training, without arms, equipment and all the essentials of warlike preparation, men sent into this awful maelstrom of war are but an incubus and danger rather than an aid.

## ONLY ONE ISSUE, BUT NOT A SPEEDY ONE

There can be but one issue to this war, but do not expect that it will be a speedy issue. I have reason to know that the results hitherto attained have been all that were anticipated by the Allies; but so far as can be foreseen there is a long struggle before us.

The justice of the Allies' cause is generally understood and recognized among our kinsmen in the great neighbouring nation, and we are proud of their sympathy. [ . . . ] The people of this Dominion are eager and determined to take their part in a struggle which involves the destiny of their Empire, and, indeed, its very existence. They are quite prepared and willing to assume all responsibilities which that action involves and they have reasonable confidence in Canada's ability to defend her territory.

[ . . . ]

## UNITY OF THE EMPIRE IS WELL DEMONSTRATED

And this war has demonstrated the essential unity of the Empire. When the book is closed and the story has been told, we shall at least owe that to the Kaiser. It was to fall asunder as soon as he girded on his shining armour. But instead it has become tense with unity and instinct with life and action. Our decadent race was to flee in terror before his victorious troops, but the plains of Belgium and France tell no story of decadence. The history of British arms contains no annals more glorious. It is our hope and our confidence that Canada's record will not be less worthy.

In the bitterness of this struggle let us not forget that the world owes much to German thought, endeavour, and achievement in science, literature, the arts and every other sphere of useful human activity. I do not doubt that the German people, misled as to the supposed designs of Great Britain, impressed for the time being by the Prussian military spirit, and not truly comprehending the real causes of the conflict, are behind their Government in this war. Nevertheless, it is in truth a war waged against the military oligarchy which controls the Government of Germany. The defeat of that military autocracy means much for the world, but it means even more for Germany herself. Freed from its dominance and inspired by truer ideals, the German people will attain a higher national greatness then before.

## CANADA BELIEVES THAT BRITAIN'S CAUSE IS JUST

Canada is united in the strong conviction that our cause is just and in an unflinching determination to make it triumphant. This appalling conflict was not of Britain's seeking. Having entered upon it, there is but one duty, to stand firmly united in an inflexible resolve to force it to a victorious and honourable conclusion. Reverses may come, but they must only inspire us with a deeper courage and greater determination. Our fortitude and our endurance must equal all demands that the future shall make upon us. All that our fathers fought for and achieved; all that we have inherited and accomplished, our institutions and liberties, our destiny as a nation, the existence of our Empire, all are at stake in this contest. The resolution, the determination, the self-reliance which never failed Canada in the stress and trials of the past will assuredly not fail her now.

## HISTORICAL INTERPRETATIONS

3   From Tim Cook, '"He Was Determined to Go": Underage Soldiers in the Canadian Expeditionary Force', *Social History* 41(81) (2008): 41–74.

Thousands of adolescents fought with the Canadian Expeditionary Force (CEF) during the Great War. Historians have overlooked their service because it has been difficult to distinguish them from their older comrades, since most of these young soldiers lied about their age in order to enlist. A sense of adventure, peer pressure, and fierce patriotism impelled young and old to serve. Most underage soldiers who enlisted were 16 or 17 (and later 18 when age requirements were raised to 19), but at least one cheeky lad enlisted at only 10 years old, and a 12-year-old made it to the trenches.[1]

As many as 20,000 underage soldiers served overseas.[2] Canadians under the age of 19 constituted an important segment of the population during the Great War, one of the most traumatic experiences in Canadian history, but their history remains largely unknown.[3] Studying the reaction of these soldiers to the war effort and their interaction with parents, society, and the military forces reveals that young Canadians were approvingly incorporated into and became a significant part of Canada's war effort.

## ENLISTMENT

The British and Canadian military had a long history of accepting into the ranks a small number of boy soldiers and sailors in apprenticeship roles, often as buglers, drummers, and young sailors. These boy soldiers and sailors, some as young as 10 or 12, were taken on strength with the regiment or ship, where they were part of the regimental family, eating, serving, and sleeping in the same barracks. Within the family officers tended to take a paternal attitude to these boys, and educational activities were offered or foisted on them to improve their lot in life.[4] Strict discipline and corresponding punishment for flouting regulations were also a part of their service in the rigid hierarchy of military service.[5] They were also in harm's way, with boy sailors fulfilling a variety of roles on a ship and drummer boys leading men into battle.

In Canada, the King's Regulations and Orders for the Canadian militia specified that boys of 'good character' between the ages of 13 and 18 could be enlisted as bandsmen, drummers, or buglers.[6] However, since the Canadian permanent force was a mere 3,000 before the war, there were very few boy soldiers, although the various and scattered militia units across the country had no compunction about turning to juveniles to fill their always thin ranks. Still, the vast majority

of the thousands of adolescents who would enlist in the Great War were not pre-war boy soldiers, but chose to serve for a variety of reasons.

To understand the role of serving adolescents in the Great War, one must acknowledge the constructed nature of childhood.[7] For much of the nineteenth century, little thought or worry was given to the emotional life of young people or the necessity of a childhood filled with play and exploration. Childhood was hard and dangerous in working-class families. All children, no matter their class or ethnicity, were sadly acquainted with death in and out of the workplace. Few families escaped the tragedy of losing children or siblings to disease or accident. Education remained a privilege for most, with youngsters often pulled from schools to support the family. Yet these pre-war working boys and adolescents were also toughened by their hardship, and it was not uncommon for them to mobilize in the workplace, demanding greater rights.[8] Despite their age, they were tough customers who eagerly embraced all aspects of their emerging masculinity, smoking, drinking, and fighting in a rough-and-tumble environment.

At the time, there was no accepted classification for what age designated a child or adolescent, although the state—both at the federal and provincial levels—attempted to define young Canadians through the creation of various forms of legislation. Since 1871, legislation had required that students stay in school until the age of 12, but by the decade before the war this had been raised to 14 or 16, depending on province, as well as on city and rural jurisdictions.[9] However, many young people left school before the legislation allowed and were employed in full-time jobs. There was legislation to control youth from flooding the market, both for their health and to defend against a dilution of the workforce, but this, too, was applied differently across the country, no doubt affected by provincial economies.[10] While labour laws varied, delinquent children and adolescents were defined and normalized in the 1908 *Juvenile Delinquents Act*, in the attempt to punish transgressive behaviour by youthful deviants. Under the act, delinquents were classified as between the ages of 7 and 16 (18 in some provinces), but children under 12 were treated more leniently under the law.[11] Thus, in the eyes of probation officers and the courts, adolescents fell somewhere between the ages of 12 and 18. While state actors attempted to define childhood, adolescence, and adulthood, the constructed nature of these classifications was also shaped by region, class, and ethnicity. Most young Canadians were involved in adult activities long before the age of 18. Any attempt to define youth invariably led legislators into contested terrain, although 21 was the required age of adult citizenship.[12]

Since the late nineteenth century, women's groups, educational reformers, and a constellation of reform-minded Canadians had aimed to improve the lot of children's and adolescents' health and spiritual wellbeing, no matter their age.[13] These groups engendered vast improvements in society and helped to shape the nature of childhood by demanding that the state and society recognize the difference between adolescence and adulthood. While many adolescents were rescued from the gutters, some would soon march straight into the trenches.

Canada went to war in August 1914, carried forward by a swell of patriotic excitement. For some boys in menial jobs or back-breaking work, the transition from a brutal, dangerous industrial profession to the military was viewed as a safe move, especially since few expected the war to extend past Christmas. Trading coal dust for healthy marching did not raise the objections of many in society. Soldiers, both young and old, spoke approvingly of having three solid, if monotonous, meals. The $1.10 a day for privates, plus the chance to serve a seemingly noble cause, were also incentives that drew lads from across the country.

Like all Canadians, adolescents had a myriad of reasons to enlist. 'When the war broke out. . . . The country went mad!' recalled Bert Remington, who immediately enlisted at age 18, but with a physical appearance, in his words, of 'five foot nothing and 85 pounds'.[14] Adolescents were just as susceptible to the hyper patriotism of the period, yet, unlike older men, most did not have good jobs or a family to temper the heady thoughts of serving King and country. Added to these factors was the inherent belief by most young people that they were nearly indestructible.[15] Others had pre-war militia training that made them more inclined to serve and fight, and before the war some 40,000 school boys had enrolled in the cadets, an institution accused by critics of militarizing childhood and adolescence.[16]

Even those youth who did not march in khaki or carry the .22 cadet Ross rifle had, for the most part, been raised at home and in school on stories of victorious campaigns that had won Britain her empire. While class mitigated some of the messages, insofar as boys and adolescents of working-class families would likely be engaged in paid work rather than education, much of the popular culture of literature, music, and toys for male children was infused with ideals of manliness. Military service in the imperial ranks caught the imagination of most boys at one time or another. Parades, marches, and flag-waving were all normal activities at school or in the community. When war came, many adolescents were eager to carve out their own heroic future.[17]

Despite the sense of naive adventure and pre-war masculine culture, one cannot discount genuine patriotism and a belief in the widely disseminated liberal ideals underpinning the British war effort. [ . . . ]

Multiple layers of masculinity thus drove adolescents to enlist. [They] ached for honour, sacrifice, and an opportunity to prove [their] manhood. Young boys instantly became men in their own eyes and those of others by signing their names to the legally binding attestation form. A 16-year-old student was treated the same as the 25-year-old baker or the

29-year-old clerk. In moving from short pants to military trousers and puttees, an adolescent moved from being a boy to a man.

This embracing of adulthood began with enlistment. Across the country, hopeful men of all ages made their way to the armouries. While militia orders stipulated that recruits were to be between the ages of 18 and 45, overage and underage Canadians provided fabricated birth dates for official documentation to serve.[18] There was a loophole, however, as adolescents under the age of 18 could enlist if they had a parent's signed letter of consent.

Many parents waived their right to veto their son's choice. Activist and author Nellie McClung was filled with fear and anger when she watched the 'first troops going away. I wondered how their mothers let them go'. But then her son, Jack, who was also there to see the soldiers off, turned to her with expectant eyes, asking, 'Mother, when will I be eighteen?'[19] It was a blow and a realization that the war would affect everyone, but especially the mothers left behind, forced to wait, worry, and watch their eager sons enlist for war. Jack would eventually serve overseas, with McClung's blessing; he survived, although in his mother's eyes he lost his youth on the battlefields of the Western Front.

Jack was lucky; thousands did not return. Percy McClare, who enlisted in April 1915, six weeks after his seventeenth birthday, wrote a pleading letter to his mother asking that she sign the consent form. He had been impressed by a recruiting sergeant who informed McClare 'that the men at the [front] are happy as can be. . . . Said they had a Jolly time. All I need is your concent [sic]'.[20] His mother eventually agreed to his service, as did many parents, who were no doubt pressured by patriotic messages in speeches and posters. As one recruitment poster aimed at the 'Women of Canada' demanded: 'When the War is over and someone asks your husband or your son what he did in the great War, is he to hang his head because you would not let him go?'[21] Many parents did not need such

shaming techniques, as they firmly believed in the war, but it is also clear that some parents allowed their underdeveloped and too-young sons to enlist because they assumed their boys could not possibly be accepted into the ranks of men.[22] Most were soon shocked to find their sons in uniform. McClare served and, as the sergeant noted, was indeed happy in the ranks; but he was killed a month after arriving on the Western Front. Many parents and adolescent soldiers spent what was left of their lives regretting their choices. Young Private Donald Gordon marched with the 8th Battalion and had lied about his age when he enlisted against his parents' wishes. On April 15, 1915, a sniper's bullet took his life. Among his personal possessions was a Bible with the inscription: 'Goodbye, Mother, Forgive me'.[23]

While adolescents showed up at recruiting stations clutching letters of consent, often they were turned down because of their size or unsuitability for soldiering. The age requirement of at least 18 seems to have been used as a guide rather than a rule, however, and no one in the heady patriotic environment of 1914 and 1915 inquired too deeply about the influx of adolescents into the ranks. Perhaps the arbitrary assignment of an age—18 and later 19—seemed at odds with the situation of most adolescents who were out of school and working in the capacity of young adults. Whatever the case, thousands of youths disregarded the rule, which was almost impossible to enforce since few recruits had birth certificates, and no one was required to produce one as proof of age. One should also not discount the prevalence of Canadians who did not know their own birth date. Nonetheless, bluster and brass often allowed many youngsters to elude serious scrutiny during the already inconsistent enlistment process, although parents had the right to pull their underage sons from the forces until the summer of 1915, when this privilege was quietly dropped after a court ruled that the militia had made a pact with a soldier, no matter his age.[24]

Queuing before the recruiting sergeant could be a nerve-wracking exercise. Forty-nine-year-olds with newly dyed hair and 16-year-olds standing erect and sweating under a borrowed jacket and bowler hat watched anxiously as recruiting sergeants jotted down their names and birth dates. Depending on the circumstances of the unit, and especially if it needed more men to hit its quota to go overseas, recruiting sergeants often turned a blind eye to an obviously too-young lad or the deeply lined face of an older man.

Some boys did not know the age requirements and so gave honest responses to the question of their birth date, revealing that they were 16 or 17, or occasionally even younger. One official CEF report noted that underage soldiers who were later questioned about how they got overseas gave consistent responses: these new recruits, when they had given their proper age, were told to 'run around the block, think over [their] age, and come back again'.[25] Most did, offering a birth date that fell within the required age range. Yet most adolescents knew that they had to be 18 or 19 to enlist. A study at the end of the war noted that, when the underage soldiers came forward with their real ages, as indicated on their birth certificates, a comparison with the initial attestation paper revealed that ages had most often been inflated to 19.[26] Another study of these soldiers indicated that the number of recruits who gave their age as 19 was out of proportion to any other age group represented in the British Expeditionary Force, likely because it consisted of several age groups, including those who were 16, 17, and 18.[27]

Not all had their wishes come true. Thomas Raddall, who would later become an eminent Nova Scotia novelist and historian, remembered wearing his first pair of trousers at age 15. Having shed his children's clothes, he walked confidently into a recruiting station. 'Several boys from Chebucto School had [already] done so and gone overseas', he recounted in his memoirs. 'One of our

neighbour's sons had enlisted at sixteen and was killed in France at seventeen. But I was recognized by the recruiting sergeant who knew my father [who would be killed overseas], and he told me bluntly to go back to school'.[28] However, even if a soldier was turned down, since there was no cross-referencing of rejected men, a determined youth could and did move from regiment to regiment in search of one that needed to fill its quota. Rejection for an obstinate youth only meant a trip down the street or re-enlisting on another day, with a different sergeant and under a new name, and it was not uncommon to find soldiers who tried to enlist two or three times before they were accepted. [ . . . ]

The act of enlistment was a two-step process, and being accepted by officers and sergeants did not guarantee service. Recruits still needed to pass a medical examination. The quality of the inspecting medical officers varied at the armouries and depots across the country. Throughout the war, several hundred thousand potential recruits were turned down by medical officers—and this number might have been as high as 40 per cent of all who attempted to enlist.[29] Anything from poor eyesight to flat feet to bad teeth could keep a man out of the service. Age was a factor, but it stopped fewer men than it should have. It was not an easy task to distinguish adolescents from men. A husky farm boy or a lad who had been working at hard labour for years might be in far better shape than a pasty 20-year-old bank clerk. A gangly boy might not stand out, especially in mid-1915 when height requirements were dropped to 5 feet to allow the malnourished and malformed to enlist. [ . . . ]

The medical screening process remained notoriously unreliable throughout the war. A cursory visual inspection of the naked body was a humiliating event: sunken chests were poked, genitals examined, flat feet kneaded, eyesight tested through distance charts.[30] Thomas Rowlett, an underage signaller, enlisted in Nova Scotia with two pals. Both naked friends were asked the same question by the medical officer: 'Are you 19 years old?' Both replied in the affirmative. To the taller one the medical officer nodded; the other he rejected with a dismissive glance.[31] While medical officers were experienced in sizing up a man or boy with a glance and a bit of prodding, this haphazard approach led to regular complaints in England that the weak, too-youthful, and aged were being accepted into the ranks. One diligent medical officer in England was nearly apoplectic about the nature of the recruits by the end of 1915. He lamented that he had examined a tunneller, C.J. Bailey, who had deformed feet, with most of the toes amputated; a J.J. McDonald of the 4th Company, Canadian Engineers, who was missing both of his thumbs; and the 79-year-old W.J. Clements, who had 'advanced arterosclerosis' and was barely able to stand erect.[32]

The problem of keeping unfits and undesirables (as the army in England called them) out of the service eventually rose to epidemic proportions, and by the end of 1916 there was a failed attempt to punish medical officers in Canada by having them pay the $120 cost of returning unfit men across the Atlantic. This was never implemented, as it was seen by military officials in Canada as detrimental to the already strained recruiting effort.[33] More successful was an order from the Overseas Ministry that a second examination be carried out on troops before they stepped off the boats in England.[34] However, this generally did not include the underage soldiers, who were often considered good troops; they would wait in England, training for battle, until the day they came of age. [ . . . ]

Searching letters from desperate parents evoking their rights under the law continued to pluck underage soldiers from their units, however, until the summer of 1915. Roy Macfie, who served with his two brothers, wrote home shortly after arriving in England: 'There are two of the Cook boys from Loring here, and their mother sent to the General and told him that they were underage, and were not to go to the front so I think they will be sent home, they won't like it'.[35] Sapper J.E. Lowe was likely even younger than the Cook brothers, having enlisted at 15 (although, of course, lying on his attestation paper, which gives his age as 18) as a bugler in a pioneer battalion. After six weeks in England, the tough little Lowe, who stood 5 feet, 3 inches but had been a pre-war miner, was sent home.[36]

While an undisclosed number of young Canadians were pulled from the ranks, either because of parents' letters or by officers who now realized that the firing line was not the place for an adolescent, hundreds and then thousands of underage soldiers pleaded and cajoled their way into overseas service. Some openly threatened that, if sent home, they would only sign up again under an assumed name. Many officers relented and allowed the adolescents to continue serving, but others would have none of it, and those under age were put on ships and sent home.

Youth has never liked to be told how to act, and this was especially true for those returned to a country gripped with hyper-patriotism as exhibited through war posters, recruiting sergeants, politicians, and patriotic groups that assaulted every young man with the same message: do your bit. One student at the University of Saskatchewan wrote to his mother that he had been pressured to enlist because the other students 'make you feel like two cents if you don't'.[37] Eminent Canadians roared that 'to live by shirking one's duty is infinitely worse . . . than to die'.[38] Many men, both young and old, would have echoed Armine Norris's statement, 'I enlisted because I hadn't the nerve to stay at home'.[39] Norris was no coward and would be awarded the Military Cross for bravery in battle before being killed during the last months of the war.

The returned patriotic youth did not last long under this pressure. Opportunities were available to fight the 'Hun' from the classroom floor through the writing of vitriolic essays, by throwing their increasing weight behind raising funds through the various patriotic movements, and, towards the end of the war, by working as 'Soldiers of the Soil' to help farmers bring in the crops, but they could not avoid the increasingly aggressive questions and disapproving stares that lumped them together with other perceived slackers. Many re-enlisted, often under assumed names and against their parents' wishes. Enlisting under a false name meant that a soldier was effectively cut off from his loved ones. There would be no letters home, no news of the family, no death benefits should the worst occur. Those at home might never know what had happened to their sons should they fall in battle.

## OVERSEAS

The Canadian Division arrived in France in February 1915 and was joined over the next year and a half by three more divisions to form the Canadian Corps, some 100,000 men strong. From the start, the Canadians soon encountered the harsh subterranean world of the Western Front. Million-man armies constructed vast trench systems in aerially eviscerated farmers' fields. The infantry had to endure rats, lice, and frozen feet in the winter and the same insect and rodent tormentors, as well as flies and thirst, in the summer. All year round there was the constant wastage of the trenches, where men were killed by shell and bullet, sickness and poison gas.

In the firing line, an underage soldier was expected to be a soldier just like his elder mates. Certainly there was no distinction for the other death-dealing weapons that indiscriminately took lives in fearful numbers. Among the ranks, however, underage soldiers sometimes were treated differently by older men who often took younger ones under their wing. Canon Scott recounted the actions of one officer, who told Scott about his encounter with a young lad in his company:

[We] had to hold on, in a trench, hour after hour, under terrific bombardment. [The officer] was sitting in his dugout, expecting every moment to be blown up,

when a young lad came in and asked if he might stay with him. The boy was only eighteen years of age, and his nerve was utterly gone. He came into the dugout, and, like a child clinging to his mother, clasped the officer with his arms. The latter could not be angry with the lad. There was nothing to do at that point but to hold on and wait, so, as he said to me, 'I looked at the boy and thought of his mother, and just leaned down and gave him a kiss. Not long afterward a shell struck the dugout and the boy was killed, and when we returned I had to leave his body there'.[40]

[ . . . ]

In the mud and misery of the front-line trenches, officers often ensured that underage soldiers were excluded from the most dangerous duties like trench-raiding, but there were few safe places at the front. Infantryman William Now remembered that his commanding officer had removed an underage soldier from the front-line trenches to carry water in the rear. One night Private Now trudged toward the forward trenches and passed the young lad's 'two horses lying dead on the cobbles and the cart all smashed up . . . the boy was not to be seen. He had evidently been picked up. I hoped that he had only been wounded and would survive but it was almost too much to expect. I could not see how he could have escaped, except by a miracle. Some Mother's Boy'.[41] While some adolescents were put in 'bomb-proof' jobs in the rear, more often underage soldiers were treated the same as their older companions. [ . . . ]

While some underage soldiers were awarded gallantry medals, including 17-year-old Tommy Ricketts of the Royal Newfoundland Regiment, a Victoria Cross recipient, more often the young soldiers simply did their duty. Herbert McBride recounted that, of the four other soldiers on his machine-gun crew, all were underage. 'Some had enlisted at sixteen and not one of them was of voting age'.[42]

None was a medal winner; nor did any ever crack in battle. All four would be killed by the end of the war. For those who survived, observed Private J.E. Cromwell, a 16-year-old in the No. 2 Construction Battalion, 'You grew up in a hurry'.[43] R.B. Henley of the 42nd Battalion enlisted at 13 years old, was caught and sent home, then re-enlisted. Finally making it to France, he reported, 'I was scared and stayed scared all the time. But a scared soldier lives longer'.[44] He survived, although he was wounded twice in battle.

Young soldiers continued to serve and endure with the help of their mates. The comradeship of the trenches was a key component in constructing and supporting the will to keep fighting through the most dire of circumstances. Not to let down one's companions drove many soldiers to hold on past their limits. It was no different for young soldiers, and perhaps even more important, since there was a desire among most adolescents to live up to the ideals of the masculine soldier. A.E. Fallen, a 17-year-old infantrymen serving with the 52nd Battalion, remembered his first time in the line, standing in mud and slush and wondering to himself, 'I hope to God I can stand this. . . . I would have hated like hell to have cracked up as a kid'.[45] He found the strength to endure, serving through some of the toughest battles of the war.

Issues of masculinity remained important for the young soldiers. There were norms and regulations to follow in emulating the masculine ideals. Young soldiers did not like to stand out as anything other than a companion in the ranks. Some obviously overcompensated. Nineteen-year-old Private John Lynch recounted that he and other young soldiers 'wanted to impress the world with their toughness. We cursed louder, drank harder and behaved in a very boisterous manner, putting on a front for the veterans of the outfit, many of whom were older than our fathers'.[46] While service conferred adulthood on young men, sometimes they felt the need to prove it. But the army saw no distinction and paid young lads as much as older men. As well, the young soldiers received the same rights and privileges in the trenches. The daily issue of rum, in itself a tool for reinforcing discipline, hierarchy, and masculinity, was not denied to underage soldiers. Signaller William Ogilvie, who had enlisted at the age of 17 from Lakefield, Ontario, testified, 'We juniors learned the ropes from our older and more experienced comrades and though we younger ones were far from serious drinkers, we were now caught up by the challenge'.[47] The act of drinking was often understood to be one of the distinguishing marks between men and boys. Army-issued rum was powerful, syrupy, over-strength spirit that burned, as one soldier remarked, as if 'he'd swallowed a red-hot poker'.[48] After the first few sputtering attempts, an infantryman learned to hold his rum, and these young soldiers soon measured up to the group's expectations.

While rum was not withheld, neither was enfranchisement. 'We had scores of fellows who had not yet reached voting age. We knew at least two who celebrated their sixteenth birthdays in France', remarked Fred Noyes, a stretcher-bearer. 'Many gave "official" ages which wouldn't have stood the test if the authorities had cared to investigate. . . . A remarkable feature of the election was the voting of our teen-old youngsters'.[49] As well, young soldiers were sometimes elevated in rank above their older peers. Although it appears uncommon, there were cases like Corporal J.G. Baker of the 15th Battalion, who, at the age of 17, would have been in charge of a dozen men, all likely older.[50] John Hensley enlisted at the age of 16 in Halifax, serving through two years of warfare before he was killed at Passchendaele at the age of 18. During that time, he had risen to the rank of captain, responsible at times for 200 men in his company.

Of course, not all young soldiers survived the emotional and mental rigours of the trenches. Lieutenant William Gray recounted watching one adolescent come unstrung during a heavy drumfire bombardment: 'He laughed rather hysterically and babbled incoherently. Suddenly he jumped up, climbed into the open, his sole thought to get away but there, a scant hundred yards, we saw him fall'.[51] While anecdotal evidence suggests that young soldiers often had a better chance of withstanding the psychological pressures of war, many soldiers eventually broke under the prolonged stress. One report on British courts martial revealed the shocking statistic that 32 minors had been executed during the war, and that 10 of them had used shell shock as a defence for why they had deserted from the front.[52] None of the 25 Canadians executed was underage, but for all soldiers, from the young in the prime of their lives to the ancient 39ers (the nickname for older men who had lied about their age), enduring the strain of war depended on the man, the circumstances, and the ability to draw on those internal and external resources.[53]

With the constant lack of sleep, the never-ending agony of scratching at lice, and the threat of dismemberment by shell fire, many soldiers eventually began to pray for their release from the front lines. Unlike older soldiers, however, underage ones had an escape route, since by 1916 trench rumours had swirled through the ranks passing on valuable information that underage soldiers could reveal their age and be pulled from the line. Corporal Harry Hillyer wrote to his sister about her son, only a few months before Hillyer was shot in the head and killed in battle:

How old is Eddie? You know if he is under 18 you can claim him out by writing to the OC of the Regiment. I think you would be wise in doing so if his age warrants it as the fighting is liable to increase in fierceness from now on, in fact, we have noticed the difference already. This has happened in 3 cases quite recently in our own regiment. One of the boys claimed

out is one of our best scouts but he is to go just the same although he was very loathe to leave us. Of course, it is immaterial to me, but if he was my brother I would not let him go through what is in store for us here.[54]

Adolescents who had enlisted and embraced the army life, who had even lied to get into it, were torn in a silent battle between doing their duty and supporting their comrades, and the release that they would have received by revealing their real age.

[ . . . ]

## CONCLUSION

The Commonwealth War Graves Commission, tasked with caring for the graves of over a million British and Commonwealth service personnel, has a total of 1,412 identified Great War Canadian adolescents under the age of 19 in its care. Of these, 1,027 were 18 years old, 296 were 17, 75 were 16, and 14 of the dead were aged 15.[55] Most were killed on the Western Front. Since only about 61 per cent of the total CWGC entries show the age of death, however, it would be logical to assume that about 2,270 underage soldiers died during the war. Of course, the number was likely higher, since soldiers who enlisted at 16 or 17 but were killed at 19 would not be classified as underage soldiers in this exercise. They warrant some acknowledgement, even if their number is unquantifiable. Since there were roughly 60,000 Canadian deaths for those in service, one in 26 was an underage soldier. Extrapolating again, of the 424,000 Canadians who served overseas, one in 26 would yield a number of almost 16,300 underage servicemen. Yet many of these underage soldiers never made it to France, and it is therefore likely that they would not have suffered the same casualty rate as those who lie buried in the CWGC cemeteries. Thus the figure of total underage enlistees under 19 was even higher, likely over 20,000. While these figures are necessarily soft, considering that underage soldiers often enlisted using a false age, it is clear that the country had relied heavily on its adolescents during the Great War.

These underage soldiers grew proficient at hiding themselves in their units to escape detection during the war. However, in the post-war years, the adolescents were left increasingly in the forefront of the ever-dwindling ranks of surviving veterans as their more elderly comrades succumbed to age. By the beginning of the twenty-first century, as the last veterans marched into history, it appeared that these now ancient heroes representing the great mass of veterans were all boys when they fought in the Great War. That, of course, is untrue: the average age of the Canadian Great War soldier was 26.3.[56] But the notion of wasted youth, of a lost generation, remains a powerful trope surrounding the Great War.[57] The war 'murdered the nation's youth and turned youth into murderers', recounted one bitter veteran in his post-war memoirs.[58] The loss of more than 60,000 Canadians, and perhaps especially those who were underage soldiers, forever marked a generation.

Most veterans survived, however. Crashing back to Canada in wave after wave in 1919, they found jobs scarce in the post-war years as a country mired in debt was little able to fulfill its promise of creating a 'land fit for heroes'. Furthermore, an 18-year-old who had seen two years in the trenches, prematurely aged and perhaps embittered, did not easily return to being a stock boy or even to live under his parents' roof and rules. There were also the wounded, among whom there would have been some 6,500 underage adolescents.[59] Some would never be the same. William Mansley had enlisted at 14 in the second year of the war. At 4 feet, 11 inches and 95 pounds, he could not deny his youth, but still he served in the trenches with the Royal Canadian Regiment, even if it was only for the last three months of the war and to escape a jail term for stealing a bike. While in the trenches he suffered no physical wounds, but remained psychologically

scarred and unable to hold down a job after the war, even though other veterans often tried to intervene on his behalf. In 1930 he wrote to Sir Arthur Currie, his former corps commander, '[O]wing to my age and sacrificing all in life, all I have now is my discharge and medals'.[60]

At least some of the underage soldiers who served in the trenches never recovered from their ordeals. These adolescents sacrificed their youth; others, their middle and old age as well. Meacham Denyes had enlisted underage and served with the 102nd Battalion in the summer of 1918 until his death on the battlefield. A post-war commemorative text reflecting on his service observed, '[N]ow that we are at peace again it seems inconceivable that young students barely on the threshold of manhood should take part in such indescribable carnage'.[61] Indeed, while these young Canadians faced the firestorm of combat, they were fully supported by a constellation of groups at home, which, despite post-war regret, had actively facilitated the service of these young soldiers. The patriotic discourse during the war encouraged and pressured young men to enlist and urged their parents not to hold them back. The increasingly unlimited war effort was supported by politicians, leaders of society, and even the clergy. The recruiting sergeants and medical officers who turned a blind eye to a nervous boy with no facial hair and an undeveloped body were clearly accountable, but they too had been pressured by their society to take all who could carry a rifle. Of course, the lads themselves must be held responsible for their own actions, as they presented themselves time and time again to enlist, refusing to be infantilized. We cannot, however, read history backwards through the lens of the twenty-first century, which includes Canada's well-respected recent record of attempting to ban child soldiers around the world and to provide support to those brutalized by war. While Canada has its own past of child soldiers, this history must be understood within the context of the time.

# NOTES

1. Desmond Morton, *When Your Number's Up* (Toronto: Random House, 1993), p. 279.

2. See the conclusion for an analysis of available data.

3. For a recent important work that offers some insight into the role of children, see Desmond Morton, *Fight or Pay* (Vancouver: UBC Press, 2004).

4. A.C.T. White, *The Story of Army Education, 1943–1963* (London: George G. Harrap, 1963), chap. 2–3.

5. A.W. Cockerill, *Sons of the Brave* (London: Leo Cooper, in association with Seceker & Warburg, 1984), pp. 41–4.

6. *King's Regulations and Orders* (1910), para. 243, 246.

7. Cynthia Comacchio, *The Dominion of Youth* (Waterloo: Wilfrid Laurier University Press, 2006), and *Nations Are Built of Babies* (Montreal and Kingston: McGill-Queen's University Press, 1993).

8. For an example of boy miners, see Robert McIntosh, *Boys in the Pits: Child Labour in Coal Mines* (Montreal and Kingston: McGill-Queen's University Press, 2000), chap. 7–8.

9. Marta Danylewycz and Alison Prentice, 'Teachers' Work: Changing Patterns and Perceptions in the Emerging School Systems of Nineteenth- and Twentieth-century Central Canada', *Labour/Le Travail*, vol. 17 (1986), p. 140; R.D. Gidney, *From Hope to Harris: The Reshaping of Ontario's Schools* (Toronto: University of Toronto Press, 1999), p. 13.

10. Robert McIntosh, 'Boys in the Nova Scotian Coal Mines, 1873–1923', in Nancy Janovicek and Joy Parr, eds., *Histories of Canada's Children and Youth* (Toronto: Oxford University Press, 2003), p. 77.

11. Joan Sangster, *Girl Trouble: Female Delinquency in English Canada* (Toronto: University of Toronto Press, 2002), pp. 15–16.

12. See Robert Mcintosh, 'Constructing the Child: New Approaches to the History of Childhood in Canada', *Acadiensis*, vol. 28, no. 2 (1999), for an overview of the literature.

13. See Ramsay Cook, *The Regenerators: Social Criticism in Late Victorian English Canada* (Toronto: University of Toronto Press, 1985); Sharon Anne Cook, *Through Sunshine and Shadow: The Woman's Christian Temperance Union, Evangelism, and Reform in Ontario, 1874–1930* (Montreal and Kingston: McGill-Queen's University Press, 1995).

14. Daphne Read, ed., *The Great War and Canadian Society: An Oral History* (Toronto: New Hogtown Press, 1978), pp. 90–1.

15. David Silbey, *The British Working Class and Enthusiasm for War, 1914–1916* (London and New York: Frank Cass, 2005), p. 81.

16. Desmond Morton, 'The Cadet Movement in the Moment of Canadian Militarism, 1909–1914', *Journal of Canadian Studies*, vol. 13, no. 2 (1978), pp. 56–69.

17. Mark Moss, *Manliness and Militarism: Educating Young Boys in Ontario for War* (Toronto: Oxford University Press, 2001); Michael Paris, *The Great War and Juvenile Literature in Britain* (Westport, CN: Praeger, 2004).

18. See Directorate of History and Heritage, 74/672, Edwin Pye papers, folder 4, Militia Order No. 372, August 17, 1914.

19. Nellie McClung, *The Next of Kin: Those Who Wait and Wonder* (Toronto: Thomas Allen, 1917), pp. 33, 48.

20. Dale McClare, *The Letters of a Young Canadian Soldier during World War I* (Kentville, NS: Brook House Press, 2000), p. 1.

21. Toronto, Archives of Ontario, C232-2-0-4-263, 'To the Women of Canada' [poster]. See also Jeff Keshen, *Propaganda and Censorship during Canada's Great War* (Edmonton: University of Alberta Press, 1996), p. 42.

22. Peter Simkins, *Kitchener's Army: The Raising of the New Armies, 1914–16* (Manchester: Manchester University Press, 1988), pp. 182–3.

23. Bruce Tascona, *Little Black Devils* (Winnipeg: Frye Publications for Royal Winnipeg Rifles, 1983), p. 77.

24. Colonel A.F. Duguid, *Official History of the Canadian Forces in the Great War, 1914–1919, General Series, Volume I* (Ottawa: J.O. Patenaude, Printer to the King, 1938), pp. 430–1; Library and Archives Canada (LAC), RG 9, III, vol. 2893, 160–33, clipping, *Montreal Gazette*, October 18, 1916.

25. LAC, RG 9, III, vol. 37, 8–2–10, 2 pts., Officer in charge of Medical Board Department,

Folkestone, to Director of Recruiting, August 22, 1916.

26. LAC, RG 9, III, vol. 1765, file U–I–13, pt. 16, Captain G.A. Dann to OC, YSB, September 13, 1918.

27. Richard Van Emden, *Boy Soldiers of the Great War* (London: Headline, 2005), p. 33.

28. Thomas H. Raddall, *In My Time: A Memoir* (Toronto: McClelland & Stewart, 1976), pp. 42–3.

29. See Ian Hugh MacLean Miller, *Our Glory and Our Grief: Torontonians and the Great War* (Toronto: University of Toronto Press, 2002), pp. 76–80.

30. Ilana R. Bet-El, *Conscripts: Lost Legions of the Great War* (Stroud, UK: Sutton Publishers, 1999), pp. 33–35.

31. Thomas P. Rowlett, 'Memoirs of a Signaller, 1914–1918' (Canadian War Museum Library, unpublished memoir, n.d.), pp. 12–13.

32. LAC, RG 9, III, 8–2–10, 2 pts., Officer in charge of Medical Board Department, Director of Recruiting to Carson, July 12, 1916.

33. Sir Andrew Macphail, *Medical Services: History of the Canadian Forces* (Ottawa: F.A. Acland, 1925), pp. 157–8.

34. LAC, RG 9, III, vol. 30, 8–1–60, Director of Recruiting and Organization to Carson, June 5, 1916.

35. John Macfie, *Letters Home* (Meaford, ON: Oliver Graphics, 1990), p. 12.

36. See LAC, RG 150, Accession 1992–93/166, box 5768–11, John Lowe; L. C. Giles, *Liphook, Bramshott, and the Canadians* (Preservation Society, 1986), postscript.

37. John Thompson, *Harvest of War: The Prairie West, 1914–1918* (Toronto: McClelland & Stewart, 1978), p. 42.

38. Quote by Robert Falconer, president of the University of Toronto, cited in Keshen, *Propaganda and Censorship*, p. 23.

39. Armine Norris, *Mainly for Mother* (Toronto: Ryerson Press, n.d. [1919]), p. 133.

40. Frederick G. Scott, *The Great War as I Saw it* (Ottawa: CEF Books, reprint 2000), pp. 94–5.

41. William Now, *The Forgotten War* (self-published, 1982), p. 30.

42. Herbert McBride, *A Rifleman Went to War* (Plantersville, SC: Thomas Samworth, 1935), p. 7.

43. Calvin Ruck, *The Black Battalion, 1916–1920:*
*Canada's Best Kept Military Secret* (Halifax: Nimbus Publications, 1987), pp. 45–46.

44. Cockerill, *Sons of the Brave*, p. 139.

45. LAC, RG 41, Records of the Canadian Broadcasting Corporation, research transcripts for radio program *Flanders Fields*, vol. 15, 52nd Battalion, A.E. Fallen, 3/1–2.

46. John W. Lynch, *Princess Patricia's Canadian Light Infantry, 1917–1919* (Hicksville, NY: Exposition Press, 1976), p. 59.

47. William Ogilvie, *Umty-Iddy-Umty: The Story of a Canadian Signaller in the First World War* (Erin, ON: Boston Mills Press, 1982), p. 40.

48. LAC, RG 41, vol. 8, 7th Battalion, J.I. Chambers, 1/7.

49. F.W. Noyes, *Stretcher Bearers at the Double* (Toronto: Hunter Rose Company, 1937), pp. 175, 183.

50. Desmond Morton and Glenn Wright, *Winning the Second Battle: Canadian Veterans and the Return to Civilian Life, 1915–1930* (Toronto: University of Toronto Press, 1987), p. 74.

51. William Gray, *A Sunny Subaltern: Billy's Letters from Flanders* (Toronto: McClelland, Goodchild & Stewart, 1916), p. 164.

52. Gerald Oram, *Military Executions during World War I* (London: Palgrave, 2003), p. 62.

53. On Canadian executions, see Andrew B. Godefroy, *For Freedom and Honour?* (Nepean, ON: CEF Books, 1998); Teresa Iacobelli, 'Arbitrary Justice? A Comparative Analysis of Canadian Death Sentences Passed and Death Sentences Commuted during the First World War' (M.A. thesis, Wilfrid Laurier University, 2004).

54. Norma Hillyer Shephard, ed., *Dear Harry: The Firsthand Account of a World War I Infantryman* (Burlington, ON: Brigham Press, 2003), p. 204.

55. I am indebted to Richard Holt for compiling and helping to interpret the information from the Commonwealth War Graves Commission.

56. Morton, *When Your Number's Up*, p. 278.

57. Jay Winter, *Sites of Memory, Sites of Mourning* (Cambridge, 1995); Jonathan Vance, *Death So Noble* (Vancouver, 1997).

58. Pierre Van Paassen, *Days of Our Years* (New York: Hillman Curl Inc., 1939), p. 81.

59. The ratio of death to wounded was about one in four during the Great War, and surprisingly consistent among most armies.

60. LAC, MG 30 E100, Sir Arthur Currie Papers, vol. 23, file 92, Mansley to Currie, January 23, 1930 and February 17, 1930; RG 150, 1992–93/166, 5904–14, W.T. Mansley.

61. Walter S. Herrington and Rev. A.J. Wilson, *The War Work of the County of Lennox and Addington* (Napanee, ON: The Beaver Press, 1922), p. 211.

4  From Tarah Brookfield, 'Divided by the Ballot Box: The Montreal Council of Women and the 1917 Election', *Canadian Historical Review* 89(4) (December 2008): 473–501. Reprinted with permission from University of Toronto Press Incorporated (www.utpjournals.com).

In January and February 1918, a special committee made of members from the Montreal Council of Women (MCW), a coalition of 44 local women's organizations, met four times to hear complaints against their president, Dr Octavia Grace Ritchie-England, and decide whether she should be impeached for her behaviour during the 1917 federal election. It was the opinion of eight affiliated clubs that Ritchie-England was no longer fit to be president of the city's largest women's organization. Her patriotism and politics had been called into question and a few members had gone so far as to call her a traitor.[1] One might assume accusations of this kind stemmed from Ritchie-England's proclaiming herself against the war. In a way this was true, since the majority of men and women considered Wilfrid Laurier, the candidate Ritchie-England supported in the 1917 federal election, to be an 'enemy', and her objections to the 'win-the-war' policies of the *Military Service Act*, the conscription of men to fight overseas, and the *Wartime Elections Act*, the temporary enfranchisement of soldiers' female relatives, as evidence that she did not support Canada's war effort. By the end of the hearings, however, Ritchie-England's name was cleared, and, only a year after these accusations, she was honoured at a soiree celebrating her long-time service in the women's movement.

The impeachment proceedings against Ritchie-England expose how Canadian suffragists' dream that their participation as electors would revolutionize politics was shattered by the reality of women's diverse political interests and the compelling election propaganda surrounding their first opportunity to vote at the federal level. This serves as a reminder of the varied and sometimes conflicting beliefs shared amongst members of the women's movement that were based on different allegiances to the ideals of maternalism, sisterhood, equal rights, nationalism, imperialism, pacifism, and party politics. In peacetime these schisms had been tolerated, but they became volatile amid the dual pressures of the war and home front politics. Women's division was further complicated by the heavy expectations placed on those who qualified as voters in the 1917 federal election. The campaign for women's votes was part of what Michael Bliss called 'the most bitter [election] in Canadian history, viciously fought on both sides. Virtually everyone's loyalty and morality were called into question'.[2] It was in this heated atmosphere that the Unionists, Prime Minister Borden's bi-partisan coalition of Conservatives and Liberals, and the remaining Liberals led by Wilfrid Laurier embroiled women, even those not qualified to vote, in a battle for their loyalty.

Women's invitation to the federal ballot box was positioned by the government and the women's movement as an opportunity to demonstrate that women could vote responsibly, an action defined differently by politicians and suffragists. The Liberals and Unionists each claimed that a vote for their party was a vote to win the war and a way to secure women's permanent voting rights. Meanwhile the National Council of Women

(NCW) warned their members not to 'merely fall in line behind two political parties' because 'their partisan vote would not help the country. Indeed it would be but an added burden by necessitating an extension of the machinery for voting and the cost of the same'.[3] Rather, the NCW advised the newly enfranchised women to rise above party politics, use their influence to sway politicians toward the best course for women, children, and Canada, and vote with a mind to women's interests. Under the popular Unionist platform, at the top of which was conscription, women's obligations to their nation, family, and sex were argued to be the same. Unionists encouraged women to follow their maternal instincts and vote as wives and mothers, thus reinforcing their boys at the front, winning the war, and having their sons and husbands come home. They explicitly made conscription a woman's issue by stating, 'To Women Voters. If your husband or father is on the fighting line, he will have less chance of being killed or injured if we send more men to help them . . . Vote to save your kin'.[4] This rhetoric positioned women as having a key role in ending the war; through their votes, they could transcend traditional wartime gender roles and become protectors as well as the protected.[5] This was a particularly attractive claim to the only body of women who had been granted the vote: the wives, mothers, daughters, and sisters of soldiers. After three difficult years of war, most of these women became convinced that to not vote Union was a betrayal of the nation, their loved ones, and the suffrage cause. Those who disagreed and instead championed the Liberal Party came under intense scrutiny for seemingly threatening Canada's chances to win the war and women's chances to win a permanent vote.

Women's wartime responsibilities were questions debated amongst members of women's organizations across the country. However, these issues consumed the MCW between the fall of 1917 and the winter of 1918. Their unique reaction, as demonstrated by the impeachment trial of their president,

is worth examining in detail, because it offers insight into the resistance of and conflicts between middle-class club women who were normally viewed as hegemonically supportive of the war. It is not coincidental that these controversial reactions to the *Wartime Elections Act* and *Military Service Act* reached their pinnacle in Montreal, a city that was at the centre of nationalistic and ethnic tensions related to the war. Focusing on the MCW, a predominantly anglophone organization operating in a predominantly francophone province, provides an opportunity to step away from the common divide of studying the history of women's suffrage as being distinct in English Canada and French Canada.[6] This allows for an examination of the influence biculturalism had on the community of English- and French-speaking Protestant, Catholic, and Jewish activist women working together and separately in Montreal during the war. An analysis of the MCW's responses to the 1917 federal election broadens our knowledge of how the war, competing definitions of feminism, and regional interests influenced women's voting patterns.

The MCW was a branch of the NCW founded in 1893. The NCW brought local, provincial, and national women's clubs together in a federation, organized charitable and educational programs, and lobbied the government for legal changes. The organization's creation reflects the growth of women's voluntary associations, predominantly joined and led by privileged women, that focused on morally, economically, and legally improving the lives of women, children, workers, immigrants, and the poor.[7] This movement coincided with resurgence in debates over women's place in society and varying opinions on how a woman could best serve her family and nation. The preamble to the NCW's constitution states that they would strive to achieve 'unity of thought' on these issues.[8] In reality, members of the NCW often found themselves at odds over interpretations of feminism, most notably between maternal feminists and egalitarian feminists. Maternal feminists insisted that their identities and experiences as mothers granted them the special responsibility and obligation to engage in public life and politics, while egalitarian feminists were adamant that women should receive political, economic, and social rights based on the their equality to men. Wayne Roberts reminds us that, even though maternal feminism might sound as if it subordinated women within the family or home, both ideologies were dedicated to enhancing the autonomy of women.[9] Among members of the MCW 'unity of thought' was further complicated by the city's diverse ethnic population. Throughout the late nineteenth and first half of the twentieth century, the MCW was placed in a unique situation, oscillating between segregation and collaboration with French-Canadian women, and when seeking reform at the federal and provincial levels, having to negotiate around British imperialism, Canadian nationalism, Catholic conservatism, and French-Canadian nationalism.

Ritchie-England (1868–1948) began her long relationship with the MCW in 1899, first assisting with the council's public health programs and later leading its suffrage crusade as vice-president and president (1911–19).[10] Ritchie first came to public attention at the age of 16 when she fought to be among the first class of girls admitted to McGill University in 1884, and later in 1891, when she was the first female physician licensed to practise medicine in Quebec.[11] In 1897 she married widower Dr Frank England, a surgeon and her former professor at Bishop's. Their only child, Esther, was born six years later. Ritchie-England was also stepmother to Murray, England's son from his first marriage, a detail that will later be relevant, given the constraints of the *Wartime Elections Act*. Although she was a mother, Ritchie-England's own feminism was egalitarian, rather than maternal. This can be seen in her choice to hyphenate her last name and her decision to continue practising medicine after marriage and motherhood.[12]

She quit her teaching job at Bishop's a year before her marriage; however, she retired as assistant gynecologist at the Western Hospital only six months after her daughter Esther's birth, and continued to operate her private practice for several more years. Despite a somewhat unorthodox lifestyle and frequent challenges to the status quo, Ritchie-England was considered one of Montreal's leading citizens, a respectable woman, well known and liked among the members of anglophone and francophone women's clubs. She was also an ardent supporter of the Liberal Party. Alongside her cousin, Sydney Arthur Fisher, a long-time Liberal Party member and the minister of agriculture in Laurier's administration, Ritchie-England frequently hosted gatherings that included Laurier and Mackenzie King.[13]

In the years leading up to the First World War, the MCW voted to make suffrage a top priority. Under Ritchie-England's leadership they organized a series of high-profile events, including the visits of British suffragettes and an exhibit of suffrage literature that featured a petition addressed to the Premier of Quebec, demanding the vote.[14] [ . . . ] In 1912 the *Montreal Daily Star* published a poll, stating that only 11.8 per cent of Montrealers were in favour of giving women the vote.[15] This finding was not surprising, given the province's Catholic majority and the church's beliefs that women did not need the vote because they were already influential in the home.

The church's opposition to suffrage was not the only reason few francophone women belonged to the MCW. Their absence has been linked to linguistic barriers and the predominance of French-Canadian women's leisure time being spent on church-affiliated charities and clubs.[16] One early French-Canadian suffragist, Marie Lacoste Gérin-Lajoie, was an active MCW member until she left in 1907 to found her own women's organization, the Fédération nationale de St Jean Baptiste (FNSJB), an association representing 22 francophone and Catholic women's clubs.[17] She believed a separate organization was necessary to represent

French-Canadian women's different interpretations of feminism and nationalism.[18] Despite these differences, the MCW and FNSJB worked closely together on suffrage and child-welfare projects. It was perhaps Ritchie-England's bonds with French-Canadian women, as well as her admiration for Laurier, that led her to join their fight against conscription during the First World War.

Living in a bilingual and bicultural city, where gender unity could at times triumph over ethnic and religious differences, offered Montreal feminists an opportunity to somewhat transcend the ethnocentric focus of the women's movement found elsewhere. Recent scholarship has criticized the leaders of this movement for upholding racist and classist philosophies. Ritchie-England's own interpretation of feminism placed little emphasis on the superiority of her race. As an egalitarian rather than maternal feminist, she described her vision as a desire for 'full liberty, perfect justice and equality of opportunity without discrimination between sexes, races and creeds', a belief that would not be compromised by the war.[19] Considering how much trouble Ritchie-England's views got her into during the First World War, it would be an exaggeration to paint Montreal and the MCW as an oasis of cross-cultural understanding.

When Britain declared war on Germany in August 1914, as a member of the empire, Canada was automatically involved. Preparations were immediately made to put together an expeditionary force.[20] As men were expected to fulfill their imperial and masculine duty by soldiering, women's wartime work was designed to literally and figuratively reinforce men's service. Working women replaced absent men in factories, offices, and farms. This employment was considered an expression of war service, as well as necessary for their own survival, particularly in households where the male breadwinner was gone. If they were nurses, they too could go overseas as part of the Canadian Army Medical Corps.[21] Middle-class women could satisfy their call to arms through volunteerism with one or more of the numerous health and welfare projects dedicated to assisting lonely, sick, and wounded soldiers, and the families they left behind.[22] Finally, the most crucial way women of all backgrounds were asked to contribute was the sacrifice of their male kin, particularly their sons. It was expected that mothers would not hold their sons back from volunteering and would encourage reluctant boys to sign up.[23] While women were also expected to transcend traditional gender roles so they could replace the absent men in the workplace and home, this came with the understanding that these changes were temporary aberrations. This mobilization gives the impression that most Canadian women, certainly those in English Canada, responded to the crisis with enthusiastic patriotism and a willingness to sacrifice.

Several groups of women did not see the war as an occasion to fall in line and salute king and country. Socialist women used the expansion of women's wartime employment opportunities to demonstrate women's economic value and rights. They spent the war lobbying the government and industry to raise women's wages and access to unions.[24] The decision to use the war as a feminist political opportunity was not fully embraced by all women on the left. Hundreds of women dropped all other activism to join the international peace movement where they publicly protested the war and the imperial politics that spawned it.[25] The war also complicated the suffrage cause, which had gathered considerable momentum right before war was declared. Some suffragists claimed that their wartime services in traditional and non-traditional roles gave them a stronger claim to full citizenship rights, while others did not think the war was the right time to fight for the vote. Canada's two main suffrage clubs, the National Equal Franchise Union and the Canadian Suffrage Association, went in separate directions, with the former temporarily abandoning suffrage in order to concentrate on causes related solely to the war.[26]

since 1902, unless they had a son, grandson, or brother in active military service.[40] It was a temporary measure that extended the franchise to approximately 450,000 new female voters while taking 50,000 to 70,000 potential male enemies off the voters list. This act was paired with the *Military Voters Act*, an equally revolutionary move, which gave the vote to any member of the military who was a British subject, including previously disenfranchised minors, female nurses, and Native Canadians. It also allowed them to cast their vote for a party rather than a candidate if they had been out of the country for more than four months. This clause was included to compensate for overseas voters being unable to follow local campaigns, but it caused speculation that soldiers would be encouraged to place their vote in ridings that needed support for conscription. Together these two acts reconstructed the definition of citizenship; certain women, those fulfilling their ultimate wartime duty, were suddenly more worthy than foreign-born men, while the most valuable citizen, the soldier, was given special privileges that defied age, race, and gender. Publicly these acts were touted by the Unionists as enfranchising Canada's most deserving men and women, those who had made the heaviest sacrifice of all. Privately, Borden confided in his diary that it was honourable that certain women could represent their fighting men, especially those prevented from casting a vote on election day due to death, injury, or engagement with the enemy; however, he also noted how his party believed these acts would prevent the election from being determined by the 'French, foreigners and slackers'.[41]

As they had with conscription, members of Montreal's women's organizations had mixed responses to the *Wartime Elections Act*. Most francophone suffragists were united against the act for nationalist and feminist reasons. The FNSJB denounced it because, as Gérin-Lajoie contended, it made 'suffrage less a privilege conceded than a right granted to

each soldier to vote several times through the intermediary of relatives'.[42] [ . . . ]

The MCW showed less cohesion in their opinions about the act, and the Montreal press fed the storm of debate by printing letters, editorials, and reports on meetings where arguments about the act broke out. Usually concerns among MCW members centred on the fairness of who was allowed to vote and who had been left out. It was apparent that under these terms a woman's political and patriotic responsibilities had nothing to do with her own achievements, labour, or beliefs. Instead it was being defined solely as having sent her husband, son, brother, or father off to war. These sentiments did not fall in line with Ritchie-England's beliefs about equality. She was outraged at this idea and was not quiet in expressing her distaste. Much to her disappointment, after a long debate about the rights of women versus the necessities of war, the MCW decided against publicly censuring the act.[43]

This MCW decision did not silence Ritchie-England. Throughout the fall and up until election day, she repeatedly condemned the *Wartime Elections Act* and the *Military Service Act*, calling them discriminatory and unrealistic.

Laurier's opposition to conscription, along with his French heritage, made him open to accusations that a vote for the Liberals was a vote against winning the war and a vote against the British Empire. These sentiments were represented in the extreme by Annie Davidson, a newly enfranchised woman voter who claimed, 'Any person who will not vote for Borden is worse than a German for the enemy is at least loyal to his country'.[44]

In addition to slandering Laurier's patriotism, Borden's campaign focused on attracting women voters by pulling at their heartstrings and playing up their accountability in winning the war and bringing the boys home. They also hinted that a vote for Union would be a vote for winning women's permanent voting rights. These two ideas were often intertwined, as in one Union ad, which implied that all women voters 'must bear the burden of proving their capacity and intelligence and patriotism of Canadian women' and suggested if they use their vote 'in the best interests of the nation, to loyally support their men folk under fire and to help in the winning of the war, the general belief will be that women as a whole can be safely trusted with the ballot . . . But if they should not show proper appreciation of the awful issues at stake—if they should be deluded by some weird wizardry into deserting their men in the trenches, then the cause of women's suffrage would be put back half a century'.[45] This rhetoric, also found in French-language Union advertisements, consistently reminded women voters that not only was Canada's chance at winning the war at stake but there was an unveiled threat that if women did not vote wisely, their vote could be taken away from them.[46]

Union supporters even appealed to women without a vote to support them. Mrs John Scott, a long-time member of the MCW, who would later be one of Ritchie-England's strongest critics, bluntly advised any ineligible women at a women's 'Win the War' meeting to keep their complaints to themselves, as they were hindering the war effort: 'You don't want the vote on the terms on which we get it? You have a wonderful chance to show us your patriotic spirit by cheerfully accepting things as they are at the present time'.[47] These statements contend that opposition to Borden based on objections to the *Wartime Elections Act* would be selfish and unpatriotic; for the sake of the war, it was time to temporally abandon the universal suffrage cause.

As with the conscription issue and the *Wartime Elections Act*, women's groups across Canada were forced to decide where they stood in the election. The NCW once again decided to sit this battle out and did not officially back the Unionists or Liberals, though its periodical, *Women's Century*, was less neutral. It had no qualms, stating even before the election had been announced, 'Women's

Century stands for Union government, winning the war and conscription'.[48] In Montreal, the FNSJB came out in support of the Liberals; however, a month before the election, the MCW executives decided not to choose sides. Ritchie-England stated to the press that the council 'has always excluded from its proceedings all questions of theological and political character on which great diversity of opinion must necessarily exist and the discussion of which would not tend to harmonious and united action'.[49] This remark caused a great deal of confusion. Why was the MCW stepping out of the political arena when it had recently debated the equally divisive topics of conscription and the *Wartime Elections Act* and had a tradition of advocating for certain candidates in municipal elections?[50] Was it because its president was a loyal Liberal and would not concede her council a chance to support the Union government? This is certainly how Unionist supporters viewed the message of neutrality. Neutrality meant that the MCW was not actively supporting the party that promised to win the war. This differed from the NCW's approach because its president and several members were known supporters of Borden and had time and time again chosen to sit on the fence on possibly incendiary matters.

On 17 December 1917 the wildly popular support for Unionists culminated in their landslide victory. The Liberals won majorities in Quebec and Nova Scotia; however, the Unionist coalition took the rest of the country, winning 57 per cent of the total vote, and 88 per cent of the vote outside of Francophone ridings. Historians argue that the Unionists would have won without the electoral changes, that in the end the specially aligned votes of 400,000 soldiers (92 per cent of whom voted for Union, compared to the 52 per cent of civilians) and 185,000 women voters were unnecessary in an election that had an outstanding 75 per cent voter turnout.[51] Nevertheless, the amount of campaign propaganda directed at women demonstrates the perceived value of their votes, especially by the Unionists. Furthermore, the intense scrutiny under which women's groups considered the election issues reveals how seriously they took their new responsibilities, even at the risk of undermining their unity and the suffrage cause. These debates continued, even after the polls closed. The Union victory did nothing to quiet the discontent over Ritchie-England's support for the Liberals, or rather her lack of support for conscription.

Leading up the election, dozens of men and women had responded to Ritchie-England's pro-Laurier/anti-Borden sentiments by writing to newspapers, referring to her as a 'sorehead', a 'grouch', and 'disloyal' for pushing the suffrage cause in spite of the war, for not supporting Borden's plans to reinforce the front, and for aligning herself with the out of touch Liberal Party.[52] Although they did not contextualize her failures in gender terms, it seems clear that her political choices marked her as unpatriotic and a potentially unreliable voter, someone who clearly did not prioritize the nation's and empire's (and therefore women's) best interests. This inspired the Montreal Women's Club, a long-time member of the MCW, to pass a resolution called 'Patriotism' that asked for Ritchie-England's resignation. They felt that Ritchie-England's beliefs, while tolerated and even respected during peacetime, were problematic during the war; consequently, it was in the best interests of Montreal women to have a less controversial figure as president of the MCW. The club executive had not been informed of the resolution prior to its reading and were shocked to see the motion carried through at the poorly attended meeting.[53] The matter was immediately brought to the MCW's executive.

Ritchie-England was at her cottage in Knowlton, QC, for the Christmas holidays when the resignation demands were made. She expresses her feelings in a letter to the council's vice-president, Kathleen Anne Chipman. Although she stated she was no longer greatly affected by public disapproval,

she was disappointed that people, regardless of their feelings about the Liberal Party, did not understand that her beliefs and goals had not changed. She was concerned only with 'fair play and equal opportunities for women in all spheres of life'. She understood how her views amid wartime despair were misinterpreted as unpatriotic, but was shocked at how people believed she was using her position as president to influence matters. She claimed to have always tried to make clear to the press or in council proceeding when she was expressing her own views. Ritchie-England was also angry at the intolerance for freedom of speech. She acknowledged that 'the desire of the crowd is to punish anyone who dares to hold a contrary opinion; it is not a thinking process nor are people at the moment being [unreadable] by reason, rather they are carried away in a frenzy of blind passion which they imagine is patriotism'. She felt resigning would not help matters and hoped to carry out her presidential duties until the following spring. She was proud to have 'resisted the temptation to follow the path of least resistance and keep silent', and concluded her letter to Chipman by declaring, 'My conscience acquits me absolutely in this matter'.[54]

It was decided by the MCW executive that Ritchie-England would publish a letter in the *Montreal Daily Star* again reasserting that her political views were not to be associated with the MCW or any of its affiliated societies.[55] Nevertheless, the letter did not quiet the storm, and before the end of January 1918, seven other affiliated associations asked that action be taken against Ritchie-England.[56] [ . . . ] As the case proceeded, Montreal was rocked by French-Canadian protests against conscription and accusations by English Canadians that even with conscription French men continued to shirk their duty. In Quebec City this conflict culminated in a major riot that saw four men killed when protesters and police confronted each other in the spring of 1918.[57]

By the time the first special meeting was held on 26 January 1918 only three groups had decided to continue their protest. The others had quietly withdrawn from the MCW or continued harmonious relations. The first meeting met with a delegation from the Montreal Women's Club and was opened by a quote from poet John Ruskin: 'Every moment of our lives we should try to see where we agree with people, and not where we differ'. This statement reflected the sympathetic attitude taken by most of the council's special committee members. The exception was Scott, who felt Ritchie-England's actions were inexcusable and thought impeachment was a suitable punishment. Mrs Murray, the author of the incriminating resolution, led the Montreal Women's Club delegation. The meeting was also attended by the president of the Montreal Women's Club, Mrs Welsh, who had voted against the resolution and spoke eloquently in defence of Ritchie-England. Despite the pledges of support for Ritchie-England, the meeting ended with the Montreal Women's Club still refusing to withdraw their protest.[58]

Ritchie-England had even fewer supporters at the second and third meetings. Delegates from the Protestant Infant's House understood that Ritchie-England had a right to her own opinion but basically felt that her opinion was the wrong one for a president of a large non-political association to hold and one that went against suffragists' hope to remain above the corruption of party politics.[59] Members of the Diet Dispensary were the most hostile toward Ritchie-England. One delegate, Mrs Rea, thought that 'Dr Ritchie-England's action was on par with pro-Germanism' and that 'she considered that Dr England was in her mind, a traitor'. [ . . . ] In conclusion to this heated meeting, Chipman asked everyone to act fairly toward 'a woman who had devoted her life for the past six years to the good of the community and refrain from calling individuals insidious epithets . . . she knew it was difficult for people with relatives at the front to view this matter in an unbiased fashion, but she hoped the delegates would bring open minds to their decision in spite of this'.[60]

Although the issue was never brought up in the press or MCW documents, it appears that Ritchie-England did not have any close relatives at the front. Her husband and brothers were in their forties and fifties and therefore generally thought to be too old to serve. Her stepson Murray, a clerk at the Bank of Montreal, was in his early twenties, but there is no record of him serving in the military. The available evidence suggests that he did not join, since one would assume if Ritchie-England had a stepson at the front it would have been used in defence of her patriotism and womanhood. The fact that she had a stepson who might have been qualified to serve, but had not, would have reflected poorly on her as a citizen and a mother. Taking either of these possible premises into consideration adds another dimension to the resentment directed toward Ritchie-England: Not only was she not fulfilling her duty as a patriot, she was failing as a mother. Given that the dominant ideology among Montreal suffragists was maternal feminism and the devastating loss of almost seventy thousand men in the war, it is understandable why Ritchie-England's opponents equated maternalistic values automatically with patriotism. As Roberts demonstrated, in this period, there had always been a conflict of interest between equal rights feminists like Ritchie-England and maternal feminists.[61] The war and the *Wartime Elections Act* furthered this conflict by declaring maternalism the victor and implying those who were not happy about getting the vote on the basis of their identities as wives, mothers, and daughters were selfish and unpatriotic. Furthermore, Murray not being overseas might also explain why Ritchie-England was particularly bitter about the *Wartime Elections Act*. If she had no close male relatives at the front, she would have been unable to vote. It is quite possible her personal absence from the voters list encouraged her vocal complaints more than her devotion to the Liberal Party. One wonders if her fight would have been as ardent if she did not feel personally snubbed by the act.

After carefully considering the evidence, the number and nature of the complaints, the MCW's bylaws, and Ritchie-England's service record, the special committee members came to this conclusion, 'Be it resolved that Dr Ritchie-England's patriotism is unimpeachable, and her private right to freedom of opinion and action absolute and unquestionable'.[62] The MCW might not have agreed with her opinions but felt they were a poor excuse to terminate her presidency, especially in light of all the past and present good she had done for women. Ritchie-England was allowed to remain president, and the Montreal Women's Club and the Diet Dispensary terminated their association with the Local Council. [ . . . ]

Ritchie-England did not appear to suffer any long-term fallout from the impeachment trial. She continued her work as president until the spring of 1918 when she did not seek re-election. Before she left office, Borden extended the franchise to all women, and Ritchie-England was invited to Ottawa for a conference to discuss women's involvement in Canada's future war plans. [ . . . ] After her retirement from the MCW executive, she continued to be active in Quebec women's rights up until her death in 1948. She remained supportive of the Liberal Party and ran in the 1930 federal election as their first endorsed female candidate. She lost but was claimed to be satisfied with her number of votes and believed that the women's rights movement was aided by her being chosen as an official candidate.[63]

Throughout the First World War, Canadian women were under great pressure to prove their value as citizens by fulfilling their gender-specific wartime obligations. Individual deviation from the prescribed norms of maternalistic sacrifice and service were seen to impede Canada's chances of winning the war. As the war progressed and casualties mounted, loyalty at home was scrutinized even more carefully, especially in a province that witnessed outbreaks of violence in protests against conscription. Against this tense backdrop, the MCW's reactions to the *Military Service Act* and the *Wartime Elections Act* led them down a path different from that of women's organizations in other provinces, a path that Ritchie-England unsuccessfully tried to align alongside the ideals of democracy and freedom, as expounded by their francophone sisters in the FNSJB, rather than maternalism and discrimination. This divergence serves as a reminder that women, even middle-class club anglophone women, reacted in multiple ways to the war. It also demonstrates that the bicultural women's movement in Montreal had unique issues to contend with that influenced the context of their activism. Ultimately, the MCW did not stray from the status quo. Nevertheless their frequent debates and the impeachment trial gave them a considerably bumpier journey. With winning the war and future suffrage rights at stake, the MCW deemed it too risky to challenge their Prime Minister's conscription plans or support a party branded as anti-patriotic. It was safer to exude the qualities associated with women's wartime responsibilities and vote for the party promising to reinforce their husbands and sons.

Yet in the end, Ritchie-England's dissenting voice was validated by most of her peers because not to do so would contradict the democratic vision many suffragists hoped their participation in politics would allow.

# NOTES

1. Grace Ritchie-England Case Papers (GRE), 8-3-A, Jan. 1918, Montreal Council of Women Fonds (MCW), P653, Quebec National Archives (QNA).

2. Michael Bliss, *Right Honourable Men: The Descent of Canadian Politics from Macdonald to Mulroney* (Toronto: HarperCollins, 1995), 84.

3. 'You Are Now Citizens!' memo to women's

organizations, n.d., Marie Gérin-Lajoie Fonds, P783 S2 S55, P2/E 02, QNA.

4. 'To Women Voters . . . ', advertisement, *Montreal Daily Star* and *Montreal Gazette*, 1 Dec. 1917.

5. Kimberly Jensen, *Mobilizing Minerva: American Women in the First World War* (Urbana: University of Illinois Press, 2008), viii–ix.

6. The history of first-wave feminism tends to be split into activities and ideology originating from English Canada or French Canada. One exception is Andrée Levesque's *Making and Breaking the Rules: Women in Quebec, 1919–1939*, trans. Yvonne M. Klein (Toronto: McClelland and Stewart, 1994).

7. Veronica Strong-Boag, 'The Parliament of Women: The National Council of Women of Canada, 1893–1929' (Ph.D. diss., University of Toronto, 1976); Mariana Valverde, *The Age of Light, Soap and Water: Moral Reform in English Canada. 1885–1925* (Toronto: McClelland and Stewart, 1991).

8. National Council of Women of Canada. Yearbook 1884, 22–7, MCW, P653, QNA.

9. Wayne Roberts, 'Rocking the Cradle for the World: The New Woman and Maternal Feminism in Toronto, 1877–1914', in *A Not Unreasonable Claim: Women and Reform in Canada 1880s–1920s*, ed. Linda Kealey, 18 (Toronto: Women's Press, 1979).

10. Esther Cushing, 'I remember, I remember . . . ', *A Fair Shake: Autobiographical Essays by McGill Women*, ed. Margaret Gillett and Kay Sibbald, 186–97 (Montreal: Eden, 1990); Margaret Gillett, *Dear Grace: A Romance of History* (Montreal: Eden, 1986); Gillett, *We Walk Very Warily: A History of Women at McGill* (Montreal: Eden, 1981); James Henry Morgan, ed., *Canadian Men and Women at the Times* (Toronto: Briggs, 1912), 377; Blanche Evans Yates, 'Through the Years', McGill News 19, no. 3 (1938): 18–20.

11. Gillett, *Dear Grace*, 199.

12. Elizabeth Milner's *Bishop's Medical Faculty Montreal, 1871–1905* (Quebec: René Prince, 1985).

13. Cushing, 'I remember, I remember . . . ', 192–3.

14. Executive meeting minutes, 19 Feb. 1913, MCW, P653, QNA.

15. Catherine Cleverdon, *The Start of Liberation:*

*The Woman Suffrage Movement in Canada* (Toronto: University of Toronto Press, 1973), 220–1.

16. Strong-Boag, 'Parliament of Women', 38–9.

17. Karine Hébert, 'Une Organisation maternaliste au Québec la Fédération Nationale Saint-Jean Baptiste et la bataille pour le vote des Femmes', *Revue d'Histoire de l'Amérique Française* 52, no. 3 (1999): 1–24.

18. Marie Lavigne, Yolande Pinard, and Jennifer Stoddart, 'The Fédération Nationale de Saint-Jean Baptiste and the Women's Movement in Quebec', in *A Not Unreasonable Claim*, 199–201.

19. Annual Report 1917–18, 8–9, MCW, P653, QNA.

20. Desmond Morton, *When Your Number's Up: The Canadian Soldier in World War I* (Toronto: Random House, 1993).

21. Debbie Marshall, *Give Your Other Vote to the Sister: A Woman's Journey into the Great War* (Calgary: University of Calgary Press, 2007).

22. Desmond Morton, *Fight or Pay: Soldiers' Families in the Great War* (Vancouver: UBC Press, 2004); Linda Quiney, '"Bravely and Loyally They Answered the Call": St John Ambulance, the Red Cross, and the Patriotic Service of Canadian Women during the Great War', *History of Intellectual Culture* 5, no. 1 (2005): 1–19; Robert Rutherdale, *Hometown Horizons: Local Responses to Canada's Great War* (Vancouver: UBC Press, 2004).

23. Suzanne Evans, *Mother of Heroes, Mothers of Martyrs: World War I and the Politics of Grief* (Montreal and Kingston: McGill-Queen's University Press, 2007).

24. Linda Kealey, *Enlisting Women for the Cause: Women, Labour and the Left in Canada, 1890–1920* (Toronto: University of Toronto Press, 1998), 151–3.

25. Barbara Roberts, '*Why Do Women Do Nothing to End the War?*' *Canadian Feminist-Pacifists and the Great War* (Ottawa: Canadian Research Institute for the Advancement of Women, 1985), 1, 3–4.

26. Kealey, *Enlisting Women*, 195–6.

27. M.H.C., 'Canadian Women and the War', *Saturday Night*, 1 July 1916, 25.

28. Strong-Boag, 'Parliament of Women', 311.

29. Morton, *When Your Number's Up*, 278–80.

30. Bliss, *Right Honourable Men*, 82–3.

31. Ray Argyle, *Turning Points: The Campaigns That Changed Canada: 2004 and Before* (Toronto: White Knight, 2004), 164–5.

32. Anne-Marie Sicotte, *Marie Gérin-Lajoie: Conquérante de la liberté* (Montreal: Les Éditions du remue-ménage, 2005), 312.

33. General and executive minutes, 15 Nov. 1916, MCW, P653. QNA.

34. Strong-Boag, 'Parliament of Women', 380.

35. 'Divided on Party Lines', *Montreal Gazette*, 17 Sept. 1917.

36. An Evaluation, Briefs, and Reports, 75th anniversary, 1968, 7, MCW Papers, P653, QNA.

37. Sicotte, *Marie Gérin-Lajoie*, 291.

38. Gloria Geller, 'The Wartimes Elections Act of 1917 and The Canadian Women's Movement', *Atlantis* 2, no. 1 (1976): 101–2.

39. Ibid., 102.

40. *Statues of Canada*, 1917, chap. 39.

41. Quoted in Bliss, *Right Honourable Men*, 83.

42. Quoted in Lavigne, Pinard, and Stoddart, 'Fédération Nationale de Saint-Jean Baptiste', 79.

43. Executive meeting minutes, 17 Oct. 17, 1917, MCW, P653, QNA.

44. 'Votes of Women Solid for Union Canvass Show', *Montreal Daily Star*, 8 Dec. 1917.

45. 'Will the Women Desert Their Men Folk?' *Montreal Daily Star*, 20 Nov. 1917.

46. Hébert, 'Une Organisation maternaliste', 24.

47. 'Business-like Meeting Is Held For Lady Voters', *Montreal Daily Star*, 24 Nov. 1917.

48. *Women's Century*, 5 Sept. 1917, MCW, P653, QNA.

49. Executive meeting minutes. 24 Nov. 1917, MCW, P653. QNA.

50. Nonpartisan, letter to the editor, *Montreal Daily Star*, 29 Nov. 1917.

51. Argyle, *Turning Points*, 177; Bliss, *Right Honourable Men*, 84.

52. Parent, letter to the editor, 18 Sept.; A Suggestion, letter to the editor, 24 Sept. 1917.

53. Montreal Gazette, Montreal Women's Club Minutes, 10 Dec. 1917, MCW, P653, QNA.

54. Ritchie-England to Chipman, 2 Jan. 1918, GRE 8-3-A, MCW, P653, QNA.

55. Grace Ritchie-England, letter to the editor, *Montreal Daily Star*, 9 Jan. 1917.

56. GRE, January 1918, 8-3-A, MCA, P653, QNA.

57. Sandra Gwyn, *Tapestry of War: A Private View of Canadians in the Great War* (Toronto: HarperCollins, 1992), 415–17.

58. Minutes from the special committee meeting on 26 Jan. 1918, GRE 8-3-A, MCW, P653, QNA.

59. Minutes from the special committee meeting on 1 Feb. 1918, GRE 8-3-A, MCW, P653, QNA.

60. Minutes from the special meeting on Feb. 4, 1918, GRE 8-3-A, MCW, P653, QNA.

61. Roberts, *Why Do Women Do Nothing?* 46.

62. Resolution, n.d., GRE 8-3-A, MCW, P653. QNA.

63. 'Results Satisfies Dr G.R. England', *Montreal Gazette*, 30 July 1930.

# Chapter 7

# Marketing the Nation

## READINGS

### Primary Documents

### Historical Interpretations

### Introduction

Most of the time, we think of artists creating their works for the purpose of depicting or inter-preting a scene, expressing an emotion, or perhaps social or political commentary. It is less common to associate artistic work with the act of 'branding', but artists have created posters and advertising materials that have become identified with a national tradition. Both of these are forms of marketing. It becomes difficult to separate the artists' work from a promotional campaign or from patriotism once that work is connected in popular or scholarly imaginations with the advertiser's message or the representation of national identity. Whether they were used specifically as advertisements or were unrelated to a particular institution or idea, we should recognize that these artworks remain valuable historically as reflections of the particular styles employed by their creators and as examples of the kinds of work that would later be dubbed 'Canadian Art'. This chapter's selected primary sources feature two-dimensional works created during the First World War and interwar period. The famous Group of Seven artists are well represented here by Arthur Lismer, J.E.H. MacDonald, and Tom Thomson. Even during their own lifetimes, most of the Group's works were considered especially evocative of 'Canadian-ness'. But one did not have to belong to such an eminent school of artists to be linked to the fortunes of the young nation. The practical requirements of the railways for passengers or the armed forces for troops gave rise to works like the anonymous poster and G.Y. Kaufman's, MacDonald's, and Arthur Wardle's, which played more direct roles in constructing the image or message their clients wanted to convey. The pieces by Lismer and Thomson convey a different kind of theme. In their translations of places they had visited, the artists associated those places with particular colours and shapes, and over time, images like these were bound up with a distinctive way of representing other Canadian (especially Ontario) places. Paula Hastings brings us back to the world of posters and advertising to remind us that more than landscape could be connected to Canada and Canadians. To set their products apart from the competition, so many advertisers played upon consumers' nationalistic tendencies that it became a cliché; but still the marketplace of proudly Canadian goods seemed to be crowded. The images of Canada promoted by these products served to reinforce the images themselves. In Lynda Jessup's article, the Group of Seven return as artists whose works resonated with observers in different ways, depending at least partially on the region those observers lived in. For Western Canadians, the Group's work was as clearly associated with convincing people to visit the West as it was with the peaceful wilderness depicted. Art could be put at the service of commerce and of national mythologies at the same time.

## QUESTIONS FOR CONSIDERATION

1. What are the main visual elements of MacDonald's work promoting an exhibition of Canadian artists in aid of the Patriotic Fund?
2. What is the man on the Bureau of Canadian Information poster doing, and who is the intended recipient of the message?
3. How does the combination of text and image in Wardle's poster compare with Yarker's poem in Chapter 4?
4. How might Lismer's depiction of Little Haven affect the observer's assumptions about Nova Scotia and its people?

## SUGGESTIONS FOR FURTHER READING

Marc H. Choko, *Canadian War Posters: 1914–1918, 1939–1945* (Ottawa: Canadian Government Publication Centre, 1994).

Marc H. Choko and David L. Jones, eds., *Posters of the Canadian Pacific* (Richmond Hill: Firefly Books, 2004).

Leslie Dawn, *National Visions, National Blindness: Canadian Art and Identities in the 1920s* (Vancouver: UBC Press, 2006).

Patrick A. Dunae, 'Promoting the Dominion: Records and the Canadian Immigration Campaign', *Archivaria* 19 (1984–85): 73–93.

Daniel Francis, *The Imaginary Indians: The Image of the Indian in Canadian Culture* (Vancouver: Arsenal Pulp Press, 1992).

Sherrill Grace, *On the Art of Being Canadian* (Vancouver: UBC Press, 2009).

Marylin J. McKay, *A National Soul: Canadian Mural Painting, 1860s–1930s* (Montreal and Kingston: McGill-Queen's University Press, 2002).

David Monod, *Store Wars: Shopkeepers and the Culture of Mass Marketing, 1890–1939* (Toronto: University of Toronto Press, 1996).

John O'Brian and Peter White, eds., *Beyond Wilderness: The Group of Seven, Canadian Identity, and Contemporary Art* (Montreal and Kingston: McGill-Queen's University Press, 2007).

David P. Silcox, *The Group of Seven and Tom Thomson* (Richmond Hill: Firefly Books, 2006).

# PRIMARY DOCUMENTS

**1**  J.E.H. MacDonald, *Exhibition of Pictures Given by Canadian Artists in Aid of the Patriotic Fund*

SOURCE: Canadian War Museum, CWM 19940018-001

2 Arthur Wardle, *The Empire needs Men! ( . . . ) Enlist Now*

3   Tom Thomson, *The Jack Pine*, 1916–1917

SOURCE: Oil on canvas, 127.9 cm x 139.8 cm. National Gallery of Canada, purchased in 1918.

4  Anonymous, *The Bureau of Canadian Information*, c.1920

5    G.Y. Kaufman, *Trans-Canada Limited*, 1924

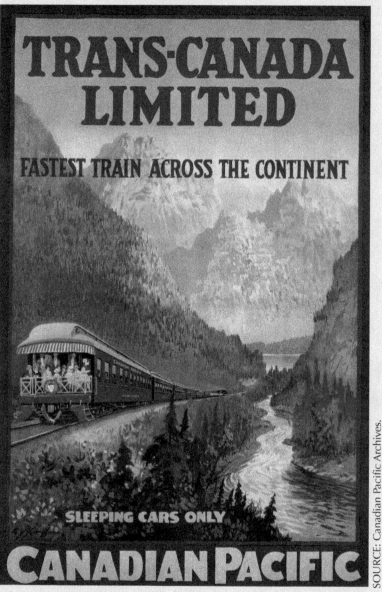

SOURCE: Canadian Pacific Archives.

6    Arthur Lismer, *Little Haven, Nova Scotia*, 1930

SOURCE: Oil on canvas, 82 cm x 102.4 cm. Montreal Museum of Fine Art. Bequest of William Gilman Cheney.

# HISTORICAL INTERPRETATIONS

7    From Paula Hastings, 'Branding Canada: Consumer Culture and the Development of Popular Nationalism in the Early Twentieth Century', in eds. Norman Hillmer and Adam Chapnick, *Canadas of the Mind: The Making and Unmaking of Canadian Nationalism in the Twentieth Century* (Montreal and Kingston: McGill-Queen's University Press, 2007), 134–58.

In the two decades before the First World War, representations of Canada permeated the language and iconography of consumer culture. Advertisers associated illustrations of the maple leaf, beaver, and Jack Canuck as well as prominent political figures, both historic and contemporary, with a variety of products. They employed images of Prime Ministers John A. Macdonald, Wilfrid Laurier, and Robert Borden to promote everything from tomato chutney to encyclopaedias.[1] The Canadian Parliament buildings appeared on labels for cherries, egg plums, and peaches.[2] L. Higgins & Company of Moncton encouraged consumers to send for a poster-size picture of the Fathers of Confederation, and the Grip Printing and Publishing Company of Toronto, for a two-dollar fee, sent consumers an 'almost life size' photograph of Laurier.[3] The Ogilvie Flour Mills Company of Winnipeg employed the image of Miss Canada as a discerning shopper and consumer authority.[4] Consumers were encouraged to eat Canada Flakes, Maple Leaf Apples, and Canada's Pride Peas and to drink Canadian Maple Leaf Malt Whisky.[5] They were urged to light their homes with Duffield's Canadian Lamp, bake with sugar from the Canada Sugar Refining Company, wash their hands with John A. Soap, chop wood with the Laurier Axe, and wear 'Canadian' Rubbers on their feet.[6]

These ubiquitous representations reflected and fuelled nationalist sentiment in Canada at the turn of the twentieth century. By the mid-1890s renewed confidence in the future of Canada had replaced the widespread disillusionment that had characterized the decades following Confederation. A changed world economy ended Canada's long depression and paved the way for national development. Unprecedented economic growth and a dramatic population increase in the West confirmed the economic viability and potential of the Canadian union. It also popularized the *idea* of Canada. Advances in print technology after 1870 provided a powerful medium for the dissemination of this idea, and mass circulation images were instrumental in the development and negotiation of a national consciousness.[7] Visual imagery reached a vast audience and promoted a common identity because it did not depend on literacy and language and could reach all social classes.

Consumer culture provides a rich framework to explore popular concepts of nationalism. Until recently, studies of Canadian identity during this period examined the ideas of prominent Canadian politicians and intellectuals.[8] Yet the shared sense of meaning among everyday Canadians characterized national self-understanding more than the ideas of an elite. Parliamentary speeches and intellectual treatises had their place in the effort to define Canada, but their significance in the development of national consciousness was secondary to the cultural influences that pervaded the everyday lives of Canadians. Other historians offer valuable insights about national consciousness from the study of celebrations, agricultural fairs, and trade shows.[9] But the impermanence of these events makes them less powerful manufacturers of cultural meaning than the images that bombarded Canadians daily. Packaged goods in particular were omnipresent in the material culture of everyday life. They lined the shelves of stores and pantries, their labels disseminating a multitude of messages about the nation.

Consumer culture expressed varied and complex nationalisms, including both explicit and implicit forms. Maple leaves, prime ministers, and the 'Canadian' brand name communicated an undeniably nationalist message; other expressions were nuanced. All comprised a consumer discourse that employed nationalist ideas to foster consumer appeal. Advertisers recognized the rising tide of nationalist sentiment in late-nineteenth- and early-twentieth-century Canada and capitalized on it in a variety of ways. The most powerful nationalist advertising constructed cultural and historical narratives that promoted a particular vision of Canada. In the effort to establish a national identity, the contours of Canadian society, past and present, were subject to reinterpretation.

Advertisers also employed rural and industrial landscapes to construct meaning about Canada. Nationalist iconography and rhetoric situated them in a national context, but they also communicated a nationalist message about Canada's economic development. Illustrations of technical innovations in agriculture and industry, for example, were thoroughly nationalist in tone. Equally important were the relationship between farm and factory in Canadian development and Canada's trade policy toward the United States. Nationalism surfaced more explicitly in consumer culture with the appearance of prime ministers, leaders of the Opposition, and the Fathers of Confederation. They were all part of a consumer discourse that relied on nationalist ideas to inspire consumer interest.

## CONSTRUCTING THE NATION WITH NARRATIVES OF CONQUEST

Constructions of nationalism in English Canadian consumer culture often appropriated and redefined histories, geographies, and cultures outside the spatial and ideological boundaries of Ontario, where the majority of these advertisements were produced. These appropriations included Native culture, French Canadian history, and the West. They were all situated in a narrative of English Canadian conquest that articulated ideas about Canada. A label for Chippewa Brand

Red Raspberries, for example, packed by the Niagara Falls Canning Company, employs the image of an imagined Chippewa to convey nationalist meaning (Figure 1). The historic presence of the Chippewa, from the Ottawa River to the plains of eastern Saskatchewan and as far north as Hudson's Bay, imbued them with national significance.[10] The snow-capped pine and the imposing white clouds in the background, symbols of the Canadian North, contribute further to the national character of the image.

By the first decades of the twentieth century, Nativeness was frequently associated with Canadian ideas of nation, and advertising provided a powerful venue to disseminate these ideas. Historian Daniel Francis demonstrates how advertisers often employed the image of the Native to promote a wide variety of products, including Pocahontas perfume, Red Indian motor oil, and Squaw Brand canned vegetables. For some products, he argues, Nativeness 'was used to associate a product with the out-of-doors, or with strength and courage, or with the simple innocence of nature', while for others it 'was used as an all-purpose symbol of Canada'.[11] The image of the Native in the Chippewa label serves both these functions. As a symbol of a 'natural' preindustrial world, the Native

**Figure 1** Chippewa Brand Red Raspberries, Niagara Falls Canning Company, c. 1910–23. Special Collections, Hamilton Public Library, Local History & Archives.

assures consumers of the purity of Chippewa Brand products.

Unique to the New World, the Native fuels a Canadian identity distinct from those shaped largely by British principles and ideas.[12] The value of this identity, however, is historical. As part of a 'disappearing wilderness',[13] the Native advances the nationalist narrative by reminding Canadians how the inexorable march of civilization shaped the nation. The historical presence of the Native furnishes Canada with a unique prehistory that predates European colonization. His (or her) importance in Canadian consumer culture is thus entirely symbolic; while the Native's *image* has a place in the nation's future, the Native himself (or herself) does not.

The French Canadian past was similarly appropriated and put in the service of English Canadian nationalism. The image of Paul de Chomedey de Maisonneuve appeared on labels for canned pears, rhubarb, and plums; the *fleur de lis* sold peaches, peas, and baked beans; Jacques Cartier's image promoted 'Canadian' Rubbers; and the image of Louis de Buade, Comte de Frontenac, recurred on labels for canned tomatoes.[14] Most of these labels, which appeared on goods packaged by English Canadian manufacturers and contained only English text, were designed to appeal to an English Canadian market.[15]

The late-nineteenth- and early-twentieth-century interest in French Canadian history likely inspired these representations. As H.V. Nelles and other historians have demonstrated, both English and French Canadians shared this interest. History was often employed to construct and negotiate ideas about the nation and to demonstrate how the past 'pointed firmly towards a collective future'.[16] Despite this shared enthusiasm, however, the selection and use of French Canadian history was divergent and often contested. Both French and English Canadians favoured figures and symbols from pre-Conquest New France, but as Colin Coates has pointed out, they employed history for different purposes. French Canadian nationalists

used historical figures to demonstrate the 'longevity of the "national" struggle', while English Canadians used them 'to appropriate the past of French Canada in order to provide a longer genealogy to the Canadian nation and to imply a continuous record of progress that linked French and English Canadians'. In this perspective, the history of New France was merely a 'prelude' to British rule, 'a romantic preface' to the more significant part of Canadian history.[17]

[ . . . ]

Among English Canadians the *fleur de lis* awoke no association with Quebec nationalism in the nineteenth century, nor was it a symbol of French Canadian difference. It invoked the quaint, nostalgic era of the old regime.[18] Just as English monarchs had inscribed the *fleur de lis* on their coats of arms to highlight their claims to the throne of France following Edward III's claim in the fourteenth century, English Canadians appropriated the *fleur de lis* for consumer culture to emphasize English Canadian authority over Quebec. History and its various reinterpretations granted English Canadians an equal claim to the symbols and figures of Quebec's historic past. The British Empire, having conquered both New France and its history, relocated the *fleur de lis* in a narrative of progress in which French culture was (and continued to be) supplanted by the unrelenting advance of British civilization.

A label for Maisonneuve Choice Egg Plums also draws from the history of New France to emphasize Canada's lengthy history (Figure 2). The label features an illustration of the Paul de Chomedey de Maisonneuve monument, erected at Montreal's Place D'Armes in 1895. Selected by the Sociéte Notre-Dame de Montréal to found a missionary colony on the Île de Montréal, Maisonneuve began the construction of Ville-Marie in 1642. An indefatigable defender of the colony against the Iroquois, Maisonneuve was a likely candidate for tribute in the late-nineteenth-century flurry to commemorate the past. Indeed, a crowd of approximately 20,000 people turned out to witness the unveiling of his statue in 1895.[19]

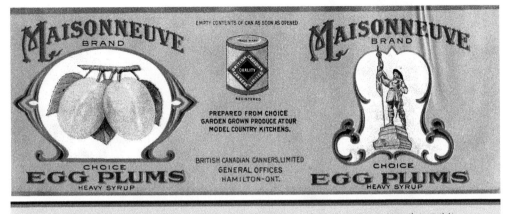

**Figure 2** Maisonneuve Choice Egg Plums, Canadian Canners Ltd, c. 1895–1915. Hamilton Public Library, Local History & Archives.

It is significant that Maisonneuve and Cartier appeared in English Canadian consumer culture while other important figures in the history of New France did not. French Canadians commemorated Maisonneuve and Cartier with enthusiasm in French Canada, but the tributes to these figures paled next to those of Samuel de Champlain and Bishop François de Laval. The images of Champlain and Laval held greater appeal in French Canada for precisely the same reason that they were absent from English Canadian consumer culture. Historian Ronald Rudin argues that Cartier's major feat, his claim to the St Lawrence Valley in 1534, 'evaporated on the Plains of Abraham in 1759'. Unlike Champlain and Laval, 'he could be celebrated only as representing a French connection that no longer existed'. Maisonneuve 'had been a founder', Rudin points out, but 'his feat was a rather local one. In contrast, the legacies left by Champlain and Laval were viewed as central to French Canadians' existence as a people'.[20] English Canadians were certainly enthusiastic about Champlain's legacy and flocked to Quebec City in 1908 to participate in the tercentenary celebrations, but the images of Maisonneuve and Cartier prevailed in English Canadian consumer culture because their legacies could be detached from the preservation of French culture. Moreover, Champlain had founded a city that was, after Confederation in 1867, 'home to the only government in North America where francophones were in control', a government that was largely French-speaking and Catholic by 1900. Maisonneuve's legacy, Montreal, had become culturally and linguistically diverse, and an English-speaking elite controlled its developing business sector.[21]

Ideas about the Canadian West, furthermore, were appropriated by advertisers and were frequently employed to construct ideas about the nation. The end of an international depression in the mid-1890s, the dramatic increase in wheat production and export after 1896, and the corresponding success in attracting more immigrants to settle farther west revived confidence in the potential of the West to transform Canada from colony to nation.[22] The disillusionment with the West that beset Canadians, especially new settlers in the late 1880s and early 1890s, was replaced with fresh enthusiasm. The utopian image of the West as a 'promised land, a garden of abundance in which all material wants would be provided and where moral and civic virtues would be perfected',[23] permeated not only contemporary literature, art, and immigration propaganda, but the iconography of consumer culture as well.

**Figure 3** Golden West Sugar Peas, Canadian Heritage Label Collection, c. 1900–10. Country Heritage Park, Milton, Ontario.

In the first decade of the twentieth century, the most popular representation of the West was that of a fertile, bountiful garden with infinite agricultural potential. A label for Golden West Sugar Peas, manufactured by the Farmer's Canning Company of Bloomfield, features an illustration of the prairie landscape of southwestern Alberta (Figure 3). In the foreground a farmer harvests a vast crop of wheat with the assistance of a modern binder and three horses. Two sheaves of wheat have been neatly bundled and left to dry in the beaming sun. Under the expansive sky, the land stretches out to the mountains in the distance. In adopting this imagery, the Farmer's Canning Company reminded consumers of the intimate association between agriculture and Golden West Sugar Peas. The idea of agriculture operates to assure consumers of the naturalness and purity of the product, but the label does not rely on antimodern ideals to construct appeal. Despite its romanticization, agriculture in this representation is not situated in the past; the agricultural landscape is not receding under the encroaching forces of urbanization but is expanding and modernizing. With the increasing association of eastern Canada with industrialization and urbanization, the West offered an appealing reference point that was simultaneously pure and modern.

[ . . . ]

## NATIONALIZING RURAL AND INDUSTRIAL SPACE

Advertisers employed images of rural and industrial Ontario to construct ideas about Canada. But the articulation of nationalism in these advertisements was more explicit than those that appropriated geographies, histories, and cultures outside the boundaries of Ontario. Rural and industrial spaces were imbued with national significance by way of textual references and visual symbols associated with the idea of Canada. Popular textual references included brand names such as Canada, Maple Leaf, and National, and the most commonly employed image was the maple leaf, followed by Jack Canuck and the beaver.

An advertisement for Canada Flakes, packaged by the Peterborough Cereal Company, features the image of a hardy farmer on a Canada Flakes cereal box (Figure 4).[24] The farmer carries a bundle of wheat under each arm and two branches of maple leaves encircle him. A banner at the bottom of each branch reads 'Made in Canada from Manitoba wheat'. The advertisement emphasizes the rural environment that harvested the wheat rather than the industrial environment in which the wheat was adulterated and packaged. This emphasis served an obvious commercial purpose in reminding consumers about the agricultural origins of Canada Flakes, but it also suggests that the farmer had greater appeal than the industrial worker in both consumer and national cultures.

Product labels at the turn of the twentieth century abound with images of rural life. In many of them the farmer plays a central role in defining and articulating national character. Rural life 'had conditioned Canadians to believe in "honest toil" and the efficacy of individual initiative for gaining a "modest competence" and social advancement',[25] and confidence in national development was based on these principles. Industrial life, on the other hand, challenged these values. As J.L. Finlay and D.N. Sprague have observed, the 'metropolitan environment that emerged in places such as Montreal and Toronto by 1911 severely challenged the ideology of success through thrift and industry. Most workers were anything but independent producers. Increasingly, they laboured for wages in large, highly mechanized establishments, at simple tasks, dictated by the pace of machinery'.[26] Moreover, industrial work was believed to threaten manly virility. Many Canadians were enthusiastic about industrial progress, but the mechanized, dehumanizing characteristics of industrial life made the industrial worker a less appealing figure in the effort to define national character. In a somewhat contradictory way, the factory was a thoroughly masculine icon that symbolized national development, while the factory worker was an 'unmanly' figure whose personal qualities were inconsistent with prevailing notions of national character. The undesirability of the industrial worker's image explains his absence in advertisements. Despite increasing industrialization in the first decade of the twentieth century, the farmer, with his hardy form and manly disposition, remained the preferred figure with whom to foster consumer appeal and project national values.

The F.F. Dalley Company of Hamilton also employed nationalist ideas to market their 2 in 1 Shoe Polish, but it relied on industrial rather

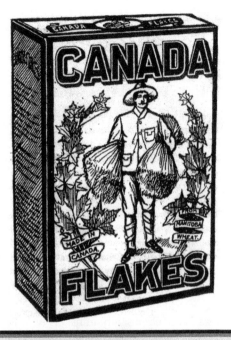

**Figure 4** Canada Cereal Flakes, *Toronto Globe*, 8 July 1905, 11. Reprinted with the permission of *The Globe and Mail*.

than agricultural imagery to articulate these ideas.[27] One of their advertisements features an illustration of Jack Canuck handing Uncle Sam a tube of 2 in 1 Shoe Polish over the Canada–United States border. Uncle Sam points to an empty box at his feet, expressing his disappointment with the meager supply of shoe polish offered by Jack Canuck. Uncle Sam's disappointment reflects his larger dissatisfaction with Canada's official disinterest in reciprocity—that is, in forming a closer economic relationship. This dissatisfaction was a common theme in early-twentieth-century advertising. An advertisement for 'Red Feather' Tea, for example, employs an image of Uncle Sam sipping 'Red Feather' Tea while he laments his failure to obtain a more regular supply.

> Quoth Uncle Sam, 'I hate to see
> Them Canucks get the draw on me.
> This here Red Feather Tea's immense—
> Makes U.S. feel like thirty cents.

I'll hike to Ottawa', says he,
'And coax for reciproci-tea'.[28]

Although these advertisements offered a somewhat critical assessment of Canada's economic relationship with the United States, they nevertheless communicated the idea of Canadian nationalism by highlighting the economic boundary between the two countries and by praising the superior products available on the Canadian side. [ . . . ]

## THE NATIONALISM OF CANADIAN POLITICAL AUTHORITY

Images of prominent Canadian political authorities were also put in the service of consumer advertising. Prime ministers and leaders of the Opposition, ministers of militia and defence, finance, and the interior, and the Fathers of Confederation all played a role in the promotion of commodities. The consumer appeal of these figures was rooted in their connection to the Canadian nation. Advertisers capitalized on contemporary nationalist sentiment by employing the images of figures who, in different ways, were icons of Canadian nationalism. These representations appeared more frequently in traditional advertisements, such as those appearing in the periodical press, than on packaged goods. The time required to package, label, and distribute canned goods made the use of political figures, whose popularity was often fleeting, a risky marketing decision. The circulation of Canadian goods in the international market may also explain the absence of Canadian political figures on packaged food labels. Unlikely to have been recognized outside Canada, their appeal was limited to the domestic market.

In the first decade of the twentieth century, L. Higgins & Company of Moncton employed an illustration of the Quebec Conference delegation of 1864 to promote their Maple Leaf Rubbers (Figure 5). The delegates, affectionately titled the 'Founders of the Dominion',

are assembled around a table negotiating the terms of union. John A. Macdonald assumes control of the room as the delegates look on with subdued interest. Papers are strewn about the table and floor, evidence of a lengthy and contested negotiation process. Seated at the end of the table, George Brown awaits his opportunity to review the benefits of union. Charles Tupper, appearing somewhat concerned about the implications of union for Nova Scotia, confers with a fellow delegate. E.P. Taché and George Etienne Cartier, confident in the course of proceedings, offer their undivided attention to Macdonald.

The characterization of L. Higgins & Company as the 'Sole Wholesale Distributors for the Maritime Provinces' suggests that this advertisement was not only produced in the Maritimes but also distributed to a primarily maritime market. This context renders the expression of nationalist sentiment in the advertisement particularly interesting. As a region of Canada often characterized as having been 'dragged kicking and screaming into Confederation', it is curious that L. Higgins & Company would employ an illustration of the Fathers of Confederation to construct consumer appeal in a maritime market.[29] In assessing the consumer appeal of the Maple Leaf Rubbers advertisement, however, the sentiments of early-twentieth-century Maritimers about their entry into union are more important than those of their predecessors in the 1860s.

Although the period from 1896 to 1911 has generally been characterized as one of national economic boom, it was a period of mixed prosperity in the Maritimes. While maritime economy experienced industrial growth, it also witnessed a transfer of financial control and a loss of capital to central and western Canada.[30] Yet despite the increased subordination of the maritime economy to central and western Canadian interests, the results of the 1904 general election revealed strong support for the Laurier government in the Maritimes. As Richard Clippingdale has

**Figure 5** Maple Leaf Rubbers Outwear all Others, c. 1905–10. Morris Norman Collection, Library and Archives Canada, C-2280341, published by L. Higgins & Co., Toronto, Ontario.

observed, Maritimers 'felt this government included them in a way no other government had since Confederation'. Laurier's popularity in the Maritimes was particularly strong after 1903 when he insisted that a 'key feature of his mammoth Grand Trunk Pacific-National Transcontinental railway scheme should be yet another line to the Maritimes, giving the region the system's eastern terminus'.[31] This enthusiasm suggests that many Maritimers had renewed optimism about their place within the nation. Advertisers could thus be assured that the nationalist tone of the Maple Leaf Rubbers advertisement would be well received.

A label for Canadian Tomato Chutnee similarly employs a powerful icon of Canadian nationalism to foster consumer appeal: the nation's first prime minister, John A. Macdonald (Figure 6). The label features both an illustration of Macdonald and his personal endorsement of the product. 'I have tried your Tomato Chutnee', the label reads, 'and found it very good'. The testimonial is

signed 'Yours very truly, John A. Macdonald'. The appearance of Macdonald's image on this label suggests that the prime minister's appeal was not confined to his role in political life. His popularity certainly originated with his formidable success in this role, but by 1891, as he neared his final election, Macdonald had transformed from a shrewd politician into a powerful icon of the Canadian nation. As an architect of Confederation, a founder of the Conservative Party, the first prime minister of Canada, and an influential force in Canadian political life for over three decades, Macdonald had become the pre-eminent figure of Canadian nationalism. Even Macdonald's opponents appreciated the magnitude of his accomplishments. As Wilfrid Laurier wrote in 1891, Macdonald's 'actions displayed unbounded fertility of resource, a high level of intellectual conception, and, above all, a far reaching vision beyond the event of the day, and still higher, permeating the whole, a broad patriotism, a devotion to Canada's welfare, Canada's advancement,

**Figure 6**  Canadian Tomato Chutnee, c. 1890s. Morris Norman Collection, Library and Archives Canada, C-148449.

Canada's glory'.[32] The immense respect and admiration that Macdonald had garnered in his political life made him a useful figure in consumer culture. Indeed, the 'Canadian' in Canadian Tomato Chutnee resonates more forcefully with the inclusion of the prime minister's image. Macdonald's political authority was effectively transformed into consumer authority.

Not until after 1896, when Wilfrid Laurier became prime minister, did advertisers find an icon comparable to Macdonald. Yet Laurier's appearance in consumer culture did not immediately follow his victory in 1896. The new prime minister needed to prove himself before advertisers gained confidence in his potential as a consumer authority.

By the first years of the twentieth century, Laurier had demonstrated that he was well-suited to the task of national leadership. Changing conditions in the international economy, coupled with domestic circumstances, quickened the pace of national development.[33] The election results of 1900

and 1904 were testaments to the popularity of the Liberal government. Laurier had established a solid reputation, and advertisers were subsequently ready to debut his image in consumer culture. In 1905 Laurier and a few of his prominent Cabinet ministers were (although probably unbeknownst to them) at the centre of a campaign to promote McClary's Sunshine Furnace. In one of the advertisements, Laurier holds a miniature-size McClary's furnace in his hands (Figure 7). His distinguished dress, complete with high Victorian collar, conveys his style and charm. A pair of spectacles sits comfortably on his nose, adding an air of learned authority to his countenance. The text, which reads 'Sunshine Furnace gives the head of the House "Sunny Ways,"' appropriates a phrase from Laurier's familiar promise to resolve divisive issues in Canada with 'sunny ways'.34 The prime minister's role as head of the national 'house' is a metaphor for the domestic house in which the Sunshine Furnace is used. Just as Laurier's commitment to national unity facilitates a

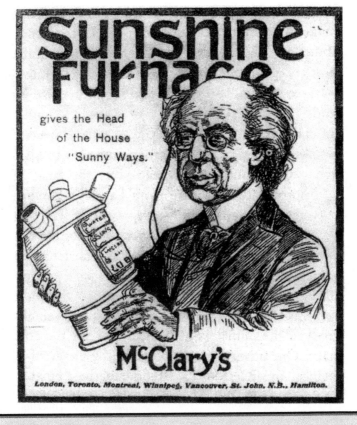

**Figure 7** Sunshine Furnace, *Toronto Globe*, 1 July 1905, 18.

'sunny' political environment in Canada, the Sunshine Furnace will ensure a 'sunny' domestic environment.

[ . . . ]

Once a prominent Canadian figure such as Macdonald or Laurier had gained popular appeal, their function in consumer culture was fairly straightforward; their image needed only to be associated with a product to inspire consumer interest. Sometimes, however, the political discourse in which prominent figures were engaged was more important than their popular appeal.

These advertisements, like those that constructed narratives of conquest and employed images of rural and industrial space, illuminate the frequency with which English Canadian nationalism, in its formative stage at the turn of the century, was often expressed in the absence of British imperialism. Images of empire were by no means absent from the iconography of consumer culture during this period and, in fact, played an equally important role in the promotion of commodities; nationalism and imperialism were often inextricably connected phenomena.[35] It is significant, nevertheless, that nationalism was often articulated in a way that highlighted the distinctly 'New World' qualities of the Canadian nation. In different ways, representations of the Native, the French Canadian past, and the West emphasized the unique features of Canadian culture, history, and geography. Images of rural and industrial space, and articulation of Canada's relationship with the United States in particular, served to forge an awareness of the economic and distinctly North American variety of Canadian nationalism. And representations of Canadian prime ministers, Cabinet ministers, and the Fathers of Confederation drew attention to the authority and autonomy of Canadian political figures in both consumer and nationalist discourses.

The prevalence of these representations highlights the importance of consumer culture in the development of Canadian consciousness at the turn of the century. Economic prosperity in the two decades before the First World War certainly revived confidence in the future of Canada and inspired nationalist sentiments, but this prosperity alone was not responsible for the development of a shared national consciousness. More significant were advances in print technology and industrial manufacture in the latter half of the nineteenth century, which produced a highly visual and material environment and subsequently provided a powerful venue for the dissemination of ideas about Canada. As commodities permeated the market and the home, a consumer discourse emerged that relied heavily on representations of Canada to foster appeal. Yet the cultural value of these representations was not confined to their ability to inspire consumer interest. They also communicated changes in the cultural, economic, and political environment while providing a means to represent, promote, and negotiate ideas about Canada. Most important, the ubiquity of these images in consumer culture provided a way for Canadians to better understand, and identify with, the nation.

## NOTES

1.  Maple Leaf Brand Pitted Black Cherries, Canadian Canners Ltd, Special Collections, Hamilton Public Library (HPL), c. 1903–23. Hygeian Brand Yellow Peaches, Canadian Canners Ltd, Special Collections, HPL, c. 1910–23; Auto Brand Greengage Plums, Canadian Heritage Label Collection, Country Heritage Park (CHP), c. 1905–10S; The Red Bird Bicycle, *Canadian Magazine*, July 1897, xxvi; Sunlight Soap, *Toronto Globe*, 5 July 1902, 21; 'Red Feather' Tea, *Saturday Night*, 8 July 1905, 11; *Encyclopaedia Britannica* advertisement, *Mail and Empire*, 1 June 1895, 12; Library and Archives Canada (LAC), Canadian Tomato Chutnee, Morris Norman Collection, C-148449, c. 1890s; and 2 in 1 Shoe Polish, *Western Home Monthly*, July 1912, 16.

2.  Parliament Brand Red Pitted Cherries, Canadian Canners Ltd, Special Collections, HPL, c. 1905–15.

3.  LAC, Maple Leaf Rubbers, Morris Norman Collection, C-2280341, c. 1905–10; The Grip Printing and Publishing Co., *Saturday Night*, 15 December 1900, 11.

4.  The Ogilvie Flour Mills Co. Ltd, *Western Home Monthly*, January 1913, 18.

5.  Canada Flakes, *Mail and Empire*, 1 July 1905, 22; Maple Leaf Brand Apples, Canadian Heritage Label Collection, CHP, c. 1903–10; Canada's Pride Peas, Canadian Heritage Label Collection, CHP, c. 1905–10; Canadian Maple Leaf Malt Whiskey, Duncan Lithography Company, Special Collections, HPL, c. 1902.

6.  Duffield's Canadian Lamp, Broadsides and Printed Ephemera Collection, Toronto Reference Library, c. 1889; The Canada Sugar Refining Company, *Monetary Times*, 1 November 1901, 553; John A. Soap, Duncan Lithography Company, Special Collections, HPL, c. 1898; Laurier Axe, Duncan Lithography Company, Special Collections, HPL, c. 1902; 'Canadian' Rubbers, *Saturday Night*, 24 December 1904, 11.

7.  See Benedict Anderson, *Imagined Communities: Reflections on the Origin and Spread of Nationalism* (London: Verso, 1983), esp. 6–7 and his chapter on 'The Origins of National Consciousness', 37–46.

8.  Ramsay Cook, *The Maple Leaf Forever: Essays on Nationalism and Politics in Canada* (Toronto: Macmillan of Canada, 1971), 197–214; Carl Berger, *The Sense of Power* (Toronto, 1970); and W.L. Morton, *The Canadian Identity* (Toronto: University of Toronto Press, 1972).

9.  E.A. Heaman, *The Inglorious Arts of Peace: Exhibitions in Canadian Society during theee*

*Nineteenth Century* (Toronto: University of Toronto Press, 1999); Keith Walden, *Becoming Modern in Toronto: The Industrial Exhibition and the Shaping of Late Victorian Culture* (Toronto: University of Toronto Press, 1997).

10. Harold Hickerson, *The Chippewa and Their Neighbours: A Study in Ethnohistory* (Prospect Heights, IL: Waveland Press, 1988); Harold Hickerson, 'The Southwestern Chippewa: An Ethnohistorical Study', *American Anthropological Association* 64, no. 3, part 2 (1962).

11. Daniel Francis, *The Imaginary Indian: The Image of the Indian in Canadian Culture* (Vancouver: Arsenal Pulp Press, 1992), 174.

12. Patricia Jasen, *Wild Things: Nature, Culture, and Tourism in Ontario, 1790–1914* (Toronto: University of Toronto Press, 1995), 80–104; Karen Dubinsky, 'Local Colour: The Spectacle of Race at Niagara Falls', in Antoinette Burton, ed., *Gender, Sexuality and Colonial Modernities*, 67–79 (London, 1999); Francis, *Imaginary Indian*, 171–2, 173–90; and Daniel Francis, *National Dreams: Myth, Memory, and Canadian History* (Vancouver: Arsenal Pulp Press, 1997), 128–51.

13. See Jasen, *Wild Things*, 43.

14. Maisonneuve Brand Flemish Beauty Pears, Canadian Canners Ltd, Special Collections, HPL, c. 1895–1915; Fleur de Lis Brand Yellow Peaches, Canadian Canners Limited, Special Collections, HPL, c. 1895–1915; and 'Canadian' Rubbers, *Saturday Night*, 24 December 1904, 11.

15. Ted Herriott, *The Canadian Heritage Label Collection* (Missassauga: Purpleville, 1982), 46, 56, 58, 62.

16. H.V. Nelles, *The Art of Nation-Building: Pageantry and Spectacle at Quebec's Tercentenary* (Toronto: University of Toronto Press, 1999), 11. Colin M. Coates and Cecilia Morgan, *Heroines and History: Representations of Madeleine de Verchères and Laura Secord* (Toronto: University of Toronto Press, 2002); and Ronald Rudin, *Founding Fathers: The Celebration of Champlain and Laval in the Streets of Quebec, 1878–1908* (Toronto: University of Toronto Press, 2003).

17. Coates and Morgan, *Heroines and History*, 44.

18. Susan Mann Trofimenkoff, *The Dream of Nation: A Social and Intellectual History of Quebec* (Toronto: Gage, 1983), 266–7.

19. Rudin, *Founding Fathers*, 6–7.

20. Ibid., 6–7.

21. Ibid., 9.

22. See Robert Craig Brown and Ramsay Cook, *Canada, 1896–1921: A Nation Transformed* (Toronto: McClelland and Stewart, 1974), 53, 75–9.

23. See R. Douglas Francis, *Images of the West: Responses to the Canadian Prairies* (Saskatoon: Western Producers Prairie Books, 1989), 107; Doug Owram, *Promise of Eden: The Canadian Expansionist Movement and the Idea of the West, 1856–1900* (Toronto: University of Toronto Press, 1980).

24. This image of the farmer was not unique to the Canada Flakes advertisement. The Canadian Cordage & Manufacturing Company, also of Peterborough, employed it in their advertisements for binder twine in the early twentieth century; see LAC, Canadian Cordage & Manufacturing Company Ltd, Morris Norman Collection, R1300–1166, c. 1900–10.

25. J.L. Finlay and D.N. Sprague, *The Structure of Canadian History* (Scarborough: Prentice-Hall, 2000), 296.

26. Ibid.

27. 2 in 1 Shoe Polish, *Mail and Empire*, 15 July 1905, 7.

28. 'Red Feather' Tea, *Mail and Empire*, 12 July 1905, 7.

29. Phillip Buckner, 'The Maritimes and Confederation: A Reassessment', in Ged Martin, ed., *The Causes of Canadian Confederation* (Fredericton: Acadiensis Press, 1990), 86.

30. See G.A. Rawlyk and Doug Brown, 'The Historical Framework of the Maritimes and Confederation', in G.A. Rawlyk, ed., *The Atlantic Provinces and the Problems of Confederation* (Halifax: Breakwater, 1979), 22–4.

31. Richard Clippingdale, *Laurier: His Life and World* (Toronto: McGraw-Hill, 1979), 85.

32. Wilfrid Laurier, as cited in Ramsay Cook, *Canada: A Modern Study* (Toronto: Clarke, Irwin, 1963), 140.

33. See Brown and Cook, *Canada, 1896–1921*, 49–50.

34. See J.L. Granatstein and Norman Hillmer, *Prime Ministers: Ranking Canada's Leaders* (Toronto: HarperCollins, 1999), 52.

35. See Berger, *Sense of Power*.

8  From Lynda Jessup, 'The Group of Seven and the Tourist Landscape in Western Canada, or The More Things Change . . . ' *Journal of Canadian Studies* 37, 1 (Spring 2002): 144–79.

Today, fifty years after the first Group of Seven exhibition of May 1920, [they] still remain the most famous, and to many people the only, 'movement' in the history of Canadian art. In terms of considered critical opinion, as far as that can be said to have existed, the measure of their importance has fluctuated. However, in the eyes of the public at large, they have steadily ascended until now they occupy a position in the Canadian cultural pantheon shared only with a few hockey stars and a handful of beloved politicians.

Dennis Reid 1970

The post-colonial dilemma confronting inter-war Canadian nationalists was how to develop a powerful set of stories and symbols through which a British 'Dominion' . . . could become a Canadian nation. . . . To meet this challenge, such cultural producers as the Group of Seven, new liberal and Laurentian historians, and political novelists . . . began to 'narrate the nation' in ways which stressed the inevitability and goodness of Canada. There was little here that any student of twentieth-century nationalism would find surprising, except, perhaps, the fact that with the exception of a few areas and people, the new definitions did not really take hold. Canadian novels did not, by and large, set the framework within which a majority of Canadians 'imagined' a new community; Canadian paintings, although frequently found on the walls of banks (as a 'natural' part of standardized corporate iconostases)

did not establish a consensus about the ultimate signifier of Canadianness. This failure to 'naturalize' Canada makes the lavish Ontario celebrations of the Group of Seven in 1995 an ironic and melancholy exercise in nostalgia—a visual homage, one might almost say, to the official nationalism of the Former Canada.

Ian McKay 2001

Things changed in the 25 years that separated the National Gallery of Canada's fiftieth anniversary celebration of the Group of Seven's formation and the gallery's 1995 extravaganza in honour of the Group's 75th anniversary. There was increasing awareness among historians of Canadian culture that the Group of Seven, and the ideas of nation advanced in and around their work, were never as fully embraced by the public at large as once assumed. The Group, and the cultural producers with whom they aligned themselves, Ian McKay points out, failed 'to construct a truly hegemonic discourse of nation, founded on both cultural consent and state coercion, in which the disparate *ethnies*, territories, provinces, regions (not merely a self-selected central Canadian elite) could all recognize themselves' (McKay, 'Handicrafts' 118). Rather, the Group's work and activities articulated an exclusive national identity based on an Anglo-Celtic ancestry, exclusive on the one hand of indigenous peoples, certainly, and on the other of the immigrant, that racialized concept occupied in Canada most conspicuously by Asians (beginning with the Japanese and Chinese immigrants of the nineteenth century) and by eastern and southern Europeans, who have also been distinguished historically from the Anglo-Celtic settler by what Matthew Frye Jacobson describes as 'whiteness of a different colour'.

The Group's was also a Canadian nationalism that in its appearance of inclusiveness—its claim to speak for the nation as a whole—was characteristic of what has been defined more precisely as Ontario regionalism. The Group's success in articulating this regional identity was, and is, such that the lack of acceptance of their work and ideas in other regions of the country (even within the realm of high culture) has never been disputed. It has simply been reconfigured as a barrier to the rightful establishment of 'a national art'. Regional opposition became part of the conventional story of the Group as a downtrodden avant-garde that enjoyed hard-won victory over its opponents in the face of criticism and resistance. That the artists enjoyed the overwhelming support of the National Gallery of Canada and the then Art Gallery of Toronto had always been part of the story as well, the inherent contradiction between their status as struggling artists and the aggressive purchase and exhibition of their work by the two major cultural institutions having been recast by the National Gallery from the outset as evidence of its willingness to assertively exercise its mandate to support art in Canada (even as it reinterpreted that mandate to mean the support of a nationalist and, as such, 'Canadian' art). Generating accusations of favouritism from artists in Montreal and resentment among artists in Vancouver at being told what Westerners should admire, the National Gallery advanced this regional perspective and, with it, a centralizing, nationalist approach to official culture that privileged Ontario to the detriment of what became by definition the eastern and western peripheries. In so doing, it contributed to the sense of alienation from central Canada that has become a defining feature of regional identities elsewhere in the country, while the painting of Canada by members of the Toronto-based Group echoed in the realm

of high culture the economic and political exploitation that had been felt to both east and west since the enactment of the National Policy in the late nineteenth century (see den Otter 208–38).

One of the reasons the Group's paintings of other parts of the country resonated most strongly, if not exclusively, with central Canadian audiences was the urban perspective reflected in the artists' work and activities, a perspective characteristic of Ontario regionalism. For Ontarian viewers, the landscape in paintings by the Group of Seven was not a place of productive labour, nor a permanent home, but rather a place of recreation—of scenic value and spiritual renewal. Much has been made recently of the fact that the Group's landscape paintings are uninhabited, that their landscape vision was tied to questions of territorialization and possession, all of them predicated on the erasure—in their case, pictorially—of the country's Aboriginal populations and, with them, Aboriginal claims to prior settlement, hereditary lands and resources (Bordo; Teitelbaum; Watson). As William Cronon points out, the removal of indigenous populations to create 'uninhabited wilderness' was part of the transformation of the wilderness concept that began in North America in the late nineteenth century. Reconfigured under the dual influence of the romantic movement and a growing antimodernist backlash to the perceived ills and artificiality of contemporary life, wilderness emerged as a recuperative environment, and, increasingly, as the preferred landscape of elite, urban tourists hoping to return to what they saw as an elemental environment untainted by civilization. Among other ironies implicit in this cultural construction of wilderness as unaffected by the culture that constructed it, is the fact that the establishment of national parks followed quickly on the subjugation of Native populations 'in which the prior inhabitants of these areas were rounded up and moved onto reservations'. As Cronon puts it, 'The myth of the wilderness as "virgin", uninhabited land had always been especially cruel when seen from the perspective of the Indians who had once called that land home. Now they were forced to move elsewhere, with the result that tourists could safely enjoy the illusion that they were seeing their nation in its pristine, original state, in the new morning of God's creation'. (79, 72–81).

In this sense, wilderness, whether in concept or in paintings of the Group of Seven, was empty as well of other tourists. It reflected a romantic notion of nature, which placed emphasis on solitude, privacy and an intimate, semi-spiritual relationship with undisturbed natural beauty; 'nature, according to romanticism', writes J.A. Walter, 'is where mankind isn't' (Walter 297; see also Cronon 72–76; Urry 1990, 45). Just as it does today, romanticism exalted a solitary experience of landscape conceived as scenery and views for visual consumption. This aesthetic experience of nature, of seeing the physical environment as landscape, is also at the root of modern sightseeing, which had taken shape as an aesthetic activity by the nineteenth century. [ . . . ]

Of course, artists have had such cultural capital in the 'general economy of looking' from the outset. Privileged players in the realm of the aesthetic, they are generally recognized as arbiters of taste and thus of picturesque scenery. This is why railway companies in Canada—specifically the Canadian Pacific and the Canadian National railways—provided Group members with free passage over their lines; they did this consistently throughout the 1920s as the artists expanded their sketching grounds from Algonquin Park and Algoma to other parts of the country.[1] In the west, the interests of the railways and the artists also converged on the national parks—on the 'CPR Rockies', which embraced what are now Banff, Yoho and Kootenay national parks, and, to the north, on Jasper National Park on the line of the CNR through the Yellowhead Pass. Even A.Y. Jackson and Edwin Holgate's trip to the Skeena River, which they made in

1926, took place in the context of the area's development as a tourist attraction and its promotion for consideration as a national park. Jackson's awareness that their activities could 'give the place some publicity' reflected the artists' easy understanding of their value to the railways.[2] Writing to request passage on the CNR to Edmonton in connection with his trip to Great Slave Lake in 1928, Jackson acknowledged this openly, arguing (unsuccessfully, it seems) that passes for his trip to Great Slave Lake would constitute a happy exception that proved the rule: 'It is not tourist country', he contended, 'but it is Can. Nat. country and the artist can help create an interest in it'.[3]

It was not that the national parks were the object of railway interest in themselves; the fact was, both companies had been working in conjunction with the National Parks Branch of the Department of the Interior to develop these tourist areas specifically as destinations, in the case of the railways, not just to increase ticket sales, but also to feed their related facilities—whether the tourist accommodations and services they had established in the parks themselves, or the company hotels they had built along their lines further west. In this sense, their reason for supporting artists who wanted to sketch along their lines was much the same as it had been since the nineteenth century, as was the nature of their support. The government-run Intercolonial Railway, for instance, had issued passes to Toronto- and Montreal-based artists to travel east between Quebec and New Brunswick almost immediately upon the completion of that railroad in 1876. Conceived as the eastern section of a transcontinental railway and built in connection with the federation of British North America in 1867, the Intercolonial had provided access to a newly articulated national landscape that artists had wanted to portray. They travelled out on the line, then returned with pictures of landmarks, scenery and salmon streams for the visual consumption of armchair travellers and elite tourists in central Canada whose participation, not only in the aesthetics of landscape but also in art patronage and collecting, deepened their claim to this landscape as their national aesthetic property (Jessup 1992, 99–146; see also Helsinger 103–25).

[ . . . ]

The CPR benefited, as well, from the location of its facilities in the country's first nature reserves, which were established in the mountains by the Canadian government in the ten years following the completion of the railroad in 1885. Although often lauded as an act by the government to preserve the picturesque mountain scenery of the region from development, the establishment of the reserves was in keeping with the conservation efforts spearheaded by sportsmen during this period. So, while the reserves protected prized tracts of 'uninhabited wilderness' from conventional development—from what the *Dominion Lands Act* described as 'sale, settlement or squatting'—the protection of the natural environment was driven as much, if not more, by the desire to preserve fish and game in the region for sport hunting and angling (Wonders 30–31). The second phase in Canada of the international development of Western conservation practices, the creation of reserves marked what MacKenzie has identified as 'the progressive conversion of game from a direct economic resource . . . into an indirect one, a means of raising revenue from "sport" and tourism' (MacKenzie 201). In this context, Cronon points out, 'one went to the wilderness not as a producer but as a consumer', hiring buggies or saddle horses to view the scenery, or 'guides and other backcountry residents who could serve as romantic surrogates for the rough riders and hunters of the frontier'(78). By negotiating special leases with the government for land on the reserves, the CPR was able to capitalize on this, which it did from the outset, actively promoting the region both as an area of unrivalled scenery and as 'a sportsman's Eden', where those kid-glove tourists could recuperate both under the stars in pursuit of blood sport and in the midst of sublime landscape in one of the railway's luxurious resort hotels. In other words, when the government created the reserves to protect these areas from development, it was from development other than that of tourism, to which the government gave the CPR almost exclusive rights.[4]

Otherwise, the early years of the CPR serve to establish the fact that the type of railway support for landscape painters offered by the Intercolonial became a convention in Canada. Just as the Intercolonial had done for eastward travel earlier, the company issued passes to Montreal- and Toronto-based painters to travel west, beginning in 1885, exploiting the artist's social authority as a judge of landscapes to promote the Rocky Mountains to what CPR general manager William Cornelius Van Horne referred to as 'the class that travels'.[5] Again, the idea was to establish the value of the region, not in the eyes of the traveller as such, but in the eyes of an urban elite that, like the artists it patronized, possessed the cultural capital necessary for discriminating between different landscapes. To facilitate such cultural legitimization, the railway avoided any perception that the company had vested interest in the artists who travelled its route, eschewing direct purchase and use of paintings by the company in favour of the benefits reaped from the artists' success among those in the best position to make appropriate judgements in taste. This worked well for the CPR, as long as landscape painting was featured prominently in art exhibitions in central Canada, and as long as the most celebrated painters of the day sought to distinguish themselves with sensational paintings of the national landscape that was now linked to central Canada (Jessup 1992, 147–248).

In this respect, the company's cultural advertising functioned in much the same way as the Intercolonial's had earlier, except in the CPR's case it operated within the new imperialistic-type relationship between central and western Canada established with the completion of the railroad west. In the realm of high culture, this relationship was expressed in the context of a shift in the immediate audience for western views from Britain to central Canada, which, in the last quarter of the nineteenth century, had developed an art scene cosmopolitan enough to vet the production of local artists who hoped to succeed internationally—most notably, of course, in Britain, which maintained its metropolitan-periphery relationship with art production in Canada in this new mediated form. Thus, paintings of the landscape along the railroad were read in both metropolitan centres as evidence of Canada's colony-to-nation trajectory, whether they were viewed as products of a developing national culture or as pictures of western scenery opened up by rail. In either case, they operated within the discourse of imperialism, which, W.J.T. Mitchell writes, 'conceives itself precisely (and simultaneously) as an expansion of landscape understood as an inevitable, progressive development in history, an expansion of "culture" and "civilization" into a "natural" space in a progress that is itself narrated as "natural". Empires move outward in space as a way of moving forward in time; the "prospect" that opens up is not just a spatial scene but a projected future of development and exploitation' (Mitchell 16; see also den Otter 5–31, 205–7). On an economic level, this was advanced with the completion of the transcontinental railway and the implementation of the National Policy, which together effected a national political economy that established central Canada as the country's urban-industrial centre and relegated outlying regions to peripheral status. As Andy den Otter summarized most recently, the establishment of this isolationist economic policy in support of the railway facilitated development of the west as a hinterland to feed central Canadian corporate interests, while the Maritime region was transformed into a branch-plant economy, the imperial ties that had linked it directly to Britain having been switched to Canada under the terms of federation (den Otter 185–238).

The Group of Seven's subsequent work and activities suggest something of the sustaining impact of this political economy; the urban perspective embodied in their work reflects both central Canadian urban-industrial dominance and the continuing vitality in Canada of a picturesque landscape tradition in which artists created views of outlying regions for consumption by this metropolitan market. What distinguishes the Group of Seven's work and activities from those of their predecessors in this regard is their relationship to the rise of middle-class tourism, which took shape in the context of what Bryan Palmer describes as 'the first act of the theatre of mass culture', a commodification of leisure time that provided growing numbers of Canadians in the 1920s, most of them members of an increasingly affluent middle class, with the same possibility of momentary escape from the perceived effects of modern-industrial capitalism that had been available to the urban elite since the nineteenth century (Palmer 229). With it came the beginnings of state involvement in the organization of the tourist industry. 'Until the 1920s', Ian McKay points out, 'it had not been a permanent part of state policy either to attract tourists or to coordinate various aspects of local culture and society as part of the "tourism plant". After that decade, however, the state aggressively intervened in civil society to construct such a plant by paving highways, developing hotels, inventing new ethnic and sporting traditions, and monitoring the steady advance of the "industry"' (McKay 1994, 33). [ . . . ]

In the national parks, this took shape as active state involvement in the commodification of the wilderness experience. It could even be argued that the operation of the National Parks Branch of the Department of the Interior was predicated from the outset on the development of this commodity. Certainly, it occupied the attention of National Parks Commissioner James Bernard Harkin, who was appointed in 1911 when the Branch was established to administer the new

Dominion (later National) parks, which were created at this time out of the earlier nature reserves. His Commissioner's Reports insistently stressed the recuperative value of what he saw as National Park wilderness; he argued that the importance of the parks lay both in the increasing revenue they generated from American and other international tourism and in what he repeatedly described as 'the service they render to the people of Canada'.[6] Conflating well-worn ideas of wilderness with a heightened sense of the parks as a national possession, Harkin consistently cast National Park wilderness as an originary environment within which humanity—in this case specifically Canadians—could temporarily escape the bureaucratic institutions and hectic work routines of everyday life in urban-industrial society to renew the 'play spirit' Harkin saw as essential to the development of nationality. In doing so, he reconciled what otherwise seem to be the contradictory aims of national park policy during this period: the conservation of 'unspoiled' wilderness from human influence on the one hand (which served to maintain the essential *idea* of wilderness, and thus its restorative value to contemporary society), and, on the other, the promotion of the parks as therapeutic 'playgrounds', in this case both for Canadians and for international tourists (who, it was argued, generated the revenue necessary to pay for infrastructure to support increased domestic use of the parks).[7]

In other words, the commodification of wilderness experience involved celebrating the pre-modern, unspoiled 'essence' of National Park wilderness while, paradoxically, looking for ways in which that essence could be commercialized in the creation of a modern tourism economy.[8] This explains why the Branch promoted conservation even as it aggressively developed infrastructure to increase the accessibility of the parks, which, almost from the beginning of the Branch's existence, meant the construction of scenic roads throughout the national park system. [ ... ]

Perhaps more important to national park development in these years than the increasing consumption of automobiles alone was the attendant popularity and almost immediate commercialization of auto camping as a leisure activity among the more affluent members of the middle class. By the mid-1920s, when Harkin was reporting that more than half the record 104,000 visitors to Rocky Mountain (later Banff National) Park were entering by car, it had stimulated not only the building of the roads in the parks, but also the construction of related facilities, which, after the early years of auto camping as simple roadside squatting, had evolved into a range of commercial accommodations for motorists, including roadside reservations, campsites and cabins, all of them capitalizing on the assertion of individual freedom, informality and ascetic self-reliance then associated with automobile travel.[9]

This is ironic because, in Canada's mountain parks, the Canadian Pacific and Canadian National railways worked closely with the National Parks Branch to encourage automobile-based tourism; because of their privileged, if not exclusive, situation in the parks, they stood to benefit most immediately from the state's efforts to develop the tourism economy in western Canada. The CPR was even committed to splitting the construction costs of the Banff-Windermere highway through what is now Kootenay National Park with the British Columbia government, shouldering the total cost of this scenic highway with the National Parks Branch, which was financing the road's construction within the boundaries of Rocky Mountain Park.[10] In the early 1920s, the CPR also introduced 'bungalow camps'— compounds consisting of small, homely cabins grouped around central dining halls—for motor tourists who sought lodgings that were comfortable yet economical. It operated these in the parks alongside the campgrounds and roadside motor parks the Branch had built to 'accommodate motorists who desire to live under canvas', as Harkin put it (Canada,

Department of the Interior 1926, 91). Such accommodations were expressive, as well, of a perceived shift in the physical experience of wilderness—a new primitivist intimacy that served to distinguish it from what had been defined as the more restricted, formal experience associated with Victorian resort hotels and rail travel. In keeping with this, the CNR used a similarly primitivist vocabulary of 'peeled logs and native boulders' when, in 1923, it constructed its new resort hotel, Jasper Park Lodge, which consisted of a luxurious central structure surrounded by what it described as smaller, 'bungalow style' log cabins.[11] By then it was also supplementing its celebrated 'motor roads' with extensive hiking trails, as was the CPR, both railways developing them in conjunction with the riding trails the Branch was building to service increasing numbers of tourists in search of the wilderness experience.[12]

[ . . . ]

In this sense, both the Branch and the railways played into what Frow has identified as one of the central tensions of modern tourism, the fact that the romantic gaze generates positional competition for a (landscape) resource rendered increasingly scarce by its vulnerability to the presence of other tourists. In the national parks, this not only motivated the initial construction of hiking and pony paths, as state and capital sought to encourage tourism; it also generated consumer demand for wilderness, which drove the construction of paths throughout the 1920s as visitors sought to escape what Harkin described as 'the beaten tourist trails' (Canada, Department of the Interior 1928–1929, 103). As Frow points out, however, the gratification of this romantic desire for a solitudinous experience of Nature was not achieved through positional competition alone. It also demanded that tourists deny, or at least repress, their awareness of the mass availability of an experience they imagined to be the privilege of a few. In the capitalist organization of such positional competition, where geographic exclusivity is tied to

economic exclusivity, this 'fantasy of achieved upward mobility' facilitated the romantic notion that one was 'getting away from it all' in a landscape increasingly occupied by other tourists.[13] This is why the work of artists continued to be of worth to the railways. In the service of an emergent mass tourism, paintings and exhibitions of scenery in the region operated in much the same way as they had in the nineteenth century. They offered the railways a means to establish the value of the landscape, where value was located in the landscape as an object of the romantic gaze and, in association with this, in ideas of class understood in terms of cultural capital.

The Branch's interest in supporting the work of artists was also predicated on the understanding that cultural capital could accrue to the parks by association. In 1923, the Department of the Interior commissioned 'A Choric Ode' to distribute as a souvenir in connection with the opening of the Banff-Windermere Highway; Harkin argued in an internal memo that 'the tourist sees through the eyes of the poet and values [the landscape] more highly on that account'. Casually conflating the tourist's gaze with that of the Canadian, he concluded as a result that such work 'would add romance and the glamour of art to the mountains and so make them more valuable in the eyes of Canadians themselves'.[14] The Branch also contributed handsomely towards the production costs of the CNR's 1927 deluxe booklet, *Jasper National Park*, an elaborate souvenir brochure featuring 21 black-and-white illustrations suggestive of charcoal drawings and six tipped-in colour reproductions of gouache paintings, most of them signed at the lower left or right—the drawings by Group of Seven members J.E.H. MacDonald, Frank Carmichael and A.J. Casson and the paintings by A.Y. Jackson (see, for example, Figures 1 and 2). Strictly a commercial production, it was designed to evoke values conventionally associated with works of fine art and the artist's response to the environment; in reality, all the illustrations were based on photographs, including the pictures by Jackson, who painted in gouache only when doing commercial work in any case (see, for example, Figures 3 and 4).[15] (MacDonald, Carmichael and Casson had never even been to the park.) Drawing on their friendship and on the artists' experience as commercial designers, the commission would have come through Carmichael, who was then art director at the commercial art firm Sampson Matthews Ltd. in Toronto, where he was supervising production of a number of CNR brochures.[16]

In other words, despite its play on the values of fine art in the promotion of National Park wilderness, the project had more to do with the Group members' contacts within the field of commercial design than it did with recognition of their status as 'bonafide artists', to use CNR president Henry Thornton's epithet.[17] An illustration by MacDonald in the 1928 CPR brochure, *Resorts in the Canadian Pacific Rockies*, in contrast, is a good example of a commercial production that acknowledged their standing as working artists (Figure 5). Following what was by then CPR convention, it is a colour reproduction of one of his sketches, a small work he probably gave to general tourist agent John Murray Gibbon as a gesture of gratitude for free passage over the railroad, which he enjoyed annually from 1924 to 1930.[18] In this brochure, his painting is one of several reproductions of works by artists who had sketched in the 'CPR Rockies'; the other artists are lesser-known today than MacDonald.[19] At the time, however, their views would have worked seamlessly with his to suggest values generally associated with landscape art, the titles of their works having clearly been adapted by the railway to serve its immediate interests. The title of MacDonald's sketch, *Lake O'Hara—seen from the Bungalow Camp*, is a case in point. Even though both MacDonald and fellow Group member Arthur Lismer stayed in the company's Lake O'Hara bungalow camp (Lismer first visiting the mountains on a pass in 1928), the titles they assigned to the products of their sketching trips do not make such

**Figure 1** Illustration in the 1927 CNR brochure, *Jasper National Park*, p. 9. Signed at the lower right, J.E.H. MacDonald. Library and Archives Canada

**Figure 2** Colour illustration in the 1927 CNR brochure, *Jasper National Park*, p. 30. Signed at the lower left, A.Y. Jackson. Library and Archives Canada.

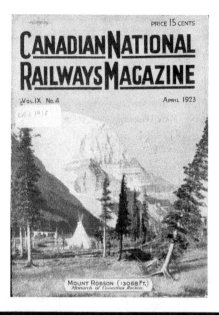

**Figure 3** *Canadian National Railways Magazine*, 11: 7 (July 1925), cover. Photo: National Library of Canada (neg. no. NL22447).

**Figure 4** *Canadian National Railways Magazine*, 9: 5 (April 1923), cover. Photo: National Library of Canada (neg. no. NL22448)

**Figure 5** Colour illustration in the 1928 CPR brochure, Resorts in the Canadian Pacific Rockies. Source: Canadian Pacific Railways Archive. 'Lake O'Hara—seen from the Bungalow Camp', J.E.H. MacDonald, colour illustration in the 1928 CPR brochure, Resorts in the Canadian Pacific Rockies. Photo courtesy of the Toronto Public Library.

explicit references to the commercial aspects of their wilderness experience.[20] The titles of their paintings make general or specific references instead to geographical locations or physical features, a work such as MacDonald's related sketch, *Lake McArthur, Yoho Park* (Figure 6), underscoring the origins of the Group's work in the picturesque landscape tradition and the seemingly private experience of undisturbed natural beauty characteristic of the romantic gaze.

The reproduction of MacDonald's painting is an isolated example of the use of a Group members' work in a railway brochure in any case, and there is no evidence to suggest that the artists were specifically interested in generating commercial art commissions in connection with their trips west to the parks. They were there to advance their work as painters and, through it, their respective careers as artists, which, if anything, made them sensitive to the potential uses of fine art in the development of a tourism economy. Their various proposals for promotional decorative schemes and murals in railway hotels and stations have been documented, along with the one decorative work of this type completed by a Group member, the Jasper Tea Room at the CNR's Chateau Laurier Hotel in Ottawa, which was undertaken by Edwin Holgate in the late 1920s using motifs inspired by his 1926 trip with Jackson west of Jasper park to the Skeena River region. There is also evidence of the artists' interest in the production of souvenirs. According to Jackson, Harris had a long talk with Thornton about 'the souvenir business', probably when the two artists returned from Jasper park in 1924.[21] At that time, Lismer was also trying to advance the idea in collaboration with National Gallery director Eric Brown, who met with J.B. Harkin ('apropos the application of Canadian Art to economic matters') to discuss a proposal by Harkin's office that the Branch sell works by Canadian artists as

**Figure 6** J.E.H. MacDonald, *Lake McArthur, Yoho Park*, 1924; oil on cardboard, 21.4 x 26.6 cm, National Gallery of Canada, Vincent Massey Bequest, 1968.

souvenirs in the parks: 'small pictures and sketches via colour prints, woodblocks, small figurines, wood carvings, pottery, metal work and many other things'. In keeping with the nationalist imperative characteristic of the artist's work and activities, Brown argued that 'this was the time for Canadian art to go forward'. He suggested that the National Gallery help by exhibiting this souvenir art and by providing loans and exhibitions to the parks in turn. 'The larger Parks might build a small and picturesque gallery', he suggested to Harkin, 'where all such objects could be sold, where lectures and talks could be given and Canadian art could be featured to the tourist'.[22]

Preliminary arrangements, which were made early the next year, included Harkin's commitment to gain the necessary approval of the scheme from the Department of the Interior, which he hoped to secure with the aid of a memorandum from Brown arguing (as Brown phrased it) 'the artistic value of the enterprise as well as the commercial and nationalistic ones'. He and Brown also devised a provisional advisory committee, which included Harkin and Brown, Group members Lismer and MacDonald and Group supporter and National Gallery Trustee, Vincent Massey. Working out of Toronto or Ottawa with start-up funds Harkin evidently anticipated along with departmental approval, they planned to discuss the organization and administration of the project, including sources of supplies, standards of excellence and designs and methods of production.[23] (Clearly inspired by the idea of a centralized, state-supervised 'souvenir industry', Brown and Lismer had already discussed the possibility of working through the established art schools, using students such as those at the Ontario College of Art in Toronto, where both Lismer and MacDonald were teaching at the time, 'if', Brown cautioned, 'they could be organized into producing the right kind of stuff'.)[24] As far as Brown was concerned, the souvenirs would need to be not only well designed and applicable to quantity production, but also

reflective of what he described in his memo as the 'Canadian nationality' seen in the art of the Group of Seven and their followers, which he characteristically conflated with Canadian art in general. 'I can imagine nothing better calculated to stimulate Canadian art and to turn it towards the development of a national spirit', he argued, casting their plans for the touristic commercialization of fine art in terms consistent with the ideas of the Group.[25] Although he did not deal explicitly with the commercial value of the scheme in his memo, it is clear that he understood the potential market for this new commodity; he wrote to Massey at almost the same time that Harkin was sure the railways would support the scheme 'both in hotels and probably on boats. Those, added to parks, ought to make a great demand when you think that about 60,000 souvenir buying visitors go to Banff Park alone each year'.[26]

As it turned out, however, the scheme was not realized—good indication, perhaps, that departmental approval was not forthcoming. Nonetheless, Harkin continued to express interest in the commercialization of fine art as souvenirs, the Branch's efforts to advance the scheme from the outset having been part of its larger involvement in the commodification of the wilderness experience and the development of a tourist industry.[27] Despite the fact that the authenticity they claimed to embody as souvenirs of the place would have been undermined by their supervised mass production in central Canada, clearly, to Harkin's mind, 'artistic Canadian souvenirs' would serve as authentic mementos of the tourist's experience of National Park wilderness insofar as they appeared to embody the individual artistic expression of the Canadian artist whose essential Canadianness was understood in relationship to wilderness landscape. On another level, the scheme was part of his ongoing efforts to structure the tourist's gaze through identification of the parks with the values of fine art and what he described as its ability 'to arouse the sort of ideas' he wanted Canadians to associate with the Rocky Mountains.[28] That Brown stood ready to use the National Gallery of Canada to help 'in any way in the working out of this idea' was important; it indicates not only that Brown understood the role of the National Gallery in the processes of cultural legitimization at the root of Harkin's scheme, but also that he was willing to use the power of the National Gallery to facilitate it.[29] Ultimately, of course, the instrumentality of this cultural authority in promoting the work and ideas of the Group of Seven to the level of 'official culture' also served to institutionalize the wilderness experience Harkin was trying to advance, bringing it into close association with the ideas of nationality in and around the work of the Group of Seven and, through the medium of elite culture, with notions of value understood in terms of cultural capital.

In this connection, it is important to remember that, in the end, the wilderness experience authorized—and nationalized—in the process was a function of the romantic gaze, with its emphasis on elitist—and solitary—consumption of undisturbed Nature. As such, the artists' expressions of this experience also work effectively to obscure what was, in the 1920s, its increasing availability for mass consumption as a commodity in the development of a tourism economy (a process that, in itself, facilitates the denial of mass accessibility essential to the tourist's experience). Even today, the artists' accounts of their sketching trips (and, thus, of their sketches) are still received at face value and accepted as chronicles of rugged engagement with an elemental, pre-modern environment, even as they are identified as a primary source for the romantic images of bushwhacker, pioneer and adventurer at the root of the Group's mythology.[30] While there is no reason to doubt the sincerity of the artists' reports (whether colourful or poetic), it is now evident that their accounts, activities, and resulting works can also be seen in terms of the anti-modern impulses at the heart of the middle-class wilderness

experience and the willing suspension of disbelief required for the restorative, solitary experience of a 'virgin', uninhabited landscape otherwise populated by other tourists (Figure 7). In this context, their wilderness images can be resituated as products of a time when they used hiking and pony trails, stayed in bungalow camps or 'lived under canvas' like other visitors to the parks, participating in the very tourist experience their work was helping to structure. Even Harris's treks to what have been seen through his paintings as increasingly remote locations in the mountains can be viewed in the context of modern tourism and the positional competition for landscape that seems to exist outside the very circuit of exchange values and commodity relations that make it accessible to the tourist. If they are, the spiritual exploration of the mountain landscape he undertook at the time takes on new meaning;

**Figure 7** Back cover of *Canadian National Railways Magazine* 18:8 (August 1932). Source: Canadian National Railways Magazine, 18:8 (August 1932), back cover. Used by the permission of the estate of Lawren S. Harris and GM Media Archives. Photo courtesy of Toronto Public Library.

among other things, it is informed by the fact that, in 1929, the year he was making sketches for his lonely *Isolation Peak, Rocky Mountains* (Figure 8), the number of visitors to National Park wilderness reached almost half a million.[31]

**Figure 8** Lawren Harris, *Isolation Peak, Rocky Mountains*, 1930; oil on canvas, 107 x 128 cm, Hart House Permanent Collection, University of Toronto.

## NOTES

1. National Gallery of Canada Library and Archives (hereafter NGC), NGC fonds, 7.1 J, 'A.Y. Jackson', Jackson to Marius Barbeau, 19 April [1927]; 7.1 V, 'F. Varley', Varley to Eric Brown, 10 August 1926 and Varley to Brown, 11 August 1926; 7.1 L, 'A. Lismer', Henry Thornton to Brown, 25 July 1927; Canadian Museum of Civilization (hereafter CMC), Information Management Services (hereafter IMS), Marius Barbeau correspondence, B197, f.: 19, 'Gibbon, J. Murray (1919, 1922–6)', Gibbon to Barbeau, 20 August 1925 and 28 April 1927; B205, f.: 23, 'Jackson, Alex. Y.',

Barbeau to Jackson [February 1926]; Jackson to Barbeau, [May 1926, early June 1926 and mid-June 1928]; B204, f.: 70, 'Howard, C.K.', Barbeau to Howard, 15 February 1927; B242, f.: 90, 'Thompson, Walter', Barbeau to Thompson, 4 February 1929.

2. CMC, IMS, Barbeau correspondence, B205, f.: 23, 'Jackson, Alex Y.', Jackson to Barbeau, 9 February 1927; A.Y. Jackson, 'Rescuing Our Tottering Totems', *Maclean's* 40 (15 December 1927): 23, 37; CMC, IMS, Barbeau correspondence, B202, f.: 22, 'Harkin, J.B. (1916–1934)', memorandum, Barbeau and

M.B. Williams to Harkin, 'National Park at Hazelton, British Columbia', 1924; National Archives of Canada (hereafter NAC), RG84, Canadian Parks Service, vol. 1981, file U2-19-1-1, 'Report re: Totem Pole Villages and Proposed National Park near Hazelton, B.C.' 29 April 1924, and, for related correspondence, vol. 1981, file U2-19-4, part 1, and vol. 184, file U2-19-4, part 1.

3.  CMC, IMS, Barbeau correspondence, B205, f.: 23, 'Jackson, Alex Y.', Jackson to Barbeau, 21 May [1928]; Jackson to Barbeau [mid-June 1928].

4.  Lothian, *History of Canada's National Parks*, vol. 3 (see, for example, 12–13, 27–8, 36).

5.  The company's London agent, Alexander Begg, referred to them more precisely perhaps as 'the better class of people such as tourists and others of that character' (NAC, Records of the Canadian Government Exhibition Commission, vol. 42, f.: 1129/1886-1143/1886, no.1233, Begg to C.C. Chipman, 7 June 1886).

6.  Canada, Department of the Interior, *Annual Report of the Commissioner of National Parks of Canada* (1914) 1.

7.  Canada, Department of the Interior, *Annual Report of the Commissioner of National Parks of Canada* (1911–20).

8.  McKay, *Quest of the Folk*, 35, makes this observation about the commercialization of the seemingly uncommercial, pre-modern 'essence' of the Folk in his discussion of twentieth-century tourism in Nova Scotia. See also Frow, 'Tourism and the Semiotics of Nostalgia', 129.

9.  Canada, Department of the Interior, *Annual Report of the Commissioner of National Parks of Canada* (1924–1925) 90–1.

10. NAC, RG84, Canadian Parks Service, vol. 169, file U109-25, Director of Publicity, National Parks Branch, Department of the Interior to W.S. Tempest, c/o *The Motorist*, 9 January 1923; Deborah Wightman and Geoffrey Wall, 'The Spa Experience at Radium Hot Springs', *Annals of Tourism Research*, 12 (1985): 401–7.

11. NAC, Canadian National Railways, MG30/34, vol. 12535, Item 645, CNR, *Jasper Park Lodge: Canadian Rockies* (1925), n.p.; CNR, *Jasper Park Lodge on Lac Beauvert* (1923), n.p. For the development of Jasper Park Lodge, see

also I.S. MacLaren, 'Cultured Wilderness in Jasper National Park', *Journal of Canadian Studies* 34 (Fall 1999): 25–31.

12. Lothian, *History of Canada's National Parks*, vol. 4, 76; Canada, Department of the Interior, *Annual Report of the Commissioner of National Parks of Canada* (1920–1930).

13. Frow, 'Tourism and the Semiotics of Nostalgia', 146–47. See also Urry, *Tourist Gaze*, 41–7, and passim.

14. NAC, RG84, vol. 169, file U109-23, memorandum from Harkin to W.W. Cory, 8 June 1923.

15. NAC, RG84, vol. 146, J-113-200 (vol. 2), W.L. Crighton to Harkin, 26 January 1927.

16. For other CNR brochure covers by Carmichael see, for example, NAC, RG30/34, vol. 12534, Item 645, CNR, *The Triangle Tour, British Columbia Canada* (1928); vol. 12535, Item 645, CNR, *Jasper National Park: Canadian Rockies* (1928); NAC, Franklin Carmichael Paper, MG30, D293, vol. 1, Item 4, CNR, *Alaska and the Yukon* (1928); McMichael Canadian Art Collection Library, Mary Mastin Donation, Item 3, CNR, *The Canadian Rockies: The Triangle Tour* (1926), with attached note: 'Cover designed by Franklin Carmichael—authenticated by CAG Matthews'.

17. NGC, NGC fonds, 7.1 L, 'Arthur Lismer', Thornton to Eric Brown, 25 July 1927.

18. Canadian Pacific Railway Archives (hereafter CPRA), CPR, *Resorts in the Canadian Pacific Rockies* (1928), opposite page 18. (The 1927 version of CPR, *Resorts in the Canadian Pacific Rockies*, which is also in the Canadian Pacific Railway Archives, does not contain a reproduction of MacDonald's sketch.)

19. The other illustrations in the brochure are reproductions of pastels by Leonard Richmond and paintings by Carl Rungius and Hal Ross Perrigard.

20. NGC, NGC fonds, 7.1 L, 'Arthur Lismer', Lismer to H.O. McCurry, 22 August 1928.

21. CMC, IMS, Barbeau correspondence, B205, f.: 23, 'Jackson, Alex Y.', Jackson to Barbeau [1935]; Jackson, *Painter's Country*, 108.

22. NGC, NGC fonds, 7.1 L, 'Arthur Lismer', Brown to Lismer, 31 October 1924. See also CMC, IMS, Barbeau correspondence, B205, f.: 23, 'Jackson, Alex Y.', Jackson to Barbeau [1935]. Harkin's assistant, Mabel B. Williams

is credited with the idea of selling such souvenirs in the parks; see NGC, NGC fonds, 7.4 C, 'Canadian National Park Branch 1925 (Outside Activities/Organizations)', Brown to Vincent Massey, 22 January 1925.

23. NGC, NGC fonds, 7.4 C, 'Canadian National Park Branch 1925 (Outside Activities/Organizations)', Brown to Massey, 22 January 1925. The memorandum from Brown that Harkin requested was written in the form of a letter. (NGC, NGC fonds, 7.4 C, 'Canadian National Park Branch 1925 (Outside Activities/Organizations)', Brown to Harkin, 23 January 1925.)

24. NGC, NGC fonds, 7.1 L, 'Arthur Lismer', Brown to Lismer, 31 October 1924.

25. NGC, NGC fonds, 7.4 C, 'Canadian National Park Branch 1925 (Outside Activities/Organizations)', Brown to Harkin, 23 January 1925. See also NGC, NGC fonds, 7.1 L,

'Arthur Lismer', Brown to Lismer, 31 October 1924.

26. NGC, NGC fonds, 7.4 C, 'Canadian National Park Branch 1925 (Outside Activities/Organizations)', Brown to Massey, 22 January 1925.

27. CMC, IMS, Barbeau correspondence, B241, f.: 41, 'Lismer, Arthur (1925–8)' Barbeau to Lismer, 10 June 1927.

28. NAC, RG84, vol. 169, file U109-23, memorandum from Harkin to W.W. Cory, 8 June 1923.

29. NGC, NGC fonds, 7.4 C, 'Canadian National Park Branch 1925 (Outside Activities/Organizations)', Brown to Harkin, 23 January 1925.

30. Teitelbaum, 'Sighting the Single Tree'.

31. Canada, Department of the Interior, *Annual Report of the Commissioner of National Parks of Canada* (1929–1930), 99.

# WORKS CITED

Bordo, Jonathan. 'Jack Pine—Wilderness Sublime or the Erasure of the Aboriginal Presence from the Landscape'. *Journal of Canadian Studies* 27 (1992–3): 98–128.

———. 'The Terra Nullius of Wilderness—Colonialist Landscape Art (Canada & Australia) and the So-called Claim to American Exception'. *Journal of Canadian Studies* 15 (1997): 13–36.

Canada, Department of the Interior. *Annual Report of the Commissioner of National Parks of Canada* (1914; 1911–1920; 1924–1925; 1926–1927).

Cronon, William. 'The Trouble with Wilderness: or, Getting Back to the Wrong Nature'. *Uncommon Ground: Toward Reinventing Nature*, ed. William Cronon. New York: W.W. Norton and Co., 1995.

den Otter, A.A. *The Philosophy of Railways: The Transcontinental Railway Idea in British North America*. Toronto: University of Toronto Press, 1997.

Frow, John. 'Tourism and the Semiotics of Nostalgia', *October* 57 (1991): 123–51.

Helsinger, Elizabeth. 'Turner and the Representation of England'. *Landscape and Power*, ed. W.J.T.

Mitchell. Chicago: University of Chicago Press, 1994.

Jackson, A.Y. *A Painter's Country: The Autobiography of A.Y. Jackson*. Toronto: Clarke, Irwin, 1958; memorial edn, 1976.

———. 'Rescuing Our Tottering Totems' *Maclean's* 40 (15 December 1927): 23, 37.

Jacobson, Matthew Frye. *Whiteness of a Different Color: European Immigrants and the Alchemy of Race*. Cambridge, MA: Harvard University Press, 1998.

Jessup, Lynda. 'Artists, Railways, the State, and "The Business of Becoming a Nation"' Ph.D. thesis, University of Toronto, 1992.

Lothian, W.F. *A History of Canada's National Parks*, 4 vols. Ottawa: Parks Canada, 1977.

MacKenzie, John M. *The Empire of Nature: Hunting, Conservation, and British Imperialism*. Manchester: Manchester University Press, 1988.

MacLaren, I.S. 'Cultured Wilderness in Jasper National Park'. *Journal of Canadian Studies* 34 (1999): 7–58.

McKay, Ian. 'Handicrafts and the Logic of "Commercial Antimodernism": The Nova Scotia Case'. *Antimodernism and Artistic*

*Experience: Policing the Boundaries of Modernity*, ed. Lynda Jessup. Toronto: University of Toronto Press, 2001: 117–29.

———. *The Quest of the Folk: Antimodernism and Cultural Selection in Twentieth-Century Nova Scotia*. Montreal and Kingston: McGill-Queen's University Press, 1994.

Mitchell, W.J.T. 'Imperial Landscape'. *Landscape and Power*, ed. W.J.T. Mitchell. Chicago: University of Chicago Press, 1994: 5–34.

Palmer, Bryan D. *Working-Class Experience: Rethinking the History of Canadian Labour, 1880–1991*. 2nd edn. Toronto: McClelland & Stewart, 1992.

Teitelbaum, Matthew. 'Sighting the Single Tree, Sighting the New Found Land'. *Eye of Nature*, ed. Dana Augaitas. Banff, AB: Walter Phillips Gallery, 1991: 71–88.

Urry, John. *The Tourist Gaze: Leisure and Travel in Contemporary Societies*. London: Sage Publications, 1990.

Walter, J.A. 'Social Limits to Tourism', *Leisure Studies* 1 (1982): 295–304.

Watson, Scott. 'Race, Wilderness, Territory and the Origins of Modern Canadian Landscape Painting'. *Semiotext(e)* 6 (1994): 93–104.

———. 'Disfigured Nature: The Origins of the Modern Canadian Landscape'. *Eye of Nature*, ed. Dana Augaitas. Banff, AB: Walter Phillips Gallery, 1991: 103–12.

Wightman, Deborah and Geoffrey Wall, 'The Spa Experience at Radium Hot Springs', *Annals of Tourism Research*, 12 (1985): 393–416.

Wonders, Karen. 'A Sportsman's Eden', *Beaver* 79 (December 1999 to January 2000): 30–7.

# Chapter 8

# Racism in Canada

## READINGS

### Primary Documents

### Historical Interpretations

### Introduction

Although Canada is often called a nation of immigrants (a description that sets aside First Nations' prior claims), for a long while these immigrants came from a rather limited slice of the world. Augmenting the colonial migrations dominated by France and Great Britain, most people who migrated to the Dominion before the turn of the twentieth century left European nations, predominantly the British Isles and Western Europe. This pattern began to shift noticeably in the 1890s, as it became more likely for southern and eastern Europeans to make the trip. The Asian workers arriving in the first couple of decades after Confederation were another notable exception to the general pattern, but their numbers remained small in comparison to the visible majority of whites around them. In terms of outward appearance and cultural practices like religion, there was not much difference between most new arrivals and families who had been in Canada for several generations. However, this demographic dominance by the 'white race' did not prevent discrimination. Racism flourished in a variety of ways, from individual acts of suspicion and disrespect to formally enacted laws and policies designed to drive out or limit the prospects of racial minorities. We've chosen sources here that highlight reactions to the presence of Asians, mainly because during the first third of the twentieth century, white Canadians saw Asians as the greatest threat to national prosperity, and partially because historians have been able to tap a rich vein of evidence detailing anti-Asian measures. Emily Murphy was a magistrate in Edmonton, and was perhaps best known for her role in promoting women's rights. She also concerned herself with the problem of drug trafficking in Canada and, despite taking some care to present her remarks as detached and scientific, had some clear opinions regarding various racial and ethnic groups and their involvement in the trade. The 1923 *Chinese Immigration Act* sets out the conditions under which Chinese migrants would be allowed to enter Canada, and the conditions exclude all but a handful of privileged groups with prior ties to Canada. This 1923 law eliminated the notorious 'head tax' of 1885 entirely, possibly in the hope that the number of Chinese eligible to pay such a tax would soon become insignificant. David Goutor's article compares attitudes toward black and Chinese workers during the period before the First World War, noting how clear differences emerged. While black workers still faced barriers to employment and social acceptance, the labour movement judged Chinese workers to be a greater threat to certain segments of the Canadian workforce. We return to the theme of drugs with Catherine Carstairs' article on the conflation of race and vice in the public imagination. Penalties for drug use increased during the 1920s, and were seemingly tailored to the sort of drug use prevalent in the Chinese community. It is important for the student of history to recognize that in the end, drugs, immigration regulations, and workplace discrimination were merely new stages on which the old script of racism was played out.

## QUESTIONS FOR CONSIDERATION

1. How does Emily Murphy represent the Chinese-Canadian community as a divided one?
2. What sort of immigrant could make it into Canada under the 1923 Act?
3. Given the effort made to discriminate between Euro-Canadians and others, what did white Canada fear?
4. Why did labour leaders seem to be more 'worried' about Chinese labourers than black ones?
5. How does Carstairs define a 'moral panic', and how does a moral panic gain momentum?

## SUGGESTIONS FOR FURTHER READING

Kay J. Anderson, *Vancouver's Chinatown: Racial Discourse in Canada, 1875–1980* (Montreal and Kingston: McGill-Queen's University Press, 1995).

Constance Backhouse, *Colour-Coded: A Legal History of Racism in Canada, 1900–1950* (Toronto: University of Toronto Press, 1999).

David Goutor, *Guarding the Gates: The Canadian Labour Movement and Immigration, 1872–1934* (Vancouver: UBC Press, 2007).

Grant Grams, 'The Deportation of German Nationals from Canada, 1919 to 1939', *Journal of International Migration & Integration* 11(2) (Spring 2010): 219–37.

Lisa Rose Mar, *Brokering Belonging: Chinese in Canada's Exclusion Era, 1885–1945* (Oxford: Oxford University Press, 2010).

Patricia E. Roy, *Oriental Question: Consolidating a White Man's Province, 1914–42* (Vancouver: UBC Press, 2003).

Harold Troper and Irving Abella, *None is too Many: Canada and the Jews of Europe 1933–1948*, 3rd edn (Toronto: Key Porter Books, 2002).

Peter Ward, *White Canada Forever: Popular Attitudes and Public Policy toward Orientals in British Columbia* (Montreal and Kingston: McGill-Queen's University Press, 2002).

# PRIMARY DOCUMENTS

**1** From Emily Murphy, *The Black Candle* (Toronto: Thomas Allen, 1922), 178–99.

## INTERNATIONAL RINGS

*Secret path marks secret foe.*—Sir Walter Scott

The Christianized Chinese in Canada and the States are also anxious to clear up crime or misbehaviour among their compatriots, and so are proceeding to make these conform to the provisions of the white man's laws.

Fussy folk, and self-opinionated ones, can be found who claim there is no such thing as a Christianized Chinaman, and that his profession is one of entire hypocrisy, just as though Jehovah's arm were shortened and His ear heavy when the suppliants' color was just a shade deeper than their own.

Knowing many men from the Flowery Kingdom who exhibit all the traits of Christian gentlemen, we are prepared to take them as such until the contrary is proven. What Sa'di, the Persian, said of the morals of the dervishes is here applicable: 'In his outward behaviour I see nothing to blame, and with the secrets of his heart I claim no acquaintance'.

We believe that the letter here following was written by a Chinaman who desires to be a good citizen, and who has the same desires for his compatriots. At any rate, he speaks to the point and is no trembler. This was received by us a few months ago, and is interesting as showing the ideals and expressions of a naturalized Oriental:—

'Magistrate Murphy,
    The Police Court,
        Edmonton, Alberta.

DEAR MAGISTRATE:—

I have information that the China Town of this City, has lots of gambling houses and opium smokers. Things around here are so quiet just now, and hard times coming soon. I do not like the people around here getting starving, because I found out lots of poor labourers lost all their money for play the Chinese gamble which is called 'fine tin'* and waste up their good money for smoking opiums and so let their families, such as their father, mother, sisters, and young brothers starving at China.

*fan-tan.

And I am also afraid that the peoples around here spoil their own condition, and spoil all business in this city too, because the peoples lost their money, but they must betting lazy, then they must go stealing any things for their lives around this town, and getting all kinds of troubles here.

I am now wish you to stop all the China gambles houses at once, and would like to show you all the gambling houses address to arrest them.

If you spent a month time for the gambling houses, I believe the all gambling houses be stop so all the gamblers have to work for their own foods and every body have take care their families. Then I say 'Amen'.

I think you would be glad to do this for me. If you want any help let me know soon.

Yours sincerely,

.............

(Chinaman)

It came about this year in Vancouver that the Chinese merchants and leading members of the colony, with the support of the Chinese consulate, joined in the citizens' campaign to clean up Chinatown both morally and physically.

Realizing that their actions might lead to reprisals and to financial loss—that 'the ungodly might bend their bow'—they still decided to wage war on those elements which had brought disrepute and opprobrium upon all Chinamen in the Province of British Columbia.

The advantages of such co-operation with the citizens has been set forth in an article in a Western daily paper by a reporter with a well-oiled mind. 'The members of the Colony' he says, 'have the inside information. They know where the drugs are coming from; who is getting them into Vancouver; the underground methods by which they are being brought in; who has the financial interest in the drug ring; the methods of distribution in this and other cities; all the ramifications of the drug traffic are known to them. And they will tell all they know to the proper authorities. It is to be open warfare and they will do all in their power to combat the drug-ring'.

It is claimed that in some of the anti-narcotic campaigns, men who have financial interest in the Ring are among the most active workers, whether these are joining for sinister purposes, or merely to divert suspicion from themselves, it would be difficult to say. Probably their purpose includes both, but, be this as it may, it was a clever move to secure the co-operation of the reputable members of the Oriental Colony as allies in this campaign.

In Vancouver and Victoria during the present year, mass meetings have been held and committees appointed to take active steps in the organization of every public service body in Canada for a fight against the activities of the Ring. The local organizations then proceeded to get in touch with all kindred branches in other cities in the Dominion, emphasizing the need of their taking a definite stand on the question.

Some of the organizations back of the movement in the cities are the Board of Trade, Ratepayers' Association, Women's Institutes, Women's Press Club, War Heroes' Association, Victorian Order of Nurses, Kiwanis, Rotary, Kwannon and Gyro Clubs, Parent-teachers' Association, Woman's New Era, and the One Hundred Per Cent Clubs, the Women's Church Temperance Union, the Imperial Order of the Daughters of the Empire, Trades and Labor Council, University Women's Club, King's Daughters, The Maccabees, Child Welfare Association, Orangemen, American Women's Club, the Great War Veterans, the Local Council of Women, the 'Y' Associations, the Medical Association, as well as the municipal and provincial authorities, and a hundred churches.

In Seattle, believing that organization is the key to success, they are also combining their forces in a drive on addictive drugs. In Seattle, they too, have a branch of the White Cross Association. This Association has done more than any other agency to combat the drug evil, and at a lesser expense. In seven months last year, one paid agent caused 275 arrests, some of the persons convicted received heavy fines and others terms of imprisonment of from one to four years. It is claimed by White Cross workers that police departments cannot appropriate the sums required for the detection of pedlars in that most of the police officials are known to the drug runners, and hence large sums must be spent to secure arrests.

The White Cross are agitating that the Harrison Anti-Narcotic law be so amended as to permit of sentences of from seven to twelve years. The organization declares that short terms and fines are no deterrent in that the Ring has abundant money with which to pay the fines while the pedlar has no fear of from thirty to sixty days imprisonment. Besides, he is well rewarded for his temporary incarceration in jail.

In January of this year, a Narcotic Drug Control League was formed in New York, this League comprising the most notable organizations and workers in the State. The secretary is Joseph P. Chamberlain, Columbia University, New York City.

The objects of their anti-drug League as set forth on the invitation sent out are as follows:— 'To marshal representative forces against the world menace of drug addiction. The Narcotic Drug Control League represents the first organized movement against this evil which has reached alarming proportions and is producing a growing horde of incompetents and criminals involving even the youth of our country'.

'Habit forming drugs are destroying and enslaving a steadily increasing number of our people. The toll of victims among the youth of the country is the striking development of recent years. The people do not know the facts. Our program is definite and constructive. Its success demands the aid of the churches, the judiciary, the medical profession, and public-spirited citizens representative of every class in the community. Patriotic people must unite to remove this scourge from our land and from the world'.

This claim that the people do not know of the terrifying growth of the narcotic evil, was referred to recently by Dr. J.A. Drouin of the State of Vermont who said, 'Most of us have been lulled to sleep by the usual so-called hospital reports, and other "official" reports, regarding the fast disappearing drug addicts in the United States, especially after the enactment of the *Harrison Narcotic Act*'.

In Canada, our federal officers declare that the people would be astounded if they comprehended the extent of the illicit traffic and the foothold it has gained.

That this method of organized public effort is a good one cannot be disputed. A Presbyterian clergyman, in Canada, speaking of this matter said the Drug Ring is successful in its operation because its brains are pooled and concentrated. Occidental ingenuity and Oriental craftiness are dangerously combined. Unless all the different public bodies become organized into a single fighting force, and the best brains of our camp centralized and concentrated as the directing mind, the fight will be futile. To carry on successfully the crusade, monetary backing is necessary also. It will take money to fight money.

In a previous chapter it was stated that white men of every clime and color were engaged in this traffic, and it was rumored that Japanese and German interests were chiefly responsible. As the Germans have not been trafficking in any goods with the people of this continent, for several years past, it would seem that the charge must be impossible of proof. Indeed, in communicating with the Chiefs-of-Police in the United States concerning the ravages of drug-intoxication, it was markworthy that those bearing German names were especially prompt and thorough in reply to my enquiries, and in making suggestions as to the applications of practical remedies.

It is true that the finest grade of cocaine in the world is manufactured in Germany and is known as 'Mercks'. Buyers claim—with what verity we cannot say—that this is now exported into Spain and shipped to this continent as 'No. I Spanish'. It is alleged on excellent authority that a kilo of cocaine (about two-and-a-fifth pounds) can, at the present time, be purchased in the Province of Alberta, Canada, for $18.00 or at about seventy-five cents an ounce. This seems incredible, in view of the prices paid by the addicts, but the Ring are not telling their secrets, nor registering their profits, so that we have no means of exactly verifying these figures.

On the other hand, we know that there are more narcotic drugs in Europe at the present time than in pre-war days, and that the market for these is in England, the United States and Canada, among the Anglo-Saxon races.

In Germany itself, the use of narcotic drugs is 'verboten', so that almost their entire traffic must be with other countries. Indeed, the same remark is practically applicable to all the European countries, a fact which is dealt with more fully elsewhere in this volume.

It is also true that while no Japanese ever becomes an addict, yet it is claimed he is the most active and dangerous of all the persons forming the Ring in that he keeps well under cover and is seldom apprehended.

We know, however, that several large seizures of contraband drugs have been made on Japanese steamers on the western coast of America. In March of this year, narcotics worth, at the wholesale price of $20,000, and a considerable quantity of Japanese whiskey were seized at Portland, on the Japanese steamer *Miegyi Maru*. The Japanese seamen hurled overboard a large number of sacks which were believed to have contained bottles.

The United States have made, this year, a formal protest to the Japanese Government against the smuggling of opium, morphine, heroin and other narcotics into America. Replying to this complaint, the Tokio foreign office has informed the American Government that efforts will be made to prevent illegal traffic in drugs and has requested Japanese ship owners to co-operate in the suppression of the same.

Returning to the matter of the alleged participation of German persons in this traffic, one of the authorities claiming this is Dr. Erwin C. Ruth, head of the Narcotic division of the International Revenue Department of Boston. He alleges that the opium and cocaine traffic is financed largely by interests in Germany and Great Britain, and that certain Germans have powerful corporations operating in South America, which deal in coca leaves, from which is produced cocaine.

Concerning the operations of Drug Rings in Asia especially in relation to opium, Dr. Ruth states that the opium traffic in Asia has grown to immense proportions and has become one of the greatest industries in the world, being organized with Standard Oil efficiency. In Persia, Turkey and India, immense plantations are operated by powerful interests, while great banking institutions for financing the drug traffic are well established.

Among the pedlars who are the agents of the Ring, the traffic is chiefly in the hands of Americans, Canadians, Chinese, Negroes, Russians and Italians, although the Assyrians and Greeks are running closely in the race.

It is claimed also, but with what truth we cannot say, that there is a well-defined propaganda among the aliens of color to bring about the degeneration of the white race.

Maybe, it isn't so, after all, the popular dictum which has something to do with a flag and a bulldog.

Oh! yes! it is the one which declares, 'What we have we'll hold'. The trouble with most bulldogs is that their heads are only developed in the region of the jaw and that any yellow terrier can hamstring them from behind.

We have no very great sympathy with the baiting of the yellow races, or with the belief that these exist only to serve the Caucasian, or to be exploited by us. Such a belief was exemplified in a film once shown at a five-cent theatre in Chicago, and was reported by Jane Addams.

In the pictures, a poor woman is surrounded by her several children, all of whom are desperately hungry, and hold out pleading hands for food. The mother sends one of the boys on the streets to beg but he steals a revolver instead, kills a Chinaman, robs him of several hundred dollars, and rushes home with the money to his mother.

The last scene portrays the woman and children on their knees in prayer thanking God for His care and timely rescue of them.

The Chinese, as a rule are a friendly people and have a fine sense of humor that puts them on an easy footing with our folk, as compared with the Hindu and others we might mention.

Ah Duck, or whatever we choose to call him, is patient, polite, and persevering. Also he inhales deeply. He has other peculiarities such as paying his debts and refraining from profanity. 'You sabe?'

The population of China amounts to 426,000,000 or one-third of the human race. Yes! it was a New York citizen who, looking up from an encyclopedia exclaimed with deadly earnestness, 'In this household, we shall not have more than three children seeing this book says every fourth child born in the world is a Chinaman'.

Still, it behooves the people in Canada and the United States, to consider the desirability of these visitors—for they *are* visitors—and to say whether or not we shall be '*at home*' to them for the future.

A visitor may be polite, patient, persevering, as above delineated, but if he carries poisoned lollypops in his pocket and feeds them to our children, it might seem wise to put him out.

It is hardly credible that the average Chinese pedlar has any definite idea in his mind of bringing about the downfall of the white race, his swaying motive being probably that of greed, but in the hands of his superiors, he may become a powerful instrument to this very end.

In discussing this subject, Major Crehan of British Columbia has pointed out that whatever their motive, the traffic always comes with the Oriental, and that one would, therefore be justified in assuming that it was their desire to injure the bright-browed races of the world.

Naturally, the aliens are silent on the subject, but an addict who died this year in British Columbia told how he was frequently jeered at as 'a white man accounted for'. This man belonged to a prominent family and, in 1917, was drawing a salary of six thousand dollars a year. He fell a victim to a drug 'booster' till, ultimately, he became a ragged wreck living in the noisome alleys of Chinatown, 'lost to use, and name and fame'.

This man used to relate how the Chinese pedlars taunted him with their superiority at being able to sell the dope without using it, and by telling him how the yellow race would rule the world. They were too wise, they urged, to attempt to win in battle but would win by wits; would strike at the white race through 'dope' and when the time was ripe would command the world.

'It may sound like a fantastic dream', writes the reporter, 'but this was the story he told in one of the brief periods when he was free from the drug curse, and he told it in all sincerity'.

Some of the Negroes coming into Canada—and they are no fiddle-faddle fellows either—have similar ideas, and one of their greatest writers has boasted how ultimately they will control the white men.

Many of these Negroes are law-abiding and altogether estimable, but contrariwise, many are obstinately wicked persons, earning their livelihood as free-ranging pedlars of poisonous drugs. Even when deported, they make their way back to Canada carrying on their operations in a different part of the country.

**2** From *An Act Respecting Chinese Immigration* (Ottawa: F.A. Acland, 1923), 301–315.

13-14 GEORGE V.
CHAP. 38.
An Act respecting Chinese Immigration.
   *[Assented to 30th June, 1923]*

His Majesty, by and with the advice and consent of the Senate and House of Commons of Canada, enacts as follows:—
[ . . . ]

## ENTRY AND LANDING

5.   The entry to or landing in Canada of persons of Chinese origin or descent irrespective of allegiance or citizenship, is confined to the following classes, that is to say:—

   (*a*)  The members of the diplomatic corps, or other government representatives, their suites and their servants, and consuls and consular agents;

   (*b*)  The children born in Canada of parents of Chinese race or descent, who have left Canada for educational or other purposes, on substantiating their identity to the satisfaction of the controller at the port or place where they seek to enter on their return;

   (*c*)  (1) Merchants as defined by such regulations as the Minister may prescribe;
   (2) students coming to Canada for the purpose of attendance, and while in actual attendance, at any Canadian university or college authorized by statute or charter to confer degrees; who shall substantiate their status to the satisfaction of the Controller at the port of entry subject to the approval of the Minister, whose decision shall be final and conclusive; provided that no Chinese person belonging to any of the two classes referred to in this paragraph shall be allowed to enter or land in Canada, who is not in possession of a valid passport issued in and by the Government of China and endorsed (*visé*) by a Canadian Immigration Officer at the place where he was granted such passport or at the port or place of departure.

6.   No person of Chinese origin or descent shall enter or land in Canada except at a port of entry.

7.    No person of Chinese origin or descent other than the classes mentioned in paragraphs (*a*) and (*b*) of section five and sections twenty-three and twenty-four of this Act shall be permitted to enter or land in Canada elsewhere than at the ports of Vancouver and Victoria.

## PROHIBITED CLASSES.

8.   No person of Chinese origin or descent unless he is a Canadian citizen within the meaning of paragraph (f) of section two of *The Immigration Act* shall be permitted to enter or land in Canada, or having entered or landed in Canada shall be permitted to remain therein, who belongs to any of the following classes, hereinafter called 'Prohibited classes':—

(a)   Idiots, imbeciles, feeble-minded persons, epileptics, insane persons and persons who have been insane at any time previously;

(b)   Persons afflicted with tuberculosis or leprosy in any form, or with any loathsome disease, or with a disease which is contagious or infectious, or which may be or become dangerous to the public health, whether such persons intend to settle in Canada or only to pass through Canada in transit to some other country;

(c)   Persons who have been convicted of, or admit having committed, any crime involving moral turpitude;

(d)   Prostitutes and women and girls coming to Canada for any immoral purpose and pimps or persons living on the avails of prostitution;

(e)   Persons who procure or attempt to bring into Canada prostitutes or women or girls for the purpose of prostitution or other immoral purpose;

(f)   Professional beggars or vagrants;

(g)   Persons who in the opinion of the Controller or the officer in charge at any port of entry are likely to become a public charge;

(h)   Persons of constitutional psychopathic inferiority;

(i)   Persons with chronic alcoholism, or addicted to the use of drugs;

(j)   Persons not included within any of the foregoing prohibited classes, who upon examination by a medical officer of the Department of Health are certified as being mentally or physically defective to such a degree as to affect their ability to earn a living;

(k)   Persons who believe in or advocate the overthrow by force or violence of the Government of Canada or of constituted law and authority, or who disbelieve in or are opposed to organized government, or who advocate the assassination of public officials, or who advocate or teach the unlawful destruction of property;

(l)   Persons who are members of or affiliated with any organization entertaining or teaching disbelief in or opposition to organized government, or advocating or teaching the duty, necessity, or propriety of the unlawful assaulting or killing of any officer or officers, either of specific individuals or of officers generally, of the Government of Canada or of any other organized government, because of his or their official character, or advocating or teaching the unlawful destruction of property;

(m)   Persons who have been found guilty of high treason or treason for an offence in connection with the late war, or of conspiring against His Majesty, or of assisting His Majesty's enemies during the war, or of any similar offence against any of His Majesty's allies;

(n)   Persons over fifteen years of age, physically capable of reading, who cannot read the English or the French language or some other language or dialect. For the purpose of ascertaining whether aliens can read, the immigration officer shall use slips of uniform size prepared by direction of the Minister, each containing not less than thirty and not more than forty words in ordinary use printed in plainly legible type in the language or dialect the person may designate as the one in which he desires the examination to be made, and he shall be required to read the words printed on the slip in such language or dialect. The provisions of this paragraph shall not apply to persons residing in Canada at the date of the passing of this Act nor to Canadian citizens;

(*o*) Persons who have been deported from Canada, or the United States, or any other country, for any cause whatsoever.

9.  The Minister may authorize the admission to Canada of any person of Chinese origin or descent without being subject to the provisions of this Act, and such admission shall be authorized for a specified period only, but may be extended or cancelled by the Minister in writing.

## POWER OF CONTROLLER.

10. (1) The Controller shall have authority to determine whether an immigrant, passenger or other person seeking to enter or land in Canada or detained for any cause under this Act is of Chinese origin or descent and whether such immigrant, passenger or other person, if found to be of Chinese origin or descent, shall be allowed to enter, land or remain in Canada or shall be rejected and deported.

[ . . . ]

11. There shall be no appeal from the decision of the Controller, as to the rejection or deportation of any immigrant, passenger or other person found to be of Chinese origin or descent seeking to enter or land in Canada when such decision is based upon a certificate of the examining medical officer to the effect that such immigrant, passenger or other person of Chinese origin or descent is afflicted with any loathsome disease, or with a disease which may be or become dangerous to the public health, or that he comes within any of the following prohibited classes, namely, idiots, imbeciles, feeble-minded persons, epileptics and insane persons: Provided always that Canadian citizens and persons who have left Canada with the declared intention of returning thereto under the provisions of section twenty-three hereof and are seeking re-entry in accordance with the provisions of section twenty-four hereof, shall be permitted to land in Canada.

12. In all cases other than those provided for in the next preceding section an appeal may be taken to the Minister against the decision of the Controller if the appellant within forty-eight hours serves written notice of such appeal upon the Controller. Such notice of appeal shall act as a stay of all proceedings until a final decision is rendered by the Minister.

[ . . . ]

15. Every person of Chinese origin or descent, brought to Canada by a transportation company and rejected by the Controller, shall be sent back to the place whence he came by the said transportation company and the cost of his maintenance while being detained at an immigrant station, as well as the cost of his return, shall be paid by such transportation company.

[ . . . ]

17. (1) The Controller shall deliver to each Chinese immigrant who has been permitted to land in or enter Canada a certificate containing a description and photograph of such individual, the date of his arrival and the name of the port of his landing, and such certificate shall be *prima facie* evidence that the person presenting it has complied with the requirements of this Act; but such certificate may be contested by His Majesty or by any officer if there is any reason to doubt the validity or authenticity thereof; or of any statement therein contained; and such contestation shall be heard and determined

in a summary manner by any judge of a superior court of any province of Canada where such certificate is produced.

(2) The Chief Controller and such controllers as are by him authorized so to do shall each keep a register of all persons to whom certificates of entry have been granted.

18. Within twelve months after the coming into force of this Act and subject to such regulations as may be made by the Governor General in Council for the purpose, every person of Chinese origin or descent in Canada, irrespective of allegiance or citizenship, shall register with such officer or officers and at such place or places as are designated by the Governor General in Council for that purpose, and obtain a certificate in the form prescribed: Provided that those persons who may, during the time fixed for registration, be absent from Canada with authority to return, may register upon their return.

19. No vessel carrying Chinese immigrants to any port in Canada shall carry more than one such immigrant for every two hundred and fifty tons of its tonnage.

20. (1) It shall be unlawful for the master of any vessel carrying persons of Chinese origin or descent, whether immigrants, passengers, stowaways, officers or crew, to any port in Canada to allow any person of Chinese origin or descent to leave such vessel until a permit so to do stating that the provisions of this Act have been complied with has been granted to the master of such vessel by the Controller. Should such master permit any such person to leave the vessel without such permit he shall upon demand pay to the Controller or officer in charge at the port of entry one thousand dollars for each such person so permitted to leave the vessel.

(2) No controller at any port shall grant a permit allowing any person of Chinese origin or descent to leave the vessel until the quarantine officer has granted a bill of health, and has certified, after due examination, that no leprosy or infectious, contagious, loathsome or dangerous disease exists on board such vessel; and no permit to land shall be granted to any person of Chinese origin or descent prohibited entry under section eight of this Act.

(3) No vessel shall be granted clearance papers pending the determination of the question of the liability to the payment of such fine, or while the fine remains unpaid; nor shall such fine be remitted or refunded unless in the opinion of the Minister a mistake has been made. Provided that clearance may be granted prior to the determination of such question upon the deposit of a sum sufficient to cover such fine.

21. (1) Every conductor or other person in charge of any railway train or car bringing persons of Chinese origin or descent into Canada shall, immediately on his arrival, deliver to the Controller or other officer at the port or place of arrival a report containing a complete and accurate list of all persons of Chinese origin or descent arriving by or being on board of the railway train or car of which he is in charge, and showing their names in full, the country and place of their birth, their occupation and last place of domicile; and he shall not allow any such persons of Chinese origin or descent to disembark from such train or car until after such report has been made.

[ . . . ]

22. Persons of Chinese origin or descent may pass through Canada in transit from one port or place out of Canada to another port or place out of Canada: Provided that such passage is made in accordance with and under such regulations as are made for the purpose by the Governor in Council.

23. (1) Every person of Chinese origin or descent, who wishes to leave Canada with the declared intention of returning thereto, and who establishes to the satisfaction of the

Controller that he was legally landed in Canada, and is lawfully resident therein, shall give written notice of such intention to the controller at the port or place whence he proposes to sail or depart at least twenty-four hours before the intended date of his departure; in which notice shall be stated the foreign port or place which such person wishes to visit and the route he intends taking, both going and returning; and such notice shall be accompanied by a fee of two dollars.

(2) The form of such notice shall be in accordance with such regulations as are made from time to time for the purpose by the Governor General in Council.

(3) The Controller shall enter in a register to be kept for the purpose the name, residence, occupation and description of the person making the declaration, and such other information regarding him as is deemed necessary under such regulations as are made by the Governor General in Council for the purpose.

24. (1) The person so registered shall be entitled on his return, if within two years of such registration, and on proof of his identity to the satisfaction of the controller, to re-enter; but if he does not return to Canada within two years from the date of such registration, he shall be treated in the same manner as a person making application for admission as an immigrant.

(2) Every person of Chinese origin or descent who leaves Canada and does not register shall be subject on his return to the provisions of this Act as in the case of a first arrival.

(3) Every person of Chinese origin or descent, who registered out between April 1st, 1914, and March 31st, 1919, and who, under the provisions of an Order in Council of the 2nd April, 1919 (P.C. 697), was accorded the privilege of prolonging his return to Canada until one year after a proclamation had been published in the *Canada Gazette* declaring that a state of war no longer exists, shall be entitled to re-enter if he returns to Canada within one year from the date of the coming into force of this Act, and substantiates his identity to the satisfaction of the Controller.

Notwithstanding the provisions of the said Order in Council P.C. 697, every person of Chinese origin or descent who registered out between April 1st, 1914, and March 31st, 1919, and who does not return to Canada within one year from the date upon which this Act comes into force shall be subject on his return to the provisions of this Act as in the case of a first arrival.

25. (1) Any person of Chinese origin or descent who has been legally admitted to Canada and who is employed as a member of the crew of any vessel which operates between Canadian and United States ports, shall in order to retain his right of re-entry to Canada on his return with such vessel from such United States ports register with the controller and obtain a certificate of registration, which certificate shall be in the form prescribed and under such regulations as may be made by the Governor General in Council, and shall be produced at any time when demanded by an officer; such registration shall be for a period not to exceed two years and a fee of two dollars shall be charged by the controller for each registration card issued.

(2) Every person who fails to register in accordance with the provisions of this section shall be subject on his return to Canada to the provisions of this Act as in the case of a first arrival.

(3) Any transportation company, master, agent, or owner of any vessel who employs on such vessel a person of Chinese origin or descent without such person having complied with this section shall pay to any controller or officer demanding the same the sum of two hundred and fifty dollars for each such person. Pending the determination

of the question of the liability to the payment of such fine, which question shall be decided by the Minister, no such vessel shall be granted clearance: Provided that clearance may be granted prior to the determination of such question upon deposit with the controller or officer in charge of a sum sufficient to cover such fine.

## OFFENCES AND PENALTIES.

**26.** Whenever any officer has reason to believe that any person of Chinese origin or descent has entered or remains in Canada contrary to the provisions of this Act or of the *Chinese Immigration Act*, chapter ninety-five of the Revised Statutes of Canada, 1906, or any amendment thereof, he may, without a warrant apprehend such person, and if such person is unable to prove to the satisfaction of the officer that he has been properly admitted into and is legally entitled to remain in Canada, the officer may detain such person in custody and bring him before the nearest controller for examination, and if the controller finds that he has entered or remains in Canada contrary to the provisions of this Act or of the *Chinese Immigration Act* or any amendment thereof, such person may be deported to the country of his birth or citizenship, subject to the same right of appeal as is provided in the case of a person applying for original entry to Canada. Where any person is examined under this section the burden of proof of such person's right to be or remain in Canada shall rest upon him. Where an order for deportation is made under this section and in the circumstances of the case the expenses of deportation cannot be charged to the transportation company, such expenses shall be paid by the person being deported if able to pay, and, if not, by His Majesty.

**27.** (1) Every person of Chinese origin or descent resident in Canada at the date of the coming into force of this Act, who was admitted under the provisions of any Act now or heretofore in force, and did not secure such admission by fraudulent misrepresentation, and does not belong to any of the prohibited classes of persons described in section 8 of this Act, shall be deemed to be entitled to continue to reside in Canada: Provided, however, that any such person who was, subsequent to the 25th day of July, 1917, admitted without payment of the head tax because of his being a merchant and who has ceased to belong to such class, shall pay into the Consolidated Revenue Fund of Canada the sum of five hundred dollars, and if he refuses or fails to make such payment he shall *ipso facto* forfeit his right to remain in Canada, and may be arrested by any officer without a warrant and brought before a Controller for examination, whereupon he shall be dealt with to all intents and purposes in the same manner and subject to the same provisions as in the case of a person apprehended under section 26 of this Act.

(2) Any person admitted under this Act who at any time after admission ceases to belong to any of the classes admissible under this Act shall, unless he is a Canadian citizen, *ipso facto* forfeit his right to remain in Canada and may be arrested by any officer without a warrant and brought before a Controller for examination, whereupon he shall be dealt with to all intents and purposes in the same manner and subject to the same provisions as in the case of a person apprehended under section 26 of this Act.

[ . . . ]

**32.** (1) Every person of Chinese origin or descent who—

(*a*) lands or attempts to land in Canada contrary to the provisions of this Act;

(b) wilfully makes use of or attempts to make use of any forged or fraudulent certificate, or of a certificate issued to any other person for any purpose connected with this Act is guilty of an offence, and liable to imprisonment for any term not exceeding twelve months and not less than six months, or to a fine not exceeding one thousand dollars and not less than three hundred dollars, or to both imprisonment and fine, and shall be deported.

(2) Every person who wilfully aids and abets any person of Chinese origin or descent in any evasion or attempt at evasion of any of the provisions of this Act is guilty of an offence and liable to imprisonment for a term not exceeding twelve months and not less than six months, or to a fine not exceeding one thousand dollars and not less than three hundred dollars, or to both imprisonment and fine, and shall be deported unless of Canadian citizenship.

[ . . . ]

34. Any person of Chinese origin or descent who fails to register as required by section eighteen of this Act or any order or regulation made hereunder shall be liable to a fine not exceeding five hundred dollars or to imprisonment for a period not exceeding twelve months, or to both. In any prosecution under this section where the accused alleges that he is not a person of Chinese origin or descent, the onus of establishing that fact shall be upon the accused.

35. Every person who takes part in the organization of any sort of court or tribunal composed of Chinese persons for the hearing and determination of any offence committed by a Chinese person, or in carrying on any such organization, or who takes part in any of its proceedings, or who gives evidence before any such court or tribunal, or assists in carrying into effect any decision, decree, or order of any such court or tribunal, is guilty of an offence and liable to imprisonment for any term not exceeding twelve months, or to a fine not exceeding five hundred dollars, or to both; but nothing in this section shall be construed to prevent Chinese persons from submitting any differences or disputes to arbitration, if such submission is not contrary to the laws in force in the province in which such submission is made.

[ . . . ]

38. No court and no judge or officer thereof shall have jurisdiction to review, quash, reverse, restrain or otherwise interfere with any proceeding, decision or order of the Minister or of any controller relating to the status, condition, origin, descent, detention or deportation of any immigrant, passenger or other person upon any ground whatsoever, unless such person is a Canadian citizen, or has acquired Canadian domicile.

[ . . . ]

41. Notwithstanding any provision of this Act or any order or regulation made thereunder, any person of Chinese origin or descent who is at the date of the coming into force of this Act en route to Canada and presents himself for admission within three months from said date, shall if admissible under the provisions of the *Chinese Immigration Act* or any amendment thereof, be permitted to enter Canada upon payment of the head tax therein provided: Provided that if he belongs to any of the exempt classes he may be admitted exempt from the head tax.

## HISTORICAL INTERPRETATIONS

**3** From David Goutor, 'Drawing Different Lines of Color: The Mainstream English Canadian Labour Movement's Approach to Blacks and the Chinese, 1880–1914', *Labor: Studies in Working Class History of the Americas* 2(1), pp. 55-76. © 2005, Duke University Press. All rights reserved. Reprinted by permission of the publisher.

'No one class can be oppressed or injured without its reaching on others', argued the *Labor Union* (the precursor to the most important Knights of Labor paper in Canada, the *Palladium of Labor*), in its March 17, 1883, editorial. 'In slavery times the degradation of the Negro implied the degradation also of the "mean white" and of all manual labor'.[1] Immediately beneath this appeal for broader solidarity, the next editorial called on local 'workingmen' to 'watch attentively the course' of a new bill to exclude Chinese immigrants. The *Labor Union* asserted that unless an exclusion law was passed soon, 'the Mongolian swarm will pour eastward and compete with the Canadian laborer and mechanic in nearly every department'.[2]

In its August 23, 1901, issue, the Winnipeg *Voice*, labour's principal press outlet in the Canadian Prairies, described British Columbia as 'New Mongolia', where the 'spirit of the few ancient Caucasians who still linger in the territory' was controlled by the capitalists with the help of 'the presence of the little brownies'.[3] Immediately below this odious outburst of racism was an editorial praising the Socialist Unity convention in the United States for bringing African Americans into the movement. The 'party's attitude towards the Negro' the *Voice* declared, 'covers [it] with honor'.[4]

In its February 1906 edition, Ontario's most significant labour paper in the early twentieth century, the *Industrial Banner*, put clear limits on who was welcome in the labour movement and Canadian society in general:

We have colored barbershops and colored laborers in large numbers in some centres, but we have never asked for an exclusion law or a poll tax to keep the colored man out of Canada. The colored man settles down and spends his money in the country and becomes a citizen. He is admitted into membership in our labor organizations and creates no feelings of antagonism. With the coolie it is altogether different. He does not aspire to citizenship. We do not admit him into our labor organizations. A coolie he was born and a coolie he will die, and while he undersells legitimate labor he hoards up his money with the intent of returning to China and spending it there.[5]

[…]

Labour presented the Chinese as 'menaces' to the job security and standards of living of white workers, 'parasites' who simply came to Canada for a short time to amass a 'small fortune' to take home, and spreaders of vice and violence in Canadian cities. Exclusion of the Chinese was therefore presented as necessary for the protection of not only the material interests of the white working classes but also the moral and social fabric of the Dominion. However, unionists rarely applied these arguments to blacks. Instead, the primary focus of labour leaders' discourse on blacks was on proclaiming support for their struggle for freedom and equality.

The divergence in labour's approaches to these two groups was largely a product of concerns about competition in the labour market. While unionists felt a 'safe distance' from any competition from blacks, they were preoccupied with the prospect of the Chinese 'flooding' into Canada and undercutting or even 'driving out' white workers. However, labour's perception of 'safety' was not entirely grounded in the realities of the Canadian labour market; much of it was rooted in labour leaders' worldviews.

Indeed, blacks and the Chinese were given essentially different roles in labour leaders' broad narrative of the struggle with industrial capitalism. The Chinese were made into embodiments of both the 'cheap', 'docile', 'unmanly', and 'slavish' workers ideally suited to an industrial system of exploitation and the 'miserly', 'ruthless', 'predatory', and 'lascivious' character traits that capitalism was said to promote. On the other hand, the struggle of blacks against the plantation slave system was upheld as a model and inspiration for organized labour in its struggle with the emerging industrial system.

Several factors further entrenched these constructions of blacks and the Chinese. Canadian unionists had a detailed knowledge of events in other parts of the British Empire, particularly the anti-Asian campaigns in other white Dominions. Still more influential were developments in the United States during the period after the Civil War, the same period in which the Canadian labour movement emerged and the Chinese began to arrive in Canada in large numbers.

The focus here is on organizations that were affiliated with, or at least allied with, Canada's largest national labour central from the 1880s to 1914, the Trades and Labour Congress (TLC). Hence the central figures here are leaders of craft unions. However, the Knights of Labor remained closely tied to the Canadian congress up to the turn of the century, with key Knights leaders such as Daniel O'Donoghue and Alfred Jury being prominent figures at TLC conventions. At the Berlin congress of 1902, the TLC was reorganized according to the wishes of American Federation of Labor president Samuel Gompers, and the Knights, along with other independent groups, were deemed 'dual unions' and expelled.[6] The

Provincial Workingman's Association in Nova Scotia, most independent labour in Quebec, the groups allied with the Socialist Party of Canada, and the Industrial Workers of the World did not align with the TLC and are thus not covered by this discussion.

## THE BOUNDS OF UNITY

The most basic difference between labour leaders' discourse about blacks and Chinese was in scale. Addressing the situation of blacks, whether it was in Canada, the United States, or globally, was not one of Canadian unionists' highest priorities. To be sure, the labour press frequently remarked on the plight of blacks and drew connections to broader social, economic, and cultural issues. But the volume of commentary on blacks paled in comparison to the gallons of ink spilled on the Chinese 'menace'.

Trade unionists presented Chinese migrants as inherently less civilized and therefore 'content' with a lower standard of living. It followed that the Chinese would, as a rule, 'accept' lower wages to support their less civilized lifestyles. 'In other words', as Lawrence Glickman puts it, 'Chinese standards were not a result of low wages but a cause of them'.[7] For Canadian labour, the differences in standards of living reflected deeply embedded differences between the races, and there seemed to be no hope of altering such differences. 'The Chinaman is the result of ages of economy', declared the *Trades Union Advocate* (which was published by the Toronto labour council in the early 1880s). 'See [in] him, with stunted stature and pinched features, a living illustration of how little one can exist on'.[8]

Competition from Chinese workers was seen as resulting in the fundamental 'degradation' of white workers, as they would be 'brought down' to the 'level' of the Chinese. The Knights of Labor local assembly for Nanaimo asserted: 'The inevitable result of [Chinese] competition with free white Labor is to lower and degrade the latter without any appreciable elevation of the former'.[9] An important part of presenting the Chinese as less than civilized was presenting them as less than men. For instance, E.E. Sheppard, the editor of Toronto's *Daily News* (the Knights' 'propagandistic outlet' in the daily press in the 1880s), claimed the Chinese were 'without manhood, without ambition, and without self-respect'.[10]

Chinese immigration was also presented as a menace to the growth and development of the Dominion. Like their American 'brothers', Canadian unionists claimed the Chinese were not consumers who would support a prosperous nation.[11] The alleged 'uncivilized standards' and low wages were only part of what made Chinese migrants 'not consumers'. The tendency of many Chinese migrants to sojourn in Canada was also presented as fundamentally rooted in the Chinese 'character', rather than as a result of laws that stripped them of rights and citizenship and thus the ability to settle—in Canada. Hence the Chinese were also presented as inherently 'draining' the economy, taking money 'out of circulation'.[12] The *Daily News* claimed that the Chinese 'salt down nearly every cent they get to take back with them to the Flowery Land'.[13] Furthermore, what the Chinese did purchase, according to Canadian labour, they did not buy from 'native' businesses but from abroad. 'They did not spend [their money] here', declared John Roney, the mover of the first anti-Chinese resolution at a national labour congress in 1883; 'they even had their clothes made in China'.[14]

Once again, gender played an important role in this part of the construction of the Chinese 'menace'. Like their American counterparts, Canadian labour reformers claimed that Chinese men had no regard for 'civilized' gender duties such as providing their families with a 'decent home' and a respectable standard of living.[15] Instead, Chinese migrants were presented as simply using the Dominion, investing nothing, and taking so much away from white workers.

As one letter to the *Labor Union* put it: 'Their wives and families being left in China, which is a great blessing, their sole aim and object is to make a stake and get back as quick as possible'.[16]

According to labour leaders, the 'uncivilized' nature of the 'Mongolians' was allegedly manifested not only in their 'degraded' standards of living but also in their 'injurious and disgusting' social 'habits'. In the same way that the 'degraded' standards of living of the Chinese were deeply ingrained, Canadian labour held little hope that the 'Mongolians' could be morally 'civilized'. The *Palladium of Labor* argued that the Chinese could only become 'parodies of Christians, which is worse than their original leprous pagan state'.[17]

In particular, labour echoed widespread claims that the Chinese were a major source of crime. The Chinese were said to have inherent talents for stealing from and defrauding trusting white Canadians.[18] Labour leaders repeatedly called attention to stories of Chinese 'opium hells'.[19] The Chinese were also purported to be responsible for much of the prostitution in Canada. Chinese migrants were accused of being content with 'importing' 'sex slaves' from the 'Orient' instead of maintaining 'civilized' family units in Canada. 'They bring no women with them but for those brought for the vilest purposes', claimed a statement from a Victoria 'workingmen's' rally.[20]

According to Canadian unionists, the 'debased morals' of the Chinese made them particularly grave 'menaces' to the virtue of the Dominion's youth, especially its 'daughters'. The *Palladium of Labor* framed the whole issue of the Chinese presence in the West using the imagery of violated female innocence. The paper lamented how British Columbia, 'the grand virgin province of our Confederation', could be 'so tamely be given up to Chinese slave Labor and Chinese lust and leprosy'.[21] Indeed, both the 'slavish' standards of living and the 'disgusting' moral habits of the Chinese also allegedly made them medical threats to white Canadians. As the *Palladium of Labor* put it: 'Chinamen breed invariably a moral and physical pestilence in the white communities into which they intrude'.[22]

Altogether, then, Canadian labour presented the Chinese as a 'danger' not only to the economic promise of the Dominion but to its social, moral, and physical vitality, and indeed to the future of 'any country having free and popular institutions'.[23] Hence labour leaders did not simply debate Chinese immigration but rather agitated ferociously for exclusion. They were not alone; a host of other groups in Canada, including social reformers, medical professionals, law enforcement authorities, and many mainstream politicians and popular newspapers also demanded action against the Asian 'menace'.[24] [ . . . ]

The federal government responded to widespread pressure by introducing a head tax of $50 per Chinese migrant in 1886, raising it to $100 in 1900, and then to $500 in 1903. In 1908 federal authorities were given further powers to exclude Chinese migrants through new amendments to the *Chinese Immigration Act*, and the passage of the *Opium Act*, which 'was designed to exclusively target the Chinese community'.[25] Nevertheless, throughout the early twentieth century, labour leaders continued to insist that Ottawa had failed to provide sufficient protection for white workers. The 1910 and 1912 TLC conventions demanded a new raft of barriers against Asian immigration, including raising the head tax to $1,000.[26] 'It is plainly apparent', declared the TLC's 'Immigration Authority' William Trotter, in late 1913, 'that the present head tax of $500 is of no avail'.[27] (After the period under review, continued broad-based agitation led to the passage of the 1923 *Chinese Immigration Act*, which declared Canada out-of-bounds for all people 'of Chinese origin or descent, irrespective of allegiance or citizenship'.)[28]

Racism against blacks was also pervasive in Canada. At the same time that Canada often served as a haven for fugitive slaves in the late eighteenth and the early and mid-nineteenth centuries, patterns of hostility and discrimination were becoming established and would endure well into the twentieth century. There were even some forms of segregation, with separate schools, for instance, firmly entrenched in southwestern regions of Canada West (Ontario after Confederation) since 1850.[29] Moreover, court records reveal that both Canadian prosecutors and defence attorneys employed and perpetuated constructions of blacks as 'child-like', lascivious, and altogether unable to control their 'baser instincts'.[30] When it came to migration, a large-scale influx of blacks rarely seemed likely—but the federal government nevertheless took preventative measures, sending agents to the United States to dampen any interest in Canada among blacks and subjecting those who did seek entry to a 'strict interpretation' of all immigration regulations. In particular, immigration authorities seized on risible pseudoscientific claims that blacks 'did not readily take to [the Canadian] climate on account of the rather severe winter' to justify turning them away on 'medical grounds'.[31] As a result, by the eve of the Great War the Canadian border was known among African Americans to be virtually impregnable, and the remaining open land in the Prairie West to be out of reach to black settlers.[32]

However, Canadian labour leaders rarely embraced or contributed to racism against blacks, or joined calls for their exclusion from the Dominion. Indeed, labour leaders' discourse on blacks was entirely different than their discourse on the Chinese. Constructions of blacks as threats to the jobs or standards of living of white workers, to the innocence of white women, or to the medical vitality of Canadian communities rarely appeared in labour sources.

On the contrary, Canadian unionists consistently portrayed blacks as people who had suffered centuries of unjust oppression and unjustifiable discrimination. Whereas unionists claimed that the 'miserable' living and working conditions of the Chinese reflected their 'inherently degraded' character, the exploitation and suffering of blacks reflected a failure on the part of societies to live up to their ideals. Thus the Toronto *Daily News* declared 'color distinctions are an anomaly in a country where all are supposed to be equal before the law'.[33]

Indeed, whereas unionists presented the Chinese as irredeemably 'uncivilized', they presented blacks as engaged in a great struggle for social equality. Unionists assailed the Chinese for their 'docile' and 'unmanly' submission to their servitude but frequently expressed admiration for blacks' determined efforts in seeking justice. For instance, the *Palladium of Labor* enthusiastically promoted the works of Frederick Douglass on labour in the US South and particularly the plight of black workers. The *Palladium of Labor* announced that Douglass's writings 'should be read by every thinking person upon the North American continent'.[34]

Hence while trade unionists scornfully dismissed attempts to educate or 'Christianize' the Chinese, let alone organize them in workplaces, they often encouraged efforts to bring blacks into the labour movement. For instance, several scholars, such as Gillian Creese, have shown that the Vancouver Trades and Labour Council was relentless in opposing Chinese immigration.[35] But the Vancouver TLC's paper, the *Independent*, also declared in 1901 that 'next to organizing themselves the wage-workers of the [American] South could do nothing better than organize their colored co-workers'. The paper added that it found it 'difficult' to 'appreciate why any trouble should be experienced on account of the colored worker'.[36]

[ . . . ]

## 'THE IMPENDING FLOOD'

What accounts for this sharp contrast in Canadian labour's approach to blacks and the Chinese? According to many labour historians, the ferocity of trade unionists' antipathy

to the Chinese stemmed from competition in the labour market. Unlike blacks, the Chinese were seen as a 'menace' because they were competing with white workers in industries like railroads, mining, and fruit farming, mostly in the Pacific west.[37]

A large body of evidence in labour sources supports this argument. Decrying 'unfair competition' from the Chinese in the labour market was indeed the primary focus of labour's anti-Chinese agitation. Job competition was the 'chief objection to Chinese immigration for the Victoria Knights of Labor and the 'marrow of the question' for the *Canadian Labor Reformer* (which was edited by Arthur Wright, Ontario's most influential Knight of Labor in the late 1880s and early 1890s).[38] Moreover, unionists periodically (and usually grudgingly) granted that were it not for concerns about competition in an industrial labour market, their approach to the Chinese might be different. For instance, the *Industrial Banner* declared that 'when capitalists adopt the Golden Rule, or when we have a better social system, or when the millennium has arrived it might be a good idea to encourage the arrival of the Chinese, but until that time has come the best plan is to keep them where they will be at home and do the least harm— in China'.[39]

On the other hand, labour leaders expressed almost no concern about a 'flood' of blacks from the United States or other areas. Whereas the Chinese were generally highly mobile, single male industrial workers in this period, most of the black population in Canada was settled in rural areas and thus largely removed from the industrial labour market. What migration there was of blacks also went mostly to rural areas.[40] Correspondingly, the *Industrial Banner* emphasized the 'colored man's' purported willingness to 'settle down' as a main reason why he 'creates no feelings of antagonism' with white organized labour.[41] More broadly, since large-scale plantation farming had never become established in Canada, black slaves were not seen as having played a major role in any part of the labour force.[42]

Indeed, the struggles of blacks seemed to take place at a 'safe distance' from the struggles of the labour movement. Note, for instance, the sense of detachment in the Toronto *Daily News*'s declaration of support for Canadian blacks: 'We cordially wish the colored people success in their struggle for the Democratic principle of equal rights and privileges'.[43]

This perception of a 'safe distance' seemed to be crucial in Canadian trade unionists' taking a more positive view of blacks. Whenever labour leaders felt blacks were encroaching on the safe space, attitudes could quickly change. In fact, the perceived encroachment did not even have to be into the labour market. For instance, the Toronto *Daily News* rejected proposals for an Imperial Confederation, not only because it clashed with the paper's desire for Canadian independence but also because it would put Canada on an equal footing with nations such as Jamaica. According to the *News*: 'A confederation in which a population of ignorant and half-civilized Negroes . . . are to be placed on a level with the intelligent and self-governing white communities, is about the wildest scheme ever broached even in these days of amateur constitution making'.[44]

Similarly, when unionists felt a safe distance from the Chinese—particularly when they contemplated the spread of European empires in Asia—they could become quite generous. While some labour leaders and newspapers, such as the Victoria *Industrial News* (endorsed by the city's Knights of Labor), supported the British Empire,[45] there was a strong anti-Imperialist strain in Canadian labour's activism. The *Palladium of Labor* was most vociferous in denouncing Britain's 'unrighteous wars' in Africa and Asia—but the Toronto *Daily News*, the *Voice*, the *Industrial Banner*, and the *Federationist* (published by the British Columbia Federation of Labour starting in 1911) all published derisive commentaries about 'Our Glorious Empire'.[46] [...]

More important, the influx of Chinese through this period was hardly massive. In the early 1880s, roughly 15,000 Chinese immigrants entered Canada, constituting only about 3.5 per cent of total immigration in those years. They were overwhelmingly concentrated in British Columbia, where they joined approximately 4,000 Chinese who remained after the influx during the gold rush of the late 1850s and early 1860s. Through to the end of the century, new immigration was small, with the annual influx exceeding 4,000 only in 1899 and 1900, and out-migration was significant, especially after the Canadian Pacific Railway was completed in 1885. Indeed, by 1902, the Chinese population in the far west was only about 16,000. The early twentieth century saw some increases in the influx, particularly from 1908 to 1914, when it averaged about 4,500. However, all Asian groups accounted for less than 2 per cent of total immigration from 1900 to the Great War.[47]

Moreover, trade unionists, particularly those east of the Rockies, consistently identified the Chinese as a massive and immediate threat—even while admitting that they had no experience with the Chinese at all. Labour leaders in Ontario and the Prairies frequently acknowledged that the Chinese had yet to arrive in their province in significant numbers.[48] To be sure, there were a few Ontario activists who claimed direct knowledge of the Chinese. The most notable were Joseph Marks, the editor of the *Industrial Banner*, and 'Ah Sin', the horrid pseudonym of the author of a series of anti-Chinese letters to the *Labor Union* and the *Palladium of Labor*.[49] However, in discussions of the Chinese 'question', labour activists usually made a point of highlighting any 'exposure' to the Chinese they had, as it was generally taken for granted that white Ontario workers had not seen the 'menace' firsthand.[50]

[ . . . ]

The continual failure of the anticipated 'hordes' to materialize did not make labour leaders feel any greater 'safe space' from the Chinese. While unionists would concede that 'we do not yet suffer acutely', the issue retained its urgency, with the 'flood' of Chinese workers always seeming to be just around the corner. For instance, it mattered little to Winnipeg labour leaders that 'in this city we have a peaceful batch of Chinamen', as they continually raised alarms that the 'hordes' were at their city's door.[51] Throughout this period, unionists in central Canada and the Prairie West commanded white workers not to 'patronize' Chinese laundries and other businesses, because any such 'encouragement' would trigger the 'impending flood'. The Ottawa *Capital Siftings* and the London *Industrial Banner* called for boycotts of local Chinese businesses, and the Montreal labour council imposed a $100 fine on any member of an affiliated union caught using a Chinese laundry.[52]

## 'SLAVERY TIMES' AND 'THE COMING CRISIS'

The contrast between labour's perception of a 'safe distance' from blacks, and a constantly 'growing menace' from the Chinese, reflects broader distinctions that labour leaders drew between the two groups. Indeed, blacks and the Chinese occupied fundamentally different spaces in the worldviews and ideological landscapes of Canadian labour leaders. The struggles of blacks and abolitionists against slavery in the United States had many positive connotations and provided many stirring points of reference for Canadian labour leaders. The Chinese, on the other hand, were closely linked with the rise of industrialization.

A favorite rhetorical tactic of Canadian labour reformers was to establish links between their campaign against industrial capitalism and the defeat of slavery, particularly, although not exclusively, the plantation system in the American South. Indeed, like their American 'brothers', Canadian labour leaders frequently compared the 'slave

system' and the capitalist or 'monopolist system'.[53] This was an especially common tactic of the Knights of Labor, with the *Labor Union* describing industrial capitalism as 'only a degree less villainous and brutalizing than Southern slavery'.[54] But unionists and labour papers in later periods frequently used this line. For instance, the *Federationist* declared that 'the world's industry is carried on now for the same purpose as it was in the days of the great slave empires of the past, and that is for the continually increasing enrichment and aggrandizement of the ruling class'.[55]

Moreover, Canadian labour leaders drew parallels between themselves and the abolitionists of 'slavery times'—and further parallels between advocates of industrial capitalism and apologists for slaveholders in the American South. 'If our information is not misleading', opined the *Canadian Labor Reformer*, 'the pro-slavery men used to denounce such men as Garrison and Wright and Phillips as demagogues and dangerous agitators. History, they say, has a habit of repeating itself'.[56]

Abolitionists were portrayed as heroes vindicated by the course of history and by the march of progress and enlightenment. In the same way, the masses would soon rally to the cause of labour, the capitalists would 'go down in blood',[57] and their exponents would fall into the same disrepute as slave owners. Phillips Thompson, Canada's leading 'labour theorist and social critic' in the 1880s, announced in his regular column for the *Palladium of Labor*: 'The day is coming, when the triumph of Labor over the tremendous arrayed odds against it, will crush capitalism as slavery was crushed and leave its hired apologists to the contempt and execration of a wiser and better generation'.[58] [...]

Labour leaders thus upheld the struggles of abolitionists and blacks as a model and inspiration. But unionists linked the Chinese with something altogether different. Indeed, [in Canada and the United States], the Chinese were 'racialized' in many distinct ways. In particular, Takaki has shown that 'in the

[American] white imagination', blacks were generally located in bygone 'slavery times' while the Chinese were 'located in the future'. 'Moreover', Takaki writes, the Chinese 'were directly identified with America as a modern industrial society'.[59] In Canada, labour leaders made Chinese immigrants into symbols of the excesses of an unrestrained industrial capitalist system.

In particular, Chinese immigration seemed to become an embodiment of labour's contention that the industrial economy would bring destitution and dependence to white workers. Chinese immigrants were presented as the type of inherently 'degraded' labour that industrial capitalism would prefer. Moreover, in the competitive labour market, it was Chinese migrants who would change the standards and conditions of white workers, not the reverse. This was essential to the argument that Chinese migration was 'degrading' to white workers. As the *Labor Union* put it, Chinese competition meant that white wages would be 'regulated' by the 'Mongolian requirements of living'.[60]

[ ... ]

Canadian labour's social and moral arguments against Chinese immigration also reflected anxieties about capitalism. Unionists regularly singled out Chinatowns as the primary source of a number of the evils of modern industrial urban centres, particularly drugs, gambling, prostitution, and diseases like leprosy.[61] [ ... ]

Moreover, labour leaders identified capitalist values of ruthlessness, materialism, and disregard for the welfare of others as the primary cause of moral degeneration.[62] As Phillips Thompson put it, in the competitive world of industrial capitalism, 'the very qualities which go to constitute true manhood are often calculated to retard success in life'. Instead, wealth and status went to those who used their 'cunning' and 'scheming' to take advantage of others.[63] A great deal of what made the Chinese such a moral and social 'menace' were 'antisocial' characteristics similar to those bred by capitalism—manifested in the extreme. 'The miser if closely studied would be found to be as near a Chinaman as was possible', claimed one speaker at an anti-Chinese meeting in Victoria.[64] For Canadian labour, the supposed extraordinary ruthlessness of the Chinese—often in the pursuit of saving money—was an especially important part of the 'disgusting habits' they introduced to white societies. [ ... ]

Several factors enhanced the tendency of labour leaders to view possible threats from blacks as more distant, but threats from the Chinese as more immediate. While unionists often denounced Imperialist military 'adventures', Canada's ties to the British Empire were an important factor. In particular, the abolition of slavery in 1834 by the British, despite resistance from interests such as Caribbean plantation owners, served as another illustration of the triumph of enlightenment over 'the great slave empires of the past'. Moreover, after abolition, indentured labour was imported en masse from China and south Asia to replace slave labour in many Caribbean plantations.[65] Although this transition was in a preindustrial setting, it amplified the sense that 'Asiatics' were supplanting blacks as the new 'class' of highly coerced and exploited labour. Indeed, in the discussion of the first anti-Chinese resolution passed by a national labour congress in 1883, the alleged impact of Chinese immigration on the West Indies was cited as an important case in point.[66]

[ ... ]

More important, Canadian labour leaders took both ideas and inspiration from anti-Chinese campaigns by white labour in other parts of the British Empire. Indeed, Canadian unionists demonstrated an impressive level of awareness of the activities of their 'brothers' in other lands. For instance, the *Trades Union Advocate* exhorted readers to take their cue from the anti-Chinese protests by workers in England in the early 1880s.[67] Even more influential were the agitations by white unionists in other British Dominions in the New World, such as Australia, New Zealand, and South Africa. Labour papers upheld the experience in these Dominions as especially compelling evidence of the impact of Chinese immigration and reported extensively and enthusiastically on their exclusion campaigns.[68]

The particular timing of both the arrival of the Chinese and the emergence of the Canadian labour movement was another crucial factor in cementing the association of blacks with the past and a struggle to emerge from an old system of oppression, and the Chinese with the future and fears about the advancement of industrialization. The American working class developed in the early and mid-nineteenth century 'in the context of a slaveholding republic', as David Roediger has put it. As a result, white workers came to view their struggle as being to remain 'free white labour' instead of becoming chattel slaves. Blacks thus became entrenched in the minds of the white labour movement as models of people who were inherently unable to maintain their independence and manhood, while whiteness meant possessing the wherewithal to maintain a respectable status in the American social hierarchy.[69]

The Industrial Revolution came later to Canada than to the United States, and the Canadian labour movement emerged mostly in the period after the American Civil War. It is worth reiterating that in the Canadian setting, no part of the economy had been based on plantations employing slave labour, and slavery had been effectively abolished (through legislation in Upper Canada, through court decisions in Lower Canada and the Maritimes) by the end of the eighteenth century, well before abolition was enacted throughout the British Empire in the 1830s. Moreover, in the post-bellum period, American labour's sympathy for blacks, and the potential for black-white labour unity, was unusually high. Open racism against blacks was seen as smacking of support for the Confederate South. Labour leaders sought out high-profile figures in the abolitionist movement 'with some success'.

Many unionists, including leaders of the AFL, spoke about 'eliminating consideration of the color line'.[70] The Knights of Labor, which was surging in America as well as Canada in the 1880s, sought to foster solidarity between black and white workers. In fact, more than 90,000 blacks had become members of the American Knights by 1887.[71]

To be sure, racism hardly vanished in this period, and the image of blacks as inherently degraded labour endured. Moreover, Glickman has shown that many labour leaders portrayed blacks as unable to provide a steady consumer base for an industrial economy because they could not control their desires for 'instant gratification'.[72] According to Eric Arnesen, blacks were commonly viewed as strikebreakers by white unionists. There was also pervasive fear that emancipated slaves would migrate north to compete with white labour.[73]

[ . . . ]

Hence the Canadian movement was establishing itself during a period when the American movement both vilified the Chinese as a 'menace' and had its antipathy to blacks influenced by some strong countercurrents. Given the close ties between the labour movements in the two countries, with American-based organizations such as the Knights of Labor and international craft unions growing across the border, it is hardly surprising that the impact of American labour leaders' attitudes was unmistakable. While adopting a sympathetic tone toward blacks and praising the struggle against slavery, Canadian labour papers endorsed and publicized the campaign against the Chinese in the United States. By volume, more than half of the anti-Chinese material published in Canadian labour papers was reprinted from American sources. Although unionists in British Columbia had much more interaction with the Chinese, they also relied heavily on outside sources. For instance, the *Victoria Industrial News* reprinted more anti-Chinese articles from American newspapers than any other Canadian source.[74] [ . . . ]

While Canadian papers described California as 'afflicted' by the Chinese, they also envied the power that its labour organizations had attained and saw their use of anti-Chinese rhetoric as 'a powerful organizing tool' as a tactic to be emulated.[75] Indeed, just as Canadian labour was gaining strength in the early 1880s, the *Trades Union Advocate* both called California 'despoiled' and described San Francisco as a 'red-hot union city' in comparison to which Toronto labour paled. The paper provided an inventory of San Francisco's labour groups as an 'incentive to our Trades Council and wage workers to perfect the work of organization here'. The paper then urged local workers to seek information and advice from their 'brothers' on the Pacific Coast.[76]

The United States and other white Dominions of the British Empire, particularly Australia, also provided recent demonstrations of ways to defeat the Chinese threat. Labour papers continually demanded exclusion legislation similar to the *Exclusion Act* passed in 1882 in the United States and the series of anti-Chinese laws enacted in Australia during the late 1870s and early 1880s.[77] The example of Australia, a fellow Dominion of the British Empire, was particularly important. In the early 1880s, the Macdonald government claimed that the Imperial Government in London would not allow Canadian exclusion laws because the British wanted to protect their trade interests in China. Labour repeatedly pointed to Australia as proof of the 'futility' of Macdonald's position. The *Palladium of Labor*, for instance, argued that Australia's laws exposed Ottawa's 'hypocritical pretext for delay'.[78] On the other hand, the Australian and especially American laws also created anxieties. The Canadian government's insistence on keeping the door open even as it was being closed elsewhere was viewed as making the Dominion—and, once again, British Columbia in particular—vulnerable to a flood of Chinese migrants.[79]

Moreover, it was in the late 1870s and early 1880s that the Chinese first began to arrive in Canada in large numbers, mostly to work on the project that was meant to spark the industrial development of the Dominion: the transcontinental railway. Indeed, the railway was a pillar of Macdonald's National Policy to expand Canada territorially and economically, and allow it to grow into a strong, independent Dominion.[80] This strengthened the association between the Chinese and Canada's advancement toward industrial capitalism. Labour leaders continually complained that 'Chinese labourers were imported by the shipload' to build the railway. More important, unionists also made broader claims that importing Chinese workers was part of the plans of 'large contractors and other monopolists' to augment their power and to 'avail themselves of the cheapest labor they can get'.[81]

Once formed in the 1880s, labour's views of the Chinese as both symbols of the excesses of industrialism and 'tools of the capitalists' would endure through the late nineteenth and early twentieth centuries. For instance, dubbing the Canadian Pacific Railway 'the Canadian Peril Route', papers like the Winnipeg *Voice*, which ran through the 1890s and 1900s, consistently described the Chinese as 'brought over' to 'assist in the carrying out of some purpose on the part of the capitalists'.[82]

## CONCLUSION

The origins of organized labour's approach to different minority groups are complex riddles that require us to explore labour's relations with immigrant and minority workers, the broader economic and political context, and labour leaders' anxieties, ambitions, ideologies, and worldviews. A particular combination of these factors led unionists to usually (though not unfailingly) reject or challenge racist constructions of blacks while consistently vilifying Chinese immigrants. Competition from the Chinese in the labour market was one of the most important factors—but that alone does not sufficiently explain labour's contrasting views of these two groups. Indeed, labour's perception of the extent of the threat to white workers from the Chinese and blacks can hardly be taken at face value.

Labour leaders located the Chinese and blacks in essentially different places in the ideological landscape. They made the Chinese into embodiments of the economic, social, and cultural damage that they expected an industrial capitalist system to produce and made blacks into examples of people who broke free of an earlier but similar, form of tyranny. These particular constructions reinforced how labour leaders defined their movement and their narrative of their struggle with industrial capitalism. The Chinese were made into opposites of the 'civilized standards', 'true manliness', and 'intelligence' that white labour should embody. On the other hand, the sympathetic portrayal of blacks by labour leaders buttressed their claims that the 'chains and shackles' of oppression, be it 'corporate bondage' or 'chattel slavery', were destined to be broken by the 'spirit of freedom'.

The association of blacks with past struggles, and the Chinese with Canada's future problems, was strengthened by unionists' awareness of both the replacement of emancipated slaves with indentured Asian workers in the British West Indies and the fierce anti-Chinese campaigns by white labour across the Empire. The fact that the Canadian labour movement emerged and the Chinese began to arrive on a large scale during the post-bellum period, a unique one in the history of race and labour relations, gave even greater strength to these constructions of blacks and the Chinese.

## NOTES

1. 'White Slavery in Toronto', *Labour Union*, March 17, 1883.

2. 'The Mongolian Influx', *Labor Union*, March 17, 1883.

3. 'Notes and Comments', *Voice*, August 23, 1901.

4. Ibid.

5. 'Oriental Competition', *Industrial Banner*, February 1906.

6. Robert H. Babcock, *Gompers in Canada: A Study of American Continentalism before the First World War* (Toronto: University of Toronto Press, 1974); Eugene Forsey, *Trade Unions in Canada, 1812–1902* (Toronto: University of Toronto Press, 1982).

7. Lawrence B, Glickman, 'Inventing the "American Standard of Living": Gender, Race, and Working Class Identity, 1880–1925', *Labor History* 34 (1993): 232; Glickman, *A Living Wage: American Workers and the Making of Consumer Society* (Ithaca, NY: Cornell University Press, 1997).

8. 'Keep Them Out', *Trades Union Advocate*, October 20, 1882, See comments of John Roney, a delegate to the 1883 congress, in *1883 Canadian Labor Congress Proceedings* (Toronto: Roddy and Nurse, 1884); 'Knights of Labour', *Victoria Industrial News*, August 14, 1886; 'Anti-Chinese Meeting', *Victoria Industrial News*, January 23, 1886; 'Oriental Competition'.

9. Statement by Nanaimo Knights, 'British Columbia: Anti-Chinese Evidence', *Palladium of Labor*, September 27, 1884 (hereafter cited as Nanaimo Knights' statement). See also 'The Chinese Question in the Senate', *Canadian Labor Reformer*, June 5, 1886; 'Pauper Immigration', *Palladium of Labor*, May 24, 1884; 'Appeal from British Columbia' (editorial), *Daily News*, June 9, 1885; 'The Labor Men: Mr Smith's Anti-Chinese Resolution Carries', *Globe*, September 17, 1896; Glickman, 'Inventing the American Standard of Living', 225–31.

10. Editorial, *Trade Union Advocate*, May 18, 1882. See also 'The Chinese Must Go', *Daily News*, October 2, 1884, 'The Chinese Question', *Daily News* March 27, 1886.

11. Glickman, 'Inventing the "American Standard of Living,"' 225–33; Editorial, *Trades Union Advocate*, May 18, 1882; Phillips Thompson's speech to the 1884 Hamilton rally, 'Indignation!' *Palladium of Labor*, October 4, 1884; 'Chinese Labor', *Daily News*; 'Never Was in Better Trim', *Industrial Banner*, April 1908.

12. Glickman, *Living Wage*, 88; Ronald T. Takaki, Iron Cages: Race and Culture in Nineteenth-Century America, rev. edn (New York: Oxford University Press, 2000), 221. See also 'The Chinese', Voice, June 6, 1897; W.M. Neil, 'Letter', *Labor's Realm* (Regina), October 1909; the letter from the Yukon Labor Protective and Improvement Union to the Dominion TLC, *TLC Proceedings, 1901*, 65–6; 'Oriental Competition'; 'Asiatic Question', Voice, October 4, 1907.

13. 'Chinese Labour', *Daily News*, January 16, 1884.

14. 1883 Convention Proceedings, 12. See also 'Ah Sin', 'Chinese Immigration', *Labor Union*, March 17, 1883; 'Labor and the Farmer', *Victoria Industrial News*, March 6, 1886.

15. Glickman, *Living Wage*, 88–89; Nanaimo Knights' statement; 'Labor and the Farmer'; 'The "Times" on Pauper Labor', *Palladium of Labor*, February 28, 1885.

16. 'Hung Wah', 'Chinese Immigration', *Labour Union*, March 24, 1883. See also Nanaimo Knights' statement; 'Chinese Immigration', *Palladium of Labor*, July 26, 1884: 'Committee on Vancouver TLC Communication', *TLC Proceedings, 1893*, 21–3; 'Communication from Vancouver TLC', *TLC Proceedings, 1896*, 11; 'The Chinese Tax', *Independent*, August 23, 1900; 'Chinese Immigration', *Independent*, May 18, 1900.

17. 'The Chinese Question', *Palladium of Labor*, June 6, 1886. See also *1883 Canadian Labor Congress Proceedings*, 13–15; Editorials, *Wage Worker*, March 15 and March 22, 1883; 'Anti-Chinese Meeting'.

18. Patricia Roy, *A White Man's Province: British Columbia Politicians and Japanese Immigrants, 1858–1914* (1989), 40–3. See also 'Ah Sin', 'Chinese Immigration', *Labor Union*, March 17, 1883; 'Washington Territory', *Palladium of Labor*, April 12, 1884; 'Chinese Beggars', *Palladium of Labor*, March 28, 1885; the comments of W.A. Robinson to an anti-Chinese meeting, 'Public Meeting', *Victoria Industrial News*, February 6, 1886; 'Victoria Knights and Sir John', *Palladium of Labor*, August 14, 1886; 'Poverty in Chinatown', *Victoria Industrial News*, January 6, 1886.

19. *1883 Canadian Labor Congress Proceedings*, 14: 'Victoria's Slums', *Palladium of Labor*, November 22, 1884; 'Hell's Horrors', *Palladium of Labor*, August 22, 1885; 'The Chinese and the Law', *Victoria Industrial News*, August 28, 1886; 'The Heathen Chinese', *Industrial Banner*, April 1907; the editorial cartoon in *Federationist*, October 26, 1912.

20. The petition from the workingmen's rally in Victoria, 'An Appeal', *Daily News*, June 8, 1885 (hereafter cited as 'Victoria petition'); 'Indignation!'; 'Chinese Prostitution', *Victoria Industrial News*, December 18, 1886.

21. 'Chinese Question'. See also Resolution 76, *TLC Proceedings, 1912*, 107; 'Trades and Labor Congress of Canada', *Industrial Banner*, February 6, 1913; 'Protection of White Girls', *Voice*, February 13, 1913.

22. 'The Mongolian Pest', August 23, 1884; 1883 *Canadian Labor Congress Proceedings*, 14; 'LEPROSY!' *Palladium of Labor*, September 6, 1884; 'Dr. C.C. O'Donnell', *Palladium of Labor*, August 9, 1884; 'Communication from the Vancouver TLC', *TLC Proceeding, 1892*, 21; 'Communication from the Vancouver TLC', *TLC Proceeding 1891*, 11–12; 'B.C. Executive Report', *TLC Proceedings, 1896*, 14; 'The Chinese', Voice, May 1, 1897; 'From Vancouver', Voice, August 12, 1898; 'Chinese Immigration', *Industrial Banner*, May 1899; 'The Chinese Question', *Independent*, April 21, 1900; 'Filthy in the Extreme', *Industrial Banner*, April 1903; 'Winnipeg's Laundries', *Voice*, January 4, 1907; 'The Menace of Chinese Laundries', *Industrial Banner*, August 1912; 'Unsanitary Shacks of the Chinese Must Go', *Federationist*, April 17, 1914.

23. Nanaimo Knights' statement.

24. Roy, *White Man's Province*; Kay Anderson, *Vancouver's Chinatown: Racial Discourse in Canada, 1875–1980* (Toronto: McClelland and Stewart, 1995); James Walker, 'A Case for Morality: The Quong Wing Files', in *On the Case: Explorations in Social History*, ed. Franca Iacovetta and Wendy Mitchinson (Toronto: University of Toronto Press, 1998), 204–23; Bruce Ryder, 'Racism and the Constitution: The Constitutional Fate of British Columbia Anti-Asian Immigration Legislation, 1884–1909', *Osgoode Hall Law Journal* 29 (1991): 619–76.

25. Ninette Kelley and Michel Trebilcock, *The Making of the Mosaic: A History of Canadian*

*Immigration Policy* (Toronto: University of Toronto Press, 1998), 152–53.

26. 'Report of the Special Committee on Immigration', *TLC Proceedings, 1910*, 74.

27. W.R. Trotter, 'Asiatic Question', *Voice*, December 26, 1913. See also the letter from W.M. McNeil, *Labor's Realm*, October 1, 1909.

28. *Canada Year Book*, 1925 (Ottawa: Dominion Bureau of Statistics, 1926), 182.

29. James W. St. G. Walker, *Racial Discrimination in Canada: The Black Experience* (Ottawa: Canadian Historical Association, 1985); Walker, *A History of Blacks in Canada: A Study Guide for Teachers and Students* (Ottawa: Minister of State Multiculturalism, 1980); Robin W. Winks, *The Blacks in Canada: A History*, 2nd edn (Montreal: McGill-Queen's University Press, 1997).

30. James Walker, *'Race', Rights, and the Law in the Supreme Court of Canada: Historical Case Studies* (Waterloo, ON: Wilfrid Laurier University Press, 1997); Barrington Walker, 'The Gavel and the Veil of Race: "Blackness" in Ontario's Criminal Courts, 1858–1958' (Ph.D. diss., University of Toronto, 2003).

31. Canadian federal minister of the interior Frank Oliver, quoted in Kelley and Trebilcock, *Making of the Mosaic*, 154–55; Harold M. Troper, *Only Farmers Need Apply: Official Canadian Government Encouragement of Immigration from the United States, 1896–1911* (Toronto: Griffin House, 1972), 127.

32. Kelley and Trebilcock, *Making of the Mosaic*, 154–55.

33. Editorial, *Daily News*, January 17, 1884; 'Black and White', *Daily News*, October 18, 1883; 'The Colored Man in the South', *Daily News*, February 1, 1884; 'Indignation!'; 'A Woman', 'Color Line' (letter), *Toiler*, June 24, 1904; 'The Negro Question in the United States', *Federationist*, April 25, 1913.

34. 'The Labor Question', *Palladium of Labor*, October 20, 1883.

35. Gillian Creese, 'Exclusion or Solidarity? Vancouver Workers Confront the "Oriental Problem,"' *B.C. Studies* (1988): 24–51.

36. 'Southern Colored Labor', *Independent*, April 13, 1901; 'Oriental Competition'; 'Asiatics Must Be Kept Out', *Industrial Banner*, March 1912; 'Negro Question in the United States'.

37. Paul Phillips, *No Power Greater: A Century*

*of Labour in British Columbia* (Vancouver: B.C. Federation of Labour Boag Foundation, 1967); A. Ross McCormack, *Reformers, Rebels, and Revolutionaries: The Western Canadian Radical Labour Movement, 1899–1919* (Toronto: University of Toronto Press, 1977); David Bercuson, 'Labour Radicalism and the Western Frontier: 1897–1919', *Canadian Historical Review* 58 (1977), 154–75; Robert Wynne, *Reactions to the Chinese in the Pacific North-west and British Columbia* (New York: Arno, 1978).

38. 'Knights of Labour'; 'The Chinese Question in the Senate'. On Wright, see Gregory S. Kealey and Bryan D. Palmer, *Dreaming of What Might Be: The Knights of Labor in Ontario* (New York: Cambridge University Press, 1982), 250–3; Christina Burr and Gregory S. Kealey, 'Wright, Alexander Whyte', *Dictionary of Canadian Biography*, vol. 14, 1911 to 1920 (Toronto: University of Toronto Press, 1998), 1084–6.

39. 'Chinese Immigration', *Industrial Banner*.

40. On the migration of black Oklahomans, see Troper, *Only Farmers Need Apply*; Kelley and Trebilcock, *Making of the Mosaic*, 154–5.

41. 'Oriental Competition'.

42. Walker, *History of Blacks in Canada*, 19–26; Winks, *Blacks in Canada*.

43. Editorial, *Daily News*.

44. 'How Jamaica Views It', *Daily News*, November 11, 1884; 'Assault on the Ballot Box', *Palladium of Labor*, May 9, 1885.

45. 'The Ties of Empire', *Victoria Industrial News*, June 19, 1886.

46. 'The Fall of Khartoum', *Daily News*, February 6, 1885; 'A Famous Victory', *Palladium of Labor*, January 24, 1885; Enjolras, 'The War Fever', *Palladium of Labor*, February 14, 1885; 'Strength for the Weak', *Palladium of Labor*, April 26, 1884; 'More Victims for the Philippines', *Industrial Banner*, July 1899; 'Our Glorious Empire', *Federationist*, July 24, 1914.

47. Roy, *White Man's Province*, 66–8, 91–3; Kelley and Trebilcock, *Making of the Mosaic*, 143–5; Peter S. Li, 'Chinese', in *Encyclopedia of Canada's Peoples*, ed. Paul Magosci (Toronto: Multicultural Historical Society of Ontario, 1999), 355–73; Gillian Creese, 'Class, Ethnicity, and Conflict: The Case of Chinese and Japanese Immigrants, 1880–1923',

in *Workers, Capital, and the State in British Columbia*, ed. Rennie Warburton and David Coburn (Vancouver: University of British Columbia Press, 1988), 56–68.

48. 'Chinese Labor', *Daily News*; 1883 Canadian Labor Congress Proceedings, 13.

49. Kealey and Palmer, *Dreaming of What Might Be*, 150; 'Reverend Dr. Johnson Has Another Brain Storm', *Industrial Banner*, April 1908.

50. *1883 Canadian Labor Congress Proceedings*, 13–16; 'Chinese Restriction', *Palladium of Labor*, March 28, 1885.

51. 'Chinese'; 'Chinese Increasing', *Voice*, October 24, 1902; Editorial, *Voice*; 'Ottawa Delegation', *Voice*, April 21, 1899.

52. 'Pig-Tail Pointer', *Capital Siftings*, July 21, 1894; 'He Will Hustle Back to China', *Industrial Banner*, September 1902.

53. David R. Roediger, *The Wages of Whiteness. Race and the Making of the American Working Class* (London: Verso, 1991), chap. 4; Glickman; *Living Wage*, pt. 1; Eric Foner, 'Workers and Slavery', in *Working for Democracy: American Workers from the Revolution to the Present*, ed. Paul Buhle and Alan Dawley (Urbana: University of Illinois Press, 1985), 21–30; David Brion Davis, 'Reflections on Abolitionism and Ideological Hegemony', in *The Antislavery Debate: Capitalism and Abolitionism as a Problem in Historical Interpretation*, ed. Thomas Bender (Berkeley: University of California Press, 1992), 162–5, 175–7.

54. 'Wage Slavery', *Labor Union*, January 20, 1883. See also 'Black Slavery', *Palladium of Labor*, November 8, 1884: untitled editorial, *Canadian Labor Reformer*, July 10, 1886; Enjolras, 'A Generation Ago', *Palladium of Labor*, September 25, 1886.

55. 'What's in a Name?' *Federationist*, December 20, 1912. See also Editorial, *Federationist*, September 28, 1912; 'Opposed to Slavery', *Industrial Banner*, January 1910; 'Manufacturing Poverty the Disgrace of Canada', *Port Arthur Wage Earner*, January 1914.

56. 'About Class Representation', *Canadian Labor Reformer*, March 5, 1887.

57. 'Coming to a Crisis', *Palladium of Labor*, July 19, 1884.

58. Enjolras, 'A Generation Ago'; Enjolras, 'The Social Future', *Palladium of Labor*, February

2, 1884. On Thompson, see Russell Hann, 'Brainworkers and the Knights of Labour: E.E. Sheppard, Phillips Thompson, and the Daily News, 1883–1887', in *Essays in Canadian Working-Class History*, ed. Greg Kealey and Peter Warrian (Toronto: McClelland and Stewart, 1976); Kealey and Palmer, *Dreaming of What Might Be*, 95, 110–11; Christina Burr, *Spreading the Light: Work and Labour Reform in Late-Nineteenth-Century Toronto* (Toronto: University Press, 1999).

59. Takaki, *Iron Cages*, 221; Timothy Stanley, 'Bringing Anti-Racist Theory into Historical Explanation: The Chinese Student Strike Revisited', *Journal of the Canadian Historical Association*, n.s., 13 (2002): 141–66.

60. 'Government Entreprises', *Labor Union*, January 27, 1883. See also 'Appeal from British Columbia'; the letter by the Moose Jaw Trades and Labor Council to the Dominion TLC, *TLC Proceedings, 1906*, 74; 'Oriental Immigration Is a Menace to Canada', *Industrial Banner*, July 3, 1914.

61. 'Victoria petition'. See also Sheppard's comments to the Hamilton anti-immigration rally, 'Indignation!'; 'One Good Result', *Industrial Banner*, June 1906; 'Chinatown in 'Frisco', *Voice*, July 6, 1906.

62. Kealey and Palmer, *Dreaming of What Might Be*, chap. 4; Burr, *Spreading the Light*, chap. 3; Karen Dubinsky and Adam Givertz, 'It Was Only a Matter of Passion: Masculinity and Sex and Danger', in *Gendered Pasts: Historical Essays in Femininity and Masculinity in Canada*, ed. Kathryn McPherson, Cecilia Morgan, and Nancy M. Forestell (Don Mills, ON: Oxford University Press, 1999), 71–2.

63. Thompson, *Politics of Labor* (Toronto: University of Toronto Press, 1975), 159; 'The Gospel of Greed and Grab', *Labor Union*, February 3, 1883.

64. 'Public Meeting'.

65. Sidney W. Mintz, *Caribbean Transformations* (Chicago: Aldine, 1974); William A. Green, *British Slave Emancipation: The Sugar Colonies and the Great Experiment, 1830–1865* (Oxford: Clarendon, 1976); Eric Foner, *Nothing but Freedom: Emancipation and Its Legacy* (Baton Rouge: Louisiana State University Press, 1983); Mary Turner, *From Chattel Slaves to Wage Slaves: The Dynamics of Labour Bargaining*

in the Americas (Kingston: Ian Randle Publishers, 1995).

66. *1883 Canadian Labor Congress Proceedings*, 13.

67. 'Chinese Must Not Come', *Trades Union Advocate*, Octobeer 12, 1882 ; 'Keep Them Out'.

68. 'The Chinese Question in Parliament'; 'Chinese Immigration', *Palladium of Labor*; Editorial, *Voice*; 'Ottawa Delegation'; 'The Chinese Tax', *Independent*, August 23, 1900; 'B.C. Acts Disallowed', *Voice*, December 1902.

69. Roediger, *Wages of Whiteness*, 79–82.

70. Alexander Saxton, *The Indispensable Enemy: Labor and the Anti-Chinese Movement in California* (Berkeley: University of California Press, 1971), 260–71; David Roediger, *Colored White: Transcending the Racial Past* (Berkeley: University of California Press, 2002), 195.

71. Robert Weir, *Beyond Labor's Veil: The Culture of the Knights of Labor* (University Park: Pennsylvania State University, 1996), 7–8, 12; Kim Voss, *The Making of American Exceptionalism: The Knights of Labor and Class Formation in the Nineteenth Century* (Ithaca, NY: Cornell University Press, 1993), 81.

72. Glickman, 'Inventing the "American Standard of Living,"' 232–33.

73. Eric Arnesen, 'Specter of the Black Strikebreaker: Race, Employment, and Labor Activism in the Industrial Era', *Labor History* 44 (2003): 319–35; Roediger, *Colored White*, 195–6.

74. 'The Sin of Cheapness', *Victoria Industrial News*, December 26, 1885, and 'Anti-Chinese Movement', *Victoria Industrial News*, February 20, 1886, which were taken from the *San Francisco Bulletin*; 'Christmas without the Chinese', *Victoria Industrial News*, January 16, 1886, which was taken from Tacoma, Washington; and 'Chinese Invasion', *Victoria Industrial News*, April 3, 1886, which was taken from a rally in Washington State.

75. Saxton, *Indispensable Enemy*, 261–2.

76. Editorial, *Trades Union Advocate*, June 29, 1882.

77. Editorial, *Wage Worker*, April 19, 1883; 1883 Canadian Labor Congress Proceedings, 13; 'A Lost Opportunity', *Daily News*, April 15, 1884: 'The Chinese Question in Victoria, B.C.', *Palladium of Labor*, August 30, 1884; Charles Old, 'Pigtails', *Palladium of Labor*, March 7, 1885.

78. 'Vetoing Anti-Chinese Legislation', *Palladium of Labor*, April 19, 1884. See also 'Anti-Chinese Legislation', *Palladium of Labor*, March 10, 1883; 'The Chinese Question in Parliament'; 'The Government and Anti-Chinese Legislation', *Victoria Industrial News*, May 1, 1886.

79. Roy, *White Man's Province*, 38; Editorial, *Trades Union Advocate*, May 18, 1882.

80. Tom Traves and Paul Craven, 'Class Politics of the National Policy, 1872–1933', *Journal of Canadian Studies* 14, no. 3 (1979): 14–38; 'Special Edition on the National Policy, 1879–1979', *Journal of Canadian Studies* 14, no 3 (1979); Pierre Berton, *The National Dream: The Great Railway, 1871–1881* (Toronto: McClelland and Stewart, 1970); and Berton, *The Last Spike: The Great Railway, 1881–1885* (Toronto: Anchor Canada, 1972).

81. 'Government Enterprises', *Labor Union*, March 10, 1883; 'The Chinese Immigration Question', *Palladium of Labor*, April 12, 1884. See also 'Argue', 'A Voice from Victoria B.C.' *Palladium of Labor*, December 8, 1883; Nanaimo Knights' statement; 'Anti-Chinese Meeting', *Victoria Industrial News*, January 23, 1886.

82. 'Fraser River Strike', *Voice*, July 27, 1900; 'Notes and Comments'. See also 'Communication from the Vancouver TLC', *TLC Proceedings, 1891*, 11; 'The Repeal Movement', *Voice*, August 17, 1906; 'The High Priest of Cheap Labour', *Industrial Banner*, January 1908; 'Asiatic Question', *Voice*, December 16, 1913.

4   From Catherine Carstairs, 'Deporting Ah Sin to Save the White Race: Moral Panic, Racialization, and the Extension of Canadian Drug Laws in the 1920s', *Canadian Bulletin of Medical History* 16(1) (June 1999): 65–88.

In the early 1920s, newspapers, women's groups, social service organizations, labour unions, fraternal societies, and church congregations all joined in a campaign to eradicate what they described as the 'drug evil'. Blaming Chinese-Canadians for degradation of white youth through drugs, they demanded harsh new drug legislation, as well as Chinese exclusion. As a result of their campaign, maximum sentences for trafficking and possession increased from one year to seven in 1921. In 1922, Parliament passed legislation that allowed judges to order the deportation of any aliens convicted of possession or trafficking. That same year, the Honourable Members decided that people convicted of possession or trafficking offences should serve jail terms of at least six months. Police were given the right to search all locations except a 'dwelling-house' without a warrant if they suspected drugs were present. In 1923, codeine and marijuana were added to the Schedule of Restricted Drugs without debate. The same legislation limited the right to appeal a conviction for possession or trafficking.[1] This legislative flurry marked a significant turning point in Canada's approach to drug use. By the mid-1920s, drug use had been thoroughly criminalized, both by the law and within the public mind.

[ . . . ]

The term 'moral panic' has been used extensively by scholars to describe periods of public alarm about deviant behaviours, such as drug use. The term was first coined by Stanley Cohen in his 1972 book, *Folk Devils and Moral Panics*. Cohen described moral panics as follows:

A condition, episode, person or group of persons emerges to become defined as a threat to societal values and interests; its nature is presented in a stylized and stereotypical fashion by the mass media: the moral barricades are manned by editors, bishops, politicians and other right-thinking people; socially accredited experts pronounce their diagnoses and solutions; ways of coping are evolved or (more often) resorted to; the condition then disappears, submerges or deteriorates and becomes more visible.[2]

[ . . . ]

Moral panics reproduce and in some cases reify or worsen the social inequalities that gave rise to them in the first place. The moral panic about drug use in the early 1920s stigmatized an already marginalized Chinese population and created legal precedents (including the right to search people and places without a warrant and limiting the right to an appeal) that potentially limited the human rights of all Canadians who interacted with the criminal justice system. For this reason, it is important to understand which social groups participated in the panic and for what reasons, whether their concern was proportionate to the actual harm involved, and why the issue of drug use gained currency at this particular point in time.

The other important term in this discussion is racialization. As Kay Anderson described in her book, *Vancouver's Chinatown*, racialization is the process by which attributes such as skin colour, language, and cultural practices are given social significance as markers of distinction.[3] The effectiveness of the drug panic depended on the creation of a racial drama of drug use that featured 'innocent' white youth and shadowy Asian traffickers who turned them into morally depraved 'dope fiends'.[4] This drama was believable because it took shape in the middle of a concerted drive to exclude the Chinese from Canada, segregate their children in West-Coast schools, and place restrictions on their business enterprises and land ownership.[5] Examining the racialization of drug panic helps explain why anti-drug crusaders called for strict penalties for possession and trafficking and at the same time wished to establish treatment facilities for the poor (white) drug addicts for whom they had so much sympathy. It also explains why parliamentarians, many of whom were trained lawyers, were willing to overlook traditional civil liberties in their desire to pass harsh legislation to counter what they regarded as a 'Chinese' menace.

## THE EARLY DEVELOPMENT OF CANADA'S DRUG LAWS

Canada's first drug law was the indirect result of anti-Asian riots on the West Coast in 1907. The government sent Deputy Minister of Labour William Lyon Mackenzie King to investigate the riots and claims for compensation. One of the claims was by several opium manufacturers who up until that time had been operating openly and legally on the West Coast. When he was in British Columbia, members of a Chinese anti-opium league called upon King and asked for the government's help in their efforts to discourage and prevent the manufacture and sale of opium. King subsequently tabled a report that warned that opium smoking was not just confined to the Chinese in British Columbia and that it was spreading to white women and girls. He quoted a newspaper clipping that told the story of a pretty young girl who had been found in a Chinese den. His report reviewed the progress of the anti-opium movement in China, the United States, England, and Japan, leaving the impression that Canada was far behind in this international moral reform movement.[6] Less than

a few weeks later the Minister of Labour introduced legislation prohibiting the manufacture, sale and importation of opium for other than medicinal purposes. The legislation passed without debate.

Three years later the government prohibited the use of opium and other drugs. In 1911, the sale or possession of morphine, opium, or cocaine became an offence carrying a maximum penalty of one year's imprisonment and a $500 fine. There was no minimum penalty. Smoking opium was a separate offence and carried a maximum term of $50 and one month imprisonment. Again, there was no minimum penalty. There were several reasons behind the new legislation. First of all, the 1908 legislation had not stopped opium smoking in Canada and the police felt that more drastic measures were needed. Chief Rufus Chamberlain, the Chief Constable of the Vancouver City Police, recommended that opium smoking and possession of opium should be offences under the law. Secondly, Mackenzie King, who introduced the legislation, had attended the 1909–10 International Opium Commission in Shanghai. The Commission was an American initiative meant to help China eradicate the opium traffic. Canada's 1911 legislation was intended to bring its legislation in line with the Resolutions passed by the international meeting.[7] [ . . . ]

The 1908 and 1911 laws were the result of a number of different factors including a growing unease about psychotropic substance use in a prohibitionist era, changing medical practices which created fewer cases of iatrogenic addiction, and the international anti-opium movement. The fact that opium was perceived to be used by working-class Chinese, and cocaine by underclass Montrealers also contributed to the notion that these drugs, like the people who used them, needed to be controlled and regulated. However, there was a significant difference between this legislation and the legislation of the 1920s. Fines were the norm in the 1910s. After the drug panic of the 1920s, an increasing number of drug users were imprisoned.

## THE CANADIAN DRUG PANIC

Canada was not alone in passing severe laws against drugs in the 1920s. Countries around the world were outlawing the use of opium and other drugs. Nonetheless, Canada's laws were among the most severe in the world, and for this reason, it is important to look at the specifics of the Canadian situation.[8] Drug crusaders claimed that the drug situation was especially troubling in Canada, but this does not seem to have been the case. In 1923–4, based on a survey of doctors and police departments, the Division of Narcotic Control estimated that there were 9,500 drug addicts in the country: 2,250 in British Columbia, 3,800 in Quebec, and 1,800 in Ontario, with small numbers in every other province except Prince Edward Island.[9] This estimate cannot be regarded as definite and did not seem to include Chinese opium smokers, but it indicated that only one in every 1,000 Canadians was an addict. Adding Chinese opium smokers, many of who seem to have smoked recreationally and were probably not addicted, would not have noticeably increased the per-capita rate of addiction.[10]

Drug scholars have generally dated the beginning of the drug panic to 1920, when the practiced social reformer, Emily Murphy, published a series of five articles in *Maclean's* magazine. Murphy was a leading suffragist, a temperance activist, and a popular writer under the pen-name 'Janey' Canuck. She was also a key player in eugenic debates, and a staunch supporter of the *Sexual Sterilization Act* in Alberta, which sterilized the mentally disabled.[11] In 1916 she was appointed police magistrate for Edmonton, and then for Alberta, becoming the first female magistrate in the British Empire. It was as a judge that she first became interested in drug use. She followed her 1920 articles with two additional articles in *Maclean's* in 1922 and her book *The*

*Black Candle*. In 1923, she nominated herself for a Nobel Prize for her work in this area.[12] Although Murphy's articles marked the beginning of a sustained anti-drug campaign, she had little impact on the Vancouver drug panic, and her importance has been overstated both by herself and by subsequent drug historians. The Division of Narcotic Control had little respect for Murphy, and the Vancouver parliamentarians who played a leading role in drug legislation paid far more attention to the anti-drug crusade in their own city.[13] Nonetheless, Murphy's articles did mark a turning point and her book, which drew heavily on the Vancouver campaign and was dedicated to the Vancouver drug investigators, brought the Vancouver drug panic to a larger Canadian audience.[14]

Murphy's first article was entitled 'The Grave Drug Menace'. The first page delineated that this was a Chinese menace. It featured a threatening drawing of a hand with long fingernails holding a Chinese tablet, a picture of a wizened Asian man with smoke coming out of his ears, and a photo of a Asian man smoking a pipe. The text itself focused primarily on white female addicts and warned that 'all folks of gentle and open hearts should know that among us there are girls and glorious lads who, without any obliquity in themselves, have become victims to the thrall of opiates'.[15] Murphy explained that drug use posed a serious threat to the white race, as it accounted for most cases of miscegenation.[16] In subsequent articles, Murphy accused the Chinese of continuing their nefarious activities behind locked doors and hidden passages despite the *Opium and Narcotic Drug Act*.[17] Several times she referred to her imaginary Chinese characters as 'Ah Sin',[18] a quick shorthand for describing the moral failures of the Chinese, and had them engage in what was clearly meant to come across as 'foreign' behaviour. In her fourth article she described one drug user's quest for religious help for a drug habit:

In this place [a joss house in Vancouver] there was a serving altar on which stood huge vases of pewter and enamel and over which hung banners and peacock feathers. These banners, the Chinese explained, were extremely efficacious in the case of opium sickness, and so were carried to the sick room whenever required. On the serving altar, there is also a rubber stamp used to impress the paper taken away by men suffering from insomnia. 'Debil, him keep China boy not sleep', explained the servitor.

Yes! It is quite certain we do not understand these people from the Orient, nor what ideas are hid behind their dark inscrutable faces, but all of us, however owl-eyed, may see pathos in the picture of the hapless drug victim—often a mere withered stalk of pain, stealing away in to the streets with his piece of sacred paper trying to make believe that, instead of the pipe, this will give sleep to his tortured eyes and still more tortured brain.[19]

Everything in this passage served to mark the 'otherness' of the Chinese—the pidgin English, the religious practices, the 'dark inscrutable faces', even the assumption that whites would be 'owl-eyed' upon observing such activities. She used her pity as a tool by which to validate her racist description of Chinese religious practices. The fact that she expressed sympathy for the Chinese drug user (something she did not do in other places) and the inability of his religion to help him highlighted what she considered to be the inadequacy and peculiarity of Chinese methods for dealing with addiction.

In her 1922 book, Murphy took care to distance herself from what she considered to be prejudice or racism. 'We have no sympathy with the baiting of the yellow races, or with the belief that these exist only to serve the Caucasian, or to be exploited by us', she wrote. 'The Chinese as a rule are a friendly people', she condescendingly pronounced 'and have a fine sense of humor that puts them on an easy footing with our folk, as compared with the Hindu and others we might mention. Ah Duck, or whatever we choose to call him, is patient, polite and persevering'. Despite her favourable assessment of what she viewed as the Chinese character, she assumed that it was her right to name the Chinese, and to tell the 'truth' of their character.

She followed this up with the statement that

> it behooves the people in Canada and the United States, to consider the desirability of these visitors—for they are visitors—and to say whether or not we shall be 'at home' to them for the future. A visitor may be polite, patient, persevering, as above delineated, but if he carried poisoned lollypops in his pocket and feeds them to our children, it might seem wise to put him out.[20]

By complimenting the Chinese and criticizing their exploitation, she gave greater credibility to her view that the Chinese were outsiders who threatened the well-being of Canadian children through drugs.

Murphy was one of Canada's best-known writers and her monthly feature in Canada's national news magazine garnered attention in newspapers across the country.[21] However, her campaign was dwarfed by a far more important anti-drug campaign in Vancouver. Vancouver was the primary location for anti-Chinese organizing, which was gathering steam in the years immediately following World War I. It also had the largest number of drug arrests and the biggest Chinese community in Canada. In 1917, an African-Canadian drug user had killed the Chief of Police, leading to a certain amount of hand wringing about the drug menace.[22] In the spring of 1920, coinciding with Murphy's campaign in *Maclean's*, the *Vancouver Sun* ran a brief campaign against the drug traffic, and in editorials, it called for the abolition of Chinatown. One declared that it is 'absolutely necessary to prevent the degrading of white boys and girls who are being recruited into the ranks of drug addicts. If the only way to save our children is to abolish Chinatown, then Chinatown must and will go, and go quickly'.[23] [ . . . ]

The catalyst for the first major anti-drug campaign occurred in March 1921, when returned soldier Joseph Kehoe pleaded guilty to eight charges of robbery with violence and was sentenced to five years in the Penitentiary and 24 lashes. According to the fast-growing *Vancouver Daily Sun*,[24] which covered the issue intensively, this unlikely 'hero' was 28 years old and came from a 'good family' in Nova Scotia. According to the paper, Kehoe had been a medical student when he enlisted at the very start of the war. In April 1915 he was gassed and taken prisoner at Ypres. The Germans put him to work in a munitions factory, but he refused to take part in work that would be used to harm his fellow allied soldiers and eventually convinced his fellow prisoners to break his arm so that he could no longer work. He was brought before a military tribunal and sentenced to 15 years imprisonment in a military prison. At the end of 16 months his health was so poor that he was sent to England in an exchange of prisoners. He was discharged in 1919 and after his return to Canada he started using drugs.[25]

[ . . . ] A few weeks later a general meeting of the Comrades of the Great War passed a resolution opposing light sentences in the case of dope peddlers.[26] As it had the previous year, the coverage quickly took an anti-Chinese turn. In a front-page article on 12 April, entitled 'Dope Peddler King Is Taken', the *Vancouver Sun* told its readers that prominent Chinese businessman Wong Way boasted that he was turning over more than half a million dollars' worth of drugs each year and that he drove one of the best limousines in the city. This fit in well with business complaints that Chinese merchants were competing unfairly with whites.[27]

A week later, Vancouverites held a mass meeting to demand 'drastic federal action' to defeat the 'dope traffickers'.[28] The meeting was organized by the Returned Soldier's Council and included the Mayor, the Chief of Police, the City Prosecutor, Oakalla Prison Farm officials, and service club representatives. A week later, a second meeting called for minimum two-year sentences for first-time traffickers and five years and the lash for a second trafficking offence. Participants demanded that all aliens convicted of selling drugs be deported, and wanted the police to have the right to search for drugs without a warrant.[29] The enormous headline proclaimed 'DEATH ON DOPE: CITIZENS PLAN BIG CAMPAIGN TO SMASH UP THE DRUG RING'. Beginning 3 May, the newspaper hired a former drug addict to carry on a special investigation into the traffic. J.B. Wilson described himself as a 'successful young businessman' before he started using drugs. Now cured, he was anxious to 'devote my talents and my energies to assisting in rescuing others who have fallen victims to the drug ring'. Wilson argued that police were doing everything they could to stamp out the drug traffic, but that the 'Chinese dope peddler is about the most cunning human being and the smartest of them all'.[30] In a later article he commended the RCMP who 'are bending their energies to rid our Canadian soil of the Oriental filth of the drug traffic'.[31]

Several weeks after the first Vancouver meeting, the Minister of Health introduced legislation to amend the *Opium and Narcotic Drug Act*. H.H. Stevens, a Conservative MP from Vancouver South who had been an active participant in the Vancouver meetings, proposed two new amendments to the Act: 1) that a person found guilty of an offence be liable on indictment to imprisonment for seven years; and that 2) a person convicted of giving or distributing to a minor be liable to whipping as an additional penalty. This was the first time the House of Commons discussed drug use as a serious social menace. Stevens introduced his amendment with the announcement that drug traffickers were distributing drugs to high school children and even to children in the higher grades of elementary school.[32] [ . . . ]

[T]he Vancouver drug panic temporarily disappeared from the headlines, but there was still considerable backstage activity. In the spring of 1921, the Rotary, Gyros, and Kiwanis Clubs established an Investigating Committee into the Drug Traffic.[33] That summer the *Vancouver Sun* published Hilda Glynn Ward's novel *The Writing on the Wall*. The plot featured wealthy Vancouver citizens who became addicted to drugs and subsequently co-operated with the Chinese in their drive for the domination of Canada.[34] At the beginning of 1922, the Investigating Committee had a great opportunity to expose their findings when the *Vancouver Daily World*, Vancouver's oldest newspaper,[35] launched a campaign that far exceeded the one launched by the *Sun* a year earlier. This newspaper highlighted the drug issue on its front page for months and increased its circulation by one third.[36] As a result, over 300 groups in Vancouver passed resolutions asking for mandatory sentences for drug possession and trafficking and the deportation of naturalized aliens who participated in the drug traffic.[37]

From the day the *World* campaign began, it was clear that they blamed Asians for the spread of the drug habit. The first day featured two front-page articles. The headline article proclaimed 'Drug Soaked Addicts Pass on the Way to Jail'. The article commenced with the case of Yung Yuen 'an ivory faced Chinese'. He was sentenced to a year in prison for procuring three packages of drugs for a 'white victim'. The next paragraph highlighted the case of Lim Gum, 'an undersized bald-headed little Chinese' who was found with four tins of opium. The descriptions of the Chinese addicts were unflattering and attempted to draw attention to the physical ways in which the Chinese were perceived to be different from whites. At his trial, Yung was said to have written his name on a piece of paper and burned it with a match while mumbling 'Chinese rigmarole to the effect

that so might his soul burn after death if he failed to tell the truth'. This depiction highlighted the 'foreign' nature of the Chinese and their customs.[38]

[ . . . ]

The anti-Asian discourse in Canada during this time period consistently emphasized the intelligence of the Chinese and their craftiness as reasons for why they should not be permitted to immigrate to Canada. The idea that the Chinese were consummate drug smugglers, on account of their ingenuity and cleverness, would not come as any surprise to the citizens of Vancouver. Most were already convinced that the business acumen of the Chinese posed a serious threat to white enterprise. The article below 'Drug Soaked Addicts' announced that 'All Boats from Asia Bring in Illicit Drugs', and was subtitled 'Oriental Crews Largely Engaged in Traffic'. Asian traffickers were described as 'wily' and the newspaper proclaimed that innocent passengers were sleeping on top of drugs hidden under berths and stitched into mattresses. Obviously, Vancouverites needed to wake up to the danger. The following day, the article 'Dying Lad Tells How Boys and Girls Are Made Drug Addicts' asserted that most of the drugs came from Chinatown. One dealer, the young addict confided, had a secret code whereby the purchaser would request drugs by number, lessening the chance of being caught over the phone.[39] Under such circumstances, it would not be easy to catch 'cunning' Asian drug traffickers. The entire community needed to unite to defend itself.

On the third day of their campaign, the newspaper announced its solution to the drug problem. The headline blared 'Deport the Drug Traffickers'. The article asserted (wrongly) that 1,778 Asians were convicted of drug offences in the Vancouver Police Court in 1921.[40] Since most received fines and only a few went to jail, they all became free again to 'commit the same sin against society'. The article concluded 'Vancouver's first move in abolishing the drug traffic must be the absolute banishment by deportation of every Oriental who lends himself to the drug ring'.[41] Over the months that followed, the *World* encouraged organizations throughout Vancouver to pass resolutions to that effect. Thousands of Vancouverites signed petitions requesting that aliens including naturalized aliens be deported if convicted of selling drugs. The measure was included in the 1922 amendments to the *Opium and Narcotic Drug Act* and in fact was even stricter than requested since deportation could be applied to people convicted of possession as well as trafficking.

The third day contained the announcement that the Child Welfare Society was joining the fight against the 'drug evil', despite the 'fact' that other officials had received threats against their lives when they opposed the 'drug ring' and that 'actual attempts have been made on the lives of government officials engaged in the fight against the big influences at work behind the scenes'.[42] [ . . . ] The frequently repeated idea that the Chinese might bring about the destruction of the white race through drug use appeared in a particularly blatant form in a front-page story about a wealthy addict who was 'dragged down by drugs'. This addict asserted that the Chinese drug sellers 'taunted him with their superiority at being able to sell the dope without using it. Taunted him by telling him that the yellow race would rule the world. That they were too wise to attempt to win in battle but that they would win by wits. That they would introduce drugs into the homes of the Caucasians; would strike at the white race through "dope", and that when the time was ripe they would take command of the world'.[43] On 29 January, less than two weeks after the start of the *World* campaign, 2,000 Vancouverites attended a meeting held at the Empress Theatre, where they passed a unanimous resolution asking for the elimination of fines as a penalty and the substitution of prison sentences of not less than six months, and not more than 10 years, with lashes, and the deportation of aliens.[44]

The *World* reported that women openly wiped tears from their eyes, as the self-styled drug investigator Charles E. Royal told the audience about young girls in their teens who sold themselves to Chinese, Japanese and 'Hindoos' to get money for drugs. The newspaper continued,

> They shuddered when he pointed out that many of them came from the best families in Vancouver and in the Dominion and when he told of a young boy of this city, himself an addict, who had, at the instigation of the Chinese traffickers, started his sister on the drug habit, and then had used her to pander to the passions of these self-same traffickers in order to get the money to buy drugs, women turned pale, while men clenched their hands and gripped their lips with their teeth to keep down the anger that fought for an outlet.[45]

The following day, the city council and the Mayor both endorsed the anti-drug campaign.[46]

[ . . . ]

In May 1922, New Westminster Unionist W.G. McQuarrie introduced a motion into the House of Commons asking for the government to take 'immediate action with a view of securing the exclusion of Oriental immigration'.[47] Vancouver South Liberal-Conservative Leon Ladner gave a long speech highlighting the discoveries of the Vancouver Investigating Committee. He concluded that the drug traffic was reason enough to stop all Chinese immigration.[48] While most members participating in this debate stressed economic issues, three other members also emphasized the dangers of the drug traffic.

The government introduced new drug legislation at the beginning of June. By this time, no parliamentarian asserted that the drug panic was overblown. Members from a variety of parties urged the Health Minister to take even more stringent steps against the drug traffic. In introducing the legislation, the Minister Henri Beland indicated that numerous requests had reached him from benevolent, charitable, and religious bodies as well as parliamentarians from both sides of the House, to abolish the option of a fine.[49] At the first reading, Progressive Archibald Carmichael, from Kindersley, Saskatchewan, asked for an amendment deporting all Asians found guilty of trafficking in drugs.[50] Vancouver MP Leon Ladner, who had spoken at several of the Vancouver mass meetings, advised the government to pass an amendment allowing for the lash.[51] [ . . . ]

In the debate that followed, the anti-Asian racism of the Vancouver campaign had a clear impact. Leon Ladner told the story of a girl of 16 who had come before the investigation committee in Vancouver. The girl was a morphine or cocaine addict. Infected with venereal disease, she worked as a prostitute with Chinese men. Ladner concluded 'this traffic is carried on in a cool and calculating way. The men who sell the drug do not themselves use it; they know its terrible effects, but they exercise all their resourcefulness and ingenuity to induce others to acquire the habit'.[52] Fully persuaded, Dr Robert Manion, who had been opposed to the lash the previous year, admitted that 'I believe that the hon. Gentlemen who represent British Columbia in this House are more familiar with this question than perhaps the rest of us, even those who are in the medical profession' and agreed to support the lash.[53] Although there were still a few such as United Farmer Oliver Gould who opposed the lash on humanitarian grounds, even he felt compelled to state that the traffic 'is one of the greatest evils extent in this country'.[54] In the discussion over deportation it was clear the 'foreigners' to be deported were Chinese. Health Minister Henri Beland pointed out that 'so far as a provision for deportation is concerned the committee will realize that it would not very well apply to Canadians. Only to Chinese who have not been naturalized could it apply'.[55] He did not even consider the possibility that citizens

of other countries might be deported by this legislation, although once the legislation was implemented, large numbers of Americans were also deported.

In 1923, not long after the passage of the 1923 *Chinese Immigration Act*, which initiated Chinese exclusion, the anti-drug consensus resulted in yet another set of revisions to the *Opium and Narcotic Drug Act*. By this time, the panic also had spread to Toronto and Montreal. That spring large meetings of prominent citizens were held at the Loew's Roof Garden Theatre in Toronto and at the Mount Royal Hotel in Montreal.[56] In the House of Commons debate that followed, the government passed legislation that restricted people's right to an appeal, increased the fine for smoking opium, and increased the maximum penalty for being found in an opium den and for the possession of opium equipment. This debate was short, but the anti-drug consensus was clear. Mr E.M. Macdonald stated that 'we are all agreed that this nefarious traffic, which saps the mind and body of the people can only be dealt with in the strongest possible way'.[57] Dr Manion, who opposed the measure to restrict appeals on constitutional grounds, made sure to indicate that his failure to support the amendment was not because he was 'soft on drugs'. 'I presume', he clarified, 'there is no member of this House, whatever may be his party affiliations who is not just as eager as my hon. friend to do away with the illicit use of any of these habit-forming drugs'.[58]

Although the 'panic' ended in 1923, the tropes that guided it had been firmly established and regularly reappeared in magazine and newspaper articles throughout the decade. In 1929, the debate over the consolidation of the Act, which added whipping at the discretion of the judge to all trafficking offences, showed how clearly the discourse of the innocent addict and the nefarious trafficker had permeated the public mind. Mr Edwards described a murderer as 'white as the driven snow in comparison with the low, degraded human beast who for a few dollars' profit will gradually murder his fellow-man by selling to him habit forming drugs'.[59] By contrast, the addict was described as a 'poor creature'.[60] Minister of Health James King declared that addicts were not being prosecuted under the Act.[61] However, in that year, more than half of the convictions under the Act were for smoking opium or for frequenting an opium den, two provisions which were clearly aimed at drug users, not at drug traffickers.[62] What he meant when he said that they did not prosecute the addict was that they did not prosecute the imaginary white 'victims' of drugs. However, they were prosecuting working-class drug users of all races.

Interestingly, in the 1929 debate, there was no mention of the race of traffickers. Did this mean that the racialization of drug use was on the decline? Perhaps, although the connection between drugs and Asians was still strong in the popular press.[63] In fact, the 1929 debate was short, and by this time parliamentarians may not have felt the need to stress the culpability of the Asian trafficker, since it was already well established in the public mind, and the *Chinese Exclusion Act* had all but ended Chinese immigration. However, the lack of attention to race in the 1929 debate also marked a transition point. By this time, the panic was over, but the public remained fully convinced that drug use was dangerous and drug traffickers immoral. Perhaps it was no longer necessary to exploit anti-Asian sentiment to pass strict laws against drugs.

The government never did act to provide treatment facilities, even for the innocent young addicts who incurred so much sympathy and who inspired such a strict legislative response to drugs. Throughout the decade, the Minister of Health and the Division of Narcotic Control asserted that treatment was a matter of provincial jurisdiction. They encouraged the provinces to pass legislation allowing for compulsory treatment of drug addicts in provincial mental institutions, but only Alberta and Nova Scotia passed such legislation and only Alberta put it into effect.[64] Ultimately, white drug users were rarely the

promising young men and women of the middle-classes who were featured in anti-drug campaigns. Many female drug users were prostitutes, and the men were often vagrants who had had previous encounters with the law.[65] These 'dope fiends' received little notice in anti-drug campaigns and police officers and health officials who came into contact with them regarded them as difficult and noisy prisoners and patients. Although 'innocent' white addicts served as an effective rhetorical tool for anti-drug crusaders who wanted stricter laws against drug use, neither the government or social service organizations were willing to spend money on the treatment and rehabilitation of the socially disadvantaged 'dope fiend'.

## CONCLUSION

The link between drug use and the Chinese was a key factor in the demonization of drugs that took place in the early 1920s. It was no accident that the most important campaign against drug use in Canada took place at the same time as a concerted drive for Chinese exclusion. In this intolerant environment, an understanding of drug use emerged in which Chinese drug traffickers were vilified, Chinese drug users were ignored or regarded as a moral contagion, and white drug users were regarded as tragic victims. This imagery provided one more excuse for keeping the Chinese out of Canada, and resulted in the passage of severe drug legislation.

Racism does not 'hurt us all', as an ad campaign declared in the mid-1990s. It hurts some much more than others. However, as Elizabeth Comack, Patricia Roy, and many others have noted, racism often divides the working class, and as such it can work to the disadvantage of people of all races. Although the middle and upper classes also used drugs, especially alcohol, to excess, by the 1920s, the drugs prohibited under the *Opium and Narcotic Drug Act* seem to have been used primarily by working-class people. The middle- and upper-class people who did use opiates and cocaine often were able to obtain supplies through doctors. They had little contact with the illicit market and rarely faced criminal sanctions for their drug use. This was not true for working-class users.

In the 1920s, as Clayton Mosher has pointed out, Chinese men convicted of drug offences often faced more lenient penalties than working-class white users of drugs. This was because they often were charged with opium smoking, or being found in an opium den, rather than possession. These charges were easier to prosecute, and served to raise revenue for the judicial system. However, Mosher's emphasis on sentencing downplays the extent to which drug laws were used to persecute the Chinese population. Between 1923 and 1932, 761 Chinese were deported as a result of the deportation provision passed in 1922, representing almost 2% of the total Chinese population in Canada.[66] On average, people deported under the Act had been in Canada for almost 17 years.[67] Moreover, the police regularly raided opium dens. In 1922, 1,117 Chinese were convicted under the Act, meaning that nearly 3 per cent of the total Chinese population was convicted under the *Opium and Narcotic Drug*

*Act* that year alone.[68] In some cities, the arrest rates were even higher. These exceptionally high rates of arrest show the extent to which the *Opium and Narcotic Drug Act* was used as a tool against the Chinese population of Canada.

Nonetheless, drug laws did hurt all drug users, and even all Canadians. By the mid-1930s opium smoking had all but died out, and the mostly white drug users caught violating the law were sentenced to at least six months in prison for possession. Moreover, the *Opium and Narcotic Drug Act* contained provisions for corporal punishment, limited the right to an appeal, and allowed the police extensive power to search without a warrant. These provisions were dangerous precedents for the human rights of all Canadians, regardless of whether or not they used drugs.

The drug panic of the early 1920s had all the hallmarks of a 'moral panic'. Concern about drug use spread widely throughout society. There was a vastly increased level of hostility towards the Chinese men associated with the traffic, the concern was disproportionate to the apparent harm caused by drug use, and it erupted quite suddenly. Most importantly, this racialized drug panic had an important impact on Canadian civil rights and liberties.

# NOTES

1. *An Act to amend the Opium and Narcotic Drug Act*, Statutes of Canada 1921, c.42; *An Act to Amend the Opium and Narcotic Drug Act*, Statutes of Canada 1922, c.36; and *An Act to Prohibit the Improper Use of Opium and Other Drugs*, Statutes of Canada 1923 c.22

2. Stanley Cohen, *Folk Devils and Moral Panics: The Creation of the Mods and Rockers* (Oxford: Martin Robertson, 1980), 9.

3. Kay Anderson, *Vancouver's Chinatown* (Montreal and Kingston: McGill-Queen's University Press, 1991), 18.

4. Catherine Carstairs, 'Innocent Addicts, Dope Fiends and Nefarious Traffickers: Illegal Drug Use in 1920s English Canada', *Journal of Canadian Studies*, 33, 3 (Fall 1998): 145–62.

5. The literature on anti-Asian racism on the West Coast includes Peter Ward, *White Canada Forever* (Montreal and Kingston: McGill-Queen's University Press, 1978); Patricia Roy, *A White Man's Province* (Vancouver: University of British Columbia Press, 1989); and Gillian Creese, 'Exclusion or Solidarity? Vancouver Workers Confront the "Oriental Problem,"' *BC Studies* 80 (Winter 1988–89).

6. 'A Report by W. L. Mackenzie King, Deputy Minister of Labour, on the Need for the Suppression of the Opium Traffic in Canada', *Sessional Papers of Canada 1908*, Paper No. 36b.

7.  G.F. Murray, 'Cocaine Use in the Era of Social Reform: The Natural History of a Social Problem in Canada, 1880–1911', *Canadian Journal of Law and Society*, 2(1987): 29–43.

8.  David Musto, *The American Disease: The Origins of Narcotic Control* (New Haven: Yale University Press, 1973); Andrew Blake, 'Foreign Devils and Moral Panics: Britain, Asia and the Opium Trade', in Bill Shwartz, ed., *The Expansion of England: Race, Ethnicity and Culutral History* (London and New York: Routledge, 1996); T.O. Reins, 'Reform, Nationalism and Internationalism: The Opium Suppression Movement in China', *Modern Asian Studies*, 25, 1 (1991): 101–42.

9.  *Annual Report of the Department of Health for the Year Ended March 31, 1924*, 36.

10. The population of Chinese in Canada in 1921 was 39,587. It is impossible to know how many of them smoked opium (Peter S. Li, *The Chinese in Canada* [Toronto: Oxford University Press, 1988]).

11. Byrne Hope Sanders, *Emily Murphy: Crusader* (Toronto: Macmillan, 1945), 186; and Christine Mander, *Emily Murphy: Rebel* (Toronto: Simon and Pierre, 1985), 117.

12. Michael Bliss, *The Discovery of Insulin* (Toronto: McClelland and Stewart, 1982), 225.

13. National Archives of Canada (NAC), RG 29, Vol. 602, File 325-1-3.

14. Murphy's dedication read: 'To the members of the Rotary, Kiwanis and Gyros Clubs and to the white Cross Associations who are rendering valiant service in impeding the spread of drug addiction, this volume is respectfully dedicated'.

15. Emily Murphy, 'The Grave Drug Menace', *Maclean's*, 15 February 1920, 9.

16. Murphy, 'The Grave Drug Menace', 11.

17. Madge Pon, 'Like a Chinese Puzzle: Constructions of Chinese Masculinity in Jack Canuck', in Joy Parr and Mark Rosenthal, eds., *Gender and History in Canada* (Toronto: McClelland and Stewart, 1996), 88–100.

18. Murphy, 'The Underground System', *Maclean's*, 15 March 1920, 55; and 'Fighting the Drug Menace', *Maclean's*, 15 April 1920, 11.

19. Emily Murphy, 'What Must Be Done', *Maclean's*, 15 June 1920, 14.

20. Emily Murphy, *The Black Candle* (Toronto: Thomas Allen, 1922), 187–8.

21. In its introduction to the second article, the editors of *Maclean's* wrote that newspapers across the country commented on the first article and commented that the editors of *Maclean's* had received a large number of letters as a result.

22. See 'Chief MacLennan Is Shot Dead in Battle with Negro Desperado', *Vancouver Daily Sun*, 21 March 1917, 1.

23. 'Chinatown—or Drug Traffic?' *Vancouver Daily Sun*, 22 March 1920, 6. See also 'Chinatown and the Drug Traffic', *Vancouver Daily Sun*, 31 March 1920, 6.

24. The *Vancouver Daily Sun* was the fastest growing newspaper in Western Canada (*The Canadian Newspaper Directory* [A. McKim, 1922], 418).

25. 'War Veteran to Be Given Lashes', *Vancouver Daily Sun*, 18 March 1921, 1.

26. 'Dope Peddlar King Is Taken', *Vancouver Daily Sun*, 12 April 1921, 1.

27. Ward, *White Canada Forever*, 124–8; and Anderson, *Vancouver's Chinatown*, 110–13.

28. 'War Opens on Drug Traffickers: Mass Meeting of Citizens Demand Federal Action', *Vancouver Daily Sun*, 21 April 1921, 1.

29. 'Death of Dope', *Vancouver Daily Sun*, 28 April 1921, 1.

30. 'Ex-Crook and Reformed Drug Fiend Aids City Police in Fight on Dope Ring', *Vancouver Daily Sun*, 3 May 1921, 1.

31. 'Drug Exposure Causes Mass Meeting to Be Called to Fight Evil', *Vancouver Daily Sun*, 12 May 1921, 1.

32. House of Commons, *Debates*, 3 May 1921, 2897.

33. 'Clubs to Report on "Dope" Probe', *Vancouver Daily Sun*, 28 January 1922, 3.

34. Hilda Glynn Ward, *The Writing on the Wall* (Toronto: University of Toronto Press, 1974, 1st edn, 1921).

35. The circulation of the *Vancouver Daily World* averaged 16,182 in 1921 (*The Canadian Newspaper Directory*, 463).

36. In an advertisement in the newspaper directory, the newspaper claimed that its circulation for February 1922 was 21,353, much higher than it had been for the year ended 30 September 1921.

37. 'Call on Liberal Executive to Take Action on Drugs', *Vancouver Daily World*, 7 March 1922, 9.

38. 'Drug Soaked Addicts Pass on Way to Jail', *Vancouver Daily World*, 16 January 1922, 1.

39. 'Dying Lad Tells How Boys and Girls Are Made Drug Addicts', *Vancouver Daily World*, 17 January 1922, 1.

40. Statistics kept by the Dominion Bureau of Statistics were for the year ended 30 September. Statistics on race were not published until 1922. In the year ended 30 September 1922, 519 Chinese were convicted of drug offences in British Columbia. For the year ended 30 September 1921, 649 people of all races were convicted of drug offences in British Columbia, meaning that the newspapers' statistics were far off.

41. 'Deport the Drug Traffickers', *Vancouver Daily World*, 18 January 1922, 1.

42. 'Waterfront Open Gate for Drugs; Child Welfare Society Joins Fight', *Vancouver Daily World*, 18 January 1922, 1.

43. 'Dragged Down by Drugs from Post Giving Big Pay', *Vancouver Daily World*, 21 January 1922, 28.

44. 'Ten Years for Drug Sellers Demanded by 2000 Citizens', *Vancouver Daily World*, 30 January 1922, 1, 13.

45. 'Ten Years for Drug Sellers Demanded by 2000 Citizens', 1.

46. 'Mayor and Council Endorse World's Anti-Drug Campaign', *Vancouver Daily World*, 31 January 1922, 1; and 'City to Join in the Drug Crusade', *Vancouver Daily Sun*, 31 January 1922, 2.

47. House of Commons, *Debates*, 8 May 1922, 1509.

48. House of Commons, *Debates*, 8 May 1922, 1529–31.

49. House of Commons, *Debates*, 15 June 1922, 3014.

50. House of Commons, *Debates*, 12 June 1922, 2824.

51. House of Commons, *Debates*, 12 June 1922, 2824.

52. House of Commons, *Debates*, 15 June 1922, 3015.

53. House of Commons, *Debates*, 15 June 1922, 3016.

54. House of Commons, *Debates*, 15 June 1922, 3017.

55. House of Commons, *Debates*, 12 June 1922, 2824.

56. Letter from F.W. Cowan to Elizabeth MacCallum, 9 April 1923, in NAC, RG 29, Vol. 605, File 325-4-7.

57. House of Commons, *Debates*, 23 April 1923, 2132.

58. House of Commons, *Debates*, 23 April 1923, 2117.

59. House of Commons, *Debates*, 12 February 1929, 62.

60. House of Commons, *Debates*, 12 February 1929, 65.

61. House of Commons, *Debates*, 29 May 1929, 2971.

62. Dominion Bureau of Statistics, *Annual Report of Criminal and Other Offences for Year Ended September 30, 1929*, 148–9.

63. Anne Anderson Perry, 'The Dope Traffic in Canada', *The Western Home Monthly*, August 1929; and Thomas Warling, 'Canada's Greatest Menace', *Canadian Home Journal*, August 1930.

64. NAC, RG 29, Vol. 326, File 324-1-2, Parts 1–3.

65. Clayton Mosher's thesis shows that 85.9 per cent of people convicted of drug offences in five Ontario cities between 1921 and 1928 were working-class or had no occupation ('The Legal Response to Narcotic Drugs in Five Ontario Cities 1908–1961', [Ph.D. dissertation, University of Toronto, 1992]).

66. *Annual Report of the Department of Pensions and National Health for 1932–33*, 70.

67. Answer to a question in the House of Commons, 27 February 1929 asking for the average length of time deported aliens had been in Canada (*Debates*, 508–9).

68. Dominion Bureau of Statistics, *Annual Report of Criminal and Other Offences for the Year Ended September 30, 1922*.

# Chapter 9

# Fighting From Home

## READINGS

### Primary Documents

### Historical Interpretations

## Introduction

When we think about war, we tend to focus on the expensive and spectacular part: sending thousands of troops across the globe or across a border to kill or otherwise harass the enemy. But in addition to the undoubtedly important work of fighting on the front, wars involve many more people who never put on a uniform. During the Second World War in Canada, those who did not qualify for combat roles because they were too young, too old, too female, physically or mentally disabled, had vital industrial or administrative skills, or were the wrong race or ethnicity nonetheless found themselves drawn into wartime rhythms of work or domestic life. This 'total war' environment was plainly discernible in Canadian society, in its economic priorities, and in the cultural lives of Canadians. Plentiful jobs in war-related industries, housing shortages, unrelenting messages to work harder and more efficiently to further the war effort, and the abandonment of at least some leisure-time pursuits were all convincing evidence. Our primary sources involve two aspects of home front life: the contributions and postwar prospects of women, and the place of the volunteer worker. Broadcaster Mattie Rotenberg reminded her listeners that the world's women stood to lose as much as any nation if the war did not end in an Allied victory. She did not call for liberation from traditional gendered family roles, but asked women to do what they could to tackle the problems of 'unemployment, housing, ignorance and want', which would continue when the war was over. In her magazine article, Anne Frances addresses the question of what might happen for volunteers after the war, and suggests that their wartime work had given them a taste for involvement that would not go away easily. She sees volunteers as capable of handling domestic and community duties at the same time, and it is worth considering that the chance for volunteers to do both would not have been possible without the trials of war. Wartime brought pressure on the household economy and, as Magda Fahrni shows, brought about a significant jump in consumer activism, despite the distractions of war and the difficulty of adjusting to a peacetime economy. We can even say that the continuation of this activism after the war indicated how wartime altered perceptions of what common citizens could do to shape their daily lives. In his study of Verdun, Quebec, Serge Durflinger describes a community grappling with wartime troubles, but also one that remained divided along linguistic and class lines. The problems of mental breakdown and delinquency highlighted here indicate that despite the efforts of local authorities to impose a necessary order, the home front could sometimes be a chaotic place.

# QUESTIONS FOR CONSIDERATION

1. How does Rotenberg depict home life under fascism?
2. Why might Frances consider the volunteer worker to be particularly suited to be a post-war community leader?
3. What would you consider to be the characteristics that would help a person or a family survive on the home front? Why?
4. What were 'purses on legs' and what does this term tell us about the way consumption was viewed in the 1940s?
5. What motivated the zoot-suiters to dress the way they did, and why did servicemen object so strongly?

# SUGGESTIONS FOR FURTHER READING

Timothy Balzer, *The Information Front: The Canadian Army and News Management during the Second World War* (Vancouver: UBC Press, 2010).

David Bercuson, *Maple Leaf Against the Axis: Canada's Second World War* (Don Mills: Stoddart, 1995).

Ivana Caccia, *Managing the Canadian Mosaic in Wartime: Shaping Citizenship Policy, 1939–1945* (Montreal and Kingston: McGill-Queen's University Press, 2010).

Magda Fahrni, *Household Politics: Montreal Families and Postwar Reconstruction* (Toronto: University of Toronto Press, 2005).

Diane G. Forestell, 'The Necessity of Sacrifice for the Nation at War: Women's Labour Force Participation, 1939–1946', *Histoire Sociale/Social History* 22(44) (1989): 333–47.

Carolyn Gossage, *Greatcoats and Glamour Boots: Canadian Women at War, 1939–1945* (Toronto: Dundurn Press, 1991).

Jeffrey A. Keshen, *Saints, Sinners, and Soldiers: Canada's Second World War* (Vancouver: UBC Press, 2004).

Ruth Roach Pierson, *'They're Still Women After All': The Second World War and Canadian Womanhood* (Toronto: McClelland & Stewart, 1986).

R. Scott Sheffield, *The Red Man's on the Warpath: The Image of the 'Indian' and the Second World War* (Vancouver: UBC Press, 2004).

Cynthia Toman, *An Officer and a Lady: Canadian Military Nursing and the Second World War* (Vancouver: UBC Press, 2007).

# PRIMARY DOCUMENTS

1 Mattie Rotenberg, 'It's a Woman's War', broadcast on *Trans-Canada Matinee*, CBC Radio, n.d. (1944). Used courtesy of Canadian Broadcasting Corporation.

Yes, it is a woman's war—in a special way. I don't mean so much that women and children are in the front line—that bombs and bullets are falling on them—though there is that, too. But this is a war to sweep Nazi tyranny from the world—to liberate the peoples who have been enslaved by it—and at the top of the list of those enslaved are women—all women. We hear a lot of what the Nazis have done to the Czechs, the Danes, the Dutch. We don't hear so much of what has happened to women under fascism, and yet, they were the first to suffer years ago in Italy, but most noticeably in Germany, because in the German Republic, women had gone far ahead in citizenship, in education, in the professions. There, the rights and privileges for which women had struggled for 50 years were swept aside within a few months—for National Socialism is a movement of men, contemptuous of women; along with the doctrine of racial superiority goes that of women's inferiority. We've heard a great deal of Jews and Socialists being driven from their jobs, forbidden to practice their professions;—but the same thing happened to women, too—just because they were women—even to Nazi women who had worked for years to help Hitler. National Socialism doesn't believe in equality of opportunity in education for everybody. It preaches the law of inequality—it says that some people are by nature inferior, and must forever be hewers of wood and drawers of water for the German master-race. And among the inferior groups are women—all women. But there's even more to it than that. Nazi treatment of women is something more than reaction and suppression—more than throwing women doctors and teachers out of work. In Nazi Germany, women are being used, relentlessly moulded to the needs and ambitions of the State,—made into unthinking, obedient robots. So this is a woman's war. On its outcome depends the answer to the question, Are we women to move forward to a position of greater freedom, or lose what we have gained? We know what the fascist answer to that question is.

In fascist countries, any woman who wants a job, an education, a profession, is told that such things are not for her—contemptuously, she is sent back to 'Kuche, Kinder, Kirche'—The kitchen, the children, the Church. These are the fields reserved for women—all other doors are closed. At first thought, this may not seem so bad—after all, for most of us women, these are our fields—but not the way the Nazis would have it.

Kuche—the kitchen—we do spend a lot of time in the kitchen, you and I, but we spend freely—we're glad to be able to provide sustenance and nourishment for our families. But we're glad to be able to give them bread that's spread with butter, and not with guns; food that is solid and nourishing, not 'crabs', imitation,—the left overs after the tanks and guns have been fed. You know how angry it would make you to have a stranger come into your kitchen and criticise what you're doing. Well, how would you like to have a lady feuhrer coming into your kitchen at any time she felt like it? Some petty official coming in, poking around to see what's in the pot, asking, where did you get that loaf of bread in the pantry, or what's this bone doing in the garbage can?—and you couldn't tell her to get out, either. That's what German women have to put up with. And that's not all. They interfere in everything. Not only tell you what to cook and how to cook it; what to wear; but if you're not married, some official calls you on the carpet and wants to know why not. If you are married, you're ordered how many children to have, and when. The Nazis need an unending stream of boys to march, soldiers to die—and they're trying to make women provide them. We know this is a war for freedom—that's rather abstract, though. But when freedom means the privacy of your own house—the right to be boss in your own kitchen—well, that does bring it home to you that this is a woman's war.

And it's even more so when we think of the children—That's the second item in women's sphere, you know. Of course we want our children, but we want to bring them up our way, not to be cogs in an insatiable war machine. We don't want them brought up in the Nazi fashion, ignorant of everything but party doctrines, contemptuous of all other races and peoples, with narrow and darkened minds, fit only for blind obedience to the Feuhrer. We want our children to live by the light of learning; we want them to carry forward the heritage of our civilization; to make some of our dreams for a better world come true—to succeed where we have failed. A war to give our children this chance—that they may live as free men, not as dumb, driven cattle—that *is* a woman's war.

And lastly, in woman's sphere, is Kirche, the church—no wonder the Nazi leaves all that to women—He is busy resurrecting the old pagan gods, who will be more at home in the barbarian world he is trying to create. And religion would hamper him, too, in his career of lawless conquest. 'Thou shalt have no other Gods before me'—against that, Hitler sets up the worship of the State. 'Honor thy father and thy mother'—how can that be for Nazi children, taught to spy and inform, even on their parents? 'Thou shalt not kill, thou shalt not steal, thou shalt not covet'—one after another the sacred tablets are smashed. Why, democracy itself, our way of life that is being challenged that's a religious idea. It's the recognition of the worth and dignity of every human life,—of the divine spark in every one of us. It is no accident, I think, that the British peoples are the ones now making the stand for the defence of democracy and religion. They have been brought up on the Bible—for centuries it has been read in their homes and churches—nurtured in its principles, theirs is the character that is now standing the test. This heritage has given them that significant spirit that made Dunkirk a modern miracle—it has given them the strength for inner self-discipline in these dark days—they don't need to be disciplined by a Duce or a Feuhrer—they can look after themselves.

And now, the very foundations of this life, this religion, are being attacked. It's been hard for people to believe such a thing—who would have thought it possible—that in the twentieth century, in our proud civilization, a powerful force would arise, deliberately bent upon dethroning the truth, abandoning justice, forsaking the rule of law—setting up brute force against the conscience of mankind? Yet, these are the issues. Shall *Mein Kampf* replace the Bible as the guide for human conduct? Shall the reign of truth give way to the reign of falsehood? We have all been taught—'Righteousness exalteth the nation'—must we forget that, to acknowledge instead that might is right? For a long time, men and women have prayed, 'Thy will be done'. Must they now bow to the dictator's 'My will be done'? It is not only the privacy of our homes and the lives of our children that are at stake—not only the liberty to choose our religion, but the whole structure and principle of religion. Realizing that these are the issues, we women know that this is our war—and that knowledge raises in every heart the unshakable resolution to hold out till victory—we just can't think of humanity plunged back to the dark ages, to start the slow, upward climb all over again.

Many people have been slow to realize that these really are the issues—they felt that Fascism and Nazism were just other political ways—of course, we preferred democracy, but perhaps they had something. You've heard people praise Mussolini,—he made the Italian trains run on time. But what good are trains *on time* if they take a people to destruction? And the Germans are efficient—yes—they're efficiently using modern science to take us quickly back to barbarism. This idea of German efficiency has spread far—their propaganda machine saw to that. Why, just this summer I was standing on the shores of a beautiful lake in Northern Ontario. Few people came there, because the road was bad. One day we were talking about how bad the road was, and a neighbour—she's no fifth columnist, she's as good a Canadian as any of us—she said to me, 'I suppose if the Germans had this country, there'd be a good road here'. Well, I felt a cold shiver go through me—because that remark showed how successful the Nazis had been in spreading the myth of themselves as supermen, of Hitler as a demigod, performing miracles with a magic wand. Have roads and buildings and a great war machine been built in his country? He had no magic wand—he used secret police and slavery, the torture chamber and the concentration camp. Nazi propaganda masks the horrible truth with fair words—they show their military pomp, but hide the slavery beneath. They want to sow doubt in our minds about democracy. To such doubts we must lock our minds, absolutely. That's what they want—to confuse us—they know that doubt and disunity are their opportunities. By appealing to ignorance and discontent, to racial and religious prejudice, they have gained entry for their ideas into every country of the world. Hitler himself says that his battles are fought with ideas, no less than with guns, and that he never attacks a nation until it has been demoralized from within. So that any hesitation, any doubt that our democratic way is better, any hospitality to racial or religious hatreds that divide our people—these open the door for the enemy.

Of course, that doesn't mean that our democracy is perfect—nobody knows that better than we women. We and our children are the ones who suffer from low wages and unemployment—we have seen people starving while food was being destroyed—living in slums while builders' hands are idle. We know we have many sicknesses to be cured—but that doesn't mean we should copy the methods of the totalitarian states. Whatever good thing they have taken—labour and unity and efficiency are good—they have corrupted, and you know the old saying, that the worst results come about through the corruption of what is good. They say they've solved unemployment but they've done it by making slaves of the people. They say they're more efficient than we are—but can their factories, where spies watch the workers and secret police watch the spies—can those factories be more efficient than ours? If every action is tangled in a web of government rules and restrictions—does that make for efficiency? With all its defects, democracy still offers the plain man and woman more security or hope than the slave states ever can. Hitler says he's introducing a new order into the world.—But there's nothing new about lawlessness, cruelty and slavery. What is new, is the new order we women want—justice, kindliness, brotherhood beyond the boundaries of race or creed—that's the new order we hope to see after the war—that's another reason why it's a woman's war.

And the time for us to start building that new order is now. Some people talk of waiting till after the war—to put our attention to it now, they say, would take away from our war effort. But they're wrong. Curing poverty and ignorance, righting injustice—that's part of our war effort. You can't put ideals into cold storage—they won't keep; unless they're put into action, made into reality, they shrivel and die. We've got to start right now to bridge the gap between our preaching and our practice; to tackle the questions of unemployment, housing, ignorance and want. Every step forward will heighten the wall of confidence and unity—will strengthen the whole nation as nothing else would.

So, in this woman's war, that's the woman's job. We want a better democracy, but we can't have it unless we make it ourselves—it won't do for a woman to say about a political question, 'Oh, I don't know anything about that. You'll have to ask my husband'. It's not easy to be a democratic citizen—there's so much to learn. You've got to study, to work, to think. But we'll have to learn to rule ourselves the way we want, or have others do it the way they want. And we've another job. In this struggle, we must muster all our resources,—and the greatest resources of a nation are its people. We have our mines and factories, our fields and forests, that's true. But what about our homes? Surely we must count the courage and cheerfulness, the tolerance and kindliness, found in every home across the land—surely we must count these among our resources—and of those resources, we women are the guardians. Oh, I know we must have the machines of war—but behind the armies and the navies stand the common people—it's their moral fibre that counts in the end. The Maginot line has proved that no material defence is worth much if the spirit behind it is feeble. And if we women can't go out and fight in the field—we can build up and guard the spirit at home. We can put on the armour of truth and of faith and in the knowledge that our homes, our children, our religion is at stake, we can resolve to stand fast, to build and endure until we can see the dawn of a clearer and brighter day. It's a woman's war! Yes! and we Canadian women are prepared to meet brute forces with the rightness of our cause, knowing that in the end it will be victorious.

---

**2**     From Anne Frances, 'Now Is the Time for Volunteer Workers to Chart the Future'. *Saturday Night* (7 October 1944): 30.

There is a great deal of speculation about the way Canadian women volunteers will behave when the war is over. Will they lose interest in community affairs and return quietly to their homes? Or will they continue to work when the stimulus of war is removed?

At present, the evidence suggests that the most intelligent women want to carry on when the war is over. For instance, the presidents of the service auxiliaries report that the women are saying: 'Can't we keep on working? Won't it be a waste of experience if we stop now?'

Again and again, I have heard canteen workers in the United Services Centre say: 'Why couldn't we run recreation centres for children and adults too when the war is over?' I've heard Salvage workers say: 'Why can't we keep on running the Salvage Corps after the war? Think what we could do with the money. We could start model apartment blocks as demonstration areas—or we could pay the salary of a psychiatrist for the Family Court. Why we could do wonderful things in peace time if we kept right on working'.

These women have learned about themselves during the last five years. They now know that they can work together. The old theory that women cannot work in a team belongs to the era of antimacassars, fainting and the legend of the 'weaker sex'. What is more important, women have found that they enjoy working together. They have also proved that they can raise money if the project is important enough. When auxiliaries needed money for welfare work among soldiers' families, or money for comforts or cigarettes, women stood on icy, windswept street corners selling tags or they organized endless silver teas, bazaars and the like. And they raised the money.

## CAN DO DOUBLE JOB

Best of all, women have proved that they can run a home efficiently or carry a professional job and still do useful outside community work. They have proved that there is no reason why housewives and business girls should not also be good citizens.

In many cases too, women have acquired special skills as well as the valuable experience gained by the actual doing of a job. Civilians have taken courses in nursery school work, social work and nursing. Women in the armed forces have been taught special trades. Naturally the most intelligent of these women want to continue to use the ability and experience gained during the war years. They want to continue working with a team which is tackling a bigger job than an individual home or family.

Of course, inevitably, there will be some women who will be tired of volunteer jobs and the dull routine which accompanies even the most interesting work. Five years of war—five years of worry and hard work and, in many cases, tragedy—are bound to take their toll of energy and enthusiasm. It will be only natural to let up when the strain is lifted. For that reason, we should expect to hear many of the old clichés when these few women begin to rationalize their normal desire to slump and leave it to Josephine. (I still refuse to believe that a woman's place is behind a bridge table in the afternoon.)

Although the most intelligent volunteers now feel that they want to go on working, there is grave danger ahead. The picture is not as rosy as it seems at first glance. After the war, the need for workers will not be as obvious as it was during the war. A woman with small children whose husband is fighting overseas does not require urging to understand the necessity for nursery schools or other family welfare work. A woman whose son was taken prisoner at Hong Kong is already convinced of the need for prisoners of war parcels. After the war it will be different. Then it will take thought and study and planning to find out what women should be doing as volunteer workers and citizens.

## BIG FIELD FOR WORK

Certainly the needs will be there. We have slums in Canada. Women can do a great deal to help liquidate slums by acting as citizens through their governments, but it will take thought and study to know the best way to approach the problem. The same holds true for education, particularly rural education. Women working in groups can raise our standards but first they will have to study and understand the problem.

In social work, women as individual volunteers as well as citizens can continue to do valuable work. They could probably make juvenile delinquency a controlled disease like diphtheria if they helped to support a series of small recreation centres where children could learn handicrafts and art as well as dance and play in the evenings. They could also support cultural centres where adults might learn to enrich their leisure.

There are hundreds of instances of things which women can do for Canada after the war. That is why the next few months are important. Now is the time for women to find out what

Canada will need when the shooting stops. Now is the time for them to learn where they belong in the post-war world.

Now is the time for the Women's Institutes, Auxiliaries to the armed forces, Red Cross groups, Alumnae societies and other organized work groups to begin a planned study of the needs of their communities. A few organizations, like the Schools for Citizenship in Winnipeg and Vancouver, have already undertaken this sort of study but, in my opinion, the matter is so important that all groups should be thinking along these lines. Women can keep right on sewing and knitting but they can also use their minds to plan their place in the future of Canada.

There are plenty of experts who will help to outline simple plans for study. The Adult Education Association is ready and eager to provide speakers as well as pamphlets and bibliographies. The National Film Board has a library of films which show how other places have tackled their problems. Several universities maintain extension departments which can give valuable assistance to rural groups. Councils of Social Agencies are only to happy to be asked to explain their philosophy of community planning in the welfare field.

## PLANS SHOULD BE MADE NOW

Now is the time, not only for study but for field trips. Field trips do more for enthusiasm than a dozen lectures. Each group of women might take as a slogan: 'Know your own community'. And knowing means seeing and smelling and feeling.

If more women visited the children's wards of their hospitals, there would be fewer arguments about the needs of children. A visit to a slum tenement in a big city would help women to understand the diseases of the body and the despair of the mind which are bred by dirt and overcrowding. A visit to a Juvenile Court should dispel any doubts about the need for recreation centres and play grounds. The point is that it is important to sell women the idea that the needs of peace are just as immediate as the needs of war.

While it is advisable to begin by studying the community problems under our noses it is also a good idea to get a picture of the needs of Canada as a whole. In June, a special committee of the House of Commons—the Committee on Reconstruction and Re-establishment—met to discuss a plan for improving the cultural life of the country. A dozen or more briefs were submitted by groups of musicians, artists and writers like the Royal Canadian Academy of Art, the Canadian Handicrafts Association, the Canadian Authors Association and the Canadian Federation of Artists. The report on the proceedings would make an admirable outline for study by any group.

# HISTORICAL INTERPRETATIONS

3    From Magda Fahrni, 'Counting the Costs of Living: Gender, Citizenship, and a Politics of Prices in 1940s Montreal', *Canadian Historical Review* 83(4) (2002): 483–504. Reprinted with permission from University of Toronto Press Incorporated (www.utpjournals.com).

Mrs. Conroy said that every woman in Canada was thinking of prices at the present time and if we intended to reach the heart of Canadian women we should give some indication that we are going to study prices very carefully.[1]

A concern with prices and a politics centred on purchasing figured prominently in Canada's urban centres in the 1940s. As Mrs Patrick Conroy, the Canadian Congress of Labour's representative to the all-women Canadian Association of Consumers, suggested, this politics of prices was thoroughly gendered. In cities across the country, women used their intimate knowledge of their household finances to demand better social welfare measures and a reasonable cost of living in the context of the Second World War and post-war reconstruction.

[ . . . ] Montreal women drew on a sense of economic citizenship cultivated over the war years to organize around consumer issues in the immediate post-war period. The federal government had encouraged a wartime consumer consciousness as part of its efforts on the home front. Rationing, price controls, salvaging and recycling drives, and the black market made the availability and distribution of goods a popular topic of discussion through the 1940s. After the war, continuing government controls, consumers' groups, and labour newspapers encouraged both middle- and working-class families to maintain their interest in prices, standards, consumer choice, and the availability of products. Montrealers, grown accustomed to the equity of rationing and worried about the rising cost of living, demanded the ability to purchase household necessities at reasonable prices as one of the rights of economic citizenship.[2]

Household management and daily shopping had long been considered the work of married women. [ . . . ] Consumer activism, then, allowed women in particular to carve out significant space in the public sphere. These women, acting in the name of wives and mothers, targeted the state as well as shopkeepers and claimed gendered citizenship rights. [ . . . ] Their efforts made the family visible in public; indeed, these women used the

claims of family as a key basis for citizenship. Moreover, in Montreal their articulation of economic citizenship took place in the context of their newly acquired political citizenship: Quebec women had secured the provincial suffrage in 1940. Consumer activists' call for the recognition of women's unpaid work, then, suggests one way that gender configured the political and the public in this period.

An examination of consumer organizing in fact nuances our understanding of the balance of 'private' and 'public' in the 1940s. The federal government's intervention in the running of households during the war, through its regulations on what and how much people could buy, what they could eat, and what they ought not to discard, threw wide open what had once been private. North American historians have argued that, at the end of the war, some citizens called for a restoration of privacy; they retreated to domesticity in an attempt to avoid engagement with public matters.[3] Yet as we shall see in this article, others took the lessons that they had learned over the course of the war and used them to transform their private household and financial situations into a kind of politics. They made a public, political statement out of what might once (during the Depression, for instance) have been regarded as a shameful situation, to be hidden at all costs.[4] In making the private public, individuals and groups who took action as consumers were taking the promise of Freedom from Want seriously and attempting to craft a more democratic public sphere. Women's consumer actions traversed the boundaries of private and public and threw into question the utility of such distinctions.

At issue here was the limited consumption of necessities such as groceries, not the high consumption of automobiles and expensive consumer durables commonly associated with post-war North America. I begin this article by exploring the dimensions and implications of the consumer consciousness developed during the war—particularly among women. I then turn to two examples of Montreal residents organizing as consumers in the immediate post-war years: women's boycott of grocers and butchers in 1947–8; and women's battle to secure the legalization of margarine as a cheaper substitute for butter. Such basic aspects of private life made headlines in the late 1940s; the margarine debate in fact made it to the Supreme Court. Middle-class families had long been units of consumption as well as production; by the 1940s this was increasingly true for Montreal's working class as well.[5] These two consumer campaigns thus had cross-class appeal and involved both French- and English-speaking Montrealers. Moreover, while such campaigns had particular class and ethnic dimensions in Montreal, they were part of a larger phenomenon in these years. Local newspaper reports on 'militant housewives' in Toronto, Chicago, and Paris lent legitimacy and increased importance to the activities of housewives at home.[6]

The prominent role played by women in these battles is not surprising: women around the world had a long history of public protests around consumption, ranging from pre-industrial bread riots to cost-of-living rallies at the close of the Great War.[7] What distinguishes the following episodes from such precedents is, first, the degree to which this consumer consciousness had been encouraged over the course of the Second World War; and, second, women's growing sense that an expanding state was accessible to them and that they were entitled to make certain demands upon it. The public claims of consumers point to some of the things to which citizens thought they were entitled in a victorious, welfare-state democracy and reveal sites where the family met the public in the period of reconstruction.

## GAINING CONSUMER CONSCIOUSNESS DURING THE SECOND WORLD WAR

In an attempt to manage the war and build a consensus on the home front, Ottawa crafted a relationship with its citizens premised on preserving scarce materials for the war effort and avoiding the inflation that might result from having more money than goods in circulation. Canadians were to save, salvage, and reuse; they were to accept rationing so that goods could be equitably distributed. They were to ensure that shopkeepers adhered to price ceilings, and they were to curb their own desires to spend.[8] Victory Bond campaigns catered to patriotic sentiment while siphoning off 'excess' purchasing power and also satisfying citizens' Depression-bred instincts to put money away in case of future need. Constant public monitoring of the cost of living meant that, despite the improved wages of the war years, Canadians were keenly aware of fluctuating costs and of the fine balance between income and expenditures.

The work of rationing, recycling, salvaging, saving, and spending wisely was seen to belong to women.[9] The Consumer Branch of the Wartime Prices and Trade Board (WPTB) in fact secured the official co-operation of 16,000 women across the country, all of whom agreed to monitor prices and report back to the board. These women, the state and the press insisted, were contributing to an Allied victory and were ensuring that the country their men came home to would be in sound economic health.[10] Women were reminded, moreover, that in wartime Canada, unlike war-torn Europe, government controls were 'inconveniences', not '"hardships" or "sacrifices"'.[11] On V-E Day the government congratulated women on their wartime efforts: thanks to them, Canadians had managed to keep inflation to reasonable levels. Now the task was to win the peace. Citizens and consumers were reminded that the worst inflation associated with the First World War had come after the end of hostilities.[12] The 'danger of inflation' was 'more real now than at any time since the war commenced'; the 'homemakers of the Nation should be on the alert, more than ever'.[13] Price controls would be lifted only gradually. Slowly, the production of peacetime consumer durables would resume and goods would return to store shelves: in the meantime, anxious consumers were to be patient.[14] Certain items would remain rationed, since Canada was allocating some of its food supplies for export to Europe.[15] Victory Bond campaigns continued through the late 1940s. As long as wages and savings exceeded supplies of consumer goods, inflation remained a threat and the black market, tempting.

Historian Jeff Keshen reminds us that cheating, 'gouging', and black-marketing co-existed with civilian compliance with wartime regulations. Black-marketing was, he claims, 'most prevalent in Montreal', a phenomenon that he attributes to 'Quebec's lukewarm support for the war'.[16] Opinions about military participation were undeniably mixed. Yet many French Canadians took pride in their co-operation with the state. Quebec women participated in the WPTB's price-watching campaign during the war, and the women of Montreal's Fédération nationale Saint-Jean-Baptiste (FNSJB) reprinted Donald Gordon's letter thanking them for their assistance with price controls in the May 1947 issue of their newsletter.[17] Mariana Jodoin, who was awarded the OBE (Order of the British Empire) for her war work with the WPTB's Consumer Branch, thanked the FNSJB for its congratulations 'en son nom personnel et au nom de toutes les Canadiennes françaises, dont cette décoration représente le dévouement pendant la guerre'.[18] Nonetheless, the federal propaganda machine may have had to work harder in Quebec than elsewhere. Maurice Duplessis's return to provincial power in August 1944 suggests significant resentment of federal policy and the appeal of Quebec nationalism as the war drew to a close. Duplessis himself regularly attacked Ottawa's wartime regulations, deriding them as 'Restrictions, vexatoires, stupides, inopportunes, intempestives' and claiming that 'la BUREAUCRATIE remplace la démocratie'.[19]

Canada-wide opposition to government restrictions intensified once the war was won and controls remained in place; the 'orderly decontrol' campaign led by Gordon and the WPTB required persistent and strategic marketing.[20] Producers, consumers, and shopkeepers alike welcomed the end of rationing.[21] The decontrol of prices, however, met with mixed reactions. La Presse noted at the end of 1945 that price controls, not surprisingly, continued to enjoy a popularity that wage controls did not.[22] Landlords, manufacturers, and some shopkeepers rejoiced as controls were gradually lifted, but tenants, workers, and consumers soon began lobbying for their re-establishment.[23] The Canadian Institute of Public Opinion claimed in 1947 that price controls were most popular among women, poor people, and unionized workers and their families. It also found that Quebec was less eager for a reimposition of price controls than other regions.[24] High taxes remained a source of grievance in the post-war period: as Gabrielle Roy's fictional bank-teller Alexandre Chenevert noted in the late 1940s, 'taxes, taxes on all sides, and the cost of living was soaring'.[25] Regular reports in the daily press on Canadians' battle with inflation, and frequent updates on price indexes, kept readers aware of the continued importance of prices in peacetime. As La Presse concluded in 1947, the public had learned a great deal about inflation over the previous three years.[26]

Most Canadians had seen their consumer consciousness raised by the war effort, but the fact that this effort had so frequently been framed as women's work had consequences for the gendered nature of post-war consumer activism. In the late 1940s, household consumers were invariably assumed to be women.[27] More specifically, they were assumed to be married women; the purchasing power of single women was largely ignored. Many Canadian wives argued that they deserved recognition for their wartime co-operation with the government's fiscal policy. Mrs Leslie Hodges, involved with Montreal's Local Council of Women and the WPTB, claimed in 1944 that Canada was 'the only country in the World where Price Ceilings are really effective, chiefly through the co-operation of the housewives and the Government'.[28] Another woman, proposing the establishment of a Women's Centre in Montreal in 1946, declared that it would be 'a tribute to the excellent work done on the home front by the ordinary housewife during the past six years': in voluntary war work, in the home, and 'as a consumer when she co-operated to maintain price ceilings'.[29] Women were aware that their ordinary work had acquired new worth during the war. As the National Council of Women remarked a half-dozen years after the war had ended, thrift had 'national importance' because of its role in combating inflation. Housewives, Montreal liberal reformer Renée Vautelet observed astutely, enjoyed a new importance as citizens of an economic democracy.[30]

Many women used the construct of the price-watching housewife to make new claims in the public sphere. . . . [R]ecipients of military Dependents' Allowances meticulously itemized their household budgets in letters to Ottawa demanding increased allowances in the context of a rising wartime cost of living.[31] Alongside such solitary letter writers were the women who organized. The Canadian Association of Consumers (CAC), an exclusively female association formed in 1947, was one example of women building on public recognition of their wartime achievements. The CAC carried on some of the work of the WPTB's Consumer Branch and represented the determination of some women to maintain a role in public life and to keep their unpaid labour in the public eye.[32] Described by one journalist as 'a permanent consumers' organization of women who "cannot sit idly by" and watch rising prices and production bottlenecks disrupt the economy of the home',[33] the CAC declared its realm of interest to be 'tout ce qui peut améliorer le statut social de la famille canadienne'.[34] It met regularly with federal politicians and civil servants and asked members to protect housewives' interests by scrutinizing prices and adhering to government controls.[35] Like the Consumer Branch and the Councils of Women that dotted the country, the CAC consisted of a national council overseeing provincial and local chapters. The Quebec division drew on institutional structures particular to the province, recruiting at the parish level.[36]

[ . . . ]

Although the CAC was the largest and most prominent of the many consumers' leagues formed in the wake of the war, some working-class women chose, instead, to participate in consumers' leagues and co-operative movements affiliated with unions and union auxiliaries.[37] The union movement's consumer activism was not the exclusive purview of women: union men also organized around prices. The Montreal Labour Council, for example, protested the increased cost of living and the lifting of price controls by the federal government, called for union label shopping, demonstrated enthusiasm for consumers' co-operatives, and invited the female representatives of the city's consumer leagues to speak at its meetings. Male members of the council made a point of inviting their wives to their 1947 conference on the cost of living and, as breadwinners, claimed an interest in prices on behalf of their families.[38] The Confédération des Travailleurs Catholiques du Canada (CTCC) likewise insisted in 1947 that the federal government's decision to abandon controls had seriously diminished the purchasing power of working families.[39]

Behind Quebec unions' objections to spiralling prices and vanishing controls was the conviction that Ottawa did not understand French-Canadian experiences: low wages, meagre budgets, and families that were sometimes larger than the English-Canadian norm. A cartoon printed in *Le Monde Ouvrier* (published by the Trades and Labor Congress–affiliated Fédération Provinciale du Travail) in January 1948, for instance, shows a tired couple sitting in the living room of a house in disarray, surrounded by eleven rowdy children. The wife reassures her husband: 'Ne te décourage pas, vieux, le docteur Pett, d'Ottawa, dit qu'on peut les nourrir pour 15½ cents par repas!'[40] In reaction to this same federal statistic, Saint-Henri's newspaper, *La Voix Populaire*, conducted an informal survey of the neighbourhood's housewives, asking them if they could feed their families on 15½ cents each per meal. The journalist was greeted with laughter and jeers, the women insisting that it was impossible to feed their husbands well enough on that sum for them to properly carry out their jobs.[41] The rickety household economies of many Montreal families in the 1940s bear little resemblance to the 'mass consumption society' assumed by most historians of post-war North America. Accustomed to frugality, many Montrealers continued to restrain themselves to careful, minimal spending for some time.[42]

[ . . . ]

## CONSUMER ACTIVISM . . .

In November 1947 shoppers across Canada loaded their baskets with fresh and canned fruits and vegetables. The federal government had recently imposed an embargo on the importation of certain goods in an effort to conserve its supply of American dollars, and consumers feared an imminent produce shortage.[43] Montreal housewives' initial response to the embargo appeared to vary by class and ethnicity. The west (or more English-Canadian and affluent) side of the city witnessed a 'course des acheteurs' (buyers' race), as shoppers made massive purchases of goods that might soon be unavailable. On the east (or largely French-Canadian and poorer) side of Montreal, women with less money, and more likely to have iceboxes than refrigerators, made small daily purchases and watched prices carefully.[44] Yet as panic buying across the country led to speculation and skyrocketing prices, housewives implemented 'buyers' strikes', refusing to purchase fruits and vegetables at outrageous prices.

From Toronto, the president of the Canadian Association of Consumers, Blanche Marshall, urged Canadian women to use their purchasing power to put an end to inflation in the produce trade. Don't pay 25 cents for a cabbage worth 10 cents, she advised. Prices would fall, she predicted, as soon as housewives stopped buying.[45] Montreal housewives took note and stayed home, 'eating the products bought in panic earlier this week and last week'.[46] Newspapers described deserted produce stands across the city; at the Bonsecours Market, women asked prices and moved on without purchasing when they heard the responses. *La Presse* reported that buyers' strikes were making farmers and merchants gloomy and that the market for fruits and vegetables was 'mort, tout a fait mort!'[47]

The housewives' strike worked, at least in the short term. Some farmers dropped the prices of their fruits and vegetables almost immediately. By the end of November, for instance, the cost of carrots and onions was falling daily. The federal government's reimposition of price ceilings on certain tinned foods and fresh produce at the end of the month contributed to the stabilization of prices.[48] By late February 1948, *La Presse* noted, Montreal housewives were loosening their purse-strings as essential foods were becoming more affordable. Cabbages that had been left on grocers' shelves at 30 cents a pound were now selling for 5 cents a pound. Shoppers' 'silent strikes' had made a serious impact, the newspaper claimed, and butchers, as well as produce-vendors, had been hard hit. Meat prices had peaked in early January: although they had dropped somewhat after the federal government threatened to impose a price ceiling, shoppers continued to exercise restraint in their purchases of bacon, beef, and sausages. By late February, butchers' iceboxes were reported to be overflowing, and meat was selling for approximately 10 per cent less than at the beginning of the month.[49] Meat consumption was especially likely to drop in times of high prices. As one labour journalist discovered, working-class mothers with numerous mouths to feed and few groceries stockpiled in their pantries could not stop buying food altogether but tended to avoid purchasing expensive items such as meat and butter.[50] Class and cultural differences were also evident in the choice of scapegoats for high food prices. While Montreal's mainstream press pointed to farmers and shopkeepers as the culprits, *Le Front Ouvrier*, a Catholic labour paper, indignantly defended rural producers and suggested that the speculation and attempted profiteering of importers, wholesalers, and distributors were more likely the cause of increased prices.[51]

The boycott of grocers and butchers in 1947–8 crossed lines of class and ethnicity and straddled the divisions between organized and informal consumer activism, between private needs and public action. In this sense it was both more widespread and more diffuse than other post-war consumer campaigns, such as the battle to secure the legalization of margarine as a cheaper alternative to butter. Margarine became news across Canada in the late 1940s, but as a city of a million consumers, Montreal was a key player in this campaign. In his legislative history of margarine, W.H. Heick argues that Canada's 1886 ban on the manufacture, importation, and sale of margarine was the result of the leverage exercised by dairy farmers and butter producers in a largely rural nation.[52] By the 1940s a more urban country faced with food rationing and a high cost of living called for margarine as a less-expensive and more easily available butter substitute. Canada's political centre of gravity had shifted: in Heick's words, 'the wishes of 150,000 producers of milk had to give way to the desires of 13 million consumers'.[53] But they were not to give way without a fight. The seemingly mundane margarine issue sparked debate not only between rural producers and urban consumers but also between Ottawa and the provinces.

In Quebec, Premier Maurice Duplessis, mindful of rural voters, chose to present the demand for margarine as an attack on the province's agrarian traditions and farmers' livelihoods. He drew support from the Union Catholique des Cultivateurs (UCC), which argued that the manufacture and sale of margarine in Quebec would deal a deathblow to the province's dairy industry and, by extension, to its entire agricultural sector.[54] Yet the massive wartime migration of rural Quebecers to industrial jobs in cities meant that, within Quebec, the balance between food producers and consumers had shifted dramatically.[55] While Duplessis catered to rural electors, the growing number of urban dwellers who called for the right to purchase margarine drew support from unions, social welfare agencies, and voluntary associations, including the Fédération nationale Saint-Jean-Baptiste, the Montreal Labour Council, Montreal's Family Welfare Association and its Local Council of Women, the Canadian Welfare Council, and the Canadian Association of Consumers.[56] At stake were questions of class and entitlement: clearly, those most in need of margarine were low-income families.[57]

Margarine advocates targeted governments rather than farmers or shopkeepers[58] and invoked free enterprise, free choice, healthy competition, and family needs in a victorious democracy. In the early post-war years, amid butter rationing and high food prices, Montreal's Local Council of Women protested the 'prohibition on the manufacture, Import and sale of Margarine' because 'a vitamin fortified substitute for butter should be available for needy Canadian families'.[59] *Le Front Ouvrier* noted in January 1948 that the cost of butter had risen steadily since price controls had been lifted; with what, the newspaper asked, would workers replace it?[60] By early 1948, polls showed that the margarine movement was gaining ground in Canada: with the notable exception of farmers, most people now opposed the ban on margarine. Although polls found that opinions on margarine did not vary much by sex, *La Presse* claimed that housewives felt the scarcity of butter most acutely.[61] Mariana Jodoin of the Fédération nationale Saint-Jean-Baptiste underlined the issue's gendered dimensions when she informed the FNSJB that, at a public assembly on margarine held in Montreal in September 1948, 'Mme [Thérèse] Casgrain a su, mieux que tous ces Messieurs, traiter la question'.[62]

The Supreme Court's widely reported December 1948 decision—that the federal government did not have the right to prohibit the manufacture or sale of margarine— was upheld by the Judicial Committee of the Privy Council in 1950 and appeared to many to confirm the consumer's right to choose.[63] Margarine lobbyists then turned their efforts to provincial authorities. In Duplessis they faced a formidable opponent: provincial anti-margarine legislation was enacted in March 1949, and margarine would remain illegal in Quebec until 1961.[64] Montreal's Local Council of Women dispatched a series of telegrams to Duplessis, arguing for the consumer's right to 'free choice in the purchase of a healthful substitute for butter'. Anti-margarine legislation, the clubwomen claimed, 'encroached on personal liberty'. How ironic that 'a government which has stood for provincial autonomy' should 'deny the autonomy of the individual in his home and household'.[65] In emphasizing free choice, personal liberty, and individual autonomy, the Local Council of Women articulated assumptions about citizenship and entitlement increasingly common in the late 1940s. As the Canadian Association of Consumers and the National Council of Women argued in 1948, if this was truly a period of free enterprise, then consumers had the right to the protection offered by competition among manufacturers, products, and stores.[66] Or, as popular Montreal performer Peter Barry sang in his post-war calypso hit, 'Margie Margarine':

My mother go to the grocery store,
To buy a pound of butter or more
But the butter price is much too high

So mother sit at home and cry . . .
This is democracy, I am told,
So why can't margarine be sold?[67]

## CONCLUSIONS

Consumer activism had considerable relevance in the post-war years in part because Quebecers, like other Canadians, were reshaping their sense of citizenship. Dominique Marshall has argued persuasively that, in the post-war years, Quebec residents came to adopt a sense of 'economic citizenship' that included new welfare state measures such as unemployment insurance and family allowances.[68] These new measures were intended, in part, to paper over the cleavages of ethnicity and politics exacerbated by war and conscription, and to build allegiance to the federal state and a common 'nation'. What Marshall calls economic citizenship has been described by other historians and sociologists as 'social citizenship'—a sense of citizenship rooted, in part, in state welfare measures.[69] In this article I have used the phrase 'economic citizenship' to mean the conviction that one was entitled to participate in a capitalist economy on reasonable terms, and, further, that the state had a role to play in facilitating this participation. This sense of economic citizenship had been fuelled by wartime propaganda which insisted that being a good citizen meant spending wisely, and it was encouraged by early Cold War rhetoric that touted the superiority of democratic capitalism.[70] Increasingly, Canadians expected the rewards of citizenship to include such tangible benefits as an acceptable cost of living.[71]

Through the years of war and reconstruction, unions, working-class branches of the Action Catholique, and unorganized men and women—members of working-class families—attempted to maintain their standards of living by calling for continued price and rent controls, and for more generous state welfare measures. Yet there existed competing visions of economic citizenship. By the later

1940s, and certainly by the 1950s, dominant understandings of democracy and economic citizenship often assumed the superiority of a more or less free market.[72] Numerous voices argued that the security provided by a healthy economy and publicly funded social welfare programs would prevent communism from taking root among the nation's citizens; economic, social, and political citizenship were linked.[73] Citizens had a role to play in fighting the Cold War and arresting communism by being disciplined consumers. In its 1950 publication *Why Be Thrifty?* the National Council of Women warned that communism grew amid 'economic collapse', but also amid regimentation and rigid controls; conversely, 'democracy's strength lies in a sense of individual responsibility and the exercise of individual initiative'.[74] Democracy needed to be carefully cultivated; citizens, including women, had responsibilities as well as rights.[75] The liberal strand of economic citizenship that seems to have won out by the 1950s drew explicit links between (gendered) consumption and political participation in a democracy. Renée Vautelet, for example, spoke of women's votes 'going to market', of 'shop[ping] on election day at the store of experience in government', of 'buying' the future.[76] In this political culture, conscientious consumer activists demanding lower prices, greater quantities of goods, and more choice in products were seen to help, not hinder, the smooth operation of the post-war economy.

A popular politics scaffolded on prices had the potential to rally large numbers of people around issues commonly thought private, ranging from margarine to monthly rent payments. Consumer activism could be seen as bringing shoppers of all classes together in a common effort to win the peace. Although working people were harder hit by the increase in the cost of living, middle-class citizens also publicly deplored increases in prices. Vautelet, for instance, declared consumption to be 'the only economic interest in Canada that speaks for all Canada . . . our common denominator

. . . the only shared Interest of the land'.[77] Yet class differences were embedded in consumer activism in Montreal. A politics of prices highlighted the fragility of working-class budgets in a city grappling with the rising cost of living. It resonated with Montreal citizens precisely because, in many cases, every penny mattered. Working-class women participated in the budget projects of the Ligue Ouvrière Catholique Féminine and in the consumer activities of union auxiliaries. Above all, they scrimped and saved at home—in non-organized forms of consumer activism. For working-class families, an emphasis on prices was clearly inadequate on its own. As Susan Porter Benson reminds us, consumption 'was always tightly tethered to earning': in a province where low wages were endemic, attempts to lower prices could only accomplish so much.[78]

The middle-class women who had forged partnerships with the federal government during the war years through the Consumer Division of the WPTB also continued their consumer efforts in the wake of the war. In insisting that governments and citizens listen to housewives, the Fédération nationale Saint-Jean-Baptiste, the Local Council of Women, and the Canadian Association of Consumers made women's unpaid work public.[79] In articulating what British historian Sonya Rose has called a 'discourse of active citizenship', these women joined other post-war North Americans involved in such family-centred causes as home and school organizations, parent-teacher associations, and battles for daycare.[80]

As Sylvie Murray has argued, a concern for issues that affected home and family was not the same thing as a retreat to the nuclear family. Members of Montreal's Notre-Dame-de-Grâce Women's Club, for instance, taught each other parliamentary procedure and held study sessions on 'Canadian Democracy in Action', took field trips to City Hall and to Parliament Hill, and invited guest speakers to lecture on such topics as 'Women Face a

Changing World' and 'Education for a New Day'.[81] Their outlook was neatly summarized in the 1948 declaration by the president of the Local Council of Women that 'as politics today have to do with the home and family[,] politics should be our business'.[82] This claim had particular resonance in a place where women had only recently secured the provincial vote. These women certainly defined themselves as active citizens; their actions call into question assumptions about post-war women's insular domesticity and suggest broader definitions of politics for this period. Moreover, they support an extensive literature demonstrating that the 'great darkness' that is supposed to have descended over Quebec during the Duplessis years was punctuated by numerous points of protest.[83]

Examining the politics of prices in a city under reconstruction points to one way that 'family' and families were mobilized in pursuit of post-war citizenship rights. Both family and consumer activism could be deployed on behalf of a variety of political beliefs and to a multitude of ends: the maternalist argument was heard in sites as diverse as the largely middle-class Canadian Association of Consumers and the Catholic labour paper *Le Front Ouvrier*.[84] Yet, while organizations as different as the Local Council of Women and the Ligue Ouvrière Catholique often had different visions of family, the families invoked by these disparate bodies were increasingly ones that purchased, rather than produced, their basic needs. And although the particular notions of family marshalled in support of consumers' rights were not always identical, family, as an abstract concept, had remarkable persuasive power in these years.

Women's consumer activity traversed the boundaries between private and public. Consumer boycotts—tellingly referred to as 'grèves silencieuses'—were markedly different from strikes, for instance, which were public, vocal, and occasionally violent. Not only did consumer activism target lower-profile establishments but, like much of women's domestic labour, decisions about what and what not to purchase were made quietly, often in private, and were acts of restraint, most noticeable in their absence.[85] Most women's consumer activism, in fact, was probably informal and unorganized: simply not buying when prices were too high.[86] Consumers' delegations and marches of women on City Hall were important exceptions: visible and newsworthy, attracting public attention similar to that garnered by strikes and men's occupation of the streets.

What we see in Montreal in the 1940s are attempts by both working- and middle-class citizens to make the public sphere more democratic by expanding its membership, but also efforts to translate public presence into political impact. In particular, the working-class families who exposed their meagre incomes and expenditures to public view were unveiling the private in an attempt to see the democratic rhetoric of wartime realized. In claiming and negotiating new post-war citizenship rights—economic citizenship, but also, for women, political citizenship in the form of the provincial suffrage, and for working-class families, especially, social citizenship in the form of new welfare-state measures—Montrealers pushed for a broader and more inclusive public and used the rhetoric of family to strengthen their claims.

# NOTES

1. National Archives of Canada (NAC), Canadian Association of Consumers (CAC), MG 28 I 200, vol. 1, file 1, Program Committee, 29 Sept. 1947.

2. This demand appears to bear out the first part of Victoria de Grazia's triple-barrelled assertion that, 'some time in the mid-twentieth century, it also became axiomatic that access

to consumer goods was a fundamental right of all peoples, that this right was best fulfilled by free enterprise, and that free enterprise operated optimally if guided by the profit motive unimpeded by state or other interference'. De Grazia, introduction to *The Sex of Things: Gender and Consumption in Historical Perspective* (Berkeley: University of California Press, 1996), 2. This article demonstrates that Canadians' opinions on free enterprise and the proper role of government in the 1940s were more varied than de Grazia suggests in the second and third parts of her statement. On American working-class skepticism about free enterprise during the Depression, see Alice Kessler-Harris, *A Woman's Wage: Historical Meanings and Social Consequences* (Lexington: University Press of Kentucky, 1990), 74–80.

3. This argument is particularly common in the American literature: see William S. Graebner, *The Age of Doubt: American Thought and Culture in the 1940s* (Boston: Twayne Publishers, 1991), 1–2; Perry R. Duis, 'No Time for Privacy: World War II and Chicago's Families', in Lewis A. Erenberg and Susan E. Hirsch, eds, *The War in American Culture: Society and Consciousness during World War II* (Chicago: University of Chicago Press, 1996), 39. For Canada, see Doug Owram, *Born at the Right Time: A History of the Baby-Boom Generation* (Toronto: University of Toronto Press, 1996), chaps. 1–3.

4. On the Depression and shame in the United States, see Duis, 'No Time for Privacy', 19–20. For Canada, consider L.M. Grayson and Michael Bliss, eds, *The Wretched of Canada: Letters to R.B. Bennett, 1930–1935* (Toronto: University of Toronto Press, 1971).

5. Denyse Baillargeon, *Ménagères au temps de la crise* (Montreal: Les Éditions du remue-ménage, 1991), 160, 196. Baillargeon emphasizes the minimal levels of consumption among Montreal's working-class families in the 1930s. The working-class family, she argues, remained a site of production rather than consumption at least until the 1940s.

6. *La Presse*, 26 mai 1947, 'Le mot d'ordre des ménagères de l'ouest', 4; 22 septembre 1947, 'Une manifestation des ménagères de Paris', 1; 20 février 1948, 'La baisse des prix continue', 1. On British women's post-war

consumer activism, see James Hinton, 'Militant Housewives: The British Housewives' League and the Attlee Government', *History Workshop Journal* 38 (1994): 128–56.

7. John Bohstedt, 'Gender, Household, and Community Politics: Women in English Riots, 1790–1810', *Past and Present* 120 (1988): 265–84; Judith Smart, 'Feminists, Food and the Fair Price: The Cost-of-Living Demonstrations in Melbourne, August–September 1917', in Joy Damousi and Marilyn Lake, eds, *Gender and War: Australians at War in the Twentieth Century* (Cambridge: Cambridge University Press, 1995); Susan Levine, 'Workers' Wives: Gender, Class and Consumerism in the 1920s United States', *Gender & History* 3, 1 (1991): 45–64; Dana Frank, *Purchasing Power: Consumer Organizing, Gender, and the Seattle Labor Movement, 1919–1929* (Cambridge: Cambridge University Press, 1994).

8. *La Presse*, 21 octobre 1944, 'Exception à la règle', 28; NAC, Marion Creelman Savage Papers, MG 30 C 92, vol. 7, file: WPTB 1933–1944 [sic], poster: 'The Story of Inflation . . . in one easy lesson'.

9. *La Presse*, 3 janvier 1944, 'L'ennemi se dresse, implacable', 4; 3 janvier 1944, 'La récupération au programme de l'année nouvelle', 4; 7 juillet 1944, 'Le marché noir est une plaie économique', 6. And see Ruth Roach Pierson, *'They're Still Women After All': The Second World War and Canadian Womanhood* (Toronto: McClelland & Stewart, 1986), chap. 1; Genevieve Auger et Raymonde Lamothe, *De la poêle à frire à la ligne de feu. La vie quotidienne des Québécoises pendant la guerre '39–'45* (Montreal: Boréal Express, 1981); Amy Bentley, *Eating for Victory: Food Rationing and the Politics of Domesticity* (Urbana: University of Illinois Press, 1998).

10. Joseph Schull, *The Great Scot: A Biography of Donald Gordon* (Montreal: McGill-Queen's University Press, 1979), 66–7; *La Presse*, 21 octobre 1944, 'Exception à la règle', 28.

11. NAC, Savage Papers, file: WPTB—*Consumer News 1944–1945*; *Consumers' News*, May 1945, 'The Price of Freedom', 1.

12. *La Presse*, 7 mai 1945, 'L'inflation, le dernier ennemi', 4; Savage Papers, file: WPTB 1944–5, Directive No.4 to Liaison Officers from Byrne Sanders, director, Consumer

Branch; File: WPTB—*Consumer News* 1944–45; *Consumers' News*, Nov.–Dec. 1945, 'Why It Could Happen Here', 4; File: WPTB 1933–1944 [*sic*], Women's Regional Advisory Committee, Montreal, Minutes, 19 Sept. 1944.

13. NAC, Montreal Council of Women (MCW), MG 28 I 164: vol. 2, Minutes, Local Council of Women, 20 Feb. 1946; vol. 5, file 6, Local Council of Women 52nd Year Book and Annual Report 1945–1946, Report of the Liaison Officer to the Women's Regional Advisory Committee (Consumer Branch) of the WPTB.

14. *La Presse*, 5 janvier 1946, 'Le Canada ne doit pas perdre patience', 22; 3 janvier 1947, 'Le retour à l'état normal', 6. Joy Parr argues that the production of household goods was deliberately given lower priority than the reconstruction of heavy industry. See *Domestic Goods: The Material, the Moral, and the Economic in the Postwar Years* (Toronto: University of Toronto Press, 1999), chap. 3.

15. *La Presse*, 27 décembre 1945, 'La lutte à l'inflation', 12; NAC, MCW, vol. 6, file 13; Letter from the LCW of Montreal [Food Conservation], 2 Jan. 1948.

16. Jeff Keshen, 'One for All or All for One: Government Controls, Black Marketing and the Limits of Patriotism, 1939–47', *Journal of Canadian Studies* 29, 4 (1994–5): 126. On the black market, see also Baillargeon, *Ménagères*, 141; *La Presse*, 29 mai 1946, 'Un juge s'élève contre les responsables du marché noir', 3; 30 septembre 1946, 'Violentes protestations contre le marché noir', 11.

17. *La Bonne Parole*, mai 1947, témoignage, 8.

18. Archives Nationales du Québec à Montréal (ANQM), P120, Fonds Fédération nationale Saint-Jean-Baptiste (FNSJB), P120/12–9, Minutes du Bureau de direction, octobre 1947–mai 1955; Bureau de Direction, 18 décembre 1948.

19. York University Archives (YUA), Maurice Duplessis Fonds, 1980–008/001, reel 7, 'Schéma—Discours' [nd], 2; reel 3, speech by Maurice Duplessis [nd, no title], 14.

20. *La Presse*, 4 mai 1946, 'Première victoire contre l'inflation', 31; 26 juillet 1946, 'Le contrôle des prix reste nécessaire', 6. See also Schull, *The Great Scot*, 59, 64.

21. *La Presse*, 27 mars 1947, 'Au Jour le Jour', 13; 4 novembre 1947, 'Au Jour le Jour', 15.

22. Ibid., 15 décembre 1945, 'Contrôle des prix', 30.

23. Ibid., 3 janvier 1947, 'Double moyen pour eviter l'inflation', 6; 5 novembre 1947, 'La lutte à l'inflation', 38; 11 novembre 1947, 'Subsides et contrôle des prix réclamés', 4; *Le Devoir*, 16 décembre 1948, 'Le contrôle des prix réclamé par deux organizations ouvrières', 3.

24. *La Presse*, 20 décembre 1947, 'Rétablissement du contrôle des prix', 30.

25. Gabrielle Roy, *The Cashier*, trans. Harry Binsse (Toronto: McClelland & Stewart, 1955), 160; *La Presse*, 28 janvier 1947, 'Va-t-on soulager le contribuable?', 1; 5 mars 1947, 'Qui va bénéficier des dégrèvements prévus?', 1; 4 fevrier 1948, 'Le fardeau restera assez lourd', 6; NAC, MCW, vol. 3, file 1A, Minutes, LCW, 19 Nov. 1947.

26. *La Presse*, 30 juillet 1947, 'L'inflation est connue', 6; see also 6 août 1946, 'Hausse accélérée du coût de la vie', 1; 5 novembre 1948, 'Le coût de la vie monte légèrement', 7; 5 juillet 1949, 'Le coût de la vie continue d'augmenter', 17.

27. NAC, MCW, vol. 3, file 1B, Minutes, Sub-Executive Committee of lcw, 1 Dec. 1948; Baillargeon, Ménagères, 146; Parr, *Domestic Goods*, 85–6. Belinda Davis notes that 'the feminization of the home front population' in Berlin during the First World War reinforced the popular perception of consumers as female; 'Food Scarcity and the Empowerment of the Female Consumer in World War I Berlin', in de Grazia, ed., *The Sex of Things*, 288.

28. NAC, MCW, vol. 2, Minutes, Local Council of Women, 17 May 1944. See also Marion V. Royce, *The Effect of the War on the Life of Women: A Study* (Geneva and Washington: World's YWCA, 1945), 62, where Royce claims that Canadian women's voluntary co-operation with the Consumer Branch of the WPTB was responsible 'in large degree for the efficient enforcement of price control'.

29. NAC, MCW, Vol. 2, Mrs E.C. Common to President, LCW, 3 April 1946. Jeff Keshen argues that voluntary war work in the realm of consumption may have led to 'enhanced recognition and self-confidence' for some women. See 'Revisiting Canada's Civilian

Women during World War II', *Histoire sociale/ Social History* 30, 60 (1997): 245.

30. NAC, MCW, vol. 12, *Why Be Thrifty?* (Ottawa: National Council of Women, 1950); Vautelet Papers, MG 30 C 196, vol. 1, 'L'association canadienne des consommateurs' (nd, but after Sept. 1947).

31. Magda Fahrni, 'Citizenship Under Reconstruction: Women's Public Claims in 1940s Canada' (presented to 'Paroles de femmes dans la guerre', Université de Nantes, 8 June 2001). On cost-of-living protests by DA recipients, see also Nancy Christie, *Engendering the State: Family, Work, and Welfare in Canada* (Toronto: University of Toronto Press, 2000), 263–4.

32. NAC, CAC, vol. 1, file 1, The Canadian Association of Consumers [Constitution]; Program [29 Sept. 1947]; *La Presse*, 20 novembre 1947, 'Les femmes du Canada s'unissent', 4; Parr, *Domestic Goods*, chap. 4

33. NAC, MCW, vol. 11, file: MCW Scrapbook, 1942–1959, part 1; newsclipping from *The Star*, 29 Sept. [1947], 'Women Meet to Organize Program'.

34. *La Presse*, 3 novembre 1947, 'Première reunion de l'Association des Consommateurs', 4.

35. Vautelet Papers, vol. 1, 'L'association canadienne des consommateurs' (nd); NAC, MCW, vol. 3, file 2, Minutes, Executive Committee of LCW, Dec. 1949; *La Presse*, 28 novembre 1947, 'Le devoir des Canadiennes', 4.

36. *La Presse*, 20 novembre 1947, 'Les femmes du Canada s'unissent', 4.

37. See, for example, Sylvie Murray, 'À la jonction du mouvement ouvrier et du mouvement des femmes. La Ligue auxiliaire de l'Association internationale des machinistes, Canada, 1903–1980' (mémoire de maîtrise, Université du Québec à Montréal, 1988), 97–8.

38. Archives de l'Université du Québec à Montréal (UQAM), Fonds d'Archives du Conseil des Métiers et du Travail de Montreal (CMTM), 103P, file: 103P–102/6, Minutes: 23 Jan., 13 Feb., 27 Feb., 10 April, 12 June, 27 Nov. 1947, 11 March 1948. Quebec's Fédération Provinciale du Travail also urged supporters to 'Buy Union-Made Goods'; *Le Monde Ouvrier*, 14 février 1948, 8.

39. *Le Front Ouvrier*, 1 novembre 1947, 'M. Abbott dit NON! POURQUOI?', 10–11; 6 décembre 1947, 'Les unions ouvrières et le coût de la vie', 3; 28 février 1948, 'Une expérience syndicale', 2.

40. *Le Monde Ouvrier*, 31 janvier 1948, 'Le Régime alimentaire d'Ottawa', 3.

41. Quoted in *Le Front Ouvrier*, 14 février 1948, 'Les ménagères n'en reviennent pas!', 3. See also *Le Front Ouvrier*, 17 janvier 1948, 'Les prix qui montent!', 17.

42. Joy Parr argues that historians of Canada's post-war economy would do well to look to the scarcity of the United Kingdom as well as to the plenty of the United States for analogies. *Domestic Goods*, 32, 64–5.

43. *La Presse*, 25 novembre 1947, 'Speculation injustifiée', 3; 26 novembre 1947, 'Organisme prêt à agir', 3; 2 décembre 1947, 'Réactions de la ménagère', 4; *The Gazette*, 20 Nov. 1947, 'Fruit, Vegetable Prices Up as Imports Cut but Modification of Law is Forecast', 13; 21 Nov. 1947, 'Grocers Scour Market for Vegetables as Price Trend Continues Upward Climb', 15.

44. *La Presse*, 26 novembre 1947, 'Organisme prêt à agir', 3; 25 novembre 1947, 'Speculation injustifiée', 3; *The Gazette*, 25 November 1947, 'Enforcement Now Feared Impossible of New Ceilings Announced by Abbott as Grocers, Others Here Hail Action', 1; 28 Nov. 1947, 'Consumer Group to Fight Panic Buying in Montreal', 4. On the lack of refrigerators and the daily shopping habits of Montreal's working-class families, see Baillargeon, *Ménagères*, 172; Sylvie Taschereau, 'Les petits commerçants de l'alimentation et les milieux populaires montréalais, 1920–1940' (thèse de doctorat, UQAM, 1992), 202, 293, 317. On the particular need for iceboxes in Quebec, given the predominance of flats without cold cellars, see Parr, *Domestic Goods*, 29.

45. *La Presse*, 22 novembre 1947, '"N'achetez pas si c'est trop cher," dit Mme Marshall', 36.

46. *The Gazette*, 29 Nov. 1947, 'Increased Prices Laid to Producers', 7.

47. *La Presse*, 25 novembre 1947, 'Les fermiers se ravisent', 3; 25 novembre 1947, 'Grèves de détaillants?', 3; 26 novembre 1947, 'Le marché mort', 3; 27 novembre 1947, 'Les acheteurs font la grève', 3.

48. Ibid., 25 novembre 1947, 'Les fermiers se ravisent', 3; 28 novembre 1947, 'Le contingent serait mince', 3; 29 novembre 1947, 'Le

commerce se stabilise', 27; 20 février 1948, 'Les réductions sur les agrumes', 29.

49. Ibid., 26 février 1948, 'Les prix se stabilisent', 3; 21 février 1948, 'Les prix maxima de la viande tout prêts', 17.

50. *Le Front Ouvrier*, 17 janvier 1948, 'Les prix qui montent!', 17. Thérèse Casgrain noted to the Canadian Association of Consumers that less milk was delivered to the poorer sections of Montreal once prices went up; NAC, CAC, vol. 1, file 1, Morning Session, September 30.

51. *Le Front Ouvrier*, 6 décembre 1947, 'Les dernières hausses de prix', 3; 6 décembre 1947, 'Qu'on laisse la paix aux cultivateurs!', 3; 6 décembre 1947, 'Lettre d'un producteur de lait à des ouvriers', 15; 13 décembre 1947, 'Qui est coupable?', 3; 10 janvier 1948, 'Beurre ou margarine?', 3; 7 février 1948, 'QUI fait monter les prix?', 1, 10, 11.

52. W.H. Heick, *A Propensity to Protect: Butter, Margarine and the Rise of Urban Culture in Canada* (Waterloo: Wilfrid Laurier University Press, 1991). See also Ruth Dupré, '"If It's Yellow, It Must Be Butter": Margarine Regulation in North America Since 1886', *Journal of Economic History* 59, 2 (1999): 353–71.

53. Heick, *A Propensity to Protect*, 73.

54. *Le Devoir*, 15 décembre 1948, 'L'U.C.C. et la margarine', 3; NAC, CAC, MG 28 I 200, vol. 1, file 2, Minutes of the Board of Directors Meeting, 10–11 Feb. 1948.

55. Vautelet Papers, vol. 2, 'The Community—Its Background and Development' (revised version, 1951).

56. *La Presse*, 21 février 1948, 'Lever l'interdiction sur l'oléomargarine', 49; UQAM, CMTM, 103P, file: 103P–102/8, Minutes, Montreal Labour Council Meeting, 22 Sept. 1949; NAC, CAC, MG 28 I 200, vol. 1, file 4, Canadian Association of Consumers, Executive Meeting, 9 March 1949. Renée Vautelet called Duplessis's treatment of the butter question 'a form of political bribe to rural voters'; Vautelet Papers, vol. 3, file: Allocution: Has butter a future? 'Has Butter a Future?' (nd).

57. Dupré, '"If It's Yellow"', 353.

58. The Montreal LCW decided not to support a butter boycott proposed by the Lachine Community Council, for instance; NAC, MCW, vol. 3, file 2, Minutes, LCW, 16 March 1949.

59. *La Presse*, 3 janvier 1947, 'Pas de changement au prix du beurre', 6; NAC, MCW, vol. 3, file 1A, Report of the Recording Secretaries, 1946–7.

60. *Le Front Ouvrier*, 3 janvier 1948, 'Speculation sur le beurre', 3.

61. *La Presse*, 21 avril 1948, 'La vente de la margarine', 6.

62. ANQM, P120, FNSJB, P120/12–9, Minutes du Bureau de direction, octobre 1947–mai 1955, Bureau de Direction, 18 septembre, 16 octobre 1948.

63. *Le Devoir*, 14 décembre 1948, 'La Cour Suprême permet la vente de la margarine', 1; 15 décembre 1948, 'Nous protegerons les droits de l'agriculture (M. Duplessis)', 10; 16 décembre 1948, 'La margarine', 1; 16 octobre 1950, 'La vente de la margarine relève des provinces', 1. See also Heick, *A Propensity to Protect*, chap. 7; Dupré, '"If It's Yellow"', 356.

64. *La Presse*, 18 décembre 1948, 'Sort incertain de la margarine dans Quebec', 1; 5 janvier 1949, 'La couleur de la margarine', 4; *Le Devoir*, 16 octobre 1950, 'La vente de la margarine relève des provinces', 1; Heick, *A Propensity to Protect*, 98, 107; Dupré, '"If It's Yellow"', 356.

65. NAC, MCW, vol. 5, file 7, LCW 55th Year Book and Annual Report 1948–49, Report of the Economics and Taxation Committee; vol. 3, file 2, Minutes, lcw, 19 Jan. 1949; Minutes, Sub-Executive Committee of lcw, 9 March 1949; vol. 7, file 25, telegram from Miss Esther W. Kerry, president, LCW of Montreal, to Maurice Duplessis, 13 Jan. 1949; vol. 7, file 25, LCW of Montreal, Third telegram to Mr. Duplessis re Margarine, 5 March 1949. Renée Vautelet also claimed that anti-margarine legislation was illegitimate because it violated principles of democratic liberty; Vautelet Papers, mg 30 vol. 1, file: Faits et chiffres, 'Le Soutien des prix favorise t'il le consommateur?'

66. *La Presse*, 9 décembre 1948, 'Concurrence qu'on juge necessaire. Les consommateurs ont droit à la protection que fournit la concurrence', 15.

67. Quoted in William Weintraub, *City Unique: Montreal Days and Nights in the 1940s and '50s* (Toronto: McClelland & Stewart, 1996), 126.

68. Dominique Marshall, *Aux origines sociales de l'État-providence, Familles québécoises,*

*obligation scolaire et allocations familiales, 1940–1955* (Montreal: Les Presses de l'Université de Montréal, 1998), 264, 274, 291.

69. See, for example, T.H. Marshall, 'Citizenship and Social Class', in his *Class, Citizenship, and Social Development* (New York: Anchor Books, 1965); Susan Pedersen, 'Gender, Welfare, and Citizenship in Britain During the Great War', *American Historical Review* 95, 4 (1990): 983–1006.

70. Vautelet Papers, vol. 1, file: Allocution–Why a Canadian Association of Consumers? (nd); Lizabeth Cohen, 'A Consumers' Republic: The Politics of Mass Consumption in America', paper presented at York University, Toronto, 2 March 2000.

71. See Davis, 'Food Scarcity and the Empowerment of the Female Consumer'; Parr, *Domestic Goods*, 10, 12.

72. *La Presse*, 4 juin 1948, 'Avantage qu'il nous faut conserver', 6; *Le Front Ouvrier*, 8 janvier 1949, advertisement for the Bank of Montreal, 3.

73. *La Presse*, 5 mai 1949, 'Le communisme est toujours dangereux', 13; Archives de l'Université de Montréal (UM), Action catholique canadienne (ACC), P16, File: P16/R64, 'Vers l'Édification de la famille de demain', Rapport des premières journées d'étude de la Commission française du Conseil canadien du bien-être social, Hôpital de la Miséricorde, Montreal, 9–10 mars 1951; Discours de Me Jean Lesage; NAC, MCW, vol. 3, file 1B, Minutes, LCW, 19 May 1948; Vautelet Papers, vol. 1, file: L'Association Canadienne des Consommateurs, St.Vincent de Paul (nd).

74. NAC, MCW, 12, *Why Be Thrifty?* See also NAC, CAC, MG 28 1200, vol. 1, file 3, Mrs F.E. Wright, president, Canadian Association of Consumers, to Presidents of National Women's Organizations, 29 Nov. 1949; Vautelet Papers, vol. 3, file: 'Notes for talk to Canadian Association of Consumers Annual Meeting', [nd].

75. Vautelet Papers, vol. 1: file: L'Association Canadienne des Consommateurs, Article pour bulletin provincial (nd); file: Social Reforms for Women, C.B.C. Xmas Eve 4.18 p.m.; file: Les droits de la femme, untitled (nd).

76. Ibid.: file: Brooke Claxton, candidat libéral, Text Radio Talk—June 24th; Radio Talk for Brooke Claxton, 1st of June; File: Assemblée Mackenzie King, election 1945. Discours Assemblée Mackenzie King Election 1945 (11 juin).

77. Ibid.: file: The High Cost of Living, Notes Lib. Women's Fed. (nd). See also Parr, *Domestic Goods*, 13.

78. Susan Porter Benson, 'Living on the Margin: Working-Class Marriages and Family Survival Strategies in the United States, 1919–1941', in de Grazia, ed., *The Sex of Things*, 236.

79. Vautelet Papers, vol. 1, 'L'industrie oubliée' (1949); 'L'association canadienne des consommateurs' (nd).

80. Drawing on the work of Jenny Hartley, who argues that the war made 'home' visible, Sonya Rose claims that the post-war emphasis on marriage and maternity for women produced an upsurge of women's activism on behalf of wives and mothers; Rose, paper presented at York University, 25 Feb. 1999; Jenny Hartley, *Millions Like Us: British Women's Fiction of the Second World War* (London: Virago, 1997), 54. For a Canadian example, see Susan Prentice, 'Workers, Mothers, Reds: Toronto's Postwar Daycare Fight', *Studies in Political Economy* 30 (autumn 1989): 115–41. For recent American work on this topic, see 'Dialogue: Reimagining the Family', *Journal of Women's History* 13, 3 (2001): 124–68.

81. Murray, 'À la jonction du mouvement ouvrier', 120; McGill University Archives, NDG Women's Club, MG 4023, container 1: 14th Record Book, Minutes, 7 Jan. 1944; 15th Record Book, Minutes of 23rd Charter Day Luncheon, 2 March 1945; 16th Record Book, Minutes, 18 Oct. 1946; 17th Record Book, Minutes, 3 Oct. 1947; 17th Record Book, Minutes, 17 Oct. 1947; 19th Record Book, Minutes, 13 April 1949.

82. NAC, MCW, vol. 3, file 1B, Minutes, Local Council of Women, 8 Dec. 1948. See also *La Bonne Parole*, novembre 1947, 'Les femmes et l'élection municipale', 2.

83. For a recent assessment of this literature, see Yves Belanger et al., dir., *La Révolution tranquille. 40 ans plus tard: un bilan* (Montreal: VLB Éditeur, 2000).

84. NAC, CAC, MG 28 I 200, vol. I, file 3, President's Remarks, Annual Meeting of Canadian Association of Consumers, 28–9

Sept. 1949; *Le Front Ouvrier*, 22 novembre 1947, 'La femme au foyer, une isolée?', 17; 6 décembre 1947, 'Editorial féminin. "Gardons" le foyer', 17.

85. Vautelet Papers, vol. 1, file: L'Association Canadienne des Consommateurs, St-Vincent de Paul (nd). But, as Dana Frank notes, shopping's 'limited visibility' meant that 'the success of a boycott was always hard to prove and observance hard to police'; *Purchasing Power*, 248.

86. There are indications, for instance, that the CAC was initially slow to attract 'the women in the home'; as Thérèse Casgrain observed, it was the majority of women who did not belong to organized consumer groups who were probably most affected by the increased cost of living; NAC, CAC, MG 28 I 200, vol. I: file 2, Minutes of the Board of Directors Meeting, 10–11 Feb. 1948; file 1, Minutes, National Conference, 29 Sept. 1947.

4   From Serge Durflinger, *Fighting from Home: The Second World War in Verdun, Quebec* (Vancouver: UBC Press, 2006), 150–68.

## FAMILY AND SOCIETY

While the Second World War may have solved some of the social and economic ills that beset Canada in the 1930s, it created, accelerated, or magnified others. The war years challenged existing social values, perhaps most noticeably those concerned with the role of women. For the families of servicemen, morale was often difficult to sustain: stress, fear, and anxiety took their toll on parents, spouses, and children. Yet the booming war economy at least helped make life more tolerable. Many families prospered, though not all Verdunites shared in this economic renewal.

Servicemen's spousal allowances and meagre service pay were often not enough for their dependants. In the autumn of 1942 the wife of an army private received a monthly Soldiers' Dependants' Allowance of $35, plus $12 each for their first two children, $10 for a third child, and $8 each for fourth, fifth, and sixth children. In addition, overseas servicemen were obliged to remit half of their pay to dependants in Canada. For a private this amounted to at least $20 a month, though rarely more than $22.50. A private's wife with three children therefore could expect $89 to $91.50 a month in allowances.[1] But the federal government's Marsh Report of 1943 calculated that a couple with three children under 12 required no less than $122.85 a month to make ends meet.[2] A serviceman's wife with children needed to supplement her income, as her Dependants' Allowance was clearly insufficient. In 1943 Robert England, who helped plan and implement Ottawa's civil re-establishment strategies during the war, admitted that the allowances, 'in the case of a small family . . . are not quite feasible if the family is resident in a large city'.[3]

### They Also Serve Who Only Stand and Wait

The Department of National Defence recognized that many young mothers and some aged parents were experiencing hardship because their husbands and sons had enlisted. It set up various administrative boards, such as the Dependants' Board of Trustees and the Dependants' Advisory Committee, to provide special and often emergency assistance to servicemen's families suffering financial or medical misfortune. Many cases came before these bodies, usually through a local welfare or social agency.

In wartime Montreal the Family Welfare Association, a Protestant charitable group, assisted and counselled needy families of overseas soldiers. In 1941 this agency helped cover medical or child-care expenses for 245 Verdun soldiers' families, often made up of aged or ill parents or unemployable spouses with children; these families also received advice on budgeting and managing debt. These 245 families accounted for some 10 per cent of Verdun servicemen at that time. The Family Welfare Association spent over $18,000 assisting Verdunites in 1941 and a similar amount in 1942.[4]

Some women sought marital and emotional advice from the association, symptomatic of their long separations from their husbands. Joan Adams, wartime head of the Women's Volunteer Reserve Corps, noted that many marriages and relationships in Verdun simply could not stand the strain. This became especially difficult for children, in her opinion, when the personal relationships entertained by some soldiers' wives, fiancées, or girlfriends became the subject of gossip at school or in community organizations. The emotional stress was very hard on these families.[5]

[ . . . ]

In March 1944 the number of Verdun servicemen's families receiving aid remained over 200. Only six families, however, had their incomes and spending strictly supervised by the Family Welfare Association. 'In view of the large number of Protestant families of enlisted men in Verdun', wrote the *Guardian*, perhaps surprised, this low figure constituted a 'tribute to the [financial] management by the wives' left behind.[6] Money management offered women enhanced social status and visibility. The view that many servicemen's wives were unable to cope with the intricacies of planning a family budget was common across Canada, however.[7] In reporting on the good works of the Family Welfare Association in Verdun, the *Guardian* regularly insinuated that many women left behind could not adequately organize family finances to supply the needs of their families. But financial difficulties rarely resulted solely from an inability to manage available funds or balance a budget.

[ . . . ]

Financial hardship was just one type of war-induced social burden for families. The war also dramatically accelerated the caseload of the Verdun Protestant Hospital, one of Canada's leading psychiatric institutions. Since Canadian troops were not committed to sustained ground combat until the invasion of Sicily in July 1943, and since relatively few Canadian casualties were incurred during the first few years of war, the stress resulting from the loss or feared loss of relatives and friends was not at first noticeably high in Verdun. In the hospital's 1940 annual report, the medical superintendent, Dr C.A. Porteus, stated that the war 'has not resulted so far in actually increasing the number of those admitted as patients to this hospital'. A year later there had been only a slight increase in admissions: 'Analysis of the individual cases does not reveal that the war, with its coincident depressing background . . . has been a specially determinant force in developing mental disorder'.[8] After three years of war, however, cracks developed. In 1942 the hospital recorded 429 new admissions—the largest number in a single year since the hospital opened in 1886. Still, Porteus downplayed these statistics. He noted that it was difficult to blame mental disorder on the war, although it might have encouraged symptoms, such as nervous breakdowns, to manifest themselves.[9]

[ . . . ]

### Crime and Juvenile Delinquency

Wartime, with its constant reminders of patriotic behaviour, was at first conducive to a 'law and order' mentality. Non-conformity or criminal behaviour, while contrary to peacetime social norms, seemed especially harmful to the national war effort. Verdun was not beset by serious crime during the war. While the incidence of crime and juvenile delinquency increased, wartime conditions permitted exaggeration of an issue widely seen as destabilizing, divisive, and unpatriotic. The press, community groups, and public officials overstated the problem.

According to police statistics and figures from Verdun's Recorder's Court, in 1939 serious criminal infractions in the city were rare. There were very few cases of burglary, auto theft (few residents owned automobiles), or assault, though there were 91 cases of loitering and 25 cases of disturbing the peace. Illicit gambling and backroom slot machines were considered Verdun's greatest criminal problems. In 1940 burglaries and auto thefts were reported to have decreased 50 per cent over the previous year. In 1941 even fewer burglaries and only 14 instances of disturbing the peace were recorded in Verdun. Few offences more serious than disturbing the peace were investigated by the police in 1942.[10] These are hardly the statistics of a crime-infested city, especially one with a population above 67,000 in 1941.

Wartime enlistment removed at least some of Verdun's older juvenile offenders from city streets. The local press had dubbed one organized group of teenagers the 'Galt Avenue Gang'. Opinions about these troublesome youths changed once they enlisted, at which time their fighting spirit and destructive energies were hailed as positive personal qualities, when applied to the proper cause. Their past misdeeds, including loitering and disturbing the peace, were explained in the press as nothing more than youthful exuberance. According to the *Guardian*, the gang could 'by no stretch of the imagination have been termed anything but young lads "full of the devil" . . . None of them had any real bad traits or tendencies to do any actual harm . . . And now the "Gang", or the greater number of them, . . . are in all the services of His Majesty's forces, in training . . . or chafing under the strain of having to wait to make the age limit'.[11] The list of gang members on active service showed ten names, all British in origin. Their ages ranged from 16 to 21, with most being 18 or 19. As evidence of the group's organized patriotism, each member received a silver disc from the gang on enlistment, a gesture much approved by the local press.

In September 1942, the *Guardian* reported, under the headline 'Evil Minded Give Verdun Wide Berth', that the city 'enjoys the enviable position of being probably the most law-abiding and peaceful community of its size . . . in the Dominion, if not on the American continent'.[12] Police spent half of their time doing 'social work': 'readjusting family troubles, giving a word of friendly warning or stricter reprimand to a young fellow slipping ever so little from the straight and narrow way, or getting off the street and into his own home without fuss or scandal a decent citizen who may have dined not wisely but too well. This type of social work . . . in Verdun often reaches an average of 50 cases a week all done without fanfare or publicity'.[13] The local perception of Verdun as a safe, conformist, and patriotic municipality seemed justified by the crime statistics as well as by the helpful attitude of the city's policemen, themselves mostly Verdunites. But this idyllic self-portrait, representative of a strong sense of community, did not last much beyond 1942.

By April 1943, a growing number of reported criminal transgressions had created apprehension in the city, and the *Guardian* suddenly took on an alarmist tone. For the first time since the outbreak of war public safety was called into question.[14] Police statistics for May 1943 showed fighting, vandalism, loitering, and disturbing the peace as increasingly common, especially among youths. The *Guardian* contended that most of these hooligans were not residents, but it offered no evidence. The local press could not or would not believe that Verdunites themselves might be responsible for local disturbances.

Serious crimes committed in Verdun in 1943 consisted of two 'highway robberies' and two hold-ups, eighty-two burglaries, twenty-seven auto thefts, fifteen cases of indecent assault, and one of carrying a concealed weapon.[15] Crime was on the rise. Rowdiness became more common, especially at night along the riverfront boardwalk. In April 1944, several serious disturbances involving gangs of youths congregating at the riverfront induced the city to institute regular police patrols of the boardwalk by two or three plainclothes officers and a motorcycle patrol.[16] City hall was determined to prevent Verdun from being a wartime battleground for disaffected youths.

The crime rate rose throughout the country during the summer of 1945. The cessation of hostilities relaxed the 'patriotic' social discipline of the early war years. The return of thousands of young servicemen from overseas signalled a rise in antisocial behaviour. Concern had been expressed in Canada that the demobilized soldiers, desensitized to violence by their training and experiences, might constitute a disruptive social force and menace to public safety. In 1946 adult offences rose 12 per cent nationwide over 1945, although they dropped 10 per cent in Québec.[17]

By early 1945, the community perceived a growing criminal problem in Verdun, widely attributed to discharged soldiers. That summer a number of assaults on women took place; without evidence, the press quickly suspected returned servicemen. Police patrols increased. Indeed, not all Verdunites were able to readjust smoothly to civilian life. In the ensuing year the *Guardian* reported a dramatic rise in the number of loiterers and panhandlers, some known to be discharged soildiers.[18] Although the war initially had been blamed for increased criminality, in the short term it was the post-war repatriation of thousands of servicemen that brought increased crime to Verdun.

Most Canadian and American studies of the home front during the Second World War refer to the rise in juvenile delinquency.[19] The contemporary perception was very strong that juvenile delinquency was the direct result of interrupted family cohesion. Hundreds of thousands of fathers had disappeared from the home and thousands of mothers were absent at jobs, sometimes employed on evening or night shifts. The lack of parental supervision was feared to encourage juvenile delinquency

among 'latch-key children' or 'eight-hour orphans'. In June 1942, as a result of enlistment and female employment, more than 5,000 children in Montreal were believed to be improperly supervised.[20] Growing delinquency was viewed as the result of overcrowded housing and the general tension and strain of wartime conditions. Stealing, vandalism, truancy, and general 'antisocial behaviour' were the usual transgressions of delinquents.[21]

Many Verdunites were disturbed to learn in April 1940 that juvenile crime had risen 19 per cent in the previous year, at the same time as adult crime was on the wane.[22] The trend continued until it was believed to have reached crisis proportions in the summer of 1943. Available statistics indicate, however, that this view was an exaggeration. National rates of juvenile delinquency peaked in 1942 and coincided with the vast increase in the employment of female labour in war industry. Yet the steady decline in the national rate throughout 1943 and 1944 preceded the return of these women into the home, indicating that the causal effect of female labour participation was overstated. Moreover, because most men 18 to 30, traditionally the most likely source of crime, were on active service, more time was devoted to policing youths. This increased the number of juvenile arrests and prosecutions (many for simple curfew violations) inflated the apparent rate of juvenile crime.[23]

In 1943 minor vandalism became common in Verdun's public parks and against private property, and the situation worsened during the summer.[24] Of 21 people arrested in Verdun in July 1943, 17 were juveniles taken into custody for relatively petty offences. In August 1943, however, a roving gang of some 50 young rowdies disrupted a 'sing-song' concert for young people at Woodland Park, near the waterfront. Police were called to quell the disorder. This incident demonstrated that an organized gang of delinquents operated in Verdun. Future wartime sing-songs were tainted by the threat of violence, and one woman, Béatrice Ste-Marie, who was a child living on Third Avenue during the war, has recalled that attendance was considered risky.[25] In January 1944, 30 of 34 people arrested in Verdun for various offences were youths. In June 1944, 40 of 52 offenders taken into custody were juveniles, most of them picked up for loitering and disturbing the peace.[26] The local press, citing police sources, alternated between alarm and reassurance. The frequency of delinquent acts depended on the season. The onset of winter lowered rates of juvenile loitering and vandalism; there was less to vandalize in winter, especially in public parks.

Boredom was viewed as a further possible cause of juvenile crime. The city hoped that sports and games would subdue mischievous young people. Sports constituted an important and inexpensive community activity and helped relax wartime tensions. In 1942 the Verdun Municipal Playgrounds Commission recorded its busiest year to that date. It issued nearly 1,500 permits for sporting matches at local parks, while 1,233 players were registered in municipally organized leagues and 305 in independent leagues.[27] The city saw to it that its playgrounds remained popular. In the summer of 1944 city hall increased the commission's budget by $5,300 to improve sporting facilities and offer more activities. Between 1939 and 1945 the number of Verdun playgrounds increased from five to eleven.[28] In co-operation with the city, Verdun's YMCA branch expanded its many youth-oriented activities, all of which the *Guardian* viewed as 'wag[ing] war on delinquency'.[29] The city's campaign met with the approval of a broad spectrum of local groups including the Greater Verdun Community Council, the Knights of Columbus, the Ligue indépendente catholique and the Société Saint-Jean-Baptiste.[30] A united response addressed a common problem.

While wartime Verdun experienced some increase in juvenile delinquency, the municipality was no hotbed of criminality. The overwhelming majority of young people were not delinquents. The city attempted to deal with juvenile crime, even though public safety was not threatened or eroded. Though the war exacerbated some social or familial circumstances that facilitated a drift to juvenile crime, it was not a substantial cause of criminal behaviour.

## The Verdun 'Zoot-Suit' Disturbances

Though not directly linked to local levels of crime or juvenile delinquency, one spectacular violent incident rocked wartime Verdun and became etched into the city's collective memory. On 3 June 1944, Verdun was the scene of a 'zoot-suit' riot that pitted more than 100 sailors stationed in Montreal against a lesser number of young civilian men and teenagers, many of them 'zooters' or 'zoot-suiters'. Zoot suits had a garish, even shocking, combination of colour, cut, and pattern. They consisted of a long, loose coat with excessively wide, padded shoulders, ballooning pants pegged at the ankles, a shirt with wide collar points sometimes accompanied by an oversized bow-tie, a wide-brimmed hat, and a long, hanging watch chain. This fad was most prominent in the United States and Canada, although some youths in Britain were also adherents.[31]

Most contemporary observers concluded that the zoot suit was foremost a symbol of youth rebellion and defiance. Antisocial behaviour such as drinking and loitering was often linked to zoot-suiters, and some roving zooter gangs were criminal and violent. Given the tense wartime atmosphere and government exhortations for social cohesion, zooters' actions and appearances seemed unpatriotic. Their attire contravened Wartime Prices and Trade Board guidelines for the rationing of fabrics and textiles, while their non-conformist attitude seemed to suggest antipathy to established social behaviour.[32] Considerable ill-will towards the apparently unpatriotic zoot-suiters developed among servicemen stationed in or near large urban areas, where concentrations of zooters could be found.

In Montreal these two groups sometimes clashed violently, and these collisions were occasionally worsened by perceptions of linguistic differences.[33] A serious outbreak of zoot-suit-related violence took place during the night of 27 May 1944 in St Lambert, on the south shore of the St Lawrence River opposite Montreal. *La Presse* noted that the zooters were mainly of Italian origin, although there were also a few French speakers among them. The soldiers and some local youths who opposed them were English speaking. Further altercations took place on 31 May, and fighting spread to the south shore landing of the Jacques Cartier Bridge, where a group of mainly French-speaking soldiers stationed in nearby Longueuil were set upon by a mixed-language band of zooters, 53 of whom were arrested.[34] Isolated incidents occurred daily in the Montreal area until at least 7 June, including the well-publicized beating of a sailor and his wife by zooters.

Meanwhile, at the end of May there had been disturbances in Verdun along the riverfront boardwalk as well as on Wellington Street. The *Guardian* referred to the incidents as 'baby riots' and 'demonstrations of racial feeling'. Although the combatants appear to have been divided by language, it is unclear whether servicemen were involved.[35] Despite nearly five years of war and several passionate election campaigns that had often divided Verdunites along ethnic lines, this was the first reported wartime incident of linguistic discord in Verdun on a scale large enough to warrant police intervention.

A much more serious outburst rocked Verdun in the late evening of Saturday, 3 June. At roughly the same time, some 400 overwhelmingly English-speaking sailors sought out and attacked zooters in downtown Montreal, especially along Ste Catherine Street. The men were apparently avenging the sailors attacked by zooters during the previous week. According to the *Guardian*, the trouble in Verdun began when 'some of the over-excited sailors . . . drifted to Verdun and

when they met with some youths who were wearing what looked like zoot suits, started to chase them. Fights developed in a pool room on Wellington Street'.[36]

Well over 100 sailors left Montreal on foot and made their way, 'en formation de parade',[37] to the Verdun Dance Pavilion on the waterfront next to Woodland Park, where they confronted perhaps sixty youths, not all of whom were zooters. Hundreds of non-zooter patrons were at the pavilion, and sailors mistook some of them, wearing pre-war, pre-WPTB suits, for zooters. Dozens of naval shore patrolmen, army provosts, and Verdun police arrived to break up the melee, watched by a large number of Verdunites. The brawl lasted for more than an hour and was over by about 11 PM.

The interior of the Dance Pavilion sustained some damage, and many minor injuries were reported. Four civilians were arrested, while the military police detained some sailors. Naval shore patrols monitored the explosive situation in Verdun long into the night. At first the local police force was overwhelmed by the magnitude of the violence, and many injured zoot-suiters, especially those who were stripped of their outfits by the sailors, were simply driven to the nearby police station to await the arrival of friends or relatives.

The *Montreal Daily Star* described the fighting in Verdun as 'vicious'. *La Presse* emphasized the language dimension, and noted that 'the brawling was serious in Verdun'.[38] The *Guardian* looked approvingly on the servicemen's vigilante actions and insisted that linguistic tensions had helped produce the violence. It treated the fighting almost as an innocent prank, accompanied 'by a number of rather humorous incidents . . . [and] some laughter'. Its account was restrained compared to the detailed report in the *Messenger*, which was far more sympathetic to the zoot-suiters and assumed them to be mostly French speakers. In an English-language article, the *Messenger* attacked the ill-disciplined sailors, who 'seemed quite willing to descend to Gestapo methods to enforce their own particular "way of life" upon fellow citizens'.[39] The *Guardian* would never have compared Canadian sailors to the Gestapo. Mirroring the views of most English-speaking Verdunites, the *Guardian* fervently opposed the zoot-suiters for what they were believed to represent: a dissenting view of the war effort, and a generally French-speaking one at that. Referring to the zoot-suiters as 'clown-like', the *Guardian* claimed the suits were the 'symbol of insolence and army evasion, frivolity in time of war' and blamed the zooters themselves for the violence.[40]

Appearances could be deceiving, however. Not all zooters attacked by the sailors were French speakers, and many did not even live in Verdun. The *Messenger* named three zooters who were arrested or injured: two were French speaking and one English speaking, while only one was from Verdun. All were between the ages of 17 and 20. One was arraigned in court and told by the magistrate to visit his tailor so as to 'avoid further trouble'.[41] No incident specific to Verdun had ignited the fighting; the sailors' march on Verdun was an outgrowth of brawling in Montreal. That the Dance Pavilion was a known haunt of zooters was sufficient to attract the sailors.

Yet Verdun's English speakers generally identified zoot-suiters as French speakers. In 1943 one grade 11 student at Verdun High School wrote a short fictional conversation (mostly in French-accented phonetic English) based on the zoot-suit craze. The piece suggested that the typical zooter was French speaking. Many Verdunites remember well the June 1944 fighting at the pavilion and usually discuss it as a language issue. One former resident, who was 15 at the time of the disturbances, recalled the events vividly and stated that the zooters were considered 'the Frenchmen'.[42] This perception encouraged a hardening of attitudes in Verdun against the unpatriotic zooters, and was a contributing factor to the fighting. But a post-riot investigation indicated that this view was mistaken.

Testimony taken at the navy's official board of inquiry into the Montreal-wide incidents, on 5 June, showed that the zooters whom the sailors attacked in Montreal and Verdun came from many ethnic backgrounds. Five of eight witnesses who were asked about the zooters' language or ethnicity insisted that they were predominantly of Italian ancestry; two claimed that the zooters were mainly French speaking, while another believed that they were of all nationalities. Several witnesses also mentioned that some zooters were 'Jewish' or 'Syrian', and most agreed that there were many English speakers among them.[43] Despite contemporary notions and enduring popular perceptions, Verdun's zoot-suit disturbances did not neatly divide French speakers from English speakers. The belief that they did so was a product of, and tainted, perceptions in Verdun of wartime social relations.

Verdun's municipal administration was alarmed at the sudden rash of violence and acted swiftly to defuse tensions. The executive committee petitioned Ottawa and the naval authorities in Montreal to investigate the matter and to take steps to prevent men under their command from engaging in renewed violence in Verdun. The city received letters of assurance from Minister of National Defence J.L. Ralston, Minister of National Defence for Naval Services Angus L. Macdonald, and MP Paul-Émile Côté, promising a thorough investigation beyond the naval inquiry. Edward Wilson, who lived only 250 metres from the Dance Pavilion and had gone to the Verdun police station at the time of the disturbances, met with Commander F.H. Davis, naval controller of the Port of Montreal. Davis promised measures to prevent similar situations in future.[44] Immediately after the fighting the navy declared the Dance Pavilion off-limits to naval personnel, cancelled leave for a week, and imposed a sailors' curfew starting at 9 PM.[45] Since civil-military relations in Montreal were becoming increasingly tense, the navy was serious about curbing further violence involving its men.

Wilson enlisted members of Verdun's Catholic and Protestant clergy to restrain latent linguistic and social animosities, even though it was known that few of the sailors and only some of the zooters of 3 June were Verdunites. Linguistic relations in Verdun were occasionally somewhat more strained than indicated by city hall's cordial façade. In a letter released to the press immediately following this incident the mayor wrote:

> In Verdun, as elsewhere, one can see more and more that youth is losing its respect towards the public . . . It follows that to efface this intolerable attitude that is now growing in alarming proportions among certain groups of young boys and even among girls, it is necessary to adopt energetic measures. Consequently, the City Council has already taken efficient steps to punish leaders of gangs . . . measures should be taken to improve community spirit in our municipality and awaken and impress our youth with the necessity of respecting our various religious beliefs. The end that we are anxious to attain is that of national unity at all times and in particular during the time of the present war. For, if there is one thing which must be safeguarded above all others, it is that spirit or mutual goodwill for which the City of Verdun has always been renowned.[46]

The French translation of this letter, published simultaneously in the *Messenger*, underscored its real intention: the phrase 'improve community spirit' was replaced with 'improve racial harmony'.

Wilson may have been acting also to ensure that non-Verdun quarrels remained that way. No further zoot-suit battles took place in the city. The brawling was an aberration and the 'mutual goodwill' between the two language groups held fast. In any event, Verdun was the scene, not the origin, of the quarrel. But the local riot was symbolic of the dichotomies inherent to Canada's war: those in uniform, those not; those English speaking, those French speaking.

Some Verdunites were outraged by the zoot-suit incidents. A frequent contributor to the *Guardian*, Reverend Ernest S. Reed, rector of St John the Divine Anglican Church, had strong opinions on the matter. Until the zoot-suit riots Reed generally had been an erudite voice of moderation on a variety of social and patriotic issues. But his 'Church Editor's Column' of 15 June 1944 was anything but moderate. He referred to zoot-suiters variously as 'hoodlums', 'hooligans', and 'chisellers of the lowest kind'. In calling for 'sterner measures' against these youths, whom he blamed entirely for the recent violence, he wrote: 'If there are those who object to military service, let them be honest . . . But young people who are making good wages in war industries and who spend their leisure time sniping at those in the armed services fall into a very different category [from conscientious objectors] . . . There may be even more sinister influences behind these disturbances. If any groups are using "zoot-suiters" to nefarious ends, let these groups be exposed. Those who, by their teaching or practice, set creed against creed, race against race or group against group are the most despicable kind of fifth columnists'.[47] Reed clearly perceived a language dimension to the disturbances; he blamed the zooters and, by extension, seemingly unpatriotic French-speaking youths for the fighting.

The owner of the Dance Pavilion, Rolland David, implied that the animosity between the sailors and the looters had more to do with social and civil-military differences since, he claimed, both sides contained English and French speakers. Rivalry for the affection of young women was also a significant contributing factor.[48] As a dance-hall owner accustomed to dealing with youths, David was familiar with the backgrounds of many of his clients. He was on the scene during the fighting and insisted that the language factor was exaggerated as an explanation for the fracas. David warned the naval inquiry that henceforth it would be dangerous for sailors to walk the streets of Verdun alone, as many local zooters and their friends and relatives would seek to avenge them. He believed that sailors risked being 'knifed or hav[ing] their heads split open'.[49]

The Montreal and Verdun zoot-suit riots became known to Verdunites serving overseas. In September 1944, one artilleryman wrote in a letter of appreciation to the Mayor's Cigarette Fund, 'at the present time Jerry is on the run and the boys arn't giving him any time to rest . . . But if our loyal friends the zoot-suiters don't want to fight for their country, we will have to do it alone . . . If you need any reinforcements in Montreal to fight the Draft Dodgers, apply for them [in] France, you will get more than you need'.[50] The view of zooters as draft dodgers was popular among servicemen and current among the civilian population. The zoot-suit disturbances constitute evidence that not all was well in the Montreal area between servicemen and civilians, between French speakers and English speakers, and between youths and their elders. Verdun was not immune from the effects of these tensions.

[ . . . ]

The Second World War affected Verdun society in a variety of ways, some more profound than others. Even though most Verdun families benefited from increased employment, the war also brought financial distress, personal hardship, emotional duress, and tragedy for many. Servicemen's families were among the city's most disadvantaged residents, a situation that wartime patriotism found particularly odious. Verdun casualties numbered in the hundreds; while hardly insignificant, they were not as heavy as the city's enormous enlistment rates might have suggested. More noticeable was the disruption of family finances and cohesion caused by the departure of thousands of men on active service.

Juvenile delinquency increased during the war, but its incidence seemed unduly magnified by its characterization as unpatriotic. The city became alarmed at this perceived rise in antisocial behaviour and provided Verdun youths with improved outlets for their energy. These initiatives were hailed in the community, which seemed satisfied with municipal responses to the social problems occasioned by the war. The local outburst of violence between zooters and sailors was the result of wider issues than those of Verdun's own making.

Despite the great potential for wartime division along class and linguistic lines, Verdun society remained generally cohesive. Hardships were borne and the social fabric remained intact. The war brought both prosperity and some dislocation, but neither in sufficient quantity to alter the city radically. Verdun was changed by the war, but Verdunites away on active service had no difficulty recognizing their home town on their return.

## NOTES

1. Robert England, *Discharged: A Commentary on Civil Re-establishment of Veterans in Canada* (Toronto: Macmillan, 1943), 149–52.

2. J.L. Granatstein and Desmond Morton, *A Nation Forged in Fire* (Toronto: Lester & Orphen Dennys, 1989), 166–7.

3. England, *Discharged*, 152.

4. *Guardian* (Verdun), 4 September 1942 and 17 September 1943.

5. R.B. Joan Adams, interview by author, 6 October 1993.

6. *Guardian* (Verdun), 2 March 1944. Catholics in Verdun were cared for by their parish Société Saint-Vincent-de-Paul or by one of over thirty groups that made up the Federation of Catholic Charities and the Federation of French Charities. *Montreal Daily Star,* 3 October 1944; *Guardian* (Verdun), 8 February 1945.

7. See also Nick Mika and Helma Mika, *Belleville: Portrait of a City* (Belleville, ON: Mika Publishing, 1983), 47–55.

8. Verdun Protestant Hospital, *Annual Report*, 1940, 33; and 1941, 33. The annual reports are located in the library of the Douglas Hospital, Verdun.

9. Verdun Protestant Hospital, *Annual Report*, 1942, 27–8.

10. *Guardian* (Verdun), 19 January 1940, 24 January 1941, 13 February 1942, and 5 February 1943. Cases brought before a local magistrate do not represent all instances of crime in the community, since not all crime is reported and not all that is reported results in court appearances.

11. *Guardian* (Verdun), 4 June 1943.

12. *Guardian* (Verdun), 18 September 1942.

13. *Guardian* (Verdun), 30 October 1942.

14. *Guardian* (Verdun), 16 April 1943.

15. *Guardian* (Verdun), 14 May 1943 and 3 February 1944. There was only one recorded murder in Verdun in the years 1939–46; see *Montreal Daily Star*, 12 September 1939 and 14 March 1940.

16. Executive Committee Minutes, 24 April 1944.

17. Desmond Morton and J.L. Granatstein, *Victory 1945: Canadians from War to Peace* (Toronto: HarperCollins, 1995), 171 and 207.

18. *Guardian* (Verdun), 12 July 1945 and 11 April 1946.

19. The Canadian literature is sparse. The best source is Jeffrey A. Keshen, *Saints, Sinners, and Soldiers: Canada's Second World War* (Vancouver: UBC Press, 2004), ch. 8. On page 213, he notes that the incidence of wartime juvenile crime nationwide was exaggerated, them and since. See also Jeffrey Keshen, 'Wartime Jitters over Juveniles: Canada's Delinquency Scare and Its Consequences, 1939–1945', in *Age of Contention: Readings in Canadian Social History, 1900–1945*, ed. Jeffrey Keshen, 364–86 (Toronto: Harcourt Brace Canada, 1997); Jay White, 'Conscripted City: Halifax and the Second World War'. (Ph.D. diss., McMaster University, 1994), passim; Geneviève Auger and Raymonde Lamothe, *De la poêle à frire a ligne de feu: La vie quotidienne des québécoises pendant la guerre '39–'45* (Montreal: Boreal Express, 1981), passim. For the United States, see Richard Polenberg,

*War and Society: The United States 1941–1945* (Westport, CT: Greenwood Press, 1980); Jack Goodman, ed., *While You Were Gone* (New York: Simon and Schuster, 1946); Francis E. Merrill, *Social Problems on the Home Front* (New York: Harper and Brothers, 1948).

20. Jean Bruce, *Back the Attack!* (Toronto: Macmillan, 1995), 67; see also *Guardian* (Verdun), 11 May 1944. White, 'Conscripted City', 339, also cites overcrowding and reduced recreational opportunities as encouraging juvenile crime in Halifax.

21. Until 3 November 1942 a juvenile delinquent was an offender aged 16 or younger. At that time the *Juvenile Delinquency Act* was amended to define juvenile offenders as 18 or younger. Executive Committee Minutes, 14 December 1942.

22. *Guardian* (Verdun), 12 April 1940. In the 1920s and early 1930s, juvenile crime rates had been very low in Verdun compared to other districts in the Montreal area. Herman R. Ross, 'Juvenile Delinquency in Montreal' (M.A. thesis, McGill University, 1932), 108.

23. Jeffrey A. Keshen, 'Morale and Morality on the Alberta Home Front', in *For King and Country: Alberta in the Second World War*, ed. Kenneth W. Tingley (Edmonton: Provincial Museum of Alberta, 1995), 154–5; Morton and Granatstein, Victory 1945, 207.

24. *Guardian* (Verdun), 18 and 25 June 1943.

25. *Guardian* (Verdun), 20 August 1943; Beatrice Ste-Marie, interview by author, 19 October 1994. Much more serious outbursts of wartime youth violence occurred in Prince Rupert, Vancouver, and Toronto, for example. Morton and Granatstein, *Victory 1945*, 208.

26. *Guardian* (Verdun), 24 February and 20 July 1944.

27. *Guardian* (Verdun), 18 December 1942.

28. Wilson municipal pre-election speech, probably 31 March 1945, box A-57, file 6, VBA.

29. *Guardian* (Verdun), 29 June 1944.

30. Council Minutes, 10 October 1944. Other Canadian municipalities noticed the importance of increasing recreational facilities to minimize delinquency. See Keshen, *Saints, Sinners, and Soldiers*, 213.

31. The precise origin of the zoot-suit fad is unclear, although it almost certainly began in New York City. For background, see Mauricio

Mazon, *The Zoot-Suit Riots: The Psychology of Symbolic Annihilation* (Austin: University of Texas Press, 1984), 6–7. Parts of this section were published in Serge Durflinger, 'Bagarres entre militaires et 'zoot-suiters' survenuesà-Montréal et à Verdun, juin 1944', in *L'impact de la Deuxième Guerre mondialesur les societés canadienne et québécoise*, ed. Serge Bernier, 7–21 (Montreal: Université du Québec à Montréal et la direction histoire et patrimoine de la Défensenationale, Ottawa, 1998).

32. Mazon, *The Zoot-Suit Riots*, passim. For a brief discussion of post-war zooter criminality in Toronto, see Mariana Valverde, 'Building Anti-Delinquent Communities: Morality, Gender and Generation in the City', in *A Diversity of Women: Ontario, 1945–1980*, ed. Joy Parr (Toronto: University of Toronto Press, 1995), 26–9.

33. Norman Bowen, a sailor, recalled that in Montreal, 'When we went ashore we'd go in a bunch', or else there was a chance 'you could wind up in the gutter'. Quoted in Keshen, *Saints, Sinners, and Soldiers*, 20.

34. *La Presse* (Montreal), 29 May 1944; *Montreal Daily Star*, 1 June 1944.

35. *Guardian* (Verdun), 1 June 1944. Information available in the Verdun and Montreal press does not pinpoint the date of these disturbances, although 29 or 30 May is most likely. These incidents followed separate gang fights along the boardwalk the previous month, although nothing suggests that these outbreaks of youth violence were linked.

36. *Guardian* (Verdun), 8 June 1944.

37. *La Presse* (Montreal), 5 June 1944.

38. *Montreal Daily Star*, 5 June 1944; *La Presse* (Montreal), 5 June 1944. Author's translation.

39. *Guardian* (Verdun), 8 June 1944; *Messenger/Le Messenger* (Verdun), 8 June 1944.

40. *Guardian* (Verdun), 8 June 1944.

41. *Messenger/Le Messenger* (Verdun), 8 June 1944.

42. Ruth Wolstein, 'L'habit zoot', in Verdun High School, *Annual*, 1943, 33, Canadiana Room, Verdun Cultural Centre; Wilson Dornan, interview by author, 21 September 1993.

43. 'Board of Inquiry', HMCS *Hochelaga*, Montreal, 5 June 1944, RG 24, vol. II, 110, File 55-2-1/423, 'Disturbances in Montreal', Library and Archives Canada (LAC).

44. *Guardian* (Verdun), 22 June 1944. The naval inquiry into the matter, which heard testimony from sailors, shore patrolmen, onlookers, zooters, and the owner of the pavilion, attempted to exonerate the sailors. These self-serving findings were rejected by the naval secretary in Ottawa and by other high-ranking officers in the Canadian Northwest Atlantic Command. Nothing came of the inquiry, and the report was simply filed away. 'Board of Inquiry', HMCS *Hochelaga*, Montreal, 5 June 1944, RG 24, vol. II, 110, file 55-2-1/423, 'Disturbances in Montreal', LAC.

45. *Messenger/Le Messenger* (Verdun), 8 June 1944; 'Board of Inquiry', HMCS Hochelaga, Montreal, 5 June 1944, RG 24, vol. II, 110, file 55-2-1/423, 'Disturbances in Montreal', LAC.

46. *Messenger/Le Messenger* (Verdun), 8 June 1944.

47. *Guardian* (Verdun), 15 June 1944. Reed was not the only Verdunite who supported the sailors. One of the few French-speaking sailors involved in the melee remarked that some of the many Verdunites who had gathered to watch the brawl openly offered the sailors drinks, indicating local sympathy for the men in uniform. 'Board of Inquiry', HMCS *Hochelaga*, Montreal, 5 June 1944, RG 24, vol. II, 110, file 55-2-1/423, 'Disturbances in Montreal', LAC.

48. William Weintraub, *City Unique: Montreal Days and Nights in the 1940s and 50s* (Toronto: McClelland and Stewart, 1996), 51–2; Keshen, *Saints, Sinners, and Soldiers*, 207, makes this point as well about a 1943 disturbance in Toronto.

49. 'Board of Inquiry', HMCS *Hochelaga*, Montreal, 5 June 1944, RG 24, vol. II, 110, file 55-2-1/423, 'Disturbances in Montreal', LAC. David forgot that Verdun was something of a navy-town: over 1,000 Verdunites were on naval service during the war. It is far from certain that local sailors and their families would have had much to fear from Verdun zooters.

50. Gunner R.I. Rowe to MCF, 14 September 1944, box A-348, VBA.

# Chapter 10

# The Welfare State

## READINGS

### Primary Documents

1   From *Report on Social Security for Canada*, Leonard Marsh

2   From *The Dawn of Ampler Life*, Charlotte Whitton

### Historical Interpretations

3   From *Contributing Citizens: Modern Charitable Fundraising and the Meaning of the Welfare State, 1920–66*, Shirley Tillotson

4   From *Social Policy and Practice in Canada: A History*, Alvin Finkel

### Introduction

In the period following the First World War, Canada, among a number of other nations, took some initial steps toward policies we now consider to be the core of the welfare state. These included enacting veterans' and survivors' benefits and proposing unemployment relief for all Canadians. During (and especially after) the Second World War, this trend accelerated. At least part of the explanation for this acceleration was that Canadians (and others) had seen how effective the national government had been during wartime, and urged governments to tackle peacetime problems using the same sort of planning and vigorous action. The basic shift involved in this development was acknowledging that complex modern societies would be more stable and prosperous if their working-age citizens did not have to fear starvation in the event of injury, illness, or unemployment, and if the aged did not have to fear poverty in their declining years. This extended, by the 1960s, to a system of health care for everyone, regardless of ability to pay. At least to some, the obvious provider of this social safety net was the state. Some people were not in favour of such drastic changes to the existing order. They feared that making life too easy for the average citizen would cause some to stop contributing to society, living on what the state provided and not seeking work. This difference of opinions is evident in our primary sources. Leonard Marsh wrote his *Report on Social Security for Canada* as a kind of blueprint for the post-war era, and he clearly patterned his plan on the system set out for the United Kingdom by Sir William Beveridge. The basic idea of Marsh's plan was to guarantee a minimum level of income for citizens and their dependents, and thus to keep the economy moving through consumer spending. Without such measures, he argued, tough economic times would become tougher as people were laid off, who then couldn't buy goods and services, so more people would be laid off. Charlotte Whitton disagreed with this idea, preferring to let local or provincial authorities take care of local welfare needs, and to let the market, rather than a board of experts, determine a decent living wage. In our secondary sources, Shirley Tillotson discusses the problems faced by private (non-governmental) charity organizations, such as the Community Chests during the 1950s, as the welfare state expanded. Donors found it difficult to support multiple charity campaigns when it seemed that the state had gotten decisively and effectively into the business of helping the destitute. Alvin Finkel tells the story of how Canada acquired a health care system that, rather than displacing doctors, figured out a way of bringing them more patients. Canada's geography played a role in this story, pushing Canadians in remote areas to demand care that a market system would be unlikely to provide. The extent to which the state should or could be involved in health care or the provision of a basic standard of living remains a current issue for debate. As our sources show, it is an issue with historical roots deep in the twentieth century.

## QUESTIONS FOR CONSIDERATION

1. Was Marsh advocating handouts to everyone?
2. Why did Whitton oppose the way that Marsh wanted to implement social security for Canadians?
3. Do Canada's size and sparse population make the welfare state a rather obvious choice?
4. What seemed to be the purpose of the private charitable organizations that Tillotson writes about?
5. What were some of the objections that doctors and other health professionals had to the idea of medicare?

## SUGGESTIONS FOR FURTHER READING

Raymond Blake, *From Rights to Needs: A History of Family Allowances in Canada, 1929–92* (Vancouver: UBC Press, 2008).

Lara A. Campbell, *Respectable Citizens: Gender, Family, and Unemployment in Ontario's Great Depression* (Toronto: University of Toronto Press, 2009).

——, '"We Who Have Wallowed in the Mud of Flanders": First World War, Veterans, Unemployment and the Development of Social Welfare in Canada, 1929–39', *Journal of the Canadian Historical Association* 11 (2000): 125–49.

Nancy Christie, *Engendering the State: Family, Work, and Welfare in Canada* (Toronto: University of Toronto Press, 2000).

Alvin Finkel, *Social Policy and Practice in Canada: A History* (Waterloo: Wilfrid University Press, 2005).

Dennis Guest, *The Emergence of Social Security in Canada* (Vancouver: UBC Press, 1985).

Antonia Maioni, *Parting at the Crossroads: The Emergence of Health Insurance in the United States, and Canada* (Princeton: Princeton University Press, 1998).

Dominique Marshall, *The Social Origins of the Welfare State: Quebec Families, Compulsory Education, and Family Allowances 1940–1955* (Waterloo: Wilfrid Laurier University Press, 2006).

Jennifer Anne Stephen, *Pick One Intelligent Girl: Employability, Domesticity and the Gendering of Canada's Welfare State, 1939–1947* (Toronto: University of Toronto Press, 2007).

James Struthers, *No Fault of Their Own: Unemployment and the Canadian Welfare State, 1914–1941* (Toronto: University of Toronto Press, 1983).

Shirley Tillotson, *Contributing Citizens: Modern Charitable Fundraising and the Making of the Welfare State, 1920–66* (Vancouver: UBC Press, 2008).

## PRIMARY DOCUMENTS

1   From Leonard Marsh, *Report on Social Security for Canada*, 1943 (Ottawa: King's Printer, 1943), 6–19.

## 1. CANADIAN PERSPECTIVE

The war, or rather the unprecedented production effort that the war has called forth in Canada, has changed the face of the Dominion so far as social needs and social security problems are concerned. It is not only that mass unemployment has been eliminated, with such unemployment as still remains limited to special problems of transferring between jobs, production hold-ups in industrial plants, and other types of interruption of working time which do not leave workers completely without prospect of further employment. In spite of the heavy demands of the Treasury for revenue to finance the war, consumer incomes have increased in several sections of the population. Earnings in many families have been brought above their previous levels through better-paid or more regular work on the part of the main breadwinner, the employment of additional members of the family, or even in some cases through the allowances now payable from state funds for the members of that family who are serving the country in uniform. There are still broken families—in some respects more than ever before—and not only because of the absence of fathers or sons overseas, but because members of the families have found work away from their hometowns, and again because many housewives are now full-time or part-time workers on one of the home fronts of the war effort. There are still problems of distress, for war bereavements have been added, and on a growing scale, to those of normal times. But full employment, whatever may be its special wartime pressures, has removed chief characteristic of the Canadian welfare picture as it was in the thirties. It has erased from the lives, if not the memories, of many thousands of families, the hopelessness and tragedy of seeing no means of making a livelihood in sight, and no means of maintenance other than doles from municipal or provincial governments, unskilled and dispiriting relief work, or assistance from the voluntary charitable agencies in the cities of Canada where these existed.

It is certain that the background of social and economic insecurity has not been entirely forgotten by many who are employed or contributing to family earnings now; and it is equally certain it must not be forgotten in projecting our minds forward to the post-war period, in planning in advance what measures should be taken to deal with the re-employment problems of that period, and on a wider plane seeking to give reality to the aspirations and hopes which the peoples of the world are more and more clearly voicing: that organized provision will be made in the post-war world for the risks and contingencies of family like that are beyond the capacity of most to them to finance adequately from their own resources.

These risks and contingencies are not solely those of unemployment. But it is understandable, against the background of the depression thirties, why unemployment should dominate most other considerations. If earning power stops all else is threatened. For the moment it is not necessary to pause to distinguish the differences in the risks of unemployment, sickness, accident, more normal but none the less serious events from the point of view of the working budget such as the increase in the number of children; and other factors. There are certain basic lessons to be learned from the experience of the thirties in which all the hazards of life—at least as they appear to the low and middle income groups—seemed to be swallowed up in the great vortex of unemployment.

The first is that provision for unemployment, both economically and socially, is the first and greatest need in a security programme designed for the modern industrial economy. A second is that in the absence of organized provision for particular categories or types of need and contingency, unemployment relief—itself the extension of provision intended only for destitution of multiple forms—draws into itself all other kinds of need: sickness, disability, widowhood, desertion, loss of residence requirements and so forth. Provision for simple destitution without any particular analysis as to cause may be barely justifiable when the scale of such assistance is small, as it was in the small parish or village of long ago when only a few persons in each community found themselves at any particular time without any means of subsistence and beyond the support of any relatives. It is completely indefensible, and of a nature to defeat efficient and constructive administration, once it attains national dimensions.

Canada has experienced all the problems of undifferentiated relief provision, and the consequence of having little or no measures designed for specific causes of distress and need. These deficiencies, in point of fact, are not solely in what is usually known as social security legislation. Some of them are due to the inability of municipal governments, whether in terms of finance or of administrative facilities, to handle many of the problems which constitutionally may still be interpreted as their responsibility. The basic framework of government itself has still not been adapted in any radical fashion—except recently for the vast effort of the war—from that which at the time of Confederation seemed proper for a country of the New World that did not know the modern problems of unemployment or public health or lack of economic opportunity, and was still in very large measure a constellation of small communities.

It would be a mistake to assume that a social security programme is entirely a matter of specific pieces of legislation, each covering a field marked off for itself alone. Social insurance involves an administrative organization, which is important for Canada not solely because it is a federal community but because of its problems of sheer distance. The proper methods for decentralization and regional administration demand the most careful consideration. None the less this much is clear. The only rational way to cope with the large and complicated problem of the insecurities of working and family life is by recognizing and legislating for particular categories or areas of risk or need. One of the contributions made by the social insurances, almost without the change being observed, is the advent of classified maintenance or treatment, or what in some countries has been called categorical provision. As will be indicated later, there is still need for development or rationalization of some of these categories. But this much may be said in advance. The establishment of organized provision for even one defensible area of need, as, for example, through the institution of unemployment insurance of health insurance, makes immensely easier the handling and the sorting out of the other types of need which still remain.

## *The Method of Social Insurance*

An explanation of these areas of social contingencies will be made in a succeeding Section. First, will be well to state simply what social insurance means, and why the approach through social insurance methods is appropriate. There are three basic reasons:

(a) In modern economic life there are certain hazards and contingencies, which have to be met, some of them completely unpredictable, some of them uncertain as to time but in other ways reasonably to be anticipated. They may be met in hit-and-miss fashion by individual families or may be met by forms of collective provision. Some of the risks may never strike any individuals or families; but we know from experience that, *collectively speaking*, these problems or needs are always present at some place in the community or among the population.

(b) For a large proportion of the population, incomes are not sufficient to take care of these contingencies through their own resources. It is no answer to this point to say that this would not be true if wage rates and earnings were higher than at present. As one of the Rowell-Sirois reports has summed up the matter, 'It is impossible to establish a wage which will allow every worker and his family to meet the heavy disabilities of serious illness, prolonged unemployment, accident and premature death. These are budget-shattering contingencies that strike most unevenly'. The inadequacy of even moderate incomes to provide for such things as major illnesses has now been measured by more than one authoritative investigation.

(c) The third principle, which really links together the first two, is that of the collective pooling of risks. Social insurance is the application on a much larger scale of the principle of pooling which has long been the basis of insurance in the more restricted sense (commercial insurance against fire, etc.). A great number of people may be liable to a certain risk, but only a few of them at anyone time. At the time the hazard strikes, they may draw on the resources gathered through the contributions of many, including their own.

The understanding of social insurance, however, is still confused because too much emphasis is placed on the second word and too little on the first word of the phrase. Social insurance brings in the resources of the state, i.e., the resources of the community as a whole, or in a particular case that part of the resources which may be garnered together through taxes or contributions. It does not mean, more particularly for phenomena subject to such variability as unemployment, that there must be a precise actuarial adjustment of premiums to risk in each individual case. The contributors who do not draw on the fund help to aid the unlucky ones who suffer unemployment or some social casualty. Some social insurance provision may have to be frankly viewed as no more than the gathering together of a fund for a contingency whose total dimensions are uncertain, but whose appearance in some form or magnitude is certain. In any circumstances it is better than having no collective reserves at all, or leaving the burdens to be met by individuals in whatever way they can. Of course, the more refinement that can be made, in the light of experience, between revenues required and current disbursements, the more systematic and economical for its particular task the social insurance fund becomes. The most important and serviceable of these devices is the provision, now written into all modern legislation, for careful annual review of the finances of the scheme, and their relation to current contribution and benefit rates. [ . . . ]

As experience with social insurance has grown, there has been increasing recognition of the advantages of this pooling of individual risks by collective means along with state control and participation. [ . . . ]

It may be questioned why, if these extensions of the pooling idea are valid, social insurance should not be financed solely by taxation, rather than the contributory method. The answer depends a good deal on practical considerations. If a widely comprehensive and unified scheme is not possible immediately, contributions serve to demarcate the section of the population for which it is intended to cater. Secondly, they have certain distinct administrative advantages, through applications, records and other ways, relating the individual directly to the service rendered or benefit received, and serving to facilitate the enforcement of conditions attached to benefit. But whatever the method of assessing the contributions, since it is in the interest of the insured person to maintain them regularly, his relation to the administration is more likely to be a responsible one. Generally speaking, the wider the area over which it is sought to make benefits available, the more important this becomes. And the proprietary interest which citizens as contributors come to feel in the satisfactory working of the scheme is not without psychological as well as administrative virtues.

None of these considerations should obscure the possibility of combining both contributory and tax-revenue methods. In effect, it is this combination which the Beveridge recommendations propose to develop extensively, and the combination has been effectively in operation in the comprehensive New Zealand system for several years. It is important to note, indeed, that state contributions or outright grants (e.g. in the form of marriage or maternity grants) administered in conjunction with an insurance system are much more likely to be payable without introducing the flavour of charity or the equal disability of irresponsible gratuity.

This is really the logical outcome of planning a better distribution of existing or anticipated income, both in point of time and as between the whole population or certain classes of it. Much of it is not necessarily additional expenditure, but the replacing of inefficient expenditures by more efficient methods. This is best recognized to-day in the case of health insurance. Large expenditures are already made both by governments and by citizens for medical care, much of it ill-advised, much of it in the later stages of an illness or disease when it is least able to be effective. Taxes in modern communities are similarly a major method of redistributing incomes, and of securing through individual contributions certain objects of collective expenditure. Social insurance administration, of course, brings to the disbursement of payments and services certain appropriate conditions. But the ability to put these conditions into effect on a fair and uniform basis is one of its major advantages. The genius of social insurance is that it enlists the direct support of the classes most likely to benefit, and enlists equally the participation and controlling influence of the state, at the same time as it avoids the evil of pauperization, and the undemocratic influence of excessive state philanthropy.

## Relation to the Post-War World

The purpose of this report is to look forward, not backward. It would not serve this purpose if it were not geared closely to consideration of the vast economic and social changes which are going on now, and which must continue only with the difference of changes in purpose and direction, once the war is over. There have been certain compelling arguments for the community types of social provision ever since the growth of large industrial communities. But there are additional reasons, and some reasons which change the force of the old ones, for planning the overhaul and extension of our social legislation at this time.

The first is that social security has become accepted as one of the things for which the peoples of the world are fighting. It is one of the concrete expressions of 'a better world' which is particularly real to those who knew unemployment, destitution, inadequate medical care and the like in the depression periods before the war. To others the idea of better social security measures may be less of a reaction from previous hard experience; but it is an intelligible recognition that it is one way of realizing nationally a higher standard of living, and of securing more freedom and opportunity through the use of such income as is available once social insurance has taken care of the minimum.

Whatever assessment may be placed on the first and rather broad interest in social security, a second one is completely realistic and timely. The end of the war means demobilization of much of the civilian as well as the uniformed population and, no matter how short may be the period of transition, there are risks and difficulties attached to the process of re-employment against which all appropriate facilities must be mobilized. It should not be forgotten, in this connection, that the re-employment problems of the post-war period include the reassembling of many thousands of families.

A third and equally realistic consideration is that the transition period will show in more marked contrast than any other, differences in respect of social provision for Canadian citizens when they are in the army or in some other branch of the services, and when in ordinary civilian life. The provisions which the state extends to its armed forces and their dependents in time of war, and to ex-service men's families after war, go far along all the avenues of what is usually comprised in 'social security'—provision for children's maintenance, widowhood, medical care, disability, unemployment, retraining, and other contingencies.

The standards and allowances and the attention given to many varieties of need will, rightly or wrongly, be measured against standards of livelihood and welfare in the civilian world. Some of these differences may be entirely justifiable. But nothing short of an objective appraisal of existing legislation, the requirements of transition, and the adjustment of such civilian deficiencies as may have been rendered more prominent by improved attention to groups affected by the pressure of war, will meet the situation.

The final point in gauging the need and validity of a social security programme in post-war Canada is only indirectly a welfare matter at all, but it is a strategic factor in economic policy generally whose importance cannot be over-emphasized. One of the necessities for economic stability is the maintenance of the flow of purchasing-power at the time when munitions and other factories are closing down and war activity in many other spheres is being liquidated. Sound social insurance, which is a form of investment in physical health, morale, educational opportunities for children, and family stability, is a desirable and a comparatively easy vehicle of expenditure. It is not only an eminently appropriate peacetime alternative for expenditures now being devoted to destruction: it is also a form of using some of the deferred backlog of consumer expenditure to which reference is so often made only in terms of radios, frigidaires and other tangible consumers' goods. In this perspective, a wide and properly integrated scheme of social insurance and welfare provision of $100,000,000 or $500,000,000 is not to be regarded with the alarm which, with inadequate understanding, it might otherwise occasion.

[ . . . ]

## Subjects Not Within the Scope of the Report

This report addresses itself particularly to those forms of individual and family need which arise when earnings are impaired or interrupted by unemployment, illness or accident; to the economic problems which are directly incurred by failing capacity through age, or loss of support through disability or death; and to the family contingencies requiring exceptional expenditure, particularly those connected with birth, death and marriage. There are, of course, a number of fields of social welfare provision which might be considered in any exhaustive survey of social facilities. Nutrition has become so important a matter in itself that it is now a separate chapter in any social welfare book. The proper provision of housing, and the elimination of bad housing, is so universally recognized as a fundamental attack on many social ills that it also is a separate topic in itself. There are certain inventories—of hospitals, sanatoria, etc. or of institutions for orphans, crippled children, etc.—which raise questions of the adequacy of our capital equipment no matter what legislative provision there may be for care. The advent of health insurance will raise some of these questions more prominently. Education is of course a fundamental not only in social welfare but for many other aspects of civilian life. Better provision for passing the young worker from school to employment, and codes governing juvenile labour, would not be fully rounded out without attention to the treatment of juvenile delinquency. These and other problems will not be forgotten by anyone who has in mind for the future the fullest utilization of our human resources.

---

**2** From Charlotte Whitton, *The Dawn of Ampler Life* (Toronto: Macmillan, 1943), 1–7, 9–10, 14–19.


## A MEMO FOR CANADA
### 1. Some Definitions and Premises

Before discussing measures of social security, it might be well to attempt to define the term itself. In recent years, in the United States, and now in the Beveridge Report, the words have been given a special interpretation. 'Social Security' is used by Beveridge to denote 'the securing of an income to take the place of earnings when they are interrupted by unemployment, sickness or accident, etc. Primarily, Social Security means security of income up to a minimum'.[1]

Surely, if Social Security is to be offered to men and women as an ideal to fire them to sacrifice and achievement it must be more than that. The world that fights this battle through will not be satisfied with anything so negative as stability or security, within or at some position to which human progress has already advanced. Its people will want a concept of dynamic action lifting life forward in a great surge of freedom and unity of purpose. To the definition of such hopes might the term Social Security more properly be applied— something offering the vision of humanity secure and happy, enjoying that peace of mind which only a sense of safety can bring. The structure of a fuller life, in a freer, better world cannot be built upon the one pier of freedom from want: it must rest upon the cornerstones of all four freedoms—with spiritual stability in freedom of worship, intellectual strength in freedom of speech, political growth in freedom from fear, and economic security in freedom from want.

What has been so generally described as Social Security is therefore really not that at all but just 'Income Security', in which narrower meaning the Beveridge Report really discusses it throughout.

Income Security calls for economic planning on the one hand and welfare planning on the other. Economic Planning should be directed to the gearing of the State's productive mechanism to assure to all, able to work, continuous gainful occupation, with such fair return for the use of the labour, skill or means of each, as to assure livelihood for the worker and the worker's dependants at a reasonable level of decency and security. Welfare Planning should seek to assure, within the State, the maintenance of such health, educational and welfare facilities as will bring the opportunity of their good use within the range of all people, but, about and behind these services, there must also be other resources, whereby in loss or impairment of income, the worker and his dependants are protected against preventable or unnecessary suffering or distress.

*Some General Premises*

Certain premises can probably be taken for granted in Canadian discussions of income security today. There will be general agreement that the purpose and organization of production, within the State, must be directed, to greater degree than in the past, to the maintenance of livelihood for all the people at a level consistent not only with survival but with decency and human dignity.

There will also be no question that this should be sought primarily by the maintenance, not so much of 'full employment' (which unconsciously assumes a national economy, predominantly industrial and using human power on a wage basis) but of 'gainful occupation' for all the population at the highest possible level, with continuity of work and remuneration, in wages, prices for goods or in other return sufficient to assure reasonable self-support.

There will be further concurrence that, no matter how well meshed or stringently controlled the organization of work opportunity, production and distribution may be, exigencies will arise to throw the system out of gear and threaten the continuance of gainful occupation on a self-supporting basis, both over large groups and for the individual worker. The force of public conviction undoubtedly recognizes and accepts the obligation of collective responsibility to keep such exigencies to the minimum and to assure community provision for them when they do arise. [ . . . ]

There will be debate but not serious disagreement in Canada as to these requisites to national well-being:

(1) The development of resources and production, geared to assurance of the highest possible level of continuous gainful occupation on a self-supporting basis for all workers, whether on wages or self-employed.

(2) A basic system of Social Utilities, affording educational, health, and welfare services for all the people, under varying auspices and available on varying bases.

(3) A correlated system of Social Assistance, paying allowances, grants, or relief against impairment of income, from non-predictable or individual contingencies, on a basis of means and need in each case, and, for circumstances and citizens, not coverable by insurance benefits or pensions.

(4) A system of Income Insurance, paying benefits and pensions to afford protection against impairment of income from predictable and insurable exigencies and applicable to insurable elements in the population.

Where real question immediately arises, is in the fundamental objective to which this planning is to be directed, the extension of protection of these varying types of provision over the respective elements of the population, and the administrative, constitutional and financial processes involved therein.

## 2. The Canadian Scene

The Dominion of Canada is the achievement of a small people with a great faith in their own strength. Initiative and enterprise meant opportunity, and opportunity, with integrity and thrift, meant security. The years between the two wars dealt, ruthlessly and cruelly, with the Canadian's superb and simple confidence in his own destiny but they did not destroy the essential vigour and buoyancy of this country. For there is vitality in the land itself, in the vibrant silence of the forests, in the quiet sense of growth in the prairie soil, the pounding power in the rushing streams. Energy, ambition and the instinct of thrift still are bred in the people, as a whole, born of their background and renewed in the necessity of preparation, always, for the sharp, harsh changes of the seasons with constant adaptation to their needs. No plan for security, with freedom and opportunity, can be well imposed upon such a people: it must be a growth from the nature and background of the land itself, a fulfilment in which each different element in our life shall have contributed its strength.

It is well that in this process Canada should draw upon the experience of other peoples, older in story and schooled in the technique of protecting life against the buffeting of its exigencies. And, among all States, it is natural that this country should look particularly to the two with whom comparison is most valid—the United Kingdom, from whom many of the basic principles of our social legislation have derived side by side with the procedures of the Quebec Civil Code; and the United States of America, the tempo of whose life beats so insistently upon our own. But this should not mean the importation of the systems of other lands, and a straining to fit them to our needs. Rather, we should seek the evolution of a Canadian wrap, with the wool thereon as distinctively the product of our own experience as our own homespun designs. This calls for knowledge and love of our land, inventive imagination and courage, if the fabric of our social planning is to afford protection against the thrusts of circumstance.

Canada must be seen for what she is, not in terms of the crowded, matured life of Europe's twenty odd States and five hundred and twenty millions of people on an area less extensive than our own; nor yet in those of the compact unified life of the United Kingdom, with almost four times our population, working 90 per cent in industry, business or commerce, on a base no larger than the average of a dozen of the larger counties of Ontario or Quebec, and affording an intimacy and efficacy of organization just unattainable in any land of our extent. Nor can the United States of America be our precept, for her great territory, continentally less than our own, is occupied by twelve times our population. Moreover, her balanced economy rests on the temperateness of the South whereas ours must meet the physical challenge of that two-fifths of our domain lying within the Yukon and the Northwest Territories and containing less population than a large USA or British town.

[ . . . ]

Across three thousand miles, from sea to sea, her population stretches in two narrow bands, contiguous to the main transportation systems, clotted at ports and junction points into heavy urban, even metropolitan, centres; dwelling, in the older farmlands, in pleasant friendly clusters; in others and in forest and hinterland as scattered, lone and isolated as the people of the Norwegian fiords or the Russian steppes. With her great water-power close to mineral and forest wealth, she supports the strange anomaly of heavy industrial development in the midst of wild, barely accessible and isolated lands, often incapable of providing the supplementary products essential to their indigenous industries. Two great cities now hold 20 per cent of all our population, while nearly a half dwells in villages of less than 500 persons or in the open country, or in these hinterlands; a third lives in the towns and smaller cities.

[ . . . ]

The relative life of the provinces varies widely. Ontario and Quebec are similar in their widely diversified and balanced activities. British Columbia also enjoys a fairly equitable economy. In the Maritime Provinces, nearly a quarter of the people are engaged in agriculture; and in the Prairie provinces, 45 per cent, Alberta and Saskatchewan having more than half, Manitoba 35 per cent of the population, agrarian.

Old and mature in their economic life, the five Eastern provinces, decades ago, developed characteristic services for the education and social protection of their people, all strongly integrated in their traditional local government on a municipal basis. Quebec incorporated the partnership of private, religious, charitable direction with a measure of public liability in finance and supervision. New Brunswick and Nova Scotia built on the public liability for the needy of the English poor laws. Ontario and Prince Edward Island modified the English practice but retained its principles and all four continued to rely upon a large measure of private citizen effort, both in administration and finance.

The Pacific Slope and the Northwest had remained for years under the direct administration of the Hudson's Bay Company. As all these great territories gradually opened to settlement, their extent, and the proportion of continental European population therein, tended to develop government along the highly centralized lines of Company administration, with the provincial authority, naturally, and to large measure necessarily, assuming many a responsibility and function which, in the older provinces, remained within municipal jurisdiction. Municipal government—and especially that extremely successful territorial intermediary between purely local and provincial government, the county—has tended to become the secondary agent in the West for many obligations and duties for which it remains primarily responsible in the East, except in Prince Edward Island where, with a small population and territory, the provincial and municipal government are peculiarly supplementary.

In such an evolution of settlement and government, the Provinces remained the primary unit in Confederation in all matters of civil rights and, so, of education, health, welfare, and the area of social assistance and protection then dimly etched but now constantly enlarging. The same enactment as constituted the sovereignty of the Dominion government, in its spheres, confirmed the sovereignty of each respective province within the area of its jurisdiction. The diversified powers and responsibilities, therefore, of three levels of government in Canada are but the reflection of the diversified character of the land, its people and their occupations.

[ . . . ]

The basic criticism of the proposals offered by Dr Marsh for Canada, is that they attempt to direct this Dominion along the blueprints of the Beveridge plan and introduce certain suggestions emerging from a different social background when all the elements of the Canadian situation demand the evolution of realistic measures, grounded deep in the character of this country and its people.

## 4. The Canadian Objective

What then should be the purpose, form, and execution of such part of the planning for income security as may lie within the framework of the Canadian state? Simply stated the objective to which the Beveridge Report and Dr Marsh's suggestions for Canada are directed is the establishment and assurance of what is described as a national social minimum, or in specific terms an actual income budget in currency values which shall be assured to every individual in the state, by supplement or substitution for earned income to the degree that the latter fails. This social minimum is to be calculated on a budgetary basis, though Sir William Beveridge leaves the gravely difficult question of rent differentials in widely varying parts of the United Kingdom unsettled, and Dr Marsh appears to rest the very complicated question of differences between costs in different types of Canadian communities on a possible variation of 15 per cent between urban and rural budgets.[2] The social minimum in the closely similar Beveridge and Marsh proposals contemplates a minimum standard living budget in terms of the single adult worker, and the adult worker with one adult dependant, these budgets varying in their relation to social aid, as to whether the cause of the income impairment is of a presumably temporary or permanent nature, the latter scales (e.g., for aged) being lower than the former (e.g., in unemployment or temporary sickness). Variation in family needs is to be met by another device, straight cash grants or allowances by the State, in the Beveridge proposals, on behalf of all children of school age, save the first (which is included, however, if the parent is in receipt of social aid), and in the Marsh suggestions for all children under 16 or 17 years of age.

Whatever the merits of the case in an industrially mature population with a declining natural increase, there seems grave doubt as to whether in a young, vigorous, rich Canada, the most dynamic ideal that can be set before her people, is the attempted mathematical calculation of a social minimum in terms of weekly income in dollars and cents, and then the organization of the national life and production to assure that. In a land of such diversity of life and occupation, the practical possibility of such a device, equitable to all parts of the country and all elements in the population seems seriously open to question, even if theoretically desirable.

There is agreement among Canadians that no one within their citizenship should be suffered to exist at less than a decent level of life, and a real anxiety and purpose to realize such economic security for all our people. But it is suggested that in this conviction Canadians are not thinking of so many dollars and cents per head being required in currency within each home: they think rather of a simple, decent, sound wholesome family life, varying with the part of the country and the occupation in which the family finds itself. They think of the shelter, food, and clothing to be acquired within their individual effort, by sale of their labour, their skill or the goods they produce; they think, too, of all the things that mean well-being and opportunity, to them,—the 'chance to make good' by development of land or fishing, or some personal enterprise, or by good training, education and employment. Health services, schools, the district or neighbourhood church—all these things are bound up together in the average Canadian's concept of what he means by a decent social minimum or standard of living; it is all something more far-reaching, vital and complex than the hope of a calculated amount of income in currency terms. Further, he wants the opportunity to provide these things by his own efforts, directly in return for what he has to sell, in so far as these individual needs are concerned and, directly, also through the creation of community services, in the provision and control of which he participates—good roads, good community facilities, good schools, hospitals, housing, etc. It is a harder way, than the calculation of a definite income, and supplementation from public funds where earnings are 'sub minimum' but it is the dynamic way, not a defeatist counsel of acceptance of things as they are, and as such, it is submitted, one more consistent with the youth and vigour of this country.

[ . . . ]

The next line of social policy should be the organization of gainful occupation on such a basis as to offer to the conscientious and efficient worker, valid hope of an income from his effort, sufficient to maintain, in reasonable decency, the family obligations which he might normally be expected to require. This premise rejects the contention that 'fundamentally insistence on relating a wage rate to family needs is illogical'.[4] It is admittedly illogical to accept the premise that the remuneration of a worker should be automatically increased, without regard to his relative value in the occupation in which he is engaged, just because his dependants increase, by birth of more children or otherwise, but to deny that the basic rate, on which the value of human power should be remunerated (in wages or fees for skills or in prices for natural products) should be grounded in decent minimum living standards, is to reject the fundamental basis on which wage standards, and the effort to control price spreads, have developed on the North American continent since the opening of this century.

Whatever the practice in other lands, in the United States and Canada the theory of wages and prices has been predicated on the earnings of an adult worker being adequate to support, in reasonable decency, his wife and a 'typical family' of two to three children of varying age. If an industry cannot be adjusted to that rate of remuneration for the human element in its relevant costs, granted the labour is efficient, the industry is deemed to require investigation to ascertain the cause of its inability to do so. Similarly, if the production of primary goods cannot yield reasonable subsistence and the hope of progress for an adult, of comparable responsibilities, it is recognized that inquiry and remedial action are required.

The encouragement and development of every occupation in the national economy should be gauged by this measurement:—Can it accord to the experienced worker therein returns adequate to the reasonable discharge of the obligations which he may reasonably be assumed to have acquired at that stage in his working life? If not, it must be submitted to inquiry and remedial policy as that inquiry may suggest.

These processes, it is submitted, should be accepted as basic in exploring greater income security for the Canadian people,—the accurate assessment of the probable peak maximum national income and of the ways and means of influencing its capacity and its distribution to afford a standard of income for the average mature worker, reasonably adequate to the minimum living needs of a typical family, and then the adjustment of all minimum wage scales and fair prices for natural products, in relation thereto.

Such proposals admittedly involve broad problems of economic policy, and of the relation of supply and demand within Canada, and internationally—all of themselves of such extent as to lie outside the limits of a discussion, centring about the maintenance of income for the Canadian at a minimum level, effected by the gearing of production to that end. Moreover, they call for technical knowledge and competence within other fields than that of social administration. But granting all this, a warning at this point is not inappropriate that, no matter what the organization of Canada's own resources and services, her ability to attain and maintain an objective of happy work and reasonable well-being for all her citizens involves interest and responsibility outside their own geographic or political frontiers. The same dynamic objective is stimulating the life of all civilized peoples. It would be culpable folly for Canadians to ignore the fact that (even with the peak demand of war's daily destruction and a large part of the highly industrialized continent of Europe occupied and partially immobilized) the productive power of this country, put into mass production, has outraced anticipated demand for many lines of goods. The extension of the Dominion's two billion dollar non-repayable credits to Britain and the Allied Nations was not only an indication of a sense of war partnership but of this rate of production outstripping presumed demand in certain lines. Industrial lay-offs in various lines, even in wartime, similarly reinforce the need of realization of this relation between our power to produce and even a greatly heightened consumer demand within the country, which is to be discounted, too, by consideration of the comparative durability of heavy consumer goods for peacetime use. The hope of continuous gainful occupation, at a decent level of security for the Canadian people, therefore seems predicated upon the integration of our life in an international pattern and in a partnership in world production and trade.

With the reservation then that Canadians cannot hope to plan for their well-being and security within the vacuum of their own state alone, discussion can proceed to that part of the economic security for the state and the individual which rests upon welfare, as reinforcing economic, planning.

## NOTES

1. Beveridge Report, p. 120.
2. For the standard budget suggested for Canada see Part II.
3. National Resources Planning Board, *After the War—Toward Security, September,* 1942, p. 4.
4. Report, L.C. Marsh, M.R. p. 26.

## HISTORICAL INTERPRETATIONS

3   From Shirley Tillotson, *Contributing Citizens: Modern Charitable Fundraising and the Meaning of the Welfare State, 1920–66* (Vancouver: UBC Press, 2008), 189–227.

### JUSTICE, INCLUSION, AND THE EMOTIONS OF OBLIGATION IN 1950S CHARITY

In addition to finding a place in the policy processes of the welfare state, the Community Chest fundraisers shifted their appeals in the 1950s to adjust to the cultural logic of the new regime. Like their predecessors in the 1930s, these social advertisers looked around them at the methods of consumer advertising and within the general culture for materials that could be used for their purposes. Their fundamental purpose—to raise money—was unchanged from the 1930s. But since the 1930s, their accumulated record of success and failure, the expansion of the welfare state, and the development of the social work profession subtly altered their campaigns' purposes and changed the emphasis on particular themes. Specifically, the chests confirmed and sought to complement rather than to criticize

the underpinning values of the universalist and socially inclusive post-war welfare regime. For the chests, a notion of inclusion had been part of their appeal from the beginning. It had been elite centred, rooted in classical notions of democracy, but it was less exclusive than particular religious or ethnic models of charity had been. In the 1950s, building on this practice, they would continue to welcome, and sometimes to arrange, the inclusion of people from diverse social backgrounds in their organizations. Universalist values underpinned rights-based, statutory forms of help, to which all were equally entitled. The chests, though not lawmakers, creatively presented equality of entitlement and the commonality of vulnerability as part of their fundraising toolkits. When they chimed in with the politicians who celebrated public programs' service to 'all the people', the fundraisers were again building on their past—namely, the base-broadening strategies of the 1930s. In their post-war use of universalist and inclusive discourse, the chests bolstered their fundraising work with cultural materials that they had helped to create.

More challenging than incorporating universalist and inclusive values was the problem of how to make charitable emotions part of a fundraising discourse that could fit with the welfare state. For the chest fundraisers, there remained an inclination to present the objects of welfare work as different: weak, pitiable, and faultlessly vulnerable, like the images of fatherless families that had been used in the interwar years. Such representations were emotional incitements to provide care—an essential element in the fundraiser's toolkit. But they were not obviously compatible with a liberal, state-centred vision of welfare as the egalitarian provision of security for all. An egalitarian vision implied that both citizens' obligations as taxpayers and citizens' rights as potential beneficiaries emerged from a single conception of individuals as generalizably alike in both responsibilities and need. In this context, could fundraisers continue to use the formerly effective images of the pitiable needy without seeming retrograde? Would Dickensian images of the poor as dangerous, horrifying, and utterly pathetic seem irrelevant and perhaps offensively sentimental to citizens who now assumed that economic growth, expanding private insurance services, and new social programs prevented or provided for real need? If the Angel of Mercy had retired to her Victorian roost, and the professional social worker had taken her place, then were appeals to modern science now inevitably more effective than emotional ones? After so many campaign failures, would a sense of futility finally harden the public to any and all appeals for the pitiable needy?

These questions point to a dilemma that may be described as the contradiction between universalist values and care values. In their struggle with this dilemma, fundraisers in the 1950s anticipated questions that, in recent years, have become politically and intellectually important. Universalist values invoke the use of abstract principle as essential to the making of policy and make fairness the central virtue of social justice. In this view, there is no real difference, except for luck, between the poor and the comfortable. This way of working toward justice in social policy is both supplemented and challenged by care values. As a supplement, care values add an awareness of the contextual specifics of need and respond to the views and values of those affected by policy. In addition, however, the care ethic casts doubt on whether blind justice is justice at all. It requires that good policy making be done with a clear eye to uneven consequences and an alert ear to a wide range of different voices. It takes as its foundational assumption that citizens are not all alike, that some groups are more vulnerable than others, and that all of us will need individualized forms of care in the course of our lives. Backed by the community work of social justice movements, the proponents of a care ethic have developed concrete improvements, such as social impact assessment tools, to help policy makers hear the voices of those whose lives their decisions affect.[1]

In the 1950s, the political context was quite different. Universalist values were in the ascendant, full of fresh promise and largely untainted by a record of perverse outcomes. The labour movement, a social force organized around the masculine role of family provider, was a key actor in the politics of social justice. Social work, though still a mainly female profession that was linked to social services, was developing ties to labour and was attracting and promoting young male leaders. Universalist values and masculine social experience were the indicators of progressive standpoints in social policy circles.[2] The 'big ticket' income programs and the government departments that administered them stood at the centre stage of policy discussions. In this context, the charities and their fundraisers could not usefully persist in presenting themselves as the agents of care against an inadequate, ploddingly rule-bound state, as they had effectively done in the 1930s. Yet they were not confident that the state would take up funding the social services, nor were they prepared to let go of those agencies' work in dealing with the peculiarities and particularities of individual need. In providing supervised play for children and social support for the isolated elderly, or counselling for families in crisis and good homes for deserted children, their agencies were doing the work of care, as yet largely unfunded by the state and practically invisible to a universalist perspective focused on the breadwinner wage.[3]

To promote charitable giving in this context required the fundraisers to describe their project and to present a notion of need in terms that could blend with welfare state discourse. By the 1950s, the agencies supported by charitable fundraising had already developed an explanation of their services as a necessary complement to subsistence maintenance of public programs: the state provides the minimum, and charity discovers and addresses other unmet needs. In the 1950s, however, this rationale to their existence encountered fresh challenges. Both at the beginning of the decade, between 1950 and 1953, and again at the end, in 1957–8, debate flared about whether or not citizens should support the chests. At each of these moments, a very thoughtful individual, well positioned in the country's social leadership, attacked the chests. In these attacks, something new was held up as the threat to private welfare: donor fatigue. At its worst, donor fatigue might become donor revolt. In these critiques, the state appeared as potentially a welcome relief rather than a threat. In this phase of the debate about the merits of public and private welfare, modern fundraising was vulnerable as much for its similarity to taxation as for its difference from it. The problem was that charity, supposedly about care and choice, was beginning to seem coercive.

## RAISING ALARM ABOUT DONOR FATIGUE

By 1950, urban Canadians were becoming accustomed to both the income tax and the Community Chest campaigns. But it would be too much to say that these systems of contribution were accepted unquestioningly. The newness of the tax system was sometimes the subject of bitter humour, as in this tidbit that was occasionally published in labour papers: 'Officials of the Income Tax Division received the following acknowledgement of a blank [i.e., an income tax form] received by a citizen: "Dear Treasury—I received your application blank, but I already belong to several good orders and do not care to join your income tax at this time"'.[4]

Ruefully, this wee joke points to the shift from a voluntary means of collective care (the fraternal order) to the compulsory one (the tax-based welfare state). Perhaps, reading this, we think, 'the poor rube! He doesn't understand that he's in a new, less free world now'. But other tax commentary of the period suggests that this joke's threat - that working-class taxpayers might not choose to 'join the income tax'—touched on a real issue of the period. What was legitimate tax avoidance, and what was criminal tax evasion? As these features of the income tax system were discovered and debated in the late 1940s, it seems clear that the new taxpayers of the new welfare state were feeling the pressures of the system, weighing its costs and benefits, and giving or withholding their consent, not just at election time but also when they were completing their tax returns.[5] In the same way, prospective donors to the Community Chests were questioning the fairness and efficiency merits of modern charity and wondering out loud whether they should continue to give.

This questioning appeared in a concentrated way between 1950 and 1953. A flashpoint came in May 1950, when a Commons-Senate committee was hearing interventions on the subject of Old Age

Security as Parliament moved toward a new federal *Old Age Pensions Act*. Speaking in favour of radical improvements to this act and a more systematic effort of the federal government to end poverty was the secretary-treasurer of the Canadian Congress of Labour, Pat Conroy. In the course of his remarks, Conroy contrasted a proper tax-funded social security system with the non-system of agencies funded by charitable donations. He called the Community Chests 'a symbol' of what was wrong with charity, which he labelled an 'organized racket'. This term was a familiar element in the left's critique of charity, by which respectable charitable fundraising was derisively associated with the more dubious sort that did nothing more than line the pockets of con artists. But the increased participation by wage earners and the union movement in chest fundraising during the war made this old critique much more consequential now than it had been in the 1930s, when it was dismissed as the inevitable communist grumbling. Conroy was an executive of an organization whose members formed a large and influential segment of Canadian employees. And they provided as much as 30 per cent of all donations made to the chests. So his critique was alarming, especially when, over the next month, it was echoed by unionists' voices in Toronto, Winnipeg, and Vancouver and reported in the national wire services.[6]

The presidents of Ottawa's chests led the local defence against Conroy's attack. According to the *Ottawa Journal's* reporter, the Protestant chest's president fulminated about how wrong it was for a 'responsible official of a responsible organization' to express such views. In a different vein, B.G. McIntyre of the Roman Catholic chest cried, 'what does he want? Does he want every charity cut to a pattern, a prescribed pattern, regardless of individual needs? The Community Chests are the last remaining evidence of human kindness, of Christian charity in our communities. It's worth a lot. It's the voluntary effort that enables us to get along without the state assuming the whole burden. Human consideration for the needs of the next-door neighbour is what pioneered this country. That's the spirit of the Community Chests'.[7] In this framing, the chests stood for care and personal relations against mere rights and bureaucratic rigidity, with religion on their side of the binary and the rights-based, tax-funded welfare state on the other.

With the teams lined up this way, Conroy had no compunction in avidly defending his side. In a long, metaphor-rich letter to the *Ottawa Journal's* editor the following day, he teasingly took credit for having incited, in the hostile reaction to his remarks, an unusual display of Catholic-Protestant unanimity.[8] He stingingly defended his view that the 'horde of agencies' financed by donations was part of a 'chaotic, inefficient and unsatisfactory' system that cost the Canadian people more than would a state-supervised welfare system designed to remove the causes of poverty rather than just tinker with its effects. Most charity workers know, he wrote, that 'they are inadequately trying to deal with a social and economic disease, and that this social cancer can only be cured by major social analysis and treatment. This disease cannot be cured by temporary applications of hot and cold poultices of voluntary charity giving'. [ . . . ]

Conroy's political rhetoric used a thumping blend of gender ridicule, class outrage, and self-congratulatory modernism and materialism to puncture the chests' balloon of equally self-congratulatory idealism. The gender element in this rhetoric flowed from a distinction between the supposedly real welfare issues, having to do with the work of breadwinning, and allegedly secondary ones, related to the maternal work of care.[9] In this scheme of things, nursing and sympathy are necessary only when the real problem, poverty, remains unaddressed. Defending working-class men against the pressures and coercions of the chests, Conroy called for them and others to exercise choice as citizens and to make rational choices rather than sentimental ones.

Of course, his discomfort with charitable emotions such as sadness and pity betrays the other emotions, such as anger and resentment, that, in a comfortably masculine way, fuelled his passion for a rationally organized system of social security. Turning around the dichotomy that makes charity about choice and tax about imposition, he appealed to the 'best value for money' discourse of efficiency. Charity is a bad choice because it costs too much. The state's role is to use taxpayers' dollars sparingly and well. 'Social analysis', not self-indulgent moaning, will produce intelligent care and genuine well-being. The well-organized, rights-based provision of services by the state constitutes true caring in this view, and emotion appears as pernicious sentiment.

As Conroy's critique was echoed and extended in the *Financial Post* and CCF-affiliated unionists in Toronto amplified his points, the pressure on chests to improve their efficiency mounted.[10] It must have seemed that a massive donor revolt was looming on the horizon. In fact, it had already begun in Detroit, as journalist Sidney Katz explained. In an article published in Maclean's on 15 November 1953, Katz assembled in one place the rallying cries of the donor revolt. The article was called 'The Unholy Mess of Our Charity Appeals'. It became essential reading for chest leaders.[11]

In his description of the problems facing charities in the post-war period, he deployed a familiar contrast. On the one (deplorable) hand was the threat of irrationality, sentimentality, and waste; on the other (hopeful) hand lay the prospect that charities might still rise to a level of efficiency, order, and fairness that would earn the respect of both business and labour and thus ensure their survival. He thought that the chests, with improved discipline, might still be the heroes of the story. In Katz's view, rational charity had as much claim to represent true caring as public provision did. But, like Conroy, Katz also called for charity's emotional content to be reformed.

[ . . . ]

To illustrate 'exorbitant expenses', Katz referred to 'the ill-fated Canadian "March of Dimes"' campaign, from which 58 *per cent* of the $360,000 raised went to campaign costs. With respect to unmet goals, he claimed that almost half (twenty-nine out of sixty) of Canada's chest campaigns failed to meet their 1952 goals. He hastened to point out that this was not a sign that federated fundraising was more vulnerable than were individual charities to failure. To support this point, he gave the example of a campaign by the new Canadian Arthritis and Rheumatism Society, whose success at raising $400,000 paled in comparison with its goal of $800,000. And he noted that the chests retained their record of superior performance in keeping collection costs low: no individual agency did as well.[12]

[ . . . ]

The 112,000 canvassers needed every year by the chests alone were getting harder to find because of 'low morale'. Giving a curious example of the fundraisers' passion for psychological expertise, Katz reported that, 'recently, a Montreal fundraiser became so worried about his volunteers that he enlisted the services of a psychologist to draw up a program that would banish their fatigue and low morale'.[13] In the short term, the risks of volunteer fatigue and donor revolt were troubling. In the longer term, Katz hinted, they threatened the very survival of the charitable sector.[14]

To Katz and the people he quoted, the problems of the charitable sector stemmed from a failure of emotional morality. Since 1945, the growth of the Canadian economy had helped to sustain more and more charitable fundraising, especially in support of health services and research: the period had seen the creation of Canadian societies for cancer, arthritis, polio, deafness, multiple sclerosis, and paraplegia. There were at least thirty national appeals of various kinds. At the same time, universities, welfare organizations, churches and temples, and hospitals were conducting capital campaigns to repair and replace buildings that had suffered decades of neglect since the 1920s. No one disputed that all, or most, of these good works were necessary. But the phenomenon of proliferating appeals raised questions about morally sound or unsound emotion. Katz pointed to a paradox: all of this altruism had a selfish side. He quoted approvingly the national Community Chest president, Montreal manufacturer Carl Reinke, castigating the leaders of non-chest charities: '[They] are guilty of rivalry, jealousy, plain selfishness, suicidal short-sightedness and a lack of team work . . . In the interest of the general welfare, it is time we stopped pussy footing about this problem for fear of offending somebody'.[15] The main targets of the Katz article were the Red Cross and the Salvation Army, which were 'deadlocked' in negotiations with the chests. These two national agencies were effective fundraisers that had, more often than not, refused membership in the chests. They believed that did not need the support of the chest apparatus, and indeed it seemed that they could raise more money on their own.[16] While their assessments of their own interests might seem rational, Reinke's series of adjectives put these supposedly altruistic agencies on the side of irrational emotions ('rivalry' and 'jealousy') and unhelpful 'competition' against the desirable emotions that underpinned regard for 'the general welfare' and the practice of 'team work'.

Katz's recommended solutions expressed what, to the chests and their supporters, was the general wisdom. One was to replace the chests with a new organization: the united fund. The exemplar of this solution was Detroit, where in 1948 business and labour had combined to limit their contributions to a single appeal and thus to force all charities to 'federate or perish'. Columbus, Ohio, had successfully followed suit in 1952. These were the foundational donor revolts. Local versions of this sort of board were also necessary, and Winnipeg was celebrated as a Canadian city that had adopted this method. Nothing in this solution called for Canadians to care more or to be more generous. These solutions simply promised that good organization would allay painful emotions—frustration, guilt, rivalrous envy—and control disproportionate emotions—'sentiment'—that seemed to produce wasted effort. And the chests, remade during the 1950s as the united appeals, were still the best mechanism for doing this work of reforming contribution. Apparently a response to rational concerns about efficiency, this was nonetheless a call for a reformed emotional morality. Selfish competition would be replaced by coordinated and well-policed means of caring, charitable emotion disciplined by rational planning.

[ . . . ]

## THE IMPERSONAL PERSONAL

In the interwar years, the struggle of the chests had been to establish their legitimacy and attract mass participation. In the war years, they felt threatened by competition from war charities and by suggestions that charity's day was over. Establishing themselves during the 1940s as part of the new welfare regime meant they served an important social function as demonstrators of need, as developers of new standards for an adequately caring society. It also meant, in reality, doing the work of promoting better income assistance policies. By the 1950s, fundraisers began to fear that their success was threatened by donor fatigue and donor revolt. And, indeed, powerful donors in business and labour were calling for the chests to live up to their promise of making private welfare efficient. 'End multiple appeals!' was the cry that condensed that demand and prompted the chests to embark on a fresh and aggressive organizational campaign. They opened their membership admission door to competing agencies and tried to redecorate their appeals with signs and symbols that would attract critical or social subaltern groups and to engage them as donors, canvassers, and participants in planning.

Among themselves, they struggled over the question of which targets could be met and how different sorts of appeals might figure in the successor failure of campaigns. From outside their committee rooms came the criticism that the chests were more like a parallel (and morally dubious) system of taxation than like true charity. The chests feared this criticism because of its potential to foment donor resistance.

The struggle around donor resistance was a new stage in the relation of charity to the welfare state. Some of the voices of donor resistance were entirely accepting of the importance of charity but thought that high-pressure fundraising was a contradiction in terms. Giving could not be giving if it was coerced. From this perspective, charity was valuable as a complement to the state, a necessary site for the expression of morally important emotion. This criticism posed no fundamental challenge to the continuation of private welfare. And the outrage about coercive fundraising was entirely compatible with a call for the creation of new, tax-funded social services. From another perspective, however, other critics of the chests' impersonality and pressure tactics meant to point to the futility of private welfare in general. This perspective, which had its roots in the traditions of labour's left, lost much ground in the 1950s as the newly expanded union movement accepted that involvement in community services offered respectability to labour and possibly political influence. In 1964, a vigorous attack on the chest by Pal O'Neal from the left wing of the BC Federation of Labour was merely a call for the reform of some chest practices and the piecemeal conversion of some agencies to management under government auspices. He publicly disavowed ever having told anyone not to donate to the united appeal or any other 'legitimate charitable campaign'.[17] Charity was no longer vulnerable to the criticism that it was a weapon against the welfare state: its demonstration function committed it wholly to encouraging the shift to public

responsibility of generally accepted services. The anti-statist hammer was no longer part of the fundraisers' toolkit, and its critics could not turn it against fundraisers.

In other ways, too, the responses made to the threat of donor revolt in the 1950s worked, like the demonstration function argument, to make the chest organization and campaigns wholly compatible with an expanded and expanding state. The organizational innovations and the inclusion practices prompted by the panic about multiple appeals expressed values that blended smoothly with public welfare discourse. Efficiency, fairness, representativeness of the community (electorate), and representation of the donor (tax-payer) were all common terms in liberal democratic welfare state talk. The chests had worked hard to blend into the political scenery. Judging from the terms in which they were criticized, they had succeeded too well for some people's taste in making the charities resemble the welfare state. Supposedly the expressions of a caring society, both the chests and the social programs of the welfare state seemed rather to be coercive and inadequate to the job of meeting needs. At the end of the 1950s, the slogan 'everyone gives, everyone benefits', might have been cynically rephrased as 'everyone is pressured, and no one is satisfied'.

In this context, fundraisers' use in annual campaigns of social events and sentiment was merely another kind of pressure tactic. Neither the mass rally launching a campaign nor the United Way movie night entailed participation in a community project in the way that, for example, actual volunteer social service did. Such fundraising events were just methods of creating a sense that 'everyone' is involved and thereby creating a norm of contribution as part of community belonging. This is a subtle coercion that had little to do with care, even though it bespoke universality and a superficial social inclusion. In addition, the abstract icons of need that the campaign ads laid out in their sweetly appealing monotony, while meant to incite feeling, were themselves quite impersonal. If the personal is about particularity, then these images were no more invitations to a personal charitable relationship than pornography is to a personal sexual one. Idealized images of need are meant to trigger emotional automatism: impulse, not moral reflection. Again it is easy to see such methods as being designed to bypass conscious choice and charity.

In their appeal to a generalized, almost biological, response to universal human vulnerabilities, these ads worked within the universalism of a liberal welfare state culture. If small children and the elderly are the needy, then we are all sometimes the needy during the span of our lives. But need actually comes in many human forms. Most make more complex demands on our emotions and moral reasoning than do innocent children. Both in fundraising and in social policy work, people ask what is a 'sellable' representation of need. The answer is rarely, for example, multiproblem adult men convicted of sex crimes. One solution to the risk that such predictable biases pose is the liberal universalist one: to wear a mental blindfold when setting up systems to meet human needs. This is a good and important solution. By that means, the goods available as human and citizen rights are distributed to the sweet and the sour alike. But

the blindfold solution has a political weakness. That weakness lies in the feature that it shares with the sentimental charity ad: its abstraction of the needy. Being represented without particular traits and getting help without particular emotions, the holders of universal rights (and the programs that confer those rights) are vulnerable to attack by opponents who effectively use images of particular unattractive, supposedly undeserving, recipients to rouse emotions of disgust envy, anger, and fear. These aversive emotions are deployed to discredit programs whose recipients' entitlements rest on the recipients being imagined as abstract citizens without traits. In the welfare state regime, it could be that fundraising for private charity might help to close off this line of attack on rights-based programs. It could be the job of fundraising to make compelling, emotionally charged representations about needs for community and caring in ways that would underscore the value both of charities and of tax-funded programs. And today's United Way advertising often does just that. But at the end of the 1950s, the fear of donor fatigue drove fundraisers to use threadbare, sentimental images of need. Designed to counter allegations of impersonality, this emotional appeal itself was impersonal.

# NOTES

1.  Olena Hankivsky, *Social Policy and the Ethic of Care* (Vancouver: UBC Press, 2004). See *Hypatia* 10, 2 (1995) in particular on two essays in that issue: Monique Deveaux, 'Shifting Paradigms: Theorizing Care and Justice in Political Theory', 115–19, and Joan C. Tronto, 'Care as a Basis for Radical Political Judgements', 141–49.

2.  Linda Gordon, 'Social Insurance and Public Assistance: The Influence of Gender in Welfare Thought in the United States, 1890–1935', *American Historical Review* 97, 1 (1992): 27–31; Shirley Tillotson, 'Dollars, Democracy, and the Children's Aid Society:

The Eclipse of Gwendolen Lantz', in *Mothers of the Municipality*, ed. Judith Fingard and Janet Guildford (Toronto: University of Toronto Press, 2004), 88–9.

3.  Nancy Christie, *Engendering the State: Family, Work, and Welfare in Canada* (Toronto: University of Toronto Press, 2000).

4.  *The Call* 1, 4 (1945): 7; *Labour Statesman*, April 1950, 16.

5.  J. Harvey Perry, *Taxes, Tariffs, and Subsidies: A History of Canadian Fiscal Development*, Vol. 2 (Toronto: University of Toronto Press, 1955), 392–5; Canadian Tax Foundation, *Report on the Proceedings of a Conference on the Income Tax Bill,*

8–9 December 1947 (Ottawa: Canadian Tax Foundation, n.d.), 21–2; William Anderson, 'Economic Security for Older Canadians', *Canadian Welfare* 25, 5 (1950): 6.

6. Clippings, 'Multiple Charity Drives Condemned', *Vancouver Sun*, 7 June 1950; and 'Says Charity Groups Growing like Weeds', *Ottawa Journal*, 13 June 1950; telegram from Betty Govan to Miss Gould [sic], 13 June 1950; Eurith Goold to R.E.G. Davis, 14 June 1950; and memo from Eurith Goold to Henry [Stubbins], 14 June 1950, Library and Archives Canada (LAC), Records of the Canadian Council on Social Dvelopment (CCSD), MG 28 I 10, vol. 77, file 564 'Labour-General'; minutes, meeting of 6 June 1950, City of Vancouver Archives (CVA), Records of the Vancouver, New Westminster, and District Trades and Labor Council, Add. Mss. 307, 269; Board of directors, executive director's report, 25 July 1950, CVA, United Way of the Lower Mainland (UWLM), Add. Mss. 849, vol. 617-B-1.

7. Clipping, 'Community Chests Hinting Libel in Pat Conroy's "Racket" Charge', *Ottawa Journal*, 12 May 1950, LAC, CCSD, MG 28 I 10, vol. 77, file 564 'Labour-General'.

8. A typescript copy of Conroy's letter, dated 13 May 1950, is in LAC, CCSD, MG 28 I 10, vol. 77, file 564 '1942–1951 Labour-General'.

9. Shirley Tillotson, 'Class and Community in Canadian Welfare Work, 1933–1960', *Journal of Canadian Studies* 32, 1 (1997): 63–92.

10. Clippings, 'Says Charity Groups Growing like Weeds', *Ottawa Journal*, 13 June 1950; and 'Unjust and Unfair' (editorial), *Toronto Star*, 17 June 1950; Henry Stubbins, report of field visit to Community Chest of Greater Toronto, 29 June 1950, LAC, CCSD, MG 28 I 10, Vol. 77, file 564 'Labour-General'; Ronald Williams, 'Is Charity Campaigning Getting out of Hand?' *Financial Post*, 5 August 1950, 1.

11. Sidney Katz, 'The Unholy Mess of Our Charity Appeals', *Maclean's*, 15 November 1953, 20, 95–99; George Hart to Henry Stubbins, 1 December 1943, LAC, CCSD, MG 28 I 10, vol. 228, file 228–17.

12. Katz, 'Unholy Mess', 95, 97.

13. Ibid., 20.

14. Ibid.

15. Ibid., 95.

16. Ibid., 98.

17. Clippings, 'Mr. O'Neal's Statements', *Vancouver Sun*, 7 October 1964; 'Good for You, Pat O'Neal!' (editorial), n.d.; and *Vancouver Labour Statesman*, October 1964, LAC, Canadian Labour Congress Papers, MG 28 I 103, reel H223.

4  From Alvin Finkel, *Social Policy and Practice in Canada: A History* (Waterloo: Wilfrid Laurier University Press, 2006), 169–92.

# THE MEDICARE DEBATE, 1945–80

'The government sponsors the TB testing of cattle, pays for loss and has blood testing every year free of charge. What about humans? Let's take our hats off to Russia as far as health is concerned'.[1] This was the conclusion of a group of farmers in Seaforth, Ontario, meeting in late 1943 to discuss the idea of a national universal medical care program. Sponsored by *Farm Radio Forum*, a CBC radio series, groups of farmers across the country responded to the proposals that were being mooted for state medical insurance. But the proposals being discussed were more radical than Canada's current medicare system. Medical care was to be removed from the private marketplace completely, and the costs of hospital care, doctors' visits, pharmaceutical costs, dental care, and eyecare were to be covered by a state-funded regime.

The farmers' groups revealed that conditions of health care in Canada, particularly in rural areas, were often grim. For example, a farmer in Elderbank, Nova Scotia, stated 'Our doctor has 275 miles of highway to travel. Many do not consult him because of cost of services. Immediate federal action is needed'. In Leader, Saskatchewan, another reported: 'Our school is never visited by either doctor or nurse. This fall one family had a child with contagious disease . . . finally the school was closed up, as teacher and all pupils were sick. Mothers here, who never have a doctor at the birth of a child, least of all pre-natal care, most of them are wrecks and old long before their time'.[2] Polls suggested that a national medicare scheme was the most popular reform discussed during the Second World War and its aftermath. In both 1944 and 1948, 80 per cent of Canadians expressed support, with the Québécois sharing this sentiment despite the claims of their provincial government and the Catholic Church that national medicare posed a threat to Quebec's traditions of individualism and Church control of social services.[3]

The dismal state of health services across the country fuelled the demand for state action. Canadians had reason to believe that they did not enjoy the full benefits of the medical knowledge of their time. While Sweden and New Zealand, both with universal state medical programs, had the world's lowest infant death rates in 1942—29 per 1,000 live births—Canada's rate was 54. In all provinces, the infant mortality rate in rural areas was higher than the urban rate, usually quite significantly, for example 79 to 51 in Nova Scotia, 76 to 43 in Manitoba, and 63 to 30 in British Columbia. Significantly, Saskatchewan, where pressure from women's groups in the interwar period had led to the hiring of municipal doctors and the creation of 'union' hospitals (hospitals operated by several municipalities uniting to pay for their construction and operation), had the country's lowest rural death rate for infants. In that province, 52 children per 1,000 died in their first year of life compared with 43 in the province's cities.[4]

Still, the State Hospital and Medical League of Saskatchewan estimated that 34 per cent of all deaths were premature and that half of all provincial residents suffering disabling illnesses could have been free of disease if preventive care had been applied. As Tommy Douglas, soon-to-be premier of that province and generally regarded as the 'father of Canadian medicare',[5] noted in a broadcast in 1943, 'If the average person were checked over by a clinic at stated intervals, and treatment were available before the illness had reached a critical stage, not only would we live longer but the cost of health services in the aggregate would be less than it is now'.[6] The National Committee for Mental Hygiene reported in 1939 that only 10 per cent of Canadians could comfortably pay for their medical services in a free-market system while 25 per cent were completely dependent on charity; the remaining 65 per cent could pay for normal services but were forced into debt or rejection of treatment if an operation or long-term care was required.[7]

Yet, despite popular support for medicare, it was not implemented in the early postwar period and, over the next two decades, pro- and anti-medicare forces were locked in constant battle. Advocates of medicare seemingly won, but the program that emerged disappointed them both in the limitations of its coverage and the structure of medical care that it embraced. This essay explores the structures of political decision-making, formal and informal, that resulted in the creation of a particular type of medicare in 1968.

## FROM THE GREEN BOOK TO HOSPITAL INSURANCE

Though the federal government balked at the potential costs of national health insurance in 1945, it recognized that Canadians expected governments at all levels to invest in health care.[8] In 1948, it announced a program of conditional health grants to provinces to build and operate hospitals, train medical personnel, and carry out health research. The wealthier provinces, in turn, also provided funding to expand their network of hospitals and to increase the number of graduates from medical schools. From 1948 to 1953 alone, 46,000 hospital beds were added across Canada.[9]

Saskatchewan had elected a CCF government led by T.C. Douglas in 1944, and it had pledged to take steps towards the creation of a universal medicare scheme. Despite the unavailability of matching federal funds, Saskatchewan forged ahead with plans to create universal hospital insurance in the province and end the distinction in hospitals between paying clients and charity cases. It immediately undertook a hospital construction project to ensure that most residents lived close enough to a hospital to receive care close to home. Then it legislated tax-funded hospitalization insurance in 1947, becoming the first jurisdiction in North America to implement such a program. The province's general revenues as well as a prepaid monthly premium levied on families and singles would pay the costs of insuring that need, and not financial means, determined who used Saskatchewan hospitals. Saskatchewan physicians largely supported this measure, while hospital administrators who opposed the legislation kept quiet after the premier threatened that the province could take control of the hospitals if the existing administrators no longer wished to run them.[10]

British Columbia's Coalition government of Liberals and Conservatives faced serious competition from that province's CCF and also decided to implement a universal hospital insurance program, financed by premiums and a 3 per cent sales tax. Claiming that it wanted to blend the concepts of private and public responsibility, it included 'co-insurance' (user fees) within its hospital insurance program, despite protests from the CCF and the labour movement. Alberta presented yet a third model for paying hospital and other medical bills. Decrying both compulsory

participation and centralization, the government established a series of health districts in 1946. District boards, which included both physician and consumer representatives, negotiated a health insurance scheme with municipalities, including the services to be covered for a maximum payment of $10 per adult. While most costs were borne by the voluntary subscriber to the insurance scheme, hospital fees were set at $1 per day, with the municipality and the province splitting the remaining operating costs. Manitoba and Newfoundland also had voluntary programs, which had been established before Newfoundland joined Canada, enrolling about half the province's population.[11]

Louis St. Laurent, like Mackenzie King, was less than enthusiastic about the federal government creating a national health insurance scheme. But he was under tremendous pressure from the five provinces that were heavily subsidizing patients' costs to implement a national program and lift at least half the burden of costs from the provinces.[12] Ontario weighed in on the provinces' side in 1955. About 70 per cent of Ontario residents enjoyed some form of hospital insurance coverage, but Premier Leslie Frost faced public pressure for the government to fund hospital insurance. This included pressure from hospital authorities. The community elites that ran the hospitals had been dealt a body blow by the Depression, as the number of paying customers dwindled while charity cases climbed. In the post-war period, they came to believe that their institutions needed the economic stability that public insurance alone could provide.[13]

Frost responded by insisting that federal involvement was required, a viewpoint he stressed at a federal-provincial conference in October 1955. St. Laurent reluctantly agreed to federal-provincial discussions on hospital insurance. These discussions led to the *Hospital Insurance and Diagnostic Services Act* of April 1957, which established a formula for federal grants to provinces that implemented a provincial hospital insurance scheme. About half of all hospital costs would be borne by the federal government. The provinces chose the method of financing for their plans, but there were penalties for provinces that levied user fees. Passage of the legislation was eased by the lack of opposition from the Canadian Medical Association (CMA), which, since 1949, had supported user-pay hospitals.[14] Their change of heart was dictated by the need to assuage public anger regarding high costs for hospital stays and to avoid more radical medicare programs that included costs of doctors' visits. The private insurance companies were the big losers in the debate, but were determined to fight to maintain the rest of their health insurance business by denouncing further state intervention in medical care.

## TOWARDS MEDICARE

If governments were to get involved in medical insurance, it was likely that they would require physicians to accept lower rates for various procedures as a means of reducing overall medical costs. In the United States, the growth of the private health insurance industry, also dominated by physicians, gave the American Medical Association (AMA) an incentive to spend lavishly to lobby politicians and propagandize Americans regarding the evils of a public health insurance program. Their efforts forestalled President Harry Truman's plans in the late 1940s to introduce a national universal medical insurance scheme despite widespread popular support for such a policy. In the context of the Cold War, the AMA painted state medicine as an exemplar of the programs that unfree Communist states imposed upon their hapless citizens, an image that was ironic in light of the introduction of state medicine in Britain and other European democracies. Supported by big business organizations, the AMA developed an impregnable opposition to state medicine in Congress that united northern Republicans with southern Democrats, the latter often wealthy conservatives elected

from pro-medicare constituencies but able to avoid the issue by making the preservation of racial segregation the key to their election strategies.[15]

At the federal-provincial conference in 1955, St. Laurent indicated that the federal government would only consider a national health insurance program when a majority of provinces representing a majority of citizens were prepared to institute provincial programs. [ . . . ]

As with hospital insurance, it was the provinces that stepped up to the plate first to offer universal programs and then put the federal government on the hot seat for failure to make such provision a national responsibility. Once again, it was Saskatchewan's CCF government that led the way. Tommy Douglas, running for re-election in 1960, announced that with the federal government now paying half of Saskatchewan's hospital bills, his government could afford to implement universal medicare. Both the urban and rural poor, including most farmers, were unable to buy medical coverage, and the Saskatchewan government, like other provincial governments, was picking up the tab for medical bills for a growing section of the poor. It argued that this was unfair, first because it stigmatized those requited to rely on state aid and discouraged them from seeing doctors, and second because it placed heavy financial burdens on the state that a universal plan would offset with the tax or premium contributions of the better-off, which the private insurers claimed for themselves. But Saskatchewan faced a huge fight in implementing its program.

Saskatchewan had played a pioneering role in the provision of medical services in Canada. Its municipal doctor schemes and union hospitals of the interwar period, the result of the work of the farm women's movement, and particularly Violet McNaughton, challenged the notion of health as a commodity to be purchased by those with the wherewithal to do so. Nonetheless, such programs relied on voluntary participation by doctors rather than state coercion. The CCF's experiments with full-state operation of medical services before the 1960s were limited to a few areas of the province in which the government was able to enlist the support of progressive-minded physicians. However, after the government announced its intentions to have a province-wide medical insurance scheme, a community clinic movement sprang up, a natural outgrowth of the populism that had produced both the major farm movements in Saskatchewan and the CCF itself. Health clinics with a holistic model of health, in which nurses, social workers, nutritionists, and dentists worked alongside doctors, enrolled about 50,000 people in 35 regional associations in a province of less than 1 million people.[16]

Most physicians had no intention of becoming salaried professionals working in state-run clinics whose policies were determined by elected boards of non-physicians. In line with the CMA, which aided them in carrying out an extensive propaganda campaign against the government's plan, Saskatchewan doctors insisted that individuals and families should pay their medical bills via private insurance. If the province insisted that all citizens should be insured, it should direct them to buy insurance from a private plan. Only the poor should have their bills paid by the state, with the state paying physician-dictated rates for services that private plans paid. In July 1962, when the government proved adamant that it would proceed with its plans, the Saskatchewan branch of the CMA organized a withdrawal of physician services.[17]

Upper- and middle-class supporters of the physicians formed 'Keep Our Doctors' committees that accused the government of imposing an unworkable policy for socialist ideological reasons. The corporate-owned daily papers, always hostile to the CCF government, terrified people by suggesting that the province might lose most of its doctors. With both the CMA and national business organizations spending extravagantly to reinforce this message through television and radio advertising, as well as by using the appearances of 'expert' witnesses on news shows, Saskatchewan residents were subjected to non-stop propaganda against state medicare. This was offset by the support for medicare from the Saskatchewan Federation of Labour and the major farm organizations, though these groups had limited access to the media.

The doctors' strike ended after twenty-two days as a result of government negotiations with the Saskatchewan branch of the CMA, in which the doctors conceded a universal state program and the government conceded many of the demands of the doctors. There would be no salaries for doctors or payments by the number of patients that they served. Instead, fee for service, the principle that governed private insurance plans, would remain sacrosanct. Doctors would continue to operate from their own private offices, and not only would doctors not be forced to participate in a community clinic, but those who chose to practise in a clinic would receive direct funding from the state rather than have to deal with the community clinic board. Finally, doctors would have the choice of participating directly in the state plan either by requiring patients to pay bills and then bill the plan or by staying out of the plan altogether and billing patients with whatever fees they deemed appropriate. This was simply a face-saving measure since both sides understood that most patients would choose to patronize doctors who were in the prepaid medicare scheme.

[ . . . ]

## MEDICARE'S OPPONENTS

Supporters of continued privatization and voluntary participation in medical insurance included the Canadian Medical Association, the Canadian Dental Association, the Canadian Chamber of Commerce, the entire private insurance industry, the pharmaceutical industry, and representatives of most other industries. The premiers of British Columbia, Alberta, Manitoba, and Ontario opposed medicare while Quebec's Premier Lesage was opposed to federal legislation in a sphere of provincial competence. The Atlantic premiers generally supported medicare but wanted the federal government to pay the lion's share of the costs and to give them time to phase in any universal program because they faced shortages of medical personnel. Only Woodrow Lloyd in Saskatchewan was an unequivocal supporter of a fully state-operated scheme.[18]

The advocates of private insurance used a variety of arguments. For example, the British Columbia Medical Association, following the lead of the CMA,[19] argued that the monies that medicare would absorb could be better spent on 'scholarships for medical students, to add rehabilitative and chronic care kids to our hospitals, to extend our mental health programme, and for many other important services'. Directing taxes instead towards paying medical insurance was 'foolhardy' because it meant 'providing a service to those who are already providing it for themselves, as most British Columbians are doing through our system of voluntary health insurance'.[20]

The CMA's brief added that the hospital insurance program, which the physicians regarded favourably, had expanded demand for hospital beds. The federal and provincial governments, it suggested, having created this demand by making hospitalization a free good, now had to cough up the money for more beds. Implicit, however, in this argument was that prior to the existence of a public program, the real health needs of the population, in the area of hospitalization, had been underserved despite the availability of private hospitalization insurance.[21] Nor did the physicians try to claim that private health insurance was meeting everyone's needs. They conceded that to achieve universal medical insurance coverage, about 3 million Canadians would have to have their bills paid by taxes collected from the rest of Canadians, who, in turn, would also have to pay for their own private insurance.

The CMA, while avoiding the Cold War rhetoric of its American counterpart in its opposition to state medicine, emphasized that doctors as a group would be hostile to state medical insurance and even more hostile to any efforts by the government to move them away from individual practice into group settings that might also include other types of medical practitioners. 'Physicians by nature and by training are strongly individualistic and it is not given to all doctors to function happily and efficiently as a member of a group'. It could lead, in any case, to 'assembly-line medicine'.[22]

The Canadian Dental Association (CDA) also claimed that state moneys could be better directed at other goals than a national insurance program. Admitting that most Canadians had little or no access to dentists, they pointed out that there was a dismal ratio of dentists to population—1 to 3,000, compared with 1 to 1,900 in the United States, with regional gaps that were best demonstrated by Newfoundland and Labrador's ratio of 1 dentist per 11,000 residents. If all Canadians suddenly had access to dental services, there would simply be too few dentists to accommodate them.

The dentists admitted that 'education and income separately and together are strongly associated with going to the dentist'. Yet the dentists largely ignored their own insight that money kept many Canadians from properly caring for their teeth, focusing instead on 'people's lack of interest in preventative measures' as the way to improve dental health. They recommended that provinces make fluoridation of water supplies mandatory for municipalities, that Canadians consume less sugar, and that more government funds go to dental research. While cool to state involvement in dentistry, outside of dental education and research, the CDA did recognize some need for governments to fund potential consumers of dentists' services. Like the physicians, they supported state funding of necessary services for destitute Canadians. If governments were going to provide state dental service programs, they should restrict their programs to children.[23]

[ . . . ]

Both pharmacists and the pharmaceutical industry strongly opposed inclusion of prescription drugs in a state medical insurance plan, since it carried the implicit threat of state regulation of drug prices. The Canadian Pharmaceutical Manufacturers' Association (CPMA) reported soothingly that competition was lively at the manufacturing and retail levels of the industry: 'The competitive aspect of research and development, combined with behaviour of prices and promotional activities, indicates that a satisfactory level of competition exists in the industry. Furthermore, this competition is directed in a manner which is socially desirable. Growth, product development and the general level of prices have been favourable rather than unfavourable to the consumer'.[24] The pharmaceutical manufacturers assured the commissioners that after-tax profits of the industry were modest and the industry's expenditures on promotion were fairly restrained and served the purpose of informing physicians and others about useful pharmaceuticals.

In fact, the industry's profits, measured as a percentage of invested capital, were double the average for Canadian industries as a whole from 1953 to 1958. A study prepared in 1961 for the federal Department of Justice by the director of Investigation and Research, Combines Investigation Act, noted that apart from making large profits, the industry was absolutely profligate in its promotion expenditures, as it worked tirelessly to press physicians to use various new drugs. Patent laws protected drug companies that developed a new pharmaceutical product, and it was the knowledge that they had a monopoly for many years over a particular drug that caused pharmaceutical companies to spend millions trying to convince physicians to prescribe their product.

[ . . . ] Health care providers, such as doctors, dentists, and pharmacy owners, had a common interest in establishing a high price

for their services, and happily confounded private provision with competition and efficient pricing.

Ultimately, the two arguments that were heard most frequently to discredit a compulsory public medical system were that it would deprive health practitioners of the freedoms that all business people ought legitimately to have in a democratic society, and that it would be so costly as to provoke crushing levels of taxation that would destroy Canada's industrial competitiveness. The CMA stated starkly: 'We consider government intervention into the field of prepaid medical care to the point of becoming a monopolistic purchaser of medical services, to be a measure of civil conscription. We would urge this Royal Commission to support our view that, exclusive of states of emergency, civil conscription of any segment of the Canadian population is contrary to our democratic philosophy.[25] Premier Leslie Frost of Ontario was prominent among anti-medicare politicians to invoke the industrial competitiveness argument. The country, he averred, 'has already become a high cost economy. And that is affecting our trading and developmental position'.[26]

## MEDICARE'S SUPPORTERS

Medicare's supporters suggested that Canadians had collective rights to the best medical treatments that were available regardless of income, and that the right of individuals to receive affordable medical service outweighed the alleged rights of medical practitioners to price their services as they deemed best. Despite the crushing majority support for medicare evident in opinion polls, few Canadians were willing to come forward as individuals and suggest that they had received second-rate medical treatment because they were poor. A careful scouring of the thousands of briefs before the Hall Commission reveals only one case where an individual Canadian denounced her doctors for providing her family mediocre care because of their inability to pay. Her physician's scathing personal attack upon her in response demonstrated why few Canadians had the temerity to reveal personal cases of receiving poor treatment or being driven to bankruptcy to obtain necessary medical attention.[27] Instead, the horror stories that the commissioners heard as well as the main arguments countering the claims of private medicine came from organizations. Trade unions, social worker and welfare organizations, farmers' federations, and the United Church of Canada convinced the commissioners that they should adopt an ambitious national program.

The Canadian Association of Social Workers placed the case before the Hall Commission that many were deterred from seeking medical assistance at clinics because several hours might be required for them to fill out forms at the accounting department. Meanwhile, many people of middle means who did not qualify for the state care available to the indigent avoided seeking needed medical care because 'it is going to come out of the food budget, or come out of the youngsters' clothing budget or something like this'. The social workers observed that the stigma of receiving a charitable service discouraged usage of the service. It also created problems regarding the proper cut-off income for recipients. Better to have medicare available to all Canadians so that no one had to see it as either a special right or a special shame.[28]

The Canadian Federation of Agriculture (CFA) and several other major farm groups appeared before the commission and indicated that the majority of farmers could not afford private health insurance.[29] The United Church of Canada, whose General Council had called for a contributory national health plan since 1952, confirmed the CFA's impressions. The United Church brief added that urban immigrants, particularly unskilled workers from southern Italy, were perhaps even more vulnerable. These people were underpaid, ill-housed, insecure about their income, and prone as a result to both physical

and mental illness. Yet they were too impoverished to be able to set aside the money for private health insurance.[30]

But the trade union movement probably proved the most effective in demolishing the arguments of industry and physicians that Canadians were gradually meeting their medical needs privately. In the post-war period, the trade union movement, which enrolled about a third of Canadian workers thanks to wartime and early post-war organizing successes, had succeeded in winning a variety of 'fringe benefits' for their members in addition to wage increases and improvements in working conditions. A medical benefits package had become a common gain for trade unionists, and such prepaid medical insurance swelled the numbers of families whom the private insurance companies could claim as they pooh-poohed the need for a public program.

Unions' characterizations of the limitations of private coverage undermined such insurance industry boasting. National, provincial, and labour federations complained that the profit-driven insurance schemes that enrolled their members tended to severely restrict or deny coverage altogether in such areas as preventive health services, rehabilitation, mental health, dental services, and social services. Prescription drugs, nursing aid, appliances, eyeglasses, and hearing aids were rarely covered. Yet most of these plans had 'costly deductible and co-insurance charges'. As the Canadian Labour Congress (CLC) concluded, 'It is too much to expect that a complete range of services can be made available on a universal basis to the Canadian people within the near future through the mere extension of the private pre-payment schemes. It is not physically, financially nor administratively possible'.[31]

## THE HALL REPORT AND THE IMPLEMENTATION OF MEDICINE

Emmett Hall and the majority of his fellow commissioners were won over, in large part, by the values and arguments of the supporters of a universal medicare program. Their 1964 report made some obeisance in the direction of business and physicians by recognizing that no doctor should be forced to join a national medicare program, and that doctors should remain in private practice even if they joined medicare rather than becoming civil servants working in government offices. Even more of a victory for the physicians was the commission's rejection of the National Health Service model of salaried physicians, which the labour movement had endorsed. Instead, the commissioners supported continuation of the fee-for-service model which was a hallmark of private insurance.[32]

However, the overall direction of the report reflected the persuasiveness of the opponents of the argument made by businesses and physicians. Wrote the commissioners: 'The achievement of the highest possible health standards for all our people must become a primary objective of national policy and a cohesive factor contributing to national unity, involving individual and community responsibilities and actions. This objective can best be achieved through a comprehensive, universal Health Services Programme for the Canadian people'. 'Comprehensive', in Hall's view, included 'all health services, preventive, diagnostic, curative and rehabilitative, that modern medical and other services can provide'.[33] This meant that governments should not only provide universal coverage for physicians' services and for hospitalization but should also cover prescription drug payments for all Canadians, home care and prosthetic services as required, dental services for children, expectant mothers, and public assistance recipients, and eyecare for children and the poor. Most of these programs would exclude user fees, though each prescription would bear a dollar user fee and adults would be expected to pay one-third the cost of eyeglasses, which would however be free for children.[34] Taxation would pay for all Canadians to be covered by the national health program.

In short, Hall had rejected the voluntary medical insurance schemes that Ontario, Alberta, and British Columbia had proposed as alternatives to the Saskatchewan plan because only the latter appeared to guarantee the potential of full coverage to all Canadians for all necessary medical services.

[ . . . ]

The Hall Report put pressure on Lester Pearson's Liberal government, which had been elected in 1963, albeit without a parliamentary majority, to live up to its medicare promises. The Liberals had promised a national medicare program that would provide comprehensive services free of charge to children till they left school and to Canadians over 65 years of age. Everyone else would have services by general practitioners, specialists, and surgeons, along with diagnostic services, covered, except for the first $25. Even the left-wingers in the government were taken aback by the scope of services that Hall wanted a national program to cover. For a year the government waffled, and even in the throne speech of 1965, the government committed itself to medicare in only the vaguest terms. The NDP, which had endorsed the Hall Report *in toto*, demanded that the government implement its fullest set of recommendations immediately.[35]

The eventual compromise reached within the government called for medicare to be introduced in phases. The first phase would add physician and diagnostic services to the existing hospitalization coverage, while other components of the Hall vision would be introduced as fiscal means became available. In practice, though few Canadians could know it at the time, there would be no second phase for medicare, at least during the twentieth century.

The Liberals called a federal election in late 1965 but narrowly failed again to form a majority government. Their commitment to a modified version of the Hall recommendations during the election left them little alternative afterwards but to legislate a medicare bill. Initially, Pearson aimed for 1 July 1967, the one hundredth birthday of the country. However, continued provincial reluctance to accept the federal principles argued against such speed, as did the change in the balance of forces in the Liberal cabinet after the election.

Walter Gordon, the progressive finance minister, took responsibility for having advised Pearson to hold an early election, and resigned from cabinet. His replacement, Mitchell Sharp, held views similar to those of organized business and appeared in no hurry to implement medicare, which he claimed could have an undue impact on the federal treasury. Robert Stanfield, the new leader of the Conservative party, denounced 'a vast new spending program'.[36] But Sharp and his supporters were only able to delay medicare's implementation by one year.[37] On 1 July 1968, funds would be available to provinces with a medicare scheme that met the four principles of medicare. Still, the division within the Pearson cabinet encouraged provinces that opposed universality and public administration to move slowly. Only Saskatchewan and British Columbia presented plans in the month after the medicare deadline and began to receive federal funding in July.

By then, the dithering Pearson had been replaced as head of the government by the more decisive Pierre Elliott Trudeau. Trudeau scotched any further attempts from within the cabinet or the provinces to allow for either delays or modification of the medicare legislation. Within a year all provinces but Quebec had announced plans that met the criteria of the *Medical Services Act* of 1968. Quebec entered the plan in 1972.[38]

[ . . . ]

The creation of a national network of provincial medicare programs, all sub-scribing to the principles of comprehensiveness, universality, portability, and public administration, represented a major victory for progressive forces in Canada, backed by overwhelming public opinion. The combination of public campaigning by important social movements, including labour, farmers, and social workers, with support from key elements of the Liberal Party and the civil service, resulted in a Tory-appointed royal commission failing to suggest some sort of public-private mix that largely subordinated health service provision to profit-seeking health insurance companies and physicians. In turn, this led the Liberal government, divided for two decades on whether to implement its promises originally made in 1919 for a national public program, to finally deliver.

Canada's 'first phase' of medicare provided far less comprehensive coverage for illness prevention and treatment than the National Health Service in Britain and similar programs in Scandinavia and Holland. The Soviet Union and its Cold War satellites in eastern Europe all provided sweeping free comprehensive medical care programs. The Hall Commission had looked to western European models rather than the United States in framing its recommendations, and the government rhetorically accepted the commission's conclusions. In practice, the desire to keep costs down resulted in a watering down of Hall's proposals that saw medicare's 'first phase' limited to coverage of visits to hospitals and physicians, and diagnostic services. Further phases were not legislated. The late 1960s represented the high point of social reform rather than a first installment on social reforms that would fundamentally redistribute wealth in Canada.

# NOTES

1. Health Study Bureau, *Review of Canada's Health Needs and Insurance Proposals* (Toronto, ON: Health Study Bureau, 1946), 41.

2. Ibid., 40–3.

3. Malcolm G. Taylor, *Health Insurance and Canadian Public Policy: The Seven Decisions that Created the Canadian Health Insurance System* (Montreal, QC: McGill-Queen's University Press, 1978), 166.

4. Health Study Bureau, *Review of Canada's Health Needs*, 3–4.

5. Georgina M. Taylor, 'Ground for Common Action: Violet McNaughton's Agrarian Feminism and the Origins of the Farm Women's Movement in Canada' (Ph.D. thesis, Carleton University, 1997).

6. 'CCF Broadcast by T.C. Douglas, MP', William Lyon Mackenzie King Papers, MG 26, J1, Vol. 346, p. 297011, Library and Archives of Canada, (LAC).

7. Ibid., p. 297809.

8. 'Resolutions, Annual Meeting, held in Regina June 6–11, 1947', National Council of Women of Canada (NCWC) Papers, MG 28 I 25, Vol. 90, File 1, LAC.

9. Malcolm G. Taylor, 'The Canadian Health-Care System: After Medicare', in *Health and Canadian Society: Sociological Perspectives*, 2nd edn, ed. David Coburn, Carl D'Arcy, George M. Torrance, and Peter New (Toronto, ON: Fitzhenry and Whiteside, 1987), 74.

10. Duane Mombourquette, '"An Inalienable Right": The, CCF and Rapid Health Care Reform, 1944–1948', in *Social Welfare Policy in Canada: Historical Readings*, ed. Raymond B. Blake and Jeff Keshen (Toronto, ON: Copp Clark, 1995), 298–302.

11. Taylor, 'The Canadian Health-Care System', 74, 84; Margaret A. Ormsby, *British Columbia: A History* (Vancouver, BC: Macmillan, 1958), 487; Alvin Finkel, *The Social Credit Phenomenon in Alberta* (Toronto, ON: University of Toronto Press, 1989), 123.

12. Eugene Vayda and Raisa B. Deber, 'The Canadian Health-Care System: A Developmental Overview', in *Social Welfare Policy*, ed. Blake and Keshen, 315.

13. David Gagan and Rosemary Gagan, *For Patients of Moderate Means: A Social History of the Voluntary Public General Hospital in Canada,* 1890–1950 (Montreal, QC: McGill-Queen's University Press, 2002).

14. Brief of Canadian Medical Association, April 1962, Canada, Royal Commission on Health Services, RG 33, Series 78, Vol. 19, File 278, LAC.

15. Monte M. Poen, *Harry S. Truman Versus the Medical Lobby: The Genesis of Medicare* (Columbia, MS: University of Missouri Press, 1979); Lawrence R. Jacobs, *The Health of Nations: Public Opinion and the Making of American and British Health Policy* (Ithaca, NY: Cornell University Press, 1993).

16. Joan Feather, 'From Concept to Reality: Formation of the Swift Current Health Region', *Prairie Forum* 16, 1 (Spring 1991): 59–80; Joan Feather, 'Impact of the Swift Current Health Region: Experiment or Model', *Prairie Forum* 16, 2 (Fall 1991): 225–48; Stan Rands, 'Recollections: The CCF in Saskatchewan', in *Western Canadian Politics: The Radical Tradition*, ed. Donald C. Kerr (Edmonton, AB: NeWest, 1981), 58–64.

17. Robin F. Badgley and Samuel Wolfe, *Doctors' Strike: Medical Care and Conflict in Saskatchewan* (Toronto, ON: Macmillan, 1967).

18. 'Discussions with Provinces on Health Services Matters', Department of National Health and Welfare Papers, Vol. 45.

19. Evidence of Canadian Medical Association, April 1962, Royal Commission on Health Services.

20. Evidence of British Columbia Medical Association, February 1962, Royal Commission on Health Services, Vol. 12, File 150.

21. Evidence of Canadian Medical Association, April 1962, Royal Commission on Health Services.

22. Ibid.

23. Evidence of Canadian Dental Association, March 1962, Royal Commission on Health, Vol. 14, Exhibit 192, 1962.

24. Evidence of Canadian Pharmaceutical Manufacturers Association, May 1962, Royal Commission on Health Services, Vol. 20, File 291.

25. Evidence of Canadian Medical Association, 16 October 1962, Royal Commission on Health Services, Vol. 6, File 67.

26. Canadian Press Report of Leslie Frost

Interview, 29 March 1961, Royal Commission on Health Services, Vol. 8.

27. Evidence of Mrs. Marguerite Miles, Toronto, n.d., File 355; Evidence of Dr. C. Collins-William, Toronto, n.d., File 375, Vol. 22, Royal Commission on Health Services.

28. Evidence of Canadian Association of Social Workers, 28 May 1962, Royal Commission on Health Services, Vol. 6, File 61.

29. Evidence of Canadian Federation of Agriculture, 27 March, 1962, Royal Commission on Health Services, Vol. 14, File 190.

30. Evidence of United Church of Canada, April 1962, Royal Commission on Health Services, Vol. 22, File 352.

31. Evidence of Canadian Labour Congress, 17 October, 1962, Royal Commission on Health Services, Vol. 6, File 68.

32. Royal Commission on Health Services, *Report*, vol. 1 (Ottawa, ON: Queen's Printer, 1964), 29.

33. Ibid., 11.

34. Ibid., 19.

35. 'Election 1963 Pamphlets', National Liberal Federation Papers, MG 28, IV-3, Vol. 1024, LAC; Bryden, *Planners and Politicians: Liberal Politics and Social Policy, 1957–1968* (Montreal, QC: McGill-Queen's University Press, 1997), 136.

36. The continued opposition of the premiers was clear in File 618.4, 'Correspondence with Premiers', Lester B. Pearson Papers, MG 26, N-4, Vol. 199, LAC.

37. Ibid., 152–63.

38. Ibid., 164–7.

# Chapter 11

# The Quiet Revolutions

## READINGS

### Primary Documents

### Historical Interpretations

### Introduction

There was no single, standard Canadian or North American way of life that Quebec suddenly caught up to in the 1960s. Life was changing in other places, too. However, when historians look at Quebec from 1960 onward, they emphasize the speed with which things seemed to change there, even though these changes resulted from the sort of place Quebec was before 1960. In other words, looking for a definitive beginning or end to the 'Quiet Revolution' is less important than acknowledging that the seeds for profound change had been present before Jean Lesage's Liberals came to power in 1960. Neither did the Liberals' defeat in 1966 bring an end to the remaking of Quebec, as we found out in October 1970 with the October Crisis, again in November 1976 with the election of the Parti Québécois, and again with the failed sovereignty referendum campaigns in 1980 and 1995. We should perhaps be speaking of Quiet Revolutions. Our first primary document is a plain-spoken, initially anonymous, call to reform Quebec's educational system, and it came from an unlikely source. Jean-Paul Desbiens, a member of the Catholic order of Marist Brothers, argued that the Roman Catholic Church played too much of an authoritarian role in education, a role he thought was hurting society's future. René Lévesque was one of the major figures in the formation of the Parti Québécois, and his 1968 work, *An Option for Quebec*, discussed the possibility of creating a new set of political relationships between Quebec and other places. This would not be a radical solution, Lévesque believed, but the realization of Quebec's destiny as the homeland of a distinct people. This would also be, he declared, something that people in Quebec would have to do for themselves. The secondary sources also take on the crucial questions of religion and politics. In his article from the mid-1990s, David Seljak chronicles the rather complex and sometimes contradictory thought of people who wanted to retain their religious ties to a Roman Catholic Church that seemed to be both a force for change and a refuge for reactionaries. The period between the late 1950s and the early 1980s brought profound shifts, but Seljak saw the church handling these with relative calm. An alternative view of this period comes from Éric Bédard, who outlines some of the political turmoil that led up to the 1970 October Crisis. The actions of the Front de Libération du Québec (FLQ), the instigators of the Crisis, could be linked to some powerful religious themes, like Millennialism, even though the FLQ itself tended to describe Quebec's problems in terms of class oppression and the dominant position of English-speaking elites. We know how this particular drama has turned out so far, but it is important to acknowledge the power of abstract ideas like independence, whether they are achieved or not.

# QUESTIONS FOR CONSIDERATION

1.   Why did 'Brother Anonymous' (Jean-Paul Desbiens) adopt a casual style rather than more formal language? Whom do you think he saw as his main readership?
2.   Who does Lévesque identify as 'we', and how does he define this group?
3.   Why do you think historians call this period the 'Quiet Revolution' when it seems that plenty of people noticed what was going on? Was there anything 'quiet' about it?
4.   Seljak paints the Catholic Church in Quebec during and after the Quiet Revolution as a dynamic institution, one that supported reform. How did an organization known for sticking to its traditions make such a transformation?
5.   Given the way it made the case for radical changes to Quebec society, how representative do you think the FLQ was of the average Quebec citizen?

# SUGGESTIONS FOR FURTHER READING

Michael D. Behiels, *Prelude to Quebec's Quiet Revolution: Liberalism versus Neo-nationalism, 1945–1960* (Montreal and Kingston: McGill-Queen's University Press, 2003).

Graham Fraser, *Sorry, I Don't Speak French: Confronting the Canadian Crisis That Won't Go Away* (Toronto: McClelland & Stewart, 2007).

Michael Gauvreau, *The Catholic Origins of Quebec's Quiet Revolution, 1931–1970* (Montreal and Kingston: McGill-Queen's University Press, 2008).

José Igartua, *The Other Quiet Revolution: National Identities in English Canada, 1945–71* (Vancouver: UBC Press, 2007).

Kenneth McRoberts, *Misconceiving Canada: The Struggle for National Unity* (Don Mills: Oxford University Press, 1997).

Sean Mills, *The Empire Within: Postcolonial Thought and Political Activism in Sixties Montreal* (Montreal and Kingston: McGill-Queen's University Press, 2010).

Bryan Palmer, *Canada's 1960s: The Ironies of Identity in a Rebellious Era* (Toronto: University of Toronto Press, 2008).

William Tetley, *The October Crisis, 1970: An Insider's View* (Montreal and Kingston: McGill-Queen's University Press, 2006).

# PRIMARY DOCUMENTS

**1** From Jean-Paul Desbiens, *Les insolences du Frère Untel [The Impertinences of Brother Anonymous* (Montreal: Harvest House, 1966) (originally published 1960), 55–63.

They say that people have had enough of religion. And the people who can't bear to hear talk about religion are the nice fat Catholics who are in fashion around here, you, you, you. Religious anxiety is not a plant that grows among us. Those who are deeply troubled by the religious question are not recruited among the ladies of Ste. Anne or the papal guards. Most French Canadians have had a bellyful of silliness and chatter on this subject. Still we have to talk about religion. There is no other serious problem. We began talking about joual and we notice that here we are describing the religious atmosphere of French Canada. That's the sign that we have but the one serious problem, that of spirituality.

However that may be, I have neither the intention nor the capacity to go into the matter exhaustively. I touched on it only indirectly in my letters to *Le Devoir*; it came about this way. The letter about speaking joual that I sent to Laurendeau and that he published started a chain reaction. For four months there was a stream of letters to *Le Devoir* about education, mostly from teachers, both religious and lay. Laurendeau noticed that nobody wanted his name printed, among all these who were protesting. 'Why all this fear?' he wondered.

The mail brings us letters all the time, mostly from teachers and most of them interesting. But four times out of five, our correspondent writes, 'Please don't publish my name. My living depends on my anonymity'.

One man recalls to us the late Paul Hébert, 'ruined by the authorities, because you published by mistake a private letter written to one of your staff'. Another speaks of 'the conspiracy of silence that surrounds our schools, as if the expression of honest discontent would shake the Church'. Every single one of them has his pseudonym all ready. Apparently the teaching Brothers live in the same stifling smog of fear. A characteristic ending says, 'Can I count on your discretion? Please don't publish this letter. My community is in enough trouble already. It gets nothing except by long struggle; I would not want to cause any more difficulties, and besides I would be the first to suffer. I'm only glad to be of service to you'.

This paragraph closes a moderate and well-informed letter, one that we would like to print because it expresses clearly opinions based on experience. One of the joys of this correspondence has been to find that there are cultured men among the teaching Brothers, whose wits are still alert in spite of the pressure on them, but who seem to exist in complete solitude.

Where does such fear arise? Sometimes very material considerations are mingled in it. One Brother writes, 'How can one explain the outrageous monopolizing tactics of some publishing houses? Real sharks, they are. We have to crawl to them, we communities who are not in the good graces of the above-mentioned publishers or of official organizations, to get a few crumbs from their table in the textbook section'.*

We get some furious letters too; we suspect they may not be all they seem, though exasperation can sometimes bring out reactions of this kind. But now I am referring to reasonable letters, obviously written by thoughtful men. Why do those who write them so seldom feel that they can permit them to appear in public? Are they imagining things? Have they a persecution complex? It seems unlikely that so many good educators should all be victims of the same mania at the same time.

Then there must be some sort of persecution, some threat to freedom? And in the most important field of human activity, that in which our youth is trained? Whence comes this weight on human spirits, this trouble in breathing? Our correspondents are too discreet on that subject. We judge that they don't admit even to themselves what authority or group of authorities restricts their liberty.

This is unwholesome, this is serious. For if they don't know what goes on in the schools, who does? Perhaps the explanation of the many open failures which show up to surprise and scandalize us all lies here. If these men think it their duty to keep quiet, is the risk so great? What is its nature? What are they afraid of, and why?

The welcome mat was out. After long hesitation and with real pain, for I could foresee where my subject might lead me, I consulted a responsible priest and decided to send my answer to the question Laurendeau was asking. Here is the whole text of the reply, which appeared in *Le Devoir*, April 30, 1960.

> Dear Mr. Laurendeau:
>
> In your Friday column you asked, addressing teachers in general, 'What are you afraid of, and why?' Do you insist on your question? I mean, do you insist on an answer? Mr. J.C. Falardeau† will tell us again to examine our consciences. How many times a week are you frightened, my child? Of whom? Why? Never mind, here I go.

The answer is simple enough. We are afraid of authority. Jean le Moyne said it in his famous article 'The Religious Atmosphere of French Canada', written in 1951 and published in *Cité Libre*, of May, 1955. I wouldn't dream of trying to add to his masterly analysis; I take up the matter here only because I am sure that repetition is an important part of our education. We are afraid of authority; we live in a climate of magic, where under penalty of death we must infringe no taboo, where we must respect all the formulas, all the conformisms.

The pervading fear in which we live sterilizes all our efforts. If we write, all our propositions must be justifiable before possible inquisitors; if we act, all our actions must be measured by the traditional standard, that is, they must be repetitions of previous actions. We choose the safest way, to say nothing, to do nothing, to stand still. *Je me souviens!* (Quebec's motto.) Our doctors of theology, our doctors of philosophy, what do they do, what do they write? Their master, St. Thomas, wrote enough, fought enough, insulted enough people: *contra pestiferam doctrinam*. And he, Thomas Aquinas, said, that every excellent master leaves some writings behind him—*excellent* master, but not frightened copycat.

---

* After 1940, when textbooks no longer came in from France, certain religious communities were given assignments to write them.
† Professor of Sociology at Laval

Nothing that is oppressive is Christian. Christianity is essentially a liberating force. One of these days French Canadians will discover that liberation. It is not Christianity that crushes us, but the triple spirit of evil. Of the three lusts which all men know, the one that scourges mankind most harshly is the third, the one of which nothing is said, the one never denounced from the pulpit, the spirit of domination. Do you know any preachers who denounce the snares of authority? Any professors who tell you to read St. Bernard's *Consideration*? Oh no, they always hammer on the same nail, as if our national vice was rebellion, as if we were not long since a dumb people, unable to express ourselves except by swearing and getting drunk.

They renounce money. They renounce sex. They never renounce power. Poor and chaste, but domineering, full of arrogance. 'The kings of the nations have lordship over them. But ye shall not be so, but he that is greater among you, let him become as the younger, and he that is chief as he that doth serve' (Luke XXIII, 25–27). This Christian revelation is the one least emphasized, this radical antithesis is skipped over. They make believe that Jesus Christ said nothing new about our relations with authority. Listen to Papini: 'To command, to dominate, to appear the greatest, the richest, the handsomest, the wisest—all the history of mankind is nothing but terror of coming second' (*History of Christ*). Lanza del Vasto says: 'The overthrow of authority is the first law of the Kingdom announced by the Messiah; for the two thousand years that he has predicted and preached this overthrow, Christianity has stubbornly pretended that nothing has been prescribed, nothing laid down on the subject' (*Commentary on the Gospel*).

They'll say, 'But Papini and Lanza are not doctors of the Church'. What about St. Peter? In the earliest days of the Church, at the moment when it was the time to assert authority, to show who was master, the centurion Cornelius appeared before Peter and knelt to him. Peter quickly raised him, saying, 'Stand up. I too am a man' (*Acts*, X, 26). St. Augustine called his faithful disciples 'Your holinesses', as we still address the Pope. We have come quite a way, but backward. In the time of St. Augustine a disciple stood up in full assembly to discuss something St. Augustine had said. Do you see any worker—or any learned man—nowadays who would get up in the cathedral to argue something with his bishop? Evidently that would mean that the man felt interested, deeply interested, in what his bishop said. It would mean too that there wasn't time for the constable to interfere. Finally it would mean that authority had a respect for man that we are not used to.

True religion is not oppressive. It is magic, it is the witchdoctors that oppress us. If at times we feel oppressed by religion, then we are dealing with a caricature of religion. Pharisaism and Jansenism are all the same. Let me give you some examples from the environment I know well, part of our general situation. Our clergy is French Canadian, our teaching Brothers are French Canadian, our superiors are French Canadian. We are all cut from the same cloth. But it is not Jesus Christ, it is not even Rome, who forces on the nuns and to a lesser degree on the priests and brothers these absurd and anachronistic costumes; it is our Jansenism, our routine, our perfectionism, our timidity, our contempt for humanity. I do believe in the necessity of a distinctive dress for our priests and nuns. The function of such clothing is not solely to mask their sex—that would be soon done—but to signify their inner spirit. But I maintain that a costume need not be an irrational encumbrance in order to signify devotion to Jesus Christ. It can be rational, functional and symbolic all at once.

Nor is it Jesus Christ who imposes on us these slightly ridiculous names by which we intend to signify our separation from the world. We don't have to be called Brother Paphnace or Pancrase, Sister Sainte-Eulalie-du-Très-Saint-Sacrement or Sister Marie-du-Grand-Pouvoir in order to belong to Jesus Christ. I exaggerate? Read the report of the Council of Instruction's 1960 meeting—'. . . the Reverend Brothers Milon, Mélène, Martinien, Martony, Modestin. . . .'

Jesus was called Jesus, a significant name, fairly common among his people. He chose to dress like ordinary folk, so much so that Judas had to agree on a sign to identify him to the soldiers sent to arrest him in the Garden.

This kindly and protective authority, sometimes becoming harsh and vengeful, never consenting to talk things over with us, this is what we are afraid of. We are afraid of inspectors and commissioners. We risk losing our jobs (or of being sent back to the sticks to shut up). This tense and monolithic authority is convinced it cannot yield on a single point without risking the collapse of the whole edifice. It stands unapproachable until it hands down a condemnation; it never discusses anything.

I said a while ago that we are our own authorities; we engender each other, paternalism and slavery producing each other. He who has never known how to be free in an inferior position will never know how to lead when he has risen from the ranks. A people which has lost its taste for liberty corresponds to a touchy authority. The loss of the sense of liberty is widespread among us, not because of Catholic doctrine, but because of our petty and security-conscious way of living Catholicism.

When the Protestants left the paternal mansion (I might as well borrow John XXIII's metaphor) they carried some good with them, a small part of the heritage. We were left with the old property, the house and the equipment; they got away with a few pennies' worth of liberty. But they knew how to make what they had bear fruit. The object of ecumenism is to capitalize on all the Christian values together. No one argues that the Protestants have not known better than we how to preserve and develop some Christian values. Let's admit that they have better preserved the sense of liberty, which St. Thomas held to so strongly, but which since his day has been somewhat suspect for tactical though not dogmatic reasons.

Historically our Catholicism is a Catholicism of counter-Reformation. Add to that the conquest (Protestant) of Quebec, and you get our shrivelled, timid, ignorant Catholicism, reduced to a morality, a sexual morality at that, and even so, negative.

You will say I am wandering from my subject—no, I'm still on it. One small incident: one day I was looking around in the Laval University Press at Quebec. On the counter was a pile of *Cité Libre*. Two Brothers were sampling the forbidden fruit. They asked the salesman, 'Is this any good, this review?' I broke in without being invited, 'It's not only good, it's indispensable.' One of them said to me, 'A priest told us it was bad.' To his mind, the case was judged; a priest had spoken.

Have you noticed, Mr. Laurendeau, that the only person who has answered your question, "What are they afraid of?" and who signed his name, was a retired lay teacher? Nobody can do anything to him, any more. Within the teaching Orders. I call see only Brother Clément Lockquell who seems to be reasonably free. I wonder how he did it and what had to confront. He must have had a bravely protective Superior, one made of gold. I know that his book, *You the Chosen*, mild enough indeed, set some old teeth on edge. Anyhow he hasn't yet been excommunicated. The Christian Brothers have a long history, since they were founded 150 years ago. Being older than the rest of us, they are more free of restraint, more grownup.

Here now is an extract from the Secondary School Program of Studies, 1958 edition. 'In order to proceed in an orderly manner, those who hold positions are requested to communicate their observations to their directors or directresses, who will transmit them to their inspectors, and these to their chiefs'. You see we have not yet got as far as God-the-Father who is in Quebec; we are only with the chiefs of the inspectors. What can be expected to remain after that filtering? No sound can pass through such a lot of stuffing, no light comes down through so many screens.

For those who have been slaves to try to be leaders is fatal. Those who have been under tyrants wait their chance to be tyrants themselves; those who are frightened wait their turn to frighten others. In the fable, the rabbit terrorizes the frogs. The teachers do not feel free, but I question if they try to free themselves. Where are the professors who not only tolerate discussion and questioning, but who provoke it? Where are the educators who are alive to the drama of our youth—the paralysis of communication—and who try to set free what struggles to break out? We shall never get anywhere if we educators do not make up our minds to liberate the captives, to do it systematically. It is so much simpler, more efficacious, more humane, more sensible even, than to wait for the slave revolt. Oppression is never perfectly watertight, personalities can never be entirely enclosed, but if they have been squeezed too long, souls find it hard not to hate. So we recover only the newly free, like the newly rich. What do we read every Saturday in *Le Devoir*? The half-quarrelsome, half-bitter confessions of those who were forbidden to read Mauriac and who read him all the same. They boast of it now, like the bold boys who whistle when the good Brothers pass by on their way to vespers. We must avoid such losses; we cannot afford to lose any talents, any brains. Instead of restricting liberty we should undertake to make it part of our education—offer Montherlant to the lad who has his eye on Mauriac, travel two miles with the man who asks us to go a mile, according to the teaching of the Sermon on the Mount.

I am still sort of unhappy, for I haven't said clearly what we are afraid of. We are afraid of authority because we haven't the courage of liberty. In place of whining, let us confess that we love the word liberty, but what we really want is security. To want both and to grumble over having security without liberty is what everybody does. Teachers ought to do better than that—that unfocused fear and unadmitted cowardice. It isn't brilliant, it isn't even French Canadian, it's just good old human nature from way back. The other evening I was talking with a bus driver— we happened to be alone. He complained of inspectors and stoolies, of abusive demoralizing controls. Who then is free? Only the man who had nothing to lose, Socrates, Jesus, Gandhi, John XXIII. (He has a sense of humour, a good sign.)

---

**2** From René Lévesque, *An Option for Québec* (Toronto: McClelland & Stewart, 1968), 14–30.

## CHAPTER 1: 'BELONGING'

We are *Québécois*.

What that means first and foremost—and if need be, all that it means—is that we are attached to this one corner of the earth where we can be completely ourselves: this Quebec, the only place where we have the unmistakable feeling that 'here we can be really at home'.

Being ourselves is essentially a matter of keeping and developing a personality that has survived for three and a half centuries.

At the core of this personality is the fact that we speak French. Everything else depends on this one essential element and follows from it or leads us infallibly back to it.

In our history, America began with a French look, briefly but gloriously given it by Champlain, Joliet, La Salle, La-Verendrye. . . . We learn our first lessons in progress and perseverance from Maisonneuve, Jeanne Mance, Jean Talon; and in daring or heroism from Lambert Closse, Brébeuf, Frontenac, d'Iberville. . . .

Then came the conquest. We were a conquered people, our hearts set on surviving in some small way on a continent that had become Anglo-Saxon.

Somehow or other, through countless changes and a variety of regimes, despite difficulties without number (our lack of awareness and even our ignorance serving all too often as our best protection), we succeeded.

Here again, when we recall the major historical landmarks, we come upon a profusion of names: Etienne Parent and Lafontaine and the Patriots of '37; Louis Riel and Honoré Mercier, Bourassa, Philippe Hamel; Garneau and Edouard Montpetit and Asselin and Lionel Groulx. . . . For each of them, the main driving force behind every action was the will to continue, and the tenacious hope that they could make it worth while.

Until recently in this difficult process of survival we enjoyed the protection of a certain degree of isolation. We lived a relatively sheltered life in a rural society in which a great measure of unanimity reigned, and in which poverty set its limits on change and aspiration alike.

We are children of that society, in which the *habitant*, our father or grandfather, was still the key citizen. We also are heirs to that fantastic adventure—that early America that was almost entirely French. We are, even more intimately, heirs to the group obstinacy which has kept alive that portion of French America we call *Québec*.

All these things lie at the core of this personality of ours. Anyone who does not feel it, at least occasionally, is not—is no longer—one of us.

But *we* know and feel that these are the things that make us what we are. They enable us to recognize each other wherever we may be. This is our own special wave-length on which, despite all interference, we can tune each other in loud and clear, with no one else listening.

This is how we differ from other men and especially from other North Americans, with whom in all other areas we have so much in common. This basic 'difference' we cannot surrender. That became impossible a long time ago.

More is involved here than simple intellectual certainty. This is a physical fact. To be unable to live as ourselves, as we should live, in our own language and according to our own ways, would be like living without an arm or a leg—or perhaps a heart.

Unless, of course, we agreed to give in little by little, in a decline which, as in cases of pernicious anaemia, would cause life to slip slowly away from the patient.

Again, in order not to perceive this, one has to be among the *déracinés*, the uprooted and cut-off.

## CHAPTER 2: THE ACCELERATION OF HISTORY

On the other hand, one would have to be blind not to see that the conditions under which this personality must assert itself have changed in our lifetime, at an extremely rapid and still accelerating rate.

Our traditional society, which gave our parents the security of an environment so ingrown as to be reassuring and in which many of us grew up in a way that we thought could, with care, be preserved indefinitely; that 'quaint old' society has gone.

Today, most of us are city dwellers, wage-earners, tenants. The standards of parish, village, and farm have been splintered. The automobile and the airplane take us 'outside' in a way we never could have imagined thirty years ago, or even less. Radio and films, and now television, have opened for us a window onto everything that goes on throughout the world: the events— and the ideas too—of all humanity invade our homes day after day.

The age of automatic unanimity thus has come to an end. The old protective barriers are less and less able to mark safe pathways for our lives. The patience and resignation that were preached to us in the old days with such efficiency now produce no other reactions than scepticism or indifference, or even rebellion.

At our own level, we are going through a universal experience. In this sudden acceleration of history, whose main features are the unprecedented development of science, technology, and economic activity, there are potential promises and dangers immeasurably greater than any the world ever has known.

The promises—if man so desires—are those of abundance, of liberty, of fraternity; in short, of a civilization that could attain heights undreamed of by the most unrestrained Utopians.

The dangers—unless man can hold them in check—are those of insecurity and servitude, of inhuman governments, of conflicts among nations that could lead to extermination.

In this little corner of ours, we already are having a small taste of the dangers as well as the promises of this age.

## A Balance Sheet of Vulnerability
The dangers are striking enough.

In a world where, in so many fields, the only stable law seems to have become that of perpetual change, where our old certainties are crumbling one after the other, we find ourselves swept along helplessly by irresistible currents. We are not at all sure that we can stay afloat, for the swift, confusing pace of events forces us to realize as never before our own weaknesses, our backwardness, our terrible collective vulnerability.

Endlessly, with a persistence almost masochistic, we draw up list after list of our inadequacies. For too long we despised education. We lack scientists, administrators, qualified technical people. Economically, we are colonials whose three meals a day depend far too much on the initiative and goodwill of foreign bosses. And we must admit as well that we are far from being the most advanced along the path of social progress, the yardstick by which the quality of a human community can best be measured. For a very long time we have allowed our public administration to stagnate in negligence and corruption, and left our political life in the hands of fast talkers and our own equivalent of those African kings who grew rich by selling their own tribesmen.

We must admit that our society has grave, dangerous, and deep-rooted illnesses which it is absolutely essential to cure if we want to survive.

Now, a human society that feels itself to be sick and inferior, and is unable to do anything about it, sooner or later reaches the point of being unacceptable even to itself.

For a small people such as we are, our minority position on an Anglo-Saxon continent creates from the very beginning a permanent temptation to such a self-rejection, which has all the attraction of a gentle downward slope ending in a comfortable submersion in the Great Whole.

There are enough sad cases, enough among us who have given up, to show us that this danger does exist.

It is, incidentally, the only danger that really can have a fatal effect upon us, because it exists within ourselves.

And if ever we should be so unfortunate as to abandon this individuality that makes us what we are, it is not 'the others' we would have to blame, but only our own impotence and resulting discouragement.

The only way to overcome the danger is to face up to this trying and thoughtless age and make it accept us as we are, succeeding somehow in making a proper and appropriate place in it for ourselves, in our own language, so that we can feel we are equals and not inferiors. This means that in our homeland we must be able to earn our living and pursue our careers in

French. It also means that we must build a society which, while it preserves an image that is our own, will be as progressive, as efficient, and as 'civilized' as any in the world. (In fact, there are other small peoples who are showing us the way, demonstrating that maximum size is in no way synonymous with maximum progress among human societies.)

To speak plainly, we must give ourselves sufficient reason to be not only sure of ourselves but also, perhaps, a little proud.

## CHAPTER 3: THE QUIET REVOLUTION

Now, in the last few years we have indeed made some progress along this difficult road of 'catching up', the road which leads to the greater promise of our age.

At least enough progress to know that what comes next depends only on ourselves and on the choices that only we can make.

The enticements toward progress were phrases like 'from now on', or 'it's got to change', or 'masters in our own house', etc.

The results can be seen on every side. Education, for us as for any people desirous of maintaining its place in the world, has finally become the top priority. With hospital insurance, family and school allowances, pension schemes, and the beginnings of medicare, our social welfare has made more progress in a few years than in the whole preceding century; and for the first time we find ourselves, in many of the most important areas, ahead of the rest of the country. In the economic field, by nationalizing electric power, by created the S.G.F., *Soquem*, and the *Caisse de Dépôts*[1] we have taken the first steps toward the kind of collective control of certain essential services without which no human community can feel secure. We also, at last, have begun to clean up our electoral practices, to modernize and strengthen our administrative structures, to give our land the roads that are indispensable to its future, and to study seriously the complex problems of our outmoded municipalities and underdeveloped regions.

To be sure, none of this has been brought to completion. What has been done is only a beginning, carried out in many cases without the co-ordination that should have been applied—and far too often in circumstances dictated by urgency or opportunity. All along the way there have been hesitations and, God knows, these still exist. In all these accomplishments mistakes have been made and gaps have been left—and whatever happens, even if we do a hundred times as much, this always will be so.

### No One Will Do It for You

But in the process we have learned certain things, things which are both simple and revolutionary.

The first is that we have the capacity to do the job ourselves, and the more we take charge and accept our responsibilities, the more efficient we find we are; capable, all things considered, of succeeding just as well as anyone else.

Another is that there is no valid excuse, that it is up to us to find and apply to our problems the solutions that are right for us; for no one else can, much less wants to, solve them for us.

## CHAPTER 4: THE BASIC MINIMUMS

On this road where there can be no more stopping are a number of necessary tasks which must be attended to without delay. Neglecting them would endanger the impetus we have acquired, perhaps would slow it down irreparably.

And here we encounter a basic difficulty which has become more and more acute in recent years. It is created by the political regime under which we have lived for over a century.

We are a nation within a country where there are two nations. For all the things we mentioned earlier, using words like 'individuality', 'history', 'society', and 'people', are also the things one includes under the word 'nation'. It means nothing more than the collective will to live that belongs to any national entity likely to survive.

Two nations in a single country: this means, as well, that in fact there are *two majorities*, two 'complete societies' quite distinct from each other trying to get along within a common framework. That this number puts us in a minority position makes no difference: just as a civilized society will never condemn a little man to feel inferior beside a bigger man, civilized relations among nations demand that they treat each other as equals in law and in fact.

Now we believe it to be evident that the hundred-year-old framework of Canada can hardly have any effect other than to create increasing difficulties between the two parties insofar as their mutual respect and understanding are concerned, as well as impeding the changes and progress so essential to both.

It is useless to go back over the balance sheet of the century just past, listing the advantages it undoubtedly has brought us and the obstacles and injustices it even more unquestionably has set in our way.

The important thing for today and for tomorrow is that both sides realize that this regime has had its day, and that it is a matter of urgency either to modify it profoundly or to build a new one.

As we are the ones who have put up with its main disadvantages, it is natural that we also should be in the greatest hurry to be rid of it; the more so because it is we who are menaced most dangerously by its current paralysis.

## *Primo Vivere*

Almost all the essential tasks facing us risk being jeopardized, blocked, or quietly undone by the sclerosis of Canadian institutions and the open or camouflaged resistance of the men who manipulate them.

First, we must secure once and for all, in accordance with the complex and urgent necessities of our time, the safety of our collective 'personality'. This is the distinctive feature of the nation, of this majority that we constitute in Quebec—the only true fatherland left us by events, by our own possibilities, and by the incomprehension and frequent hostility of others.

The prerequisite to this is, among other things, the power for unfettered action (which does not exclude co-operation) in fields as varied as those of citizenship, immigration, and employment; the great instruments of 'mass culture'—films, radio, and television; and the kind of international relations that alone permit a people to breathe the air of a changing and stimulating world, and to learn to see beyond itself. Such relations are especially imperative for a group whose cultural connections in the world are as evident and important as ours.

Our collective security requires also that we settle a host of questions made so thorny by the present regime that each is more impossible than the next. Let us only mention as examples the integrity of Quebec's territory, off-shore rights, the evident in acceptability of an institution like the Supreme Court, and Quebec's need to be able to shape freely what we might term its internal constitution.

That collective personality which constitutes a nation also cannot tolerate that social security and welfare—which affect it daily in the most intimate ways—should be conceived and directed from outside. This relates to the oft-repeated demand for the repatriation of old-age pensions, family allowances, and, when it comes into being, medicare.

By the same token, and even more so, it relates to the most obvious needs of efficiency and administrative responsibility. In this whole vast area there are overlapping laws, regulations, and organizations whose main effect is to perpetuate confusion and, behind this screen, to paralyze change and progress.

## The Madhouse

*Mutatis mutandis*, we find similar situations with equally disastrous results in a multitude of other areas: the administration of justice, jurisdiction in fields such as insurance, corporations, bankruptcies, financial institutions, and, in a general way, all economic activities which have become the most constant preoccupations of all men today and also the aspect of society in which modern states have seen their sphere of action grow most dramatically in the last couple of generations.

## A Strong State

How can it be carried out? Let us mention only what is clearly obvious. Order must be re-established in the chaos of a governmental structure created at a time when it was impossible to foresee the scientific and technical revolution in which we now are caught up, the endless changes it demands, the infinite variety of things produced, the concentration of enterprises, the crushing weight that the greatest of these impose on individual and collective life, the absolute necessity of having a state able to direct, co-ordinate, and above all humanize this infernal rhythm.

In this up-dating of political structures that are completely overtaxed by an economic role they cannot refuse to play, the action demanded of the Quebec government, to be specific, would require at the very least new jurisdictions over industrial and commercial corporations, fiduciary and savings institutions, and all the internal agencies of development and industrialization, as well as the power to exercise a reasonable control over the movement and investment of our own capital.

So as not to belabour the obvious, we shall mention only for the record the massive transfer of fiscal resources that would be needed for all the tasks this State of Quebec should undertake in our name—not counting the tasks it already has, tasks that daily grow more out of proportion to its inadequate means: *i.e.*, the insatiable needs of education, urban problems without number, and the meagreness or tragic non-existence of the tools of scientific and industrial research.

Very sketchily, this would seem to be the basic minimum of change that Quebec should force the present Canadian regime to accept in order to reach both the collective security and the opportunity for progress which its best minds consider indispensable.

We could certainly add to the list. But nothing could be struck from it easily.

For us, this is, in fact, a true minimum.

## CHAPTER 5: THE BLIND ALLEY

But we would be dreaming if we believed that for the rest of the country our minimum can be anything but a frightening maximum, completely unacceptable even in the form of bare modifications or, for that matter, under the guise of the constitutional reform with which certain people say they are willing to proceed with.

Not only the present attitude of the federal government, but also the painful efforts at understanding made by the opposition parties and reactions in the most influential circles in

English Canada all give us reason to expect that our confrontation will grow more and more unpleasant.

From a purely revisionist point of view, our demands would seem to surpass both the best intentions displayed by the 'other majority' and the very capacity of the regime to make concessions without an explosion.

If we are talking only of revision, they will tell us, our demands would lead to excessive weakening of that centralized state which English Canada needs for its own security and progress as much as we need our own State of Quebec. And they would be right.

And further, they could ask us—with understandable insistence—what in the world our political representatives would be doing in Ottawa taking part in debates and administrative acts whose authority and effectiveness we intend so largely to eliminate within Quebec.

If Quebec were to begin negotiations to revise the present frame of reference, and persisted in this course, it would not be out of the woods in the next hundred years. But by that time it is most likely that there would be nothing left worth talking about of the nation that is now trying to build a homeland in Quebec.

During the long wait we would soon fall back on the old defensive struggle, the enfeebling skirmishes that make one forget where the real battle is, the half-victories that are celebrated between two defeats, the relapse in to divisive federal-provincial electoral folly, the sorry consolations of verbal nationalism and, above all, ABOVE ALL ELSE—this must be said, and repeated, and shouted if need be—above all the incredible 'split-level' squandering of energy, which certainly is for us the most disastrous aspect of the present regime.

And as for this waste of energy, English Canada suffers from it, too. And there, too, the best minds have begun to realize this fact, let there be no doubt of that.

## Two Paralyzed Majorities

For the present regime also prevents the English-speaking majority from simplifying, rationalizing, and centralizing as it would like to do certain institutions which it, too, realizes are obsolete. This is an ordeal which English Canada is finding more and more exhausting, and for which it blames to the exaggerated anxieties and the incorrigible intransigence of Quebec.

It is clear, we believe, that this frustration may easily become intolerable. And it is precisely among the most progressive and 'nationalist' groups in English Canada, among those who are concerned about the economic, cultural, and political invasion from the United States, among those who are seeking the means to prevent the country from surrendering completely, that there is the greatest risk of a growing and explosive resentment toward Quebec for the reasons mentioned above.

And these are the very men among whom we should be able to find the best partners for our dialogue over the new order that must emerge.

We are seeking at last to carve out for ourselves a worthy and acceptable place in this Quebec which has never belonged to us as it should have. Facing us, however, a growing number of our fellow-citizens of the other majority are afraid of losing the homeland that Canada was for them in the good old days of the Empire, when they at least had the impression that they were helping to rule, and that it was all within the family. Today the centres of decision-making are shifting south of the border at a terrifying rate.

In this parallel search for two national securities, as long as the search is pursued within the present system or anything remotely resembling it, we can end up only with double paralysis. The two majorities, basically desiring the same thing—a chance to live their own lives, in their own way, according to their own needs and aspirations—will inevitably collide with one another repeatedly and with greater and greater force, causing hurts that finally would be irreparable.

As long as we persist so desperately in maintaining—with spit and chewing gum or whatever—the ancient hobble of a federalism suited to the last century, the two nations will go on creating an ever-growing jungle of compromises while disagreeing more and more strongly on essentials.

This would mean a perpetual atmosphere of instability, of wrangling over everything and over nothing. It would mean the sterilization of two collective 'personalities' which, having squandered the most precious part of their potential, would weaken each other so completely that they would have no other choice but to drown themselves in the ample bosom of 'America'.

## CHAPTER 6: THE WAY OF THE FUTURE

We think it is possible for both parties to avoid this blind alley. We must have the calm courage to see that the problem can't be solved either by maintaining or somehow adapting the status quo. One is always somewhat scared at the thought of leaving a home in which one has lived for a long time. It becomes almost 'consecrated', and all the more so in this case, because what we call 'Confederation' is one of the last remnants of those age-old safeguards of which modern times have robbed us. It is therefore quite normal that some people cling to it with a kind of desperation that arises far more from fear than from reasoned attachment.

But there are moments—and this is one of them—when courage and calm daring become the only proper form of prudence that a people can exercise in a crucial period of its existence. If it fails at these times to accept the calculated risk of the great leap, it may miss its vocation forever, just as does a man who is afraid of life.

What should be conclude from a cool look at the crucial crossroads that we now have reached? Clearly that we must rid ourselves completely of a completely obsolete federal regime.

And begin anew.

Begin how?

The answer, it seems to us, is as clearly written as the question, in the two great trends of our age: that of the freedom of peoples, and that of the formation by common consent of economic and political groupings.

### A Sovereign Quebec

For our own good, we must dare to seize for ourselves complete liberty in Quebec, the right to all the essential components of independence, i.e., the complete mastery of every last area of basic collective decision-making.

This means that Quebec must become sovereign as soon as possible.

Thus we finally would have within our grasp the security of our collective 'being' which is so vital to us, a security which otherwise must remain uncertain and incomplete.

Then it will be up to us, and us alone, to establish calmly, without recrimination or discrimination, the priority for which we are now struggling feverishly but blindly: that of our language and our culture.

Only then will we have the opportunity—and the obligation—to use our talents to the maximum in order to resolve without further excuses or evasions all the great problems that confront us, whether it be a negotiated protective system for our farmers, or decent treatment for our employees and workers in industry, or the form and evolution of the political structures we must create for ourselves.

In short, this is not for us simply the only solution to the present Canadian impasse; it also is the one and only common goal inspiring enough to bring us together with the kind of strength and unity we shall need to confront all possible futures—the supreme challenge of continuous progress within a society that has taken control of its own destiny.

As for the other Canadian majority, it will also find our solution to its advantage, for it will be set free at once from the constraints imposed on it by our presence; it will be at liberty in its own way to rebuild to its heart's desire the political institutions of English Canada and to prove to itself, whether or not it really wants to maintain and develop on this continent, an English-speaking society distinct from the United States.

## —and a New Canadian Union

And if this is the case, there is no reason why we, as future neighbours, should not voluntarily remain associates and partners in a common enterprise; which would conform to the second great trend of our times: the new economic groups, customs unions, common markets, etc.

Here we are talking about something which already exists, for it is composed of the bonds, the complementary activities, the many forms of economic co-operation within which we have learned to live. Nothing says that we must throw these things away; on the contrary, there is every reason to maintain the framework. If we destroyed it, interdependent as we are, we would only be obliged sooner or later to build it up again, and then with doubtful success.

Now, it is precisely in the field of economics that we feel the pinch most painfully. In our outmoded constitutional texts and governmental structures, we flounder hopelessly over how to divided between our two states the powers, the agencies, and the means for action.

On this subject any expert with the slightest pretension to objectivity must certainly endorse the following statement by Otto Thur, Head of the Department of Economics at the University of Montreal (in a special edition of *Le Devoir*, June 30, 1967): 'It is not the wording of a constitution that will solve problems [in the field of economics], but rather enlightened and consistent action, which brings about a progressive betterment of existing reality'.

It seems to us, given a minimum of wisdom and, of course, self-interest—which should not be beyond the reach of our two majorities—that in the kind of association we are proposing we would have the greatest chance of pursuing jointly such a course of 'enlightened and consistent action' worth more in economic affairs than all the pseudo-sacred documents with their ever-ambiguous inflexibility.

Such an association seems to us, in fact, made to measure for the purpose of allowing us, unfettered by obsolete constitutional forms, to pool our stakes with whatever permanent consultation and flexible adjustments would best serve our common economic interests: monetary union, common tariffs, postal union, administration of the national debt, co-ordination of policies, etc.

And nothing would prevent us from adding certain matters which under the present system have never had the advantage of frank discussion between equals: the question of minorities, for one; and also the questions of equal participation in a defence policy in proportion to our means, and a foreign policy that might, if conceived jointly, regain some of the dignity and dynamism that it has lost almost completely.[2]

We are not sailing off into uncharted seas. Leaving out the gigantic model furnished by the evolution of the Common Market, we can take our inspiration from countries comparable in size to our own—Benelux or Scandinavia—among whom cooperation is highly advanced, and where it has promoted unprecedented progress in the member states without preventing any of them from continuing to live according to their own tradition and preferences.

## Making History Instead of Submitting to It

To sum up, we propose a system that would allow our two majorities to extricate themselves from an archaic federal framework in which our two very distinct 'personalities' paralyze each other by dint of pretending to have a third personality common to both.

This new relationship of two nations, one with its homeland in Quebec and another free to rearrange the rest of the country at will, would be freely associated in a new adaptation of the current 'common-market' formula, making up an entity which could perhaps—and if so very precisely—be called a Canadian Union.

The future of a people is never born without effort. It requires that a rather large number of 'midwives' knowingly make the grave decision to work at it. For apart from other blind forces, and apart from all the imponderables, we must believe that basically it is still men who make man's history.

What we are suggesting to those who want to listen is that we devote our efforts, together, to shape the history of Quebec in the only fitting direction; and we are certain that at the same time we shall also be helping the rest of the country to find better future of its own.

## NOTES

1. S.G.F. is *la Société Générale de Financement* (General Investment Corporation), an investment, holding, and management company designed to promote business and industry in the province, and financed by both public and private sectors. *Soquem* is *la Société Québécoise d'Exploration Minière* (Quebec Mining Exploration Co.), government-owned and the largest in the province. The *Caisse de Dépôts* is the investment arm of the Quebec Pension Plan.

2. In this paragraph some people have felt obliged—and others have hastened—to find a far-too-strict limitation imposed on Quebec's sovereignty. This would indeed be true if we proposed really to include Defence and External Affairs in the areas of actual association. These two are among the most important means through which a people can express its personality. But such is not our proposal.

## HISTORICAL INTERPRETATIONS

3    From David Seljak, 'Why The Quiet Revolution Was "Quiet": The Catholic Church's Reaction to the Secularization of Nationalism in Quebec After 1960', *CCHA Historical Studies* 62 (1996): 109–24.

Writing about the rapid secularization of Quebec society in the 1960s and 1970s, Hubert Guindon remarks: 'In every respect except calendar time, centuries—not decades—separate the Quebec of the 1980s from the Quebec of the 1950s'.[1] A similar observation might be made about the Church of Quebec and its development between 1960 and 1980. Before 1960, the Church exercised a virtual monopoly over education, health care, and the social services offered to French Quebecers who formed the majority of the population. During his years as premier from 1944 to 1959, Maurice Duplessis had declared Quebec a Catholic province and actively promoted the Church's welfare. In 1958, more than 85 per cent of the population identified themselves as Catholic and more than 88 per cent of those Catholics attended mass every Sunday.[2] A virtual army of nuns, priests, and brothers, which by 1962 numbered more than 50,000, oversaw the Church's massive bureaucracy.[3] This semi-established status and public presence was legitimated by the traditional religious nationalism, which united a conservative, clerical version of Catholicism and French-Canadian ethnic identity.

By 1980, the situation had changed dramatically. The Quebec state had taken over the Church's work in education, health care, and the social services. This 'Quiet Revolution' meant that the state and not the Church was to be 'the embodiment of the French nation in Canada'.[4] While the roots of the Quiet Revolution could be seen in the rapid economic growth and the growth of state power of the 1920s,[5] the changes of the 1960s were experienced as a dramatic shift. Thus the Church had to react both to its loss of real power and to its loss of control over the important symbols, stories, and values carried by traditional religious nationalism. By 1980 no nationalist group sought to promote a Catholic political culture or to remake Quebec's economy in conformity with the Church's social teaching. No one imagined that Quebec was a Catholic state. Like its control over schools, hospitals, and social services, the Church leadership saw its control over nationalist movements evaporate in two decades.

Remarkably, the Church reacted to the secularization of Quebec society with relative serenity. Certainly, the bishops and other religious leaders objected to the government's plans for the secularization of education and the religious communities opposed the reforms which turned their hospitals into public institutions.[6] But generally, Quebec society avoided the tragic cultural schism that marked the movement into secular modernity

of Catholic countries like France and Italy. In Quebec, the Church did not withdraw into a 'Catholic ghetto', anathematize the new society, and work towards a restoration of the old order.[7] Part of the reason for this was that many of the supporters of the reforms were members of the Church.

In Catholic societies, it is natural that opposition to the regime [has] its origins within the Church. The important question becomes how did Quebec avoid the history of schism experienced by France, Italy, Mexico, Spain and other Catholic countries? For although the Quiet Revolution was inspired by and promoted some complaints against religion, even anti-clericalism, there was no massive rejection of religion on behalf of the modernizers. Even today [1996], while only 29 per cent of Catholics attend mass on Sunday, most have retained their Catholic identity and insist on Catholic religious education for their children.[8]

The Quiet Revolution coincided with the reforms of the Second Vatican Council, which radically altered the Church's self-definition, and the emergence of a faith and justice movement in the late 1960s and 1970s. José Casanova has argued that the Council rejected any vision of religious establishment, that is, the use of state power to impose a Catholic religious monopoly on society.[9] Thus just as the Quebec state was declaring its autonomy from the Church, the Church was itself affirming the autonomy of political society, the freedom of individual consciences in political matters, and the need for citizens to involve themselves in the important debates and projects of their societies. Because of this coincidence, Gregory Baum has argued that Catholics in Quebec could be critical of the old Quebec and its religious nationalism, and still remain good Catholics. Despite misunderstandings, heated disagreements, and personal grievances, the Quebec Church and state learned to co-operate and compromise in a spirit of pluralism, reform, and tolerance.[10] This is not to say that the Second Vatican

Council and the emergence of a faith and justice movement were the direct causes of the Church's acceptance of the new society and the new nationalism, but these developments allowed the Church to become more open to compromise and undermined the position of Catholic conservatives who dreamed of a restoration of the old society.

One of the most important issues was the Church's acceptance of the secularization of French-Canadian nationalism. If the Quebec state had the power to make the reforms of the 1960s 'revolutionary', then the Church had the power to make the revolution 'quiet'—or not. Its reconciliation to the new nationalism has helped to determine the shape of Quebec culture and society after 1960.

While the *British North America Act* implicitly gave the Catholic Church a semi-established status in the province of Quebec, the two most important motors of modernization, democratic political structures and capitalist economic institutions, remained outside of its control.[11] Consequently, despite its important role in Quebec society, the Church was most often in the position of reacting to social change. From 1900 to 1930, the Church responded to industrialization and modernization with what Guindon has called an 'administrative revolution', an unprecedented campaign to create new institutions and bureaucracies to meet the needs of French Catholics in every realm of modern urban life.[12] Besides multiplying its institutions which provided education, health care, and social services, the Church promoted the growth of Catholic labour unions, farmers' co-operatives, credit unions, pious leagues, newspapers, radio and television shows, films, and Catholic Action groups for workers, students, women, farmers, and nationalists. Conservative Catholics dreamed that these bodies would eventually reclaim all those functions in society that had been wrenched from the Church's control.[13]

While other peoples met the challenges of industrialization and modernization with programs of what sociologist Karl Deutsch has called 'nation-building',[14] French-Canadian nationalists embarked on an aggressive program of 'church-building' with the goal of creating an '*Église-nation*' (nation-Church) rather than a nation-state. While they encouraged state intervention in specific projects (such as the *colonization* of the hinterlands of Quebec), French-Canadian nationalists usually preferred to resolve conflicts by creating religiously inspired social structures rather than appealing to state power. For example, in the Church's corporatist response to the Depression, the actions of the state were limited to those realms where the first agents of society (the family and the Church) were as yet incapable of fulfilling their responsibilities. Typically, French-Canadian nationalism was marked by a certain *anti-étatisme* and *apolitisme*.[15] Because it was rooted in a profoundly conservative, clerical, Catholic triumphalism, this nationalism could be xenophobic, intolerant, and repressive, as evidenced by its crusades against Jews, socialists, and Jehovah's Witnesses in the name of religious and national solidarity. Despite the anti-modern discourse that its authors employed, this bureaucratic revolution ironically promoted the modernization of French Quebec society including that of the Church itself and French-Canadian nationalism.[16] This modernization was certainly problematic. Critics drew attention to the gulf between the modern, multicultural, urban, industrial reality of Quebec society and a conservative Catholic ideology centred on rural values, ethnic solidarity, religion, and a rejection of politics and the state.[17] [ . . . ]

The rapid changes of the 1960s, known as the Quiet Revolution, grew directly out of the type of society that was formed in Quebec after 1867. After World War II, a 'new middle class' of university-trained bureaucrats increasingly occupied important positions in the immense bureaucracy that the Church had created. While educated in Catholic culture and values, members of this clerically dominated bureaucracy were simultaneously socialized into modern, rational and democratic values. Thus, they were uncomfortable with the conservative, undemocratic practices of the Duplessis regime and with the complicity of the Church in those practices.[18] They demanded the rationalization of the bureaucracy that oversaw education, health care, and social services. They also demanded its democratization and protested against its 'clericalism', understood as the best positions being reserved for Church officials.[19] Consequently, the new nationalism was defined as much against the Catholic Church as the anglophone business elite.[20]

The ascent to power of these elites was assured when the Parti liberal du Québec (PLQ) took power in June of 1960. Inspired by a secular and modernizing nationalism, the Lesage government introduced a number of measures that radically redefined the role of the state. It took over the functions of the Church in education, health care, and social services. Through the nationalization of hydroelectric utilities and the creation of Crown corporations, the PLQ sought both to expand the influence of the government in the economy and to increase the presence of French Canadians in the upper levels of that economy.[21] The state bureaucracy increased at a tremendous rate, growing by 42.6 per cent between 1960 and 1965.[22] While the changes adopted by the Lesage government mostly satisfied the interests of the new middle class and francophone business people, some sought to promote a more democratic, humane, and participatory society. The Liberal government introduced more progressive labour legislation and important social welfare reforms. Supporters of the government's reforms attacked both traditional religious nationalism and laissez-faire liberalism. In doing so they created a new political nationalism that was adamantly secular, state-centred, and optimistically oriented to Keynesian liberalism or even social democracy.[23]

While accepting these reforms, Catholics attempted to find ways of adapting Church structures and Catholic thinking to the new context. Given the history and theology of the Catholic hierarchy in the 1950s, this reaction was by no means the obvious route to take. Even in the early 1960s, the bishops condemned the attack on traditional French-Canadian nationalism in the very popular book, *Les insolences du Frère Untel*.[24] Even though, led by Cardinal Paul-Émile Léger, they had accepted the urbanization of Quebec society and reluctantly had given up the strategies of colonization and corporatism, the bishops' traditional paternalistic attitude, obedience to Rome, moralizing spirit, and confusion between Catholicism and conservative ideology had remained intact.[25] Yet by 1970, the bishops had largely reconciled themselves to the autonomy of the state, the liberty of individual consciences in political questions, and the legitimacy of the new nationalism. The early opposition and later reconciliation of the bishops was paralleled in many sectors in the Church.

This reconciliation would have been impossible without the coincidence of the Quiet Revolution with the Second Vatican Council. In Quebec, the Church's redefinition of its relationship to modernity had three immediate consequences. First, it took the wind out of the sails of the conservative rejection of the new society. It made the project of the traditional nationalists impossible—since the Church hierarchy now refused its designated role as spiritual and cultural leaders of the attack on modernity. Second, it allowed Catholics—and even clergy and bishops—to support some projects of the Quiet Revolution in spite of their 'laicizing' agenda. Finally, it inspired a new concern for development and social justice among Quebec Catholics. The Council affirmed the new direction of Catholic social teaching laid out by Pope John XXIII. Catholics sought to remain relevant to Quebec society and to participate, as Christians, in the important struggles of their society. This new social teaching, along with the reflections of the Catholic Church in Latin America, would lead to the emergence of a faith and justice movement in the 1970s. Influenced by this teaching, the Church in Quebec could develop a sustained ethical critique of the new society and the new nationalism while affirming their liberating aspects. Taken together these three developments meant that Quebec society avoided the painful cultural schism between Catholics and modernizers (both liberal and radical) that has marked other Catholic societies.

Within the Quebec Church, there were varying reactions to the new society and its new nationalism. Many Quebecers were no more interested in the religious reforms of Vatican II than they were in the political reforms of the Quiet Revolution.[26] For example, rural Catholics remained loyal to the traditional religious nationalism and continued to support the Union nationale. When that party adopted a political program similar to that of the PLQ, many of these voters shifted their support to the provincial wing of the Social Credit party, the Ralliement créditiste. The Ralliement wrestled with the question of independence and even absorbed two overtly independentist parties. While its conservative supporters were federalists, the party leaders pursued independence in order to protect the traditional social arrangement defined by religious nationalism from the incursions of the secular, modernizing, federal government.[27]

What was important about the Catholic nationalist groups and political parties which sought to redefine Quebec society along the lines of Catholic social teaching in the 1960s was that virtually all of them disappeared by 1970. Earlier in the twentieth century, nationalist movements had failed because they were politically irrelevant. In the 1960s, when the Catholic nationalist groups disintegrated, no new Catholic groups emerged to take their place, for they had become religiously as well as politically irrelevant. The Church no longer wanted to define its public presence

in opposition to the new democratic society. Conservative Catholics who refused to adapt to the new society have limited their conceptualization of the public presence of the Church to its role in the school system, charity, community celebrations, pastoral services, and certain single-issue ethical debates such as abortion, pornography, and sexual morality. They have remained silent on the national question.

Not all those who rejected the new society and its new nationalism abandoned public life. After a long struggle, many conservatives came to accept the new state while maintaining their fidelity to the old nationalism. Particularly important voices were those of François-Albert Angers and the Jesuit priest Jean Genest who attacked the supposed anti-clericalism of the Quiet Revolution in the pages of *l'Action nationale*. They argued that the growth of the state represented a new form of dictatorship and a violation of the rights of the Church. In 1965, Angers wrote:

> When the state is master in every domain, the people are masters in none. The phrase, 'We are the state!', which we have not ceased repeating here, is the greatest load of rubbish ever proposed to put the people to sleep and to give the dictatorial green light to all [government] ministers who are, by definition, budding little dictators.[28]

Angers and Genest cast their arguments in nationalist terms: without the service of the Church, the nation was surely doomed to tyranny by the state on one hand and social and moral disintegration on the other. The sexual revolution, the feminist movement, and the youth culture of the 1960s, they thought, were surely signs of this degeneration.[29]

This position was also taken by the Jesuit journal *Relations*. Père Richard Arès railed against the reforms as a violation of the democratic rights of French Canadians. He found Bill 60, which promised to secularize and modernize the school system, especially threatening. In a 1964 editorial entitled 'Le bill 60 et la democratie totalitaire', he argued that liberal democracy could become totalitarian because it sought to eliminate all intermediary bodies between the state and the individual. Naturally these bodies included the Church which, he argued, the Catholic families of Quebec had created and voluntarily put in charge of education, health care, and social services.[30] [ . . . ]

By the late 1960s, these conservatives were finally converted by the effectiveness of the new political nationalism. They translated their conservative values into a communitarian ethos that continued to inspire the Mouvement national des Québécois (formerly the Fédération des Sociétés-St-Jean-Baptiste), the journal *l'Action nationale*, and an important constituency within the Parti québécois (PQ). In the Church, they insisted that Catholicism maintain a public role and rejected the privatization of religion. They insisted that the Church be concerned with the national question and that it continue to contribute to Quebec culture. Conversely they also demanded that secular nationalist groups recognize the unique contribution that Catholicism had made to Quebec culture in the form of a communitarian ethos.

Conservative Catholics could not rally the rest of the Church behind their cause. On every important issue, from the debate on education reform to abortion, there was a Catholic presence on both sides of the issue. Consequently, it was impossible to identify Catholicism with the conservative rejection of the new society. For example, the contributors to the Dominican journal *Maintenant* consistently supported attempts to modernize Quebec society and reform the education system. [ . . . ]

In September 1967, *Maintenant* declared itself in favour of independence and socialism. Citing the domination of the economy by foreign capital and the low rate of participation of francophones in the upper echelons of the Quebec economy, the editorial team of *Maintenant* argued that only state intervention would allow French Quebecers to participate in the definition of their society. The editor, a Dominican priest named Vincent Harvey, argued that they were searching for 'a democratic socialism of participation'.[31] To use Fernand Dumont's term, they sought to define *'un socialisme d'ici'*, that is, a socialism which would reflect the culture, values, and social reality of French Quebecers. While rooted in French-Canadian reality, this nationalism could not be isolationist; independence had to represent a first step in opening up Quebecers to a new participation in the modern world.[32]

[ . . . ]

The Jesuit journal *Relations* changed dramatically when most of the editorial team was replaced in 1969 and Père Irénée Desrochers became the editor. The new team rejected the conservatism of its predecessors and accepted the new society. It also became more sympathetic to the growing faith and justice movement within the Church. *Relations* dedicated itself to the theme of liberation, a term that had religious, social, and political meanings. Religiously, the Jesuits promoted the themes of democratization and reform within the Church, liberty of conscience, and new forms of Christian expression. Socially, the journal, an advocate of interventionist government and workers' rights since its inception in 1941, became more radical. Politically, *Relations* adopted a socialist position. Besides becoming a forum for the network of Christian Marxists known as the Reseau des politisés chrétiens, the Jesuits reported on and welcomed the development of liberation theology in Latin America and the ecclesial documents it inspired.

When they turned their socialist analysis to the situation of French Quebecers, the writers of *Relations* applied the insights of liberation theology and the Church's new social teaching. Of course, they did not consider French Quebecers to be colonized or oppressed to the same degree or in the same manner as aboriginal peoples or poor nations. But the writers of *Relations* did judge that the teaching outlined in the 1971 World Synod of Bishops' document *Justice in the World* on the rights of peoples to development, self-determination, and social justice was relevant to the situation of French Quebecers.[33] In 1973 the editorial team of *Relations* declared its support for independence but only if it was tied to 'the construction of a new type of society and to the blossoming of a real community'.[34] Political independence was a first, necessary, but not sufficient, step towards the construction of a socialist society.

After a purge of the more radical element on the editorial board in 1976, *Relations* adopted a more reform-oriented, social-democratic position. However, it never wavered in its support for the transformation of Quebec society and for the right of Quebecers to self-determination. The journal welcomed the 1980 referendum as a step towards a more participatory society; the democratic procedure in itself, they believed, served the common good. The staff supported a 'yes' vote for several reasons. First they believed that sovereignty could be the first step towards building a more egalitarian and open society. Second, they wanted to lend their support to progressive groups in Quebec society—especially the labour unions and popular action groups—who saw the referendum as the best chance at democratizing Quebec's political institutions and transforming its socioeconomic structures.[35] Finally, they wanted to send a message to English Canadians that Quebecers were not happy with the constitutional status quo. A yes vote would lead to more equal, just, and friendlier relations with the rest of Canada.[36]

The 1980 referendum was also the catalyst that induced the most important contributions by the Quebec bishops to the national question. The mood created by the Second Vatican Council had encouraged them to rethink the relationship of the Church to society and of the laity to the hierarchy. An important step in this evolution had been the creation of the Commission d'étude sur les laïcs et l'Église in 1968. The Dumont Commission, as it was known, firmly rejected the old Church and old Quebec and accepted the disestablishment of the Church in the Quiet Revolution as an irreversible development. It argued that the Church would have to become a 'compagnon de route' with the people of Quebec.[37] This was a radical change from the ultramontanist view of the 1950s, which saw the institutional church as the framework of the *Église-nation*. According to the report, the Church would have to serve Quebec society while adopting a critical or prophetic stance towards its injustices. Influenced by liberation theology and the papal teaching on social justice, the bishops became critics of Quebec society, calling society and the state to task on such issues as unemployment, regional disparity, aboriginal rights, the plight of refugees and immigrants, the environment, and others.[38]

The bishops released two widely read and well-received letters during the referendum debate. In their first letter, they affirmed the right of the people of Quebec to determine their future collectively and the responsibility to decide important questions about their development democratically. They also insisted that nationalism had to be respectful of individual and community rights and defined 'le peuple québécois' as all residents of Quebec, including French Quebecers, anglophones, immigrant minority groups, and the aboriginal peoples. Furthermore, they hoped to foster an atmosphere of respect and tolerance and warned against the demonization of one's opponents, ethnic isolationism, prejudice and stereotyping, insulting rhetoric, and discriminatory practices.[39] Finally, they argued that the national question could not be abstracted from the search to create a more just social order in Quebec and the world.[40] [ . . . ]

The style of the bishops' teaching on nationalism was just as important as its content. The bishops stated that, while the Church affirmed Quebecers' right to self-determination, the hierarchy did not have the authority to tell them how to vote. Neither sovereignty-association nor federalism could be identified directly with the gospel message of liberty and responsibility. The role of the Church was to defend basic Christian values, which demanded that people decide their future in a mature, respectful, fraternal, and peaceful manner.[41] During the referendum campaign itself, the bishops ensured that the Church was not identified with either side. They warned the clergy to remain discrete; they could take sides but they had to present their opinions as their own and not as the Church's.[42]

While the principles laid out by the bishops may have been violated by individuals during the heat of the 1980 referendum debate, Catholic groups and institutions were remarkably disciplined during the campaign and consistent in emphasizing that their choices were based on political analyses that were open to democratic debate.[43] The style of their participation reflected a consensus on the Church's new attitude to secular Quebec and its new nationalism, which affirmed that the people of Quebec had the right to determine their own future through the democratic process and neither outsiders nor the Church itself could interfere. By taking this position, the Church affirmed the fact of its political and social 'disestablishment' and accepted that the old Quebec had passed away. During the referendum, and perhaps for the first time in Quebec political history, no group sought to define Quebec as a Catholic society or proposed that Catholicism could provide a political culture or economic system for a pluralist, modern, industrial society. While this separation of Church and state was affirmed, no major Catholic groups supported the separation of the Church from Quebec society—either in the form of creating a Catholic ghetto (as in France after its secularizing revolution) or in allowing Catholicism to be defined as a purely private religion. Because of the Church's long history at the very centre of French-Canadian

civil society, Catholics felt that the Church had to maintain a public presence.

In reaction to the new society and its nationalism, the Church maintained its moral authority and public presence by creating a sustained ethical critique that integrated its traditional commitment to Quebec society with the new social teaching coming from Rome, Europe, and Latin America. Nationalist claims had to be measured against two sets of criteria. The first was supplied by the Catholic teaching on the 'common good'. Did a nationalist movement promote the welfare of all citizens and not just one group? Was it democratic? Did it encourage mature, responsible citizenship and a balance between the rights and duties of individuals? Did it promote isolationism, racism, or xenophobia? The second was supplied by the new Catholic teaching on social justice. What was the 'projet de société' attached to the nationalist movement? Did the nationalist project respect the rights of minorities and of the aboriginal peoples? Did it seek to create a more just distribution of wealth? Was it open to participation by the poor and the marginalized? Would it promote a more just and open society? This position, while interpreted differently, was taken seriously by every Catholic group active in the nationalist debate after 1970.

The teaching carried an explicit limitation of the public role and authority of the Church itself. Even the Church could not define itself above the Christian values that it now recognized as inherent in the democratic process. The Church could, however, remind society of its commitment to democracy and denounce attitudes and practices that ignored the dignity and rights of individuals and communities. This teaching represented a dramatic turnabout of the Church's attitude to the democratic process. Catholics affirmed that even the heated and sometimes divisive debate around the 1980 referendum was a positive process in and of itself. The debate encouraged a 'prise de conscience', an awakening to one's dignity, responsibility, and liberty as a citizen and person. In a society that Catholics had analyzed as encouraging people to become self-interested, depoliticized consumers, the nationalist debate came to be seen as encouraging serious reflection on issues of identity, common values, solidarity, and social justice.[44]

The Church's support for democratic participation, responsible citizenship, and individual liberty was remarkable when contrasted with its former opposition to those very features of modernity. It was the religious revolution inspired by Vatican II, the emergence of a faith and justice movement, and the struggles of Quebecers, that allowed the Church to adapt to the secular society created by the Quiet Revolution. This extraordinary shift leads to the conclusion that 'centuries—not decades'—separate the Church of Quebec of the 1980s from that of the 1950s.

# NOTES

1. Hubert Guindon, *Quebec Society: Tradition, Modernity, and Nationhood*, eds. Roberta Hamilton and John L. McMullan, (Toronto: University of Toronto Press, 1988), 138.

2. Reginald Bibby, *Unknown Gods: The Ongoing Story of Religion in Canada* (Toronto: Stoddart, 1993), 6, table 1.1.

3. Jean Hamelin, 'Société en mutation, église en redéfinition, le catholicisme québécois contemporain, de 1940 à nos jours', dans *La croix et le nouveau monde. Histoire religieuse des francophones d'Amérique du nord*, dir. Guy-Marie Oury (Montréal: Editions C.L.D./C.M.D., 1987), 224.

4. Guindon, *Quebec Society*, p. 104.

5. Jean Hamelin et Nicole Gagnon, *Histoire du catholicisme québécois. Le XXe siècle. Tome 1. 1898–1940* (Montreal: Boréal Express, 1984), pp. 442–3.

6. Hamelin et Gagnon, *Histoire du catholicisme*, pp. 245–59.

7. Gregory Baum, *The Church in Quebec* (Ottawa: Novalis, 1991), pp. 15–47; David Martin, *A General Theory of Secularization* (New York: Harper and Row, 1978).

8. See Micheline Milot, 'Le catholicisme au creuset de la culture', *Studies in Religion* 20, 1 (1991): 51–64.

9. José Casanova, *Public Religions in the Modern World* (Chicago: University of Chicago, 1994), 71–3.

10. Baum, *The Church in Quebec*, 38–47.

11. Guindon, *Quebec Society*, 103–4.

12. Ibid., 20–1.

13. Hamelin et Gagnon, *Histoire du catholicisme*, pp. 175–291; Nive Voisine, André Beaulieu, et Jean Hamelin, *Histoire de l'Église catholique au Québec (1608–1970)*, Première annexe au rapport de la Commission d'étude sur les laïcs et l'Église (Montréal: Fides, 1971), 55–72.

14. Karl W. Deutsch and William J. Foltz, eds, *Nation-building* (New York: Atherton Press, 1966).

15. See André-J. Bélanger, *L'Apolitisme des idéologies québécoises: le grand tournant de 1934–1936* (Québec: Presses de l'Université Laval, 1974), 3–5.

16. See William F. Ryan S.J., *The Clergy and Economic Growth in Quebec, 1896–1914* (Québec: Presses de l'Université Laval, 1966); Guindon, *Quebec Society*, pp. 107–9; and Hamelin et Gagnon, *Histoire du catholicisme*, 290.

17. Pierre Trudeau, 'The province of Quebec at the time of the strike', in *The Asbestos Strike*, ed. Pierre Trudeau, trans. James Boake (Toronto: Lewis and Samuel, 1974), 1–81; Michael D. Behiels, *Prelude to Quebec's Quiet Revolution: Liberalism versus Neo-nationalism 1945–1960* (Kingston and Montreal: McGill-Queen's University Press, 1985), 98–9.

18. Guindon, *Quebec Society*, 21–4; Kenneth McRoberts, *Quebec: Social Change and Political Crisis*, 3rd edn (Toronto: McClelland & Stewart, 1988), 147–69.

19. Guindon, *Quebec Society*, 48–9; McRoberts, *Quebec*, 149–50.

20. McRoberts, *Quebec*, 148–51.

21. Ibid., 132–4.

22. Ibid., 136.

23. Guindon, *Quebec Society*, 40–3, 58; Léon Dion, *Nationalisme et politique au Québec* (Montréal: Hurtubise HMH, 1975), 54–119.

24. Hamelin, *Histoire du catholicisme*, 238–43.

25. Hamelin, 'Société en mutation', 223.

26. McRoberts, *Quebec*, 169–72.

27. Paul-André Linteau, René Durocher, Jean-Claude Robert, et François Ricard, *Histoire du Québec contemporain. Tome 2. Le Québec depuis 1930* (Montréal: Boréal, 1989), 128.

28. 'Hauteur et mauvaise foi envers nous de "l'État c'est nous!"', *L'Action nationale* 55(3) (novembre 1965): 331. Translation by the author.

29. Jean Genest, 'Jusqu'à la lie?', *L'Action nationale* 60, 3 (novembre 1970): 184.

30. Richard Arès S.J., 'Le bill 60 et la démocratie totalitaire', *Relations* no. 279 (mars 1964): 65–6.

31. Vincent Harvey, O.P., Pierre Saucier, Hélène Pelletier-Baillargeon, André Charbonneau, Louis Racine, et Yves Gosselin, 'To be or not to be', *Maintenant* no. 68–9 (août–septembre 1967): 236.

32. Ibid., 237.

33. Irénée Desrochers S.J., 'Le principe du droit à l'autodétermination du Québec: amorce d'une réflexion pré-politique', *Relations* no. 366 (décembre 1971): 334–7; and 'Le droit du Québec à l'autodétermination: les évêques se sont-ilsprononcés?', *Relations* no. 372 (juin 1972): 163–8.

34. 'Relations et l'avenir du Québec', *Relations* no. 386 (octobre 1973): 259; emphasis in the original.

35. Irénée Desrochers S.J., 'La FTQ et le référendum', *Relations* no. 455 (janvier 1980): 11–14; 'Le référendum et la question sociale', *Relations* no. 457 (mars 1980): 67, 93–5; 'La CSN, la question nationale et le oui au référendum', *Relations* no. 459 (mai 1980): 155–7.

36. Albert Beaudry, 'Le référendum: un pas dans la bonne direction', *Relations* no. 459 (mai 1980): 131–3.

37. Commission d'étude sur les laïcs et l'Église, *L'Eglise du Québec: un heritage, un projet* (Montréal: Fides, 1971).

38. Gérard Rochais, *La justice sociale comme bonne nouvelle: messages sociaux, économiques et politiques des évêques du Quebec 1972–1983* (Montréal: Bellarmin, 1984).

39. Baum, *The Church in Quebec*, 164.

40. 'Le peuple québécois et son avenir politique: message de l'Assemblée des évêques du Québec, sur l'évolution de la société québécoise, le 15 août 1979', dans Rochais, *La justice sociale*, 137–44.

41. Assemblée des évêques du Québec, 'Le peuple québécois', dans Rochais, *La justice sociale*, 137–44.

42. Jean Martel, 'L'Église se fera discrète', *Le Soleil*, 26 avril 1980, B2; Jules Béliveau, 'Mgr Gregoire est satisfait de la discrétion des prêtres', *La Presse*, 9 mai 1980, A12.

43. Dossiers 'Vie ouvrière', 'Oui à un projet de société', *Dossiers 'Vie ouvrière'* 30, 141 (janvier 1980): 2–9 and Mouvement des travailleurs chrétiens, *La question nationale* (Montréal: Mouvement des travailleurs chrétiens, 1979).

44. Jacques Grand'Maison, *Nationalisme et religion. Tome 2. Religion et idéologies politiques* (Montréal: Beauchemin, 1970), 200–1.

---

4   From Éric Bédard, 'The Intellectual Origins of the October Crisis', in Magda Fahrni and Robert Rutherdale, eds., *Creating Postwar Canada: Community, Divesity, and Dissent* (Vancouver: UBC Press, 2008), 45–60.

Future historians, writing at a greater distance from the 1960s than us, will no doubt view the decade as the theatre of an unprecedented cultural revolution. Youth embarked on a radical contestation of traditional norms and of the institutions that had until then held authority.[1] Among these institutions was the Catholic Church, which despite its efforts at reform through Vatican II, was considered by most baby boomers to be an archaic, outdated institution. In the era of the consumer society and an infinite quest for freedom, of structuralism and the birth control pill, the Catholic Church, even reformed, seemed to offer no satisfactory responses to those who sought to take up the challenges of modern life. Thus in all Catholic countries, churches were increasingly empty, fewer and fewer priests were ordained, and many clerics returned to civil life.[2] We must not, however, be misled by this cultural break with religion. If the church, as an institution, no longer seemed to respond to the expectations of the population, did this necessarily mean the disappearance of the sacred? Or should we instead see the 1960s, as philosopher Marcel Gauchet has argued,[3] as a period in which the sacred was transferred to other spheres, as a 'revolution in faith'? Did spiritual expectations disappear, or were they invested in other goals? The study of the most radical Quebec nationalism of the 1960s, situated in its context, can provide several avenues of reflection on this question.

## QUEBEC'S QUIET REVOLUTION AND ITS CONSEQUENCES

The coming to power of Jean Lesage's Liberals marked the beginning of Quebec's Quiet Revolution. This period of dramatic political change brought about highly important reforms ranging from the nationalization of Quebec's private hydroelectric power utilities to the establishment of a Ministry of Education. Quebec's late transformation into a welfare state—some 15 years after most other Western societies—was due largely to conservative resistance within the Union nationale government, which had been in office since 1944, and to the dominance of the Catholic Church, which staffed and operated a large part of the school network and most institutions responsible for the care of the ill and the needy. Together, these conservative powers had long persuaded a majority of French Canadians to put their trust in the laws of the free market and the social teachings of the church. By the end of the 1950s, however, their views no longer seemed to convince much of the Quebec electorate. On the one hand—as the Laurendeau-Dunton Commission showed in 1968—the economic lot of French Canadians remained glaringly inferior despite thirty years of exceptional prosperity following the Second World War. On the other hand, owing

to the breakdown of the tradition of mutual support within the extended family, institutions of social welfare could no longer keep up with growing needs.[4] In June 1960, under new influences spread mostly by television, a majority of French Canadians decided to support a political party that proposed to make the Quebec state the engine of economic recovery for French Canadians as well as the instrument of a new form of social solidarity.

These economic and social transformations brought about the development of a new Québécois nationalism that was distinct from the type of nationalism traditionally espoused by the Union nationale and the Catholic Church. In the new nationalist way of seeing and labelling things, the idea of 'Quebec' as a nation gradually came to replace the notion of 'French Canada' as an ethnic community. The new Québécois nation now defined itself by reference to territory rather than culture and claimed to be more inclusive since belonging to Quebec no longer depended on one's ethnicity or religion. Followers of this new nationalism practically all came around to supporting the goal of Quebec independence. Their particular paths varied considerably, however. Some, like René Lévesque and Jacques Parizeau, became *souverainistes* because they wished to see the state in charge of all the tools required for the full development of the Quebec nation. These 'reform' nationalists who launched the Parti Québécois in 1968 were mostly born before the Second World War, belonged to a new middle class whose outlook was shaped by the study of the social sciences, and were opposed to the Union nationale regime in their youthful twenties. Others, referred to as *indépendantistes* rather than souverainistes, believed in an independent Quebec for altogether different reasons. For the indépendantistes, the struggle to be waged by the Québécois was akin to the struggles of the Algerians, Vietnamese, or Afro-Americans against the forces of colonialism. Children of the baby boom, a number of these noisy young *indépendantistes* held that, since the British Conquest in 1760, the Québécois—the 'White Niggers of America' to borrow the notorious phrase of the leftist activist Pierre Vallières—constituted a people colonized, economically and politically. To put an end to this domination, some advocated resorting to the same violent methods as the Front de libération nationale (FLN), which after a long war of attrition against the French Army, had succeeded in securing in dependence for Algeria in 1962. It is therefore not by mere coincidence that the following year a handful of Quebec *indépendantistes* set up the Front de libération du Québec (FLQ), a clandestine organization that fully expected to overthrow Anglo-Saxon colonialism through tried and true revolutionary methods.

Between 1963 and 1970 FLQ actions often attracted public attention. In the beginning the clandestine group would mostly set off bombs at night in Montreal locations symbolizing the Canadian government (e.g., mailboxes) or big 'Anglo-Saxon' capital (e.g., the Stock Exchange). In 1970 the FLQ's most dramatic actions sparked what has become known as the October Crisis. The crisis was set off when a British diplomat was kidnapped and held in confinement for two months and Quebec's vice premier assassinated by FLQ kidnappers. To end the crisis, the Canadian government, headed by Pierre Elliott Trudeau, invoked the *War Measures Act*, temporarily suspending the rights and freedoms of citizens. During the troubled weeks of the October Crisis, armoured vehicles of the Canadian army patrolled Montreal streets in order, it was said, to ensure the security of the people. The police proceeded, without warrants, to arrest over 500 persons, all on the grounds of their alleged association with the *indépendantiste* movement. Even today, the exact number of Québécois who belonged to the FLQ is difficult to tally since, as a clandestine association, the FLQ did not keep up-to-date membership lists. At most, a few hundred activists and around a thousand sympathizers were involved in this underground organization.

The events of the 1970 October Crisis deeply marked the Québécois and Canadian psyches. In Quebec literature and cinema, there are countless references to these few troubled days. Among the most prominent *felquistes*,[5] as well as among those who sought to track them down,[6] several have borne witness. Furthermore, both levels of government published important enquiry reports offering a better grasp of what really happened.[7] Despite what the authorities of the day may have let the public believe, one of the things that stands out in all this testimony and these investigations is the improvised nature of the FLQ's actions. Contrary to other revolutionary movements, the FLQ of October 1970 did not have an 'armed branch' at its disposal, nor did it even benefit from a very strong organization. Why, then, move into action at that particular moment?

To answer this difficult question, it is most helpful to read *La Cognée* attentively.[8] Published at regular intervals between 1963 and 1967, this newspaper is a very rich source. Beyond tracing the many ups and downs of FLQ activists, it enables us to follow their assessment of the Quebec situation at the time, to analyze their proposed means of improving the lot of the people, and to understand the dilemmas that they faced when the time came to act. Published with insignificant means, this tiny voice was in no way designed to formulate some new doctrine of social action nor indeed to win over a wide public. *La Cognée* was published twice a month. At the beginning 100 copies of each issue were printed. By the mid-1960s around 3,000 copies of each issue were printed.[9] First and foremost, *La Cognée* was a liaison bulletin aimed at ensuring that activists were informed of the movement's directives. Even so, it is no less valuable a resource inasmuch as clandestine and violent activism was a new phenomenon in French Canada's history. The activists wrote up this bulletin in the heat of action, with little concern for coherence. Its purpose was mainly to galvanize energies, not to build a thought system. The identities of the contributors to *La Cognée* are still unknown. All of the newspaper's writers published under pseudonyms and took great care not to reveal any information that might have allowed the police to identify them.[10]

A glance at *La Cognée* shows that, even if the *felquistes* used the same idiom as the *indépendantistes* concerning the need to decolonize Quebec, two waves can be identified within the FLQ. The first, which dominated until the mid-1960s, set revolutionary action in the context of the long term: the individual strove to be faceless within the group, the structure, the 'Party'. A servant of the 'Cause', he practised obedience to the movement's enlightened hierarchy. In such a context, life counted little when measured against the success of the 'Final Struggle', a grand victory that would be made possible only by methodical preparatory work to bring together the 'objective conditions' for the 'Revolution'. The second wave, which imposed itself in the end, is termed *spontanéiste*. Inspired by Latin American guerrillas and the heroic action of Che Guevera, the *spontanéistes* were in greater haste to commit acts that would strike the imagination. In their eyes, every spectacular deed would be another call to revolutionary action. Spontaneity put the valiant activist in the forefront: only the most courageous are capable of the great deeds that success requires. The high spirit of a courageous activist, or even that of a cell imbued with a sense of history, sets an example of bravery to be followed in resisting bourgeois and colonial forces.

While the first wave of the FLQ was moved by a millennialist spirit, the second came closer to, or even blended in with, the countercultural landscape of the late 1960s. If militant FLQ activists moved into action in October 1970, it is because they were more committed to the *spontanéiste* view. This hypothesis is empirically fragile because the first wave seems to have been composed of activists more inclined to reflect and to write, while adherents of spontaneous action seem

to have preferred handling explosives to wielding the pen.

## THE FIRST FLQ: THE MILLENNIALIST WAVE

At first glance, a quick reading of *La Cognée* would lead us to believe that its ideology was breaking with the past, in tune with the era launched in 1964 by Parti pris, Quebec's first truly *indépendantiste*, socialist, and secular review. Like most radical activists in the 1960s, it nurtured violent resentment toward the Catholic Church. Far more than in its portrayal of Duplessis, the late authoritarian leader of the Union nationale whose name it rarely mentioned, *Parti pris* depicted parish priests as the true 'rois nègres'[11] responsible for keeping the French Canadian folk in the dark. Here, one easily recognizes the vulgate of *la grande noirceur*, or 'great darkness', which had wide currency at the time and consisted of describing the period prior to 1960 as one of gloom and reaction.

These activists felt that, thanks to Marxism, they—more than anyone else—had in hand a most potent analytical tool. Masters of a new truth, they judged older clerics severely for preaching a life away from politics: as for themselves, they had no fear of conflict. The days of resignation were definitely over. 'Never has a generation been so thoroughly politicized', wrote the earliest FLQ leaders. Never, they believed, had a generation better understood the dynamics of colonial exploitation and, hence, the need to act. Referring to the action of the new *indépendantiste* parties who accepted the rules laid down by the democratic regime, one activist wrote: 'The new generation knows full well what to make of this silliness. It has figured out that it isn't through banquets and debates that one will kick the ass of the dispensers of patronage, throw them out and take their places'.[12] This view, with its vindictive, fearless tone and sharp complaints about the church's role, seemed to show that the *felquistes* were breaking with French Canada's religious past. Indeed, by trashing its religious heritage, they were putting forward an ideology of 'rupture'. Their analysis of the situation opened new vistas focused on the future. Resolutely modern, the ideology of the FLQ served to prove that all things religious had been left behind.

Upon closer inspection of their language, we quickly see that these activists were drawing from the mythological universe of millennialism, specifically Judeo-Christian eschatology, according to which History has an absolute finality and time is slipping away irreversibly. In this view, according to the Book of Revelation, after an age of oppression during which Evil will reign as master, Liberation will follow. Before this can occur, however, a prophet will renew the hope of the downtrodden. He will give meaning to the death of many martyrs, victims of the forces of Evil. On the day of Liberation, the martyrs will all rise from the dead and Peace will settle upon Earth for a thousand years. From this narrative, which the Roman Church swiftly declared heretical, the earlier *felquistes* retained the idea of a wait. Radical dissatisfaction with the world is a harbinger of a period of intense revolt. When experienced as sacrifice and filled with faith in happier tomorrows, the wait is rewarded by the arrival of a golden era. For the believer, salvation will not necessarily come during his own lifetime but as a result of the achievement of a new earthly order in which peace and justice will reign.[13] Earlier sacrifices will then be recognized: the wait will not have been in vain.

Scattered throughout the first pages of *La Cognée* was the millennialist hope, harboured by *felquiste* activists, of a new Quebec freed of its oppressors and harmoniously united in a classless world celebrating its courageous prophets. We are a long way, here, from the combative, albeit good-natured, eagerness of the old Catholic Action activists. This organization was violently rejected, and the crudest possible language was used to indict those seen as having persistently kept the people in the dark. If the prose was different, however, and if action took other, far more extreme forms, existential angst was no less acute, determination to create a radically new world no less sincere. [ . . . ]

As was seen in the early years of *La Cognée*, while the first wave of the FLQ did not borrow from traditional religious speech, here and there one detects elements of a variety of millennialism new to French Canada. I have identified a few: the relationship to the past and to the future, the role of learning and knowledge in the march of History, the place of the individual in relation to the group.

Although harsh toward the bourgeois and clerical elite, FLQ activists of the first wave seldom used the expression 'grande noirceur'. While believing themselves entrusted with a new mission, and considering themselves more enlightened about the true meaning of the course run by the Québécois, they didn't see themselves as having been generated spontaneously, like titans coming out of the earth, to save a debased people. This was hardly a complete and definitive break with the past: on the contrary, the new activism sought to respond to a new perspective on the past. During its early years *La Cognée* insisted repeatedly on carrying forward the 'ancestral combat' and recalled 'the struggle of our fathers' to give better meaning to the battle in progress. In its first issue announcing the program of the Front de libération du Québec, one can read: 'We are struggling in memory as much of Asbestos, Murdochville, and Louiseville, as of conscription in 1917 and 1943, Saint-Eustache and the Plains of Abraham'.[14] One was therefore not required to start from scratch and sweep away the past. Quebec's history teems with heroic battles, courageous personalities of distinction, resolute characters. Accordingly, respect was owed to the heroes of the Plains of Abraham and to the courageous forefathers who died, pitchfork at the ready, in the 1837 Rebellions because, before anyone else and despite their era, they had understood the true direction of History. On the other hand, those who consistently blocked 'the path of progress' were traitors. Here, the notion of progress was of paramount importance, referring, as it did, to a linear and teleological view of History. Indeed, history was spelled with a capital 'H', being the History of people making their way toward liberation. Great movements were those able to discern the right time to move into action so that History could achieve its true destiny.

It was easy to figure out, however, that it was not enough to know the laws of History and to have at hand the techniques required to bring about Revolution. Unquestioning faith in science would never suffice to cause the new Québécois to break out of his shell. National liberation would be possible only if Quebec's most courageous sons agreed to sacrifice their lives for the salvation of all. Before there could be a harmonious synthesis of new beginnings, the enemy would have to be conquered physically, in hand-to-hand combat, never to rise again. In their 1963 program, the *felquistes* highlighted the following from Chénier: 'Some of ours will be killed; you will pick up their guns'.[15] Later, *La Cognée* returned again and again to this idea of the possibility of sacrifice and the unavoidable death even of brothers, insisting that at times the honour of *la patrie* is the daughter of tragic necessity. Accordingly, life counted for little measured against the collective work to be accomplished, and its sacrifice could even prove useful to the victory of the Nation. Thus the FLQ was not a movement of Romantic adventurers in pursuit of powerful emotions: it presumed to embody the people as a whole, and all its members were meant to take a backseat to the common cause. Those who agreed to sacrifice everything—freedom, life—would some day enter the pantheon of the liberators of the people. Recollection of their heroic deeds would be their highest reward.

In response to those who accused the FLQ of being a terrorist group, *La Cognée* replied that it was not FLQ activists who were terrorizing the people but those who had taken advantage of them ever since the Conquest. FLQ terrorism introduced itself as a new form of humanism, 'a vast front of love and fraternity'.[16] Conquering one's fears and resorting to violence to follow the course of revolutionary logic were made necessary by love for a group of men and women so alienated that they had come to mistake their material and political inferiority for moral superiority. The salvation of the group, and it alone, would enable individual members to unshackle themselves from their chains.

[ . . . ]

These earlier FLQ activists seemed to be saying that the wait for *le Grand Soir* would be a long one. Before ridding Quebec of its clique of exploiters, there would have to be much sacrifice, a few martyrs, and many setbacks. While the wait would be long, difficult, and filled with traps, triumph would be all the more glorious for the enlightened vanguard that had anticipated Liberation. This millennialist variety of *felquiste* rhetoric illustrates very well how misleading it is to view the Quiet Revolution as marking a definitive break with all things religious. A new gnosis emerged to fit new premises. Some, the reformers, shifted their focus toward the state,[17] while others, the radicals, pinned their hopes on a nation freed from its perceived exploiters. The first wave of the FLQ is an interesting case in point. Inspired by Third World ideologies of decolonization mentioned above, the earlier *felquistes* communed in a millennialist hope of a new kind.

## THE SECOND-WAVE FLQ: COUNTERCULTURAL SPONTANEITY?

The patience needed to wait for *le Grand Soir*, a sense of anonymous sacrifice, and faith in History were not to everybody's liking. Here and there, somewhat different noises were heard about the actions required, the future of the movement, and the meaning of daily struggle. Those uttering these divergent opinions were hardly preoccupied with mastering the science of revolution. They had little use for laws of History and wanted nothing to do with objective conditions: all they sought was to act, to strike at those who were keeping the people alienated. It was through spontaneous action that the masses would recognize their true defenders, not in obscure theories about Marxism. If the end seemed the same, namely to free Quebec from perceived colonial oppression, there was a change in the nature of the means to achieve it. At first glance, it is clear that this new praxis coincided with a new way of conceiving revolutionary action, or so at least the last few issues of *La Cognée* (published before it disappeared in 1967) would seem to indicate. This transformation had less to do, however, with some new philosophy, matured at length, than with a context in which a therapeutic view of society had attracted numerous followers among the French Canadian elite of the 1960s.[18] In light of the 1966 and 1970 election results, many FLQ activists concluded that the wait had lasted long enough. In 1966, after six years of Quiet Revolution, the Union nationale regained power. Four years later, the Liberal Party returned to office, while the Parti Québécois, which ran candidates for the first time in its history, managed to elect only seven members despite gathering 23 per cent of ballots cast. It was obvious that many *indépendantistes* were greatly disappointed with the outcome and felt that the Québécois feared real change. According to some, the time had come, after the early days of millennialist mysticism, to apply real shock therapy to this people unaware of its true alienation. In order to understand this, it is necessary to draw on the rich context of protest of the late 1960s.

Less given to reflection than the activists of the millennialist sort, the second wave, labelled *spontanéiste*, was rather anti-intellectual. Deeply hostile toward the guiding spirits of *Parti pris*, whom they accused of preferring poetry to revolutionary action, the *spontanéistes* could not stand these youths who 'waste

their time in idle chatter'.[19] According to them, the activist's abundant energy did not need to be intellectualized in order to yield real results. Moreover, theories about revolutionary action were often ephemeral and contradictory, whereas actions themselves left a deep imprint on the mind. Exactly four days before the October Crisis, they wrote that 'any doctrine can be, and is, virtually overtaken'.[20]

Without doubt, 1966 was a turning point for nationalist activists of the revolutionary left. In their eyes, the election in June of the Union nationale was a distinct step backward, even a return to the Duplessis years. During the election campaign, Daniel Johnson, leader of the Union nationale, had severely criticized the expansion of the Quebec state for contributing to the dissolution of 'intermediate bodies' (e.g., family, church). For many, the victory of the Union nationale marked a return in strength of the clericalism of yore, a significant 'flip-flop' from the preceding years.[21] This 'clerical reaction' was perceived as a crisis of the Quebec conscience. There could be no revolution, however, without real secularism. Some of the guiding lights of *Parti pris* asked themselves whether before changing society, before proposing new structures, it might not perhaps first be necessary to change Man. To achieve a socialist and independent society, might it not be necessary to re-educate the Québécois, to instill in them a new conscience? To get there, *Parti pris* proposed stressing cultural leadership at the grassroots level. The disalienation of a nation comes, at first, from the reform of consciences, not from the transformation of structures that constitute society's framework.

The election of the Union nationale affected FLQ activists in like fashion. This return to the past supplied munitions to proponents of immediate, direct action. Not only did the 'objective conditions' of revolution seem out of reach, but one also had the feeling of witnessing the retrogression of national awareness. The confluence of these circumstances was all that was needed to intensify the sense of urgency of the *spontanéistes*. The people were more alienated than had even been imagined and had to be awakened to reality. Following the election of 5 June, an activist described 'the growing uneasiness in Quebec'.[22] As he saw it, agricultural stagnation, labour discontent, student dissatisfaction, and the crisis in the political system were all signs of an imminent breakdown. The FLQ had to move into action and fulfill its vanguard role. The last issues of *La Cognée* stated the urgency of doing so in many ways. In December 1966 it condemned 'the prodigious mess of the Estates General'[23] of French Canada, which it likened to yet another exercise in largely useless 'chatter' and 'palaver'. Only force and direct action would enable the Québécois to escape from this dead-end. In the next-to-last issue of *La Cognée* available to us (dated 15 January 1967), FLQ activists vowed to carry on 'clandestine combat' and 'political agitation' throughout 1967. Most of all, warned one FLQ activist, 'don't expect fantastic explosions or spectacular D-Days . . . it's quite sure we aren't relying on a reserve army of 100,000 guerilla fighters in secret camps to act'. Above all, it was necessary to set up an 'authentic organization' capable of moving into action swiftly. *La Cognée* published its last issue on 15 April 1967.[24] It is therefore not possible to follow the evolution of the ideas of the *spontanéistes* beyond this point, a sign perhaps that, from then on, FLQ activists were staking everything on direct action. As well, we now know how drastic their actions would be and what mark they would leave on the national imagination of the Québécois.

While from April 1967 onward there are no written traces whatsoever of the evolution of FLQ *spontanéisme*, the context of the late 1960s offers the view of a clear convergence toward direct action. There is every reason to believe the *felquistes* of the *spontanéiste* school saw this as confirming their predictions. The student leaders of the day also seemed weary of 'idle chatter'. Following the October 1968 walkouts, the wind of radicalization blew away everything in its path. At the beginning

of 1969 the leaders of the Association générale des étudiants de l'Université de Montréal (AGEUM) decided to scuttle their association. Among the reasons put forward was a concern to return to their roots, a way of 'fostering the development of a responsible man's conscience within everyone'.[25] Almost at the same time, the same thing occurred at the Union générale des étudiants du Quebec (UGEQ). At a final stormy convention, the UGEQ also decided to dissolve itself after students opted for the most radical of courses. Proponents of this view reckoned that the UGEQ was duplicating the elitist structure prevailing in Quebec. But, the activists insisted, it was important for them to return to their roots. Before defending their own well-being, student activists had a duty to concern themselves with 'politicizing the masses' and 'setting up a self-managing revolutionary society'.[26]

Ideas such as 'returning to grassroots', 'politicizing the masses', and 'developing revolutionary awareness' gave rise to new organizations typical of the times. Political action committees (*comités d'action politique*, or CAPs), whose mission was to support workers striving to break free, appeared in Montreal working-class neighbourhoods. Associations of the same nature (e.g., the Travailleurs étudiants du Québec, or Quebec Student Workers, and the Front de libération populaire, or People's Liberation Front) proliferated. The Mouvement syndical politique (Political Movement of Trade Unions, or MSP) was born at the young Université du Québec à Montréal (UQAM), which opened in September 1969. These activists and would-be revolutionaries saw themselves as a seminal group—a *minorité agissante* to borrow a term that enjoyed wide circulation at the time. In no way did the MSP intend to replace the UGEQ, for it was 'at the grassroots that the real work is done'.[27]

Revolution had yielded to revolt; the sacrifice of some for the salvation of all had given way to a glory trip. Yesterday's institutions (e.g., AGEUM, UGEQ) were cast aside for immediate revolutionary activism. Ties to a past that no longer had anything to offer were severed; the time had come to jump into action. From hope in human renewal, revolutionary militancy seemed to have become an end in itself, no longer embedded in the long march of History. One felt justified in behaving this way because the past had crippled the alienated people. The task of healing minds, a mission of the vanguards and minorités agissantes, was far beyond their means. Still, it was necessary to seize the opportunity, capture the imagination, and shake the prevailing torpor.

Against this background, to liken the FLQ's October 1970 action to shock therapy is no exaggeration. After the April electoral victory of Robert Bourassa's Liberals and the very disappointing results obtained by the Parti Québécois, the FLQ felt the need to strike a sharp blow. In the summer that followed, a few activists organized a kidnapping plan, although it didn't secure unanimous approval among *felquistes*. Nevertheless, on 5 October 1970 the Libération cell went into action and kidnapped commercial attaché James Richard Cross of the British Consulate General in Montreal from his Westmount home. The members of the Chénier cell learned of the news over the radio on their way back from the United States. In *Pour en finir avec Octobre*, Francis Simard recalls the disappointment that he felt at the time.[28] He, the Rose brothers, and Bernard Lortie totally improvised an attack of their own by kidnapping Quebec's vice premier, Pierre Laporte, whom they assassinated a few days later. The events that followed are well known. Incapable of following these improvised acts coherently, the FLQ was rapidly neutralized and its leaders jailed or sent to Cuba.

Weary of theoretical discussions and tiny isolated bombs that no longer stirred anyone, several *felquistes* decided that the waiting had lasted long enough. Yet they could rely only on a handful of activists, had no influence over any large media, and could call upon no organized armed group. In this context, how could they expect to win? 'We weren't really ready in terms of organization to deal with events like that', said Paul Rose in an interview that he gave several years later. 'It was suicidal, after all, to come and do kidnappings, just like that, and then not be able to follow up with others'.[29] Charles Gagnon, active in the FLQ from the movement's very beginning and a leader of Quebec's Marxist-Leninist left during the 1970s, explained in a recent text that might be seen as a kind of testament, 'the FLQ remained a movement that was essentially *spontanéiste*, in which one mythologized immediate, direct action, rather than political reflection and strategic thinking . . . Rebellious youth . . . didn't want anything to do with debates about the path of socialism, about strategy, about objective and subjective conditions, etc. Young people wanted action, they acted, and they collided headfirst with the established order'.[30]

The evolution in the thought and actions of FLQ activists during the 1960s tends to confirm the intuitive observations made by François Ricard in 1984, at a point when the *souverainiste* movement was at its lowest. Having determined that many activists, full of enthusiasm for the cause not long before, now seemed to have withdrawn into private life, Ricard wondered whether the drift in *souverainiste* ideals might not be due to its basically 'narcissistic' inspiration. In the 1960s, he argued, the *indépendantiste* ideal had undergone a 'vast turnaround in meaning'. The restless humanism of predecessors like Hubert Aquin and Gaston Miron, and of the journals *Liberté* and *Parti pris*, might have yielded its place to a 'new spirit', to 'the expression of undiluted yearning for liberation without object', to a 'vague taste for Quebec'. According to Ricard, the seriousness of the first *indépedantistes*, their earnestness in the face of the collective effort to be marshalled, had been replaced by an overflowing lyricism in which activism had become a huge narcissistic *trip*. From a scheme to provide French Canadians with a structure to overcome their cultural fatigue, independence had been transformed into a massive celebration, a big party.[31] In short, said Ricard, as preached by the Parti Québécois, sovereignty had been stripped of its sacred character. Defended in the beginning by a handful of committed activists willing to sacrifice their own lives to bring about *le Grand Soir*, the *indépendantiste* ideal had, little by little, become 'laid-back'.

Because there are too few indicators to support the idea, it would be imprudent to confirm the hypothesis that the *spontanéistes* were narcissistic. Likewise, it would be a mistake to draw parallels between the *souverainisme* of the Parti Québécois in 1968 and the radical *indépendantisme* of the FLQ. Yet, like Ricard, we can observe a 'turnaround in meaning' of 1960s FLQ militancy and share his impression that the 1963 activists did not give the same meaning to their actions as would, later on, the activists of 1970. Without knowing it, early FLQ activists practised the three mythical virtues described by Jean-Marc Piotte, namely devotion, faith in a new ideal, and hope for a radically new world to come. Piotte's hypothesis was that the new type of activists were seeking to reconstitute the 'original community'—the village—held together by stability, warmth of affection, sharing, and some constraints.[32] Later activists, however, did not seem cut from the same cloth. Their action was not designed for the long term and their determination to do something seemed to have overtaken their determination to succeed. At the origin of this transformation was a feeling of urgency fired up, or so it would seem, by a therapeutic conception of society. For FLQ activists, the 'politicization of the masses', or the freeing-up of their awareness, called for a particular kind of therapy. After two general elections—those of 1966 and 1970—the people needed an electroshock of sorts. The effects of such therapy were unimportant: before anything else, what was needed was to act, to shake this sick body in order, at long last, to awaken it.

The discovery of the corpse of Pierre Laporte would have extraordinary reverberations. It would indeed seize the imagination of many. Although it remains noteworthy, the event did not bring about the expected effect. On the contrary, it marked the end of *spontanéisme* and of a certain revolutionary romanticism.

## NOTES

1.  Doug Owram, *Born at the Right Time: A History of the Baby-Boom Generation* (Toronto: University of Toronto Press, 1996), 159–215.

2.  Denis Pelletier, *La crise catholique: Religion, société. politique en France (1965–1978)* (Paris: Payot, 2002), 52, 59.

3.  Marcel Gauchet, *La religion dans la démocratie* (Paris: Gallimard, 1998).

4.  Daniel Fournier, 'Que s'est-il passé au Québec? La fin du Canada français', *Société* 20, 21 (Summer 1999): 57–93.

5.  Louise Lanctôt, *Une sorcière comme les autres* (Montreal: Québec/Amérique, 1981); François Schirm, *Personne ne voudra savoir ton nom* (Montreal: Quinze, 1982); Francis Simard, *Pour en finir avec Octobre* (Montreal: Stanké, 1982); Pierre Vallières, *Nègres blancs d'Amérique* (Montreal: Parti pris, 1969).

6.  Robert Côté, *Ma guerre contre le FLQ* (Montreal: Trait-d'Union, 2003); Carole DeVault, *Toute ma vérité* (Montreal: Stanké, 1981); Gérard Pelletier, *La crise d'Octobre* (Montreal: Les Éditions du Jour, 1971).

7.  Jean-François Duchaîne, *Rapport sur les événements d'Octobre* (Quebec: Gouvernement du Québec, ministère de la Justice, 1981); Jean Keable et al., *Rapport de la commission d'enquête sur des opérations policières en territoire québécois* (Quebec: Gouvernement du Québec, ministère de la Justice, 1981); D.C. Macdonald et al., *Royal Commission of Inquiry into Certain Activities of the RCMP*, vol. 1 (Ottawa, 1981).

8.  *La Cognée* translates as 'The Hatchet'.

9.  Louis Fournier, *FLQ—Histoire d'un mouvement clandestin* (Montreal: Lanctôt éditeur, 1998), 55.

10. Ibid., 58.

11. Literally, 'negro kings', a concept introduced in 'La théorie do roi nègre' (*Le Devoir*, 4 July 1958) by André Laurendeau, the journalist and intellectual (and later co-chairman of the B&B Commission), to describe the servile attitude of Maurice Duplessis toward Anglo-American suppliers of capital.

12. *La Cognée*, February 1964.

13. Yves Couture, *La terre promise* (Montreal: Liber, 1994), 44.

14. *La Cognée*, October 1963.

15. *La Cognée*, October 1963.

16. *La Cognée*, 31 May 1964.

17. E.-Martin Meunier and Jean-Philippe Warren, *Sortir de la 'Grande noirceur': L'horizon personnaliste de la Révolution tranquille* (Sillery: Septentrion, 2002).

18. Stéphane Kelly, 'La critique du clérico-nationalisme: La veine teutonne', *Société* 20, 21 (Summer 1999): 189–212.

19. *La Cognée*, 24 February 1964.

20. Ibid.

21. André J. Bélanger, *Ruptures et constances* (Montreal: Hurtubise, 1977), 182.

22. *La Cognée*, 16 June 1966.

23. *La Cognée*, 10 December 1966.

24. Louis Fournier, *FLQ: Histoire d'un mouvement clandestin* (Montreal: Québec/Amérique, 1982), 59.

25. Aldéï Darveau, 'La dissolution: Hara-kiri ou mort naturelle', *Quartier latin*, 18 February 1969, 7.

26. François Béland, 'L'anti-congrès', *Recherches sociographiques* 13, 3 (September–December 1972): 380–91 at 383.

27. *Bulletin de liaison du MSP* 2, 1 (August 1969).

28. Simard, *Pour en finir avec Octobre*.

29. Marc Laurendeau, *Les Québécois violents* (Montreal: Boréal, 1990), 62.

30. Charles Gagnon, 'Il était une fois . . . Conte à l'adresse de la jeunesse de mon pays', *Bulletin d'histoire politique* 13, 1 (Fall 2004): 43–56 at 45–46.

31. François Ricard, 'Quelques hypothèses à propos d'une dépression', *Liberté* 153 (June–July 1984): 40–8. This reading is strongly influenced by Christopher Lasch, *The Culture of Narcissism* (New York: Norton, 1977).

32. Jean-Marc Piotte, *La communauté perdue* (Montreal: VLB Éditeur, 1987).

# Chapter 12

# Immigration and Multiculturalism

## READINGS

### Primary Documents

1   From 'Cultural Democracy', W.M. Haugan

2   From 'Announcement of Implementation of Policy of Multiculturalism within Bilingual Framework', Pierre Elliott Trudeau, Robert L. Stanfield, David Lewis, and Réal Caouette

### Historical Interpretations

3   From *Gatekeepers: Reshaping Immigrant Lives in Cold War Canada*, Franca Iacovetta

4   From 'The Roots of Multiculturalism: Ukrainian-Canadian Involvement in the Multiculturalism Discussion of the 1960s as an Example of the Position of the "Third Force"', Julia Lalande

## Introduction

While the end of the Second World War did not introduce Canada to immigration, it did mark the beginning of a period in which a new and more diverse series of immigrant 'waves' began to land. Entrenched ideas and stereotypes about newcomers from various nations survived the war, but it became more difficult for the Canadian government to enact laws restricting immigration, to favour certain potential immigrant groups, and to uphold existing discriminatory or exclusionary policies. In the late 1940s, following a war fought to defeat the sort of overt racism and ethnic biases that defined Nazi Germany, Canada, like other Western nations, portrayed itself as a welcoming place, especially to people fleeing countries that were in danger of 'falling' to Communism. Even though Canada's 'founding peoples'—those of British and French origins—sought to retain their positions as social leaders, their respective shares of the population decreased when immigration laws changed in 1962 to end discrimination based on national origin, race, or religious allegiance, and changed again in 1976 to accommodate refugees and re-unite families. As a result of these changes, the proportion of African and Asian immigrants increased. So far, historians are behind geographers and sociologists in studying the effects of these profound shifts. In the midst of those developments in immigration law, Canada adopted multiculturalism as an official policy in 1971. The policy explicitly stated that the Canadian government would acknowledge the contributions of all its various ethnic communities and, wherever possible, enact laws and policies that would respect the diversity of the Canadian population and the cultural differences between its various constituent groups. This counted as a big reversal, considering that the previous expectation was that newcomers would adapt their lives to a vaguely British/Canadian set of norms. Throughout the whole post-war era, the road to a more equitable multicultural society encountered obstacles, and the official vision masked the ongoing private tensions between individuals and communities in both urban and rural settings. In other words, hopes for an accommodating multicultural society sometimes differed drastically from reality. We feature the optimistic vision here in our primary sources. First, W.M. Haugan's call for pluralism is a call to reject old hierarchies and stereotypes, and foreshadows the multicultural policy that would be adopted over two decades later. Canadians should stop trying to make newcomers change to suit their new environment, Haugan argued, and instead recognize that retaining 'foreign' traditions can only help newcomers feel at home. The material from the House of Commons debates shows political party leaders (Liberal, Progressive Conservative, New Democratic Party, and Créditiste) more or less on the same page in their support of the basic idea of multiculturalism. Everyone, beginning with Prime Minister Trudeau, chimed in to remind Canadians that perhaps Canada's two founding peoples still rated a little extra merit in that multicultural would not mean multilingual. Trudeau's commitment to the rights of the individual no doubt contributed to his support for this ideal. The secondary material deals with two different processes: integrating immigrant 'foodways' with Canadian norms, and defining multiculturalism during the 1960s and early 1970s amid the worry over nationalism in Quebec. Iacovetta's contribution addresses the topic of immigrants' cooking as a part of the various immigrant cultures and as apart of home life that established Canadians saw as a threat to their own culture. These 'gatekeepers'—established Canadians who were well connected in government and community circles—mixed the sort of pluralism that Haugan advocated with a dose of caution. They wanted Canada's cuisine to be more diverse, but not too distant from what Canadians were used to consuming. Above all, they urged immigrant cooks to adjust their culinary habits to Canadian practices, especially to post-war abundance. Julia Lalande looks at the role of Ukrainian community members as representatives of a 'third force' influencing the Bilingualism and Biculturalism Commission during the 1960s. As a group whose career in Canada pre-dated the First World War, Ukrainians saw themselves as having a claim, even a right, to speak along with or on behalf of other immigrants who did not want to see Canada defined rigidly as a British/French creation. As norms changed in the post-war period, so did the expectations of newcomers, and so did the vision of harmony in diversity that Canadians proclaimed.

## QUESTIONS FOR CONSIDERATION

1. What do you think Haugan means by 'good Canadians'?
2. Even though they're mostly in agreement with the general principle of multiculturalism, what were some of the cautions or complaints the other party leaders had regarding the Trudeau government's policy?

3. Why might it be difficult to conduct historical research regarding some of the more recently arrived immigrant groups?
4. Why did the gatekeepers consider food so important to the process of helping immigrants see themselves as Canadian?
5. What were some of the items that representatives of the Ukrainian-Canadian community wanted to see as part of Canada's multiculturalism policy? Why do you think some were not adopted?

# SUGGESTIONS FOR FURTHER READING

Stephanie Bangarth, *Voices Raised in Protest: Defending North American Citizens of Japanese Ancestry, 1942–49* (Vancouver: UBC Press, 2008).

Neil Bissoondath, *Selling Illusions: The Cult of Multiculturalism in Canada* (Toronto: Penguin Books, 1994).

Richard J.F. Day, *Multiculturalism and the History of Canadian Diversity* (Toronto: University of Toronto Press, 2000).

Marlene Epp, Franca Iacovetta, and Frances Swyripa, eds., *Sisters or Strangers? Immigrant, Ethnic, and Racialized Women in Canadian History* (Toronto: University of Toronto Press, 2004).

Ninette Kelley and M. Trebilcock, *Making of a Mosaic: A History of Canadian Immigration Policy* (Toronto: University of Toronto Press, 1998).

Patricia Roy, *The Triumph of Citizenship: The Japanese and Chinese in Canada, 1941–67* (Vancouver: UBC Press, 2007).

# PRIMARY DOCUMENTS

1 From W.M. Haugan, 'Cultural Democracy', *Food for Thought* 10(1) (October 1949): 13–16, 50.

*What kind of cultural pattern do we wish to develop in Canada?*

Since the end of World War II, approximately a quarter of a million immigrants have come to this country. What do they expect and hope for in Canadian life? On the other hand, what do Canadians expect of them?

Most immigrants want freedom persecution and fear, a right to live as free persons. All want homes, jobs, and above all, social acceptance in the community to which they go. Most of all, they want to feel that they will not only enjoy, but actually be able to contribute something to, our community and national life. Canada is the first choice of many Displaced Persons as a re-settlement country partly because it is a relatively new country in the building of which they will be able to play a part and so prove their worth.

Canada wants immigrants who will add new skills and techniques to our industrial development, who will perform labour, skilled and unskilled, which will increase our national income, individuals who will be an asset and a valuable addition to our population. Most of all, we want immigrants who will become 'good Canadians'.

A good Canadian is not necessarily one who speaks, dresses and thinks as his neighbour, but one who shares with other Canadians a common understanding of the principles of Canadian democracy, confidence in her institutions, and faith in her people. He may still retain an interest in his former home and be a good Canadian. He may bring critical attitudes to the consideration of Canadian policies and he may contribute from his background to the solution of our problems.

If the pressure of social attitudes tends to influence the immigrant to drop his connections with his ethnic group, he is likely to resist. Then he is forced to find all his social contacts with his ethnic group and he develops a feeling of being different and isolated. His contribution to our country is lost. The man who can be an active member of a Service Club or a Board of Trade and at the same time a member of an ethnic group will find a more complete means of expression and will therefore be in a position to make a greater contribution to the community.

The present movement of immigrants to Canada does not create a new cultural problem, though it does serve to emphasize an already existent situation. This situation needs clarification. It requires the formulation of a policy which will permit all Canadians to enjoy the best possible way of life and yet contribute most to the common weal. With the varied origins of the people in mind, the question which presents itself to us is this: Are we to adopt a program of assimilation or uniformity in our cultural life, or of cultural pluralism, that is, the encouragement of a variety of cultural patterns? The factor which will guide us in any program for assisting immigrants in their adjustment to new values and standards must be determined by the method we choose for our own cultural development.

The cultural background of the Canadian people is just as varied as is the number of ethnic groups in our population. We recognize two major ethnic groups, but very often forget that our neighbours have come from every country in the world. Because of the fact that two dominant groups come from different origins, we are inclined to believe that these original cultures have remained unchanged. In reality the cultural contributions of these two dominant groups have been modified radically since they were brought to the shores of North America. Whether we like to admit it or not, modifications have come principally as the result of two major impacts. One was the necessity for adapting these cultures to new conditions found in North America. The other was the intermingling of cultural patterns brought to this country by the large number of non-Anglo, non-French people, and to some extent by the intermingling of the French and British cultures.

Much of the difficulty in discussing this subject arises from confusion of thought in the use of the word 'culture'. Culture is defined as the total result of human invention and discovery and the accumulated results of human effort which have been built up during man's continued struggle to satisfy his needs. The world is ever changing, and with it human behaviour. Therefore, culture is a dynamic concept of development and variation which, through the incorporation of new methods and the modification of old practices, is never static. It is continually changing as it is transmitted by social contact between the individuals who make up the total society. In reality culture is an expression of the life of a people and changes with that life.

Every group in Canada has a background in a way of life brought from some other part of the world. Each has a contribution peculiarly its own to make to a Canadian way of life. These cultural differences can be likened to the facets of a diamond. The beauty comes only when the stone is shaped with a number of facets. It is the facets which give life, sparkle and radiance to the stone. They vary with the light and the point of view of the observer.

A great deal is said about the contribution of the dominant groups to the growth and development of Canada, but at the same time recognition of the contribution of the less known groups is often, consciously or unconsciously, denied them. In reality each individual and group has added to the growth and development of this country. It may have been during the early settlement of Canada, through building our railroads, or by playing a part in confederation. It may be in more recent times in the opening up of our frontiers and industries or through the institutions they brought with them and developed here. We would lack something today had they not come.

In Canada we have at our disposal the cultural background of all who make up our Canadian population. We Canadians should draw upon this wealth for the benefit of all. Too often the use of this varied cultural reservoir is hampered by the false belief that we should not encourage the non-Anglo, non-French groups to retain their cultures because it will weaken the culture of one of the dominant groups. Nothing could be further from the truth. We must recognize, if we view it realistically and honestly, that the growth of Canadian culture is a result of the social intermingling of individuals of many different groups.

The tendency of people to form groups according to their own interests is recognized the world over. This has its basis in the family but usually the life of an individual must also revolve through many other groups—social, economic, political, religious, ethnic, language, as well as national and international. No one group can consider itself an entity, even though it be a community, but only as one of the integral parts of the nation, and that as part of mankind.

Dominant groups often have a tendency to criticize a minority for its grouping which is, in effect, a denial to that minority of social forms which are taken for granted by the dominant group. Criticism such as this tends to make the group boundaries rigid and forces members of each group to attach a disproportionate importance to their own group. At this point the harmful effects of social grouping appear: contact between groups becomes more difficult and the feeling develops within each group that its own values are the only ones that are right, and that those of all other groups are wrong.

Attitudes such as this prohibit the possibilities for any common bond between groups. It is not until the members of each ethnic or cultural group recognize and respect the origins and values of all other groups that intermingling can be accepted and encouraged. Only when this recognition and respect are given can all groups work together for a common purpose and the general benefit of all. Ability to work towards a common goal is the real indication of unity of purpose among groups, and people. As people learn to accept each other and work together, the capacity for development of the individual and of the nation is enlarged.

Language differences are often held to be the cause of the segregation of groups. This is true only so far as it makes communication between groups difficult. Any demand that a group give up its language is asking that group to give up one of the most vital parts of its culture. Without its own language a culture would lose much of its significance. The language of a cultural group provides the means of expression for beliefs, values and customs. Respect for others comes, not so much from knowing their language, as from the understanding of their beliefs, customs, and social organizations.

The worth of any nation is in her people and in this Canada is no exception. We believe that the inherent value of the individual is a basic principle of democracy. Therefore, the individual must be free to choose the group with which he wishes to be identified and still retain his equality of status. Some people are consciously or unconsciously drawn towards the dominant group while others hold tenaciously to their ethnic background. This should be their right. It is only when people can choose without fear of prejudice the path they wish, that there can be a free interchange of ideas which will stimulate cultural growth. This in turn, increases the scope and range for the development of the individual.

Cultural assimilation would mean reduction of all to one common form and expression, while, on the other hand, cultural pluralism would mean many more or less rigid divisions. Midway between is a cultural freedom, a cultural democracy, which will permit individuals to remain part of a minority group, to merge with a dominant group, or to unite with others to form new variations of the cultural theme. Cultural democracy is a pattern which is possible in a community, both large and small, where all individuals and groups are integrated on a basis of unity of purpose and mutual respect.

With the centripetal forces of common interest in Canadian democracy, with the cohesive effect of participation in community activity, and with the free interplay of socially equal groups, Canadian culture can be enriched and will continue to develop to limitless achievement. Only in such a pattern is there opportunity for fulfillment of the creative power and potential growth of the human personality.

2   From Pierre Elliott Trudeau, Robert L. Stanfield, David Lewis, Réal Caouette, 'Announcement of Implementation of Policy of Multiculturalism within Bilingual Framework', *House of Commons Debates*, October 8, 1971, 8545–8.

HOUSE OF COMMONS
Friday, October 8, 1971

ROUTINE PROCEEDINGS

CANADIAN CULTURE

ANNOUNCEMENT OF IMPLEMENTATION OF POLICY
OF MULTICULTURALISM WITHIN BILINGUAL FRAMEWORK

**Right Hon. P.E. Trudeau (Prime Minister):** Mr. Speaker, I am happy this morning to be able to reveal to the House that the government has accepted all those recommendations of the Royal Commission on Bilingualism and Biculturalism which are contained in Volume IV of its reports directed to federal departments and agencies. Hon. members will recall that the subject of this volume is 'the contribution by other ethnic groups to the cultural enrichment of Canada and the measures that should be taken to safeguard that contribution'.

Volume IV examined the whole question of cultural and ethnic pluralism in this country and the status of our various cultures and languages, an area of study given all too little attention in the past by scholars.

It was the view of the royal commission, shared by the government and, I am sure, by all Canadians, that there cannot be one cultural policy for Canadians of British and French origin, another for the original peoples and yet a third for all others. For although there are two official languages, there is no official culture, nor does any ethnic group take precedence over any other. No citizen or group of citizens is other than Canadian, and all should be treated fairly.

The royal commission was guided by the belief that adherence to one's ethnic group is influenced not so much by one's origin or mother tongue as by one's sense of belonging to the group and by what the commission calls the group's 'collective will to exist'. The government shares this belief.

The individual's freedom would he hampered if he were locked for life within a particular cultural compartment by the accident of birth or language. It is vital, therefore, that every Canadian, whatever his ethnic origin, be given a chance to learn at least one of the two languages in which his country conducts its official business and its politics.

A policy of multiculturalism within a bilingual framework commends itself to the government as the most suitable means of assuring the cultural freedom of Canadians. Such a policy should help to break down discriminatory attitudes and cultural jealousies. National unity if it is to mean anything in the deeply personal sense, must be founded on confidence in one's own individual identity; out of this can grow respect for that of others and a willingness to share ideas, attitudes and assumptions. A vigorous policy of multiculturalism will help create this initial confidence. It can form the base of a society which is based on fair play for all.

The government will support and encourage the various cultures and ethnic groups that give structure and vitality to our society. They will be encouraged to share their cultural expression and values with other Canadians and so contribute to a richer life for us all.

In the past, substantial public support has bean given largely to the arts and cultural institutions of English-speaking Canada. More recently and largely with the help of the royal commission's earlier recommendations in Volumes I to III, there has been a conscious effort on the government's part to correct any bias against the French language and culture. In the last few months the government has taken steps to provide funds to support cultural educational centres for native people. The policy I am announcing today accepts the contention of the other cultural communities that they, too, are essential elements in Canada and deserve government assistance in order to contribute to regional and national life in ways that derive from their heritage yet are distinctively Canadian.

In implementing a policy of multiculturalism within a bilingual framework, the government will provide support in four ways.

First, resources permitting, the government will seek to assist all Canadian cultural groups that have demonstrated a desire and effort to continue to develop a capacity to grow and contribute to Canada, and a clear need for assistance, the small and weak groups no less than the strong and highly organized.

Second, the government will assist members of all cultural groups to overcome cultural barriers to full participation in Canadian society.

Third, the government will promote creative encounters and interchange among all Canadian cultural groups in the interest of national unity.

Fourth, the government will continue to assist immigrants to acquire at least one of Canada's official languages in order to become full participants in Canadian society.

[*Translation*]

Mr. Speaker, I stated at the outset that the government has accepted in principle all recommendations addressed to federal departments and agencies. We are also ready and willing to work co-operatively with the provincial governments towards implementing those recommendations that concern matters under provincial or shared responsibility.

Some of the programmes endorsed recommended by the Commission have been administered for some time by various federal agencies. I might mention the Citizenship Branch, the CRTC and its predecessor the BBG, the National Film Board and the National Museum of Man. These programmes will be revised, broadened and reactivated and they will receive the additional funds that may be required.

Some of the recommendations that concern matters under provincial jurisdiction call for coordinated federal and provincial action. As a first step, I have written to the First Ministers of the provinces informing them of the response of the federal government and seeking their co-operation. Officials will be asked to carry this consultation further.

I wish to table details of the government's response to each of the several recommendations.

It should be noted that some of the programmes require pilot projects or further short-term research before more extensive action can be taken. As soon as these preliminary studies are available, further programmes will be announced and initiated. Additional financial and personnel resources will be provided.

Responsibility for implementing these recommendations has been assigned to the Citizenship Branch of the Department of the Secretary of State, the agency now responsible for matters affecting the social integration of immigrants and the cultural activities of all ethnic groups. An Inter-Agency Committee of all those agencies involved will be established to co-ordinate the federal effort.

[*English*]

In conclusion, I wish to emphasize the view of the government that a policy of multiculturalism within a bilingual framework is basically the conscious support of individual freedom of choice. We are free to be ourselves. But this cannot be left to chance. It must be fostered and pursued actively. If freedom of choice is in danger for some ethnic groups, it is in danger for all. It is the policy of this government to eliminate any such danger and to 'safeguard' this freedom.

I am tabling this document, Mr. Speaker, but it might be the desire of the House to have it appended to *Hansard* in view of its importance and long-lasting effect.

**Mr. Speaker:** Is that agreed?

**Some hon. Members:** Agreed.

**Hon. Robert L. Stanfield (Leader of the Opposition):** Mr. Speaker, these are excellent words in the Prime Minister's statement. I am sure this declaration by the government of the principle of preserving and enhancing the many cultural traditions which exist within our country will be most welcome. I think it is about time this government finally admitted that the cultural identity of Canada is a pretty complex thing.

[*Translation*]

I wish to state immediately, Mr. Speaker, that the emphasis we have given to multiculturalism in no way constitutes an attack on the basic duality of our country. What we want is justice for all Canadians, and recognition of the cultural diversity of this country.

[*English*]

It is about time the government finally recognized the validity of what we were trying to say in June of 1969 at the time of the debate on the official languages bill in the amendment we put forward then proposing recognition of the right to speak other languages and the importance of assisting in the development and preservation of these other cultures. The amendment said that we can accept the official duality of the country without denying the rights of other cultural groups. Our amendment was put forward for that purpose. It is pleasing to note that the government this morning is recognizing the importance of the rights of other cultural groups, although at that time our amendment was rejected out of hand. I am pleased the government has seen the light. But I must also say that, although this is all to the good, I regret that this statement was not made much more promptly.

Apart from what members of our party, among others, have been saying, it is a fact that the fourth volume of the B and B report has been available since early 1970, and I say in all sincerity that the failure of the government to endorse these principles earlier has created some suspicion, some doubts, in the minds of the members of these other cultural groups about the importance the government of Canada has attached to them. I must say that if the effectiveness of the government's action in encouraging the cultural self-fulfilment of the native peoples of Canada can be taken as any kind of an indication of what the practice will be in this broader field, apart from the statement of principles, then there is not a great deal of hope for the various non-French and non-British ethnic groups within Canada. With regard to the native peoples there have been many statements about high principles but very little in the way of results and there is some doubt, to mention one example, concerning whether the government is doing enough in northeastern Alberta to help the native peoples study their own language.

It is fine to announce a principle, but perhaps the most important thing is what the government is going to do to implement this principle. When the Prime Minister uses a phrase such as 'within available funds' we must keep in mind the importance of a balance here. There is no indication whatsoever in the Prime Minister's statement this morning that there will be any substantial implementation. I fully agree that a good deal of money must be expended for the encouragement of the development of bilingualism in this country, but I do not think that members of the other cultural groups with other cultural traditions are at all happy with the relatively pitiful amounts that have been allocated to this other aspect of the diversity about which the Prime Minister spoke this morning, multiculturalism.

The Prime Minister has announced the principles. We expect the Prime Minister and his colleagues to give those principles life and meaning, and we will look forward most anxiously to the implementation of these principles.

**Mr. David Lewis (York South):** I must say, Mr. Speaker, that it is a pleasure to be able to comment on an important aspect of Canadian life that does not have to do with the economy or with unemployment, and it is equally a pleasure to be able to agree with the statement that the Prime Minister made this morning.

As members of this House know, I have not hesitated to criticize government policy, and no doubt a great deal can be said about tardiness and other aspects of the problem which the Prime Minister has put before us. But I propose this morning merely to express our support and our hopes in order to indicate to the people of Canada that this Parliament is united in its belated determination to recognize the value of the many cultures in our country.

[*Translation*]

Mr. Speaker, it is with a deep appreciation of both aspects of our Canadian cultural life, official bilingualism and multiculturalism, that my party warmly supports the principles set forth this morning by the Prime Minister.

I have often said that one of the most striking wealth of our country is the fact that it has been founded by two distinctive groups having two distinctive languages well known throughout the world. However, another wealth is also important, since we find in Canada some representatives of almost all the cultures in the world. To all Canadians, whatever their ethnic origin, I say that they must be proud of those two enriching aspects of our country.

[*English*]

Every society has its own cultural treasures which it cherishes with pride. It is a fact of man's history that his preoccupations have been too frequently centred on material development and that his spirit has too often been embittered by conflict and by prejudice. The result has been throughout the world—and this is true of Canadians as well—a failure to appreciate the values of diversity, a tendency to resent rather than to welcome enriching differences. For Canada this attitude is particularly destructive. The diversity of cultures across the land is a source of our greatness as a people.

As a representative from Toronto I could perhaps say that even a serious subject permits of a little lightness. There was a time not so very long ago when there were jokes made all across Canada about spending a month in Toronto last weekend, and other remarks of that sort. But it is a fact that the influx of people of Italian origin, of Greek origin, of West Indian origin, of origins from many other parts of the world, has made Torontonians proud of their city in a way in which they were not before, and makes some of them even suggest that it is now a viable rival to the city of Montreal.

Yet, Mr. Speaker, it is a fact of society that every minority has a problem of survival. It has a problem of assimilation. It has a problem of keeping alive.

[ . . . ]

**Mr. Lewis:** Mr. Speaker, if I may become serious again, I suggest that the important point that faces us is that in every society a minority has a problem, the problem of survival, the problem of keeping alive its history, its language, its traditions, its songs, its legends, its identity. When the majority in a society is as cruel as majorities have often been, not only are minorities crushed but the spirit of that society, the soul of that society is destroyed. It is in that spirit, therefore, that on behalf of my party I welcome the Prime Minister's statement without any reservations.

I make only these two short comments in conclusion. I suggest that our failure in this area in the past was not the fault of any one government or any one level of government in Canada. It has been a failure of all our people across this country, a failure of Canadians to appreciate the importance of these things, a failure of Canadians in their neglect of the native peoples of this country. I am not saying this to needle the Prime Minister or the government but I say, because I believe it to be true. The statement of principles will be a mockery and a betrayal of high ideals and objectives unless collectively we provide the funds to make the principles meaningful in the lives of the minorities in Canada, and unless we develop programs in consultation with the minorities, giving them every opportunity to participate in the development of programs rather than imposing such programs on them. Democracy requires this kind of consideration, and with all my heart I hope that the statement of principles will be followed with action which will make us all proud of our country.

[*Translation*]

**Mr. Réal Caouette (Témiscamingue):** Mr. Speaker, even if I do not always agree with the Prime Minister on various points, I fully agree with the statement he made this morning. Indeed, I have been repeating for 30 years, to those who will hear me, and those who won't, that we have one Canadian nation and not two, three or ten, that we have two official languages, English and French, and that we have a multiplicity of cultures which are the wealth of our country.

Mr. Speaker, my colleagues and myself are happy the Prime Minister made that statement. However, I find this statement somewhat confusing. The Prime Minister has stated and I quote:

For although there are two official languages, there is no official culture, nor does any ethnic group take precedence over any other. No citizen or group of citizens is other than Canadian . . .

Mr. Speaker, if there is no official culture in Canada, I do not see how we could succeed in really becoming a nation while we would be endowed with only a few cultures unable to get on among themselves or at war with one another. I am positive that we have in Canada a culture peculiar to us. We French Canadians have one that is not at all that of France, just as English-speaking Canadians have a culture which is different from that of Englishmen from England. We have our own Canadian culture. We have our history. Our traditions and customs may differ from one area or ethnic group to another. However, if we cannot change an Englishman into a Frenchman, or vice versa, we can nonetheless make good Canadians out of members of all ethnic groups in Canada.

Ukrainians, Italians and Germans must be able to attain self-fulfilment in Canada.

I am absolutely convinced that Canadians in general share the views expressed this morning by the Prime Minister. So there is no reason to worry. There is trouble in Quebec and elsewhere in Canada. Some say that if things are going wrong, it is the fault of French Canadians or English Canadians, or because we welcome too many immigrants, and so on.

[*English*]

What I said in French was that we do not want to have in Canada a little France, a little England, a little Italy or a little Russia. We want in Canada a great country for all the people of Canada, for all the ethnic groups in our country. Through that channel we will achieve unity and we will reinforce our position in the whole world.

# HISTORICAL INTERPRETATIONS

3    From Franca Iacovetta, *Gatekeepers: Reshaping Immigrant Lives in Cold War Canada* (Toronto: Between the Lines, 2006), 137–69, 323–9.

## CULINARY CONTAINMENT? COOKING FOR THE FAMILY, DEMOCRACY, AND NATION

In those post-war years the struggle to win the hearts and minds of the newcomers was contested on another less immediately apparent terrain: the culinary front. As the gatekeepers well understood, the culture of food—the newcomers' kitchens and family meals, and women's shopping and cooking methods—was no less political than were the workings of the ethnic organizations and press. People's foodways were shaped not simply by choice but by a constellation of forces: material circumstances, educational and cultural backgrounds, the mass media, including the saturation advertising of food corporations and appliance manufacturers, and even government campaigns. As a result, Canada's post-war food and nutritional gatekeepers—a group including professional dietitians, public health nurses, social workers, food writers, and fashion-makers as well as Citizenship Branch officials—were at the ready to assess and shape the newcomers' nutritional profiles and food practices—and thereby to promote a pro-capitalist and pro-democracy ideal of family and kitchen consumerism.

Just as they were concerned about Canadianizing and democratizing—and also containing—the ethnic press, the gatekeepers' approach to the newcomers' food customs reflected a mix of democratic ideals, Cold War politics, and cultural pluralism. In this case the pro-capitalist democratic discourse stressed the paradoxical ideal of the democratic but patriarchal family. It also played with notions of affordable abundance tempered by Cold War anxieties and the challenge of helping harried and financially strapped mothers feed their families properly on limited family incomes.

The greater emphasis on cultural pluralism as opposed to Cold War politics largely reflected the gatekeepers' view that ethnic foodways could be more easily contained and were less threatening to the Canadian state or mainstream culture than were the subversive activities of either the ethnic left or far right. As they did with ethnic craft shows and international music nights, the gatekeepers endorsed, mined, and appropriated ethnic foodways as part of their nation-building strategy of promoting national unity through an embrace of cultural diversity. There was also a significant gender difference: whereas the state's dealings with the ethnic press occurred within a largely male world, the food gatekeepers included large numbers of women, and they primarily targeted their own sex on the grounds that a better informed and Canadianized wife and mother would have a positive influence over the rest of her family.

Working within this complex realm of foodways—and its class, gender, and cultural dynamics—the post-war health and food campaigns would become the site of conflicts and accommodations between, on one side, the experts who promoted good health and modern cooking and family lifestyles and, on the other, the newcomer mothers from war-torn or impoverished regions of Europe. These mothers, having had little access to convenience foods or the latest kitchen technology, were now told to abandon their folkways for 'modern' shopping and homemaking techniques. Canada's post-war food gatekeepers would also make pronounced efforts to bring certain ethnic foods into the mainstream, and even celebrate multi-ethnic foodways as a nation-making device.

# FROM FAMINE TO WELL-STOCKED KITCHENS AND SHOPS

When the gatekeepers articulated the dominant family values and heightened domesticity of the early post-war era, they frequently invoked images of 'wholesome' and 'modern' family living. These images were premised upon a dominant and highly influential bourgeois model of a breadwinner husband and homemaker wife and mother—though this model was far from universal, even within Canada. Indeed, the model privileged middle-class ideals that had never entirely reflected most people's lives.[1]

This ideal, whose celebration also reflected a conservative reaction again women's increased freedoms and economic gains in wartime, focused attention on women's primary responsibility for feeding and nurturing healthy families, managing modern, efficient, and well-equipped households, and raising well-adjusted children.[2] It was also the ubiquitous subject of contemporary debates over women's roles engendered by the growing presence of working mothers, day-care lobbies, increasing divorce rates, and other signs of women's changing status in post-1945 society.[3]

The dominant homemaker ideology called for the 'domestic containment' of women—which necessarily included the many European women who would enter the Canadian workforce, in very large numbers, in Toronto. At the same time, as the IODE illustrated in its image of the woman sweeping out communism, both old and new Canadian women could practise democracy and fight communism from their kitchens.

The Canadian post-war discussions of the ideal homemaker often made much of the differing economic situations prevailing in post-war Europe and Canada. For example, even in the late 1940s, when Canadians faced continued rationing, spiralling inflation (after the lifting of wartime price controls), and an acute housing crisis, various gatekeepers drew comparisons between a Europe of scarcity and a Canada of abundance. Canadian relief workers posted overseas emphasized that Canadian homemakers, though struggling, were still better off than those in Britain and Europe. In 1948 a Canadian nutritionist posted in England with the United Emergency Fund for Britain noted the particularly horrid plight of the British housewife, who was still lining up for long hours to get her paltry weekly family rations (lamb chop, egg, bits of bacon, cheese, some milk) and perhaps a bit of unrationed meat (heart, kidney, tripe). By comparison, she said, Canadian women lived 'in a land of plenty', and should donate to the British fund.

The impact of the Cold War does not in and of itself explain the renewed popularity of the nuclear family and the homemaker ideal as post-war ideology. But insofar as the homemaker ideal also symbolized the stability and superiority of Western democratic families, the Cold War did have an important effect. Just as the Communist alerts and fact sheets of the time tended to emphasize the contrast between claims about the quality of life under Communism and the difficult realities of workers' lives in the Soviet Union, the Cold War versions of the homemaker ideology stressed the huge gap in the quality of life between North America and the Soviet Union. In Canada, as in the United States (and Canadians were regularly exposed to US propaganda), mothers were portrayed as the beneficiaries of an economic system that ensured them a decent standard of living, good health, the resources to raise children properly, and opportunities for personal and cultural fulfilment. By contrast, Soviet women were depicted as beasts of burden brutalized by heavy work and acute scarcity, as people denied the opportunity to ensure 'a wholesome family life'.

[ . . . ]

Following a group tour in the Soviet Union, Rev. James F. Drane wrote a scathing report in the *Canadian Register*, describing the shocking presence everywhere of white-kerchiefed peasant women who, far removed from their families, performed heavy, filthy, and dangerous (male) jobs on railway work crews, in construction and farm work, and factories producing heavy machinery. With wages that were inadequate to meet their families' needs, their masculinized bodies, 'with muscles hardened', were a fitting 'tribute' to the harsh 'doctrine of Bebel, Engels, Marx and Lenin'.[4]

Far from being merely rhetorical devices or cultural by-products of the Cold War, these propaganda materials were carefully constructed, gendered ideological weapons meant to promote Western capitalism's superiority and to cultivate loyalty and conformity to North American ideals. Once again, however, some social critics, including liberal Cold Warriors, warned that rampant consumerism and the planned obsolescence (including of appliances) that was becoming a hallmark of capitalism might produce entirely materialistic citizens.[5] [ . . . ]

When Canadian gatekeepers introduced European women to 'Canadian ways', including Canadian food customs and households, they promoted a Canada of middle-class affluence and modernity, promising the women that they too could have the resources required to meet all of their family's needs. They used teaching tools that, whether produced by government departments or corporate capital, featured consumer images of the ideal homemaker and the many modern conveniences that supposedly defined the Canadian way of life.

Front-line social workers and nutritionists also made use of commercial magazines, newspapers, and government publications, as well as NFB films produced with the Citizenship Branch for the purpose of educating the staff of social service agencies working with new Canadians. These materials presented the usual image of the Canadian homemaker as a white, slim, attractive, well-dressed and nicely coifed middle-class woman pushing an overflowing grocery cart down store aisles between well-stocked shelves. At home she was at work in a well-appointed modern kitchen using canned, frozen, and other items from her well-stocked shelves, fridge, and freezer. She might whip up a family snack or impromptu cocktail party using the latest tabletop appliances, such as blenders and bun warmers. She could use the brightly coloured plastic Tupperware containers to store leftovers or for packing a child's school lunch.[6]

# DIETETIC GATEKEEPERS: FATTENING UP THE BODY POLITIC

Health lobbyists, nutritionists, and social workers drew links between ensuring a healthy body politic and a healthy nation and Western democracy in the Cold War. Even the act of fattening up thin and malnourished newcomers was celebrated as a moral and political victory. When writer Ronald Williams praised Thorold, Ontario businessmen for fighting Communism through an aggressive refugee reception program, he used a Ukrainian DP [displaced person] woman's body as one indicator of success: 'When Daria left the camp, she was a skinny 86 pounds. Today she's a plump 150 pounds'. He was referring, perhaps too flippantly, to how hearty portions of Ukrainian dishes such as borscht and dumplings (served with thick gravy or sour cream) and high-fat sausages could do the trick.[7] [...]

Given that a healthy body politic meant ensuring the health of the entire population, the newcomers' health was not discussed in isolation. With declarations that Canada, like the United States, was falling behind the Soviet Union in promoting health, Canadian health advocates lobbied for more public funding to teach everyone, especially mothers, the importance of stringent health standards, healthy food habits, and 'modern' eating regimes. Professional dietitians, social workers, and public health nurses used the

flexible *Canada Food Guide* to raise awareness about nutrition, illness prevention, and the importance of early diagnosis and treatment.[8] A good diet, they stressed, improved children's growth rates and physiques, built up resistance to diseases, and meant longer lives. A faulty diet from early in life might not show immediate results, but could produce far greater damage than a vice such as adult drinking. [ . . . ]

In keeping with the era's sense of liberal pluralism, in evaluating immigrant food customs Canadian nutritionists counselled flexibility (not assimilation). They cast themselves both as the experts with the scientific authority to assess foods and as the cultural interpreters who could 'coax' newcomers into adapting their food habits to Canadian conditions. Both themes are captured in a post-war guidebook, *Food Customs of New Canadians*, produced by the Toronto Nutrition Committee. Aimed at health workers dealing with newcomer clients across Canada, the book reflected the basic principles of the post-war food and health campaigns: it emphasized efficient and economical food shopping and preparation, with a focus on nutrition (and variety).[9]

*Chatelaine* magazine also proved to be a valuable source in the post-war food campaigns. A team of professional home economists staffed the magazine's Institute Kitchen, where they created recipes and meal plans and tested their readers' recipes, all in the service, once again, of promoting healthy, efficient, and economical food shopping and cooking. A common piece of advice for consumers was to avoid expensive out-of-season fruit and vegetable imports in winter, and instead purchase tinned foods or, if they could afford it and had the freezer space, the slightly more expensive frozen foods. Predictably, given the magazine's dependence on advertising, it sometimes gave its seal of approval to the products of corporate sponsors—as no doubt suggested by the business department. This practice illustrates one of the ways in which food corporations fashioned taste, that is, by saturating the popular media with their products.[10] But the *Chatelaine* experts did enjoy a degree of autonomy and sometimes refused to promote the advertisers' products (many of them processed convenience goods) on the grounds that they were too expensive. Their food features highlighted affordable and healthy meals based on economical cuts of meat, including hamburger. They might suggest a quick potato or rice side dish and vegetables, or the ubiquitous casserole, which stretched modest amounts of meat mixed with potatoes, rice, or other starches. A popular feature with readers, including the admittedly small number of immigrant and ethnic Canadian women who wrote in to say so, was 'Meals of the Month', a month-long table of daily menu plans that provided the new, busy, or unimaginative cook with ideas for making a variety of nutritious meals on a modest budget. Some front-line health workers used this and other Chatelaine guides, as well as supplementary publications such as *A Bride's Guide to Cooking*, in their work with female and family clients, who would have included the European newcomers.[11]

Canadian food experts thus promoted a scaled-down version of affluence, one that recognized the modest incomes of many new and old Canadian mothers, though they certainly celebrated democratic living by extolling the virtues of affordable abundance and capitalist modernity. In England, Canadian Red Cross dietitians had told the British war brides that the greater array of foods in Canada meant they could produce the all-Canadian well-balanced diet, which included fresh salads and homemade fruit pies—and in the process save them from doctor and dentist bills.[12] [ . . . ]

These kinds of efforts to improve and modernize women's culinary skills also nicely served the interests of Canadian capitalists, who were well aware that the establishment of tens of thousands of new Canadian households would involve the purchase of countless kitchen and other appliances as well as furniture and other household items. (An irony of the latest 'labour-saving' devices was that the constantly escalating standards of homemaking meant that few women ever enjoyed the promised leisure that was to come with the purchase of a new stove, fridge, washing machine, or vacuum cleaner.) Similarly, Canadian dietitians used definitions of Canadian ways and standards that were as much about class and capitalist notions of efficiency, budgeting, and time management as about nutrition and food. They held that the North American pattern of three square meals per day was sacrosanct, for example, on the grounds that it perfectly suited the normal school and working hours.[13]

## NEGOTIATING AND RESISTING HOMEMAKER TRAINING

In handling the pressures placed on them by the gatekeepers' food and homemaking campaigns and by their husbands and children, newcomer women took on their responsibilities with alacrity. Their activities reveal general patterns, and the many anecdotes highlight the importance of choice and circumstance.

While their capacity for exercising individual choice or resistance to outsiders could differ greatly, they generally responded in selective and pragmatic ways to Canadian health experts and to the homemaking campaigns, even if they could not entirely control the terms of these encounters. Some of them also found particular ways of negotiating family culinary conflicts, especially between husband and children. Many women were able to reproduce old world family dishes and diets fairly soon after their arrival, and they also gradually integrated Canadian foods, though the timing and degree differed across households. The many different hybrid family cuisines that emerged as a result reveal a variety of patterns that defy easy categorization. Alongside the many immigrant mothers who steadfastly stuck to 'traditional' meals were some mothers who deliberately experimented with certain Canadian recipes or convenience foods. Canadian nutritionists would have happily applauded Dagmar Z., a Czech woman who said she had maintained a 'traditional Czechoslovakian kitchen' but 'altered it' to be 'more nutritious and healthy', as she had 'learned' to do in Canada.[14]

Newcomer women were exposed to Canadian foodways in different contexts. The British war brides, for instance, were encouraged to attend nutrition and cooking lectures in Britain before sailing for Canada. In Canada, Red Cross personnel and others taught them how to make muffins, tea biscuits, cream sauces, salads, and cakes, and showed them canning techniques, while public health workers ran nutrition classes and made home visits to advise them about 'meal planning and budgeting'. In their positive reports, Red Cross workers noted that the British 'girls' learned to use Canadian equipment and measurements, got practical cooking experience, enjoyed the chance to socialize with other women, and liked their 'Canadian' gift of a set of plastic measuring spoons. Some British women were encouraged by their husbands (and in-laws) to make Canadian meals, while others complained that Canadians failed to appreciate the differences between British and Canadian foodways.[15] The Dutch war brides had a reputation as healthy and hearty eaters. Their favourite meals included beef or pork pot roasts and stews (which could be made with cheaper cuts of meat), smoked sausages, or herring, served with potatoes, vegetables, and gravy.[16]

[ . . . ]

The frequency and intensity of the European women's encounters with Canadian nutritionists, dietitians, or nurses varied greatly, but generally these occasions were not of lengthy duration. In Toronto some women discussed their children's health needs in a new Canadian mother's club or local nursery school. Others used the baby clinics staffed by public health nurses. After giving birth, a mother might be visited by a nurse, at the hospital or at home, who tried to counsel her about meal planning, nutrition, and family budgets. Some settlement houses arranged field trips to stores and supermarkets. In this and other ways, the women picked up information or advice and could choose how and when to use it.[17]

The women's encounters with the 'experts' cannot be separated from their material conditions upon arrival or from their family dynamics. Wherever they settled, their household conditions were often far from ideal. In contrast to the boosterish and consumer images of 'typical' Canadian dining rooms, modern kitchens, and suburban houses, many of Toronto's newly arrived Europeans lived in crowded, even substandard flats, or in equally unappealing rooming houses. A woman and her family might share a bathroom or kitchen with other families, or boarders, and perhaps make do with makeshift sleeping arrangements. A Greek woman's description of her first family home in the west end of Toronto applied to many of the newcomers' first rental flats. Since it had 'no kitchen', her mother cooked on an electric hot plate in a room that also did for a bedroom. She washed the dishes in the bathroom sink. A lack of hot water meant a lot of boiling, and the absence of a refrigerator meant daily shopping to purchase fresh milk and other perishables. [ . . . ][18]

## ETHNIC APPROACHES TO FEEDING FAMILIES

Despite their less than ideal early households, many European women in Toronto needed either to learn new cooking skills or, when necessary, modify existing skills in order to feed their families and reproduce traditional meals. They could do so largely because of the presence of ethnic food shops and markets established by the members of earlier migrations. Whatever their class background, many European women shopped for food not in the splashy new supermarkets, but in the many ma and pa ethnic shops, with their pungent smells, lopsided aisles, unwrapped foods, and old-fashioned cash registers. These stores had what they wanted. In west-end Toronto, Italians and Portuguese flocked to the tiny shops and outdoor stands of Kensington Market just off Spadina Avenue, where they could find everything from bread and oil-drenched olives (much preferred to the 'tasteless' tinned black or bottled green varieties) to rabbits and pigeons. [ . . . ] With increased migration, new shops, as well as restaurants, were established.[19]

When European women said they found Canadian meat 'unappetizing', they largely meant that they preferred their own well-seasoned dishes, which, again, could be made on a budget. For example, German, Czech, and Polish women frequently cooked pork or beef along with seasoned potatoes and vegetables. They might cook everything in a one-pot, stovetop stew. If they could afford it, they would top the dish off with a cream sauce, or sour cream, or a gravy made from the meat juices. The same vegetables, cooked in a variety of ways, produced a range of European dishes. For example, women used cabbage in homemade sauerkraut, a common German, Austrian, Dutch, Polish, and Ukrainian dish. Or they made cabbage rolls stuffed with rice or meat, a favourite dish among Latvians, Estonians, and Lithuanians. Soups and vegetables cooked with roasted flour produced a flavour characteristic of meals made in parts of Hungary and surrounding regions.

[ . . . ]

## CANADIAN APPROACHES TO FEEDING FAMILIES

Significantly, Canadian food experts, including the Toronto nutritionists who designed the post-war food guide *Food Customs of New Canadians*, acknowledged the capacity of European newcomer women to manage, in their new environment, to cook traditional or familiar meals that were relatively inexpensive and reasonably nutritious. But they also found plenty to criticize, especially with respect to ensuring children's health. In keeping with its liberal slant, the guide did not give any one group an entirely negative or positive evaluation.

On the positive side, the guide reported that in their family diets most of the European groups had a good mix of vegetables, including lettuce, cabbage, carrots, spinach, kale, turnips, beets, cauliflower, tomatoes, peas, leeks, parsnips, and mushrooms. The guide recognized that many European women from modest rural backgrounds, and even urban ones, knew about stretching economical cuts of meat with starches and vegetables and producing one-dish meals using meat alternatives such as fish. Comments made about the Polish homemaker, that she could make 'a small amount of inexpensive meat' go 'a long way in soups and stews' and that she often substituted meat for 'legumes, eggs and fish in all forms', were echoed in the assessments of the other European groups. The guide also observed that many of the women had adapted easily to the availability of certain foods, such as citrus fruits, that had been prohibitively expensive back home.

On the negative side, the nutritionists made specific criticisms and recommendations for each group. Some of their advice applied as much to old Canadian as to new Canadian mothers, as in the case of teaching the value of canned or frozen fruits, vegetables, and fruit juices as substitutes for fresh but expensive and out-of-season imports. The call to cook more hearty breakfasts was another common piece of advice. In this case, European women who cooked milk-based mushes with bread or oatmeal-type breakfasts (such as the Portuguese) or pancakes with fruit (such as the Dutch) scored well in comparison to many Canadian mothers. But those who stuck to their 'continental-style' breakfast of crusty bun, or toast, and coffee had to be reformed.

As newcomers' children quickly became too fond of candy, sweet carbonated pop, and sugared cereals, the guide also instructed front-line workers to discourage the mothers from purchasing these items. Again, Canadian mothers, especially working mothers who did not have the time to make cooked cereals or other dishes, faced similar criticism. In other cases the advice was specific to a group. For example, the guide stated that Polish women had to learn to cook their vegetables for less time in order to preserve the nutrients.

Furthermore, the guide established a hierarchy of ethnic groups based on the principle of who could most easily make the transition to Canadian food customs. The hierarchy bore a strong resemblance to Canada's traditional ethnic preference ladder, with the biggest winners being the Germans and Dutch. The 'similarity of foods in the home countries and Canada', the guide observed of Germans and Austrians, 'makes adjustment relatively easy'. The most positive evaluation of all went to the 'Dutch housewife', who 'prizes culinary skill combined with economy and these abilities enable her to make a smooth transition in any adjustment of foods and food customs necessitated by changed environment'. Her generous use of cheese and milk, fruits, and a wide variety of vegetables, and her limited use of candy and soft drinks, were 'particularly commendable'. [ . . . ] But even the Dutch homemaker could improve her skills: the guide advised a greater use of liver and organ meats. It also made specific recommendations for other highly rated groups. The Czechs adapted comparatively easily to Canadian foodways and used a healthy array of food groups, but they had a propensity to be overweight because of their love of dumplings—which they often ate together with potatoes—as well as sweetened beverages and high-fat meats. The adults needed to drink more milk and eat more cheese. The Austrians ate too many sweets.

The southern Europeans (as well as the few non-European groups profiled), particularly the Portuguese and Italians, came in for more critical comments and recommendations, but the guide praised Greek mothers for producing 'a happy combination of both Greek and typically Canadian dishes'. The guide approved of dishes such as moussaka, described as 'a casserole with ground beef and potatoes', as well as of bean and lentil soups and tomato and cucumber salads. As the supposedly most humble rural newcomers, Portuguese and Italian women were portrayed as the furthest removed from modern Canadian foodways. Not only did they need to be introduced to the necessary tools of a modern household (a gas or electric stove, refrigerator, and storage space), but they had to reform their food-shopping regimes. According to the experts, these women foolishly spent too much of their meagre family budgets on expensive imported goods, such as olive oil, meats, and cheeses for the Italians and fresh fish for the Portuguese. These were particular food no-nos given the availability of cheaper Canadian alternatives, such as corn oil and frozen fish, respectively. Front-line workers were instructed to encourage these women to forgo familiar items, now dubbed expensive luxury foods, in favour of more affordable Canadian products. The experts' family-budget focus trumped their respect for the newcomers' cultural preferences even though the items in question were healthy. For no group was alcoholism identified as a problem, though all of them, save Jews, were described as regular consumers of beer or wine. But Italian mothers were scolded for permitting children to drink a bit of wine (with water or pop) with meals. The *Food Customs* guide recommended carbonated soft drinks as the lesser evil.

Certain class and cultural biases also emerge in the nutritionists' negative evaluations of European women's frequent food-shopping habits, attributing them entirely to poverty (lack of storage or refrigeration) or rural underdevelopment, while ignoring the cultural and social significance. In the bakeries, butcher and fish shops, and other specialty stores of old world towns and villages, women had developed important lines of trust and credit with shopkeepers and critical networks of information and support. For Canadian nutritionists, however, North American middle-class notions of efficiency and cleanliness predominated (access to clean, well-stocked, modern stores meant shopping less frequently and more efficiently), and indeed were equated with modernity. But in the post-war years the celebrated modern supermarket that was being promoted—large chain stores such as Dominion, Loblaws, and Power—were hardly places in which immigrant women well versed in marketplace 'haggling' could practise their craft. For these women the ethnic shops and open markets made better economic sense: the frequency of contact helped low-income women to forge bonds of trust with local shopkeepers, who often extended credit to families in financial straits. Even for the middle-class Europeans who had lived in the world's most historic cities, the assumption that daily shopping was 'backward' revealed an ignorance of food and shopping customs that involved daily or frequent trips to local bakeries, coffee bars, butcher shops, or greengrocers.

[ . . . ]

## RESISTING CONFORMITY

Generally speaking, European mothers were both preserving and, in some cases, modifying their food habits in Canada. In certain cases they clearly resisted the pressures to adopt Canadian foodways. When the medical health of a child was not at stake, some women tried to draw boundaries around what they, as mothers and food providers, were prepared to 'give up' to the gatekeepers. To the frustration of the public health nurses who staffed the baby clinics in Toronto neighbourhoods, for example, immigrant mothers willingly brought their children in for their vaccination shots, weigh-ins, and free milk, but comparatively few of them stuck around for the

lectures on nutrition and child-rearing, which at any rate were in English. Women from a variety of European countries responded in this pragmatic way, although the Italian mothers were singled out as the worst offenders.[20]

Like all mothers, European women had to negotiate the daily pressures that emerged within their own families, and their responses influenced the various family dynamics and cuisines that developed. While most European couples generally preferred familiar foods, various intriguing patterns, as well as some divergent patterns, did emerge. When husbands insisted that, at home, the family was 'to eat Estonian' or Greek or German, they usually did so as a bold, even manly, declaration of their pride in their culture. This gender and cultural dynamic could also overlap with class politics, as in the case of left-wing Ukrainian Canadians. The men believed as strongly as the women that 'eating Ukrainian' was critical to their twinned cultural and political identity as progressive Ukrainian Canadians, but they left the women to make the meals. The women's willingness to shop and prepare such favourite dishes as *holubtsi* (cabbage rolls) and *pyrohy* reflected their own commitment and emotional attachment to those foods. Their labour also saved costs at their various community events, so that it was also a form of kitchen activism.[21] By the same token, the husband who encouraged his wife to incorporate Canadian foods into their family rituals usually constructed himself as the family's representative in the outside world, the one who would guide his own family's accommodation to Canadian ways. At times this feature also related directly to the man having obtained Canadian citizenship, an act that many men linked to their role as the family head.[22]

By far the greatest pressures on women to experiment with Canadian foods came from their children, especially those who were exposed to the vastly different lunches of their Canadian schoolmates. At school, many a European child quickly became embarrassed by the spicy salami or sausage sandwiches that mother made with crusty or dark bread. They dreaded opening up their bags lest the smells offend the other children and prompt insulting remarks. They looked with envy at the neat 'Canadian' sandwiches of white bread with peanut butter and jam, or at the bright orange slices of cheese that had little or no odour. Along with sugar-coated cereals, immigrant children's favourites were hot dogs, hamburgers, and the airy buns served with them. Many a Polish, German, Hungarian, Greek, and Portuguese mother first experimented with store-bought hot dogs (as opposed to 'real sausages'), tinned soups, Kraft singles, hamburgers and hamburg buns, mayonnaise, Spam, Jell-O, and sugared cereals because of her children's persistent requests. Getting this food sometimes required going to a Loblaws or Dominion store, so that both changes occurred in tandem. The issue of food could also cause mothers embarrassment or emotional hurt. During her *Chatelaine* interview with Edna Staebler, Alda Pilli was visibly embarrassed when her son Luigi declared his love of 'Canadian' food—'hamburgers, hot dogs, potato chips', and Coke. His brother Paul added 'chewie gum'. It was only when her husband said, 'I still like best how my wife cook—spaghetti, pizza, radicchio, lasagne', that she smiled in relief. But many newcomer mothers agreed to include 'Canadian' foods because many of them were convenient (an important facet for the many working mothers), inexpensive, and reasonably healthy as well as being a hit with the kids.[23]

## HYBRID ETHNIC-CANADIAN MEALS

These modest efforts at experimentation led to a variety of hybrid family diets, though the timing and degree differed across households. A common early pattern in many families was one in which the mother cooked a 'Canadian meal' for her children while she and her husband stuck to familiar old world fare. She could thus placate the children without totally upsetting her husband, and she could also

exercise a measure of control over the process of change. A mother's shopping budget could influence her decision to indulge her children's desire for the more expensive convenience items, such as sugar-coated cereal. Furthermore, a concession to a 'Canadian breakfast' for the children (even one that the experts disliked), or lunch, was not a serious threat to cultural traditions when the evening and weekend meals included traditional fare.

[ . . . ]

Families that were the result of mixed ethnic marriages between newcomers from different European countries also produced hybrid diets. An Austrian woman who married an Italian man in Toronto in the 1950s said that they had developed 'international' tastes and outlook. She also stressed that her daughter, also a cosmopolitan eater, identified entirely as a Canadian.[24] At holiday times the tendency among mothers to mix the old with the new became more pronounced. For instance, the Canadian wife of a Budapest man made his favourite chicken paprika dish for the holidays, but instead of the traditional Hungarian Christmas fish dinner (eaten on Christmas eve), she prepared 'the good old English turkey'. A Canadian woman married to a Greek man learned to make baklava (a sticky pastry with chopped walnuts, honey, and cinnamon) using ready-made phyllo pastry bought at a store. Such stories can be seen as a form of culinary pluralism from the bottom up. By the 1960s some European families had begun to incorporate 'ethnic foods' from other origins, with common examples being takeout Chinese meals and (among non-Italians) lasagne and pizza.[25]

[ . . . ]

## POPULARIZING AND CONTAINING ETHNIC FOOD CULTURES

As with other cultural activities, the gatekeepers used food as a social device and ethnic dinners as an integration device that could encourage cultural exchange and thus contribute to nation-building and national unity. Food did break the ice with some malnourished children like Abbie, a 'very sad' European boy at the St. Christopher nursery school. Abbie, fortunately, brightened up at the sight of milk and biscuits. While eating remained his favourite part of the nursery program, he learned to speak some English and enjoyed singing the children's songs and doing gymnastics.[26]

Ethnic banquets were used as social icebreakers or catalysts for cultural exchange. At St. Christopher House the staff invited ethnic groups to host dinners featuring some of their popular food, with other ethnic group members to attend. While the staff probably exaggerated the success of these events and their role in promoting 'integration', the participating European women and their families clearly enjoyed them. In 1954 the 'New Canadian party' was the biggest event of the year at St. Christopher, attracting more than 150 people. Indeed, the crowd was far too big for the space provided because the members had all brought friends along. [ . . . ] But when some of the newcomers stayed seated during the singing of 'O Canada', the organizers were not amused. Rather, they lectured the group on the necessity of standing up. They then used the incident as an example of just how helpful they could be 'in showing our Canadian way of life and customs to these people and preparing them towards integration'.[27]

On other occasions the St. Christopher staff acknowledged the independent capacity of peoples from different homelands to co-exist peacefully. In 1955, at the first in a series of ethnic dinners initiated by a St. Christopher female social worker, the Italian House members prepared a Calabrian-style spaghetti dinner for the Portuguese members . . . [who] agreed to host the next dinner, which would feature their 'national food'—probably an islander's cod fish stovetop dish or casserole, with potatoes and vegetables. For the social worker the event showed that 'friendship and understanding' had developed between the two groups, and she hoped to see more of this. Dinners like this one took place in service clubs and community halls across the country, representing a form of culinary exchange and encouraging cultural pluralism.[28]

[ . . . ] While many newcomers enjoyed these events, and helped to organize them, the showcasing of ethnic cuisine, like the celebration of ethnic crafts and folk dancing, was also part of a strategy by which the gatekeepers mined ethnic culture to serve the larger goal of consolidating the post-war Canadian nation. The promotion of ethnic foods provided a way of stripping the immigrants of their more threatening features, or reducing ethnicity to entertainment and novelty. A form of ethnic containment, the approach created a safe and confined context in which cultural diversity could be endorsed.[29]

In keeping with these cultural politics, the Citizenship Branch gave its backing to cookbook projects featuring ethnic recipes. [ . . . ]

At this time European women and more 'ethnic' recipes began appearing in *Chatelaine*, along with more stories on working wives and mothers. One of the first feature-length articles on the newcomers, Janine Locke's 1957 piece on a Hungarian couple, Katey and Frank Myer, was a classic Cold War escape narrative that ended in a modern Canadian paradise. The caption accompanying a photo of a slim and smiling Katey described her as having the 'inconspicuously attractive' good looks typical of the average Canadian housewife. Katey's domestication is telling, given that she had a professional background and had just landed a bank-teller job. The article offers a lighthearted story of how this couple, having lost so much in Communist Hungary, could truly appreciate Canada's abundance and North American middle-class standards.

In Budapest the couple had shared a three-room apartment with three other family members; they had no electrical household appliances and had endured a 'perpetual chill' due to the scarcity and high cost of fuel. In Toronto, their patrons, a doctor and his family, had given them commodious accommodations: a suite of two rooms, a new refrigerator and stove, and their own bathroom. During her first trip to a Canadian supermarket, Katey happily loaded up with many 'newly discovered delicacies' (sardines, instant coffee, canned soups, ham, chicken legs) and with so much ice cream that 'they used it in great scoops even in their coffee'. She enthused, 'There is everything you could want . . . in the supermarket . . . not like the little shops at home where there was little to buy and what we wanted we could never afford'. As a treat to celebrate her husband's acceptance to the University of Toronto and her new job, Katey had gone to a department store to buy a practical item, a slip. But once there she could not resist some high-heeled red leather pumps (at $35 they cost about a week's salary for Frank). She 'limped, painfully but persistently' in them until she could wear them proudly in public. The Myers were planning to save for a car and a suburban home.

[ . . . ]

One way of reading this piece is to say that the tension between the newcomers' adaptation to Canadian ways and the gatekeepers' liberal nod to European customs is not completely resolved. Another is to say that it fits with the often ambiguous, even contradictory, assumptions that informed the gatekeepers' cultural pluralism.[30] By comparison Staebler's 1965 piece on Italian Alda Pilli (also slim and attractive) and her family was a sadder tale of struggle. Yet Staebler's evocative descriptions introduced readers to various Italian specialties still foreign to most Canadians, such as radicchio ('a bitter tasting' salad green that is reportedly 'very good for the blood'). In discussing Alda's preference for the ethnic stores in her neighbourhood (in the newer Little Italy further north on St. Clair Avenue West), Staebler presents daily food shopping as a viable alternative to

the weekly Canadian supermarket model (this way, 'everything is fresh'). Staebler evocatively describes the shops ('Italian butcher shops have gutted kids and fleecy black lambs hanging in their windows, with salami and mortadella sausages') and features Alda's simple specialties: spaghetti, thin slices of veal, green salad dressed with lemon and olive oil, cauliflower or eggplant or broccoli 'dipped in a batter and fried golden brown'. In describing the meat servings ('usually thin slices of fried veal or boiled chicken'), Staebler explains that in Toronto Alda can afford to serve more beef than she had been able to do in Italy, where it was tough and expensive. On Sundays they had homemade pizza, made from dough and dotted with anchovies, olives, and sauce. As for dinner, Staebler noted that they all drank the husband's homemade wine, even the boys, who took some wine in their glasses of water.[31] Staebler's approach to the Pillis' foodways was typical of the magazine in the 1960s, when the *Chatelaine* Institute staff and a variety of food writers were featuring more ethnic recipes and more strongly encouraging Canadian mothers to try them out.

[ . . . ]

We should not exaggerate this important nod to cultural pluralism, however, or exaggerate the impact of ethnic foods or multicultural eating in the early post-war decades. As with other cases of the increasingly mainstream ethnic foods in North America and elsewhere, the ethnic recipes meant to add 'spice' to the family meals were hardly 'authentic'. The homogenizing process is apparent in a 1960 recipe for 'Easy-to-Make Pizza Pin Wheels' (small individual pizzas), which had substituted Canadian for Italian ingredients. [ . . . ] Even by end of the 1960s *Chatelaine* was promoting Canadian foods by invoking the budget-conscious Canadian homemaker who cooked updated classics such as 'hamburgers with class' or 'ten ways with a pound of hamburg'.[32] Indeed, a Canadian centennial cookbook project called *Discovering Canadian Cuisine* was dominated by 'Canadian' recipes for flapjacks, seafood salad, biscuit cheese squares, pies, turkey, French-Canadian pea soup, and venison. For those Torontonians who could afford it, 'dining out' still meant patronizing high-end WASP restaurants. [ . . . ][33] When devising their weekly or monthly family meals, or preparing for family picnics and holidays, many mothers turned to their tried and trusted recipes. For Canadian mothers, that meant the clipped pages of *Chatelaine* or the glossy-coloured *Joys of Jell-O* recipe books put out by the General Foods Corporation. For European mothers, it meant old world favourites, especially in the case of holiday specialties. In some cases mothers indulged their children by adding some of their favourite 'other' foods.[34]

[ . . . ]

Indeed, the relationship between the nutritional and food gatekeepers and newcomer mothers is perhaps best understood as a series of negotiations and encounters that transformed both food cultures, though not equally. The gatekeepers had the power and position to define 'ethnic' food as un-Canadian, while the *Food Customs* guidebook and similar projects suggest that nutrition experts and food fashion-makers, like other gatekeepers, sought to modify, not obliterate the food (and other) cultures of emigrating groups, even though their liberal intentions did not eliminate a rampant cultural chauvinism. If the recent allure of multicultural and conspicuous dining has brought immigrant food cultures into the forefront of North American standards of 'taste', the 1950s and 1960s were a much more tentative, contested terrain—and, of course, class and cultural conflicts over food continue. But we are still left with a final conundrum, namely that culinary pluralism, even when practised in positive and affirming ways, always involves a degree of cultural appropriation, an act of 'eating the other'.[35]

# NOTES

1. Doug Owram, *Born at the Right Time: A History of the Baby Boom Generation* (Toronto 1996), chapters 1–3; Mona Gleason, *Normalizing the Ideal: Psychology, Schooling and the Family in Postwar Canada* (Toronto 1999); essays in Joy Parr, ed., *The Diversity of Women: Ontario 1945–1985* (Toronto 1985); Marlene Epp, *Women without Men: Mennonite Refugees of the Second World War* (Toronto 2000).

2. Cynthia Comacchio, *Nations Are Built of Babies: Saving Ontario's Mothers and Children, 1900–1940* (Montreal and Kingston 1993); Kathryn Arnup, Andrée Lévesque, and Ruth Pierson, eds., *Delivering Motherhood: Maternal Ideologies and Practices in the 19th and 20th Centuries* (London and New York 1990); J.R. Miller, *Shingwauk's Vision: A History of Native Residential Schools* (Toronto 1996); Donna L. Gabaccia, *We Are What We Eat: Ethnic Foods and the Making of Americans* (Cambridge 1998); and Harvey A. Levenstein, *Paradox of Plenty: A Social History of Eating in Modern America* (New York 1993). Parr, ed., *Diversity*

of Women; Mary Louise Adams, *The Trouble with Normal: Postwar Youth and the Making of Heterosexuality* (Toronto 1997)

3. Susan Prentice, 'Workers, Mothers, Reds: Toronto's Postwar Daycare Fight', *Studies in Political Economy* 30 (1989); Veronica Strong-Boag, 'Home Dreams: Canadian Women and the Suburban Experiment', *Canadian Historical Review* 72(4) (1991); Jeff Keshen, 'Wartime Jitters over Juveniles: Canada's Delinquency Scare and Its Consequences, 1939–1945', in Jeffrey Keshen, ed., *Age of Contention: Readings in Canadian Social History, 1900–1945* (Toronto 1997); Ruth Roach Pierson, 'They're Still Women After All' The Second World War and Canadian Womenhood (Toronto 1986); Valerie J. Korinek, *Roughing It in the Suburbs: Reading Chatelaine Magazine in the Fifties and Sixties* (Toronto 2000).

4. *Canadian Register* 19 May 1962; Julia Guard, 'Women Worth Watching: Radical Housewives in Cold War Canada', in Gary Kinsman, Dieter K. Buse, and Mercedes Steedman, eds., *Whose*

*National Security? Canadian State Surveillance and the Creation of Enemies* (Toronto 2000), 73–88; Reginald Whitaker and Gary Marcuse, *Cold War Canada: The Making of a National Insecurity State, 1945–1957* (Toronto 1994), ch. 4.

5. Belmonte, 'Mr and Mrs America'; Karal Ann Marling on the 'Kitchen Debate', in Marling, *As Seen on TV: The Visual Culture of Everyday Life in the 1950s* (Cambridge, MA 1994), 243; Elaine Tyler May, *Homeward Bound: American Families in the Cold War Era* (New York 1988, 2008); Whitaker and Marcuse, *Cold War Canada*.

6. Korinek, *Roughing It in the Suburbs*; Franca Iacovetta and Valerie Korinek, 'Jello Salads, One Stop Shopping and Maria the Homemaker', Marlene Epp, Franca Iacovetta, and Frances Swyripa, eds., *Sisters or Strangers? Immigrant, Ethnic and Racialized Women in Canadian History* (Toronto 2004); Alison J. Clarke, *Tupperware: The Promise of Plastic in 1950s America* (Washington, DC 1999). Marling, *As Seen on TV*, 266–67.

7. Williams, 'How to Keep Red Hands off Our New Canadians', *The Financial Post*, Dec. 3 1949; Thelma Barer-Stein, *You Eat What You Are: A Study of Ethnic Food Traditions* (Toronto 1979), 132–7, 524–32. Dora Wilensky, 'From Juvenile Immigrant to Canadian Citizen', *Canadian Welfare* 26 (January 1950).

8. Nutrition Division of the Department of Health and Welfare, *Canada Food Guide* (Ottawa 1950).

9. Archives of Ontario (AO), International Institute of Metropolitan Toronto (IIMT), MU 6410, file: Cookbook Project, booklet: Toronto Nutrition Committee, *Food Customs of New Canadians*. Published with funds from the Ontario Dietic Association.

10. Korinek, *Roughing It in the Suburbs*; Levenstein, *Paradox of Plenty*, ch. 12; Joanne Jay Myerowitz, ed., *Not June Cleaver: Women and Gender in Postwar America, 1945–1960* (Philadelphia 1994).

11. AO, Maclean Hunter Records Series (MHRS), F-4-1-b, Box 432, Elaine Collett to DHA (Doris Anderson), LMH (Lloyd Hodgkinson), and J. Meredith, 'Western Trip', 2 Oct. 1961. Korinek, *Roughing It in the Suburbs*; Iacovetta and Korinek, 'Jello Salads'.

12. Canadian Red Cross (CRC), Ontario Division, *News Bulletin*, September-October 1945, 1, May 1946.

13. Toronto Nutrition Committee, *Food Customs of New Canadians*; Korinek, *Roughing it in the Suburbs*.

14. Multicultural History Society of Ontario (MHSO), Oral History Collective (OHC), Interview with Dagmar Z.

15. *News Bulletin* (CRC, Ontario Division), September 1946. Baird, 'British War Brides'. Script of a Canadian Broadcasting Corporation broadcast, Halifax, 25 Oct. 1944. CRC Publications, National Headquaters, Ottawa.

16. 'Vows Bananas Will Fatten 'Peg Hubby Freed from Japs', *Toronto Star* 23 Feb. 1946; Depoe, 'Why Dutch War Brides Came to Canada and How They Survived', Major Research Paper, Department of History, University of Toronto, 1996; Barer-Stein, *You Eat What You Are*, ch. 15.

17. City of Toronto Archives (CTA), St Christopher House, SPC 484, IA1, Box 1, Folder 3, Minutes 1947–1948, Minutes 10 June 1948, Mrs. Donna Wood, Nursery School Report. See also United Church Archives (UCA), Women's Missionary Society (WMS), Toronto Conference Branch, Annual Report, 1959, Box 156, File 8, Miss Mamie Gollan, Report, Queen Street, Church of All Nations; Miss Annie B. Bishop and Mrs. Pearl Budge, Report on Immigration and Community Work.

18. MHSO, OHC, Interview with Carol A (who came to Canada in 1951 as a ten-year-old) and interviews with Jose A, Mails A, Mr. and Mrs. Unis M., and Alfredo F.; Franca Iacovetta, *Such Hardworking People: Italian Immigrants in Postwar Toronto* (Montreal and Kingston 1992); Depoe, 'Why Dutch War Brides Came to Canada and How They Survived'; 'Victims of Gouging Landlords', *Toronto Star* 6 Feb. 1963; Parr, 'Introduction', in Parr, ed., *Diversity of Women*; Korinek, *Roughing It in the Suburbs*; Trudi Bunting and Pierre Filion, eds., *Canadian Cities in Transition: The Twenty-First Century* (Toronto 1991); Sean Purdy, 'Scaffolding Citizenship: Housing Reform and National Formation in Canada, 1900–1950', in Adamoski, Chunn, and Menzies, eds., *Contesting Citizenship*.

19. MHSO, OHC, Interviews; essays in Special Theme Issue on Toronto's People, *Polyphony*

6(1) (Spring/Summer 1984); Christiane Harzig, 'When You Are a New Immigrant You Are Just Half and Half', in Doris Eibl and Christina Strobel, eds., *Selbst und andere/s: Von Begegnungen und Grenzziehungen* (Augsburg 1998). Also, Gabriele Scardellato and Manual Scarci, eds., *A Monument for Italian-Canadian Immigrants* (Toronto 1989); NFB Archives, *A Million and A Half of Us*, revised script, September 1958.

20. CTA, SCP, SCHO, Box 6, File 22: Interpretation, Immigrants 1958, A Cecilia Pope to Doris Clarke, 15 April 1958, with enclosed report, 'Civic Action in a Well Baby Clinic', 16 April 1958.

21. Rhonda Hinther, '"Sincerest Revolutionary Greetings": Progressive Ukrainians in Twentieth Century Canada', Ph.D. thesis, McMaster University, 2004, ch. 2; Frances Swyripa, *Wedded to the Cause: Ukrainian-Canadian Women and Ethnic Identity, 1891–1991* (Toronto 1993) chs. 4–5.

22. Personal conversations. The lower rates of citizenship among women for many groups also put them at a disadvantage vis-à-vis the Canadian state.

23. Edna Staebler, 'Other Canadians', *Chatelaine*, March 1965; personal conversations with men and women who, as children, found themselves in this situation. See also Jo Marie Powers, ed., *Buon Appetito! Italian Foodways in Ontario* (Toronto 2000).

24. MHSO, OHC, interview with Annemarie H.; Powers, *Buon Appetito!*

25. MHSO, OHC, interviews; Vancy Kasper, 'Use National Dishes to Build Christmas Recipes', *Toronto Star* 7 Dec. 1957; Iacovetta and Korinek, 'Jello Salads'; personal conversations.

26. CTA, St Christopher House, SPC 484, IA1, Box 1, Folder 3, minutes 1947–1948, minutes 10 June 1948, Mrs. Donna Wood, Nursery School Report. For similar food stories see: UCA, WMS, Toronto Conference Branch, Annual Report, 1959, Box 156, File 8, Miss Mamie Gollan, Report, Queen Street, Church of All Nations; Miss Annie B. Bishop and Mrs. Pearl Budge, Report on Immigration and Community Work, and other entries on Toronto work in annual reports.

27. CTA, St. Christopher House, SPC 484 IA1, Box 1, Folder 6, Minutes 1953–54, 28 Jan. 1954.

28. CTA, St. Christopher House, SPC 484, 1A1, Box 1, Folder 6, minutes, report of New Canadian Adult Programme Worker, 1955.

29. 'World's Tastiest Dishes Tempt Appetites at First International Cooking School', *Toronto Star* 1 Nov. 1954. Eric Geiger, 'New Canadians' column, 'Had 15 Cents in 1956, Buys Café', *Toronto Star*, 28 Dec. 1957.

30. Jeannine Locke, 'Can the Hungarians Fit In?' *Chatelaine*, May 1957. Mrs. M. Filwood, Toronto, *Chatelaine*, July 1957; letter from a new reader, Halifax, NS, August 1957; Rev. G. Simor, SJ, St. Elizabeth of Hungary Church, Toronto, September 1959.

31. Staebler, 'Other Canadians'; Marlene Epp, 'Semiotics of Zwieback: Feast and Famine in the Narratives of Mennonite Refugee Women' in Epp, Iacovetta, Swyripa, eds., *Sisters or Strangers?* 314–40; Louise Di Iorio, 'Pasta, Polenta, Ice Cream and Won Tons', York University, Toronto, April 2003.

32. Marie Holmes, 'Easy-to-Make Pizza Pin Wheels' (1961), 'Meals off the Shelf' (February 1955), and 'Seven Dinners on the Double' (1961); Elaine Collett, 'Ten New Ways of Cooking with a Pound of Hamburg' (September 1961), 47, and '98 Cent January Specials' (January 1960); all in *Chatelaine*; Levenstein, Paradox of Plenty, Gabaccia, *We Are What We Eat*.

33. AO, MU6410, IIMT, File: Cookbook Project, *Discovering Canadian Cuisine* (Canadian Gas Association 1966); Holiday issues of popular women's magazines such as the *Everywoman's Family Circle* 57(6) (December 1960).

34. *The Joys of Jell-O* (published by General Foods, White Plains, NY).

35. The phrase 'eating the other' is from bell hooks. Lisa Lowe, *Immigrant Acts: On Asian American Cultural Politics* (Durham, NC 1996); and Lawrence Grossberg, Cary Nelson, and Paula Treichler, eds., *Cultural Studies* (London 1992).

4   From Julia Lalande, 'The Roots of Multiculturalism: Ukrainian-Canadian
Involvement in the Multiculturalism Discussion of the 1960s as an Example of the
Position of the "Third Force"', *Canadian Ethnic Studies* 38(1) (2006): 47–64.

## INTRODUCTION

On 8 October 1971, Prime Minister Pierre
Trudeau announced the first Canadian policy
of multiculturalism to the House of Commons
and only one day later addressed an audience of Ukrainian Canadians at a Ukrainian
Canadian Congress convention in Winnipeg.[1]
This public appearance is often interpreted as
a sign that Trudeau acknowledged the strong
contribution of Ukrainians during the multiculturalism discussions of the 1960s. Even
today, Ukrainians are generally hailed as having been one of the most active participants
in the entire debate on multiculturalism
(Isajiw 1983, 113; Ferguson 1991, 307–08;
Burnet and Palmer 1988, 224). However,
the specifics of their positions in the debate
have not, thus far, been thoroughly studied.[2]
As Marcel Martel points out, research in the
area of politics usually focuses on politicians
and largely ignores ethnic and other interest
groups (2004, 1), but these groups are very
important in the context of the multiculturalism debate. This article offers insight into
Ukrainian Canadians' position in the debate
and thus an impression of the hopes and concerns of the third force. The third force consisted of the 'other ethnic groups', because at
the time of the debate, the Royal Commission
on Bilingualism and Biculturalism (hereafter
B&B Commission) divided Canadian society
into three categories: the Founding Nations
consisting of British and French Canadians,
other ethnic groups, and First Nations.
However, the B&B Commission only dealt
with the first two categories (Government
1967, XXI–XXII).

Ukrainians are an interesting example of
the position of the third force because they
were (numerically) one of the largest of the
other ethnic groups in Canada. According to
the B&B Commission, they were also the best
organized and most active group and could
potentially lead the discussion.[3] Why were
they so actively involved in the debate, and
what did they hope to achieve? What kind of
demands did they make, and how did they
rationalize them? To what extent can we apply
their position to the third force in general?
How did the contribution of the other ethnic
groups shape the discussion? [ . . . ]

## DEFINITION OF MULTICULTURALISM

Multiculturalism is an important aspect of
contemporary Canadian society, but it is often
not quite clear what is meant by multiculturalism, and different authors have pointed
out the ambiguity of the term. Will Kymlicka
makes us aware that terms like multiculturalism, citizenship, federalism, or cosmopol-
itanism 'are all normatively-laden, and while
we often think we know what they mean,
they are surprisingly ambiguous and vulnerable to misuse and inconsistent application'
(Kymlicka 1998, 8). The ambiguity of the
terminology is further influenced by the fact
that the concept of multiculturalism can be
divided into three components. On one hand,
we have what Evelyn Kallen calls 'social reality' (Kallen 1982, 51), meaning that people
of different ethnic backgrounds live together
in one society. Then there is the ideology of
multiculturalism, the interpretation of which
depends on the respective individual or institution. Finally, there is the policy of multiculturalism that depends on the respective
government. Ideology and policy are not
necessarily mutually exclusive. They can be

intertwined, thereby influencing each other (Bociurkiw 1978; Kallen 1982). This article deals only with two of the three components of multiculturalism—the ideology and the policy, or rather, with their roots, which are embedded in the discussion of the 1960s. That was a time when multiculturalism was a very modern concept, and Canadians were searching for their meaning of multiculturalism, their ideology, and eventually, their policy. This process of developing an idea of a multicultural Canada started at a time of crisis and change in the country.

## THE 1960s IN CANADA AND THE CREATION OF THE COMMISSION ON BILINGUALISM AND BICULTURALISM

Throughout the western hemisphere, the 1960s were a decade of revolution and change. In the United States, for example, the Vietnam War ignited protest movements that were further influenced by the civil rights and women's movements as well as a whole new youth culture. These developments swept across the border into Canada where they had a profound effect, especially on the younger generation (Owram 1996, 159–84; 216–47). However, the discussion on bilingualism and biculturalism (which later evolved into a debate on multiculturalism) was triggered by one of the major events of the 1960s specific to Canada—the Quiet Revolution in Quebec. During the 1960s, a new French Canadian elite emerged that was no longer tied to the church, thereby developing a new kind of nationalism (Taylor 1993). The Quebec question gained especially strong attention from the media owing to the rise of violence, in particular in connection to the emergence of the Front de Liberation du Quebec. In order to tackle the increasing problems affecting Canadian society—the threat of secession and the unrest in

Quebec in general—the Royal Commission on Bilingualism and Biculturalism was established in 1963. Its task was to examine the state of bilingualism and (initially) biculturalism in Canada, focusing on the federal administration and on public and private organizations as well as opportunities for bilingualism in Canada (Government 1965, 143–44). Many groups that were part of the third force (the most vocal of which was the Ukrainian-Canadian community) were exasperated by the commission's focus on bilingualism, but talk of biculturalism frustrated them even more.

## DEMANDS OF UKRAINIANS

For Ukrainian Canadians, the early years of the discussion on multiculturalism coincided with the seventy-fifth anniversary of Ukrainian settlement in Canada in 1966.[4] By this time, Ukrainians had evolved into a strong community very much interested in the preservation of its language and traditions. In the 1960s, this concern with conserving their culture was expressed in their strenuous involvement in the multiculturalism debate. For example, Ukrainians made the most submissions to the B&B Commission, and they actively discussed the issue in the community and in their newspapers (Bociurkiw 1978, 105).[5] Their submissions to the hearings of the B&B Commission, letters to politicians, speeches and addresses, as well as resolutions at community meetings offer insight into their position. The ideas—one could even call them demands—outlined in these sources can be classified into demands for participation, recognition, and equality.

Demands in the area of participation were often connected to the political sphere. At the end of the 1950s, the Diefenbaker government had already taken some steps to incorporate women or members of the third force into the administration. For example, the Minister of Labour Michael Starr was the first Ukrainian appointed to the federal cabinet (Momryk 1987). Encouraged by some preliminary successes, Ukrainians in Canada demanded more political representation for the 'smaller ethno-cultural groups', often arguing that 'only a person from a given cultural milieu can properly present his group's case, because of his total association and acquaintance with it'.[6] In this context, they wanted the community's umbrella organizations—the Ukrainian Canadian Congress (UCC)—to be acknowledged as the official voice of the Ukrainian-Canadian community. As such, the UCC could advise the Canadian government and have more influence on day-to-day politics. As this proposal shows, the quest for more political influence was often connected to the achievement of greater recognition by the government.

Recognition was another catchphrase at the time, and this was a very broad term linked to several areas. Some proposals, such as the one made by Jaroslav Rudnyckyj, a prominent Ukrainian academic representative and a member of the B&B Commission, were rather far-reaching. He stated that Canada should be officially English/French bilingual at the federal level. However, he took into consideration so-called regional languages that also deserved protection, among them Ukrainian, German, and Italian. He proposed an amendment to the *British North America Act* stating that 'notwithstanding anything in this section, any language other than English and French used by 10 per cent or more of the population of an appropriate administrative district of a province or territory shall have the status of a regional language; the legislation of the provision for regional languages shall be vested in the governments concerned' (Rudnyckyj 1969, 155–69). Other recommendations were often made in the sphere of education—one of the major foci of the discussion due to its connection to language development and preservation. Demands were made that Ukrainian (or the other ethnic groups' languages) should be offered as a credited subject in schools where demand existed and should receive

matriculation status in universities.[7] The recognition of languages other than French and English was an important issue, because language itself was commonly regarded as the vehicle of culture, especially important for the preservation of religious identity.[8] Having Ukrainian recognized in schools was often seen as one way of ensuring the survival of the language as well as the survival of traditions.

Language was not the only factor considered important in education. School curricula and textbooks were criticized for their western European focus: it was argued that they should have a more international outlook.[9] Especially when it came to writing Canadian history, Ukrainians insisted that the contribution of the other ethnic groups should be taken into consideration. This would, of course, make more research necessary and go beyond the school's realm (Ukrainian National Youth Federation 1966, 14–22). Apart from educational issues, the media also played an important role. Groups recommended that the contribution of the third force should be more visible in the media,[10] such that the community could reach the wider Canadian public.[11] The media was a topic widely discussed in Canada, since the Canadian Broadcasting Corporation (hereafter the CBC) continually refused to broadcast in a language other than French or English (Ryan 1975, 151). All these demands in the sphere of language, education, and the media had one thing in common: they were directed toward a general recognition of the contribution of the other ethnic groups to Canada's development.

Another central aspect of such demands was the quest for equality. Ukrainians feared that they were not on quite the same footing as members of the Founding Nations. They were afraid that their aspirations were not accepted as equal to those of the British or the French Canadians. Walter Tarnopolsky, a writer on multiculturalism, law, and human rights and one of the many active Ukrainian-Canadian representatives, expressed this feeling of inequality and the hope that the new policy of multiculturalism might change the situation for Canadians of non-British, non-French origin. Referring to an editorial in the *Toronto Telegram* in which he was criticized for urging the ending of the monarchical tradition (as a Canadian of non-British descent), Tarnopolsky stated:

> The editorial in typical fashion said: 'Why doesn't he go home where he came from?' Well home, of course, is Gronlid, Saskatchewan—and I do go home as frequently as I can. The point that I want to emphasize is that until the multiculturalism policy was adopted, and until this policy is effectuated, the fact that I was born in Canada would never put me on quite the same basis as someone who might have been born in the United Kingdom, and who had just immigrated to Canada.[12]

[ . . . ]

## THE PIONEERING ARGUMENT

From the time of the first Indian-European contact in 1497 to Confederation in 1867, two groups determined Canadian history—the British and the French who explored and settled the country (Kelley and Trebilcock 1998, 21–60). Owing to this history, the B&B Commission saw the term 'founding races' as 'an allusion to the undisputed role played by Canadians of French and British origin in 1867 and long before Confederation' (Government 1967, XXII). During the 1960s, it became obvious that parts of the organized faction of the Ukrainian-Canadian community intended to jump on the bandwagon. They tried to make the case that they also had a special position in Canada owing to their experience as settlers. This argument—put forward by organizations encompassing members of all waves and generations—could only be made by linking the entire community to the first wave, whose many members

had settled in dense compact blocks on the prairies and had a significant impact on the land and its surroundings (Darlington 1991; Lehr 1991; Martynowych 1991). During the debate on multiculturalism, the early settlement experience was used as an argument to support claims for recognition, participation, and equality. One could even say that the Ukrainian-Canadian community created a 'pioneer myth' at this time.

## THE PIONEER MYTH

The pioneer myth that dominated Ukrainian-Canadian literature after 1970 encompassed the initial hardships of settlement, the isolation of the early settlers, the discrimination they faced, as well as their constant efforts to succeed in the new country (Mycak 1996, 68ff).[13] The roots of this pioneer myth can be seen during the debate on multiculturalism. In the opinion of the Ukrainians of the 1960s, the early Ukrainian settlers were role models, even heroes, and the allegory of Ukrainians as pioneers was evoked and perpetuated throughout the discussion.[14] Ukrainians were often referred to as having pioneered the prairies: they had turned wilderness into fertile land through hard physical work. Emphasis was given to the Ukrainian contribution in the area of agriculture, such as prize-winning wheat cultivation.[15] Characteristics attributed to Ukrainian pioneers—such as 'a long and intimate contact with the soil' or the 'love of freedom'—were often celebrated[16] and sometimes even transferred to the present community. For example, John Yaremko, a lawyer and politician of Ukrainian descent, stated that 'if there is a single characteristic common to those of us of Slav descent in this country, it is a burning love of freedom and democracy'.[17] In the eyes of many Ukrainians, the pioneering qualities and the hard work of the early settlers put Ukrainians on the same footing as the British or French Canadians.[18] Rudnyckyj went so far as to state that at least some Ukrainians saw themselves as the 'founding races' of the prairies[19]—however, as Rudnyckyj himself pointed out this view could not be generalized for the entire community. Nonetheless, as Sonya Mycak states, 'this national role—their ordination as a founding people of the Canadian nation—is the fourth motif which marks the prairie pioneer myth' (Mycak 1996, 68). In addition to the mostly agricultural work on the prairies, the Ukrainian involvement in the early Russian exploration missions was also cited in order to create a picture of 'true pioneers'.[20] As the historiography has shown, features of this myth, such as the hardship of settlement, the struggle to succeed in the country, and the discrimination that early settlers faced were rooted in the historical experience of Ukrainians in Canada (Martynowych 1991; Darlington 1991; Lehr 1991). However, it became a myth once it was generalized for all Ukrainians in Canada and once certain demands were connected to this pioneering experience (at least by part of the community). This implies an exclusive claim that does not take into consideration that Ukrainians were not the first, nor the only, ones to settle the prairies (Friesen 1987).

The 1960s also saw a spread of information on Ukrainians in Canada, further perpetuating the pioneer myth. Generally, publicizing these contributions was meant to celebrate Ukrainian cultural heritage, shed light on the historical roots of Ukrainian settlement in Canada, and reveal the Ukrainian contribution to the development of the country.[21] The third Ukrainian-Canadian senator Paul Yuzyk, for example, wrote *Ukrainian Canadians: Their Place and Role in Canadian Life* in order 'to provide Canadians and visitors in Canada during the Centennial Year with all the important, authoritative information, in concise treatise form, about a leading dynamic Canadian ethnic group—the Ukrainian Canadians' (Yuzyk 1967, preface). Dr Vladimir Kaye[22] contributed a study on the early settlement period, thereby providing the first scholarly examination of Ukrainians in Canada (Kaye 1964). Publications such as booklets (often in the context of M.A. or Ph.D. theses) came from

Ukrainian Canadians in different corners of the country. They dealt with the contribution of Ukrainians to Canada and also with aspects of maintaining one's identity—and the corresponding struggle—(Gregorovich 1964; Darcovich 1967; Woycenko 1964). Furthermore, different aspects of Ukrainian-Canadian community life were brought to the attention of a wider audience; for example, the church (Trosky 1968), political life,[23] or the developments of particular communities.[24] In addition to publications focusing exclusively on Ukrainian Canadians, information about them could also be found in the general context of 'the contributions of the other ethnic groups', for example, in publications by conferences such as the First National Conference on Canadian Slavs, where the Ukrainians also took a leading role (Slavutych 1966). The 1960s truly saw a very diverse range of publications concerning Ukrainian Canadians. For the first time, the community researched and expressed its contributions to Canadian history on a larger scale. This literature was often seen as a tool 'to fight for the truth about Ukraine and to take credit for our part in Canadian history'.[25] The focus was generally on the contribution of Ukrainians to Canadian society and history, often specifically referring to Ukrainians as pioneers in this context.

Although government officials often referred to Ukrainians as pioneers, they rejected the idea of a special position for Ukrainians in Canada. Using the same argument, Canadian government officials could acknowledge the contribution of Ukrainian settlers and still argue against special rights for them. Additional arguments had to be found to underscore the demands made on behalf of the Ukrainian-Canadian community.

# THE IMPORTANCE OF THE SITUATION IN THE HOMELAND

A frequent position taken to reinforce the desire to preserve their heritage was related to the situation in the homeland. Community leaders, especially, viewed activities in Canada in reference to what was going on in Ukraine. As Senator Paul Yuzyk said: 'Ukrainians cherish Canadian freedom and democracy, as they are conscious of Ukraine's subjugation and bondage'.[26] Indeed, Ukrainians in Canada, whether they were born in Canada or emigrated, had never been able to look back to a free homeland. Furthermore, all of Ukraine was part of the Soviet Union after 1945, and its inhabitants were subject to measures of Russification (Subtelny 2000, 521–6). Ukrainians in Canada, especially those who came as 'Displaced Persons' after the Second World War, saw their role as preservers of Ukrainian culture, especially language, in the diaspora.[27] Members of the community felt they had to preserve what they had in Canada,[28] and it was often noted that this task was so much more important to Ukrainians than to other ethnic groups like the Italians or Germans because these groups had the opportunity 'to go back' if they desired, an option that did not exist for Ukrainians in Canada.[29]

This 'mission' to preserve Ukrainian culture in the diaspora was complicated by the fact that there had been no new wave of Ukrainian immigration since the late 1940s/ early 1950s, and Ukrainian language usage and community participation were declining in Canada (Reitz and Ashton 1980; Darcovich 1980). The preservation of language and heritage was only possible, it was argued, if there was enough money to fund organizations, language classes, and other activities. It was often assumed that the number of people speaking Ukrainian as their mother tongue, for example, would not decline further if there were more interest in minority languages in general and if greater encouragement were given (Woycenko 1964, 13f). In addition to language and culture preservation in Canada, Ukrainians also hoped to influence Canada's foreign policy regarding the Soviet Union, so that the country would 'do everything to support and encourage the struggle of the captive nations for liberation'.[30] This hope was almost realized when Prime Minister John Diefenbaker openly criticized the Soviet Union in his speech at the United Nations in 1960 (Palmer 1991, 20f; Hilliker 1986, 188f). Although there were other groups in Canada who had their homeland behind the Iron Curtain and who also fought for recognition and for their homeland's liberation, Ukrainians still saw their position as unique in Canada. Manoly Lupul, an education professor at the University of Alberta, made this clear when he stated: 'In Canada the Baltic peoples are not numerous, and so it is to Canadians of Ukrainian descent that a phrase made popular by French Canadians in recent years best applies: "We are not a people like the other(s)". For truly we are not'.[31]

## PARALLELS TO THE FRENCH CANADIANS

Parallels to the French-Canadian case become obvious upon comparative examination of both groups' position. Aspects like geographical density, the concept of French Canadians as a nation, coupled with the displayed desire and drive to survive were important for French Canadians throughout the multiculturalism discussion (Anderson 1981, 86–93). One argument Ukrainian Canadians presented to have their group share this category was to indirectly compare their case to that of French Canadians. Ukrainians were presented as pioneers, and their strong bloc settlements in the prairies were offered as a reason for special language rights. Furthermore, it was stressed that they had a strong desire to survive (owing to the situation in the homeland), and maintaining their language was an important component. However, it must be stated that the comparison to the French was seldom directly made. Very few people openly asked that those 'who have also concretely contributed to the building, development, and defence of Canada' should receive the same rights as the French Canadians,[32] or stated that the preservation of language was as important to Ukrainians as it was to the French Canadians.[33]

## ARGUMENTS AGAINST A SPECIAL STATUS

A different, underlying rationale was put forth in direct co-operation with members of the other ethnic groups; that special status—for anybody—was unconstitutional and contrary to human rights. It was deemed unfair to select only two groups for survival, while the other groups were singled out for eventual assimilation. The case made was that 'in democracy, one cannot apply one set of standards and moral principles to one group of citizens, and a different standard for another group of Canadians',[34] because that would eventually lead to discrimination and devaluation. It was further argued that children would be discouraged from learning their mother tongue if they perceived it as unrecognized or devalued. Tarnopolsky, for example, stated that 'a child who sees that the language of his ancestors is not important enough to be studied as a subject will inevitably feel that his forefathers were not quite equal'.[35] Furthermore, the question of discrimination often came up in the context of civil service. Community activists feared that people of non-French, non-British background would be disadvantaged because they had to learn two additional languages.[36]

## APPLICATION TO THE 'THIRD FORCE'

These demands and arguments offer insight into the fears and hopes of the community. Ukrainians in Canada were afraid of being reduced to 'second class citizens'[37] and demanded opportunities equal to those of the Anglo and French Canadians. Owing to the situation in the homeland, many Ukrainians in Canada were eager to preserve their heritage and culture, fearing that this might not be possible in the future without the implementation of multiculturalism. They also wanted their contribution to the building of Canada recognized and valued. Parallel to arguments for special status, it was alternately noted that there should be no special group rights because this might be considered unconstitutional. To what extent were these demands and arguments made on behalf of the Ukrainian-Canadian community representative of other groups of the third force?

Certainly, the Ukrainian-Canadian community was the most active participant in the discussion, and some arguments, for example, pioneering or the issue of the homeland, cannot be generalized to all groups, especially not in that combination.[38] Nonetheless, there are common aspects that hold true for many members of the third force. Many groups had an interest in preserving at least part of their heritage, whether it was just for personal reasons or in the context of a personal mission, as many Ukrainians saw it. In addition, many members of the third force feared being reduced to second-class citizens, thus facing discrimination in public life. An aspect that also interested many groups beyond the Ukrainians was the contribution made by other ethnic groups to the development of Canada as a country. Although most (including the majority of the Ukrainian-Canadian community) did not question the concept of two founding nations, they did know that they had made, and continued to make, an important contribution to the country, and they wanted this acknowledged through a multiculturalism policy.[39] Which demands made during the multiculturalism discussion were actually addressed in the policy? [ . . . ]

## THE FOCUS OF THE MULTICULTURALISM POLICY OF THE 1970s

The language issue was high on the Ukrainian-Canadian agenda, and it was answered in 1969 with the *Official Languages Act* that made English and French the official languages in all federal institutions. The idea of regional languages, brought up by the Ukrainian community during that discussion, was not implemented by the Canadian government. However, the multiculturalism policy acknowledged in 1971 that Canada was a bilingual country with a multicultural character. The government saw its task as assisting all groups to overcome cultural barriers so that they would have the opportunity to 'share their cultural expression and values with other Canadians'. In order to reach this goal, the government would support the promotion of cultural encounters and help members of all cultural groups to acquire at least one official language. Furthermore, support would be given to research proposals, art displays, and projects that fought racism.[40] Comparing this policy and the first steps taken during the 1970s to appease the Ukrainian-Canadian community, it becomes obvious that the biggest changes and developments took place in the field of recognition. This is especially true for school curricula, textbooks, and the media, as well as general recognition of the contribution of the ethnic groups to the country through more research in this area.[41] However, the new multiculturalism policy confined the preservation of heritage to the private sector. Groups had the chance to preserve their heritage through government programs, but they had to apply for grants, and all efforts to mobilize their members had to come from within the community itself. The multiculturalism policy did not guarantee the ethnic groups' survival, instead focusing more on inter-group relationships.

Many Ukrainians were originally very content with, one could even say excited about, the multiculturalism policy.[42] Most importantly, something was finally implemented: it was officially stated that Canada was a multicultural country and the contribution of the other ethnic groups to Canada was officially recognized. Furthermore, the community now had the possibility of acquiring funds outside their own community, thereby widening their opportunities for survival. However, as the years went by and the make-up of Canadian society changed owing to a large influx of visible minorities, the focus of multiculturalism in Canada changed as well. Combating racism and helping people find their place in Canadian society (for example, through language courses) gained in importance, whereas cultural encounters were no longer a top priority (Burnet and Palmer 1988, 226–27; Avery 1995, 213–18). Many Ukrainians were dissatisfied with these changes, especially since they meant a shortage in budgets for cultural festivals and encounters (Bociurkiw 1978, 110–20). Ukrainians were more interested in preserving the status quo, whereas the multiculturalism policy adapted to changes in Canadian society and thus shifted its focus.

## NOTES

1. Library and Archives Canada (hereafter LAC) MG31 D58 Vol. 8, File 27: Notes for the remarks by the Prime Minister to the Ukrainian-Canadian Congress, Winnipeg, Manitoba, 9 October 1971.

2. Bociurkiw 1978, Jaworsky 1979.

3. LAC MG31 E55 Vol. 10, File Secretary of State, Resumé of the Report of the Royal Commission on Bilingualism and Biculturalism, Book Four; The Cultural Contribution of the Other Ethnic Groups, 8–15.

4. Martynowych 1991.

5. LAC RG26 Vol. 76, File 1-5-11, Part 4, *Ethnic Scene*, September 1964: A review of opinions, trends, and activities among the ethnic groups in Canada, 5–8; LAC MG31 E55 Vol. 10, File Multiculturalism 1971–1975: Notes for an address to be delivered by the Honourable John Munro, Minister Responsible for Multiculturalism, to the Ukrainian Canadian Committee Congress in Winnipeg, 12 October, n.d., 1.

6. LAC MG31 E55 Vol. 10, File Multiculturalism 1971–1975: Submission to the Joint Parliamentary Committee of the Senate and the House of Commons on the Constitution of Canada by the Ukrainian Alumni Association Toronto, 6ff.

7. LAC MG31 E55 Vol. 9, File Multiculturalism 1964–1971: Bohdan Bociurkiw, Bilingualism and Biculturalism as Seen by Western Canadians of Other Ethnic Origins, an address presented at the Community Seminar on Bilingualism and Biculturalism at the University of Alberta in Edmonton, 23 April 1964, 5; LAC MG31 D58 Vol. 7, File 3: Submission to the Manitoba Advisory Committee for the Discussion of Bilingualism and Biculturalism, 30 January 1964, by the Ukrainian Catholic Brotherhood of Manitoba, 2f.

8. LAC MG31 E55 Vol. 9, File Multiculturalism 1964–1971: Bohdan Bociurkiw, Bilingualism and Biculturalism, 4; LAC MG31 D58 Vol. 7, File 3: Submission to the Manitoba Advisory Committee for the Discussion of Bilingualism and Biculturalism, 30 January 1964, by St. Andrew's College in Winnipeg, 2f.; LAC MG31 D58 Vol. 7, File 9: Bohdan Krawchenko, Toward a Development of Multiculturalism, an address presented at the Ukrainian Canadian University Students' Union, 8 August 1970, 4.

9. LAC MG31 E55 File Multiculturalism 1964–1971: Brief submitted to the attention of those assembled at the meeting held 19 March 1971, 'YHO' Hall, Saskatoon, between representatives of the Saskatoon Ukrainian Community and Mr. A. Lapchuk, Secretary of State's Office (brief prepared by the National Executive Canadian Ukrainian Youth Association), 8–9.

10. LAC MG31 E55 Vol. 9, File Multiculturalism 1964–1971: Bohdan Bociurkiw Bilingualism and Biculturalism, 5f; Ukrainian National Youth Federation of Canada 1966, 17f; LAC MG31 D58 Vol. 7, File 3: Submission to the Manitoba Advisory Committee for the Discussion of Bilingualism and Biculturalism, 30 January 1964, by the Markian Shashevich Society of Ukrainian Catholic Teachers, 5–7 (this brief also supported the abovementioned steps concerning language and history in schools).

11. LAC MG31 D58 Vol. 7, File 3: Submission to the Manitoba Advisory Committee for the Discussion of Bilingualism and Biculturalism, 30 January 1964, by the Ukrainian Catholic Women's League of Manitoba, 2.

12. LAC MG31 E55 Vol. 10, File Multiculturalism 1971–1975: The New Policy of Multiculturalism for Canada, an address delivered in Winnipeg at the Conference of Ukrainian Canadian Business and Professional Men's Clubs on Sunday, 10 October (n/d), following the prime minister's elaboration of the Federal Government's Multiculturalism Policy given at the Congress of Ukrainian Canadians the evening before by W.S. Tarnopolsky, 2.

13. Sonia Mycak points out that the perpetuation of this myth was dependent on government funding through multicultural programs as well as the multicultural ethic in general.

14. Swyripa 1993, 225ff.

15. UNYFC, Canada's Culture, 11–14; LAC MG31 E55 Vol. 9, File Multiculturalism 1964–1971: Debates of the Senate. Maiden speech of the Honourable Paul Yuzyk, Senator, Canada: A Multicultural Nation, 3 March 1964, 6. Members of the first and second wave were also often labelled pioneers (see, for example, the obituary for John Swystun: LAC MG32 C67 Vol. 20, File 9: V. John Swystun, Q.C).

16. LAC MG31 E55 Vol. 9, File Multiculturalism 1964–1971: An address by the Honourable John Yaremko to the Inter-University Committee on Canadian Slavs Conference, 23 May 1971, 2; LAC MG32 C67 Vol. 20, File 10: Complete resolutions passed 14 October 1968, Ukrainian Canadian Congress, Winnipeg, 5f.

17. LAC MG31 E55 Vol. 9, File Multiculturalism 1964–1971: An address by the Honourable John Yaremko to the Inter-University Committee on Canadian Slavs Conference, 23 May 1971, 1.

18. LAC MG31 D58, Vol. 9, File 12 (1): Paul Yuzyk, The Emerging New Force in the Emerging New Canada, at the Thinkers' Conference on Cultural Rights, 13–15 December 1968), 3–4.

19. LAC MG31 D58, Vol. 6, File 8: Rudnyckyj, Remarks regarding the texts of Dunton, Dion, and Hawkins—and additional comments regarding interim report, 19 September 1964, 1f.

20. LAC MG31 D58, Vol. 6, File 8: Rudnyckyj, Ethno-Lingual Groups in Canada, 30 January

1964, 3f; LAC MG31 D69, Vol. 6, File 14: *Vancouver Sun*, 6 December 1973, Ukrainians earned rights in Canada (letter to the editor by Michael Huculak); Subtelny 1988, 539.

21. Swyripa, *Ukrainian Canadians* (1978, 88–117).

22. LAC MG31 D69, Reel 2997, KAYE.

23. LAC MG32 C67 Vol. 18, File 4: Dr. Kaye, Golden Jubilee of the Participation of Ukrainians in the Political Life of Canada, 1913–1963.

24. UCC Hamilton Branch, *Salute to Canada, 1867–1967*. Hamilton: UCC, 1967.

25. LAC MG 31 D58 Vol. 6, File 7: Andrew Gregorovich, Ukrainian Canadian University Students, 2.

26. LAC MG31 E55 Vol. 9, File Multiculturalism 1964–1971: Maiden Speech of the Honourable Paul Yuzyk, Senator: Canada: A Multicultural Nation, 3 March 1964, 6f.

27. LAC MG31 D58, Vol. 6, File 7: Andrew Gregorovich, Ukrainian Canadian University Students, 2; LAC MG31 D58 Vol. 7, File 3: Submission to the Manitoba Advisory Committee for the Discussion of Bilingualism and Biculturalism, 30 January 1964, by the Ukrainian Catholic Women's League of Manitoba, 1. See also Lalande, 2006.

28. LAC MG31 D58 Vol. 8, File 10 (Multiculturalism): Panchuk on Multi-lingualism and Multiculturalism, no date given (Ukrainian Canadian Veterans Association), 4; LAC MG31 E55 Vol. 10, File Multiculturalism 1971–1975: The New Policy of Multiculturalism for Canada, an address delivered in Winnipeg at the Conference of Ukrainian-Canadian Business and Professional Men's Clubs on Sunday, 10 October, following the Prime Minister's elaboration of the Federal Government's Multiculturalism Policy given by W.S. Tarnopolsky at the Congress of Ukrainian Canadians the evening before, 3.

29. LAC MG31 D58 Vol. 8, File 17: Lupul, The Federal Government, Multiculturalism, and Education in Canada, 9.

30. LAC MG32 C67 Vol. 20, File 10: Complete Resolutions passed 14 October 1968, Ukrainian Canadian Congress, Winnipeg, 5–6.

31. LAC MG31 D58 Vol. 8, File 17: Lupul, The Federal Government, Multiculturalism, and Education in Canada, 7f.

32. LAC MG31 D58 Vol. 7, File 3: Mr. V. Solman, Grand Knight, St Josephat Council 4138, Knights of Columbus, to the Manitoba Com-mittee on Bilingualism and Biculturalism, 2.

33. LAC MG31 D58 Vol. 7, File 12: UNF, Montreal Branch, to the Commission of Inquiry on the Position of the French Language and on Language Rights in Quebec, September 1969, 3.

34. LAC MG31 D58 Vol. 7, File 12: UNF, Montreal Branch, to the Commission of Inquiry on the Position of the French Language and on Language Rights in Quebec, September 1969, 3; LAC MG31 E55 File Multiculturalism 1964–1971: Brief submitted to the attention of those assembled at the meeting held 19 March 1971, 'YHO' Hall, Saskatoon, between representatives of the Saskatoon Ukrainian Community and Mr. A. Lapchuk, Secretary of State's Office (Brief prepared by the National Executive of the Canadian Ukrainian Youth Association), 3.

35. LAC MG31 E55 Vol. 9, File Multiculturalism 1964–1971: *Saskatoon Star Phoenix*, 5 July 1971, Tarnopolsky sees multi-culture future for Canada.

36. LAC MG31 E55 Vol. 9, File Multiculturalism 1964–1971: Bociurkiw' speech at the Community Seminar on Bilingualism and Biculturalism at the University of Alberta in Edmonton, 23 April 1964; MG31 D58 Vol. 8, File 17: Lupul, The Federal Government, Multiculturalism, and Education in Canada, 6f.

37. This term often appears in the submission to the B&B Commission.

38. The Germans were numerically larger than the Ukrainians. However, owing to two world wars and other factors (e.g., a strong tendency for assimilation), interest in the preservation of heritage was not as strong (LAC MG31 E55 Vol. 10, File Secretary of State: Resume of the Report of the Royal Commission on Bilingualism and Biculturalism, Book Four. The Cultural Contribution of the Other Ethnic Groups), 8.

39. Based on an evaluation of issues of the *Ethnic Scene*, a press organ of the Canadian govern-ment examining the ethnic press in Canada, and publications and correspondence by the Ethnic Press Federation.

40. LAC MG31 E55 Vol. 10, File Secretary of State: Statement by the Prime Minister, House of Commons, 8 October 1971, 1–6.
41. Findlay, Oliver, and Solberg 1974.
42. MG31 D58 Vol. 8, File 17: Lupul, The Federal Government, Multiculturalism, and Education in Canada), 1f.

# REFERENCES

Anderson, Alan. 1981. *Ethnicity in Canada: Theoretical Perspectives*. Toronto: Butterworths.

Avery, Donald. 1995. *Reluctant Host: Canada's Response to Immigrant Workers, 1896–1994*. Toronto: McClelland & Stewart.

Bociurkiw, Bohdan. 1978. Federal Policy of Multiculturalism and the Ukrainian-Canadian Community. In *Multiculturalism, Separatism, and Ukrainian Canadians: An Assessment*, ed. M. Lupul, 98–128. Edmonton: Canadian Institute of Ukrainian Studies Press.

Burnet, Jean R., and Howard Palmer. 1988. *'Coming Canadians': An Introduction to a History of Canada's Peoples*. Toronto: McClelland & Stewart.

Darcovich, William. 1967. *Ukrainians in Canada. The Struggle to Retain their Identity*. Ottawa: Ukrainian Self-Reliance Association.

———. 1980. The 'Statistical Compendium': An Overview of Trends. In *Changing Realities: Social Trends among Ukrainian Canadians*, ed. R. Petryshyn, 3–17. Edmonton: Canadian Institute of Ukrainian Studies Press.

Darlington, James. 1991. The Ukrainian Impress on the Canadian West. In *Canada's Ukrainians* ed. L. Luciuk and S. Hryniuk, 53–80. Toronto: University of Toronto Press.

Ferguson, Barry. 1991. British-Canadian Intellectuals, Ukrainian Immigrants, and Canadian National Identity. In *Canada's Ukrainians*, ed. L. Luciuk and S. Hryniuk, 304–25. Toronto: University of Toronto Press.

Findlay, Peter, Michael Oliver, and Janet Solberg. 1974. 'The unpublished research of the Royal Commission on Bilingualism and Biculturalism', *Canadian Journal of Political Science* 4(7): 709–20.

Friesen, Gerald. 1987. *The Canadian Prairies: A History*. Toronto: University of Toronto Press.

Government of Canada. 1965. A Preliminary Report of the Commission on Bilingualism and Biculturalism. Ottawa: Queen's Printer.

———. 1967. Report of the Royal Commission on Bilingualism and Biculturalism. Book 1. General Introduction. The Official Languages. Ottawa: Queen's Printer.

Gregorovich, Andrew. 1964. *The Ukrainians in Canada*. Toronto: Ukrainian National Youth Federation of Canada.

———. 1991. Ukrainians in Metro Toronto. In *Narys istorii kongresu ukraintsiv Kanady v Toronto*, ed. W. Didiuk, 39–48. Toronto: Ukrainian Canadian Congress.

Hilliker, John F. 1986. 'Diefenbaker and Canadian External Relations', in *Canadian Foreign Policy. Historical Readings*, ed. J.L. Granatstein, 183–97. Toronto: Copp Clark Pitman.

Isajiw, Wsevolod. 1983. Multiculturalism and the Integration of the Canadian Community. *Canadian Ethnic Studies/Etudes ethniques au Canada* 15(2): 107–17.

Jaworsky, John. 1979. A Case Study of the Canadian Federal Government's Multiculturalism Policy. M.A. Thesis. Department of Political Science, Carleton University.

Kallen, Evelyn. 1982. Multiculturalism: Ideology, Policy, and Reality. *Journal of Canadian Studies* 17(1): 51–63.

Kaye, V.J. 1964. *Early Settlements in Canada, 1895–1900. Dr Josef Oleskow's Role in the Settlement of the Canadian Northwest*. Toronto: Ukrainian Canadian Research Foundation/University of Toronto Press.

Kelley, Ninette, and Michael Trebilcock. 1998. *The Making of the Mosaic. A History of Canadian Immigration Policy*. Toronto: University of Toronto Press.

Kymlicka, Will. 1998. *Finding Our Way. Rethinking Ethnocultural Relations in Canada*. Toronto: Oxford University Press.

Lalande, Julia. 2006. 'Building a Home Abroad'—A Comparative Study of Ukrainian Migration, Immigration Policy and Diaspora Formation in Canada and Germany after the Second World War. Ph.D. dissertation, University of Hamburg.

Lehr, John. 1991. Peopling the Prairies with Ukrainians. In *Canada's Ukrainians. Negotiating an Identity*, ed. L. Luciuk and S. Hryniuk, 30–52. Toronto: University of Toronto Press.

Luciuk, Lubomyr, and Stella Hryniuk, eds. 1991. *Canada's Ukrainians: Negotiating an Identity*. Toronto: University of Toronto Press.

Martel, Marcel. 2004. 'Managing Ethnic Pluralism: The Canadian Experience, 1860–1971', In *Meeting Global and Domestic Challenges*, ed. T. Greven and H. Ickstadt, 110–24.

Martynowych, Orest. 1991. *Ukrainians in Canada: The Formative Period, 1891–1924*. Edmonton: Canadian Institute of Ukrainian Studies Press.

Momryk, Myron. 1987. 'Mike Starr: From Mayor to Cabinet Minister', *Archivist* 14(4): 10–12.

Mycak, Sonia. 1996. 'A Different Story' by Helen Potrebenko: 'The Prairie-pioneer Myth Revisited', *Canadian Ethnic Studies/Etudes ethniques au Canada* 28(1): 67–88.

Owram, Doug. 1996. *Born at the Right Time: A History of the Baby-boom Generation*. Toronto: University of Toronto Press.

Palmer, Howard. 1991. *Ethnicity and Politics in Canada since Confederation*. (Canada's Ethnic Groups, Booklet No. 17).

Petryshyn, Roman, ed. 1980. *Changing Realities: Social Trends Among Ukrainian Canadians*. Edmonton: Canadian Institute of Ukrainian Studies Press.

Reitz, Jeffrey G., and Margaret A. Ashton. 1980. Ukrainian Language and Identity Retention in Urban Canada. *Canadian Ethnic Studies/Études ethniques au Canada* 12(2): 33–54.

Rudnyckyj, Jaroslav. 1967. Separate Statement. In Report of the Royal Commission on Bilingualism and Biculturalism. Book 1. *General Introduction. The Official Languages*, ed. Government of Canada. Ottawa: Queen's Printer.

Ryan, Claude. 1975. Canada: Bicultural or Multicultural? Speech given at the Heritage Ontario Congress, 2 June 1972. Reprinted in *Immigration and the Rise of Multiculturalism*, ed. H. Palmer, 147–51. Vancouver: Copp Clark.

Slavutych, Yaroslav, et al., eds. 1966. *Slavs in Canada*. Vol. 1, Proceedings of the First National Conference on Canadian Slavs, 9–12 June 1965, Banff, AB. Edmonton: Inter-University Committee on Canadian Slavs.

Subtelny, Orest. 2000. *Ukraine. A History,* 3rd edn. Toronto: University of Toronto Press.

Swyripa, Frances. 1978. *Ukrainian Canadians: A Survey of their Portrayal in English-language Works*. Edmonton: University of Alberta Press.

———. 1993. *Wedded to the Cause: Ukrainian-Canadian Women and Ethnic Identity, 1891–1991*. Toronto: University of Toronto Press.

Taylor, Charles. 1993. 'Nationalism and the Political Intelligentsia: A Case Study', in *Reconciling the Solitudes*, ed. G. Laforest, 3–22. Montreal/Kingston: McGill-Queen's University Press.

Trosky, Odarka S. 1968. *The Ukrainian Greek Orthodox Church in Canada*. Winnipeg: Bulman Bros.

Ukrainian National Youth Federation of Canada. 1966. *Canada's Culture. Views of Canadian Youth of Ukrainian Origin*. A brief submitted to the Royal Commission on Bilingualism and Biculturalism, Toronto, June 1964. Toronto: UNYFC.

Woycenko, O. 1964. *Canada's Cultural Heritage: Ukrainian Contribution*. Winnipeg: n/a.

Yuzyk, Paul. 1967. *Ukrainian Canadians: Their Place and Role in Canadian Life*. Toronto: Ukrainian Canadian Business and Professional Federation.

# Chapter 13

# First Nations— Contemporary Issues

## READINGS

### Primary Documents

1 From *Statement of the Government of Canada on Indian Policy, 1969* [the White Paper], Jean Chrétien

2 From *Citizens Plus* [the Red Paper], The Indian Chiefs of Alberta

### Historical Interpretations

3 From 'Making Aboriginal People "Immigrants Too": A Comparison of Citizenship Programs for Newcomers and Indigenous Peoples in Postwar Canada, 1940s–1960s', Heidi Bohaker and Franca Iacovetta

4 From '"Our City Indians": Negotiating the Meaning of First Nations Urbanization in Canada, 1945–1975', Evelyn J. Peters

### Introduction

The historical episodes highlighted here were chosen to illustrate some of the ways in which First Nations and others have interacted in what we consider the 'contemporary' era. We can certainly recognize some of the challenges referred to in both the primary and secondary readings because band members live off-reserve in cities like Calgary today, or because the Trudeau government's 1969 plan to dismantle the Department of Indian Affairs might gather both sympathy and opposition if proposed again. The current relationship between Aboriginal and non-Aboriginal people in Canada is affected by many of the same concerns that have troubled leaders in both communities for about 60 years. In particular, the need for Canada's various levels of government to fulfill longstanding promises to Aboriginal Canadians ties the past to the present. It is important to see the 1950s through the 1970s as an era in which both groups acknowledged the needs of 'modern' Aboriginal people, even though distrust and discomfort remained. The primary sources here are a matched set. In the 'White Paper' (a name given to all similar proposals before they become legislation for debate) the Canadian government suggested the eventual end of the bureaucracy that administrated several aspects of life for indigenous people. Prime Minister Trudeau wanted them to take up a standard kind of citizenship, rather than being afforded special rights. He told Aboriginal people he wanted to give them the 'power to change your own condition' by conferring individual rights in place of the collective rights negotiated in treaties. In their response, the 'Red Paper', the Indian Chiefs of Alberta contended that Aboriginal people should be 'citizens plus'. They feared that Trudeau's set of suggestions would wipe away the obligations that the government had undertaken but never quite fulfilled. They wanted First Nations to remain distinct from the multicultural consensus (see Chapter 12) that was gaining momentum during the 1960s. Our secondary sources also tackle assimilation and resistance to it. Heidi Bohaker teams up with historian of immigration Franca Iacovetta to argue that Aboriginal people had to deal with considerable pressure to become citizens of Canada in the same way that immigrants to Canada were expected to become citizens. The combining of two federal ministries (Citizenship and Indian Affairs) for about a decade reflected a simplistic view of the attachments that people had to their own communities and cultures. In our other secondary source, Evelyn Peters discusses the urban environment, particularly in the context of the struggles that many First Nations people had as they tried to fit into cities that were unfamiliar and often inhospitable. Nonetheless, authorities did not do a great deal to ease this transition, other than finding ways for the 'urban Indian' to assimilate to the dominant culture more gradually. The problem of Aboriginal poverty, the rise of limited forms of indigenous self-government, and the ongoing question of land claims are but a few examples of the contemporary developments that are connected to the complex historical relationship between Aboriginal people and other Canadians. This relationship today remains in need of improvement.

# QUESTIONS FOR CONSIDERATION

1.   What did the 1969 proposals from the federal government recommend regarding land claims? Status?
2.   What does 'citizens plus' mean?
3.   Is there an issue that has been more important to the recent history of Canada's Aboriginal people than assimilation and resistance to it?
4.   Why did the Department of Citizenship and Immigration see immigrants and Aboriginal people as threatening?
5.   Were the problems faced by urban Aboriginal people caused, as Father Renaud suggested, by their inability to cope with modern society?

# SUGGESTIONS FOR FURTHER READING

John Bird, Lorraine Land, and Murray MacAdam, eds., *Nation to Nation: Aboriginal Sovereignty and the Future of Canada*, new edn (Toronto: Irwin, 2002).
John Borrows, *Canada's Indigenous Constitution* (Toronto: University of Toronto Press, 2010).
Robin Jarvis Brownlie, *A Fatherly Eye: Indian Agents, Government Power, and Aboriginal Resistance in Ontario, 1918–1939* (Toronto: Oxford University Press, 2003).
Alan C. Cairns, *Citizens Plus: Aboriginal Peoples and the Canadian State* (Vancouver: UBC Press, 2000).

Canada, Royal Commission on Aboriginal Peoples, *Report of the Royal Commission on Aboriginal Peoples*, 5 vols. (Ottawa: The Commission, 1996).

Ken Coates, *The Marshall Decision and Native Rights: The Marshall Decision and Mi'kmaq Rights in the Maritimes* (Montreal and Kingston: McGill-Queen's University Press, 2000).

Tom Flanagan, *First Nations? Second Thoughts*, 2nd ed. (Montreal and Kingston: McGill-Queen's University Press, 2008).

——, Christopher Alcantara, and Andre Le Dressay, *Beyond the Indian Act: Restoring Aboriginal Property Rights* (Montreal and Kingston: McGill-Queen's University Press, 2010)

Janet Silman, *Enough Is Enough: Aboriginal Women Speak Out* (Toronto: Women's Press, 1987)

Annis May Timpson, *First Nations, First Thoughts: The Impact of Indigenous Thought in Canada* (Vancouver: UBC Press, 2010)

# PRIMARY DOCUMENTS

1   From Jean Chrétien, *Statement of the Government of Canada on Indian Policy, 1969* [the White Paper], 3, 6–11. http://www.ainc-inac.gc.ca/ai/arp/ls/pubs/cp1969/cp1969-eng.pdf. p. 1. Reproduced with the permission of the Minister of Public Works and Government Services Canada, 2011.

To be an Indian is to be a man, with all a man's needs and abilities. To be an Indian is also to be different. It is to speak different languages, draw different pictures, tell different tales and to rely on a set of values developed in a different world.

Canada is richer for its Indian component, although there have been times when diversity seemed of little value to many Canadians.

But to be a Canadian Indian today is to be someone different in another way. It is to be someone apart—apart in law, apart in the provision of government services and, too often, apart in social contacts.

To be an Indian is to lack power—the power to act as owner of your lands, the power to spend your own money and, too often, the power to change your own condition.

Not always, but too often, to be an Indian is to be without—without a job, a good house, or running water; without knowledge, training or technical skill and, above all, without those feelings of dignity and self-confidence that a man must have if he is to walk with his head held high.

All these conditions of the Indians are the product of history and have nothing to do with their abilities and capacities. Indian relations with other Canadians began with special treatment by government and society, and special treatment has been the rule since Europeans first settled in Canada. Special treatment has made of the Indians a community disadvantaged and apart.

Obviously, the course of history must be changed.

To be an Indian must be to be free—free to develop Indian cultures in an environment of legal, social and economic equality with other Canadians.

## SUMMARY

### 1 Background

The Government has reviewed its programs for Indians and has considered the effects of them on the present situation of the Indian people. The review has drawn on extensive consultations with the Indian people, and on the knowledge and experience of many people both in and out of government.

This review was a response to things said by the Indian people at the consultation meetings which began a year ago and culminated in a meeting in Ottawa in April.

This review has shown that this is the right time to change long-standing policies. The Indian people have shown their determination that present conditions shall not persist.

Opportunities are present today in Canadian society and new directions are open. The Government believes that Indian people must not be shut out of Canadian life and must share equally in these opportunities.

The Government could press on with the policy of fostering further education; could go ahead with physical improvement programs now operating in reserve communities; could press forward in the directions of recent years, and eventually many of the problems would be solved. But progress would be too slow. The change in Canadian society in recent years has been too great and continues too rapidly for this to be the answer. Something more is needed. We can no longer perpetuate the separation of Canadians. Now is the time to change.

This Government believes in equality. It believes that all men and women have equal rights. It is determined that all shall be treated fairly and that no one shall be shut out of Canadian life, and especially that no one shall be shut out because of his race.

This belief is the basis for the Government's determination to open the doors of opportunity to *all* Canadians, to remove the barriers which impede the development of people, of regions and of the country.

Only a policy based on this belief can enable the Indian people to realize their needs and aspirations.

The Indian people are entitled to such a policy. They are entitled to an equality which preserves and enriches Indian identity and distinction; an equality which stresses Indian participation in its creation and which manifests itself in all aspects of Indian life.

The goals of the Indian people cannot be set by others; they must spring from the Indian community itself—but government can create a framework within which all persons and groups can seek their own goals.

### 2 The New Policy

True equality presupposes that the Indian people have the right to full and equal participation in the cultural, social, economic and political life of Canada.

The government believes that the framework within which individual Indians and bands could achieve full participation requires:

1    that the legislative and constitutional bases of discrimination be removed;
2    that there be positive recognition by everyone of the unique contribution of Indian culture to Canadian life;
3    that services come through the same channels and from the same government agencies for all Canadians;
4    that those who are furthest behind be helped most;

5    that lawful obligations be recognized;
6    that control of Indian lands be transferred to the Indian people.

*The Government would be prepared to take the following steps to create this framework:*

1    Propose to Parliament that the *Indian Act* be repealed and take such legislative steps as may be necessary to enable Indians to control Indian lands and to acquire title to them.
2    Propose to the governments of the provinces that they take over the same responsibility for Indians that they have for other citizens in their provinces. The take-over would be accompanied by the transfer to the provinces of federal funds normally provided for Indian programs, augmented as may be necessary.
3    Make substantial funds available for Indian economic development as an interim measure.
4    Wind up that part of the Department of Indian Affairs and Northern Development which deals with Indian Affairs. The residual responsibilities of the Federal Government for programs in the field of Indian affairs would be transferred to other appropriate federal departments.

In addition, the Government will appoint a Commissioner to consult with the Indians and to study and recommend acceptable procedures for the adjudication of claims.

The new policy looks to a better future for all Indian people wherever they may be. The measures for implementation are straightforward. They require discussion, consultation and negotiation with the Indian people—individuals, bands and associations—and with provincial governments.

Success will depend upon the co-operation and assistance of the Indians and the provinces. The Government seeks this co-operation and will respond when it is offered.

### 3 The Immediate Steps

Some changes could take place quickly. Others would take longer. It is expected that within five years the Department of Indian Affairs and Northern Development would cease to operate in the field of Indian affairs; the new laws would be in effect and existing programs would have been devolved. The Indian lands would require special attention for some time. The process of transferring control to the Indian people would be under continuous review.

The Government believes this is a policy which is just and necessary. It can only be successful if it has the support of the Indian people, the provinces, and all Canadians.

The policy promises all Indian people a new opportunity to expand and develop their identity within the framework of a Canadian society which offers them the rewards and responsibilities of participation, the benefits of involvement and the pride of belonging.

## HISTORICAL BACKGROUND

The weight of history affects us all, but it presses most heavily on the Indian people. Because of history, Indians today are the subject of legal discrimination; they have grievances because of past undertakings that have been broken or misunderstood; they do not have full control of their lands; and a higher proportion of Indians than other Canadians suffer poverty in all its debilitating forms. Because of history too, Indians look to a special department of the Federal Government for many of the services that other Canadians get from provincial or local governments.

This burden of separation has its origin deep in Canada's past and in early French and British colonial policy. The elements which grew to weigh so heavily were deeply entrenched at the time of Confederation.

Before that time there had evolved a policy of entering into agreements with the Indians, of encouraging them to settle on reserves held by the Crown for their use and benefit, and of dealing with Indian lands through a separate organization—a policy of treating Indian people as a race apart.

After Confederation, these well-established precedents were followed and expanded. Exclusive legislative authority was given the Parliament of Canada in relation to 'Indians, and Lands reserved for the Indians' under Head 24 of Section 91 of the *British North America Act*. Special legislation—an *Indian Act*—was passed, new treaties were entered into, and a network of administrative offices spread across the country either in advance of or along with the tide of settlement.

This system—special legislation, a special land system and separate administration for the Indian people—continues to be the basis of present Indian policy. It has saved for the Indian people places they can call home, but has carried with it serious human and physical as well as administrative disabilities.

Because the system was in the hands of the Federal Government, the Indians did not participate in the growth of provincial and local services. They were not required to participate in the development of their own communities which were tax exempt. The result was that the Indians, persuaded that property taxes were an unnecessary element in their lives, did not develop services for themselves. For many years such simple and limited services as were required to sustain life were provided through a network of Indian agencies reflecting the authoritarian tradition of a colonial administration, and until recently these agencies had staff funds to do little more than meet the most severe cases of hardship and distress.

The tradition of federal responsibility for Indian matters inhibited the development of a proper relationship between the provinces and the Indian people as citizens. Most provinces, faced with their own problems of growth and change, left responsibility for their Indian residents to the Federal Government. Indeed, successive Federal Governments did little to change the pattern. The result was that Indians were the almost exclusive concern of one agency of the Federal Government for nearly a century.

For a long time the problems of physical, legal and administrative separation attracted little attention. The Indian people were scattered in small groups across the country, often in remote areas. When they were in contact with the new settlers, there was little difference between the living standard of the two groups.

Initially, settlers as well as Indians depended on game, fish and fur. The settlers, however, were more concerned with clearing land and establishing themselves and differences soon began to appear.

With the technological change of the twentieth century, society became increasingly industrial and complex, and the separateness of the Indian people became more evident. Most Canadians moved to the growing cities, but the Indians remained largely a rural people, lacking both education and opportunity. The land was being developed rapidly, but many reserves were located in places where little development was possible. Reserves were usually excluded from development and many began to stand out as islands of poverty. The policy of separation had become a burden.

The legal and administrative discrimination in the treatment of Indian people has not given them an equal chance of success. It has exposed them to discrimination in the broadest and worst sense of the term—a discrimination that has profoundly affected their confidence that success can be theirs. Discrimination breeds discrimination by example, and the separateness of Indian people has affected the attitudes of other Canadians towards them.

The system of separate legislation and administration has also separated people of Indian ancestry into three groups—registered Indians, who are further divided into those who are under treaty and those who are not; enfranchised Indians who lost, or voluntarily relinquished, their legal status as Indians; and the Métis, who are of Indian ancestry but never had the status of registered Indians.

## THE CASE FOR THE NEW POLICY

In the past ten years or so, there have been important improvements in education, health, housing, welfare, and community development. Developments in leadership among the Indian communities have become increasingly evident. Indian people have begun to forge a new unity. The Government believes progress can come from these developments but only if they are met by new responses. The proposed policy is a new response.

The policy rests upon the fundamental right of Indian people to full and equal participation in the cultural, social, economic, and political life of Canada.

To argue against this right is to argue *for* discrimination, isolation and separation. No Canadian should be excluded from participation in community life, and none should expect to withdraw and still enjoy the benefits that flow to those who participate.

### 1 The Legal Structure
*Legislative and constitutional bases of discrimination must be removed.*

Canada cannot seek the just society and keep discriminatory legislation on its statute books. The Government believes this to be self-evident. The ultimate aim of removing the specific references to Indians from the constitution may take some time, but it is a goal to be kept constantly in view. In the meantime, barriers created by special legislation can generally be struck down.

Under the authority of Head 24, Section 91 of the *British North America Act*, the Parliament of Canada has enacted the *Indian Act*. Various federal-provincial agreements and some other statutes also affect Indian policies.

In the long term, removal of the reference in the constitution would be necessary to end the legal distinction between Indians and other Canadians. In the short term, repeal of the *Indian Act* and enactment of transitional legislation to ensure the orderly management of Indian land would do much to mitigate the problem.

The ultimate goal could not be achieved quickly, for it requires a change in the economic circumstances of the Indian people and much preliminary adjustment with provincial author-ities. Until the Indian people are satisfied that their land holdings are solely within their control, there may have to be some special legislation for Indian lands.

### 2 The Indian Cultural Heritage
*There must be positive recognition by everyone of the unique contribution of Indian culture to Canadian society.*

It is important that Canadians recognize and give credit to the Indian contribution. It manifests itself in many ways; yet it goes largely unrecognized and unacknowledged. Without recognition by others it is not easy to be proud.

All of us seek a basis for pride in our own lives, in those of our families and of our ancestors. Man needs such pride to sustain him in the inevitable hour of discouragement, in the moment when he faces obstacles, whenever life seems turned against him. Everyone has such moments. We manifest our pride in many ways, but always it supports and sustains us. The legitimate pride of the Indian people has been crushed too many times by too many of their fellow Canadians.

The principle of equality and all that goes with it demands that all of us recognize each other's cultural heritage as a source of personal strength.

Canada has changed greatly since the first *Indian Act* was passed. Today it is made up of many people with many cultures. Each has its own manner of relating to the other; each makes its own adjustments to the larger society.

Successful adjustment requires that the larger groups accept every group with its distinctive traits without prejudice, and that all groups share equitably in the material and non-material wealth of the country.

For many years Canadians believed the Indian people had but two choices: they could live in a reserve community, or they could be assimilated and lose their Indian identity. Today Canada has more to offer. There is a third choice—a full role in Canadian society and in the economy while retaining, strengthening and developing an Indian identity which preserves the good things of the past and helps Indian people to prosper and thrive.

This choice offers great hope for the Indian people. It offers great opportunity for Canadians to demonstrate that in our open society there is room for the development of people who preserve their different cultures and take pride in their diversity.

This new opportunity to enrich Canadian life is central to the Government's new policy. If the policy is to be successful, the Indian people must be in a position to play a full role in Canada's diversified society, a role which stresses the value of their experience and the possibilities of the future.

The Indian contribution to North American society is often overlooked, even by the Indian people themselves. Their history and tradition can be a rich source of pride, but are not sufficiently known and recognized. Too often, the art forms which express the past are preserved, but are inaccessible to most Indian people. This richness can be shared by all Canadians. Indian people must be helped to become aware of their history and heritage in all its forms, and this heritage must be brought before all Canadians in all its rich diversity.

Indian culture also lives through Indian speech and thought. The Indian languages are unique and valuable assets. Recognizing their value is not a matter of preserving ancient ways as fossils, but of ensuring the continuity of a people by encouraging and assisting them to work at the continuing development of their inheritance in the context of the present-day world. Culture lives and develops in the daily life of people, in their communities and in their other associations, and the Indian culture can be preserved, perpetuated and developed only by the Indian people themselves.

The Indian people have often been made to feel that their culture and history are not worthwhile. To lose a sense of worthiness is damaging. Success in life, in adapting to change, and in developing appropriate relations within the community as well as in relation to a wider world, requires a strong sense of personal worth—a real sense of identity.

Rich in folklore, in art forms and in concepts of community life, the Indian cultural heritage can grow and expand further to enrich the general society. Such a development is essential if the Indian people are again to establish a meaningful sense of identity and purpose and if Canada is to realize its maximum potential.

The Government recognizes that people of Indian ancestry must be helped in new ways in this task. It proposes, through the Secretary of State, to support associations and groups in developing a greater appreciation of their cultural heritage. It wants to foster adequate communication among all people of Indian descent and between them and the Canadian community as a whole.

Steps will be taken to enlist the support of Canadians generally. The provincial governments will be approached to support this goal through their many agencies operating in the field. Provincial educational authorities will be urged to intensify their review of school curriculae and course content with a view to ensuring that they adequately reflect Indian culture and Indian contributions to Canadian development.

## 3 Programs and Services

*Services must come through the same channels and from the same government agencies for all Canadians.*

This is an undeniable part of equality. It has been shown many times that separation of people follows from separate services. There can be no argument about the principle of common services. It is right.

It cannot be accepted now that Indians should be constitutionally excluded from the right to be treated within their province as full and equal citizens, with all the responsibilities and all the privileges that this might entail. It is in the provincial sphere where social remedies are structured and applied, and the Indian people, by and large, have been non-participating members of provincial society.

Canadians receive a wide range of services through provincial and local governments, but the Indian people and their communities are mostly outside that framework. It is no longer acceptable that the Indian people should be outside and apart. The Government believes that services should be available on an equitable basis, except for temporary differentiation based on need. Services ought not to flow from separate agencies established to serve particular groups, especially not to groups that are identified ethnically.

Separate but equal services do not provide truly equal treatment. Treatment has not been equal in the case of Indians and their communities. Many services require a wide range of facilities which cannot be duplicated by separate agencies. Others must be integral to the complex systems of community and regional life and cannot be matched on a small scale.

The Government is therefore convinced that the traditional method of providing separate services to Indians must be ended. All Indians should have access to all programs and services of all levels of government equally with other Canadians.

The Government proposes to negotiate with the provinces and conclude agreements under which Indian people would participate in and be served by the full programs of the provincial and local systems. Equitable financial arrangements would be sought to ensure that services could be provided in full measure commensurate with the needs. The negotiations must seek agreements to end discrimination while ensuring that no harm is inadvertently done to Indian interests. The Government further proposes that federal disbursements for Indian programs in each province be transferred to that province. Subject to negotiations with the provinces, such provisions would as a matter of principle eventually decline, the provinces ultimately assuming the same responsibility for services to Indian residents as they do for services to others.

At the same time, the Government proposes to transfer all remaining federal responsibilities for Indians from the Department of Indian Affairs and Northern Development to other departments, including the Departments of Regional Economic Expansion, Secretary of State, and Manpower and Immigration.

It is important that such transfers take place without disrupting services and that special arrangements not be compromised while they are subject to consultation and negotiation. The Government will pay particular attention to this.

## 4 Enriched Services
*Those who are furthest behind must be helped most.*

There can be little argument that conditions for many Indian people are not satisfactory to them and are not acceptable to others. There can be little question that special services, and especially enriched services, will be needed for some time.

Equality before the law and in programs and services does not necessarily result in equality in social and economic conditions. For that reason, existing programs will be reviewed. The Department of Regional Economic Expansion, the Department of Manpower and Immigration, and other federal departments involved would be prepared to evolve programs that would help break past patterns of deprivation.

Additional funds would be available from a number of different sources. In an atmosphere of greater freedom, those who are able to do so would be expected to help themselves, so more funds would be available to help those who really need it. The transfer of Indian lands to Indian control should enable many individuals and groups to move ahead on their own initiative. This in turn would free funds for further enrichment of programs to help those who are furthest behind. By ending some programs and replacing them with others evolved within the community, a more effective use of funds would be achieved. Administrative savings would result from the elimination of separate agencies as various levels of government bring general programs and resources to bear. By broadening the base of service agencies, this enrichment could be extended to all who need it. By involving more agencies working at different levels, and by providing those agencies with the means to make them more effective, the Government believes that root problems could be attacked, that solutions could be found that hitherto evaded the best efforts and best-directed of programs.

The economic base for many Indians is their reserve land, but the development of reserves has lagged.

Among the many factors that determine economic growth of reserves, their location and size are particularly important. There are a number of reserves located within or near growing industrial areas which could provide substantial employment and income to their owners if they were properly developed. There are other reserves in agricultural areas which could provide a livelihood for a larger number of family units than is presently the case. The majority of the reserves, however, are located in the boreal or wooded regions of Canada, most of them geographically isolated and many having little economic potential. In these areas, low income, unemployment and under-employment are characteristic of Indians and non-Indians alike.

Even where reserves have economic potential, the Indians have been handicapped. Private investors have been reluctant to supply capital for projects on land which cannot be pledged as security. Adequate social and risk capital has not been available from public sources. Most Indians have not had the opportunity to acquire managerial experience, nor have they been offered sufficient technical assistance.

The Government believes that the Indian people should have the opportunity to develop the resources of their reserves so they may contribute to their own well-being and the economy of the nation. To develop Indian reserves to the level of the regions in which they are located will require considerable capital over a period of some years, as well as the provision of managerial and technical advice. Thus the Government believes that all programs and advisory services of the federal and provincial governments should be made readily available to Indians.

[ . . . ]

In many situations, the problems of Indians are similar to those faced by their non-Indian neighbours. Solutions to their problems cannot be found in isolation but must be sought within the context of regional development plans involving all the people. The consequence of an integrated regional approach is that all levels of government—federal, provincial and local—and the people themselves are involved. Helping overcome regional disparities in the economic well-being of Canadians is the main task assigned to the Department of Regional Economic Expansion. The Government believes that the needs of Indian communities should be met within this framework.

2  From The Indian Chiefs of Alberta, *Citizens Plus* [the Red Paper], 1–9.

## A. THE PREAMBLE

To us who are Treaty Indians there is nothing more important than our Treaties, our lands and the well being of our future generation. We have studied carefully the contents of the Government White Paper on Indians and we have concluded that it offers despair instead of hope. Under the guise of land ownership, the government has devised a scheme whereby within a generation or shortly after the proposed *Indian Lands Act* expires our people would be left with no land and consequently the future generation would be condemned to the despair and ugly spectre of urban poverty in ghettos.

In Alberta, we have told the Federal Minister of Indian Affairs that we do not wish to discuss his White Paper with him until we reach a position where we can bring forth viable alternatives because we know that his paper is wrong and that it will harm our people. We refused to meet him on his White Paper because we have been stung and hurt by his concept of consultation.

In his White Paper, the Minister said, 'This review was a response to things said by Indian people at the consultation meetings which began a year ago and culminated in a meeting in Ottawa in April'. Yet, what Indians asked for land ownership that would result in Provincial taxation of our reserves? What Indians asked that the Canadian Constitution be changed to remove any reference to Indians or Indian lands? What Indians asked that Treaties be brought to an end? What group of Indians asked that aboriginal rights not be recognized? What group of Indians asked for a Commissioner whose purview would exclude half of the Indian population in Canada? The answer is no Treaty Indians asked for any of these things and yet through his concept of 'consultation', the Minister said that his White Paper was in response to things said by Indians.

We felt that with this concept of consultation held by the Minister and his department, that if we met with them to discuss the contents of his White Paper without being fully prepared, that even if we just talked about the weather, he would turn around and tell Parliament and the Canadian public that we accepted his White Paper.

We asked for time to prepare a counter proposal. We have received assurances that the implementation process would not take place. However, the Federal rhetoric has not been substantiated by action. In fact, there is every indication that the implementation process is being carried as fast and as fully as possible. For example, the Departmental officials have prepared their budgets so as to make implementation possible. They rationalize this action by saying that if the White Paper on Indians is implemented their programs must be set whereby they can achieve the implementation within five years or if it does not come about that they can have better programs. Where is the moratorium that we have asked for on activities on the implementation on [sic] the White Paper?

The Minister of Indian Affairs has stated publically [sic] that he is not attempting to throw the Indians over to the provinces in spite of what is contained in writing in his White Paper. Yet, while maintaining this contradictory position he writes a letter to the Premier of Alberta dated February 20, 1970 stating that the Federal Government would transfer funds to the Province for the extension of provincial services to reserves; but these funds would be gradually phased out with the assumption that at this point the Provincial Government would bear full financial responsibility for the provision of these services.

Where is the consistency of the Minister's position when he tells Indians verbally that their reserves will not come under the Provincial tax system but his White Paper and his letter of the Premier say otherwise.

The Indian Chiefs of Alberta meeting in Calgary addressed a letter to the Honorable Pierre E. Trudeau dated January 22, 1970. That letter said:

'This assembly of all the Indian Chiefs of Alberta is deeply concerned with the action taken by the Minister of Indian Affairs and Northern Development, the Honorable Jean Chrétien, regarding the implementation of the Indian policy.

Time and time again, on the one hand, the Minister has declared publically [sic] to the Canadian people that the Indian Policy contained proposals to be discussed with the Indian people. On the other hand, Indian Affairs officials have been recruited for implementation teams to go ahead with the implementation of the policy paper.

We find this double-headed approach contradictory. A glaring example is the appointment of the Claims Commissioner.

Another example is the concentrated public relations program being conducted to impose the White Paper on the Canadian public. We find this incompatible with the Just Society. Discussions between the Federal Department of Indian Affairs and provincial governments have also been initiated.

This assembly of all the Indian Chiefs of Alberta reaffirms its position of unity and recognizes the Indian Association of Alberta as the voice of all the Treaty Indian people of this province. As representatives of our people we are pledged to continue our earnest efforts to preserve the hereditary and legal privileges of our people. At this meeting of Alberta Indian Chiefs, we have reviewed the first draft of our Counter Policy to the Chrétien paper. We plan to complete our final draft in the near future, for presentation to the Federal Government.

We request that no further process of implementation takes place and that action already taken be reviewed to minimize suspicions and to make possible a positive and constructive dialogue between your government and our people'.

In his reply, dated February 19, 1970, to telegrams sent by the Chiefs' Conference of January 22nd, the Minister states that 'the policy proposals, which were put forward in quite general terms will require modification and refinement before they can be put into effect.' In a preceding sentence attempting to explain his Consultation and Negotiation Group which we know as the implementation team, he says, 'I believe that the policy that has been proposed is a correct one, I expect that my Consultation and Negotiations officers will also try to persuade the Indian people, and Canadians generally, that the direction of the policy proposals is indeed in the best interest of all concerned'.

If this is his belief, where is his so called flexibility, especially, when Indian people disagree with his mythical concepts of him leading the Indians to the promised land?

# B. THE COUNTER POLICY

## B.1. *Indian Status*

The White Paper Policy said 'that the legislative and constitutional bases of discrimination should be removed'.

We reject this policy. We say that the recognition of Indian status is essential for justice.

Retaining the legal status of Indians is necessary to be treated justly. Justice requires that the special history, rights and circumstances of Indian People be recognized. The Chrétien Policy says, 'Canada cannot seek the just society and keep discriminatory legislation on its statute books'. That statement covers a faulty understanding of fairness. Professor L.C. Green found that in other countries minorities were given special status. Professor Green has concluded:

'The 1969 Statement of the Government of Canada on Indian Policy is based on the assumption that any legislation which sets a particular segment of the population apart from the main stream of the citizenry is ipso facto conducive to a denial of equality and therefore discriminatory and to be deplored. Such an attitude indicates a complete lack of understanding of the significance of the concept of equality, particularly in so far as the law concerning the protection of minorities is concerned.

'. . . It is perhaps not easy to define the distinction between the notions of equality in fact and equality in law; nevertheless, it may be said that the former notion excludes the idea of a merely formal equality. . .

'Equality in law precludes discrimination of any kind; whereas equality in fact may involve the necessity of different treatment in order to obtain a result which establishes an equilibrium between different situations. . .

'To attempt to maintain that the rights of the Indians result in discrimination against them or are evidence of a denial of their equality in the sense that their status is reduced thereby, is to indulge in an excessively narrow view of the meaning of words, of the purpose of equality and of the nature of discrimination'.[1]

The legal definition of registered Indians must remain. If one of our registered brothers chooses, he may renounce his Indian status, become 'enfranchised', receive his share of the funds of the tribe, and seek admission to ordinary Canadian society. But most Indians prefer to remain Indians. We believe that to be a good useful Canadian we must first be a good, happy and productive Indian.

## B.2. *The Unique Indian Culture and Contribution*

The White Paper Policy said 'that there should be positive recognition by everyone of the unique contribution of Indian culture to Canadian life['].

We say that these are nice sounding words which are intended to mislead everybody. The only way to maintain our culture is for us to remain as Indians. To preserve our culture it is necessary to preserve our status, rights, lands and traditions. Our treaties are the bases of our rights.

There is room in Canada for diversity. Our leaders say that Canada should preserve her 'pluralism', and encourage the culture of all her peoples. The culture[s] of the Indian peoples are old and colorful strands in that Canadian fabric of diversity. We want our children to learn our ways, our history, our customs, and our traditions.

Everyone should recognize that Indians have contributed much to the Canadian community. When we signed the treaties we promised to be good and loyal subjects of the Queen. The record is clear—we kept our promises. We were assured we would not be required to serve in foreign wars; nevertheless many Indians volunteered in greater proportion than non-Indian Canadians for service in two world wars. We live and are agreeable to live within the framework of Canadian civil and criminal law. We pay the same indirect and sales taxes that other Canadians pay. Our treaty rights cost Canada very little in relation to the Gross National Product or to the value of the lands ceded, but they are essential to us.

## B.3. Channels for Services

The White Paper Policy says 'that services should come through the same channels and from the same government agencies for all Canadians'.

We say that the Federal Government is bound by the *British North America Act*, Section 9k, Head 24, to accept legislative responsibility for 'Indians and Indian lands'. Moreover in exchange for the lands which the Indian people surrendered to the Crown the treaties ensure the following benefits:

(a) To have and to hold certain lands called 'reserves' for the sole use and benefit of the Indian people forever and assistance in the social[,] economic, and cultural development of the reserves.

(b) The provision of health services to the Indian people on the reserve or off the reserve at the expense of the Federal government anywhere in Canada.

(c) The provision of education of all types and levels to all Indian people at the expense of the Federal government.

(d) The right of the Indian people to hunt, trap and fish for their livelihood free of governmental interference and regulation and subject only to the proviso that the exercise of this right must not interfere with the use and enjoyment of private property.

These benefits are not 'handouts' because the Indian people paid for them by surrendering their lands. The Federal Government is bound to provide the actual services relating to education, welfare, health and economic development.

## B.4. Enriched Services

The White Paper policy says 'that those who are furthest behind should be helped most'. The policy also promises 'enriched services'.

We do not want different treatment for different tribes. These promises of enriched services are bribes to get us to accept the rest of the Policy. The Federal Government is trying to divide us Indian people so it can conquer us by saying that poorer reserves will be helped most.

All reserves and tribes need help in the economic, social, recreational and cultural development.

## B.5. Lawful Obligations

The White Paper Policy says 'that lawful obligations should be recognized'. If the Government meant what it said we would be happy. But it is obvious that the Government has never bothered to learn what the treaties are and has a distorted picture of them.

The Government shows that it is willfully ignorant of the bargains that were made between the Indians and the Queen's Commissioners.

The Government must admit its mistakes and recognize that the treaties are historic, moral and legal obligations. The redmen signed them in good faith, and lived up to the treaties. The treaties were solemn agreements. Indian lands were exchanged for the promises of the Indian Commissioners who represented the Queen. Many missionaries of many faiths brought the authority and prestige of whiteman's religion in encouraging Indians to sign.

In our treaties of 1876, 1877, 1899 certain promises were made to our people; some of these are contained in the text of the treaties, some in the negotiations, and some in the memories of our people. Our basic view is that all these promises are part of the treaties and must be honored.

*Modernize the Treaties*

The intent and spirit of the treaties must be our guide, not the precise letter of a foreign language. Treaties that run forever must have room for the changes in the conditions of life. The undertaking of the Government to provide teachers was a commitment to provide Indian children the educational opportunity equal to their white neighbors. The machinery and livestock symbolized economic development.

The White Paper Policy says 'a plain reading of the words used in the treaties reveals the limited and minimal promises which were included in them . . . and in one treaty only a medicine chest'. But we know from the Commissioners' Reports that they told the Indians that medicine chests were included in all three.

Indians have the right to receive, without payment, all healthcare services without exception and paid by the Government of Canada.

The medicine chests that we know were mentioned in the negotiations for Treaties Six, Seven and Eight mean that Indians should now receive free medical, hospital and dental care—the same high quality services available to other Canadians.

[ . . . ]

The Indian people see the treaties as the basis of all their rights and status. If the Government expects the co-operation of Indians in any new policy, it must accept the Indian viewpoint on treaties. This would require the Government to start all over on its new policy.

[ . . . ]

# NOTE

1.   L.C. Green, *Canada's Indians—Federal Policy* (Edmonton: Government of Alberta, 1969).

# HISTORICAL INTERPRETATIONS

3    From Heidi Bohaker and Franca Iacovetta, 'Making Aboriginal People "Immigrants
     Too": A Comparison of Citizenship Programs for Newcomers and Indigenous
     Peoples in Postwar Canada, 1940s–1960s', *Canadian Historical Review* 90(3)
     (September 2009): 427–61. Reprinted with permission from University of Toronto
     Press Incorporated (www.utpjournals.com)

When a journalist asked Liberal prime minister Louis St Laurent in 1950 why, as a follow-up to the passage of the *Canadian Citizenship Act* in 1947, he had brought the Canadian Citizenship Branch and Indian Affairs Branch together in a new Department of Citizenship and Immigration (DCI), he replied that the goal was 'to make Canadian citizens of those who come here as immigrants and to make Canadian citizens of as many as possible of the descendants of the original inhabitants of this country'.[1] This essay explores the contested nature of the new category of Canadian citizenship by focusing on the period when the Canadian state strategically chose to combine its management of immigrant admission and settlement with its Indian Affairs policies under the rubric of one federal ministry. Within the new DCI, the Citizenship Branch (CB) influenced and helped develop integration programs for both newcomers and Aboriginals until 1966, when Indian Affairs moved to a new ministry.[2]

We argue that the DCI's dual mandate was part of a deliberate policy to deal with two populations perceived by the federal government to be potentially threatening: Ottawa viewed immigrants and status Indians (especially those living on reserves) as marginal and foreign groups who had to be brought into the Canadian mainstream. The promotion of white middle-class society's dominant family ideals, rigid gender codes, and pro-capitalist values informed both programs, for example, but the programs aimed at Aboriginal peoples were far less respectful of Indigenous cultural traditions and political autonomy than were the immigrant campaigns of European customs. Indeed, the Aboriginal programs showed plenty of continuity with a much older state policy of assimilation that predated Confederation.

[ . . . ]

## INDIGENOUS PEOPLES, IMMIGRANTS, AND A MADE-IN-CANADA CITIZENSHIP

Citizenship is a complex concept and Canadian citizenship is a relatively young official category of belonging. As a white settler society and immigrant-receiving country, Canada has portrayed itself as an enlightened nation while downplaying its history of immigrant restrictions, institutionalized racism, and mistreatment of Aboriginal peoples.[3] The tension between liberal nationalist discourses and repressive practices is readily apparent when Canadians discuss citizenship and belonging more broadly. [ . . . ]

Canada's citizenship regime began after the Second World War, when Mackenzie King's Liberal government drafted legislation to establish a category of national citizenship independent from that of Britain. By doing so, it was acting on initiatives taken in the latter stages of the war by Secretary of State Paul Martin Sr and by senior officials who had spent the war years managing, manipulating, and, in specific cases, interning Canada's ethnic groups as well as mediating ethnic tensions between the country's majority and minority groups. As the Bill's acknowledged architect, Martin Sr accentuated the advantages of promoting a Canadian citizenship defined in terms of a common set of values—democracy, freedom, liberalism—with which a diverse population could be made to identify and support.[4] In seeking to shed the colonial vestiges of a citizenship system, Martin and his colleagues were in no way rejecting the country's British heritage. Indeed, it was to this British and Christian heritage, they argued, that Canada owed its superior values (including respect and tolerance) and institutions (parliamentary democracy).[5] Rather, as Ivana Caccia observes, this largely Anglo-Protestant elite was advocating a symbolic institution of Canadian citizenship that could serve as the primary signifier of belonging to a Canadian community without reference to specific racial, religious, cultural, or linguistic characteristics. But the act also affirmed a vision of a nation composed of two charter groups, English and French, and an array of other (mostly European) ethnic groups.[6] The act became law on 1 January 1947 amid much official fanfare.[7] [ . . . ]

The creation of a legal category of citizenship alone could never have produced the intended sense of common Canadian-ness or belonging, given post-war social realities. These included the challenges of resettling veterans, delivering on the promises of welfare capitalism, and managing a cold war. There was also the anticipated immigrant boom that would further diversify Canada's already ethnically diverse (albeit white) population—and renew age-old fears, especially among Anglo-Celtic Canadians, that their way of life would be threatened unless these inferior 'others' were Canadianized. Equally threatening was the significant increase in the Aboriginal population—another historically 'othered' social group. For decades, successive federal governments had assumed that what they called 'the Indian problem' would eventually disappear on its own, the product of demographic decline. But after reaching a low of 100,000 people in 1900, the population

of 'status Indians' began a remarkable recovery. By the late 1930s, this population had grown 18 per cent; Indian Affairs officials were increasingly worried about the strain that such growth would place on government coffers.[8]

Although 'status Indians' clearly met the *Citizenship Act*'s simple requirement for citizenship of birth on Canadian soil, they were not considered to have the rights of legal citizenship. In fact, the *Citizenship Act* makes no mention of Indians or Aboriginal peoples more generally. It was the *Indian Act* that denied them the right to vote; legally they remained wards of the federal government.[9] In light of their growing numbers, however, Ottawa viewed these 'unassimilated' status Indians as much of a potential threat to Canadian unity as immigrants from traditionally 'non-preferred' southern and eastern European locales. The solution, as King's successor Louis St Laurent explained when he created the DCI to implement the *Citizenship Act*, was to target both groups with similar citizenship programs that would foster an explicit sense of Canadian identity.[10]

In the ensuing years, a new discourse emerged among government officials and others engaged in immigrant reception and Aboriginal education work: Our identity as Canadians is rooted in a shared experience of immigration. In speeches, publications, and organized activities, DCI staff reinforced their message that Aboriginal people were 'immigrants too' in various ways. One was to emphasize the growing numbers of 'Indians' migrating from reserve life to employment in urban centres and to predict that more would follow until few if any were left on reserve communities. Another was to portray Aboriginal people as historic or ancient migrants through repeated attention to the Bering Strait Theory. In a 1952 address to a group of mostly European newcomers in Ottawa who had completed their citizenship course, Vladimir Kaye, chief liaison officer of the DCI's Citizenship Branch, typically declared that 'all Canadians originated from immigrant stock' as even the Indians were 'immigrants to this country in some earlier stage of settlement of Canada'.[11] A DCI immigrant booklet, *The Canadian Scene*, even pointed to archaeology for evidence of migrations across the Bering Strait 'many thousands of years past'.[12]

The DCI's Indian Affairs liaison officers and their colleagues working with First Nations also spread this message. In a 1954 article entitled 'From Oldest to Newest: Our Indian Citizen', André Renaud, an Oblate priest with experience in Indigenous education, stressed that 'our oldest Canadians must be given the status of New Canadians or else they may never become true Canadians like the rest of us'. (In 1957 he co-founded the National Commission on the Indian Canadian, a project of the Canadian Association for Adult Education that liaised with the CB.) Renaud insisted that movement off reserves and assimilation into white settler society would not only end government paternalism and save the state large sums of money but reverse the sad fact that most 'off-reserve Indians' in Canada's cities ended up 'on the fringe and margin of our community, if not physically, at least socially and economically'.[13] For Renaud, as for the DCI officials and other activists, this policy involved applying the programs being developed for training, settling, Canadianizing, and 'modernizing' newcomers, especially rural men and women from peripheral Europe accustomed to 'primitive' living conditions, to Indigenous peoples, who, from the government perspective, had lived too long in the more-or-less foreign world of the rural-based, underdeveloped, and often isolated reserve. Citizenship campaigns also demand conformity to dominant norms, or moral regulation,[14] and here, too, officials, experts, and volunteers intended that, like their immigrant counterparts, Aboriginal youth and adults would adopt Canadian social mores, including pro-capitalist values. [ . . . ]

# MAKING CANADIANS OUT OF ABORIGINAL PEOPLES

In the 1960s, the population of 'Indians with status' was roughly one-tenth of Canada's immigrant population, or 190,000 persons. But Aboriginal peoples nevertheless remained the fastest growing 'ethnic group' in Canada (to use the government's problematic term).[15] As the title of a 1955 film that Ottawa produced with the National Film Board put it, Indians were *No Longer Vanishing*.[16] Like their DCI colleagues involved in the immigrant programs, the Indian Affairs Branch staff took very seriously their citizenship mandate to Canadianize ('modernize') Indigenous peoples.[17] They celebrated what they viewed as successful transformations in the gender dynamics of family and community life: speaking of the Shamattawa Band in northern Manitoba, for instance, Indian Affairs officials reported with approval that 'formerly it was the women's job to provide the fuel while the men hunted and trapped. Shamattawa men have realized that this is not suitable women's work'.[18] However, there were also critical differences between the immigrant and Aboriginal campaigns, including the virtual absence of any explicit discourse of cultural pluralism or unity-in-diversity in the Aboriginal programs for the period under review. Instead, these programs were characterized by a more marked policy of racial assimilation into white society.

Our exploration of the DCI-era programs reveals that the Indian Affairs Branch concentrated many of its assimilation efforts on specific educational programs: formal schooling for children, and leadership and vocational training for adults. A sample of the headlines that appeared in the branch periodical *Indian News*, which beginning in 1954 was distributed free to status Indians across Canada, reveals how staff defined progress through a celebration of people who participated in mainstream Canadian society 'Indian Accomplishments Increase

Admiration of Canadian Public', 'Miss Hoff Proves Valuable Clerk', 'Shalath Girl Receives Nursing Diploma', 'Sales Manager Found Life Varied, Never Dull in Successful Career', 'Indian Magistrate Holds Respect of All', 'Career in RCAF', 'Ambitious Mohawk Actress Studies Radio, Television', and 'Handicapped Indian Fine Barber Says Boss'. A 1964 article titled 'Domestic Service Proves Useful Step' explained how 54 'Indian girls from Southern Alberta' found jobs as 'domestics, babysitters and housekeepers' in Calgary. As in the case of immigrant domestic schemes, the job training was also expected to equip these young women for eventual marriage and modern homemaking. Another article, simply titled 'Achieves Success by Hard Work', featured a couple who had saved enough money from various jobs to purchase their own farm outside of the reserve—thereby becoming what the government desired: property-owning and capitalist-oriented Indians. In every issue of *Indian News*, at least one article addressed off-reserve employment possibilities and profiled people in those jobs: a 1962 instalment was entitled 'Why I Became a Nurse'.[19]

The importance of education to the project of moving people off reserve and assimilating them into Canadian society was clearly understood by the entire Department of Citizenship and Immigration. In a 1961 DCI publication, Minister of Citizenship and Immigration Ellen Fairclough was quoted as saying that 'the fundamental aim of the government's policy towards Indians is the gradual integration of our country's fastest growing ethnic group into the Canadian community'. Education, she felt, was 'the key to a promising future for the Indians'. The author of the piece, Douglas Leechman, went on to underscore the government's intention to use education and training as part of a tool to depopulate reserves: 'It is anticipated that, by 1970, two-thirds of our Indian people will have left the reserves. Some of the elderly ones, born and brought up there, can obviously never leave, but their children can, and their grand-children will'.[20]

The theme of education as the key to children's success dominated *Indian News*. Students were praised for winning scholarships, perfect attendance prizes at residential schools, and one for achieving 'the Grand Award for Residential School pupils in the Tuberculosis Poster Competition'. The president of the Edmonton Indian Residential School reported in 1954 that 'Indian children rated high in tests of mental ability compared to other Canadian boys and girls of the same age'.[21] Students who acquired post-secondary education were singled out for praise, as were those who entered the military or undertook careers in policing, nursing, and social work.[22] As with the immigrants, an acknowledgement of individual accomplishments reinforced the state's mandate to promote pro-capitalist and liberal ideologies. The stakes involved were far greater for status Indians, however, because until the *Indian Act* was amended in 1961, any person with Indian status who achieved post-secondary education could be deemed 'enfranchised' by Indian Affairs and thus would be removed from the register and no longer be a legal member of their band.[23]

That Canadian officials and their network of professional and volunteer colleagues hoped to encourage Indigenous women (like immigrant women) to aspire to emulate a largely bourgeois-defined domesticity is clearly indicated by the favourable coverage in *Indian News* of the Homemakers' Clubs in reserve communities. Having grown out of similarly named clubs created for newcomer prairie women in the early 1900s and the Women's Institutes of Ontario (begun in 1897), these clubs aimed to bring the science of home economics to rural women, and to extend middle-class values into the countryside. By the 1950s, many of the Saskatchewan Homemakers' Clubs began outreach to First Nations reserves on the grounds that, as Jennifer Milne observes, programs of 'personal improvement and community service' could help Indian 'integration into mainstream society' and 'ultimately lead them out of a life of poverty'.[24] The clubs were relatively popular with Aboriginal women—for example, the number of Aboriginal clubs on Saskatchewan reserves increased from one to twenty-five between 1937 and 1954. These clubs, according to *Indian News*, were committed to service, 'to make life on the reserves better and happier'.[25] [ . . . ]

Notwithstanding the lofty language of integration and success, there was a clear class component to the DCI's citizenship programs for Natives; they promoted Aboriginal assimilation to the Canadian working class. Government officials had specific and limited ideas of how Aboriginal peoples would be permitted to exercise their right to Paul Martin Sr's 'full partnership in the fortunes and in the future of the nation'.[26] As superintendent of Indian Affairs, J.W. Pickersgill elaborated on these ideas in 1956, when he described his department's training opportunities. The boys would be trained for farm work and parcelled out to farmers, while girls would receive instruction in 'the rudiments of household science, with a view to equipping them to take employment as domestic workers or as workers in hospitals or institutions'.[27] As many *Indian News* features made clear, the most basic vocational training would be the norm while post-secondary training would be the exception. In addition to the 'three R's', girls at Portage la Prairie Indian Residential School learned 'domestic science—cooking, sewing, handcrafts' to become 'good homemakers' while the boys practised 'building an open-air rink and painting and decorating the rooms of the school'. In addition, the 4-H Clubs had 'the school farm to practice on, with 16 fine cows to milk and eggs to gather from 150 hens'.[28]

As these examples suggest, Indian Affairs encouraged the adoption of white middle-class cultural values but structured educational opportunities to ensure that these young people remained firmly in the working class and were best 'qualified' to work in essentially unskilled positions. [ . . . ]

The Onion Lake Residential School garnered particular attention in *Indian News* for its novel approach to teaching 'home economics'. The school had constructed a special three-room house in which the girl students could take turns playing 'housewife'. The house was equipped

> with a wood and coal stove, hot water reservoir, gasoline-operated washing machine, sewing machine, ironing boards and hand irons, all of the type which can be purchased easily by a young couple on a budget suited to their means . . . Subjects they are taught include cleanliness, laundry, sewing (including Indian handicrafts) and cooking (family-sized meals).[29]

This description highlights another important racial divide: while both Indigenous and newcomer women faced campaigns of domesticity, the model house at Onion Lake was far removed from the celebrated modern homes that CB officials and others encouraged new Canadians to aspire to eventually purchasing. Indeed, it more resembled the conditions of wartorn or impoverished European regions. One could argue that Indigenous peoples were not expected to aspire to the same level of modernity as white Europeans. In part these lower expectations of potential to 'modernize' may have reflected the more rural and dispersed nature of reserve populations, especially compared to the more concentrated urban focus of post-war immigration.

[ . . . ] Another long-standing cornerstone of government policy towards status Indians specifically was to encourage relocation from reserve communities to urban centres. Such a policy was attractive for three reasons. First, income earned off-reserve is generally taxable, especially if the employee also lives off-reserve. Second, off-reserve employment was preferable to and easier than encouraging economic development on often isolated reserves. Third, off-reserve employment increased the likelihood that people would meet and marry non-status people and stay put in urban centres, and thus they (or their children) would no longer be the financial responsibility of the federal government.[30]

In the 1950s, DCI officials spoke of promoting 'immigration' to the cities by providing, through the Indian Affairs Branch, a placement officer in a number of major cities to 'help make the changeover from reserve to city as easy and as successful as possible'. The branch also provided very short courses of two to three weeks' duration in a variety of low-skilled trades and occupations. (Immigrant training courses were longer or involved several courses.) At one such Indian Affairs program 'devoted to homemaking and agriculture' in Prince Albert, SK, the 38 men and 17 women attendees were grouped by gender into a training course: the men reportedly studied 'motors and machinery, care of livestock, and welding and carpentry' and the women 'homemaking with cookery, laundering, sewing and family health emphasized'. Indian Affairs officials steered members of reserve communities towards employment off-reserve in lower-skilled working-class positions as farm labourers, lumberjacks, miners, construction workers and (low-level) mechanics as well as domestic servants and fish plant and cannery workers. The expressed hope was that those trained in a trade or service would relocate to urban settings and establish themselves as 'property-owners and wage earners', albeit at the bottom end of the socio-economic spectrum.[31]

As for teaching the lessons of democratic citizenship, Indian Affairs officials stressed the need to inculcate 'leadership skills' by running 'leadership courses' where students were exposed to recreational planning or community development programs based on mainstream 'Canadian' values. In this regard, the leadership courses developed for Indigenous peoples, like those targeting immigrants, were part of a larger post-war recreational movement and its aim of encouraging a participatory form of liberal democracy.[32] Topics at typical Aboriginal leadership courses, such as health, education, recreation, home management, and family relationships, echoed those featured in immigrant leadership camp and other programs. In addition, the Aboriginal courses addressed such topics as 'the role of Indian leaders and the part credit unions and co-operatives could play in the economic development of reserves'.[33] There were leadership training programs that focused on how to run social clubs or cottage industries or covered topics such as 'the new problems which have resulted from changing family life and customs' and 'the proper relationship of the Homemakers' Club to the band council'.[34] Articles in *Indian News* continually reported 'great interest' on the part of bands for such training.[35] All of this suggests that while Indian Affairs hoped to ultimately eliminate reserves, it was nonetheless compelled to provide some response to the needs and demands of Aboriginal reserve communities.

Predictably, given the alarmist declarations of officials and experts who railed about declining families and spreading immorality, Indigenous youth, like their immigrant counterparts, were targeted by state-supported programs that sought to prevent juvenile delinquency with organized recreational programs. Particularly in regard to female sexuality, however, it must be noted that while the racism and sexism of the day made both 'non-preferred' newcomer girls and Indigenous girls more vulnerable than others to moralizing judgements, the latter faced far greater gender stigmatization, as evidenced by the shameful history of rape, murder, and excessive incarceration of Aboriginal women in Canada.[36] As for the proposed remedies to youth problems, the experts relied on familiar methods, such as recruiting Indigenous teenagers into youth training courses, which also stressed leadership skills. Here, too, 'leadership' was a trope for the inculcation of white, middle-class values, including gender expect-ations (girls cooked and sewed, boys fished and farmed), though, in certain cases, girls as well as boys could choose elective subjects such as weaving, leather-work, film projec-tion, photography, and dramatics.[37]

Other activities were explicit in their aims of reshaping Aboriginal cultures. In an effort to inculcate more capitalist values, a course set up to teach Cree and Chipewyan youth in northwest Saskatchewan 'how to care for their home and improve its appearance', for example, trained the men in 'the preparation and preservation of pelts for the best mar-kets' without regard to the traditional role of women in this task.[38] The women's famil-iar domestic program also included lessons on how to can and preserve fruits and vege-tables, suggesting a plan to introduce healthy 'Canadian' items into what nutritional experts considered to be an inferior Indigenous diet. Similar efforts were made with immigrant women. But, as Krista Walters shows, the fol-low-up campaigns to 'modernize' Aboriginal women's food customs would involve highly intrusive social surveys that dismissed the value in Indigenous diets and pathologized them as the most 'backward' or 'ignorant' of mothers in Canada.[39]

By the late 1950s, the Citizenship Branch, which had been carving out new roles for itself within the government bureaucracy, and instigating more collaborative ventures with Indian Affairs, switched its main focus from reception to social adjustment, a pro-ject that easily incorporated work meant to prepare Aboriginal peoples for their eventual assimilation into the Canadian mainstream. Initially, this meant concentrating on meet-ing the needs of status Indians who moved to urban environments and were under-serviced by Indian Affairs programs. By the mid-1960s, the CB was also loaning leader-ship experts to Indian Affairs for projects on reserves, sponsoring voluntary agencies, and getting directly involved in on-reserve projects.[40] CB liaison officers, quick to seek

opportunities to expand their influence, strove to develop an expertise on Aboriginal peoples that could parallel their knowledge of immigrants. In 1957, the head of the branch's Research Division entered into discussions with the University of Toronto, proposing a survey of Ontario Indians. Regional liaison officers were soon making direct contact with Indigenous people who had moved to cities; the regional officer based in Saskatoon, for instance, familiarized himself with vocational programs in order to offer guidance services to status Indians leaving reserves. At the end of 1957, the CB's work among status Indians was mentioned in the department's Annual Report for the first time. By 1959, CB officials were also being invited to Indian Affairs Branch functions, such as the Regional Conference of the Indian Homemakers' Club held in Toronto. In Alberta, officials of each branch 'met frequently to coordinate their programs with respect to Indian integration and settle-ment in various communities'. The depart-ment's Annual Report for 1958–9 formally acknowledged co-operation between the two branches, especially in liaising with 'voluntary organizations interested in the settlement of Indians in urban communities'.[41]

Throughout the 1960s, the CB extended its efforts well beyond the social integra-tion of status Indians who had relocated to urban areas. The Alberta liaison officer 'held discussions with the psychology and sociol-ogy departments of the University of Alberta concerning possible further research on Indians and Immigrants'. Staff members were also loaned to Indian Affairs. Despite its tiny budget, the CB's activities were now continu-ally highlighted at the front of the DCI's Annual Report, and the 1961 report first mentions on-reserve activity by the branch. By 1963, the branch was planning 'a number of co-oper-ative projects' in Saskatchewan to promote 'wider areas of co-operation between Indians and non-Indians'. The department published a booklet, *Citizenship Projects among Indians*, that described particularly successful joint programs, such as Camp Gold Eye, where 20 Aboriginal and non-Aboriginal youth were taught citizenship skills.[42]

Beginning in the 1950s, but accelerating rapidly in the 1960s, the Citizenship Branch was involved in sponsoring, funding, and monitoring the activities of voluntary groups (such as church organizations) and volunteer agencies and academic experts dealing with Aboriginal people in urban settings.[43] Voluntary groups such as the Indian Eskimo Association, the Canadian Welfare Council, and the Friendship Centers had tremendous power over the lives of Aboriginal people: Their executives often testified before the Special Joint Committees on Indian Affairs. As their briefs from the early 1960s suggest, these groups were committed to encouraging—and, if necessary, cajoling—people to leave the reserves and assimilate into white settler society.[44]

Government and voluntary associations saw little if anything wrong with their programs for transforming Aboriginals into Canadian citizens. To a considerable degree, the views of even the best-intentioned citizenship educators reflected a familiar politics of nation-building—one predicated on a two-founding-nations construction of Canada—that excluded all Aboriginal peoples from that nation-building project. (By contrast, 'ethnic Canadians', especially of European origins, belonged to that category of 'the others' whose contributions to Canadian development also deserved recognition.) Despite the geography of their birth, in order to be considered citizens, Aboriginal Canadians had to 'immigrate' from peripheral reserves to mainstream Canadian communities in a manner metaphorically similar to the journey taken by the refugees who left Europe's DP camps and immigrants who fled its impoverished regions. Furthermore, just as citizenship officials and activists encouraged social mingling among old and new Canadians and among different groups of newcomers, the staff of both the Indian Affairs and Citizenship branches

emphasized the value to be gained from ensuring association between Indigenous and immigrant persons and promoted contact between the two groups. An issue of *Indian News* reported that 'the Indian's pride in his heritage and his privileges as a Canadian citizen were well illustrated one evening at a Vancouver YMCA when Indians attending part of a leadership training course there decided to visit with a group of new Canadians who had just finished a course in the English language'. 'The occasion', it continued, 'became a warm and friendly one as the Indian group made friends with the newcomers and told them of the fine things Canada holds for them'. The same issue also featured a photo of a 1960 dance at the Toronto Indian Youth Club that showed a young woman from the Sarnia Reserve dancing modestly with a male immigrant from Italy. Citizenship activists considered dance an effective tool of integration, and such photos visually recreated a Canadian state discourse linking Aboriginals to immigrants.[45] So, too, did the multi-ethnic folk festivals celebrating the Canadian mosaic: alongside the colourfully costumed Ukrainian folk dancers, Hungarian choral singers, and Scottish bagpipers could be Iroquois dancers who 'show us some of the traditions and customs of our Indians of Ontario' and prairie Indians performing the 'dances and folklore from BC, the Plains, and southwest Indians'. While delivering a liberal message of pluralism, these cultural spectacles, which enjoyed CB support, had the effect of reducing Native peoples to one of Canada's many 'ethnic groups' and both groups to primitive 'folk' bearing quaint customs.[46]

Still, government officials did have to face the reality that Aboriginal people were born in Canada, and this finally led to some refinement of thinking. Whereas in 1949 St Laurent clearly stated that Canadian citizenship was something status Indians needed to acquire, by 1956 Pickersgill, as head of Indian Affairs, was noting that, while technically 'the Canadian Indians were already citizens of Canada', they were 'citizens with a difference' because 'the Indians have privileges, which other Canadians do not have, and other citizens have privileges and responsibilities, which are not shared by the Indians'.[47] For Pickersgill and others, citizenship was linked to taxation. Since status Indians living on reserves did not pay tax, by Pickersgill's reasoning they were citizens who were not entitled to certain citizenship (legal) rights, such as the franchise. This logic had to be abandoned in 1960 when John Diefenbaker's Conservative government, responding in part to the rise of human rights movements within Western nations and the international community's criticism of Canada's treatment of

Aboriginal peoples, granted the federal vote to status Indians with no loss of status and no impact on treaty rights or obligations. As a newly middle-ranked nation keen to increase its international status, Canada had at least to give its Indigenous peoples the semblance of full political partnership by granting status Indians the franchise. Suddenly, all Aboriginal people were transformed by key political figures like Minister Ellen Fairclough into 'our oldest citizens . . . these ancient Canadians', who now needed to acquire specific skills in order to ensure their 'economic survival'.[48] Nevertheless, the government's assimilationist goals remained the same.

## NOTES

1. St Laurent cited in A.O. Cole, 'Make Canadians New Policy Aim, Will Admit More', *Toronto Star*, 3 Dec. 1949; Valerie Knowles, 'Towards the Canadian Citizenship Act', in *Forging Our Legacy: Canadian Citizenship and Immigration, 1900–1977* (Ottawa: Citizenship and Immigration Canada, 2000), chap 5, 63–77.

2. The new ministry was the Department of Northern Affairs and Natural Resources. At that time, Ottawa also created a Department of Manpower and Immigration, and the Citizenship Branch was placed under the jurisdiction of the department of the Secretary of State. Freda Hawkins, *Canada and Immigration: Public Policy and Public Concern* (Montreal and Kingston: McGill-Queen's University Press, 1972), 89–118.

3. Introduction and essays by Bonita Lawrence and Mona Oikawa in *Race, Space and the Law: Mapping a White Settler Society*, ed. Sherene Razack (Toronto: Between the Lines, 2002).

4. Norman Hillmer, Bohdan Kordan, and Lubomyr Luciuk, eds., *On Guard for Thee: War, Ethnicity, and the Canadian State, 1939–1945* (Ottawa: Canadian Committee for the Second World War, 1985); Paul Martin, 'Citizenship and the People's World', *Belonging: The Meaning and Future of Canadian Citizenship*, ed. William Kaplan, 64–78 (Montreal and Kingston: McGill-Queen's University Press, 1993).

5. Canada, *House of Commons Debates* (22 Oct. 1945), pp. 1335–7 (Paul Martin, Sr, MP). See also Hawkins, *Canada and Immigration*, 96.

6. Ivana Caccia, 'Managing the Canadian Mosaic: Dealing with Cultural Diversity during the World War Two Years' (Ph.D. diss., University of Ottawa, 2006).

7. *Canadian Citizenship Act*, 1946 (10 Geo. VI).

8. For 1900, see Russell Thorton, *American Indian Holocaust and Survival: A Population Hisotry since 1492* (Norman: University of Oklahoma Press, 1990), 242. Data for 1939 compiled from Canada, *Census of Indians in Canada* (Ottawa: 1939).

9. John Leslie and Ron Maguire, eds., *The Historical Development of the Indian Act* (Ottawa: Treaties and Historical Research Centre, Research Branch, Corporate Policy, Indian and Northern Affairs Canada, 1978); Robin Brownlie, '"A Better Citizen than Lots of White Men": First Nations Enfranchisement—an Ontario Case Study, 1918–1940', *Canadian Historical Review* 87(1) (2006): 29–52.

10. A third 'target' was youth. In creating the DCI, the Citizenship Branch (originally the wartime Nationalities Branch) and the Citizenship Registration Branch were moved from the Secretary of State while the Immigration

Branch and Indian Affairs Branch were moved from Mines and Resources.

11. 'Address by Dr. V.J. Kaye to graduating class of new Canadians at the High School of Commerce', Ottawa, 21 Mar. 1952, file 1952, vol. 11, Vladimir Julian Kaye Fonds, Canadian Citizenship Branch series, MG31 D69, Library and Archives Canada (hereafter LAC).

12. DCI, *The Canadian Scene* (Ottawa: DCI, 1963).

13. André Renaud, 'From Oldest to Newest: Our Indian Citizen', in *Food for Thought*, repr. (Canadian Association for Adult Education, 1954), box 270, file 5, American Federation of International Institutes Collection, Immigration RG3, Immigration and Refugee Services of America Records, Immigration and History Research Centre Archives, University of Minnesota.

14. Franca Iacovetta, *Gatekeepers: Reshaping Immigrant Lives in Cold War Canada* (Toronto: Between the Lines, 2006); Adele Perry, *On the Edge of Empire: Gender, Race, and the Making of Empire* (Toronto: University of Toronto Press, 2001); Mariana Valverde, *The Age of Light, Soap, and Water: Moral Reform in English Canada, 1885–1925* (Toronto: University of Toronto Press, 1991).

15. Speech of Minister Ellen Fairclough, in Douglas Leachman, 'The Meeting of the Ways', in *The Indian in Transition: The Meeting of the Ways, Learning for Earning*, DCI (Indian Affairs) (Ottawa: Queen's Printer, 1961), 10.

16. National Film Board, *No Longer Vanishing*, 1955; DCI, *Annual Report, 1955–6*, 45; DCI, *The Indian in Transition: The Indian Today* (Ottawa: Queen's Printer, 1962) 3; and DCI, *The Indian in Transition: The Meeting of the Ways; Learning for Earning* (Ottawa: Queen's Printer, 1963), 6.

17. Immigration and Citizenship Committee, pt 1, file 1-24-1, vol. 26, MG 28 I 17, LAC.

18. 'Once Northern Nomads: Woodcutting Operation Helps to Settle Band', *Indian News* 3(3) (Mar. 1959): 8.

19. H.M. Jones, 'Indian Accomplishments', *Indian News* 1(1) (Aug. 1954): 3 (Jones was then director of Indian Affairs) and the following in *Indian News*: 'Miss Hoff', 1(2) (Jan. 1955): 5; 'Shalath Girl', 1(2) (Jan. 1955): 7; 'Sales Manager', 1(3) (Apr. 1955): 1; 'Indian Magistrate', 1(4) (July 1955): 1; 'RCAF', 2(1)

(Jan. 1956): 3; 'Mohawk Actress', 2(3) (Mar. 1957): 6; 'Handicapped Indian', 2(4) (Sept. 1957): 11; 'Why I Became a Nurse', 6(2) (1962): 4; 'Domestic Service Proves Useful Step', 7(2) (Mar. 1964): 7; 'Achieves Success', 7(3) (July 1964): 7.

20. Leachman, 'The Meeting of the Ways', 10.

21. 'The Grand Award' and 'Tests of Mental Ability', *Indian News* 1 (Aug. 1954): 7.

22. *Indian News*: 'The Professions', 1(4) (July 1955): 2; 'Heads Branch at High School', 1(4) (July 1955): 3; 'Indian Nurse', 2(1) (Jan. 1956): 5; 'First Indian to Join the Mounties', 3(1) (June 1958): 7; 'Indian Students at University of British Columbia', 7(2) (Mar. 1964): 8.

23. Olice Patricia Dickason, *Canada's First Nations: A History of Founding Peoples from Earliest Times*, 3rd edn (Toronto: Oxford University Press, 2002), 327; 'Compulsory Enfranchisement Now No Longer Possible', *Indian News* 4(4) (Apr. 1961): 3.

24. Jennifer Milne, 'Cultivating Domesticity: The Homemakers' Clubs of Saskatchewan, 1911 to the Post-War Era' (M.A. thesis, University of Saskatchewan, 2004), 59–60; Dorinda Stahl, 'Marvelous Times: The Indian Homemaking Program and Its Effects on Extension Instructors at the Extension Division, University of Saskatchewan' (M.A. thesis, University of Saskatchewan, 2002).

25. 'Homemakers Clubs Hold Three Regional Conventions This Year', *Indian News* 1(1) (Aug. 1954): 3.

26. When introducing the Citizenship Act, Martin declared that Canadian citizenship 'means more than the right to vote' and 'to hold property' and 'to move freely under the protection of the state' but also 'the right to full partnership in the fortunes of the nation'. Cited in Pierre Boyer, Linda Cardinal, and David Headon, 'Introduction', in *From Subjects to Citizens: A Hundred Years of Citizenship in Australia and Canada* (Ottawa: University of Ottawa Press, 2004), 2–3.

27. 'The Future of the Canadian Indian', *Indian News* 2(2) (May 1956): 1.

28. 'Portage La Prairie Students Are Happy, Boys and Girls Have Busy Program at Indian Residential School', *Indian News* 2(3) (Mar. 1957): 12.

29. 'Household Study Real to Students', *Indian News* 1(3) (Apr. 1955): 1.

30. Bonita Lawrence, *'Real' Indians and Others: Mixed-Race Urban Native People, the Indian Act, and the Rebuilding of Indigenous Nations* (Lincoln: University of Nebraska Press, 2004).

31. 'Employment Horizon Broadens for Indians, New Placement Service Aids Jobhunters', *Indian News* 3 (Sept. 1957): 1–2.

32. Shirley Tillotson, *The Public at Play: Gender and the Politics of Recreation in Post-War Ontario* (Toronto: University of Toronto Press, 2000); Allan Irving, Harriet Parsons, and Donald Bellamy, *Neighbours: Three Social Settlements in Downtown Toronto* (Toronto: Canadian Scholars Press, 1995), chaps. 13–14.

33. 'They're Learning . . . to Be Leaders', *Indian News* 3(3) (Mar. 1959): 6.

34. 'Leadership Courses Continued to Interest Indian Bands', *Indian News* 1(4) (July 1955): 7.

35. See 'Leadership Courses'; see also 'These Adults are Learning by Doing', *Indian News* 5(1) (June 1961): 1.

36. 'Aboriginal Women' in *The Justice System and Aboriginal People*, vol. 1 (Winnipeg: Provincial Inquiry, 1991); Jean Barman, 'Taming Aboriginal Sexuality: Gender, Power, and Race in British Columbia, 1850–1900', *BC Studies* 115–16 (1997–98): 237–66; Sarah Carter, *Capturing Women: The Manipulation of Cultural Imagery in Canada's Prairie West* (Montreal and Kingston: McGill-Queen's University Press, 1997); Joan Sangster, 'Domesticating Girls: The Sexual Regulation of Aboriginal and Working-Class Girls in Twentieth-Century Canada', in *Contact Zones*, ed. Katie Pickles and Myra Rutherdale (Vancouver: UBC Press, 2005); Christine Welsh, *Finding Dawn* (Ottawa: National Film Board, 2006).

37. 'They're Learning', 6.

38. 'Course for Home Improvement, Families Learn at School', *Indian News* 3(2) (Oct. 1958): 8; Sylvia Van Kirk, *Many Tender Ties: Women in Fur-Trade Society in Western Canada, 1670–1870* (Winnipeg: Watson & Dwyer, 1980).

39. 'Course for Home Improvement', 8; 'Northern Diet Improves as Some Bands Begin Growing Vegetables', *Indian News* 2(2) (May 1956):

1; Krista Walters, 'A National Priority Food, Health and Colonizing Bodies in Nutrition Canada's National Survey, 1965–75', paper presented to the Canadian Historical Association, Vancouver, June 2008.

40. DCI *Annual Report*, 1953–4, and *Annual Report*, 1964–5.

41. Kaye reports, file 1959, vol. 11, Citizenship Branch series, MG31 D69, Vladimir Julian Kaye Fonds, LAC; files 1955, 1957, 1960, vol. 12, Citizenship Branch series, MG31 D69, Vladimir Julian Kaye Fonds, LAC; DCI, *Annual Report 1962–63*; Canada, *Citizenship Projects among Indians: A Collection of Articles Reprinted from Citizen* (Ottawa: Department of Citizenship and Immigration, 1965).

42. Kaye 1960 report, file 1960, vol. 12, Citizenship Branch series, MG31 D69, Vladimir Julian Kaye Fonds, LAC; Citizenship Branch series, DCI, *Annual Report*, 1962–3.

43. Walter M. Hlady, 'Directed Social Change and the Agencies Involved', Indian-Eskimo Association, Learned Societies Meeting, 1960, 5; 'Indian Research Seminar', Queen's University, sponsored by Indian-Eskimo Association, June 1960; Indian-Eskimo Association of Canada, *The Urban Indian Canadian: A Handlist of Voluntary Organizations Working with People of Indian Background in Canada's Towns and Cities* (City: Indian-Eskimo Association of Canada, 1962); *A Moon in His Moccasins* (United Church pamphlet), Emmanuel Library Collection, Victoria University.

44. Canadian Welfare Council, *Submission to the Joint Parliamentary Committee on Indian Affairs*, 22 Mar. 1961; Indian-Eskimo Association of Canada, *Report of Executive Director to the Sixth Annual Meeting*, 21 Oct. 1965.

45. *Indian News* 4(2) (May 1960): 2, 3.

46. Program, 'Eighth Annual John Madsen Folk [School] Festival, 23 June 1956', and program, 'Seventh Annual John Madsen Folk Festival, 25 June 1955', both in file 1957 Folk Festival, International Institute of Metropolitan Toronto, MU6416, Ontario Archives.

47. J.W. Pickersgill, 'The Future of the Canadian Indian', *Indian News* 2(2) (May 1956): 2.

48. 'A Review of Indian Affairs', *Indian News* 4(4) (Apr. 1961): 6.

4    From Evelyn J. Peters, '"Our City Indians": Negotiating the Meaning of First Nations Urbanization in Canada, 1945–1975', *Historical Geography* 30 (June 2002): 75–92.

Contemporary cultural criticism has celebrated the potential of the idea of the 'travelling native' for disrupting cultural assumptions about the modern 'nation'. The focus has been on movements across contemporary national borders and boundaries—fundamentally, on transnationalism. However, nations also make sense of themselves through internal spatial and social divisions. Challenging these divisions also disrupts definitions of 'nation'. The urbanization of First Nations people in Canada provides a telling illustration of this point.[1]

First Nations people were systematically dispossessed of their lands, which were 'emptied' for colonial resettlement.[2] Colonial constructions of the Canadian 'nation' involved the creation of narrowly circumscribed native territories or reserves, separate from metropolitan centres.[3] Arguably, reserves were viewed as temporary enclaves, places where First Nations people would either be civilized through agriculture, Christianity, or education to take their place in emerging Canadian society, or where First Nations people could live in peace while their 'races' died out. The invention of reserves as temporary and 'primitive' spaces of First Nations culture and history, secured a 'place' for First Nations people in the spatial order of the Canadian nation.

By the early decades of the [twentieth century], almost all First Nations people were settled on reserves, and almost all reserves were located at a distance from urban centres. Through a variety of mechanisms, many of which remain to be fully documented, these largely segregated patterns of settlement persisted unaltered into the 1950s (Table 1). Increasing population pressure and a chronic lack of economic possibilities on the small and often resource-poor reserves resulted in a gradually rising number of First Nations people migrating from reserves to cities after mid-century. Despite their initially very small numbers, non-Aboriginal people perceived First Nations peoples' presence in urban centres as extremely problematic.[4] The conference referred to in the title of this paper, one of a number of events during this period involving a variety of non-governmental organizations and representatives from three levels of government, attested to the discomfort that emerged when First Nations people became known as 'city Indians'.[5] Governments and First Nations representatives responded to widespread concern over the presence of First Nations people in cities, and by 1975 the main dimensions of government policy for urban First Nations people had taken shape.

[ . . . ]

As government agencies struggled to make sense of First Nations urbanization, they were influenced by a colonial history that relegated First Nations people and cultures to spaces separate from modern and, particularly, urban society. [ . . . ] Despite contradictions in government-program development, and despite First Nations representatives' attempts to influence the definition process, policies and programs that emerged during this period reinforced colonial interpretations of the place of First Nations people and cultures in the Canadian nation.

## DIMENSIONS OF URBANIZATION

Inconsistent patterns of data collection make it difficult to document the movement of First Nations people to cities or to relate urban population numbers to the growing public interest in their situation with any

## Table 1  Canadian Census Counts of Urban Populations, Canadian and Indian Ancestry* Populations, 1871–1981†

| Date | Canadian Population Living in Urban Areas | | Indian Population Living in Urban Areas | |
| | Number | Per cent | Number | Per cent |
|---|---|---|---|---|
| 1871 | 712,465 | 19.6 | 1,740 | 1.7 |
| 1881 | 1,111,475 | 25.7 | 651 | 0.6 |
| 1891 | 1,537,098 | 31.8 | N/A | N/A |
| 1901 | 2,021,799 | 37.6 | 4,765 | 5.1 |
| 1911 | 3,280,444 | 45.5 | 3,905 | 3.7 |
| 1921 | 4,350,299 | 49.5 | 3,531 | 3.2‡ |
| 1931 | 5,573,798 | 53.7 | 5,056 | 3.9 |
| 1941 | 6,252,416 | 54.3 | 4,469 | 3.6 |
| 1951 | 8,628,253 | 61.6 | 11,015 | 6.7 |
| 1961 | 12,700,390 | 69.6 | 28,382 | 12.9 |
| 1971 | 16,436,850 | 76.2 | 90,705 | 30.7 |
| 1981 | 18,215,440 | 75.6 | 150,675 | 36.4§ |

Sources: Canada, Statistics Canada, *1981 Census*, cat. 92-.0911, Table 3; *1971 Census*, cat. 92-723, Table 3; Dominion Bureau of Statistics, *1961 Census*, cat 92-553, Table 82; *1951 Census*, vol. II, Table 4; *1941 Census*, Table 10; *1931 Census*, vol. IV, Table 44, *1921 Census*, vol. I, Table 23; W.E. Kalbach, 'Growth and Distribution of Canada's Ethnic Populations, 1871–1981', in Leo Dreidger, ed., *Ethnic Canada. Identities and Inequalities* (Toronto: Copp Clark Pitman, 1987): 102.

* Census counts for ethnicity refer to racial or ethnic origins or ancestry, which do not necessarily capture the groups with which the respondents identify.
† The term 'Indian' is used because that is the terminology of the census. The counts and percentages of Indians are not comparable between census years because of differences in geographic coverage, changing definitions of urban, and varying question format and instructions to enumerators.
‡ Data for 1921 to 1961 include Inuit people.
§ Includes Indian, Métis, and Inuit.

precision.[6] Table 2 shows the number of registered Indians living off of the reserve between 1959 and 1981. The small number living off the reserve suggests that throughout this period, urbanization rates were very low, even though they were increasing. The greatest absolute increase in Indians living off reserve was between 1966 and 1971, but even if all of these were urban migrants, this represents an increase of only a little over 5,000 individuals per year in Canada's cities. While some may have migrated to cities through 'enfranchisement', the term used to describe the process through which First Nations people were encouraged to give up their legal status as Indians and become ordinary citizens of the country, data on the historically low number of enfranchisements shows that this was not a common route First Nations people used to leave their reserve communities.

Census statistics also suggest that the total number of First Nations people in major Canadian cities remained low, both in terms of absolute numbers and as a percentage of the total population (Table 3). At the same time, population estimates from various non-governmental organizations and individuals concerned with urban Aboriginal populations were much higher than census counts. At a 1962 conference on urban Aboriginal people involving federal, provincial, municipal, and non-governmental organizations, the latter estimated that there were more than 5,000 Indians living in Winnipeg and approximately 3,000 living in Edmonton.[7] In

## Table 2  Total and Off-Reserve Registered Indian Population, 1959–1976

| Year | Registered Indian Population | Off-Reserve† (Number) | Off-Reserve† (Per cent) | Enfranchisements* Per 5-Year Period |
|------|------|------|------|------|
| 1959‡ | 179,126 | 30,372 | 16.9 | — |
| 1961 | 191,709 | — | — | 2077 |
| 1966 | 224,164 | 43,746 | 19.5 | 3216 |
| 1971 | 257,619 | 69,106 | 26.8 | 3009 |
| 1976 | 288,938 | 79,301 | 27.4 | 1094 |

Sources: Canada. Indian Affairs Branch, *Indian Affairs Facts and Figures* (Ottawa: Indian Affairs Branch, 1967): 5; Canada. Statistics Canada, *Perspective Canada: A Compendium of Social Statistics* (Ottawa: Ministry of Industry, Trade and Commerce, 1974): 244.

* Figures for 1961 and 1966 are estimates based on the Department of Indian Affairs' fiscal year; figures for 1971 and 1976 are based on the calendar year.
† This number does not include individuals living on Crown land.
‡ Statistics on off-reserve residency began to be collected in 1959.

## Table 3  Aboriginal People in Major Metropolitan Centres, 1951–1981

| | 1951 | 1961 | 1971* | 1981 |
|------|------|------|------|------|
| Montreal | 296 | 507 | 3215 | 14450 |
| Ottawa-Hull | — | — | — | 4370 |
| Toronto | 805 | 1196 | 2990 | 13495 |
| Winnipeg | 210 | 1082 | 4940 | 16575 |
| Regina | 160 | 539 | 2860 | 6575 |
| Saskatoon | 48 | 207 | 1070 | 4350 |
| Calgary | 62 | 335 | 2265 | 7310 |
| Edmonton | 616 | 995 | 4260 | 13750 |
| Vancouver | 239 | 530 | 3000 | 16080 |

Sources: Department of Indian Affairs and Northern Development (DIAND) *Customized Data, 1981 Census* (Ottawa: Indian Affairs Branch, 1985). Statistics Canada, Perspective Canada (Ottawa: Information Canada, 1974): 244.

* The 1971 data do not include the Inuit.

1980, journalist Larry Krotz reported non-governmental-agency estimates of 25,000–80,000 Aboriginal people in Winnipeg[,] over 25,000 in Regina, and 30,000–40,000 Aboriginal people in Edmonton.[8] Part of the difference between these estimates and census figures may be the result of under-counting of Aboriginal populations, either because respondents did not identify them-selves, or because they were in living situa-tions not easily accessible to census takers. However, the magnitude of the difference between census counts and agency estimates suggests that other factors were involved. Moreover, they hint at the high levels of concern that had emerged about the urban migrant situation, and a sense of being over-whelmed by the challenges this migration involved. Some of these perceptions arose from the prospect of incorporating a rela-tively poor, undereducated population into city life. The debate and concern centering on First Nations migration suggest that the response to their presence was shaped in no small part by the sense that First Nations were 'out of place'—that their presence in urban areas represented a transgression into what had been defined as a space for non-Aboriginal peoples and cultures.[9] As Jean Lagassé indicated in a 1959 study for the Manitoba Ministry of Agriculture, 'the belief that an Indian's place is on the reserve is still very strong among the Canadian people'.[10]

Although policy-makers, researchers, and politicians of this period clearly focused their attentions on the move from the reserve to the city, it is clear that patterns of migration were not so simple. For many First Nations people living in cities, the reserves and rural areas of their genesis were places that still represented home, places that were important for their sense of cultural identity, and places to which they wished to return to raise their children or to retire.[11] An analysis of First Nations migration patterns between 1966 and 1971 found that while in-migration to urban centres accounted for 22 per cent of Aboriginal relocation in that period, 31 per cent of migration could be attributed to moves from one reserve or rural area to another, 22 per cent were moves from one city to another, and a significant 17 per cent of moves were return migration from cities back to reserves and rural areas.[12] In addition, surveys documented the fact that migrants to cities often kept contact with relatives and friends on reserves and there were steady flows of visitors in both directions.[13]

Almost all surveys of First Nations people living in cities during this period found that the main reason individuals and families moved to urban areas was to find employment, effectively escaping the economic limitations inherent in the reserve system.[14] Other common reasons for migration were for education, medical care, 'family reasons', or because of problems on the reserve. A national study that examined off-reserve migration in relation to reserve characteristics, found that reserves with greater resources in terms of employment and educational opportunities, services, and stronger local governments, had

lower rates of out-migration.[15] These findings underscored the continued attachment of many First Nations people to their reserves despite the sometimes dramatic demographic changes of this period.[16]

It is difficult to follow settlement patterns of First Nations migrants following their arrival in urban areas. A common assumption has been that they settled in the inner city or 'skid row',[17] and some of the studies that explored Aboriginal location within cities seemed to confirm this assumption.[18] It is also apparent that some migrants, socially and economically marginal, created 'shanty-towns' at the geographic margins of urban areas, although the extent of fringe settlement during his time period is not known.[19] Still, it is clear that in some cities, First Nations populations were scattered throughout urban areas, and that a significant number of First Nations migrants moved directly to more suburban locations rather than to inner-city housing.[20] Despite these varied settlement patterns, and despite their small numbers, non-Aboriginal people largely saw the presence of First Nations people in cities as problematic.

## DEFINING URBAN INDIANS

The negative perception of growing urban First Nations populations put increasing pressure on governments to respond. Before government agencies could formulate responses, they faced the challenge of defining the nature of the population toward which government programs should be directed, and the nature of the problem that required remediation. Building on Michel Foucault's 1978 lecture entitled 'Governmentality',[21] researchers have demonstrated that the way in which subjects are represented—what concepts are invented or deployed to render them governable—is a prerequisite for policy intervention.[22] First Nations urbanization challenged government agencies to define the meaning of First Nations urbanization and the nature of the urban First Nations population. The definitions that emerged through this process proved revealing.

The idea that First Nations urbanization represented a larger process of culture change soon became dominant in government agencies.[23] This interpretation was championed by the Indian-Eskimo Association, a largely non-Aboriginal and non-governmental organization with a mandate to improve the condition of native people in Canada. The Indian-Eskimo Association exerted considerable influence over government departments responsible for programs for urban First Nations people during this period.[24] Father André Renaud, one of the original organizers of the association, summarized this perspective at a 1957 Calgary conference on Aboriginal people in urban areas:

> Our Indian Canadian is faced or hampered with . . . his own personality. The Indian Canadian is different from his fellow Canadians of European descent. . . . These differences have nothing to do with his blood or heredity but are from his cultural heritage. . . . For instance, his concepts of time, money, social communication, hygiene, usefulness, competition and co-operation are at variance with our own and can prove a stumbling block to successful adjustment. . . . Our duty is to establish: (1) Where do these cultural traits interfere with smooth adjustment? At work, in recreation, at home etc. In other words where does be get into trouble because he is an Indian and what can he done about it? (2) Where does he make the most successful adjustment and cultural contribution to our society and how could we expand or open these areas?[25]

The assumption underlying Renaud's interpretation was that First Nations migrants to the city faced difficulty because they came from reserves characterized by cultures with behaviours, values, skills, and institutions suitable to pre-modern society, but antithetical to life in modern urban settings.[26] This framework, then, reaffirmed the spatial ordering underlying the colonial construction of the Canadian nation—the identification of reserves and their residents as minute islands of traditional and primitive culture amidst a growing tide of modern and modernizing Canadian society. Reserves were defined as existing in a different timeframe.[27] The clearest statement of this position is arguably found in a 1967 address by the Honorable Arthur Laing, minister of Indian Affairs and Northern Development to a convention of the Native Brotherhood in Vancouver. '[T]he reserves will have to continue to be centers of Indian Community life for many years to come. . . . The reserves must provide an essential time-cushion while Indian people make their own decision as to the kind of life they want to lead'.[28]

The movement of First Nations people to cities was interpreted by most policy-makers of the post-war period as a decision to integrate into the Canadian mainstream. This interpretation rendered First Nations people in cities categorically distinct from First Nations people on reserves. In 1962, R. Alex Sim, chief liaison officer in the Citizenship Branch of Canada's Department of Citizenship and Immigration, produced a paper proposing the definition of a new 'category' of Indian—the 'urban Indian':

> It is time that the expression 'Urban Indian' began to take its place with others—the Plains Indian, the Woodlands Indian, the Enfranchised Indian, and the Half-breed or Metis [sic]. . . . From the point of view of the Citizenship Branch, an urban Indian is anyone who is living off the reserve in a setting where there are industrial and commercial job opportunities, and who identifies himself as an Indian.[29]

[ . . . ] One comes to assume that individuals living in a certain area share the same attributes. Categorizing First Nations people by place of residence redefined them as two distinct but internally homogeneous populations—urban Indians and reserve Indians. Urban First Nations people were represented as possessing different qualities, perspectives, values, and behaviours from their relatives on the reserve. They were viewed as being a transformational ethnic category, in the process of shedding their traditional cultures and identities and becoming Canadian citizens.

The invention of the population category of 'urban Indian' introduced new possibilities for administration and provided a rationale for the involvement of government departments not historically associated with the administration of First Nations affairs. According to Sim, 'It seems that we are prepared to pursue these two goals: one of first-class citizenship off the reservation, the other to maintain the principle of trusteeship implicit in the present reservation system'.[30] While reserve Indians had historically been administered by the Department of Indian Affairs (later termed the Indian Affairs Branch), the Citizenship Branch of Canada, an agency customarily in the business of aiding international immigrants, was to take precedence for policy and program development for First Nations people in cities.[31] In this way, the Citizenship Branch introduced new programs, services, and administrative structures that were associated, not with the historic responsibility of the crown for Aboriginal peoples, but with efforts at integration and the forging of new citizens. For the Citizenship Branch, First Nations urbanization was a matter of 'internal migration', an analogue of overseas immigration, representing 'a new phase where the skills that were applied to immigrant groups can be used with Indians who migrate to the cities'.[32] The Indian Affairs Branch could maintain its historic role with respect to reserve residents, a population to which these goals still did not apply.

Defining rural-to-urban migration as a process of culture change, government agencies depicted urbanization as inevitably damaging and disturbing. Represented in terms of their past and pre-urban cultures, First Nations migrants were expected to uniformly experience culture shock upon their departure from the reserve. The threat urban lifeways posed to First Nations cultures was assumed to make it difficult for migrants to create opportunities for themselves, creating a rationale for direct government intervention. This intervention would ultimately take myriad forms.

## CREATING PROGRAMS

The frameworks of meaning that government agencies used to understand First Nations urbanization affirmed the assignment of separate spaces for First Nations and majority Canadian cultures. While both the Indian Affairs and Citizenship branches agreed that 'urban Indians' represented a distinct population category, the two branches advanced different policy and program-development goals for this population. Program development was a complex process, affording opportunities for the destabilization of spatial categories both through internal contradictions in branch programs and through initiatives from First Nations representatives.

### Indian Affairs Branch Placement Program

Beginning in the early 1960s, the Indian Affairs Branch had identified the increasing involvement of provincial governments and other federal government departments in providing services to First Nations people as important to the integration process. Indian Affairs maintained that provinces and municipalities were constitutionally responsible for providing social assistance to First Nations people once they left the reserve.[33] During this period, though, the development of Indian Affairs Branch programs for urban First Nations people was contradictory. In its 1956–57 Annual Report, the branch announced a program addressing the urbanization issue. In response to what it called the 'problems of adjustment to the standards of the non-Indian community', the branch created a placement program that worked in co-operation with the National Employment Service.[34] Indian Affairs placement officers were responsible for selecting individuals from reserves to be placed in urban employment, and for providing these individuals with focal and administrative support during the initial phases of their employment. The goal of integrating Indians into the national mainstream appears to have been their guiding motive.

Placement officers became deeply involved in individual cases, and at times officers intervened extensively in their clients' lives in an effort to facilitate permanent urban employment and residence.[35] Careful selection of First Nations candidates for this program, and intensive supervision and control after their placement, suggest that the program represented the extension of the historic wardship role of the Indian Affairs Branch off of the reserve and into the city.

The placement program could be easily reconciled with the long historical mandate of the Indian Affairs Branch's to intervene in the interest of assimilating First Nations people, but simultaneously it was at odds with an administrative perspective that employed the spaces of reserve and city to define different categories of Indians.[36] As a result, there was considerable debate and discussion within the branch about the desirability of involvement in the placement program. The debates were brought to a head in 1972, when an urban Blackfoot group in Calgary introduced a placement program similar to that of the Indian Affairs Branch, with support from local Indian Affairs officials.[37] As the Blackfoot initiative gained publicity, other First Nations groups began to request support for similar initiatives, creating increasing conflict within the Indian Affairs Branch over policies, practices, and jurisdictions. The Indian Affairs Branch could

not reconcile First Nations control over their own service delivery in the city with its long-standing definition of First Nations people as either wards or as ordinary citizens. The Indian Affairs placement program was largely abandoned by 1975.[38]

## Citizenship Branch Friendship Centres

While the Citizenship Branch, like the Indian Affairs Branch, viewed urbanization in terms of both the threats and assimilationist potentials of culture change, it approached program development in its own way. Drawing on its experience facilitating the adjustment of immigrant groups, the Citizenship Branch promulgated a model of urban ethnicity for First Nations Groups in the city. For the Citizenship Branch, the assumed inevitable loss of traditional culture in the urban environment was seen as a disabling experience on the short term, which must be counteracted with strategies to allow migrants to retain or regain aspects of their identity during the period of transition. As J.H. Lagassé, later director of the Citizenship Branch, informed the audience at an Edmonton conference on urban Aboriginal people:

> A way must be found by which cultural values from the native culture remain until values of the larger culture can be taken on. People who make a satisfactory adjustment are those who can maintain their own culture long enough to learn the new culture.[39]

Friendship Centres comprised the main mechanism through which the Citizenship Branch became involved with native people in urban areas.[40] In a 1965 address at the Vancouver Friendship Centre, Minister of Citizenship and Immigration J.R. Nicholson emphasized their cultural role:

> It is your avowed purpose, the task of all in the Indian Friendship Centres, to

assist [migrating Indians] to make the adjustment to a way of life which is in strong contrast to the traditional Indian culture of the reserve. It is up to you to help soften the blow. Unless such a service is available to him, the Indian who has newly arrived in the city often finds that he is being asked to reject completely everything that has been dear to him for generations, in favour of a way of life about which he knows little or nothing. It is up to you, in the Indian Friendship Centre, to provide a place where the harassed city-migrant can find a sheltered haven where he can rest and take stock of himself during the hectic process of adjustment to city life.[41]

This was 'culture as therapy', facilitating integration by providing a temporary if somewhat superficial sense of identity, a reprieve and a source of self-esteem.[42] For the Citizenship Branch, then, the boundaries differentiating reserve and city were not absolute, and urban and reserve lifeways were not completely exclusive. Some aspects of First Nations cultures (still associated with past times and distant reserve places) could be accommodated and even prove beneficial in city life. However, according to Citizenship Branch policy, the place of First Nations culture in urban life was highly circumscribed, and was destined for replacement. Generally seen as antithetical to urban life ways, it should be contained and diffused within the walls of the Friendship Centre through special celebrations and contact with other natives.

Certainly, the benefit of First Nations culture in the city was limited to its role in facilitating the initial adjustment of migrants. The branch emphasized the responsibility of Friendship Centres to promote the 'full utilization of, and referral to, existing services to prevent segregation'. Migrating First Nations people were to be referred to provincial and municipal agencies for social assistance,

employment and financial information, personal counselling, justice issues, and any other social needs.[43] Centres were seen as essential for narrowly defined cultural programming, but the major role in facilitating integration was to remain with the institutions of the dominant society.

## First Nations Perspectives

The available material suggests that many First Nations people understood the process of urbanization through different frameworks of meaning than did the Citizenship and the Indian Affairs branches.[44] One theme threading through the First Nations material contradicts the distinction between 'urban Indians' and reserve communities. A 1976 proposal by the Federation of Saskatchewan Indians to conduct a survey in urban areas clearly contradicts the assumption that urbanization reflected a rejection of the reserve community of origin and an attempt by migrants to adopt a new cultural identity. In the proposal the federation characterized urban migrants as 'treaty Indians who belong to the different Indian bands in the province'.[45] The 1978 report based on the survey emphasizes: 'Throughout the entire report, the reader should bear in mind that this is not a report on Urban Natives. It is a report on band members living off-reserve'.[46] The report noted that:

Although a large number of Indians have left their home reserves, and it is likely that larger numbers will continue to do so, this cannot reasonably be interpreted to mean that these people are rejecting their Indian culture and traditions, their home reserves or their fellow band members. While this assumption may be true in a limited number of cases, the general discussions that interviewers held indicate that the vast majority of Indians living in cities still consider themselves to be members of their band—not urban Indians.[47]

The definition of urbanization as a problem of culture change was also challenged. For Calgary Friendship Centre Executive Director Andrew Bear Robe, culture was only one of many more important factors affecting the ability to succeed in the city:

> An Indian moving into an urban community does not always find it difficult. It depends on many tangible and intangible factors such as the amount of education and skilled training a person has acquired; single or married, and if married—how large is the family; a student or a person looking for permanent employment; a Treaty, non-Treaty or a Metis [sic] person, a drinker or a non-drinker; an Indian thinker with typical habits and attitudes, or an Indian who has become acculturized to the dominant white society; good personal appearance accompanied by the important ability to express oneself articulately and distinctly, or a person with poor grooming and withdrawn personality—the availability of a car or no transportation at all, and many other factors which make a person more or less employable.[48]

In a report commissioned by the Citizenship Branch, Bear Robe linked difficulties native migrants had in the city directly to the economic impoverishment of the reserves from which migrants had come, rather than to some traditional culture that was supposedly incompatible with urban life.[49] Refusing to define First Nations migrants only in terms of their supposedly pre-urban culture, Bear Robe's argument contradicted the association of urbanization and culture shock. It also pointed out the heterogeneity of the migrating population, and suggested that the issue of urbanization required a much more nuanced analysis from one that used the spatial categories of urban and reserve to define distinct populations for policy and program development.

In contrast to perspectives that emphasized the inability of urban First Nations migrants to develop adequate coping strategies without non-native intervention, and that prescribed a limited role for Aboriginal cultures in urban areas, First Nations people argued that they had an essential role in meeting the needs of urban Indians. The Federation of Saskatchewan Indians explained that band councils continued to feel responsible for the welfare of band members who migrated to off-reserve areas:

> The bands to whom [migrants] belong, and the Federation as their representative, have serious concerns about what is happening to the people who make up this migration. As well, the Federation and the bands feel a deep responsibility for these people and wish to find ways of extending this concern by offering them help and support with the problems resulting from their move.[50]

First Nations representatives increasingly pressured for First Nations involvement and control of Friendship Centre boards and programs during this period. They also rejected the narrow scope and place for First Nations cultures in the city defined by the Citizenship Branch. They noted that mainstream service organizations did not have the skills or knowledge to provide appropriate assistance; that First Nations migrants preferred to receive assistance from Aboriginal Friendship Centre personnel; and that because of their lack of knowledge of First Nations cultures and circumstances, social service organizations often referred clients back to Friendship Centres.[51] Bear Robe's argument went further, suggesting that the issue was not limited to service provision, but First Nations representation in political and economic systems:

> This haphazard concern for the general welfare of the native people of Canada will not change until Indian leaders

themselves demand the change. They will not effect the change unless they become involved with the main political and economic pulse of this country, either as city aldermen, members of the Provincial Legislative, members of Parliament, businessmen or leaders of organizations promoting social change for all people concerned. . . . Until we actually have Indian people assuming important, influential and responsible roles in society, either in government or in business, the Indian voice and demands will never get top priority or have an adequate hearing.[52]

[ . . . ] The frameworks of meaning through which First Nations migrants interpreted the process of urbanization emphasized a continuity of culture, identity, and relationships between city and reserve. They also asserted a strong role for First Nations representatives in defining a response to the urbanization process. In this way, First Nations put forward an alternative categorization of space, one that was not constructed on the basis of contrasts between First Nations and settler space that were rooted in the cold terrestrial calculus of colonialism.

## CONCLUSIONS

In the 1940s, almost all First Nations people lived on reserves and very few lived in Canadian cities. These patterns reflected and perpetuated colonial attitudes based on constructed dichotomies of First Nations people and Canadians, primitive and modern, historical and contemporary, on which the spatial order of the Canadian nation was founded. The migration of First Nations people to cities upset the colonial geographies of isolated and bounded native territories separate from the metropolitan centres of the nation. These movements challenged First Nations and non-First Nations people to formulate frameworks for understanding the 'place' of

First Nations people in the Canadian nation. Interpretations of First Nations urbanization between 1945 and 1975 are particularly interesting in this respect. Anthropologist Nancy Lurie argued that First Nations people saw the process of urbanization less as one of moving from reserve to city than as travelling within their traditional territories or equivalent spaces—performing, in contemporary times, historically familiar patterns of movement and migration.[53] First Nations representatives' rejection of 'urban' and 'reserve' as meaningful categories upon which to construct indigenous identities or to base responses to First Nations urbanization is consistent with a mapping of identity based on traditional territories, rather than on colonial spaces of bounded and isolated native reserves. First Nations representatives' arguments about providing services to community members living in cities was consistent with their traditional responsibilities over economic and social life within traditional territories. This idea was nascent between 1945 and 1975, but it would be developed much more fully in later decades.[54] The idea of traditional territories challenges representations of the Canadian nation that are built on containing and bounding First Nations people and cultures and that separate them from the metropolitan centres of population and power. Traditional territories underlie all of what is now called Canada, including all of its urban areas. First Nations' ideas about traditional territories subvert colonial representations of the internal spaces through which the Canadian nation creates its identity.

The response of government agencies to First Nations urbanization, worked out over several decades, was complex and often contradictory, and provided opportunities for First Nations people to attempt to define the significance of urbanization in ways which fit their own frameworks of meaning. Clearly the introduction of Friendship Centres and, to a lesser extent, the Indian Affairs Branch Placement Program provided a toehold for

First Nations representatives to begin to challenge hegemonic definitions of First Nations cultures in relation to urban places and cultures. Between 1945 and 1975, these efforts were largely ineffectual, though, and the resulting policies and programs did not significantly challenge the colonial representations of First Nations people and cultures that were embedded in dichotomous social and spatial divisions. First Nations representatives were unable to effectively insert their interpretations into the dominant discourse—a sobering reminder of the difficulty marginalized peoples face in forcing an understanding, let alone a serious consideration, of counter-hegemonic perspectives.[55]

Government responses to the First Nations urbanization involved the re-affirmation of reserves as First Nations territories, separate in time and space from the centres of the modern nation where First Nations people existed only precariously as mainstream citizens. They also involved, through Friendship Centre programming, the creation of narrowly circumscribed spaces for native cultures *within* the city, but limited only to an initial period of adaptation to urban life. Both of these responses bounded and located First Nations people and culture, and both reproduced a nation divided into 'primitive' spaces of native culture and the 'modern' space of mainstream Canadians. In this period, the colonial organization of space perpetuated the colonial ordering of society. Government policy toward First Nations migration would continue to reaffirm this time-honoured division uncritically; only gradually and reluctantly would policy-makers begin to consider the Aboriginal perspectives on this important dimension of their modern history.

## NOTES

1. The Canadian constitution defines Indians, Métis, and Inuit peoples as the Aboriginal people of Canada. Each of these three groups has a different history as well as a unique set of rights as defined in Canadian legislation and jurisprudence. My focus here is on Indian people. Indians are the descendants of the indigenous peoples of Canada, registered under Canada's *Indian Act*. I prefer to use the term 'First Nations' because of the colonial overtones the term 'Indian'. However, I employ 'Indian' when this term was the common usage at the time. I also recognize that many First Nations people choose to identify themselves by their cultural origins—for example, Cree, Gwitchin, or Algonquin—rather than by the homogenizing term 'First Nations'.

2. Kenneth G. Brealey, 'Mapping Them "Out": Euro-Canadian Cartography and Appropriation of the Nuxalk and Ts'ilhqot'in First Nations' Territories, 1793–1916', *The Canadian Geographer* 39 (1995): 140–156; R. Cole Harris, *The Resettlement of British Columbia: Essays on Colonialism and Geographic Change* (1997); Bruce Willems-Braun, 'Buried

Epistemologies: The Politics of Nature in (Post)colonial British Columbia', *Annals of the Association of American Geographers* 87 (1997): 3–31.

3. In Canada, the policy that was supposed to accompany this process was treaty-making through which First Nations people relinquished title to their lands in exchange for small reserves and promises for a variety of services and material provisions. Clearly, this policy was often disregarded. The basic assumptions about the nature of Aboriginal title and the place of Aboriginal people in the nation that are reflected in this policy, however, differ from those of other nations. The construction of the Australian nation, for example, was based on an idea of 'terra nullius' or empty land.

4. Neils W. Braroe, *Indian and White: Self-Image and Interaction in a Canadian Plains Community* (Stanford: Stanford University Press, 1975); Hugh Brody, *Indians on Skid Row: The Role of Alcohol and Community in the Adaptive Process of Indian Urban Migrants* (Ottawa: Department of Indian Affairs and Northern Development,

1965); Mitsuru Shimpo and Robert Williamson, *Socio-Cultural Disintegration Among the Fringe Saulteaux* (University of Saskatchewan: Centre for Community Studies, 1965); David Stymeist, *Ethnics and Indians* (Toronto: Peter Martin Associates, 1975); Yngve G. Lithman, *The Community Apart: A Case Study of a Canadian Indian Reserve Community* (Winnipeg: University of Manitoba Press, 1984).

5.   The phrase comes from the title of an early conference on urban Indian issues. Regina Welfare Council, *Our City Indians* (Regina: Saskatchewan House, 1958).

6.   Census data are problematic because definitions and categories change, and in different years ancestry is traced through the father, the mother, and through both parents. An estimate of urban Indian populations can be made from the Indian Register kept by the Department of Indian Affairs. While the department kept treaty pay lists prior to 1951, these do not identify place of residence of those receiving payments. Beginning in 1959, the department began to collect information about individuals living 'off reserve', that is, neither on reserves or crown land. These data can be used as a proxy for urbanization, but the numbers must be interpreted cautiously.

7.   Gordon K. Hirabayashi, Anne J. Cormier, and Vincent S. Billow, *The Challenge of Assisting the Canadian Aboriginal Peoples to Adjust to Urban Environments* (Edmonton: Report of the First Western Canada Indian-Métis Seminar, 1962).

8.   Larry Krotz, *Urban Indians: The Strangers in Canada's Cities* (Edmonton: Hurtig Publishers Ltd., 1980).

9.   Tim Cresswell argues, 'The occurrence of "out-of-place" phenomena leads people to question behaviour and define what is and what is not appropriate for a particular setting'. Tim Cresswell, *In Place/Out of Place: Geography, Ideology and Transgression* (Minneapolis: University of Minnesota Press, 1996): 22.

10.  Jean H. Lagassé, ed., *A Study of the Population of Indian Ancestry Living in Manitoba* (Winnipeg: Department of Agriculture and Immigration, Queen's Printer, Winnipeg, 1959): 141.

11.  Walter E. Boek and Julius K. Boek, 'The People of Indian Ancestry in Greater Winnipeg' in Lagassé, ed., *A Study of the Population*; Trevor Denton, 'Strangers in Their Land: A Study of Migration from a Canadian Indian Reserve', (Ph.D. thesis, University of Toronto, 1970); Larry Ellis, Elaine Pinacie, Velma Turner, and Hilda Swiftwolfe, *Survey of Band Members living Off Reserve* (Prince Albert: Federation of Saskatchewan Indians, 1978); Nancy O. Lurie, 'The Indian Moves to an Urban Setting', *Resolving Conflicts—A Cross-Cultural Approach* (Winnipeg: Department of University Extensions and Adult Education, University of Manitoba, 1967): 73–86; Donald N. McCaskill, 'The Urbanization of Canadian Indians in Winnipeg, Toronto, Edmonton, and Vancouver: A Comparative Analysis', (Ph.D. thesis, York University, 1979); William T. Stanbury, *Success and Failure: Indians in Urban Society* (Vancouver: University of British Columbia Press, 1975).

12.  Andrew J. Siggner, 'A Socio-Demographic Profile of Indians in Canada', in J.R. Ponting and R. Gibbins, eds., *Out of Irrelevance* (Toronto: Butterworth and Co. Ltd., 1986): 31–65.

13.  Stanbury, *Success and Failure*; Union of Ontario Indians, *Indians in the City Project* (Toronto, 1972); David B. Vincent, *The Indian-Metis Urban Probe* (Winnipeg: Indian-Métis Friendship Centre and Institute of Urban Studies, University of Winnipeg, 1971); Denton, 'Strangers in their Land'; Jeanne Guillemin, *Urban Renegades: The Cultural Strategy of American Indians* (New York: Columbia University Press, 1975); Evelyn J. Peters, 'Native Households in Winnipeg: Strategies of Coresidence and Financial Support', *Research and Working Papers No. 5* (Winnipeg: Institute of Urban Studies, University of Winnipeg, 1984).

14.  Indian Association of Alberta, *Native Migration Survey, Edmonton* (1971). Frank Maidman, *Native People in Urban Settings: Problems, Needs and Services* (Toronto: A Report of the Ontario Task Force on Native People in the Urban Setting, 1981); McCaskill, 'Urbanization of Canadian Indians'; Stanbury, *Success and Failure*; National Association of Friendship Centres and the Secretary of State, *A Survey of Native People* (Ottawa, 1977); Vincent, *Indian-Métis Urban Probe*.

15. Linda Gerber, *Trends in Out-Migration from Indian Communities Across Canada* (Ottawa: Department of the Secretary of State, 1977).

16. While few surveys differentiated between men and women in examining reasons for migration, those that did found that men were more likely than women to cite employment as the reasons for moving, while women were more likely than men to cite 'family reasons' or problems on reserves as the main reason for migration to the city. Stewart Clatworthy, *The Demographic Composition and Economic Circumstances of Winnipeg's Native Population* (Winnipeg: Institute of Urban Studies, 1980); Clatworthy and Jeremy Hull, *Native Economic Conditions: Regina and Saskatoon* (Winnipeg: Institute of Urban Studies, 1983); Stanbury, *Success and Failure*; Evelyn J. Peters, 'Subversive Spaces: First Nations Women and the City', *Environment and Planning D: Society and Space* 16 (1998): 665–85.

17. Brody, *Indians on Skid Row*; John Melling, *Right to a Future: The Native Peoples of Canada* (Toronto: T.H. Best Printing Co. Ltd., 1967).

18. Boek and Boek, 'People of Indian Ancestry'; Clatworthy, *Demographic Composition*; Arthur K. Davis, *Edging into Mainstream: Urban Indians in Saskatchewan* (Bellingham: Western Washington State College, 1965); Edgar J. Dosman, *Indians: The Urban Dilemma* (Toronto: McClelland and Stewart, 1972); Mark Nagler, 'Status and Identification Groupings Among Urban Indians', in Mark Nagler, ed., *Perspectives on the North American Native* (Toronto: McClelland and Stewart, 1972): 280–8.

19. Davis, *Edging into Mainstream*; Peter D. Elias, *Metropolis and Hinterland in Northern Manitoba* (Winnipeg: Manitoba Museum of Man and Nature, 1975).

20. Dosman, *Indians*; Krotz, *Urban Indians*.

21. Michel Foucault, 'Governmentality', in Graham Burchell, Colin Gordon, and Pete Miller, eds., *The Foucault Effect: Studies in Governmentality* (London: Harvester Wheatsheaf, 1991).

22. Burchell, et al., *Foucault Effect*; Pete Miller and Nikolas Rose, 'Governing Economic Life', *Economy and Society* 19 (1990): 1–31; Mariana Valverde, 'Despotism and Ethical Liberal Governance', *Economy and Society* 25 (1996): 357–72.

23. Dosman, *Indians*; Family Service Association of Edmonton, *Adjustment Factors in the Indian Moving to the Community: A Descriptive Study* (Edmonton: Family Service Association of Edmonton, 1969); John J. Honigmann, Social Disintegration in Five Northern Communities *Canadian Review of Sociology and Anthropology* 2 (1963): 199–214; Henry Zentner, 'Reservation Social Structure and Anomie: A Case Study', in Nagler, *Perspectives*; Henry Zentner, *The Indian Identity Crisis* (Calgary: Strayer Publications Ltd., 1973); Braroe, *Indian and White*; Canadian Corrections Association, *Indians and the Law* (Ottawa: Canada Welfare Council, 1967); Elias, *Metropolis and Hinterland*; Lithman, *Community Apart*, p. 7.

24. Citizenship Branch Director Jean H. Lagassé, *Memorandum* (Canada: National Archives of Canada, Record Group 6, Volume 661, File 2-4-8, 23 March, 1966).

25. Father André Renaud, 'The Indian in the Community', *National Commission on the Indian Canadian* (Toronto: National Commission on the Indian Canadian, 1957): 3.

26. James Clifford, 'Of Other Peoples: Beyond the Salvage Paradigm', in H. Foster, ed., *Discussions in Contemporary Cultures* (Seattle: Bay Press/Dia Art Foundation, 1987): 121–30; Johannes Fabian, *Time and the Other: How Anthropology Makes Its Object* (New York: Columbia University Press, 1983); Anne McClintock, *Imperial Leather: Race, Gender and Sexuality in the Colonial Context* (New York: Routledge, 1985): 40.

27. A.P. Asimi, 'The Urban Setting', *Resolving Conflicts—A Cross Cultural Approach* (Winnipeg: University of Manitoba Department of University Extensions and Adult Education, 1967): 89–96; J. Jameson Bond, *A Report on the Pilot Relocation Project at Elliot Lake, Ontario* (Ottawa: Department of Indian Affairs and Northern Development, 1967); Melling, *Right to a Future*; Mark Nagler, *Indians in the City* (Ottawa: Canadian Research Centre for Anthropology, Saint Paul University, 1970); Joan Trudeau, 'The Indian in the City', *Kerygma* 3 (1969): 118–23; Vincent, *Indian-Metis Urban Probe*; Lous Zeitoun, 'Canadian

Indians at the Crossroads: Some Aspects of Relocation and Urbanization in Canada', Unpublished Report (Ottawa: Department of Manpower and Immigration, 1969).

28. Arthur Laing, 'Address to the Convention of the Native Brotherhood, Vancouver', (Ottawa: Department of Indian Affairs Library, 25 February 1967): 4, 8.

29. R. Alex Sim, 'What is Meant By "Urban Indians,"' National Archives of Canada, Record Group 29, Portion of 60 File 2-38-6 1, n.d., [1962]: 1.

30. R. Alex Sim, 'Perspectives', in Hirabayashi, *Challenge of Assisting*, 26.

31. Canada. House of Commons, *Debates* (26 November 1949): 2285. In 1949, the Department of Citizenship and Immigration was created as part of the process of dismantling the last vestiges of wartime government organization. The new department combined the Citizenship Branch, which was previously under the Secretary of State, and the Immigration and Indian Affairs branches, previously under Department of Mines and Resources. In 1966, the Indian Affairs Branch was moved to the Ministry of Northern Affairs and Northern Development. To avoid confusion, the terminology used here will be either 'Indian Affairs Branch' or 'Indian Affairs'.

32. R. Alex Sim to R. England, 14 August 1962. National Archives of Canada, Record Group 30, Volume 2, File 19.

33. Harry Bostrom, 'Recent Evolution of Canada's Indian Policy' in Raymond Breton and Gail Grant, eds., *The Dynamics of Government Programs for Urban Indians in the Prairie Provinces* (Montreal: Institute for Research on Public Policy,1984): 519–544; Sally Weaver, *Making Canadian Indian Policy: The Hidden Agenda 1968–1970* (Toronto: University of Toronto Press, 1981).

34. Canada, Indian Affairs Branch, *Annual Report* (1956–57): 50.

35. Canada, Indian Affairs Branch, *The Indian News* (1957): 2; Dosman, *Indians*, 84–98 and 101–106; and Carl R. Latham, *Indian Placement Programme Administered by the Indian Affairs Branch of the Department of Citizenship and Immigration*, Master's report (Toronto: University of Toronto School of Social Work, 1958).

36. Jones to Lagassé (23 May 1962) National Archives of Canada, Record Group 26, Series A-1-b Vol. 69 file 2-38-6.

37. Joan Ryan, *Wall of Words* (Edmonton: Hurtig Publishers, 1972).

38. Most of the costs were incorporated into general programs developed by the Department of Manpower and Immigration. Indian Affairs programs covered only occasional supplementary assistance for items and costs not covered under Manpower and Immigration programs.

39. Jean H. Lagassé, 'The Cultural Implications in Leaving the Reserve' in Hirabayashi, et al., *Challenge of Assisting*, 13.

40. The first centre opened in Winnipeg in April 1959. By 1962, the Citizenship Branch indicated there were similar developments in 19 urban areas.

41. John R. Nicholson, Address to the Indian Friendship Centre in Vancouver, (12 June 1965): 5–6.

42. Margaret Wetherell and Jonathan Potter, *Mapping the Language of Racism: Discourse and the Legitimation of Exploitation* (Brighton: Harvester Wheatwheaf, 1992): 131.

43. Susanne Johnson, *Migrating Native Peoples Program Evaluation Summary* (Ottawa: National Association of Friendship Centres, 1976).

44. Isaac Beaulieu, 'Urbanizing the Indian', *Ontario Housing* 6 (1964); Walter Currie, 'Urbanization and American Indians', Address to Mid-Canada Development Corridor Conference (Toronto: Indian-Eskimo Association, 1979).

45. Federation of Saskatchewan Indians, *Indian Urban Development Project. Phase I. A Proposal to Undertake an In-Depth Survey of the Circumstance of Treaty Indians Living in Urban Areas* (National Archives of Canada, Record Group 10, Volume 12712, File 1/1-19-4, 2 November 1976): 1.

46. Ellis, et al., *Survey of Band Members*: 3.

47. *Ibid.*, 22.

48. Andrew Bear Robe, *A Study Tour of Canadian Friendship Centres, June 1 August 31, 1970*, prepared under the auspices of the Steering Committee for the National Association of Friendship Centres (1971): 28.

49. *Ibid.*, 1–2.

50. Federation of Saskatchewan Indians, *Indian Urban Development*, 1; Harold Cardinal, ed.,

The Rebirth of Canada's Indians (Edmonton: Hurtig Publishers, 1977).

51. Standing Committee on Indian Affairs and Northern Development, Minutes of Proceedings and Evidence No. 17 (Ottawa: Queen's Printer, 1969): 568, 570–71, and 582.

52. Bear Robe, Study Tour, 30–31.

53. Lurie, Indian Moves.

54. Canada, Report of the Royal Commission on Aboriginal Peoples (Ottawa: Canada Communications Group, 1996).

55. Matthew Sparke, 'A Map that Roared and an Original Atlas: Canada, Cartography, and the Narration of Nation', Annals of the Association of American Geographers 88(3) (1998): 463–96.

# Chapter 14

# Canada in a Globalizing World

## READINGS

### Primary Documents

### Historical Interpretations

## INTRODUCTION

With our ability to access goods, services, and especially cultural products across borders or oceans more quickly and conveniently than ever, the world may not actually be smaller, but it seems that way. Worldwide publishing deals have made Swedish detective novels a recent sensation and, thanks to satellite and web services, Canadians can more easily keep up with Filipino news or Latin American *telenovelas*. In the springtime, huge retail stores draw crowds by selling Chinese-made patio sets at prices that even Canadian workers laid off from their jobs making patio sets can afford. Economic and cultural globalization are here, but if we think historically about it, studying the arrival of a phenomenon like globalization rather than probing its contemporary effects should be more illuminating. In other words, for historians, studying the process of becoming globalized beats just telling stories about being global-ized. For Canada, one important step toward this new global order was the Canada–US Free Trade Agreement, which came into effect in the late 1980s. For Americans, it was an eco-nomic deal. For Canadians, it was also a cultural one, as a closer economic relationship would make it more difficult to protect the Canadian cultural 'industries' that had been struggling for decades to compete with the output of the big American publishers, studios, and networks. Mexico joined the North American free trade club in the early 1990s, and the trend since has been toward opening up world markets through the World Trade Organization. Resistance to these changes has tended to come from citizens' groups and non-governmental organizations, and it is the voice of one of these groups that provides our first primary source. Maude Barlow's Council of Canadians wanted to demonstrate the varied ways in which the free trade deal of the late 1980s would alter the lives of Canadian workers and consumers. The picture she paints here is one combining statistical evidence that free trade has already significantly affected Canada with the suggestion that there are more profound economic and social changes to come. David Crane's newspaper column from the mid-1990s is a compact indictment of global developments. He contrasts the optimism of those who see market forces as liberating with the reality of the self-interest that has kept wealthy nations wealthy. Still, the promise of tapping into these wealthy markets drove developing nations to get into the global game. Dimitry Anastakis tells the story of Volvo's venture into Canadian manufacturing, showing us that globalization has a history before the free trade era. In fact, the tariffs and duties on high value goods like cars often prompted multinational companies to invest in manufacturing plants so they could compete in more countries. Nova Scotia, not a place known for its industrial might, gained a factory that failed to give the automaker a strong presence in the North American market but shows us how interconnected and complex global trade can be. Shifting the focus to cultural differences, Diane Pacom emphasizes perhaps one of the most fundamental: language. Historically, this language difference had protected and isolated Quebec from a dynamic and powerful American culture, but in the post–Second World War period this barrier began to break down, especially in urban Quebec, as elites began to equate a global perspective with freedom from a repressive past. The resulting hybrid culture that Pacom describes resembles the sort of culture that Canadians have become used to in the globalized era: one that seems less and less homemade.

# QUESTIONS FOR CONSIDERATION

1. According to Barlow, what are some of the downsides of the Canada–US free trade deal, and how will these be worsened under a free trade agreement that embraces Mexico as well?
2. Why does Mr Johnston (the man interviewed in Crane's article) think that globalization will benefit the world's poorer countries? What assumptions are behind his reasoning?
3. Has the process of globalization ended, or will we see greater levels of economic and cultural exchange than we see today?
4. What were some of the problems that plagued Volvo's plant in Nova Scotia? Were all of these problems the result of globalized industry?
5. Think about some of the musical acts that Pacom mentions. Why might these be considered as threatening to the identity of young French speakers? Would the young people even care?

# SUGGESTIONS FOR FURTHER READING

Abigail B. Bakan and Daiva K. Stasiulis, *Negotiating Citizenship: Migrant Women in Canada and the Global System* (London: Palgrave Macmillan, 2003).

Maude Barlow, *Too Close for Comfort: Canada's Future within Fortress North America* (Toronto: McClelland & Stewart, 2005).

Stephen Clarkson, *Uncle Sam and Us: Globalization, Neoconservatism, and the Canadian State* (Toronto: University of Toronto Press, 2002).

Murray Dobbin, *The Myth of the Good Corporate Citizen: Canada and Democracy in the Age of Globalization*, 2nd edn (Toronto: Lorimer, 2003).

Diane Francis, *Who Owns Canada Now? Old Money, New Money and the Future of Canadian Business* (Toronto: HarperCollins Publishers Ltd., 2008).

L. Ian Macdonald, ed., *Free Trade: Risks and Rewards* (Montreal and Kingston: McGill-Queen's University Press, 2000).

Winfried Siemerling and Sarah Phillips Casteel, *Canada and Its Americas: Transnational Navigations* (Montreal and Kingston: McGill-Queen's University Press, 2010).

Thom Workman, *Social Torment: Globalization in Atlantic Canada* (Black Point, NS: Fernwood Books Ltd, 2003).

# PRIMARY DOCUMENTS

**1** From Maude Barlow, 'The Free Trade Agreement Fails Canada', *American Review of Canadian Studies* 21(2/3) (Summer–Autumn 1991): 163–9.

The Canada–US Free Trade Agreement has been a failure in Canada. While some argue that three years is too short a time in which to judge a trade deal of this magnitude, most Canadians remember the extravagant promises of immediate rewards made by the Mulroney government—rewards of jobs, savings, and prosperity—and rightly hold their government accountable for the massive deterioration of the Canadian economy.

Free trade is a misnomer. It implies simply a trade deal in which both sides agree to liberalize trade between them by bringing down barriers to that trade. But this deal did far, far more. It is a sweeping economic harmonization agreement that covers resource sharing, services, standards, and the movement of people and capital. So far, Canada is doing all the harmonizing. The free trade agreement is, in fact, the foremost tool used by the governments of the two countries to realign the historic balance in Canada between public and private enterprise. It has shifted economic power from elected governments to the private sector and locks future Canadian governments into this model. For Canada the issue goes beyond the traditional public versus private debate. For Canada the issue goes to the heart of our identity, our culture, and our very existence.

The histories of Canada and the United States are very different. Because our country is so vast and geographically harsh, and because we had and have such a sparse population, mostly strung along the US border, we had to develop a distinct economic model of sharing for survival. We entrusted our government to develop a mix of public and private enterprise to provide services in areas business alone would not have been able to enter or maintain profitably. This distinct economy not only served to foster a different way of life in Canada but also prevented us from being absorbed into the United States. To have permitted the marketplace to dictate all economic decisions would have doomed the young country.

So we developed a railway, an airline, a national broadcasting system, and some of the finest national social programs in the world. We also developed mechanisms to maintain some measure of economic control in the face of massive foreign (mostly American) domination of our industry and resources. We implemented protections for our cultural industries to ensure that we would have Canadian perspectives on the world and to make room for the work of Canadian artists and writers. Without such protections, Canada is overwhelmed by the dominant, mass entertainment industry of a neighbour ten times our size.

The free trade agreement, in effect, challenges every single part of this distinct Canadian system and, in so doing, threatens the very survival of our country. In leaving undefined for future talks what the United States considers to be unfair subsidies, the deal has exposed every Canadian government practice that helps foster our economic independence. Our constitutional requirement to provide equal opportunities and services to all regions of Canada is being challenged. Our marketing system to regulate farm supplies in order to give some measure of security to our farmers is under the axe. It is not that Canadian farmers are not as smart or resourceful as American farmers. But they operate in different conditions. As one Manitoba farmer explains, 'My "level playing field" is under snow for eight months of the year'.

Now battered by a recession that increasingly resembles the depression of the thirties, Canada has been stripped by the free trade agreement of its ability to respond with programs that would kick-start the economy and protect those sectors most hurt. For a branch-plant economy like Canada, this reality is devastating. Big transnationals, who now make all the financial choices for the country, are 'rationalizing' their production out of Canada, and government is powerless to stop them. Canada is losing its manufacturing base and, with it, its ability to continue providing universal social programs.

The numbers are wrenching. Flooded by cheaper American imports, hundreds of Canadian companies have shut down. With no reason to stay, many hundreds of others have moved to the United States. In the first year of free trade, 92 per cent of all new businesses set up in Buffalo, New York, were Canadian. US corporate parents, no longer required to create employment in Canada, converted Canadian plants to warehouses. By the spring of 1991, there were at least 350,000 manufacturing jobs lost in Canada. (The equivalent in the United States would be 3,500,000 jobs.) This is just the tip of the iceberg. In 1990, Canada's manufacturing output decreased by 10 per cent—depression-level statistics. In the same year, the manufacturing workforce shrank 11 per cent. Everyone agrees now that many of these jobs will never return. In Ontario, the industrial heartland of the country, well over half of the layoffs of the last two years have been due to plant closures. This contrasts to the recession of 1982 when less than one-quarter of the layoffs were related to plant closures.

Free trade is not the sole reason for this disaster. Linked is the relatively high price of the Canadian dollar against the American, a situation many Canadians believe was an unwritten part of the free trade deal. Our former low dollar would have helped offset the manufacturing losses of free trade, but it was clearly an important irritant to American industry, who made it plain that a higher Canadian dollar was prerequisite to a deal. Free trade, cheaper goods, and a tough new consumer tax [are] driving millions of Canadians south of the border to shop, placing hundreds of retailers in peril.

But free trade has failed to secure Canadian producers market access to US consumers, and US industry interests continue to punish Canadian products with quotas and countervailing duties. As well, Canada did not gain exemption from US trade law. Since the free trade deal was signed, US harassment of Canadian exporters has increased. Canada has won only one of the sixteen cases that have come before the binational dispute panels set up under the deal—a dispute over pork—and the US trade negotiator, Carla Hills, refused to abide by it, thus politicizing what was supposed to be a non-political way for the partners in the free trade agreement to come to the resolution of trade disputes between them. Canadians were sold the free trade deal on the basis that we needed it to secure a dispute settlement mechanism. We can be forgiven for asking if it was worth destroying our manufacturing base to create what is arguably a more vulnerable situation for Canada. After all, the United States implementing legislation (Section 409) created a new weapon to assist producers to harass Canadian exporters suspected of using unfair subsidies.

The free trade–driven corporate restructuring has been a one-sided affair. Record mergers, takeovers, closures, downsizing, and rationalizations have destroyed thousands of jobs, and the promised high-value jobs have not materialized. And the takeover of the Canadian economy continues unabated. The Mulroney government scrapped Pierre Trudeau's Foreign Investment Review Agency in 1985 and replaced it with an agency that has not turned down one single application for a takeover in the six years of its existence. In the two years ending in the spring of 1990, a record 1,403 Canadian companies were taken over, at a price of over $35.5 billion. Only 8 per cent of this is new investment in Canada. These takeovers are directly connected to job loss. For every billion dollars of profit made by a Canadian firm in Canada, 765 jobs are created. For every billion dollars of profit made by a US firm in Canada, seventeen jobs are created.

Now, the free trade agreement is about to be extended to Mexico, and eventually to all of Latin America, creating the greatest military and economic trade block the world has ever known. Dependent on American capital and technology, Canadian resources (secured in the Canada–US Free Trade Agreement) and the cheap labour of Mexico and points south, this block is intended to balance the growing economic clout of Europe and Japan. The model, however, is very different. Free trade, North American style, is based on cheap, plentiful labour and the willingness of Latin American countries to look the other way when Fortune 500 companies abuse the environment, which they do often. Mexico and Canada will be required to enrich the core economy of the United States and their continued political acquiescence will be expected.

Canadians are very wary of the next round of free trade talks, and the polls show it. At the heart of this fear is our perception that, as a model for international economic agreements, it is fundamentally incompatible with Canadian interests. To support the extension of free trade would be to legitimize the Canada–US deal, and its critics seek its abrogation, not its enlargement. Canadians are also wondering what promises our government gave to the United States to be included in this round. It is apparent that the United States preferred to negotiate separate bilateral agreements with a number of countries but reluctantly allowed Canada to sit at the table, so long as we didn't become a 'spoiler' at the talks.

Already, US negotiators have declared that Canada cannot maintain the protections for its cultural industries that it managed to safeguard in the Canada–US deal. A standstill clause (which many criticized as giving Canada no future power to bring in any new measures as needed to sustain Canadian cultural integrity), it nevertheless protected current Canadian content regulations, which, for instance, are the underpinnings of our national public broadcasting system, the Canadian Broadcasting Corporation. This exemption will be doomed, however, in the trilateral negotiations, leaving Canada totally vulnerable to bullying by American entertainment giants, such as Jack Valenti, who wants to crush any obstacles in his bid for international free trade in the film business. 'The prospect of pain must be inserted into the equation, else the solution will never be suitable,' he once said.

Quite simply, US corporate interests want to make the hemisphere safe for business. They want uniform rules for investment and services, an end to any screening of foreign investment by member countries of this trade block, and restrictions on their ability to set any rules governing the behaviour of American transnationals. Such agreements rob a country of economic sovereignty. Most transnational companies located in the United States now view Canada as just another domestic market, one about the size of California. Rendered the political equivalent of a regional interest, Canadian branch plants have neither autonomy nor clout: what is good for them, or Canada, is irrelevant. The few rights that Canada maintained to regulate foreign investment in the Canada–US Free Trade Agreement are slated for elimination in the trilateral talks.

And the job losses that started in 1988, when Canada signed the free trade agreement with the United States, will accelerate under hemispheric free trade. Canada's manufacturing industries are now adding Mexico to their choices of relocation, and the process is well under way. Forty-five companies, which collectively shed some 15,000 jobs in Canada in 1989–90 (well before the trend was really started) were active in the *maquiladora* of Mexico. Whole sectors of our economy are vulnerable. Our workers simply cannot compete with the wages paid to the workers of Mexico. Auto parts, plastics, furniture, food processing, appliances, chemicals, and textiles—all will likely be wiped out.

Most disturbing, our automotive sector will not survive. Governed by the Canada–US Auto Pact, this key sector was threatened by a weakening of its enforcement measures by the first free trade deal. Under a trilateral deal, the remaining enforcement measures will be erased, and Canadian auto makers will be in a head-to-head battle for survival against massive, cheap production of the *maquiladoras*. The argument that Canada will lose the low-end jobs, and that we will keep the high-technology jobs does not hold water. It is cheaper by far for a company to locate its high-skilled labour in an American plant bordering Mexico, and ship the components a short distance across that border for assembly, than to develop the products in Canada and ship them all the way to Mexico. Besides, business leaders admit that a well-run *maquiladora* can attain the productivity of a 'first-world' plant in several years.

The options for Canadians will be to accept a dramatic lowering of standards, wages, and working conditions to keep businesses here. The threat of Mexico is already a silent partner at every employee-employer negotiation. Because no protections—social, environmental, or wage—are being established, it will be as if someone placed a huge funnel on the North American continent. Not only will the jobs slide relentlessly south, there will be enormous pressure to downgrade standards, laws, and working conditions to the lowest common denominator.

Canadians are rightly angry and frightened by this process. We have been told that we have to become more competitive, and we accept that. There are, however, different ways to become competitive. A country can slash spending, taxes, wages, social programs, communication and transportation infrastructures—in fact, government itself—in the hopes of attracting foreign investment because it is cheap to do business in such a system. Or, it can invest—in people, in education, in research and development, in communications—in short, in all of the areas that require an active nation-state and strong government-business co-operation.

Mexico has done the former, destroying its agricultural industry and driving wages to historically low levels. Canada has chosen this route as well, and the downward spiral has no bottom. As a result, we are beginning to resemble our American neighbours: deep divisions between rich and poor, food banks, inner-city violence, and a weakest-to-the-wall, survival-of-the-fittest mentality that is not only destroying our culture but threatening to destroy our actual existence.

This should matter to American friends for several reasons. A destabilized, impoverished northern neighbour would serve no American interest. If Canada's economy is converted to a third-world status, we will lose much of our value as a trading partner.

For American environmentalists, it is essential to understand that the concern is not only the fact that Mexico is a haven for acts of corporate environmental crime. Extensive job losses to Mexico in the manufacturing sector will force Canada to turn increasingly to the production of raw resources, deepening our dependence on their exploitation. Canada is now losing its resource policy on massive, guaranteed exports of fossil fuels, foreign ownership and the destruction of our forests, and deregulation of our energy production. The whole continent will suffer as a result.

Finally, for many Americans, Canadian social programs have been held up as a model. Our medical system, for instance, is not only universal, it is delivered more cheaply than health care in the United States. Surely the pursuit of prosperity must be linked to a rise in the standard of living for all, or we must ask what such a search is for. And surely it must place value on the unique contributions and characteristics of the different players. Canada is an exceptional friend and neighbour to the United States. It would be to no one's advantage to go any further with a trade arrangement that aims for the lowest common set of standards and in the bargain may destroy at least one of the participants.

---

**2**   From David Crane, 'Myopia Could Wreck Global Trade Dream'. *Toronto Star*, 14 December 1996, E2. Reprinted with permission of Torstar Syndication Services.

Any doubts about the globalization of the world economy had to be put to rest this week as trade ministers and officials from around the world agreed on an agenda for freer world trade in the twenty-first century.

The World Trade Organization (WTO), created barely two years ago, now has 128 members (Niger became the latest member yesterday).

And another 28 countries are anxiously seeking to join as soon as possible. Some are big, such as China and Russia. Others are mid-size, such as Ukraine, China-Taipei and Saudi Arabia. And some—such as Estonia and Croatia—are small.

Today, almost 75 per cent of the world's people live and work within the WTO universe. As new members join over the next two to three years, the WTO will become virtually universal.

The WTO plays a crucial role in the expanding system of governance in this enlarging economy. While there is no move to world government, the global economy can't work without institutions that help run the system.

With the extension of trade into services and growing linkages with policies that used to be considered purely domestic, such as investment, competition policy and, in a tiptoe way, even labour standards and the environment, the WTO is moving to centre stage in the governance of the world economy.

Its key functions are to provide and enforce a clear set of rules, to resolve trade disputes through a legally binding dispute settlement system and to expand freer world trade through negotiations.

Don Johnston, the former Trudeau cabinet minister who is now the secretary-general of the Organization for Economic Co-operation and Development (OECD), gave the global challenge a key perspective when he spoke to the WTO summit earlier this week.

Noting that historians will probably call this period the 'dawn of the Age of Globalization', he said it was up to world leaders to make sure that future historians have a 'good story' to tell about the end of the twentieth century and the start of the twenty-first.

It should be, Johnston said, 'a story of how world leaders seized this moment to harness unprecedented opportunities, not just for the developed world, but for the world community.'

It should be a story, he continued 'of how poverty, misery and disease in many parts of the developing world were put on the fast track to eradication through multilateral free trade and investment.'

It should be a story as well 'of how the prosperity of the developed world was sustained through the evolution of the global market and how, in turn, economic growth was firmly established in the developing world through the transfer of capital, technology and know-how, combined with unfettered access . . . to the markets of the developed world'.

And it should be a story 'of how the widening gap between the rich and the poor in the world . . . was arrested and then began to narrow'.

In their own declaration here, the trade ministers optimistically declared that 'the scope and pace of change in the international economy, including the growth of trade in services and direct investment, and the increasing integration of economies offer unprecedented opportunities for improved growth, job creation and development'.

But they also acknowledged that these developments 'require adjustment by economies and societies'.

And there's the rub.

Market forces by themselves simply won't write the 'good story' that the OECD's Johnston hopes future historians will find.

In countries such as Canada, there's an urgent need to continue to upgrade the kind of economy we have by investing in people, in new ideas and technology, in infrastructure, in training and in programs for young children and families.

In developing countries, where population growth is higher and poverty much greater, the challenges are even more difficult.

While these countries will do most of the work, they will still need our help.

This is essential in order to maintain what Renato Ruggiero, director general of the WTO, has called the 'fragile unity' of the global community, consisting of developed countries such as Canada, developing countries such as Malaysia and Mexico, the least-developed countries, such as Bangladesh and Haiti, and the transition economies, such as Russia and Ukraine.

Unfortunately, the rich countries seem less willing to help these days. Foreign aid is being slashed.

And the rich countries, including Canada, are also blocking the growth of the developing countries by maintaining highly protectionist policies in products where poorer countries have an obvious comparative advantage, such as clothing and textiles, footwear and leather goods.

Yet, if the WTO is to succeed in bringing world prosperity by expanded trade and investment to all members of the world community, its efforts will have to be backed by supportive policies from its richest members. We don't have that today, so the great potential of the WTO trading system may founder on the rocks of rich nations' myopia.

# HISTORICAL INTERPRETATIONS

3     From Dimitry Anastakis, 'Building a "New Nova Scotia": State Intervention, The Auto Industry and the Case of Volvo in Halifax, 1963–98', *Acadiensis* 34(1) (Autumn 2004): 3–30.

When the first Volvo 'Canadians' rolled out of the company's new assembly facility in Dartmouth, Nova Scotia in the summer of 1963, the event was heralded by Premier Robert Stanfield as the harbinger of a 'New Nova Scotia', which would quickly vault the province to the forefront of the manufacturing age. This sentiment was echoed by Volvo officials as well, who saw the plant as a crucial beachhead into an important foreign market. As the earliest non-North American–owned automotive facility built on this continent (Honda opened its first American facility in 1982), the plant emerged as a result of the federal and Nova Scotia governments' efforts to actively encourage industrial development. Yet Volvo's experiment in North America fell far short of the governments' lofty goals: operated as a simple assembly venture, the facility reached a maximum production of never more than a few thousand vehicles and employed only hundreds of workers in the province. After its initial burst of enthusiasm, the Volvo Corporation itself exhibited a lukewarm attitude towards the plant, providing only limited investment and support for its Canadian offspring. By the late 1990s, overcapacity in the auto industry in Europe and North America, reorganization of Volvo and the new realities of the quickly changing global auto industry resulted in the parent company's decision to close the plant. In 1999 Volvo was purchased by Ford of the United States, allowing the company to import the cars directly from Sweden duty-free under the 1965 *Canada-United States Automotive Products Trade Agreement* (Auto Pact). A year

later in 2000, this arrangement ended with the demise of the Auto Pact at the World Trade Organization.[1]

The story of the Nova Scotia Volvo plant is part of the end of 'national' auto strategies and auto companies and the emergence of a world industry. The Volvo experiment is also the story of state intervention in the Canadian auto industry from a regional perspective. Provincial and federal government industrial policies provided incentives to the company to locate in Nova Scotia during a particularly activist period of state initiatives in industrial development. The federal government's auto policy was shaped by determined civil servants in Ottawa who were keen to generate as much economic activity as possible in this important sector of the Canadian economy. Interventionist industrial policy was central to the new Liberal government of Lester Pearson, and the creation of the 1965 Auto Pact, a key driver in encouraging automotive production, reflected this new approach. In Halifax, provincial politicians and policymakers were also keen to develop Nova Scotia's industry beyond traditional resource extraction, and utilized the newly created Industrial Estates Limited (IEL) to foster their activist bent. This new attitude was epitomized by the provincial government of Robert Stanfield. Volvo's experience in Nova Scotia points to some obvious questions: How did Volvo fare at the hands of the federal government in comparison with the rest of the automotive industry, which was overwhelmingly located in central Canada—principally Ontario? On balance, given that the venture lasted for nearly four decades, could the

Volvo plant be considered a successful venture? Why did Ontario plants thrive under the Canadian state's central automotive policy—the Auto Pact—but the Volvo plant did not? How did the Halifax plant fit into Volvo's corporate strategy? In the final analysis, were the policies implemented by the two governments to persuade Volvo to locate and remain in Nova Scotia a success?

[ . . . ]

In a period characterized by the federal government's efforts to improve Canadian industry and the economic status of the Atlantic provinces through the creation of the departments of Industry and Regional Economic Expansion—and similar efforts by the Nova Scotia government such as IEL and the Voluntary Economic Planning Board— the establishment of Volvo in Dartmouth-Halifax stands out as a fascinating case in the industrial evolution of both Canada and the Maritimes. Although both the federal and provincial governments were instrumental in facilitating the establishment of Volvo in Nova Scotia, the operation was beset by numerous difficulties, including issues surrounding the plant location and operation of the facility, a changing market that put Volvo products at a disadvantage and the failure to achieve new or a broader range of production in the facility. In the end, however, these problems only partially contributed to the demise of the plant. The story of Volvo Halifax is a unique tale that illustrates the limits of 1960s-era federal and provincial industrial development initiatives in the rapidly changing and highly competitive global auto sector. Although instrumental in luring the plant to Nova Scotia, limited tariff reduction measures, small-scale direct infrastructure concessions and local boosterism could not sustain Volvo's small Halifax operation, a reflection of changing trade regimes, the large economies of scale required by the evolving automobile industry and the shifting worldwide strategy pursued by Volvo by the 1990s.

## FEDERAL AND PROVINCIAL INTERVENTION IN THE CANADIAN AUTO INDUSTRY: 1958–65

Between 1962 and 1965, Canadian policymakers sought new methods to encourage industrial development in the automotive sector, primarily through the use of duty-remission schemes that were export incentives.[2] Responding to demands for change in the industry from workers, firms and academics, the governments of Progressive Conservative John Diefenbaker and Liberal Lester Pearson created these programs in an effort to spur auto industry production and solve an increasingly difficult balance-of-payments problem. In October 1962, the Diefenbaker Conservative government created a special 'remission plan' for automatic transmissions, an item which had been predominantly imported by Canadian industry until that time. Manufacturers were now forced to pay the 25 per cent duty on automatic transmissions (a measure that had not been enforced previously), but received a 100 per cent rebate (and a 100 per cent rebate on up to 10,000 imported engine blocks as well) for every dollar increase in the amount of Canadian goods they exported over and above a 12-month base period. The plan worked well, and by the time the Liberals came to power in 1963, the rebate scheme was having a positive impact on the industry.[3]

The newly elected minority Liberal government, also searching for ways by which to reduce the massive deficit on current account goods, took aim directly at the auto industry. In October 1963, C.M. 'Bud' Drury, the minister of the newly created Department of Industry, introduced a plan that was intended to both alleviate the balance-of-payments burden and boost production even more than the Conservative plan had. The Liberals' new plan was a drastic expansion of the Conservatives' rebate scheme. Now, for every dollar of exported goods over and above the base year, manufacturers would be allowed to remit an equal amount on dutiable exports; the plan was also extended to all automotive exports. It was expected to run for three years and could, according to Drury, lead to an increase of between $150 and $200 million dollars in exports, a substantial chunk of the expected $500 million deficit for 1963–4.[4]

While the Conservative plan had raised few American eyebrows, the Liberals' broad, far-reaching scheme provoked an immediate response. The Americans were dismayed at the Canadian unilateral action, and chided the Canadian government that 'any measures adopted to deal with Canada's balance-of-payments problems should not artificially distort the pattern of trade or interfere with the normal exercise of business judgement'. The US State Department warned that American trade laws left open the possibility that a private interest might take exception to the plan, which could force the American government to take retaliatory measures.[5] By April of 1964, the American predictions were realized. That month, the Modine Manufacturing Company of Racine, Wisconsin initiated a complaint with the US Treasury Department that, under US trade law, the Canadian program constituted an unfair trade advantage. With a private corporation forcing the US government's hand because of Canadian unilateral actions (while the Canadian government steadfastly defended the program), relations between the two governments became strained. Both governments quickly realized that unless they resolved the issue, a trade war in the important automotive sector would be unavoidable.[6] As a result, the two sides negotiated the far-reaching and innovative Auto Pact, which erased tariffs for automotive trade between the two countries as long as each side achieved certain requirements.

Volvo's interaction with the Canadian state emerged parallel to and as a part of the federal government's automotive policy. As we shall see, Volvo asked for and achieved special status within the Canadian government's automotive policy and then continued to receive special treatment under the new automotive regime that governed automotive-state relations after 1965. Canadian state planners were willing to 'bend the rules' to ensure that Volvo could operate in this country; in exchange, the presence of the company provided jobs and investment and promised to be a catalyst for further industrial development.[7]

While this explains the federal government's interventionist role in the auto industry, it does not explain the efforts of Nova Scotia's government to play a role in luring Volvo to Nova Scotia nor the motives and policies of the Nova Scotia government concerning provincial intervention in the auto industry. [ . . . ]

In 1956 Conservative Robert Stanfield won the Nova Scotia provincial election on a platform that espoused industrial renewal based on effective state intervention in a number of sectors in the Nova Scotia economy. Stanfield was determined to diversify the province's economy, which had suffered the collapse of traditional Nova Scotia industries—especially coal. Since the end of the Second World War, Nova Scotia had faced increasing unemployment and slowly declining economic prospects. As part of its platform, Stanfield's new government implemented a host of economic policies designed to assert government planning more forcefully in directing the provincial economy. These policies began to take a clear shape after 1960, and chief among them were the *Voluntary Planning Act* of 1963, which was intended to improve business-government communication, and IEL, the provincial development Crown corporation.[8]

IEL's first president was Frank Sobey, the scion of the supermarket chain, who was appointed in 1957. Considered a titan amongst Nova Scotia's business elite, Sobey worked at the unsalaried position until 1969, during which IEL attracted numerous businesses to the province, including textile, rubber, food processing and, of course, automotive companies.[9] [...] By 1968, more than

60 firms had been supported by IEL initiatives, and Sobey boasted that nearly 10,000 jobs had resulted from IEL agreements and projects, adding $40 million to the province's revenue.[10]

In the case of Volvo, both provincial policies (IEL's direct support for plant and investment) and federal policies (tariff concessions) were key to attracting it to the Dartmouth-Halifax region in the early 1960s. Yet Volvo's decision to come to Nova Scotia stemmed from more than just the incentives offered by the two governments.

## VOLVO ARRIVES IN CANADA: 1962–65

Volvo, which means 'I go' in Latin, was founded in 1924 by Assar Gabrielsson and Gustaf Larson, two employees of ball-bearings maker SKF, and it became an independent company in 1935. From the first hand-built model in the 1920s, the company grew impressively. By 1962 Volvo production reached over 100,000 cars, buses and trucks at 13 facilities in Sweden employing 18,000 workers. The company's ethos was very conservative and focused on quality: there were only 15 different vehicle designs in Volvo's history, the vehicles were offered in only seven different colour choices and 11 per cent of its employees were involved with product inspection. As one excited Volvo Canada employee later reported, 'Volvo rejects more component parts than any other car maker in the world'.[11]

Volvo Canada was incorporated on 21 July 1958, a year after the first importation of Volvos to Canada by a British Columbia firm which arranged to distribute the cars nationwide. After 1959 Volvo sales increased dramatically, and the company responded by setting up its Canadian administrative headquarters in Toronto, which established a dealer network. With the nationwide growth in Canadian sales, in early 1962 the company began to consider setting up a plant in Canada. The company's president of Canadian operations, D.W. (Pat) Samuel, a New Zealander, was key to hatching the agreement that saw Volvo arrive in Canada.[12] Samuel was dispatched by the parent company to negotiate with the federal and provincial governments towards gaining better terms for the company to facilitate the establishment of a plant and ease its initial production.

Samuel arrived in Ottawa in October of 1962 to begin discussions with Diefenbaker's Minister of Finance George Nowlan. Volvo had decided upon setting up their operation in Nova Scotia, Samuel told Nowlan, due to the province's relative proximity to Sweden and its year-round ice-free ports, a prerequisite for a venture which was to be heavily dependent on imports from the home country. The company was keen to begin production as soon as possible, Samuel argued, but the current content regulations for automotive production were unrealistic for an operation as small as Volvo. Under the 1936 *Tariff Act*, which still governed the auto trade in 1962, the most-favoured-nation (MFN) tariff rate was 17.5 per cent for all autos and most parts. In order to gain duty-free access for imported parts, a company was required to achieve 40 per cent Commonwealth (essentially Canadian) content for companies producing 10,000 units, 50 per cent for companies producing between 10,000 and 20,000 units and 60 per cent for companies producing over 20,000 vehicles.[13] In Ontario, the tariff schedule had the effect of facilitating much Canadian production by the established US-owned manufacturers, but would be punitive for any other company in its initial production stages. For a company like Volvo, which had the added cost of importing from the distant locale of Sweden, it was impossible to reach the 10,000 vehicle mark in the first period of production. In other words, without some special dispensation, Samuel argued, Volvo could not make a go of it.

Moreover, Samuel informed the minister that Volvo's initial plan was to be a barebones operation, one in which the company simply reassembled partially knocked-down (PKD) vehicles. There would be few Canadian parts added to the major vehicle components shipped from Sweden and bolted together in Nova Scotia. The Canadian plant would not even paint the vehicles, as the parts would arrive already coloured in Volvo's famous seven-colour range of choices. The operation was to employ Canadian labour and include some Canadian parts (headlights, bumpers and perhaps tires) but, again, the scale and size of the operation made it difficult to reach even basic Canadian content levels. While the facility would be an important step in Nova Scotia industrial development, Volvo in Nova Scotia was not going to be the next Windsor, Oshawa or Oakville—at least not yet.[14]

Nowlan was sympathetic. As a native Nova Scotian and a 'red tory', he believed in the utility of interventionist programs that could help areas such as his home province.[15] The Volvo idea also fit well within federal plans for the entire Canadian auto sector. A 1961 Royal Commission on the Automotive Industry chaired by University of Toronto economist Vincent Bladen pointed to the need for exports in the industry, which was hampered by short production runs designed for a small market and a dependence on US parts imports.[16] This dependence on US parts imports stemmed from Canadian tariff law, which allowed duty-free imports for any parts of 'a class or kind' not made in Canada. The almost entirely US-owned Canadian assembly industry took advantage of this situation to import massive amounts of vehicles and parts. As a result, the Canadian industry faced a difficult situation: If the market for autos in Canada performed poorly, employment and production declined. If the market performed well, massive US parts and vehicle imports would send the Canadian trade balance spiralling downward. By 1962, auto imports accounted for 90 per cent of Canada's nearly $500 million trade deficit. In response, the government had created the duty-remission scheme that

allowed companies to increase their imports of transmissions and engines duty-free if they increased their exports of other parts from Canada.[17]

While Volvo could not take advantage of the transmission/engine program (the company did not yet have facilities in Canada), Nowlan was eager to find some relief for Volvo so that it could begin production in Canada. Thus, the company was granted a number of tariff concessions from the Diefenbaker government to ease their way into production, as Volvo represented a 'special case' that involved the establishment of new enterprise in Canada. In return for assurances that Volvo train 500 Canadians as mechanics and hire at least 400 workers at their new plant, the company received remission of duties on bodies, engines and parts through a process similar to the transmission/engine program. The company's Canadian content requirements were to be slowly increased as Volvo adapted to the Canadian market.[18] In Nowlan's view, Volvo gained the benefit of 'temporary tariff arrangements', and would be 'increasing their purchases in Canada quite quickly once they become well established'. Initially, Volvo was allowed to begin production with virtually no Canadian content while importing their parts duty-free.[19]

[ . . . ]

The site for a plant was also to be supported by Nova Scotia tax dollars through the granting of loans to the company to secure a facility. Samuel and company representatives investigated a number of sites in late 1962, and decided that Halifax-Dartmouth was the best location: since the company was dependent on shipments from Sweden, and Halifax was the closest major North American port to Sweden, it made sense to locate there.[20] The city's good road and port infrastructure also helped to convince Volvo. In January 1963 Samuel informed IEL that the company had leased a 55,000 sq. ft. dockside former sugar refinery owned by Acadia Sugar Refineries Co. in Dartmouth for $2 million for three years.

For its part, IEL loaned the company funds for the lease at very favourable terms (8 per cent) until a plant could be built 'to order' by the Crown corporation.[21] The new Volvo facility was little more than a converted warehouse. With the rail transportation issue and lease with IEL worked out, Volvo began working closely with Nova Scotia trade minister Manson to identify Nova Scotia companies as potential suppliers.[22]

Halifax was also ideal because of its lower labour costs, especially in comparison to those in the traditional Canadian automotive-producing communities in Ontario. Volvo officials were well aware that the average hourly industrial wage in Halifax in 1963 was $1.86 while the average hourly wage of a GM worker in Oshawa was between $2.16 and $2.29.[23] Thus, Nova Scotia's proximity to Sweden was not the only locational benefit bestowed upon the company as the Halifax location would produce a significant labour cost advantage. By February 1963, Canadians were being trained in Sweden in anticipation of the plant's opening.[24]

On 21 February 1963, the announcement of Volvo's Nova Scotia plant was made simultaneously in Halifax and Ottawa. Publicly, Samuel and the company enunciated a number of reasons for Volvo's decision to locate in Nova Scotia. In interviews with the financial press, Samuel stated that Volvo's move was because of the potential for both the market in Canada and production in Nova Scotia: 'The main one is that we think we have a car that is suitable for the Canadian market and Canadian conditions. . . . I also believe that to sell a car in volume in Canada you must build it in Canada'. He also saw a 'growing nationalistic spirit' among Canadians, and that the plan was an 'experiment' for the parent company.[25] Samuel boldly predicted that the plant would produce 5,000 vehicles in its first year and 7,500 in its second. Dartmouth Mayor I.W. Akerley's efforts in the final negotiations was also pointed out by Samuel as being pivotal to Volvo's decision to locate in

the area as was the help of the provincial government—especially IEL.[26] While he did not mention IEL's role in facilitating the export of Volvo cars to central Canada, Samuel did state that Halifax's excellent rail connections to central Canada and the eastern United States had played a role in the company's decision.[27]

[ . . . ]

The Volvo announcement sparked a burst of Nova Scotia pride. Volvo's arrival was likened to an 'economic miracle' by Stanfield in the legislature, an event he 'could hardly believe. . . . For years we have all dreamed of something like this, and now the dream has become a reality'.[28] The Halifax *Chronicle-Herald* also captured the spirit unleashed by the announcement: 'All Nova Scotians should rejoice in the good fortune of Dartmouth, chosen yesterday as the location for a branch assembly plant of the giant Swedish car manufacturer, Volvo'.[29] Volvo's Samuel heralded the choice of Nova Scotia as a testament to the 'inherent traditions of quality of workmanship dating back to Nova Scotia's period of eminence as one of the world's biggest builders of wooden ships'. Nova Scotia was, according to Samuel, 'The cradle of Canadian craftsmanship'.[30] Samuel himself was feted by the *Chronicle-Herald* as a man of 'confidence' who helped embody the spirit that Volvo was bringing to Nova Scotia.[31]

[ . . . ]

The arrival of Volvo prompted an economic mini-boom in the region. Within weeks of Volvo's start-up, a number of other automotive and automotive-related companies announced their intentions to establish operations in Halifax, including Continental Can Co. and Surrette Battery.[32] Within months, William Docsteader, sales manager for the company, stated publicly that he expected many different firms to follow Volvo to Dartmouth. The company's move to the area was, in his opinion, not only big news in Canada, but 'big news all over the world'.[33] In an effort to spur such growth, Volvo worked with Nova Scotia trade minister Manson to organize a Volvo-oriented trade show for prospective firms to understand the company's supplier needs.[34]

Volvo's arrival also generated interest from other non-North American auto companies about the possibility of setting up facilities in the province. In March 1963, IEL General Manager R.W. Manuge quietly held talks with Reneault and Peugot, and the province was actively recruiting Toyota through Canadian Motor Industries Limited, an outfit fronted by Toronto entrepreneur Peter Munk, which was also trying to establish auto assembly in the province.[35] In April it was reported that the United Kingdom's main auto association, the Society of Manufacturers and Traders Limited (SMMTL), was canvassing Nova Scotia locations for potential future sites. While the Volvo move had turned some heads in Europe, a 10 per cent surcharge on European imports by the Diefenbaker government had also generated newfound interest by British companies in Volvo-like knock-down operations in Canada.[36]

Notwithstanding the initial enthusiasm for the prospects of the Volvo plant and the development it might generate, the plant's beginnings were humble. The first crew of Volvo Nova Scotians received 12-weeks training. None had any experience in automotive assembly, yet many had backgrounds as mechanics. Assembly operated on a one-station system as opposed to a fully automated assembly line.[37] Only 5 of the first 100 employees were from Sweden. Initially, the company produced 15 to 20 vehicles a day. The company assembled imported body shells from Sweden, which were matched with Canadian-assembled Swedish engines and mechanical parts plus some parts supplied by Canadian manufacturers.[38]

[ . . . ]

The company quickly took advantage of the US market under the scheme as well. Gunnar Engellau, president of parent company AB Volvo, who appeared at the Dartmouth grand opening, stated that the company was 'definitely interested in the export market'. He was hopeful that the company could develop a market for its Canadian-built cars among Commonwealth countries, and that the Nova Scotia plant would produce for the US market.[39] In December 1963 Volvo Canada announced that 75 Volvos would be sold in New England. Although Volvo already sold 18,000 vehicles in the US, Canadian sourcing was seen as a way to boost production in Canada and a way to save on tariffs by taking advantage of the export-incentive nature of the duty-remission scheme. Moreover, Volvo had faced continuous product shortages in the United States.[40]

Notwithstanding the initial production increases and potential for the export market in the US, Volvo's output in Canada fell far from the company's early, optimistic predictions of Volvo Canada President D.W. Samuel. Instead of 5,000 vehicles in 1963 and 7,500 in 1964, Dartmouth had not even broken the 4,000 vehicle mark by 1965. By June 1965, Canadian content was up to approximately 40 per cent and Volvo was producing 75 cars per week, boosting its annual production to 3,500 cars.[41] Employment, which had originally been targeted at 300–400, had stalled at 101 employees. Faced with the difficulties of slow production and disappointed expectations, the company also faced the uncertainty created by a significantly altered automotive trade and regulatory regime after 1965.

## VOLVO UNDER THE AUTO PACT, 1965–95

On 16 January 1965 Prime Minister Lester Pearson and President Lyndon Johnson signed the *Canada-United States Automotive Products Trade Agreement* at Johnson's 'L.B.J. Ranch' in Texas.[42] The agreement aimed to rationalize the North American industry for the benefit of producers and consumers alike, cement the strong continental ties and spirit of co-operation between the two countries and resolve a difficult issue in the US-Canadian trade relationship. The creation of the Auto Pact was precipitated by the unilateral Canadian efforts in 1962–64 to boost Canada's flagging auto industry and redress its rapidly deteriorating current account balance, a deficit that was largely the result of massive auto and parts imports from the United States. When the US and Canadian governments realized that the issue might deteriorate into a full-fledged trade war between the two countries, negotiations began in earnest.[43]

By the fall of 1964, the two sides came to an agreement. Duty-free trade in autos and parts was to be limited only by the different provisions governing each country. The agreement stipulated that imports to the US could come only from Canada and required 50 per cent North American content. In Canada, only certain bona fide manufacturers that maintained a ratio of production to sales and a base Canadian value-added rate were allowed to import from any country, though the US was the most likely country of origin. This intergovernmental agreement was complemented by a series of agreements between the Canadian government and the US-owned Canadian subsidiaries of the major auto producers referred to as 'letters of undertaking'. The companies promised to boost their investments in Canada over the next three years and to increase the Canadian content of their production by 60 per cent of whatever increase might occur in their sales in a given year. Instead of unrestricted free trade, the Auto Pact provided for a tightly managed limited sectoral trade area in autos and parts.

As the two governments and the American Big Three auto makers had been the instigators of the new agreement, it was primarily designed to benefit the US-based companies, largely to the exclusion of offshore manufacturers. While the Canadian government consulted extensively with the Canadian Big Three presidents, Volvo's representatives did not participate in the Auto Pact discussions. But with Volvo in mind, the Auto Pact did include a part which stipulated that

the government of Canada could designate a manufacturer 'not falling within the categories' in the Annex as being entitled to duty-free treatment. This allowed the government to designate Volvo under the agreement at a 40 per cent Canadian value-added (CVA) rate (being the dollar amount of Canadian labour or parts added to a vehicle), which was in keeping with the company's previous content commitments and did not preclude the company's participation in the new regime.[44]

Although the new agreement provided immense benefits for GM, Ford and Chrysler, as they could now import and export across the border tariff free as long as they maintained their commitments in Canada and content requirements in the US, Volvo would benefit as well. The company could now import duty-free from Sweden, as the Canadian negotiators had ensured that the Canadian aspects of the agreement applied to third countries. In other words, Volvo could import parts from Sweden duty-free if they continued to maintain their Auto Pact commitments. This meant massive savings, and provided an opportunity for further growth as long as Volvo increased its Canadian presence.[45]

In its first years of operation, the Auto Pact proved to be immensely successful as expansion in the auto sector was impressive. The main players in the industry, the American Big Three, expanded their facilities greatly in the period immediately following the agreement's signing. One Department of Industry official estimated that of the over 50 major automotive-related projects announced by October of 1965, nearly half were by subsidiaries of US companies. The official noted that in many instances, the companies specifically declared that the reason for the growth was the automotive agreement, though many had been planned before 1965 because of growing Canadian demand.[46] During the first two years of the Auto Pact, every major manufacturer, including Volvo, opened or expanded at least one major facility in Canada, which accounted for much of the $260 million target in the letters of undertaking.[47] By the late 1960s, the Big Three had all boosted production and increased their investments. In 1969, the Canadian auto industry produced over one million vehicles for the first time, a massive increase over the 325,000 total vehicles produced in 1960.

[ . . . ]

While the tariff relief was welcomed by the company, continued disappointing production figures sparked stories that Volvo intended to flee to greener pastures. Compounding these rumours was the fact the company's lease at the Atlantic Sugar Refineries Plant was expiring in 1967 and that the company did not wish to renew the lease with Volvo.[48] Moving the company's head office to Toronto in 1966, and setting up a major parts depot at a new $1.2 million facility in Toronto, did not help matters. In early 1966 Volvo Canada President Kohler was forced to quell rumours that the company was moving to Quebec; he publicly stated the company was eager to remain in Nova Scotia.[49]

Volvo did move, but only to a new facility across the harbour from Dartmouth. After difficult deliberations over choosing a new site and a host of false starts, in 1966 Volvo took possession of a new and larger plant on Halifax's Pier 9. Built by IEL and leased to Volvo, the facility was a 190,000 sq. ft., $1 million investment by the Crown corporation.[50] Incentive was further provided by the Halifax City Council, which offered a 10-year tax-benefit package. The plant's location allowed Volvo to load shipments directly into the facility.[51] Again, this move by Volvo was heralded as a signal that the company was in Nova Scotia to stay, although the company did not own the building outright.

By 1968 Volvo, like the rest of the industry in Canada, had improved its position. That year, the new plant produced nearly 5,000 Volvo 140 Series vehicles and had increased turnout from 360 cars a month to over 420; in November, in fact, the company boosted production at the Halifax facility from 120 to 130 cars a week. However, this optimism for Volvo's prospects did not stop company president Kohler from reminding Nova Scotia Premier G.I. Smith that the plant required provincial assistance 'to further strengthen our position in Canada, and thereby create more jobs and opportunities for your area'.[52]

[ . . . ]

Nonetheless, rumours continued to persist that the plant's position was precarious, a situation which was exacerbated by labour difficulties. In 1974 UAW Local 720, in a strike position following the end of their contract, were locked out by the company after negotiations broke off over the issue of overtime rates. Volvo representatives made it clear to Nova Scotia officials that they could not operate the facility under the overtime provisions being demanded by the union; Volvo executives were, in the view of IEL President Dean Salsman, 'very disturbed and concerned about the negotiations'.[53]

[ . . . ]

A number of other problems beyond the plant's control hindered its operation during the early 1970s. A 1971 report from the Centre for Automobile Safety in Washington, DC claiming that Volvo's cars were not as safe as advertised was widely publicized, and prompted the Halifax *Mail-Star* to question the reliability of Volvo Canada vehicles.[54] In its critique of Volvo safety, the paper also erroneously stated that the company was receiving 'advances' from IEL. In response, Volvo Canada strenuously defended the quality of its cars and the integrity of its workforce, and vehemently repudiated the assertion that it had received any inappropriate 'advances'.[55] In the fall of 1973 a strike that closed the Port of Halifax led to production delays and the eventual closure of the Volvo plant for two weeks in November.[56] Both incidents added to the difficulties the company faced during that period.

Notwithstanding these setbacks, in 1975 the company reached its peak production and assembled more than 13,000 units. For the remainder of the decade, the plant produced between 7,000 and 12,500 vehicles every year.[57] By 1980, while the rest of the automotive industry was in the depths of a severe recession, Volvo representatives were cautiously optimistic of the plant's long-term prospects. Although output usually remained less than 10,000 vehicles per year, Volvo's sales in Canada were increasing, which led to further production increases and underlined the importance of consistent output to meet that domestic demand.[58]

By the mid-1980s, however, Volvo Canada was producing only a fraction of what had been expected in 1963. In-vehicle Canadian content was barely 5 per cent and the vast majority of the Canadian value added at the Halifax plant resulted from labour costs. Ironically, tires from Michelin, which had been the other significant provincial effort to attract new industry to the province, were used on Nova Scotia Volvos—but they were imported from Germany rather than being delivered from the province's own plants in Pictou County and Bridgewater.[59]

This lack of content curtailed Volvo exports from Halifax to the United States. While Canadian officials gave the company preferential treatment to import from Sweden without achieving its content requirements, it was prohibited from exporting to the US if it did not achieve a 50 per cent 'North American Content' threshold, which it never attained. As a result, the company was unable to use Halifax as a source for exports to the US which, by the mid-1970s, had become its largest market.

A new Halifax plant did not really provide the production that was necessary for the Canadian market either. In 1987 Volvo and IEL announced that the company would leave the Halifax plant at Pier 9 to move to an entirely new facility constructed at a cost of $13.5 million by Volvo at Bayer Lake Industrial Park. Volvo's move was sweetened by further tax breaks given by the municipal government, which required the company to pay only a fraction of its municipal tax bill for the next ten years. While some municipal councillors voiced concern about the continuing breaks for the company, especially after it was reported that Volvo Canada had been increasingly profitable during the 1980s, the municipal measures passed with little dissent.[60] During the move to the new facility, Volvo planned to reduce its workforce, which led to further labour difficulties at the plant as a wildcat strike ensued. Production reached near-record lows, and Volvo workers recall the move with bitterness.[61] Their bitterness would reach a breaking point only a few years later. By the mid-1990s, the company faced new challenges in its North American strategy—one which required drastic changes to its Halifax plant.

## THE END OF VOLVO'S CANADIAN ADVENTURE, 1995–98

On 8 September 1998, Volvo announced that it was closing the Bayer Lake assembly plant, stating that it was no longer 'economically viable' to produce cars in Halifax for the Canadian market. Volvo Canada President Gord Sonnenberg stated that the facility was simply too small for the long-term plans of the company. A plant that produced less than 10,000 vehicles was no match for one that produced over 100,000. Moreover, the company argued that economies of scale were key to their tariff concerns. Even with the 6.1 per cent Canadian tariff for complete vehicles, it was still more efficient to build the cars in Sweden at the large-scale plants and ship them to Canada. This was particularly true for the US export market. The closure also provoked rumours that Volvo was in greater financial trouble than the company was letting on and that the Halifax facility was being shuttered in part to address its over-capacity problems in Europe.[62] There was also speculation that the company was being pursued as a takeover target.

On 11 December 1998, the last Volvo assembled in Canada, a four-door S70 sedan, quietly rolled out of the facility and was donated to the IWK Grace Health Centre by the company and the workers.

Why did the Volvo venture in Canada, which had begun with such optimism and enthusiasm, end so sadly? The project, which was heralded as representing the start of a 'New Nova Scotia' in 1963, ended with an unhappy and very public labour dispute and plant takeover. How did a venture which had the benefit of federal and provincial programs to spur industrial development come to such an ignominious end? Notwithstanding the plant's uneven existence, on balance can Volvo's Canadian venture be considered a success?

Some have viewed the story of Volvo in Canada as an example of corporate exploitation. Critics of the company argue that 'Volvo did not "bring a little bit of Sweden" to Nova Scotia; instead the company quickly adapted to and exploited the peripheral conditions of its new location'.[63] The company took advantage of a weakened economic jurisdiction and lower labour costs, and gained the benefit of preferential treatment in tariff, capital and infrastructure policies from federal and provincial governments—all in exchange for the promise of booming employment and increased industrial development. But that promise never materialized. Volvo never employed more than 200 people directly in the plant; its partial-knock-down system resulted in few secondary jobs in either parts or assembly; the plant produced barely 10,000 vehicles in an average year, a shadow of the over 100,000 vehicles produced at Volvo's European operations.

Others might compare the shortcomings at Volvo in Nova Scotia with the success of other assembly facilities in Ontario, and place the blame at the feet of a central Canadian-oriented federal government. After all, provincial representatives often felt slighted at the hands of the federal government when it came to government contracts—such as the

military truck order—or felt that Ontario conditions were dictating the terms of Nova Scotia labour. When Volvo announced the Halifax closure, local reporters noted that the executives came to the press conference 'with their Ontario public relations experts in tow'.[64] Criticism towards the federal government, however, or its automotive policy could not be too harsh. After all, Volvo had been included in the Auto Pact, something not even the Honda and Toyota facilities in Ontario could boast.[65] Furthermore, Volvo had been given preferential tariff treatment by the federal government from the outset and had even gained further concessions under the Auto Pact. Instead, when it came to federal automotive policy, Volvo's status as a 'regional' producer actually resulted in beneficial treatment. Volvo's demise was not a result of regional discrimination in favour of Ontario.

The end of Volvo's Canadian venture can also be seen as a failure in corporate strategy. Although Volvo was keen to exploit a new market, it never committed adequate resources to the plant or made a concerted financial investment in the Halifax operation. Such an effort may have paid off in far greater sales in Canada and a significant growth in Volvo's overseas market, but the company's managers were unwilling to commit wholeheartedly to their Canadian facility. Volvo's reluctance to boost its facility in Canada contrasted sharply with the Canadian Big Three plants in Ontario and Quebec, particularly after 1965: the GM, Ford and Chrysler facilities received billions of dollars in new investment, not only in response to the companies' requirements under the Auto Pact but because these firms understood the benefits of sourcing production in Canada.[66]

Volvo faced constraints, of course, that largely precluded it from taking more advantage of its Canadian facility. First, Volvo did not have the benefits of proximity that the Big Three boasted. Windsor, where much of the Canadian auto industry was located, was only across the river from Detroit, America's 'Motor City'. Halifax, on the other hand, was thousands of miles from Sweden—there was no chance of developing 'just-in-time' production techniques or of merging production schedules and operational plans of Volvo's Canadian and Swedish facilities, as happened with the Big Three after 1965. By the 1990s, the Halifax operation remained a far-flung outpost of the company, a remnant of a bygone era where a niche independent auto company such as Volvo had attempted to build its own multinational presence.[67] While Volvo's other 'foreign' plants established during this period—Ghent, Belgium in 1965 and Kuala Lumpur, Malaysia in 1967—continued to function, their survival reflected local considerations (European integration and tariff requirements to be in Southeast Asia) rather than any coherent international policy.

Second, Volvo's Halifax plant was caught in a proverbial catch-22. The plant originated under tariff rules designed for small-scale production for the Canadian market. It lacked the economies of scale necessary to take full advantage of its Auto Pact status to export into the US market; doing so required hitting the necessary 50 per cent North American regional content guarantees under the agreement, a prohibitively expensive undertaking for a company of Volvo's size at a plant of Halifax's stature. Volvo's corporate managers likely saw little benefit in boosting investment or production in a facility that was originally intended as a beachhead into the Canadian market and which remained as such for all of its existence. With the concessions and incentives provided by the federal, provincial and municipal governments, it cost the company little to maintain the facility. In return for these generous inducements, Volvo provided nominal employment and minimal Canadian value added while gaining a measure of good corporate citizenship.

Indeed, in providing continued preferential treatment, both the federal and provincial governments showed that they could only do so much in an automotive industry that experienced so much change during the period under examination. Tariff concessions and

plants built for Volvo did provide an incentive for the company to set up operations in Nova Scotia but governments could not control the market or the management decisions of the company. In this case, state intervention was beneficial in attracting the firm to Nova Scotia but could do little after the plant was established in the face of the vagaries of the marketplace or the quickly changing world auto industry. State intervention can be successful, but it can only be as successful as the partners with which it is dealing.

At its core, the departure of Volvo from Halifax did not happen because Nova Scotia was a poor choice for an auto plant or because Nova Scotia auto workers were not capable or effective. Nor did Volvo's departure hinge upon unrealistic tariff rules or overly demanding content regulations by the federal government. While many of the location and labour difficulties the plant faced certainly curtailed the growth of its production, Volvo left Halifax because of a rapidly changing world automotive industry, because it could not take advantage of new trade regimes to exploit its largest market, and because the economies of scale, which were realistic in 1963, were utterly unrealistic in 1998.

In the end, the plant itself may not have been a success, but it did provide employment for hundreds of workers in the Halifax area for over three decades. The plant takeover illustrates how valued those jobs were by the employees. As Anders Sandberg noted before the closure of the facility, 'There are several reasons why Volvo workers stay in what appear to be less than satisfying jobs. The wages are high by Nova Scotia standards. There is little else to do. The workers are relatively old and know few other skills; in 1994, the average age was close to 50 years. These are facts of which the workers are critically aware and constantly reminded by management'.[68] For these people, Volvo's Halifax venture had nothing to do with corporate exploitation: the company provided jobs where none had existed before, and the governments' willingness to use taxpayer funds to provide incentives was not a case of Volvo 'taking advantage' of Canadian largesse but a genuine effort at economic development that did not, in the end, have a lasting effect.

In the long run, the battle over the closure of Volvo Halifax may have been moot. In 1998 the Ford Motor Company purchased the auto assembly operations of Volvo of Sweden. With the new arrangement, it is highly unlikely that Ford would have continued to operate the facility, given that they could import Volvo cars directly from Sweden into the United States duty-free under the Auto Pact because of the change of ownership. Even the demise of the Auto Pact, following the 2000 World Trade Organization ruling that the agreement was contrary to international trade laws, would have likely led to the end of the plant. Without the preferential tariff treatment afforded by the agreement, Volvo would not have continued to build cars at its tiny Canadian operation. Corporate consolidation and the globalization of the automotive industry would have quickly shuttered the plant, something that sporadic production and uncertain facilities had not managed to do in nearly four decades.

# NOTES

1. Dimitry Anastakis, 'Requiem for a Trade Agreement: The Auto Pact at the WTO, 1999–2000', *Canadian Business Law Journal*, 34, 3 (February 2001), pp. 313–35.

2. Dimitry Anastakis, 'Auto Pact: Business and Diplomacy in the Creation of a Borderless North American Auto Industry, 1945–1971', Ph.D. thesis, York University, 2001.

3. John Holmes, 'From Three Industries to One: Towards an Integrated North American Automobile Industry', in Maureen Molot, ed., *Driving Continentally: National Policies and the North American Auto Industry* (Ottawa, 1993), p. 27.

4. Simon S. Reisman to Walter Gordon, 'Proposals to Reduce Trade Deficit in Automobile Industry', 28 August 1963, RG 19 (Department of Finance), vol. 3946, file 8705-1-1, National Archives of Canada [NA] and Canada, *Debates of the House of Commons*, 25 October 1963, pp. 3999–4000.

5. 'United States Aide Memoire: Confidential', 24 October 1963, RG 19, vol. 3946, file 8705-1-1, NA.

6. 'Time Bomb May Lie Under Exports; Opposition Intensifies', *Globe and Mail*, 31 July 1964; 'U.S.–Canada Trade War Feared in Wake of Auto Export Row', *Globe and Mail*, 4 August 1964; Charlotte Yates, *From Plants to Politics: The Autoworkers Union in Postwar Canada* (Philadelphia, 1993), p. 118.

7. Canada, Cabinet Conclusions, 27 December 1962, RG 2, vol. 6193, 1962, NA; *Ward's Automotive Reports*, 12 November 1962 and 4 March 1963.

8. James Bickerton, *Nova Scotia, Ottawa and the Politics of Regional Development* (Toronto, 1990), pp. 142–3.

9. Bickerton, *Politics of Regional Development*, pp. 236–7.

10. Frank Sobey, 'Industrial Estates "prepared for risks"', *Financial Times*, 15 October 1968.

11. 'Volvo a "Go" Company Similar to GM in U.S.', *Financial Post*, 23 February 1963; Eric Dennis, 'Volvo Expanded Rapidly', *Chronicle-Herald* (Halifax), 22 February 1963. Lindholm and Norstedt, *The Volvo Report*, pp. 5–13.

12. 'D.W. Samuel—A Man of Confidence', *Chronicle-Herald*, 12 June 1963; D.W. Samuel, interview by author, telephone and letter, Toronto, 20 May 2002.

13. In August 1945, Order-in-Council P.C. 5623 modified the 40 per cent content bracket by raising the level to 15,000 units. This was intended to ease the way for Nash (later American) Motors, which planned to begin production in Canada. The order remained in effect until the 1965 tariff changes.

14. Samuel, interview by author, 20 May 2002.

15. Bickerton, *Politics of Regional Development*, pp. 140–1.

16. Bladen, *Royal Commission on the Automotive Industry*.

17. Anastakis, 'Auto Pact', ch. 2.

18. Canada, Cabinet Conclusions, 27 December 1962, RG 2, vol. 6193, NA; *Ward's Automotive Reports*, 12 November 1962 and 4 March 1963.

19. 'First Plant in Canada', *Chronicle-Herald*, 21 February 1963; 'Changes in Tariff aid to company'; *Chronicle-Herald*, 22 February 1963; Samuel, interview by author, 20 May 2002.

20. 'Will Provide Building', *Chronicle-Herald*, 21 February 1963; Lauchie Chisholm, 'Maritimes' "New Sweden" Gulps its "Second Wind"', *Financial Post*, 15 June 1963.

21. Minutes of the IEL Executive Committee, 5 December 1962, 18 December 1962, 23 January 1963 and 11 February 1963, RG 55, Trade and Commerce, vol. 11, file 7, Nova Scotia Archives and Record Management [NSARM].

22. Minutes of the IEL Executive Committee, 18 December 1962 and 1 February 1963, RG 55, Trade and Commerce, vol. 11, file 7, NSARM; 'Canadian Volvo Month Away, Green Workers Being Trained', *Financial Post*, 11 May 1963.

23. 'Canadian Volvo Month Away', *Financial Post*, 11 May 1963.

24. 'First in Dominion', *Chronicle-Herald*, 21 February 1963.

25. '200–300 Workers, Mostly Canadian, Will be Employed', *Chronicle-Herald*, 21 February 1963; Carlyle Dunbar, 'What Volvo Bid Means to Maritimes', *Financial Post*, 23 February 1963.

26. 'Mayor's Efforts in Getting Plant Are Praised', *Chronicle-Herald*, 11 April 1963.

27. 'Why Volvo Went to Dartmouth', *Chronicle-Herald*, 11 June 1963.

28. Nova Scotia, Debates of the Legislative Assembly, 25 February 1963, pp. 174–5.

29. Editorial, 'Surest Way', *Chronicle-Herald*, 22 February 1963.

30. 'Why Volvo Went to Dartmouth', *Chronicle-Herald*, 11 June 1963.

31. 'D.W. Samuel—A Man of Confidence', *Chronicle-Herald*, 11 June 1963.

32. 'Volvo Has Broken the Trail', *Financial Post*, 29 June 1963; 'N.S. firms to be offered Volvo parts production', *Chronicle-Herald*, 4 April 1963.

33. 'Volvo Sales Manager Outlines Company Plans', *Chronicle-Herald*, 11 April 1963.

34. 'N.S. firms to be offered Volvo Parts Production', *Chronicle-Herald*, 4 April 1963; 'Volvo opens "opportunity show" for N.S. producers', *Chronicle-Herald*, 11 April 1963.

35. Minutes of the IEL Executive Committee, 12 March 1963, RG 55, Trade and Commerce, vol. 11, file 7, NSARM.

36. Eric Dennis, 'U.K. auto firms taking second look at Maritimes', *Chronicle-Herald*, 4 April 1963; Eric Dennis, 'Volvo's Lead May Induce More Firms to Come to Canada', *Chronicle-Herald*, 22 February 1963.

37. 'Canadian Volvo Month Away', *Financial Post*, 11 May 1963.

38. 'Swedish Industrial Giant Gets Beachhead in Canada', *Financial Post*, 23 February 1963.

39. Chisholm, 'Maritimes' "New Sweden"', *Financial Post*, 15 June 1963.

40. After 1965, however, Volvo was unable to ship cars from its Halifax plant due to tariff rules under the Auto Pact. See 'Volvo, too, plan export of Canadian cars to U.S.', *Financial Post*, 21 December 1963.

41. 'Second Company to Assemble Cars', *Financial Post*, 26 June 1965.

42. Lester Pearson, *Memoirs, Volume 3, 1957–1968* (Toronto, 1975); Lawrence Martin, *The Presidents and the Prime Ministers, Washington and Ottawa Face to Face: The Myth of Bilateral Bliss, 1867–1982* (Toronto, 1982) and J.L.G. Granatstein and Norman Hillmer, *For Better or For Worse: Canada and the United States to the 1990s* (Toronto, 1991).

43. Greg Donaghy, 'A Continental Philosophy: Canada, The United States and the Negotiation of the Auto Pact, 1963–1965', *International Journal*, 52, 3 (Summer 1998); James F. Keeley, 'Cast in Concrete for all Time? The Negotiation of the Auto Pact', *The Canadian Journal of Political Science*, XVI, 2 (June 1983) and Anastakis, 'Auto Pact'.

44. Lyndon Watkins, 'Monday Make or Break for Canadian Volvo', *Chronicle-Herald*, 15 January 1965; 'Puts Volvo "Fully in Trade Plan"', *Chronicle-Herald*, 12 February 1965.

45. Dimitry Anastakis, 'The Advent of an International Agreement: The Auto Pact at the GATT, 1964–1965', *International Journal*, 55, 4 (Autumn 2000), pp. 583–602.

46. K.W. Burke (Officer, Mechanical Transportation Branch) to C.D. Arthur, 18 August

1965, K.W. Burke to File, 19 August 1965 and K.W. Burke to File, 20 August 1965, all in RG 20, vol. 1826, 1022–17, part 3, Automotive Agreement Enquiries, August–December 1965, NA; 'Facts Relating to Expansion of Automotive Industry in 1964 and 1965', Department of Industry, 8 October 1965, RG 20, vol. 1793, file Automotive Correspondence, NA; K.W. Burke, 'Quarterly Report on the Auto Industry', 19 November 1965, RG 20, vol. 1775, file V.8001-260/A4, part 2, MTB, Auto Industry, 1965–1968, NA.

47. The exact nature of Big Three spending on plant and parts has never been disclosed by the corporations.

48. Minutes of IEL Executive Committee, 17 November 1965, RG 55, Trade and Commerce, vol. 12, file 6, NSARM.

49. 'Volvo Disappointed, May Pull Out of Here', *Chronicle-Herald*, 17 January 1966; David Crane, 'Kohler Kills Rumours about Volvo Pull-out', *Financial Post*, 22 January 1966; 'Chances of Volvo Staying Brighten', 'Volvo President, Mayor of Quebec Meet in Hotel' and 'Nova Scotia Has Good Chance to Keep Volvo', *Chronicle-Herald*, 19 January 1966.

50. K. Kohler to G.I. Smith, 19 January 1968, RG 100, vol.41, file 14.1, Trade and Industry, NSARM.

51. 'Volvo Considers Shift to Halifax', *Chronicle-Herald*, 25 May 1966; Lyndon Watkins, 'New 10 Year Agreement Signed by Volvo Plant', *Chronicle-Herald*, 1 June 1966; 'Volvo Looks For Space', *Chronicle-Herald*, 15 April 1967; 'Volvo plant nears single shift capacity', *Financial Post*, 5 October 1968.

52. K. Kohler to G.I. Smith, 19 January 1968, RG 100, vol. 41, file 14.1, Trade and Industry, NSARM; 'Volvo boosts production in Nova Scotia', *Financial Post*, 2 November 1968.

53. Dean Salsman to George Mitchell, 9 July 1974, RG 55, Trade and Commerce, vol. 5, file Volvo, NSARM.

54. 'Check-Up for Volvo', *Mail-Star* (Halifax), 9 September 1971.

55. Ove P.F. Lindblad (Volvo Canada) to Finlay MacDonald (IEL), 15 September 1971, RG 55, Trade and Commerce, vol. 5, file Volvo, NSARM.

56. Gunnar K.G. Jennegren (Volvo Canada) to George M. Mitchell, 13 December 1973, RG 55, Trade and Commerce, vol. 5, file Volvo, NSARM.

57. Anders Sandberg, 'Missing the Road: Working Life at Volvo Nova Scotia', in Ake Sandberg, ed., *Enriching Production: Perspectives on Volvo's Uddevalla Plant as an Alternative to Lean Production* (Brookfield, US, 1995), p. 270.

58. Patricia Best, 'Volvo Canada: Making it in Halifax', *Financial Post*, 2 August 1980.

59. Volvo Research Group, 'The Volvo Story in Nova Scotia', *New Maritimes: A Regional Magazine of Culture and Politics*, VII, 5 (May/June 1989): pp. 16–7.

60. At the Pier 9 site, Volvo was paying only 27 per cent of its annual municipal tax bill of $130,000. The new Bayer's Lake deal was similar. Sandberg reports that the company made profits of between $8–$12 million between 1984 and 1989. See Volvo Research Group, 'The Volvo Story', p. 18 and Sandberg, 'Missing the Road', p. 277.

61. Sandberg, 'Missing the Road', p. 275.

62. Roger Taylor, 'Volvo plant closure shocking but not unexpected', *Chronicle-Herald*, 15 September 1998.

63. Sandberg, 'Missing the Road', p. 278.

64. Roger Taylor, 'Volvo plant closure shocking but not unexpected', *Chronicle-Herald*, 15 September 1998.

65. By the early 1990s, Toyota and Honda were producing over 200,000 vehicles annually at their Ontario plants and employing over 3,000 workers yet did not have official Auto Pact status. Volvo, with less than 10,000 vehicles produced yearly and barely 200 workers, had Auto Pact status.

66. One Department of Industry official estimated that Auto Pact investment in the 1965–70 period was over $1 billion.

67. Kenneth Good and Skye Hughes, 'Globalization and Diversification: Two Cases in Southern Africa', *African Affairs*, 101, 402 (2002), pp. 39–59.

68. Sandberg, 'Missing the Road', p. 277.

4   From Diane Pacom, 'Being French in North America: Quebec Culture and Globalization', *American Review of Canadian Studies* 31(3) (Autumn 2001): 441–8.

The main focus of this analysis will be on understanding how 'Americanity' (l'Americanité) has been integrated into Quebec's collective Social Imaginary.[1] It is important to stress that the American influence on Québécois cultural identity has always been a very important, yet divisive issue in Quebec's cultural, social, and political reality. The acceptance of American influence by the urban working-class masses was doubled because of its fierce rejection by the rural masses and their traditional elites. The urban masses saw America's influence as a tool of emancipation from the conservative ideological hold of that past. The rural masses and their elites, on the other hand, saw this as a negative, regressive influence that was evil, morally corrupt and, overall, dangerous to Quebec's identity and cultural survivability. It is important to stress that, while Québécois society has always been critical of and reluctant about the Americanization of Quebec, Americanity was recognized even though its acceptance generated a fierce and lengthy debate through modern Quebec history. This particular characteristic of Quebec's culture puts it in a different cultural space than the rest of Canada, which tries to build an identity to resist American cultural influence. Contrary to Anglo-Canadian culture, which tries to insulate itself from its Americanity, Québécois society, especially since the 1950s, has accepted, integrated and, in many ways, bypassed this question, which continues to haunt Anglo-Canadian society and its elites.

A creative political tension has always prevailed in Quebec concerning this particular aspect of its reality. This tension stems from the dialogue between the forces that fought in order to bring Québécois culture to accept the American component of its identity, and those who insisted on keeping Quebec outside of the continental cultural sphere. I also wish to underline that the topic of Québécois culture's particular rapport with American culture remains at worst an unknown dimension (especially for a non-Québécois public), and at best immersed in and/or subordinated to the topic of Quebec's politics. It also seems that the only time Québécois culture draws the attention of the international (that is, non-francophone) media is when the question of Quebec's possible separation from Canada comes to the forefront, as it did most recently with the October 1995 Referendum on independence.

Discussing Québécois culture implies, therefore, the acknowledgement and the necessity of moving beyond this political determinism, which renders peripheral other important aspects of its social reality. And although it is very hard to transcend the political question, which has mobilized the passions, not only of Quebec's population, but also of the rest of Canada, the imperative to understand Quebec society's totality remains an important task. This importance stems from the fact that most of the partisan political arguments concerning Québécois distinctiveness as a society are based on the belief that Québécois culture is different from the culture that prevails in the rest of Canada. Therefore, 'culture' remains ultimately the principal domain on which the political discourse (being separatist or federalist) is constructed. At another level, it is important to stress that Québécois politics—whichever side is advocated—have always insisted on a continuous and sustained effort to safeguard Québécois cultural values and institutions, and more recently, as we shall see in the following pages, to keep them in tune with the global and international reality.

## QUÉBÉCOIS CULTURE: A COMPLEX AND PARADOXICAL STATE OF AFFAIRS

Québécois culture in its high and low manifestations is a rich, complex, dynamic, and often paradoxical reality full of meaning and contradictions. [O]ne of the pre-eminent Québécois scholars, the late sociologist Marcel Rioux (Rioux, 1971)[ . . . ] noted that the 1970s were governed by an ideology of 'dépassement'. Indeed, at that particular moment in Quebec's history, Quebec society was bypassing its own traditional limits set in its colonial past and becoming part of North America, part of modernity, and part of the world. [ . . . ].

At [that time], Québécois youth culture distinguished itself from other francophone youth cultures around the world by its vitality, creativity, and openness. At the same time Québécois culture underwent a process of deconstruction that gave it tremendous creative energy. Rock-and-roll and pop bands such as Harmonium, Offenbach, Beau Dommage; singers, songwriters, and performing artists such as Diane Dufresne, Robert Charlebois, Plume Latraverse; writers such as Michel Tremblay; and cinematographers such as Denis Arcand and Jean Pierre Lefebvre set the tone for a whole generation of francophone artists around the world.

The vitality of that particular generation of Québécois young artists was fuelled by the after-effects of a socio-historic era that, according to Marcel Rioux's book *La Question du Québec*, was governed by a new perspective on the world. This era was crowned by Quebec society's effort to transcend the conservatism of its traditional civil society and enter a more liberal era characterized by openness to North American, continental, and cosmopolitan values. According to Rioux, a rigid conservatism from the original French culture (*idéologie de conservation*) characterized the first period. French culture, Catholicism, and rural values dominated. Criticism of these values characterized

the second period (*idéologie de rattrapage*, the 1950s and 1960s). Quebec civil society, at that moment [ . . . ] was going through a dramatic cultural explosion critically questioning its past and catching up with the rest of the western world. At all levels, in this effort to reshape its identity beyond Catholicism and its traditional puritan, natalistic, rural, and overall conservative vision of life, Québécois society ended up reassessing the validity of all the essential aspects of its reality.

Following World War Two, a comprehensive and sustained effort to transcend the morality and values set up by the clergy put the Québécois family, for example, through a radical restructuring (Dandurand, 1988). Along with that went a revision of the relationships between men and women.[2] At that point, any power struggle that would prove costly divided society into two camps. On the one hand stood the traditional elites, faithfully attached to French colonial cultural values. On the other hand stood the urban working-class masses that became increasingly fascinated by American values expressed in cinema, vaudeville theatre, and country music, for example. French-Canadian country music performers Willy Lamothe and Le Soldat Lebrun became at that time the most important symbols of the Québécois country music scene. Cars, fast-food restaurants, dance halls, and poolrooms competed with the austere lifestyles of the rural habitant population. French-Canadian folk music, as embodied by Ti-Jean Carignan and Oscar Tiffault, remained for a long time the voice of the rural population. And this rural culture was totally subordinated by hegemonic Catholic religious values.

Naturally, the clergy was violently opposed to the intrusion of these American urban values, which were considered impure, sinful, and detrimental to Quebec's French identity (Bouchard and Courville, 1993). Condemnation targeted specifically American urban popular culture as the source of all evil. It would be cured by the antidote of French high culture. French Catholic literary figures, poets and writers such as Chateaubriand, Rene Bazin, Victor Hugo, and Louis Veuilot, a royalist, fundamentalist nineteenth-century French writer, were used to exorcise the growing influence of American popular culture on the Québécois Social Imaginary. Since the 1950s, despite the Church's sometimes repressive efforts at containment, North American urban values have become increasingly influential. This liberalization movement of Québécois civil society, which many scholars have labelled The Quiet Revolution (*La Révolution Tranquille*), created a new Québécois culture proud of its unique status within the Canadian federation. This movement also brought awareness of the triple nature of its Social Imaginary. It became not only French (*la Francité*), but also Québécois (*le Quebecité*) and American (*l'Americanité*). By absorbing international culture from not only the media, but also from any other sources, Québécois culture developed a unique particularism.

## THE TRIADIC NATURE OF QUEBEC'S IDENTITY

Despite innumerable essays, books, articles, and reports produced and in process by French-Canadian and Canadian scholars and writers, the question of Québécois identity remains unresolved. Constructing and deconstructing the many facets of Quebec's civil society remains one of the most controversial topics of Canadian politics, as the amount of funding and scholarship invested in this process attests. Quebec's cultural identity also remained an enigmatic puzzle that the rest of Canada found threatening, dangerous, and seductive. It is hard to discuss this topic in Quebec, and in the rest of Canada, in a cool and unemotional manner. Experience taught me that, sooner or later, feelings and ideology get in the way of even the most scientific and rational exchange. [ . . . ]

Generally, the discourse on Québécois identity has been polarized between those who would like to reduce it to its French component and those who have tried to recognize in it other sources of influence. And, at this level, the division adopts a class connotation. Laval University's Gerard Bouchard, the brother of Quebec's ex-Prime Minister Lucien Bouchard, has investigated Québécois social history and cultural identity closely (Bouchard and Courville, 1993, Bouchard and Lamonde, 1995). He underlines the fact that in Quebec there has, until recently, been a discrepancy between the governing elites and the masses concerning the interpretation of what constitutes Québécois identity. Bouchard and his colleague Yvon Lamonde argue that the clergy that formed the ruling caste of traditional Quebec society, and the liberal intellectuals that defined the parameters of the civil society in Quebec during and after the Quiet Revolution, despite their opposed political and ideological perspectives, agreed on one particular dimension: the hegemony and prevalence of French culture in the life of Québécois society (Bouchard and Lamonde, 1995). Ironically, the arguments invoked against 'American imperialism' at the cultural level by the new liberal, and often socialist, elite coincided with the extreme right's arguments against the opening up of Quebec to the larger world.

Gerard Bouchard and his research team suggest that this anachronistic, unidimensional construction of Québécois culture has been radically transformed since the 1950s. Globalization and mass culture, the power of the media, urbanization, and the changing Québécois demographics because of increasing numbers of immigrants had slowly eroded the traditional image of the Québécois identity as being solely shaped by Franco-French culture (*la Francité*). A powerful shift has occurred in Quebec's Social Imaginary over the last five decades that has imparted a broader sense of self-construction around the three poles that Marcel Rioux defines in *The Quebec Question*: la Francité, l'Americanité, and la Quebecité. The traditional discrepancy between the highbrow, traditional version of Québécois culture being exclusively nourished by French culture, and the more Americanized version of popular culture has been, according to Bouchard and Lamonde, sidestepped. Today's cultural and political elites seem to accept wholeheartedly this triadic version of Quebec's identity.

## TOWARDS A HYBRID QUÉBÉCOIS IDENTITY

At the beginning of the twenty-first century, Quebec society has come a very long way from its beginnings in French colonization. Increasingly multilingual, industrialized, and scientifically, economically, and culturally advanced, it now confronts all the challenges of post-modern times. As is the case in most modern post-industrial societies, for the younger generation, technology replaces ideology as the biggest challenge. Through the Internet the door to the world opens ever wider. Some of the conservative elites wonder again about Quebec's capacity to retain its French identity. Again, the question of the French language becomes important. Will the Internet Anglicize French-Canadian society? Even if by now at the institutional level (political, cultural, or economic) the Francization of Quebec reality leaves no doubt, many scholars and politicians wonder about this new virtual space that opens up in its Social Imaginary. Thus the spectre of Americanization emerges yet again.

At the same time, Quebec confronts through immigration the challenge of becoming an ever more multicultural society. *Possibles*, a Montreal-based radical journal, has dedicated some of its most recent issues to this problem. As they plead for an intercultural society, the contributors attempt to tackle the new set of problems that face Québécois society. The questions of racism and intolerance on the face of this new, hybrid Québécois reality, the role of the media, of the intellectuals, Quebec's new identity politics, the specificity

of modern Québécois society, all become the centre of a new, collective reflection. Quebec moves toward a future that remains culturally uncertain. As it confronts new economic, political, cultural, and spiritual challenges, what will become of its quest to remain—as the slogan on automobile licence plates suggests, *Je me Souviens* (I remember)—always aware of its past and its French cultural legacy?

Paradoxically for the scores of young people growing up today in Quebec, almost all of whom by now can speak, read, and write French fluently, this is a difficult task. Their identity is not only French Canadian, but also that of Quebec-born sons and daughters of immigrants arriving from all the corners of the world. For them learning French, and living in French, is not, as it was for the more homogeneous generation of Quebecers before them, an issue. At the same time, most have grown up under the rule of the Parti Québécois and its strict linguistic rules. So they did not have to fight in order to live in French. They struggle more about safeguarding their hybrid identity as part Québécois, part Haitian, Greek, African, North African, or East European. Furthermore, these young Quebecers perceive themselves as citizens of the new global reality within which American popular culture rules. Nike, Tommy Hilfiger, Eminem, 'N Sync, Christina Aguilera, and the Backstreet Boys transmit the same message every day to thousands of young people: American culture is cool and sexy! Québécois rap, like Québécois rock and roll, blues, and country music before it, has adopted the task of building new cultural bridges.

At this juncture, is it even legitimate to ask how this new generation will resist seduction by America? How will this generation maintain a balance among its Americanity, its Quebecity, and its Francity? Whatever the outcome, the future will soon offer signs of Quebec culture's inexhaustible creative capacities.

# NOTES

1. The concept of Social Imaginary derives from Cornelius Castoriadis's theory in *The Imaginary Institutions of Society*. The term refers to the symbolic constitution, cultural significance, and social representations of a certain society.

2. High divorce rates, low birth rates, single-parent families, and an overall malaise at the family level are today's expression of the radical transformation of the French-Canadian family that has taken place since the 1960s.

# REFERENCES

Bouchard, G., and S. Courville. 1993. *La construction d'une culture: Le Québec et l'Amérique: Française*. Saint-Foy: Laval University Press.

———— and Y. Lamonde. 1995. *Québécois et Américains: La culture Québécoise aux XIXe et XXe Siècles*. Saint-Laurent: Fides.

Castoriadis, Cornelius. 1987. *The Imaginary Institutions of Society*. Cambridge, MA: MIT Press.

Dandurand, R. 1988. *Le mariage en question: Essai socio-historique*. Québec: Institute Québécois de Recherche sur la Culture.

Rioux, M. 1971. *Quebec in Question*. Toronto: J. Lewis and Samuel.